IDS DEVELOPMENT STUDIES SERIES

North–South Trade,
Employment and Inequality

IDS Development Studies Series

The Institute of Development Studies at the University of Sussex was established in 1966 as the British national research and training centre in development studies. In this series members of the Institute aim to bring the results of their most interesting research projects to the widest possible audience. The books are drawn from a number of social science disciplines and have their origins in research projects, reflective work by IDS Fellows, or conference papers. The series reflects the broad range of IDS Fellows' expertise on development and encompasses both the traditional concerns of this interdisciplinary area of study and new theoretical debates.

North–South Trade, Employment and Inequality

Changing Fortunes in a Skill-Driven World

ADRIAN WOOD

CLARENDON PRESS · OXFORD
1994

Oxford University Press, Walton Street, Oxford OX2 6DP

Oxford New York Toronto
Delhi Bombay Calcutta Madras Karachi
Kuala Lumpur Singapore Hong Kong Tokyo
Nairobi Dar es Salaam Cape Town
Melbourne Auckland Madrid

and associated companies in
Berlin Ibadan

Oxford is a trade mark of Oxford University Press

Published in the United States
by Oxford University Press Inc., New York

British Library Cataloguing in Publication Data
Data available

Library of Congress Cataloging in Publication Data
Wood, Adrian.
North–South trade, employment and inequality: changing fortunes
in a skill-driven world | Adrian Wood.
p. cm.—(IDS development studies series)
Includes bibliographical references and index.
1. Labor market—Developing countries. 2. Labor Market.
3. Developing countries—Commerce. 4. Income distribution—United
States 5. Unemployment—Europe. 6. International division of
labor. 7. International trade. I. Title. II. Series.
HD5852.W65 1994 93–30541
331.12'09172'4—dc20
ISBN 0–19–828352–0

1 3 5 7 9 10 8 6 4 2

Typeset by Hope Services (Abingdon) Ltd.
Printed in Great Britain
on acid-free paper by
Bookcraft Ltd. Midsomer Norton

To Joyce, Dora, and Lucy

Readers' Guide

To get access to the contents of this long book in the shortest possible time, the best way to begin for almost all readers would be to read the first chapter, which is a non-technical summary of the whole book.

The first chapter also contains signposts to later chapters, to make it easier to follow up in particular areas. In addition to the usual index, there are two tables of contents, one a simple list of chapter titles, the other showing the headings of all sections and subsections within chapters. Each of the later chapters concludes with a brief summary of its contents.

The later chapters are more technical than the first chapter, but not technically demanding by the standards of contemporary economics books. The book spans three specialised fields of economics: trade, labour, and development. However, it should be fully accessible to all professional economists, whatever their special field, and mainly accessible to anyone with (or close to getting) an undergraduate degree in economics.

Preface

I started to think about this book while working on a World Bank report (1985a) which encouraged China to follow the examples of Korea and Taiwan in expanding labour-intensive manufactured exports. In discussing that report, some of my Chinese friends asked me questions about the long-term economic relationship between the North and the South, and about how China would fit in, which I was completely unable to answer. Back in Washington, I began to wonder whether the increasing economic polarisation of American society, all too evident in that city, might have something to do with the expansion of those manufactured exports from the South whose volume we were urging China to swell. This concern was sharpened when I returned to academic life in England, my supposedly tolerant and civilised country, to find mobs of unemployed youths stoning the police.

As I knew, the economic literature utterly rejected any such connection. The idea that low-wage workers in the South posed a threat to high-wage workers in the North was protectionist nonsense, as I had helped to explain in another World Bank report (1980). Theoretically unsound, this idea was also inconsistent with all the empirical evidence, which showed that the impact of the South's exports on the labour markets of the North was tiny, and that Northern unemployment did not have the characteristics (of mismatch by skill and sector) that a trade explanation would imply.

But somehow I could not put the idea out of my mind. The flame was fanned during my first year at IDS by listening to Manfred Bienefeld (the most articulate of all pessimists), by reading an important book by Michael Beenstock (1984), and by talking to Martin Wolf (the most articulate of all scourgers of protectionism). This encouraged me to start serious research. During 1987 and 1988, I looked much more closely at the empirical evidence, found what seemed to be some serious flaws in its methodology, and produced new results using other methods. This work, on which Part A of the book is based, was exposed during 1989 to the criticism of friends, colleagues, and journal referees. Some parts of it did not survive, but the main result—that the impact of North–South trade on labour markets was far larger than earlier estimates had suggested—weathered the storm.

I then moved on to the second phase of the research, represented by Part B of the book, investigating the effects of trade on wages and employment in both the North and the South. In the course of that work, in early 1991, while I was struggling to make sense of profitability trends in the North, I realised that I was making a mistake in treating (physical) capital and skill (or human capital) as essentially similar—a common assumption, but one with which I had long been uncomfortable, as a result of my learning and teaching in Cambridge (England). Though related in some ways, skill and capital need to be treated separately in the analysis of trade, and in the context of North–South trade, it is skill that matters. This insight led me to rethink the theoretical framework of the book (in Chapter 2), and to reconsider a lot of earlier empirical work, my own and other people's.

By the end of 1991, I had a complete draft of the book, including Part C, which addresses the vital question of what Northern governments should do about the problems uncovered by my research, while leaving their markets open to further expansion of Southern exports. By this time, other people were thinking along similar lines. A few US economists had suggested that changes in trade might explain the increasing inequality of wages in the 1980s. There had also been published the important book by Robert Reich (1991), whose argument, though not couched in the language of economists, parallels that of this book in remarkably many respects. During 1992, I restructured, shortened, and rewrote the book, in accordance with Hollis Chenery's rule that all books should be written twice, the first time to work out what one is trying to say, the second time to say it.

Even now, I consider the work far from finished. There are some major issues which this book hardly touches, for example international migration and gender differences in the labour market (though see Wood 1991a). Also missing is a proper exploration of the implications for policy in the South, on which the next phase of my research will focus. And within the scope of the book, on almost every page, I can see ways in which the research could and should be extended, or done better, using new data and more powerful analytical tools. But one has to stop somewhere.

It is also likely, despite the comments of many colleagues and my efforts to respond to them, that the book still contains a fair number of mistakes. Among other things, I expect criticism from specialists in the three fields of economics which it spans—international, labour, and development—for failing to be aware of some previously published work. For such omissions, I apologise, but would plead in my defence that it is now impossible for any single person to fully master the literature in more than one field of economics—though I hope the length of the list of references will show that I did try—and that it would be unfortunate if research spanning more than one field had to be avoided for this reason.

Acknowledgements

The research for and writing of this book were largely financed by the UK Overseas Development Administration, through ESCOR grant R4258 and through its financial support for IDS, and by the UK Economic and Social Research Council, through grant R000231829. The views expressed in the book are of course those of its author, not of either of these organisations.

My list of intellectual debts is far longer. First, I should thank those who worked with me on this project. Trevor King was a most dedicated and industrious research officer for the first two years. Terence Moll also worked with me in this capacity for six months, and continued to provide helpful comments on draft chapters, including many editorial suggestions which made the book much more readable. Short-term research assistance of high quality was provided by Mark Adams, Jane Bailey, Kersti Berge, Rachel Lambert, and Krishnan Sharma. The library staff of the IDS were also extraordinarily supportive, and I had the benefit of some excellent secretaries: Nadine Beard, Margaret Harding, Judi Minost, Glenis Morrison, and Mary Shiner.

Second, I must thank the colleagues and friends who gave time to reading and commenting on drafts of substantial parts of the book, enabling me to make huge improvements: Christopher Bliss, Chris Clague, Chris Colclough, Jaime de Melo, David Evans, Chris Freeman, Jamie Galbraith, Martin Godfrey, James Howard, Carolyn Jenkins, Ad Koekkoek, Anne Krueger, Michael Lipton, Jim Malcomson, Christian Morrisson, Keith Pavitt, Jim Pemberton, Sherman Robinson, Bob Rowthorn, Dieter Schumacher, Alasdair Smith, Chris Stevens, John Toye, Robert Wade, John Wells, Alan Winters, Michael Wolfson, and several anonymous journal referees. Unpublished papers and data were also generously supplied by Gary Fields, Andrew Glyn, David Grubb, Jan Haaland, Ken Hanson, Farrukh Iqbal, David Marsden, Toshiyuki Mizoguchi, John Rhee, Paul Richards, Gugliemo Wolleb, and Young Rin Cho.

Many other people gave me comments and suggestions at various stages. I am especially grateful to John Black, Mike Faber, Reg Green, Charles Harvey, Richard Jackman, Ravi Kanbur, Raphie Kaplinsky, Richard Layard, Steve Lewis, Alasdair MacBean, Simon Maxwell, Sheila Page, George Psacharopoulos, Graham Pyatt, Kunibert Raffer, Clark Reynolds, Alan Roe, Christopher Saunders, Hans Singer, Nick Stern, Gene Tidrick, Jean Waelbroeck, and Martin Williamson. Also to be thanked in this category are other participants in seminars at the universities of Cambridge, Oxford, Manchester, Reading, and Warwick, at the London School of Economics, at the Netherlands Development Economics Seminar at Erasmus University, and at several seminars in IDS.

The editors of the *Development Policy Review, Weltwirtschaftliches Archiv*, and the *World Bank Research Observer* have kindly permitted the inclusion in this book of some material from articles by me in their journals.

Finally, my deepest thanks go to my wife and two daughters, to whom the book is dedicated, for putting up with my preoccupation with this project for such a long time, and for making me enjoy the other aspects of life.

A. W.

January 1993

Contents

Detailed Contents

Part A
Patterns and Magnitudes

Part B
Causes and Consequences

Part C
Prospects and Policies

Appendices

List of Figures

List of Tables

1

Summary and Conclusions

Expansion of trade has linked the labour markets of developed countries (the North) more closely with those of developing countries (the South). This greater economic intimacy has had large benefits, raising average living standards in the North, and accelerating development in the South. But it has hurt unskilled workers in the North, reducing their wages and pushing them out of jobs. Northern governments must take action to solve this problem. Otherwise, the North will continue to suffer from rising inequality and mass unemployment, and the South from barriers to trade.

That, in one paragraph, is the argument of this book. The rest of this chapter will provide a fuller statement, with references to the detailed discussion and evidence in the following nine chapters. Why are so many chapters needed for such a simple argument? Part of the reason is its broad scope. The main reason, though, is that the argument is rather controversial—which means that less can be taken for granted.

1.1 Trends and Disputes

There is no disagreement about the changes in the pattern of North–South trade over the past few decades, during which developing countries have ceased to be merely exporters of primary products. The South's exports of manufactures to the North, which were negligible in the 1950s, had risen to about $250 billion by 1990, involving growth of about 15 per cent per year in real terms.[1] These extra earnings have financed a big increase in the North's manufactured exports to the South. However, the labour-intensive parts of Northern manufactured exports have vanished, as developing countries have learned to make these goods for themselves.

[1] In current dollars, using the sources and definitions in Table 1.1, the South's manufactured exports to the North were less than $1bn. in 1955 and $232bn. in 1989 (the latest year available from this source at the time of writing). Estimates for 1990 from other sources range from $238bn. (GATT *International Trade* 90–91, Table A3) to $287bn. (World Bank 1992, indicators table 17, adding Israel, Hong Kong, and Singapore to the low-and-middle-income country total). The variation is due to the way in which the two country groups are defined and the data are obtained. In constant 1980 dollars, using the data in Fig. 1.1, the annual average 1960–90 growth rate was 14.6% (calculated by regression).

TABLE 1.1. *Composition of North–South merchandise trade, 1955–1989* (%)

	1955	1970	1980	1989
A. North's exports to South				
Primary and processed primary	19.8	19.0	19.4	17.7
Manufactures	73.2	78.1	78.6	79.4
TOTAL	100.0	100.0	100.0	100.0
B. South's exports to North				
Primary and processed primary	94.8	84.1	84.1	45.3
of which: fuels	20.4	33.1	66.4	24.8
Manufactures	5.0	15.6	15.2	53.3
TOTAL	100.0	100.0	100.0	100.0
Manufactures as % non-fuel exports	6.3	23.4	45.1	70.9

Notes: (1) North is 'developed market economies', South is 'developing countries and territories' plus 'socialist countries of Asia'.

(2) Primary and processed primary are SITC 0 to 4 plus 68. Fuels are SITC 3. Manufactures are SITC 5 to 8 less 68 (non-ferrous metals). Unclassified exports are excluded, hence components do not sum to totals.

Source: UNCTAD *Handbook of Trade and Development Statistics* 1976, 1990, 1991 (annexe tables).

Table 1.1 shows the commodity composition of North–South merchandise trade over this period, in both directions. The North's exports have continued to consist mainly of manufactures. The composition of the South's exports has fluctuated with the price of oil, but the share of manufactures in non-fuel exports has risen steadily, from 6 per cent in 1955 to 71 per cent in 1989. The old pattern of trade, in which manufactured goods from the North were exchanged for primary products from the South, has thus largely been replaced by a new pattern, in which the North and the South each specialise in different sorts of manufactured goods.

Manufactures, incidentally, are defined here rather narrowly, excluding 'processed primary' products such as canned food and refined oil. Table 1.1 also excludes (for lack of data) trade in services. But fragmentary evidence suggests that North–South trade in services is quite large, and has changed in much the same way as trade in manufactures.[2] The old one-way flow from North to South has been replaced by a two-way flow, with the South as a substantial exporter of services such as shipping, tourism, and even routine key-punching. In a basic economic sense, moreover, traded services resemble narrowly defined manufactures—both are produced mainly by labour and capital, with a low natural resource content.

[2] See Sect. 4.4.3.

So the term 'manufactures' will be used below to embrace also traded services.

Optimists versus pessimists

The controversy is over the *consequences* of this change in the pattern of North–South trade. There are actually two controversies, one about the North and the other about the South. In both cases, there is a range of opinions, partly reflecting the widely varying circumstances of particular countries within these coarse groupings. But broadly speaking, the dispute in both cases is between those who view the consequences of these changes in trade as predominantly good ('optimists') and those who view them as predominantly bad ('pessimists').[3]

In the South, the optimistic view—based on the remarkable success of Korea and Taiwan—is that expansion of labour-intensive manufactured exports offers an ideal path to prosperity for developing countries. It is ideal in that it promises not only rapid growth but also, by creating many jobs and pulling up wages, less inequality. The pessimists, by contrast, regard export-oriented manufacturing as exploitation by foreigners, with abysmally low wages and miserable working conditions. The optimists point to the increasing number of developing countries adopting their strategy. The pessimists see this compliance as more the result of arm-twisting by external creditors than of enthusiasm for the strategy.

In the North, the optimists emphasise the efficiency gains from more trade with the South. Increased imports of labour-intensive manufactures release workers from low-productivity sectors. These imports also provide the South with more foreign exchange to spend on sophisticated exports from the North, which raises employment in high-productivity sectors. The changes in the structure of employment are acknowledged by the optimists to be painful for workers in contracting sectors, but this problem is seen as localised and temporary. It can thus be satisfactorily handled by some help in moving to new jobs, aid to blighted regions, and vigorous efforts to make labour markets more flexible.

The pessimistic view is that there is a vast global labour surplus. More trade with the South exposes workers in the North to the consequences of this surplus, driving down their real wages and degrading their

---

[3] The optimistic view, in both the North and the South, has consistently been taken by the World Bank (e.g. 1987) and the OECD (e.g. 1979, 1985, 1989), as well as by many others, some of whose works are cited later in this book (esp. in Ch. 3). Pessimistic views are often expressed—by politicians, union leaders, and members of the public—but rarely set out in a formal or academic way. Exceptions are the articulate statements of Bienefeld (1982, 1986) and Godfrey (1985), both influenced by Seers (1983), and of Gray (1985). Beenstock (1984) also argues that the South's manufactured exports have adversely affected the North, though he opposes protection. The diversity of views expressed by both optimists and pessimists should be reiterated. The summary in this section is condensed and simplified for the sake of brevity and clarity.

conditions of work. Moreover, so long as wages in the North remain superior to those in the South, job losses from rising imports cannot be fully offset by job gains from rising exports, and hence unemployment tends to increase. There may be gains from trade with the South, but they accrue to the owners of capital, while labour loses. Adjustment assistance is cosmetic, and labour market flexibility makes matters worse. What pessimists advocate instead is protection—barriers against imports from the South.

An intermediate position

Where does this book stand in relation to these disputes between optimists and pessimists? On the South, its conclusion is one of qualified optimism. Export-oriented industrialisation is a good development strategy, which can reduce inequality. For this reason, it is essential that the South should have access to Northern markets for its manufactured exports. However, not all developing countries currently have the human resources needed for this strategy. Nor do more open trade policies necessarily accelerate growth or reduce inequality.

On the North, the conclusion of this book is that the optimists and the pessimists have each got hold of a vital part of the truth, but that each of them is also in important respects wrong. The optimists are right to emphasise the efficiency gains from trade with the South, but they greatly underestimate the adverse side-effects of this trade on income inequality in the North. The pessimists are right that there is a large and enduring distributional problem, but they are wrong about its nature: it is not that capital gains and labour loses, but that skilled labour gains and unskilled labour loses. The pessimists are also advocating the wrong solution: protection is the most costly of the alternatives, even from the standpoint of the North—leaving aside the damage it inflicts on the South.

1.2 Skill as the Basis of North–South Trade
(see Chapters 2 and 3)

To understand the consequences of North–South trade in manufactures, it is essential to understand its causes. The most fundamental question is why this trade exists at all—what is the source of the economic gains from exchange of manufactures between North and South? The answer is that the North has a relatively large supply of skilled labour, while the South has a relatively large supply of unskilled labour. It thus makes economic sense for the North to specialise in producing skill-intensive items, exporting these to the South in exchange for (unskilled-)labour-intensive items which the South can produce relatively more cheaply.

This answer is in some ways extremely conventional. It conforms with the most widely taught (Heckscher–Ohlin) theory of trade. Moreover, many other economists have argued—with empirical evidence—that skill availability is an important basis of trade. It is agreed by all that the labour force in the North contains a far larger proportion of skilled workers than in the South. Indeed, most people would probably accept that differences in the availability of skills—or human resources—are the most fundamental of all the differences between developed and developing countries.

What is unconventional about this answer is what it leaves out. The most notable omission is capital, which is usually seen as one of the main bases of North–South trade in manufactures. More specifically, the North is said to be well-endowed with capital and hence an exporter of capital-intensive goods to the South, which, because it is poorly endowed with capital, has a comparative advantage in labour-intensive (meaning non-capital-intensive) production. However, this interpretation of North–South trade appears, on closer investigation, to be theoretically unsound and empirically untrue.

Even this conclusion should not come as a surprise. Interest rates and profit rates are much the same in the South as in the North, largely because financial capital is mobile. Most capital goods, moreover, can be moved freely around the world (machinery) or constructed anywhere in a year or two (buildings). So there is no particular reason why the North should have a comparative advantage in capital-intensive production. An important exception to this proposition concerns infrastructure. The difference in the availability and quality of this sort of capital is the second most basic economic difference (after skill supplies) between developed and developing countries.

The conclusion that capital is not at the root of North–South trade in manufactures is of more than academic interest, because it assuages one of the main concerns of the Northern pessimists. For if this trade is based on the availability of skills, rather than of capital, then expansion of trade with the South does not tend to drive down the average real wage in the North, nor to pull up the share of profits at the expense of labour, nor to push workers in general into unemployment. What it does, instead, is to widen the economic gap between skilled and unskilled workers.

Skill categories

Before going much further, it is necessary to explain what is meant by 'skilled' and 'unskilled' workers. There are of course many types and gradations of skill. A proper analysis of North–South trade and labour markets requires a minimum of three categories. One includes all workers with more than a basic general education, which makes it a mixed bag of professional and technical workers, managers, and craftsmen, all of whom have advanced education or substantial training or work experience. (In later chapters, this category is given the ugly label *SKILD* as a constant reminder of its crudity.)

The second category consists of workers who have a primary or general secondary education, but no more. (In later chapters they are labelled *BAS-EDs*—pronounced *base*-eds, by the way, rather than *bass*-eds.) The third contains those who have little or no education (labelled *NO-EDs*). Both these sorts of workers are often loosely referred to as 'unskilled'. In the North, this conflation is acceptable, because there are so few *NO-EDs*. But the distinction between them is important in the South. This is because *NO-EDs* are unemployable in modern manufacturing, where the work requires at least literacy or primary education. Thus for many of the least developed countries, where *NO-EDs* still outnumber *BAS-EDs*, the common suggestion that their 'abundance of unskilled labour' gives them a comparative advantage in labour-intensive manufacturing is misleading.

Skill formation

The relative sizes of these skill categories are not fixed, except in the short run. The supply of skilled labour can change over time in two ways that affect the argument of this book. One is that Southern countries can accumulate skills (reduce the shares of *NO-ED* and *BAS-ED* workers in their labour forces), which tends to shift the pattern of their exports towards more skill-intensive goods. The other point is that skill supplies can respond to, as well as shape, trade flows. In particular, the harm done to unskilled workers in the North by expansion of trade with the South is to some extent automatically undone by the stronger incentive that it creates for people to acquire skills—moving themselves from the losing category into the gaining category.

In both respects, though, the malleability of the skilled labour supply should not be exaggerated. For a developing country, skill accumulation is at best a slow process. This is partly because of increasing returns (the more skills you have, the easier is it to acquire new ones), partly because of externalities (the more skilled the people around you, the more you learn). Similarly, the supply of skilled labour in the North can respond only slowly and partially to worsening pay and job prospects for unskilled workers. This is partly because individuals and families, like countries, are subject to increasing returns and externalities in skill acquisition, partly because capital markets are imperfect (it is hard for many people to finance the necessary investment in education and training), and partly because not everyone has the ability to acquire a high level of skill.

1.3 Causes of the Change in North–South Trade
(see Section 5.1)

Enduring differences in skill availability are the underlying reason for North–South trade in manufactures. But why has the pattern of this trade changed in recent decades from a limited one-way flow to a larger two-way flow? The answer varies somewhat, among countries and time-periods, but the main cause appears to have been a lowering of barriers to trade, both natural and artificial.

International transport and telecommunications have become much cheaper, quicker, and of better quality—shrinking the world, as it is often said. Northern import restrictions and exchange controls were liberalised, and tariffs drastically reduced, in the 1950s and 1960s, though this was later partly reversed by the introduction of quantitative limits on imports from the South (and Japan). In the South, a series of countries have followed Korea and Taiwan in shifting to export-oriented industrial trade regimes.

These barrier reductions have done more than simply ease the flow of goods from the South to the North. Just as important has been easier movement of inputs from the North to the South—components, machinery, finance, and information, including visits from technical and marketing experts. More generally, Northern companies have learned how to manage globally dispersed production and procurement activities. Somewhat paradoxically, increases in barriers have also played a part in changing the pattern of North–South trade: initial protection of Southern industry stimulated the investment and learning needed to start producing labour-intensive manufactures.

The conclusion that reduction of barriers was the main cause makes it possible to argue—as this book does—that the change in trade has been an autonomous influence on labour markets, both in the North and in the South. In principle, this argument could be stood on its head. The change in trade might not have been autonomous; it might have been caused by changes in labour markets, and in particular by changes in the relative supplies of (or relative domestic demands for) skilled and unskilled labour. For example, the rise in imports of manufactures from the South might have represented for the North not an unskilled-labour-displacing intrusion but a response to increasing scarcity of unskilled labour.

There was in fact some reverse causation—from labour markets to trade—especially in the earlier part of the post-war period. Korea and Taiwan both greatly raised their literacy rates in the 1950s, prior to their rapid expansion of labour-intensive exports in the 1960s. And in the North there were shortages of unskilled labour in the 1960s, as evidenced by the influx of guest workers into Western Europe. These shortages probably contributed to the reduction of trade barriers by triggering interest in procurement from the South. However, the deteriorating economic position of unskilled workers in the North since the 1970s is clearly inconsistent with the idea of imports from the South being sucked in by unskilled labour shortages.

1.4 Size of the Impact on Labour Markets

This account of the causes of North–South trade in manufactures makes the nature of its impact on labour markets quite clear. Countries in the South have increased their production of labour-intensive goods (both for export and domestic use) and their imports of skill-intensive goods, raising the demand for unskilled but literate labour, relative to more skilled workers. In the North, the skill composition of labour demand has been twisted the other way. Production of skill-intensive goods for export has increased, while production of labour-intensive goods has been replaced by imports, reducing the demand for unskilled relative to skilled workers.

That expansion of North–South trade should have these symmetrical effects on the relative demand for skilled and unskilled labour in the two groups is in accordance with the standard economic theory of trade. Such effects have also consistently been identified in earlier empirical studies of both developed and developing countries, as well as in the new calculations in this book.

However, although there is little dispute about the *pattern* of the impact on the composition of labour demand, there is a lot of disagreement about its *magnitude*. This is a crucial question. For if the effects of North–South trade on labour markets were small, they would not be worth worrying about. It is also a most difficult question to answer, partly because this requires an assessment of what would have happened in the absence of trade, and partly because of a shortage of relevant data.

Previous work (see Chapter 3)

In the South, advocates of export-oriented industrialisation assert that their strategy greatly increases the demand for unskilled labour. These claims that the impact is big are not, in general, based on formal studies (most of which have been confined to the *pattern* of trade), but they are highly plausible. This is because even casual observation reveals that many millions of unskilled and semi-skilled people are indeed working in factories in developing countries producing goods for export to the North.

In the North, there have been numerous formal studies of the magnitude of the impact of trade with the South, but almost all of them have concluded that this impact is tiny—to be measured in hundreds of thousands rather than millions of workers, even when the effects on all developed countries are added together. On the face of it, such a small impact is puzzling—difficult to reconcile with casual impressions that the effect has been much larger (and with the consequent strength of political pressure for protection). The smallness of the estimated impact in the North also sits uncomfortably with the seemingly far larger impact in the South.

Such results, however, have been accepted by most economists, and by the Northern governments and international organisations they advise. Their confidence that the impact of trade with the South on the labour market is small has been reinforced by the fact that this conclusion emerges from two entirely different methods of analysis, each of which has been supposed to provide a cross-check on the results of the other. It transpires, though, that *both* methods are subject to severe downward biases. The errors are so important that they merit a brief explanation here.

The first method is to calculate the *factor content of trade*. This means figuring out how much skilled and unskilled labour is required to produce the goods that are exported to the South, and how much would have been required to produce domestically the goods that are imported from the South. The effect of trade is then estimated as the difference in skilled and unskilled labour content between exports and imports. In principle, this approach is sound, but the way it is usually applied involves one seriously misleading assumption. This is that imports of manufactures from the South 'compete' with identical goods made in the North, and hence that their labour content can be estimated from data on Northern industries that produce goods in the same statistical categories as the imports.

In reality, however, firms in the North no longer manufacture many of the labour-intensive items imported from the South. To use a technical term, many manufactured imports from the South are 'noncompeting'. As a result, the usual method of calculation, using actual Northern input coefficients in industries now producing more skill-intensive items, gives much too low an estimate of the unskilled labour content of these imports. The extent to which trade with the South reduces the relative demand for unskilled labour is thus greatly understated. (The same problem arises in the South, whose manufactured imports from the North are also largely noncompeting, but in this case what is understated is the net *increase* in the relative demand for unskilled labour.)

The other commonly used method, which is applied to sectors rather than skill categories, is *accounting decomposition of the sources of change in employment*. The first step is to separate the (negative) effects of labour productivity growth from the (usually positive) effects of output growth. The second step is to split up the sources of output growth, distinguishing domestic demand from export demand (which tends to raise domestic output) and import flows (which tend to lower it). By this method, the net effect of trade with the South on employment appears significant in some sectors, such as clothing, but tiny for industry as a whole.

The main weakness of this method is that it assumes changes in labour productivity to be unrelated to foreign trade. There are in fact two important ways in which expansion of trade with the South has raised labour productivity in Northern industry (implying that this method must be understating its impact on employment). One is changes in product mix, which occur when competition from the South forces firms in the North to abandon labour-intensive activities, either by eliminating particular products altogether or by splitting up the production process so that only the skill-intensive stages are performed domestically.

The second way in which trade with the South raises productivity in the North is by inducing unskilled-labour-saving technical progress. In other words, a common reaction of Northern firms to Southern competition has been to seek new ways of producing with less unskilled labour. In some cases this has not proved possible, and domestic production has been replaced by noncompeting imports, but in other cases defensive innovation has kept Northern firms competitive. Even in the latter cases, however, the demand for unskilled labour has been reduced—an effect captured neither by the accounting method nor by the factor content method.

New estimates (see Chapter 4)

This book's reassessment of the magnitude of the impact of North–South trade on the demand for labour is based on a modified version of the factor content of trade approach, allowing for noncompeting manufactured imports and estimating their labour content in a new way. The positive impact on the demand for unskilled labour in the South appears to be about five times as large as the conventional calculations suggest, the negative impact on unskilled labour in the North about ten times as large.

For Northern manufacturing as a whole, the cumulative reduction up to 1990 in the demand for unskilled labour caused by expansion of trade with the South is estimated by this method to have been between 6 and 12 million person-years. The increase in the demand for skilled labour was small, so that the total demand for labour in manufacturing was reduced by about the same amount as the demand for unskilled labour. The central estimate of 9 million person-years implies a reduction in the economy-wide demand for unskilled relative to skilled labour of about 5 per cent.

This initial estimate, however, omits the effects of defensive unskilled-labour-saving innovation. There is no satisfactory way to quantify this omission. But case study and anecdotal evidence suggests that the impact of defensive innovation on the level and skill composition of the demand for labour has been at least as large as the relocation and reallocation effects measured by the factor content method. This assessment receives some support from calculations of the rise in the proportion of skilled workers in Northern manufacturing, relative to nontraded sectors, in the recent past. So the tentative conclusion is that allowance for defensive innovation would require the initial estimate to be roughly doubled.

A further source of understatement is that the modified factor content estimates are confined to manufacturing. Increased trade with the South has had qualitatively similar effects in other sectors, particularly in traded services. In addition, there is the impact on the relative demand for skilled and unskilled labour in the nontraded sectors from which the traded sectors buy intermediate inputs. There is again no accurate means of quantifying these effects, but the limited data available suggest that inclusion of traded and nontraded services would approximately double the impact estimated for manufacturing alone.

This combination of calculation and guesswork—starting from the factor content estimates, and doubling them twice—leads to the conclusion that up to 1990 the changes in trade with the South had reduced the demand for unskilled relative to skilled labour in the North as a whole by something like 20 per cent. This estimate is subject to a wide range of error (plus or minus about 8 percentage points). The shift in demand, it should also be stressed, did not happen suddenly, but over three decades. However, it was concentrated towards the end of the period, because the absolute size of the annual increases in imports from the South became ever larger. As Fig. 1.1 indicates, about 70 per cent of the total real increase in the South's manufactured exports to the North during 1960–90 occurred in the 1980s.

1.5 Sectoral Effects of the Change in Trade (see Sections 5.3 and 5.4)

An incidental consequence of the shifts in relative demand for skilled and unskilled labour caused by the change in North–South trade has been shifts in the sectoral composition of labour demand. The increased specialisation of the North in skill-intensive activities, and of the South in labour-intensive activities, has involved internal restructuring of manufacturing and other traded sectors. It has also altered the total demand for labour in traded sectors relative to nontraded sectors, reducing it in the North and increasing it in the South.

Summary and Conclusions

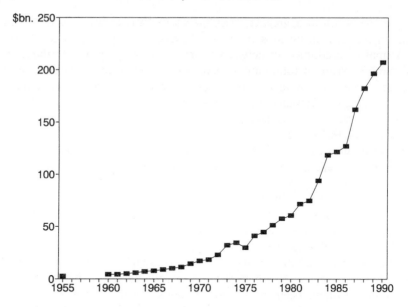

FIG. 1.1 Manufactured exports of the South to the North (billions of constant 1980 dollars)

Notes and sources: Data in current dollars for 1955 and 1960–88 from UNCTAD *Handbook of Trade and Development Statistics* 1976, 1983, 1982–90. Definitions and coverage as in Table 1.1.

Conversion to constant 1980 dollars based on world manufactured export unit value index from GATT *International Trade* 85–86 and 89–90 (table A1). However, the prices of the South's manufactured exports rose more slowly over this period than those of the North, the difference being about 1% per year (Ventura-Diaz and Sorsa 1985; Sarkar and Singer 1989). So the GATT index was adjusted downward by a uniform 0.8% per year. (The world index is in effect a weighted average of the North and South indices, and the weights were about 0.8 and 0.2 respectively at the end of the period.)

The 1980 dollar index was extended from 1988 to 1990 on the basis of the growth rates in the UNCTAD *Trade and Development Report* 1991 (table 11), which refer to the South's manufactured exports to all destinations.

Absolute reductions in the demand for labour in particular sectors devalue skills specific to those sectors. Thus in the North, some of the skilled workers in labour-intensive sectors have been even harder hit than their unskilled colleagues. Wage levels in sectors exposed to more competition from imports have also been depressed relative to other sectors. However, because most sorts of workers are fairly mobile among sectors, the largest and most enduring effect of changes in the sectoral composition of labour demand is on the sectoral composition of employment.

For the South in aggregate, the changes in trade created more than 20 million manufacturing jobs by 1990. But the proportional effect of this was small—an addition of between 1 and 2 percentage points to the share of manufacturing in total employment—simply because the South's overall labour force is so vast. A different impression emerges from comparisons among individual developing countries: there is a strong positive correlation between expansion of North-bound manufactured exports and increases in the share of manufacturing in total employment. Indeed, countries which did not raise these exports (as a ratio of GDP) did not on average achieve any increase in their manufacturing employment shares.

The absolute size of the effect on manufacturing employment in the North was much the same as in the South, but its proportional effect was greater—a reduction of at least 4 percentage points in the share of manufacturing in total employment for the North as a whole. Thus expansion of trade with the South was an important cause of the deindustrialisation of employment in the North over the past few decades. However, it does not appear to have been the sole cause: some decline in the manufacturing employment share would have occurred for other reasons, even in the absence of the changes in North–South trade.

These changes in trade probably also contributed to the reduction in Northern profit rates between the late 1960s and about 1980, which seems to have been confined largely to manufacturing. For even though capital is not an important basis of North–South trade (and hence this trade does not have enduring effects on the aggregate rate of profit), the North started this period with a large stock of installed capital in labour-intensive industries, whose profitability was reduced by competition from the South. Eventually, most of this capital was scrapped, but during the transition the average profitability of manufacturing was dragged down.

1.6 Skill Differentials and Inequality in the South
(see Chapter 6)

The optimistic view of export-oriented industrialisation suggests that it reduces inequality within developing countries. This book supports that proposition, but with some strong qualifications.

Expansion of manufactured exports raises the demand for—and hence the wages of—unskilled but literate (*BAS-ED*) labour relative to other sorts of labour. It thus tends to narrow the wage differential between *BAS-EDs* and (higher-paid) skilled workers, reducing inequality. It also tends to widen the wage differential between literate and (lower-paid) illiterate workers, and thus to increase inequality. But there are comparatively few illiterates in the countries which account for most of the

South's exports of manufactures to the North. So the reduction in inequality should have predominated.

It is not easy to test this hypothesis empirically, partly because of a lack of data, and partly because it is hard to control for simultaneous changes in other influences on inequality. However, the hypothesis seems consistent with most of the evidence, including a (weak) correlation across Southern countries between growth of North-bound manufactured exports and changes in income inequality.

Closer examination of the leading East Asian exporters of manufactures confirms that their adoption of export-oriented policies narrowed the wage gap between skilled and unskilled workers, and so reduced overall income inequality. However, these case studies also corroborate the theoretical prediction that a change in trade policy will have only a one-shot effect on income inequality—spread out in practice over about a decade. There were in fact more sustained reductions in wage differentials in these East Asian economies (as well as some periods in which inequalities increased), but the main contributor to this trend appears to have been expansion of higher education, increasing the relative supply of skilled labour.

All this evidence, however, leaves open a much more basic question about the optimistic view. For although there is a fairly consistent association between expansion of manufactured exports and reduction of inequality, it does not necessarily follow that a switch to more liberal trade policies (which is what the optimists usually advocate for developing countries) would lead to more manufactured exports or to less inequality. The result of such a change of policy would depend on the availability of human and natural resources in the country concerned.

It is no coincidence that the successful East Asian exporters had literate populations and few natural resources. Because illiterates are of little use in manufacturing, countries with low literacy rates are less likely to have a comparative advantage in that sector. Countries with more farmland or minerals per person are also less likely to export manufactures. And as other authors have shown, exporting primary commodities may increase or decrease income inequality, depending on the pattern of ownership of the resources concerned.

1.7 Skill Differentials and Inequality in the North
(see Chapter 7)

The expected effect of the changes in North–South trade on inequality in the North is more straightforward than in the South, because there are so few illiterate workers. The decline in demand for literate but unskilled labour, relative to skilled labour, tends to widen the wage differential between these two groups, and hence to increase inequality.

A complication in the North, however, is that wider wage differentials tend to be resisted, especially in Europe. The resistance arises partly from the power and egalitarianism of labour unions, partly from minimum wage legislation, and partly from minimum income provisions in social security systems (which make people unwilling to accept low-wage jobs). In so far as these institutional forces reduce relative wage flexibility, the pressure for wider skill differentials emerges in a different form—as shortages of skilled labour and surpluses of unskilled labour.

Trends in skill differentials

There is compelling evidence that skill differentials widened in the North during the 1980s, reversing a long-term trend in the other direction. The availability of data varies, but the widening is observable to some degree or in some form in almost every developed country.

The wages earned by workers with higher education rose relative to those of workers with secondary education or less (after falling during the 1970s, because of rapid expansion of the supply of college graduates). In most cases, unemployment rates among people with less education also increased relative to rates among people with more education. People who were both ill-educated and inexperienced fared particularly badly, though the decline in the relative economic position of younger workers had started earlier, in the 1970s.

Occupational wage statistics also reveal widening skill differentials in many developed countries during the 1980s—between white-collar and blue-collar workers, between professional and clerical workers, and between skilled and unskilled manual workers. But the variation among countries and occupational groups was considerable. The widening was strongest and most consistent in the USA and the UK, weaker and less consistent in other European countries, notably France. Movements in the relative wages of skilled and unskilled manual workers were particularly diverse, probably because unions and other institutions have most influence in this domain.

The allocation of the unemployed among occupational categories is subject to some obvious problems, and the data on relative unemployment rates by occupation do not all point in the same direction. However, most of the available series suggest a widening of skill differentials during the 1980s, with unemployment rates in less skilled occupations rising relative to those in more skilled occupations. The same conclusion emerges from most of the data on vacancies and shortages, with skilled workers becoming harder to find, relative to less-skilled workers.

The dispersion of the size distribution of wages among full-time workers, both male and female, increased during at least part of the 1980s in all the developed countries for which data exist, apparently because of the widening of skill differentials. This rise in wage dispersion contributed to greater inequality in the distribution of all income among households, which deteriorated in the majority of countries during this period.

Competing explanations of these trends

The widening of skill differentials in the North is clearly consistent with the anticipated impact of the change in trade with the South. There are other possible explanations of this trend, but most of them are much less plausible.

The political shift to the Right in many countries during the 1980s was significant in two respects. Measures to weaken unions and minimum wage laws, and to make unemployment benefits less generous, helped to widen skill differentials in wages. Redistribution through the tax system was also reduced, amplifying the effects of widening wage and unemployment differentials on inequality of living standards. But a purely political explanation is inadequate. Skill differentials in unemployment and vacancy rates widened even where wage differentials did not, indicating a more basic shift in the balance between relative demand and relative supply.

It is also clear that this shift occurred predominantly on the demand side rather than the supply side. In the 1970s, bulging cohorts of young people helped to widen skill differentials in some countries. During the 1980s, however, the relative supply of skilled workers increased, as did their share of total employment. The concurrent widening of skill differentials in wages, unemployment and vacancy rates is therefore symptomatic of an upward shift in the demand for skilled relative to unskilled workers.

Several features of the evidence support the view that the main cause of this demand shift was the change in trade with the South. One is its *timing*: the impact of this trade was concentrated in the 1980s, which is when the widening of skill differentials occurred. Another is the general *magnitude* of the widening of skill differentials, which is consistent with the estimated size of the trade-induced demand shift. A third is the pattern of *cross-country variation*: the relative position of unskilled workers apparently deteriorated more in countries with larger increases in Southern import penetration.

North–North trade is unlikely to have been a major contributor to the widening of skill differentials. The differences in the skill intensity of trade flows among developed countries are much smaller than those of North–South trade flows. In principle, moreover, trade arising from intra-

North differences in skill intensity cannot explain why skill differentials in all Northern countries moved in the same direction.

By far the most plausible of the alternative explanations of the decline in the relative demand for unskilled labour in the 1980s is the spread of new technology based on microprocessors. The timing and pervasiveness of this wave of innovation are clearly consistent with the view that it caused the widening of skill differentials, which is supported also by a few formal studies. But microprocessors have displaced skilled as well as unskilled workers, and even where new technology has been linked with falling demand for unskilled labour, the underlying cause may often have been competitive pressure from the South (in other words, defensive innovation). It is also difficult to reconcile the new technology explanation with the slow-down of aggregate productivity growth, and with the apparently smaller widening of skill differentials in countries with more industrial robots—Japan and Sweden, in particular.

The available evidence does not permit a proper comparative appraisal of the trade and technology explanations, but suggests that both these forces contributed to the widening of skill differentials in the North. The main effect of more trade with the South was probably to reduce the demand for unskilled workers, while the autonomous diffusion of microprocessors acted mainly to boost the demand for skilled workers. The relative size of the impact of these two forces cannot be accurately determined. The evidence is consistent with the view that trade with the South had a larger role, but leaves open the possibility that new technology was more important.

1.8 Unemployment in the North (see Chapter 8)

Where relative wages are rigid, as explained above, a rise in the relative demand for skilled labour tends to cause shortages of skilled workers and surpluses of unskilled workers. This aggravates the macroeconomic problem of reconciling low inflation with low unemployment. In technical language, it raises the equilibrium rate of unemployment or the NAIRU (the rate of unemployment that would be needed to prevent inflation from accelerating).

What happens to the *actual* rate of unemployment depends on government policy towards inflation. Skill shortages speed up inflation, since they cause money wages to rise faster, not only for skilled workers but also for unskilled workers (whose wage rises follow those of skilled workers because of the institutional pressure for relative wage rigidity). So if the government wants to stop inflation accelerating, it must deflate the economy to eliminate the shortages of skilled labour. This deflation amplifies the increase in unemployment among unskilled workers.

Expansion of trade with the South could thus explain two major features of recent trends in unemployment rates in the North. One is that in most developed countries the unemployment rate rose between the 1960s and the 1980s, a period over which their imports of manufactures from developing countries greatly increased. The other is that this rise in unemployment was much greater in Europe, where institutional pressures causing relative wage rigidity are much stronger, than in the USA.

A complete history of unemployment during 1960–90 would have to bring in other influences, such as the oil shocks of the 1970s, to explain shorter-term movements. However, this would not involve any conflict with the present explanation of these two major features, which other economists have been unable to explain satisfactorily. The best of the alternative explanations is that high unemployment in Europe persists because skills and motivation, and hence the chance of re-employment, are eroded by long-term unemployment (encouraged by European social security systems). The weakness of this 'hysteresis' explanation, though, is that the long-term unemployed are not a random sample of the work-force: most of them lacked marketable skills even when they entered unemployment.

If the present explanation is correct, the gap in unemployment rates between skilled and unskilled workers should have widened in recent decades: that is, there should have been an increase in skill 'mismatch'. Most economic research has rejected this proposition, contrary to popular opinion and casual observation, but the data and methods used are open to serious doubt. The evidence on trends in unemployment and vacancies by skill category is limited and mixed. Most of it, however, suggests an increase in skill mismatch, and most of the apparent discrepancies can be accounted for in ways that are consistent with the present explanation.

Two other sorts of calculation support the view that expansion of trade with the South contributed to the trend rise in unemployment in the North. First, the average *magnitude* of this rise appears consistent with that of the trade-induced reduction in the relative demand for unskilled labour (about half of which emerged instead as wider wage differentials). Second, *variations* in this unemployment trend among Northern countries are strongly correlated with variations in Southern import penetration and relative wage rigidity. The countries where unemployment increased most were in general those with a combination of above-average rises in import penetration and below-average wage flexibility.

1.9 Will the Future be like the Past? (see Chapter 9)

Most of this book is about history—what happened in the period 1960–90. To derive implications for policy, however, it is necessary to think also about the future. There can be no hope of accurate predictions. But with an understanding of the causes of past trends, one can make some informed guesses. Thus if reductions in barriers to trade (broadly defined) were the main cause of the recent change in the pattern of North–South trade, a vital question is what will happen to these barriers in the future. And if differences in skill availability are the main basis of North–South trade in manufactures and services, it is also vital to ask about (autonomous) future changes in relative supplies of skilled and unskilled labour.

To think sensibly about the future—and about the present—one must go beyond the crude division of the world into North and South, and split the South into three sub-groups. First, there are countries whose natural and human resources tend to restrict their exports to primary and processed primary products (to be labelled the P group). The rest of the South can then be divided between countries (labelled L for low) whose comparative advantage lies in unskilled-labour-intensive manufactures, and countries (labelled M for middle) whose larger supplies of skilled labour make them specialise in intermediate-skill-intensive items. For example, Korea and Taiwan now belong to the M group. So, after a period of adjustment, will most of the countries of Eastern Europe and the former Soviet Union.

For the North, the key issue is whether trade with the rest of the world will cause further reductions in the relative demand for unskilled labour. The answer could be no: in principle, a lowering of trade barriers tends to have a one-shot effect on the domestic labour market, and barriers may now be as low as they ever will be. In practice, too, it is clear that many unskilled-labour-intensive manufacturing activities have already departed in their entirety to the South, so that there is no need for concern about their future shrinkage. If this were generally the case, the North would still have to face the consequences of the past reduction in the demand for unskilled labour, but at least the problem would not get any worse.

However, there are two sorts of reason why the demand shift is likely to continue—perhaps more slowly than in the past, but not necessarily so. One is further reduction of trade barriers. Transport and communications facilities will continue to improve, and firms will think of new ways to use them, and of new ways to split up production processes. The future course of artificial barriers to trade in the North is much less certain, but some decline seems probable, especially in services. An increasing range of the North's unskilled-labour-intensive activities will thus be exposed to Southern competition.

The other reason is fast growth of the global supply of intermediate-skill-intensive goods, as a result both of expansion of the skilled labour supply in the South, and of the enlargement of the M group as the ex-Soviet block countries integrate themselves into the world economy. Some of these goods are produced both in M countries and in the North, where they are now the least skill-intensive parts of the traded sector. A supply-driven fall in the world price of these goods, relative to skill-intensive goods, would tend to reduce the relative demand for unskilled labour in the North.

The effective size of the L group, too, is likely to increase, as more developing countries liberalise their trade regimes, expanding the global supply of labour-intensive manufactures, and driving down their relative price. This will have little effect on the demand for unskilled labour in the North, which no longer produces these goods. However, the M countries produce labour-intensive, as well as intermediate-skill-intensive, goods. The enlargement of the L group will thus tend to lower the relative demand for unskilled labour (and increase inequality) within the M group. This already seems to be happening in the four little East Asian tigers, under pressure from their newly exporting but poorer neighbours.

1.10 Policy Implications in the South[4]

This book touches on many issues relevant to policy choices in developing countries, but examines only a few of them in depth. A proper assessment of its implications for policy in the South must await further research. In two important respects, though, the analysis in the book supports what is now conventional wisdom in policy advice.

(1) Improvement of human resources is crucial for both growth and equity. What mainly distinguishes a developed from a developing country is the average skill level of its workers. Reducing the proportions of the labour force in low-skill categories, through education, training, and work experience, is essential for sustained economic growth, and for moving up the global income ladder. Such reductions also tend, by making unskilled labour relatively scarcer, to shrink the wage differentials between more and less skilled workers, and thus to improve distributional equity.

(2) Reform of the foreign trade regime can also contribute to both growth and equity. In particular, where incentives for manufacturers are biased against exports, movement to a more neutral trade regime may cause expansion of labour-intensive industrial exports, improving efficiency and raising national income. By increasing the relative demand for unskilled labour, such trade reform may also improve distributional equity.

At the same time, the analysis summarised above suggests some important qualifications concerning the second of these two pieces of advice.

---

[4] This section draws on Chs. 2 (esp. Sects. 2.1.4, 2.4.2), 5 (Sect. 5.1.2), 6 (esp. Sects. 6.1.3, 6.3.5, and 6.3.6), and 9.

The general point is that the outcome of this sort of trade reform is likely to vary widely among developing countries, depending on the skill structure of their labour forces and on their natural resources and infrastructure.

In some developing countries, greater neutrality of incentives will not cause expansion of labour-intensive manufactured exports, and may even cause industrial output and employment to contract. These are what were labelled above P countries, with low ratios of human to natural resources. In some of them this ratio is low because they are richly endowed with agricultural land or minerals, in others it reflects more meagre natural resources and a high illiteracy rate. Either way, such countries will not normally export manufactures, other than processed primary products.

Even in countries where the introduction of a more neutral trade regime would tend to increase manufactured exports, the increase in exports will not necessarily be large. Nor will income inequality necessarily decline. As explained earlier, greater demand for unskilled but literate workers to produce manufactured exports narrows the wage gap between them and skilled workers, but widens the wage gap between literate and illiterate workers. Where illiterates form a substantial share of the labour force, the net effect on inequality is thus ambiguous.

Widening the wage gap between literate and illiterate workers might have some benefits, by strengthening the incentive for families to send their children to school. This would be especially likely to help girls, since manufacturing for export tends to employ a lot of female labour, and since in most countries the majority of boys already attend school. But changes in trade policy can make only a small contribution to improving education in developing countries. Better educational policies and greater public expenditure are of more fundamental importance, along with the commitment to persist in a process whose returns are bound to be spread over decades and generations (Colclough 1993).

Experience—learning by doing—is also essential to the acquisition of skills, and in this regard too the lessons for developing-country trade policy are not simple. Trade brings knowledge as well as goods, so that countries which limit their economic contacts with the rest of the world deny themselves opportunities to learn new skills. In this sense, more open trade policies offer the prospect not only of a one-shot increase in income by making better use of existing labour force skills, but also of a faster rate of learning, which is probably of far greater importance for sustained development.

At the same time, one must recognise that the countries which have been most successful at catching up in skills—France, Germany, and the USA in the nineteenth century, Japan, Korea, and Taiwan more recently—have not practised free trade. Especially in the East Asian countries, judicious selection and development of infant industries with temporary protection and subsidies appear to have made a major contribution (Wade 1990).

1.11 Policy Implications in the North (see Chapter 10)

On average, people in the North have gained substantially from the change in trade with the South, but it has caused two sorts of problems for particular groups. One, which is well-recognised, is that trade-induced contraction of particular industries hurts the workers concerned. It is generally agreed that governments should help them to move or retrain.

The second sort of problem, on which this book focuses, is less widely recognised, but more pervasive and enduring. It is that unskilled workers throughout the economy have been hurt by the reduction in demand for their labour, relative to that of skilled workers. In countries where wages are flexible, such as the USA, this problem has emerged mainly in the form of a decline in the relative wages of unskilled workers. Where this widening of wage differentials has been resisted, as in Europe, the demand shift has emerged largely as higher unemployment among unskilled workers.

Governments should take action to solve this second sort of problem, too. Why? Partly because it is inequitable that the poorer members of Northern society should suffer as a result of changes in trade which have benefited the North as a whole; partly because the resulting unemployment is a waste of human resources; and partly because the decline in demand for unskilled labour has aggravated some serious social problems—crime, rioting, drug abuse, and racial conflict.

A 'solution' with strong popular appeal is protection—raising artificial barriers to imports from the South. This must be resisted. It would help unskilled workers in the North, but would be more costly than other ways of doing so, and would hurt much poorer workers in the South. However, the political pressure for protection makes it all the more important to help unskilled workers in better ways. In other words, failure to implement an alternative policy could amount to choosing protection by default.

Education and training

The most attractive response to falling demand for unskilled labour would be government action to expand the supply of skilled labour—moving some workers out of the unskilled category, while benefiting those who remained by making their sort of labour relatively scarcer. This would shrink wage differentials between skilled and unskilled workers, and reduce unskilled unemployment. It could also raise average incomes in the North, because market forces alone tend to cause underinvestment in skill acquisition.

Improvement of education and training is therefore a vital part of the solution. However, the scope for expanding the skilled labour supply is more limited than usually recognised, not for want of ways of spending more public money on schools and colleges, but because it would be hard to finance this extra spending. Raising taxes on *unskilled* workers would cut their living standards even further, while higher taxes on *skilled* workers would diminish the incentive for people to acquire skills, and so tend to cancel out the extra spending. Thus it is only worth pursuing measures which would have a large effect on the skill supply per dollar spent.

The education and training approach would also yield results only slowly, since it would probably not be cost-effective to turn many of the people who are now unskilled workers into skilled workers, largely because they were initially poorly educated. It should be possible to raise the share of skilled workers among new entrants to the labour force by giving young people better schooling and training (subject to limits imposed by natural ability). However, this would mean at best a gradual fall in the share of unskilled workers in the labour force as a whole.

Government action to increase the skilled labour supply is thus unlikely, on its own, to provide a quick or complete solution to the problems caused by the fall in demand for unskilled labour. But improvements in education and training could be combined with two other sorts of action: boosting the demand for unskilled labour, and redistributing income from skilled to unskilled workers. The appropriate mix of policies varies between America, where relative wages are flexible, and Europe, where relative wages are more rigid.

America

The greater flexibility of relative wages in America is a symptom of less concern about income inequality than in Europe. However, there is concern about poverty, especially when its causes are outside the control of those afflicted, as in this case, since the fall in demand for unskilled labour was unanticipated, and since it is now too late for most unskilled workers to become skilled. Measures to reverse the deterioration in the economic position of unskilled workers, by reducing crime and other forms of social decay, would also improve the quality of life for skilled workers, their families and other Americans.

To be politically acceptable, measures to help unskilled workers must be demonstrably linked with effort on the part of the beneficiaries, though with concessions for their dependent children. One useful approach would thus be for the government to create more unskilled jobs on projects to improve infrastructure, or in maintenance or community work. However, the economic and political limits to expanding public employment are probably quite tight.

A more comprehensive approach would be to supplement the earnings of low-wage workers in both public and private employment. The supplements would consist of tax relief and cash grants, for which all workers in low-paying jobs would be eligible, though more would be given to those with children. They would have to be financed by raising personal income taxes on skilled workers, which would impose a real economic cost by reducing the incentive to acquire skills. The benefit of the scheme, though, would be a rise in the living standards of unskilled people who were willing to work—in the spirit of workfare—without diminishing the incentive to employ unskilled labour that is provided by low wages.

Europe

The principal motive for going beyond education and training measures in Europe would be to reduce the high rates of unemployment among unskilled workers. The impact of this unemployment on poverty is limited (in most European countries) by permanent income support for people who are out of work. But it is inefficient not to use part of the labour force, and the enforced idleness and sense of rejection among the unemployed are a major cause of vandalism, violence, and other forms of social corrosion.

The main need in Europe is thus for action to increase the relative demand for unskilled labour. Public employment projects with a high proportion of unskilled workers could contribute to this objective. However, to achieve a large enough impact in a reasonably efficient way, it would be better to apply a progressive payroll tax to both the public and the private sectors. Under such a scheme, which could be implemented by modifying the structure of employers' social security contributions, employers would pay a higher proportional tax rate, the higher the wage of the worker concerned (perhaps with subsidies for the lowest-paid workers). This would correct the bias towards employing too low a ratio of unskilled to skilled labour that is created by narrow and inflexible wage differentials.

1.12 Costs of Being Wrong (see Section 10.5)

These suggestions for policy stem from this book's analysis of the effects of North–South trade. But what if the analysis is wrong? The empirical evidence on some important points is unsatisfactory, and further research is needed. It is thus important to ask, with respect to four key areas of uncertainty, about the consequences of error—in both directions. Would it be worse for policy-makers to act on the assumption that this book is right, when in fact it is wrong, than for them to act on the assumption that the book is wrong, when in fact it is right?

(1) This book may have overestimated the reduction in the relative demand for unskilled labour in the North. If so, the implementation of its policy suggestions would have some costs: economic efficiency would be lowered by excessive spending on unskilled job creation and redistribution. But the costs of *underestimating* the reduction in the demand for unskilled labour would probably be larger: more hardship would be inflicted on the poorest parts of Northern society, aggravating the social decay and conflict that now blight most developed countries; and unremitting demands for barriers to trade would rob many millions of people in the South of the chance to work their way out of much more serious poverty.

(2) This book may have exaggerated the contribution of trade with the South to the reduction in the relative demand for unskilled labour in the North, and underestimated the contribution of new technology. However, this possible error would make little difference to its policy suggestions, because these do not involve interference or linkage with trade flows. The recommended policies for the North are designed to respond to an autonomous decline in the demand for unskilled labour, regardless of its cause.

(3) This book attributes the high level of unemployment in Europe to mismatch: a decline in the relative demand for unskilled labour, in conjunction with rigidity of relative wages. Others attribute this problem to hysteresis: de-skilling caused by long-term unemployment. The policy responses implied by these two explanations overlap, but differ in one respect, which is that hysteresis unemployment could be cured by temporary measures, whereas those needed to cure mismatch unemployment would be permanent. It clearly would be costly to take permanent measures when only temporary ones were actually needed. But in the long run, it would probably be more costly to implement a succession of temporary measures when permanent ones were needed.

(4) This book takes for granted that the choices of people and countries about acquiring skills are heavily constrained by forces over which they have no control—luck and history. Other economists, by contrast, see skill acquisition as simply a matter of individual choice. If the free choice view were correct, a decline in the relative demand for unskilled labour could not cause serious or enduring problems, and the policies suggested for the North in this book would be unnecessary and inefficient. But it would be a worse mistake to do nothing on the basis of an incorrect belief in the free choice view, thus hurting the poor both in the North and (through greater pressure for protection) in the South.

The policy suggestions of this book can thus be defended even in the face of uncertainty about some of its conclusions. The empirical evidence on all four of the points mentioned above is inadequate, but tends to support these conclusions. Moreover, the likely costs of wrongly rejecting these conclusions appear greater than the costs of wrongly accepting them.

2

Theoretical Framework

The argument of this book, summarised in the previous chapter, is largely empirical. Beneath the numbers, however, is a theory. The purpose of this chapter is to explain what the underlying theory is, and how it relates to other theories of trade, labour, and development.

2.1 A Skill-Based Model of North–South Trade

We begin with the shortest and simplest possible statement of the present theory. The rest of the chapter elaborates and qualifies this statement— relaxing some of its simplifying assumptions, but defending others.

2.1.1 Initial sketch

Consider a textbook Heckscher–Ohlin model, with two countries (North and South), two factors (skilled and unskilled labour), and two goods (skill-intensive and labour-intensive manufactures). The North is more abundantly endowed with skilled labour: it has a larger (inelastic) supply of skilled, relative to unskilled, workers than the South. Both sorts of workers are mobile between sectors within each country, but internationally immobile. The North thus has a comparative advantage in the production of the skill-intensive good, which needs a higher ratio of skilled to unskilled workers than the labour-intensive good. And vice versa for the South.

To begin with, barriers of various kinds prevent trade in manufactures between the North and the South. These barriers are then reduced, with familiar consequences. In the North, the output of skill-intensive goods for export expands, while production of labour-intensive import substitutes contracts. The domestic price of the labour-intensive good falls relative to that of the skill-intensive good. The opposite happens in the South, which starts to export labour-intensive manufactures and to produce fewer skill-intensive import substitutes. The domestic price of the skill-intensive good falls relative to that of the labour-intensive good.

Within each country, the gains from this expansion of trade accrue to the abundant factor, while the scarce factor becomes worse off. In the

South, expansion of labour-intensive production increases the demand for unskilled workers and hence raises their wages, while the demand for (and wages of) skilled workers fall. This decreases income inequality, because it reduces the wage differential between higher-paid skilled workers and lower-paid unskilled workers. In the North, conversely, skilled workers become better off and unskilled workers worse off, which increases income inequality. Unskilled workers may resist this widening of wage differentials: in so far as their resistance is successful, what emerges instead is a combination of excess demand for skilled workers and unemployment among unskilled workers.

2.1.2 Relative factor price convergence

This model is clearly rooted in 'old' trade theory. The insights of the 'new' theories of trade remain in the background, because their emphasis on the exchange of differentiated products in oligopolistic markets seems more relevant to North–North trade.[1] The North and South, by contrast, mainly exchange different *sorts* of product, in competitive international markets, with primary commodities and labour-intensive manufactures being traded for skill-intensive goods and services. Moreover, the economic basis for this exchange lies not in scale economies and history (which explain much of the pattern of North–North trade), but in fundamental differences between North and South in the comparative costs of producing these sorts of goods.

The present model clearly also stems from one particular version of 'old' trade theory—the Heckscher–Ohlin (H–O) version, in which differences in relative production costs are determined by differences in relative factor abundance.[2] However, not all the assumptions and deductions of H–O theory are relevant or helpful in the present context. To begin with, one of the four core H–O propositions, namely the factor price equalisation theorem, will be rejected, as it has been by others who have observed the enormous differences between the wages of similar types of workers in the North and the South (Krueger 1977; Bliss 1989: 1206; Leamer 1984: 11–12).

What is rejected here is the standard strong form of this theorem, in which trade equalises the absolute price of each factor across countries. Vital to the argument, however, is the weaker proposition originally advanced by Ohlin, who thought in terms of relative as well as absolute prices, and of tendencies toward (rather than strict) equalisation.[3] The

---

[1] See the surveys by Helpman (1984*a*, 1989) and Venables (1985).

[2] Jones and Neary (1984) provide a concise taxonomy of trade theories, and summarise the four core propositions of the H–O version. See also Evans (1989*b*).

[3] See Ohlin (1933, 1967: 24–8), whose position in this regard is made clear in the articles

impact of North–South trade, as described above, is to narrow the skilled–unskilled wage ratio in the South, and to widen it in the North. This outcome, which may be labelled 'relative factor price convergence', requires less restrictive assumptions. So long as a greater relative supply of skilled labour gives the North a comparative advantage in skill-intensive goods, and vice versa for the South, reduction of trade barriers will tend to have this effect.

Relative factor price convergence differs from absolute factor price equalisation in two respects. One is the absence of equalisation, since it would be possible for relative factor prices not merely to converge but to be strictly equalised.[4] The other is the difference between equalisation of relative and of absolute factor prices. The wages of most skilled as well as unskilled workers are absolutely lower in the South than in the North. So although trade tends to make the skilled–unskilled wage ratios in the North and South more similar, and to narrow the North–South gap in the absolute wages of unskilled workers, it tends to widen the absolute North–South gap in skilled wages. (The wages of the initially higher-paid skilled workers in the North rise, whereas those of the initially lower-paid skilled workers in the South fall.)[5]

It is important to understand why the tendencies recognised by Ohlin might exist and yet fail to cause strict absolute equalisation. One reason is *specialisation*. In H–O theory, if the variation of factor endowments among countries is large, relative to the variation of factor intensities among goods, some countries will produce some goods, other countries other goods, and factor prices will not be equalised by trade (e.g. Leamer 1984: 18–20).[6] Moreover, Krueger (1977; 1983, ch. 4) has pointed out that this theoretical possibility is of practical importance in the present context, namely North–South trade in manufactured goods.

She argues that countries on different rungs of the ladder of development tend to specialise in different sorts of manufactures. At any given time, each country produces the goods which lie within the narrow band

by Samuelson (1948, 1949) which first stated the theoretical conditions under which strict equalisation of absolute factor prices would occur. It is unfortunate that most subsequent attention has been paid to this strict case, whose seemingly unrealistic nature has tended to detract from Ohlin's important insight. A recent exception is Davis (1992: 18–22), whose argument is similar to that of the present section (originally put forward in Wood 1991*f*).

[4] This would occur if, within an otherwise strict set of H–O assumptions, the South's technology were assumed to be Hicks-neutrally inferior (rather than identical) to that of the North, as can be shown using the standard Lerner diagram (exploited for other purposes by Leamer 1984, ch. 1).

[5] Ohlin (1933, 1967: 31, 34) argued that trade would not necessarily make the scarce factor absolutely worse off, because of the economy-wide gains from trade. But on the assumptions that are now standard in H–O theory, the Stolper–Samuelson theorem suggests that Ohlin was too optimistic about the scarce factor's fate.

[6] Specialisation need not be complete: there can be small overlaps between the sets of goods produced in different countries. However, with only two factors, and no transport costs, no more than one good can be produced in common (Krueger 1977: 4–5, 16–19).

of factor intensities in which its current factor endowments give it a comparative advantage, while also consuming a wide range of other goods imported from countries at higher and lower levels of development. In the simple model presented in the previous subsection, reduction of barriers to trade would thus result in the North producing only skill-intensive goods, the South only labour-intensive goods. This division of labour would alter, but not equalise, the wages of skilled and unskilled workers in the two regions.

Specialisation, it should be noted, is not sufficient to explain all the observed facts about wages. For if skilled and unskilled labour were the only two factors of production, and the other standard assumptions of H–O theory applied, the absolute (as well as the relative) wages of skilled workers would be lower in the North than in the South, which is generally not the case.[7] Further modifications are thus needed to explain why *both* sorts of labour earn more in the North (see especially Section 2.4.4).

2.1.3 Transport costs

Another reason for the incompleteness of factor price equalisation is transport costs, which prevent the relative prices of goods from being equalised across countries. For most material goods, transport costs are now small, but some goods are too heavy or bulky to be worth shipping, and poor transport facilities in many developing countries severely limit the trading opportunities of large sections of their populations. In addition, transport costs remain prohibitively large for most services, which account for a large share of output and employment in all countries. Some services are traded, and these are important in North–South trade, but for simplicity, traded services will be included in the definition of 'manufactures'.

Although in reality goods and services lie along a continuum of transport costs, it is conventional to divide them into two categories—traded and nontraded. Nontraded goods can have a variety of effects in theoretical models, and need not prevent complete factor price equalisation (Jones and Neary 1984: 5–6; Leamer 1984: 23 and n. 11; Evans 1989*b*: 33–7, 101–6). For present purposes, nontraded goods must be subdivided into three groups: intermediate inputs; capital goods; and final consumption goods. As is appropriate in a H–O model, nontraded *intermediates* will be made to vanish, both theoretically and, where possible, statistically (Krueger 1983: 94; Deardorff 1984*a*: 479). In other words, the factor intensity of traded goods—and nontraded final outputs—will be defined to include the direct and indirect factor content of nontraded

---

[7] This point was impressed upon me by Alasdair Smith. See also e.g. Romer (1992: V.1).

intermediate inputs. Nontraded *capital goods* will be discussed later (in Section 2.2.2).

Nontraded (household or government) *consumption goods*, which in practice are mainly services, are important in the context of this book. There is no general reason why they should alter the direction of the impact of trade on skilled and unskilled wages, but they do affect its magnitude. In particular, the existence of large sectors producing non-traded consumer services tends to muffle the effects of trade on inequality. In the North, for example, continuing demand from the service sectors would make the economy-wide reduction in the demand for unskilled workers (and hence the decline in their wages) proportionately smaller than the trade-induced reduction in the demand for such workers in manufacturing.

2.1.4 Land

The initial model contained only two factors—skilled and unskilled labour—and made no mention of land and capital, inputs which feature prominently in most theoretical discussions of trade. Land (defined to include all natural resources) plays a major role in North–South trade. Primary and processed primary products still account for nearly half the South's total merchandise exports to the North (Table 1.1), and for many developing countries remain the sole source of foreign exchange earnings. Moreover, both casual observation and serious research (e.g. Leamer 1984) suggest that trade in primary products is shaped by differences in natural resource endowments, in accordance with the general principles of H–O theory.

However, land is of much less concern in the narrower context of this book. For the book is about *changes* in North–South trade, and the main change has been in manufactures, not in primary products. Of course, all manufactures contain some primary products (and what are called here 'processed primary' products are classified as manufactures in production and employment data). Possession of a particular natural resource may therefore give a country a comparative advantage in manufactured goods embodying the primary product concerned. But this is not necessarily or generally the case, even for processed primary products, since most raw materials are internationally traded with low transport costs (Krueger *et al.* 1981: 15; Jones and Neary 1984: 31–2). Only where bulk or perishability are serious problems is the location of manufacturing governed by that of the natural resource.

Another reason why land plays only a small part in this book is that the economic difference between the South and the North is not fundamentally a matter of natural resource availability. On average, the South probably has *fewer* natural resources per person than the North, and most of the developing countries which depend heavily on primary exports do so not because they have absolutely abundant natural resources, but because they have few other resources. In some respects, then, the most illuminating way to introduce land into the simple model sketched above would be not as a third factor, but as a third country, which supplied primary intermediate inputs to the manufacturing sectors of both the North and the South.

This formulation would be misleading for some purposes, because natural resources can affect comparative advantage in manufacturing (in general, not only in resource-processing activities). Countries with more natural resources tend to export *fewer* manufactures, since they can produce (and export) primary commodities relatively more cheaply than other countries.[8] However, natural resource abundance need not affect a country's comparative advantage *within* manufacturing. This is clear from the model in Section 2.1.1 above. Whether a country exports skill-intensive or labour-intensive manufactures depends simply on the ratio of skilled to unskilled workers in its labour force, regardless of the extent of its natural resources. (This point is considered further at the end of Section 2.2.4.)

2.2 Capital

The omission of (physical) capital from the initial model in Section 2.1.1 may seem even more curious than the omission of land. Not only is capital one of the two factors in most textbook presentations of H–O theory, but it is also usually seen as one of the fundamental bases of North–South trade in manufactures. The North is said to be well endowed with capital and thus an exporter of capital-intensive manufactures to the South, which, because it is poorly endowed with capital, has a comparative advantage in labour-intensive (meaning non-capital-intensive) production.

But this capital-based view of North–South trade is misleading. Machines and financial capital are internationally mobile, most buildings can be put up anywhere in a year or two, and rates of interest and profit are much the same in the South as in the North. In these circumstances, theory tells us (as does common sense) that capital cannot be a basic source of comparative advantage, though the capital-based view of North–South trade contains one important element of truth, which concerns infrastructure. There is thus actually little reason to bring capital into the present model.

[8] This proposition is well supported by empirical evidence, both for developing countries (Syrquin 1988, sects. 4.4, 5.2) and for developed countries (Rowthorn and Wells 1987, ch. 3).

Readers who are persuaded on this point, which is not controversial in a theoretical sense—although its empirical assumptions might be disputed—should probably skip on to Section 2.3 (page 41). Other readers, whether strongly disagreeing or merely doubtful, are invited to join a brief tour of the caves of capital theory, which will explain in greater detail why capital is omitted from the model.

2.2.1 Nature of capital

Implicit in the capital-based view of North–South trade is a simplified treatment of capital, which is common to most expositions and applications of the H–O version of 'old' trade theory. The simplification is to regard capital as an exogenously given aggregate, analogous to land, of which some countries have relatively larger endowments than others, giving them a comparative advantage in relatively capital-intensive products. This approach has been subjected to two quite different sorts of criticism.

The first criticism is that capital goods are *reproducible*.[9] Given some time, machines and buildings can be multiplied without physical limit, and are thus not at all like land. On the contrary, it is more helpful to think of capital goods as a special class of intermediate goods: made to be used up in production, albeit over a longer period than other intermediate goods. It is also helpful to think of both intermediate goods and capital goods as forms of *indirect labour*: work done at earlier stages of the process of production, as contrasted with the direct labour of current production.

This way of thinking is helpful because it reminds one constantly that capital goods are not an independent primary factor of production, but a reflection of the phasing or time-pattern of the input of labour. It also helps in explaining how the prices of capital goods are determined, and hence makes it easier to interpret value aggregates of capital, which in practice are usually based on the purchase prices of the capital goods concerned. In particular, this view of capital goods makes it clear that their prices must depend on the cost of producing them, which in turn must depend largely on the amount of labour (directly and indirectly) used in their creation, and on the wages of the labour concerned.

Of course, the cost of a capital good also includes an element of profit or interest on the part of the labour that was contributed in earlier periods, as well as some rent on natural resource inputs. But the bulk of the cost of most capital goods consists of (direct and indirect) wages. This wage element can be decomposed into (*a*) the number of hours of labour

---

[9] This is put forcefully by neo-Ricardian theorists (Steedman 1979*a*, *b*; Pasinetti 1981; Metcalfe and Steedman 1981), but is also recognised in rigorous expositions of H–O theory (e.g. Smith 1984; Evans 1989*b*).

involved and (*b*) the average hourly wage. The latter clearly depends on the ratio of skilled to unskilled labour used in producing particular capital goods. It also depends on *where* these goods were produced. So if wages are lower in the South than in the North, the price of a capital good will tend to be lower if it is produced in the South than if it is produced in the North.

The second criticism of the 'given-endowment-of-capital' version of H–O theory is that many capital goods are internationally *tradeable*. Capital goods can be divided into two categories, traded and nontraded. These will be referred to as 'machines' and 'buildings' respectively, although in reality some machines are too bulky to transport, and some buildings are erected by internationally mobile construction firms. There are of course transport costs on machines, and tariffs and other artificial barriers to trading them. But in theory, if machines are traded, it is natural to assume that their prices will be similar in all countries.[10] It is also an empirical fact that the average price of machines is much the same in poor countries as in rich countries (Kravis *et al.* 1982, table 6.8).

Moreover, if machines are traded, it is reasonable to suppose that any country can buy any machine, in unlimited amounts, provided it is able and willing to pay the going price. (Some exceptions will be discussed below.) If this is so, then possession of particular types or amounts of machinery cannot give a country an enduring comparative advantage in the production of particular goods, any more than a comparative advantage in cotton spinning can be obtained simply by purchasing a lot of ginned cotton on the international market. Thus whether machines are labelled a 'middle good' or a 'footloose factor', all theorists would agree that this type of input cannot in itself affect the pattern of trade (Jones 1980; Leamer 1984: 22–3; Jones and Neary 1984, sect. 3.1).

2.2.2 Nontraded capital goods

This logic does not apply to buildings. They cannot be moved around the world, nor are their prices similar in the North and the South. As theory predicts, most buildings are much cheaper in poor countries (Kravis *et al.* 1982, table 6.8.) However, the existence of buildings need not damage the conclusion that possession of capital goods cannot in itself constitute an enduring source of comparative advantage. This is because even non-traded capital goods are reproducible. It takes only a year or two to

---

[10] This similarity is not logically inconsistent with the proposition in the previous paragraph that the price of capital goods depends on where they are produced, since most machines will tend to be produced either in the North or in the South, but not in both regions. This is an example of the tendency mentioned earlier for the North and the South to specialise in different sorts of manufactured goods.

build a factory, construction materials are usually either available locally or importable, and there are plenty of construction workers. So the mere presence or absence of factories is not, either in theory or in reality, a basic determinant of comparative advantage in manufacturing.

What may be important is the differing skill content of different sorts of buildings. Some products can be made in factories that are no more than sheds to keep the machines and the workers dry. Other products require sophisticated structures whose construction involves a high proportion of skilled workers—architects, engineers, technicians, and craftsmen. In the North, where skilled labour is cheaper relative to unskilled labour, the price of skill-intensive buildings is lower, relative to low-skill-content buildings, than in the South. The North thus has a comparative advantage in goods whose production requires more skill-intensive buildings, and vice versa for the South.[11] This point, however, can easily be accommodated in the two-factor model sketched in Section 2.1.1, by defining the skill-intensity of goods to include the skill content of the nontraded capital goods used in their production, this being the convention adopted in Section 2.1.3 with respect to nontraded intermediate inputs.

By equating buildings with factories, the discussion so far has avoided the important issue of infrastructure. So let us now divide 'buildings' into two distinct sub-categories. 'Factories' are individual buildings, often tailored to the production of specific goods, which can be constructed in a fairly short time. 'Infrastructure' (transportation, communications, and electricity generation and distribution facilities) takes much longer to construct, partly because it usually involves a network, whose components are of limited use until the system is complete. Infrastructure is also usually not product-specific (for example, the production of most goods requires electricity and transport).

In all countries, infrastructure is a large share of the capital stock (typically about two-fifths of fixed assets other than housing; Syrquin 1988, fig. 7.2). Moreover, one of the most obvious economic differences between developed and developing countries, on average, is the extent and quality of their infrastructure. One may argue about the extent to which improvement of infrastructure in the course of development is an autonomous cause of, rather than a response to demands arising from, other aspects of economic growth. But it would be hard to deny that the large and enduring gap in the availability of infrastructure constitutes a basic element of truth in the simple H–O proposition that the North is relatively well-endowed with capital, and the South poorly endowed.

---

[11] It should be recalled that 'building' is defined here to mean a nontraded capital good. It is sometimes economically worthwhile to use international construction firms to erect skill-intensive factories in developing countries, but such factories are in effect traded capital goods and hence defined here as 'machines'.

This difference in infrastructure helps to explain why wages (skilled and unskilled) are lower in the South. It also gives the North a comparative advantage, and the South a comparative disadvantage, in infrastructure-intensive traded goods and services, i.e. those whose production requires, for example, a reliable supply of electricity or a sophisticated domestic telecommunications network. A detailed empirical explanation of the commodity composition of North–South trade should thus take account of differences in the availability of infrastructure (Clague 1991). In the present context, however, it seems unlikely that the gain in accuracy from incorporating infrastructure explicitly into the skill-based model of Section 2.1.1 would be worth the loss of expository simplicity.[12]

2.2.3 Scarcity and profitability

The simple H–O proposition about the effects of differing endowments of capital on comparative advantage assumes not only that the South has a smaller endowment, but also that this causes capital to be scarcer and hence more expensive. This is true of infrastructure, whose shadow price, relative to that of labour, is higher than in the North. However, the usual assumption that greater scarcity of capital causes the interest rate—and the profit rate on machines, factories, and inventories—to be higher in the South than in the North is apparently incorrect.

It is important to emphasise that if this assumption *were* correct, the essence of the simple H–O view that the North has a comparative advantage in relatively capital-intensive goods would survive both the criticisms noted in Section 2.2.1 concerning the reproducibility and tradability of capital goods. In other words, this simple statement about comparative advantage could in principle be reformulated in a more sophisticated and defensible way. There is no theoretical dispute on this point: if the profit or interest rate were higher in the South, other things being equal, the autarky relative price of capital-intensive goods would also be higher, and hence the South would have a comparative advantage in non-capital-intensive goods (e.g. Smith 1984; Evans 1989*b*, ch. 6).

What *is* disputed is the view that a country's rate of interest (or profit) is governed by the size or scarcity of some exogenously given aggregate of capital. This view is rejected by most theorists, even neoclassical ones, who prefer, following Irving Fisher, to explain the interest rate as the outcome of intertemporal optimisation decisions, and view the profit rate as simply the interest rate plus a risk premium. Empirically, too, the

[12] In the North, the reduction of trade barriers should in theory have increased the price of infrastructure and tended to reduce that of labour (skilled and unskilled), and vice versa in the South. However, in practice most infrastructure does not have a market-determined price.

proposition that the South has scarce capital and high profit rates, by comparison with the North, appears false. The most striking feature of interest and profit rates in the North and the South is their *similarity*, which is documented in Section 3.2.3, and has been acknowledged by economists of widely differing theoretical persuasions (Pasinetti 1981: 195; Bliss 1989: 1206).

It thus seems realistic, as well as analytically convenient, to proceed on the assumption that rates of interest (or profit) are the same, on average, in the South as in the North.[13] However, it is also necessary to provide some theoretical explanation of what determines these rates, and why they are similar in the two regions. In particular, it is important to argue that these rates are *exogenous*. The minimum requirement in this regard is that they should not be passively determined by the changes in trade with which the present discussion is concerned, as would be the case, say, if their similarity were due to the factor price equalising effects of trade. It is convenient, though, to go further, by assuming that these rates are *strictly* exogenous—not to any substantial extent affected by North–South trade—since this avoids the complications of simultaneous causation.

The most persuasive justification for assuming equal and exogenous profit or interest rates is international mobility of financial (debt and equity) capital. There have long been flows of this kind, but in the past few decades they have become much larger, with the lowering of many sorts of barriers to international financial transactions. There is now a global capital market, into which the countries of the North and many (though not all) countries in the South are integrated. The actual extent of capital mobility continues to be debated (e.g. Sinn 1992), but most people would agree that it is now sufficient to impose a tight limit on differences in national interest rates.

Although international mobility of financial capital provides sufficient justification for the assumptions made here, there are some other possible theoretical reasons for similar interest or profit rates. These reasons could explain why the similarity apparently existed prior to the creation of a global capital market, and why it exists even in countries which are not well integrated into that market. Neoclassical economists might argue that rates of time preference are similar world-wide. Neo-Keynesians might emphasise that rates of growth do not differ much, on average, between the North and the South (Kaldor 1956, 1966; Wood 1975). These two approaches might even be reconciled by arguing that rates of growth depend on rates of time preference.

---

[13] Interest and profit rates do vary among individual countries within these regions, e.g. because of differences in risk and taxation. Moreover, sustained variations of this sort should affect the commodity composition of trade, e.g. a country which subsidised interest rates would tend to export more capital-intensive goods.

2.2.4 Comparative advantage and capital intensity

In combination, the seemingly realistic assumptions that finance and machines are internationally mobile, and buildings reproducible, destroy the logic of the usual presumption that the North has a comparative cost advantage, and the South a comparative disadvantage, in the production of capital-intensive goods. This is why capital was left out of the initial simple H–O model in Section 2.1.1.

Readers who are satisfied with the preceding explanation may now wish to move on to Section 2.3. For those who still find the omission of capital odd, it may be worth trying another theoretical tack, asking how so many economists have arrived at the contrary view—that North–South trade is based on differences in the scarcity of capital—and explaining why this view cannot be correct if the interest rate and the price of machines are similar in the North and in the South. The premiss of the argument which follows, in other words, is that there is no North–South difference in the 'rental' of internationally traded capital goods (the price of such goods times the profit rate, gross of depreciation).

This premiss is accepted by most of the economists who argue that North–South trade is based on differences in the availability of capital. But these economists point out (correctly) that wages, and hence *wage–rental ratios*, are much lower in the South than in the North. They then infer from this that the South has a comparative advantage in activities which use a relatively low ratio of capital to labour. This last step in the argument is wrong, but seductive, since it appears to follow the logic of cost minimisation, as in the textbook diagram with capital and labour on the axes, a wage-rental line tangential to the convex unit isoquant, and another wage-rental line showing that a relatively more labour-intensive technique will be chosen if labour is relatively cheaper.

In the present context, however, this textbook diagram is irrelevant, because it is addressing a different issue.[14] International comparative advantage arises, in the simplest possible case, from differences in the

---

[14] This diagram has also been attacked by neo-Ricardian economists, but their usual criticisms do not apply under the present set of assumptions. The main criticism, which in other contexts is of fundamental importance, is that the price (and so the rental) of capital goods is not independent of the wage rate. Thus, at a given rate of profit, a lower wage tends to cause an equiproportionate lowering of the price of capital goods, leaving the wage–rental ratio and the choice of technique unaltered (Pasinetti 1981: 194–7). However, it is assumed here that machines, which account for about half the capital stock, are internationally traded: their prices must thus be the same in all countries, regardless of local wage rates, and so wage–rental ratios must vary among countries according to their wage levels, though not in direct proportion, since the other half of the capital stock is nontraded and hence cheaper in low-wage countries. Moreover, since the rate of profit is assumed here to be the same in both regions, there need be no concern about reswitching—the point that at a lower rate of profit there is no general reason to suppose that a more (rather than a less) capital-intensive technique will be chosen (Pasinetti 1981: 193).

autarky *relative prices of two different goods* in two countries. The cost-minimisation diagram, by contrast, shows how the *choice of technique for a single good* would differ between two countries with different relative factor prices. The diagram does not include a second good, and so cannot say anything about the effect of different factor prices on the relative prices of different goods. Nor, indeed, can its multi-product multi-factor algebraic equivalent, namely that marginal rates of substitution between factors are equated with relative factor prices. This tells us that in a country with a lower wage-rental ratio and identical technology, *all* goods will be produced by more labour-intensive techniques, but not *which* goods are relatively cheaper and hence (if there is trade) exported.

There is thus no inconsistency between the standard analysis of cost-minimising choices of technique and the standard trade theory result that comparative advantage cannot be conferred by a factor such as machines whose cost is the same in all countries. Take ginned cotton as another example of such a factor. Relative to labour, this internationally traded input is more expensive in low-wage countries. In a Southern textile mill, by comparison with a Northern textile mill, one would therefore expect to find more workers engaged in recovering and recycling waste cotton. But this in itself would not tell one whether textile mills were lower-cost, relative to (say) steel mills, in the South or in the North.

Now for a more formal answer to the question of why higher wages do not confer a comparative advantage in capital-intensive manufacturing. This question cannot even be posed in the usual framework of a model with two inputs (reproducible capital goods and homogeneous labour) and identical technology. For in such a framework, with equal rates of profit in the North and the South, the wage rates in the two regions would also have to be equal. To explain the lower wage in the South, while keeping the H–O assumption of identical technology, another factor must be added, of which the South has a smaller fixed endowment (Bliss 1989: 1206). The obvious candidate here is skilled labour. However, to retain the simplicity of a single wage rate in each country, and to pursue the discussion of Section 2.1.4 about the effect of natural resources on comparative advantage in manufacturing, the third factor may be taken initially to be land.

This land is assumed to produce a costlessly transportable intermediate input to two manufacturing sectors, one of which is more capital-intensive than the other (and one of which produces the capital goods for both of them). Because the primary intermediate input is available at the same price in both countries, it cannot cause the relative prices of the two manufactured goods to differ between the two countries. So the North's more abundant land confers no comparative advantage in processing this input, but makes the Northern wage higher than in the South. Does this higher wage give the North a comparative advantage, within manufacturing, in the capital-intensive good? If so, the relative price of the capital-intensive good would have to be lower in the North in a situation of manufacturing autarky (with trade only in the intermediate). This last proposition can be disproved, on the standard assumptions of neoclassical non-substitution theorems (Johnson 1968: 27; Salvadori 1987), which are made also by neo-Ricardian theorists (Pasinetti 1981: 194–7).

The economic logic of the disproof may be conveyed intuitively by thinking of capital as indirect labour. Production of the capital-intensive manufacture thus requires a higher ratio of indirect labour (L_I) to direct labour (L_D) than the other manufacture. With given technology, the least-cost choice of technique for each good (reflected in L_D/L_I) depends on the rate of profit, which governs the relative cost of L_D and L_I, the former being simply the wage, the latter the wage plus a profit mark-up (because the indirect labour was contributed earlier). Since technology and the rate of profit are by assumption the same in the two regions, the same technique (the same L_D and L_I) is chosen for each of the goods in both regions, and the proportional profit mark-up on the wage of L_I is the same in both regions. The higher wage in the North makes the cost of L_D greater than in the South, but also the cost of L_I, and by the same proportion. So although both manufactures cost more in the North, the relative price of the two goods is the same as in the South. The North's higher wage does not give it a comparative advantage in the capital-intensive good.

The same logic can clearly be applied within the South to show (following up the argument in Section 2.1.4) that developing countries with abundant natural resources, though they are likely to export fewer manufactures in total, do not necessarily export more capital-intensive manufactures than developing countries with few natural resources.[15] And in the context of North–South trade, the same conclusion can also clearly be obtained with other assumptions (than less land) about what causes wages to be lower in the South. The 'third factor' could be infrastructure. Or 'labour' could be redefined as unskilled labour, with skilled labour as the third factor, although the analysis becomes more complicated unless it is assumed that the two manufactures are equally skill-intensive.

---

[15] Contrary to the suggestion of Krueger (1977: 15). See also Deardorff (1984b: 736) and Leamer (1987: 983–4). Krueger further argues (1977: 12–13) that land-rich countries use more capital-intensive techniques in manufacturing. In a closed economy, on standard (non-substitution-theorem or neo-Ricardian) assumptions, this too would be incorrect. Given the profit rate, the ratio of direct to indirect labour (or the *capital–output* ratio) is independent of the real wage. The *capital–labour* ratio would be higher in a more land-abundant economy, but this would simply be because the same set of physical capital goods was higher priced because of the higher wage (Pasinetti 1981: 180–97). When machines and other goods are traded, however, Krueger's proposition about the dependence of the choice of technique on land availability contains an important element of truth: if two countries produce the same good, the country with the higher real wage will use a more capital-intensive technique for producing that good, even at the same profit rate.

2.3 Knowledge, Skill, and Technology

In summary, Sections 2.1.4 and 2.2 have sought to justify the omission of land and capital from the skilled-unskilled labour model of North–South trade in manufactures, at least as a first approximation to reality. Raw materials and machines are internationally traded with low transport costs, buildings are reproducible, and financial flows tend to equalise interest and profit rates. Apart from infrastructure, labour is thus the only internationally immobile factor of production (some exceptions to this immobility are discussed in Section 2.4.4). But labour is not homogeneous: there are, rather, two distinct immobile factors—skilled and unskilled workers. The North–South difference in the relative supply of these two factors provides the main basis for trade in manufactures.

Many economists have emphasised the importance of skills and human capital in international trade (e.g. Ohlin 1933; Johnson 1968; and Leamer 1984; see the survey in Deardorff 1984*a*: 482–90, 496–7). This idea has also featured in many studies more specifically of North–South trade in manufactures, for example, Lary (1968), Balassa (1979*a*, 1986*b*), Krueger (1983), Schumacher (1983, 1989*a*), and Evans (1989*b*). The argument of this book, which is that North–South trade in manufactures is based *solely* on skill differences, is more unusual, but essentially the same proposition can be found in Keesing (1965, 1966), Findlay and Kierzkowski (1983), and Minford (1989).

2.3.1 Heckscher–Ohlin assumptions

The theoretical discussion above has been conducted on fairly standard H–O assumptions. Some supplementary assumptions have been made, about trade in intermediate and capital goods, and about profit rates. The treatment of capital is unconventional, but not incompatible with H–O theory (Smith 1984; Leamer 1984: 41–4). The only significant divergence from standard H-O assumptions so far has been to invoke specialisation, transport costs, and differing infrastructure to explain the absence of strict factor price equalisation, i.e. North–South differences in skill-specific wage rates.

Since the standard assumptions of H–O trade theory are widely regarded as 'incredible' (Leamer 1984: 45), the consistency of the preceding argument with them will probably be interpreted by some readers as a vice rather than a virtue. The use of these assumptions thus needs to be defended. The most important part of the defence is the empirical evidence in later chapters, but a number of basic points can be made at once. The initial restriction to two goods, two factors, and two countries can be relaxed without much alteration of economic content (Ethier 1984). Nor is the usual strong assumption of identical homothetic preferences needed when factor prices are not equalised (Helpman 1984*b*).

The economic content of an H–O model is more dependent on the absence of factor intensity reversal, which in the present context requires different manufactured goods to be unambiguously rankable by the skill-intensity of their production processes. Otherwise, the alternative methods available for producing a particular good might be such that at one skilled–unskilled wage ratio a relatively (to other goods) skill-intensive technique would be chosen, while at another wage ratio the best technique would be relatively labour-intensive. This could upset the neat and tidy H–O vision of skill-intensive countries exporting skill-intensive goods. However, instances of this kind seem to be rare, at least within manufacturing (Section 3.5.1).

Constant returns to scale is another assumption of H–O theory that is not generally accurate. Scale economies explain why small countries produce a narrower range of traded goods (and hence tend to be more open), and why only large countries can produce certain goods competitively. Increasing returns to scale also underpin the 'new' theories of trade, and are the main basis of most North–North trade. For present purposes, however, the constant returns assumption is probably not too misleading (Minford 1989: 198; Clague 1991: 372–3). Only for a few products do scale economies explain the North–South division of labour in manufacturing.

The most contentious H–O assumption in the present context is that the North and the South have identical technology. This refers only to the availability of possible production techniques, not to the particular techniques in use (which may differ because of differences in relative factor prices). But even the premiss that developed and developing countries have *access* to the same technology would be regarded by many people as empirically absurd, if not logically self-contradictory. There are models of development which revolve around 'technology gaps' (starting with Gershenkron 1966), and entire theories of trade based on international differences in technology (surveyed by Jones and Neary 1984; Evans 1989*b*; Dosi, Pavitt, and Soete 1990).

Yet if it is carefully articulated, the assumption of identical technology can be defended as a reasonable simplification in the present context, and as compatible with some apparently conflicting points of view. The first step is to define some terms more precisely. This is important because the word 'technology' has been used by different economists to mean different things, resulting in confusion and unnecessary disagreement. No monopoly of correctness is claimed for the definitions below, but they accord quite well with common usage.

2.3.2 Direct and indirect skill

The highest-level concept, KNOWLEDGE, is defined to include all sorts of economically relevant information—scientific, technical, commercial, and organisational.[16] But knowledge contributes to production only in so far as it is embodied either in people or in material objects—intermediate and capital goods. Knowledge embodied in people is defined here as SKILL, while knowledge embodied in material means of production is the present definition of TECHNOLOGY. (The word 'technique', however, will still be used to refer to a particular combination of productive inputs.)

Knowledge is embodied in material objects through the prior application of skill. So technology can also be thought of as *indirect skill*, in contrast to the skill directly applied by people in production. (This distinction corresponds precisely to that between direct and indirect *labour* mentioned earlier.) The idea of knowledge embodied in capital goods is familiar from 'vintage' growth models (Hahn and Matthews 1965, sect. II.3). But the technical quality of intermediate goods is also vital, as anyone who has worked on an industrial project in a developing country can attest.

This definition of technology gives a particular meaning to the assumption that the North and the South have access to the same technology. It also makes this assumption essentially equivalent to one that has already been made above, namely that most machines and intermediate goods are freely traded internationally. There are exceptions: some goods are kept for the exclusive use of their patent-holders, or their use by others restricted by the terms of licensing agreements, or their sale to particular countries legally prohibited. But these conditions apply to only a tiny proportion of all producer goods. Many other goods are *expensive* because of patents, licensing fees, and royalty payments, but this does not matter. Equal access to technology requires only that producer goods be available at the *same* ex-factory price to any firm in any country which can pay for them. There are many producer goods which firms in developing countries want but cannot get, but the obstacle is usually that they cannot afford them.

The present definition of technology, it should be emphasised, would be grossly misleading without the present definition of skill, or if it were used in a model which treated labour as homogeneous and unskilled. When people say that the South is 'technologically backward', they are

---

[16] It is not necessary to specify here how knowledge is generated, but Kaldor (1957), Arrow (1962), and Scott (1989) have argued persuasively that the creation of new economically relevant information is not autonomous, but involves an endless cycle of learning-by-doing and doing-from-learning, whose pace and direction are partly shaped by economic pressures.

talking about something real and important, but what they mainly mean, in terms of our definitions, is that the South has a *less-skilled labour force*. They may also mean that the producer goods used in the South on average embody less indirect skill. This is correct, but the underlying reason is again usually the scarcity of skilled labour. For the capacity to make economic use of technology frequently depends on the availability of workers with complementary skills.

This last proposition about complementarity between skill and technology (or between directly and indirectly applied skill) is widely acknowledged, and illustrated by examples such as the uselessness of a computer to an illiterate peasant. But it is vital to recognise that this proposition is not always true. In some activities, relatively unskilled workers use equipment or materials embodying a high level of indirect skill—primary school graduates assembling circuit boards in factories, or using new seed varieties or solar pumps on their farms. Conversely, some highly skilled workers work with tools embodying little indirect skill—cabinet-makers with hammers, or professors with pieces of chalk. To put it another way, all production activities could in principle be fitted into a matrix with direct skill on one axis and technology (or indirect skill) on the other axis. Most activities lie on or close to the main diagonal, but others are scattered all over the matrix, often far away from the diagonal.

So the South's comparative advantage, which derives from its relatively low ratio of skilled to unskilled workers, can now be more precisely identified as lying in activities with relatively low *direct* skill requirements. Some such activities also have low indirect skill requirements; hence the South also has a comparative advantage in producing most of the intermediate and capital goods needed. Other low-direct-skill activities have high indirect skill requirements: thus most of their intermediate or capital goods are produced in (and imported from) the North. But in so far as producer goods are freely traded, the indirect skill requirements of a particular activity do not affect whether the South or the North has a comparative advantage in that activity. In this sense, technology is neutral, as in H–O theory.

As discussed earlier, some producer goods are nontraded. Technologically inferior factories put the South at a comparative disadvantage in some activities, as does the low quality or unavailability of some intermediate services. But in all such cases the disadvantage stems fundamentally from a shortage of skilled labour. So it is realistic as well as analytically convenient to maintain the convention introduced above of defining the skill intensity of an activity to encompass both its direct and its nontraded indirect labour inputs. The word 'direct' in the two previous paragraphs therefore needs to be interpreted in this special sense.

2.3.3 Ricardian theory reinterpreted

To assume that technology is neutral may seem greatly at variance with the Ricardian view that trade is based on uneven international differences in technology. In this view, a country has a comparative advantage in activities whose technology, by local standards, is relatively advanced, though perhaps inferior to that of the trading partner, and a comparative disadvantage in activities which are relatively backward. This is because the unevenness of the differences makes the products of the more advanced activities relatively cheaper than in the trading partner. However, the present version of neutrality and the Ricardian view are not necessarily contradictory, since the meaning and causes of international differences in technology are not precisely specified in most Ricardian models (Johnson 1968: 8), and since most such models treat labour as homogeneous.

Trade which appeared in a Ricardian framework to be based on uneven international differences in labour productivity among sectors might thus arise not from differences in technology as defined here, but from the combination of (*a*) differences among sectors in skill intensity and (*b*) differences among countries in the relative availability of skilled and unskilled labour. In other words, the higher relative productivity of labour in certain sectors in a particular country might be due to these sectors being more skill-intensive and the country concerned having a relatively large skilled-labour supply, or vice versa. Minford (1989: 197) notes the Ricardian affinities of the present type of model. This interpretation of neo-Ricardian theory is also consistent with the strong emphasis which Pasinetti (1981) places on the economic contribution of human knowledge, skills, and learning.

Even with the present definition of technology, the assumption that all activities in all countries have equal access to technology should not be pushed too far. Exclusive or restrictive patents do confer a comparative advantage on the countries which hold them. Even in the absence of such restrictions, new types of producer goods take time to diffuse around the world. And there are illuminating models of trade based on diffusion lags—product cycle and North–South technology transfer theories (Posner 1961; Vernon 1966; Findlay 1978; Krugman 1979; Grossman and Helpman 1991; see also Johnson 1968; Deardorff 1984*a*; Jones and Neary 1984; and Dicken 1986). However, there are three reasons for abstracting from diffusion lags here. One is that the object is not to explain the detailed commodity composition of trade. The second is that our focus is on changes over decades rather than years.

The third reason is that the pace and pattern of technological diffusion are not exogenous, but dependent on skill availability. Consider, for example, the basic hypothesis of product cycle and technology transfer theories, which is that as goods mature, and production methods become standardised, so their production is relocated from North to South. The evidence is consistent with this hypothesis: the South's manufactured exports do consist mainly of items with standard or mature production methods.[17] But the hypothesis is closely related to the present argument that the South's comparative advantage lies in goods whose production is not skill-intensive. For the essence of a standard or mature technology is that it can be operated by a labour force containing a relatively small proportion of engineers and other highly trained workers.

It would be grossly wrong, of course, to argue that *all* cases in which people or firms in the South use producer goods embodying less indirect skill than in the same activities in the North can be explained simply by the unavailability or high relative price of complementary direct skills in the Southern labour force (or because a lower-quality and cheaper output is preferred by poorer consumers: Stewart 1978). On the contrary, alas, there are many cases in which Southern producers who could put modern means of production to good economic use are denied access to them, by artificial barriers to foreign trade, by discriminatory rationing of foreign exchange or credit, by lack of electricity, or by high internal transport costs.

Obstacles of this sort are most common in certain sectors (notably peasant agriculture), in places with poor infrastructure, and in countries which have artificially closed themselves to foreign trade. These obstacles help to explain why average incomes in the South are low, and they undoubtedly affect the extent and pattern of North–South trade. But at a theoretical level, these obstacles can conveniently and reasonably be reconciled with the identical-technology assumption by classifying them all as barriers to trade. It is also notable that obstacles of this kind have been of least importance in the manufacturing sectors of those developing countries whose exports have transformed the pattern of North–South trade over the past few decades—the phenomenon with which this book is primarily concerned.

In summary, the standard H–O assumption that technology (or the production function) is identical in all countries cannot be literally true. There are many possible reasons for differences, and for some purposes it would be extremely misleading to assume these differences away. In the present context, however, provided that technology is appropriately defined, this H–O assumption appears to be a reasonable theoretical simplification, and the evidence in Chapters 3 and 4 gives it strong support. Whatever may be the differences in production functions between

[17] See e.g. Fröbel *et al.* (1980: 35–6, 328) and Ballance, Ansari, and Singer (1982: 150–2).

North and South, they do not appear to overwhelm the effects of different factor endowments on the pattern of trade.

2.4 Skill Further Considered

Thus far, it has implicitly been assumed that 'skill' is a unidimensional and measurable characteristic, of which some workers possess more than others, and of which some activities require more than others. This is a tremendous simplification. There are innumerable different types and gradations of skill. Even in principle, there is no ideal way of reducing them all to a common denominator. Moreover, any division of the labour force into a few skill categories is bound to be rather arbitrary. This section outlines the approach to these problems taken in this book. Later chapters address various statistical difficulties in more detail.

2.4.1 Common denominators of skill

There are two contending common denominators of skill: (*a*) the wage levels of the workers concerned; and (*b*) the amounts of education, training, and experience they possess, which are to some extent reflected in occupational categories. The two measures are often correlated, but they can also diverge widely. Each measure also has its own strengths and weaknesses, which makes it desirable in practice to use both of them.

The wage level is the cleaner of the two. In a competitive labour market, differences in wage levels among workers could provide an economically meaningful index of all types, amounts, and qualities of skill, regardless of how these skills were acquired. The correspondence between specific physically defined skills and the wages of workers with these skills would not in general remain constant over time, since the pattern of supply and demand for particular skills changes continually. But this is as much a strength as a weakness, because it keeps the skill index up to date.

However, the wage common denominator has three limitations. One is that even in a perfectly competitive labour market, not all wage differences would reflect differences in skill. For example, average hourly earnings vary among industries and activities because of differences in the non-pecuniary attractiveness or unattractiveness of the work involved (Rosen 1986). Wages also vary among individual workers because of differences in diligence and effort. The second limitation is that wages are not always determined by competitive pressure (see Section 2.5.1).

The third limitation is that the wage common denominator requires labour mobility. Even within a country, there are impediments to the movement of workers from one industry or locality to another, which cause differences in wages to exist among workers with identical skills (Taubman and Wachter 1986). Between countries, the impediments to mobility are far greater, and have been assumed so far in this chapter to be absolutely prohibitive. The wages earned by workers with specific skills may thus vary widely from one country to another, for many reasons, including differences in the supply of complementary and competitive skills, in the composition of the demand for labour, and in natural resources and infrastructure. International trade tends to shrink such wage differences. But it would be risky, for example, to base a North–South comparison of skill levels on wage rates.

The amount of training, the other common denominator of skill, is usually measured as the *length of time* needed to acquire the skills concerned, i.e. the number of years of schooling, formal training, and experience (often gauged by the worker's age). The amount of training can also be measured by the *cost* of skill acquisition (cash outlays and forgone earnings), for which the length of time involved is a rough proxy. Choice and competition tend to cause the differing costs of acquiring specific skills to be compensated by variations in wages. And within countries the two common denominators of skill (wages and length of training) are strongly correlated. But in international comparisons of skill levels, the length-of-training index is more likely to diverge from—and is more reliable than—the wage index.

The limitations of the length-of-training index are fairly clear. Above all, the extent and economic usefulness of the skills acquired in a given number of years of training can vary enormously, depending on the ability of the trainee, the quality of the instruction, the subjects studied, and the fields in which experience is acquired. Within countries, there is wide variation of earnings within education and age groups, much of which reflects differences in skill levels. There are also major differences between countries, and especially between the North and the South, in the quality both of educational facilities and of opportunities for learning outside school, which mean that even the length-of-training index has to be used very cautiously for international comparisons of skill.

2.4.2 Skill categories

Although skill can be conceptualised and applied as a continuous variable, it is often convenient to divide the labour force into a small number of distinct skill categories. To understand North–South trade and labour markets, a minimum of three skill categories appears to be essential.

The first category contains workers with no (or virtually no) schooling, called *NO-EDs* for brevity. There are few such workers in the North, but they account for about two-fifths of the total labour force in the South.

These uneducated people work mainly in agriculture and other traditional activities, and are generally unsuited to manufacturing and other modern activities, which require at least literacy or primary schooling. Workers who have such a basic general education, but no more, are the second skill category, and will be labelled *BAS-EDs* (pronounced *base*-eds, not *bass*-eds, incidentally). They are described as 'unskilled' in the North, but in the South this term is ambiguous, because it fails to distinguish *BAS-EDs* from *NO-EDs*.

The third category, with the ugly label *SKILD* to remind us constantly of its crudity, includes all workers with substantial post-basic education and training. Exactly where the dividing line should be drawn is open to debate, but in principle this category encompasses not only professional and technical workers with advanced education and training qualifications, and experienced managers and supervisors, but also manual craftsmen who have undergone extended and structured training such as an apprenticeship. The *SKILD* category is therefore much more heterogeneous than the other two categories: it spans a wide range of skill levels; and its composition, including the average skill level of the workers within it, varies over time and among countries. For many purposes it would thus be better to subdivide the *SKILD* category, and at some points in subsequent chapters this will be attempted.

The use of three skill categories requires some modification of the initial simple model in Section 2.1.1, which had only two skill categories. In the North, where *NO-EDs* are so few that there are effectively only two skill categories, all that has to be changed are the labels, from 'skilled and unskilled' to *SKILD* and *BAS-ED*. In the South, too, since *NO-EDs* are of little use in modern manufacturing, there are effectively only the same two skill categories (*SKILD* and *BAS-ED* workers) in that sector—the one which is central to the changes in North–South trade that are the focus of this book. The comparative advantage of the South within manufacturing thus continues to depend, as in the initial model, simply on the relative supply of these two categories (*SKILD* and *BAS-ED* workers), and is not affected by the proportion of *NO-ED* workers in the labour force.

However, the presence of many *NO-ED* workers in the South matters in other respects. The size of the *NO-ED* labour supply does not affect comparative advantage *within* manufacturing, but it does affect whether or not a country has a comparative advantage in manufacturing as compared with other sectors such as agriculture. (From an analytical point of view, *NO-ED* workers are thus similar to land, and it is often helpful to consider these two anti-manufacturing factors in conjunction with one another.)[18]

---

[18] On land, see the last paragraph of Sect. 2.1.4. The similarity between land and *NO-ED* labour arises because manufacturing is both more education-intensive and less land-intensive than agriculture (and other primary production). On this point, see also Sects. 6.3.6, 9.1.2, and 9.3.2.

In a country with a high proportion of *NO-EDs* in its labour force, the wages of educated (*BAS-ED* and *SKILD*) workers tend to be higher, relative to the wages of *NO-EDs*. This tends to raise the price of manufactures, relative to agricultural products (because manufacturing is more education-intensive than agriculture), and hence to put the country at a comparative disadvantage in manufacturing. In other words, a country with a lot of *NO-EDs* is less likely, other things being equal, to export *any* manufactures. However, such manufactured goods as it does produce might in theory be mainly skill-intensive, if there were a high ratio of *SKILD* to *BAS-ED* workers in the non-*NO-ED* minority of its labour force.

The presence of *NO-ED* workers also complicates the effects of reduced barriers to North–South trade in manufactures on income inequality in the South. Consider for example a Southern country with (as is typical) a low ratio of *SKILD* to *BAS-ED* labour, and suppose that the barriers had consisted mainly of tariffs and quotas on all manufactured imports, which were then abolished. This reduction of barriers, as in the initial model, would tend to shift the composition of manufacturing output away from *SKILD*-intensive activities towards *BAS-ED*-intensive activities. But the abolition of protection would also tend to shrink manufacturing, relative to agriculture. This second tendency would be stronger, the larger the share of *NO-EDs* in the labour force (and hence the smaller the country's comparative advantage in manufacturing). Three sorts of outcome may be distinguished.[19]

(1) In a country where the share of *NO-EDs* was 'large', the demand for *BAS-ED* as well as for *SKILD* labour in manufacturing would fall, since the rise in the *BAS-ED*-intensity of manufacturing would not be enough to offset the decline in the relative demand for all labour in manufacturing. Income inequality would be reduced, because the wages of *SKILD* workers would fall relative to those of *BAS-ED* workers, and the wages of *BAS-ED* workers would fall relative to those of *NO-ED* workers, the lowest-paid category. But this reduction in inequality would be associated with contraction rather than expansion of manufacturing employment.

(2) In a country where the share of *NO-EDs* was 'moderate', the demand for *BAS-ED* labour would increase, but the effect on income inequality would be ambiguous. For the wages of *BAS-ED* workers would rise relative both to *SKILD* workers, who are richer, and to *NO-ED* workers, who are poorer. The net effect would depend on the relative

---

[19] The labels 'large', 'moderate', and 'negligible' for the *NO-ED* share of the labour force in these three cases are deliberately vague. The exact dividing lines depend upon other variables and parameters not explicitly specified here, including the extent of natural resource endowments.

numbers of workers involved, the extent of the changes in their wages, and the measure of inequality used.

(3) In a country where the share of *NO-EDs* was 'negligible', the initial two-skill-category model would apply without any substantive modification. The demand for *BAS-ED* labour would increase, as in the 'moderate' case, but the effect on inequality would be unambiguously favourable, since, with few *NO-ED* workers, a decline in their wages would not have a noticeable effect on the overall outcome. This case is not representative of the South in general, where *NO-EDs* are still numerous. But the four leading East Asian exporters of manufactures started with unusually high literacy rates (as is shown in Table 5.1).

2.4.3 Skill formation

The initial simple model, like most H–O trade theory, assumed that the supplies of skilled and unskilled labour in the North and the South were given and completely inelastic. This assumption is not acceptable in the context of the present book, which is concerned with change over a long period. Most skill is *acquired*, not innate, and much of it is *purposively* acquired, as a result of decisions and deliberate actions by individuals, parents, employers, or governments. So not only is it obviously true that the relative supplies of workers in different skill categories can change, but it is also certain that the skill formation decisions of people and firms, and the provision of education and training facilities (public and private), are to some degree responsive to relative wages and employment opportunities in different skill categories.

The initial model thus needs to be modified to allow for some elasticity of supply. The effect on the outcome is straightforward. The reduction in barriers to North–South trade in manufactures still shifts the relative demand function for *SKILD* and *BAS-ED* labour in each region in opposite directions. But because the relative supply function is now elastic, these shifts in demand are partly accommodated by parallel movements of relative supply. The induced changes in relative wages are thus smaller than they would have been with completely inelastic supply.[20] For example, in the North the reduction in the demand for, and hence in the wages of, *BAS-ED* labour induces some *BAS-ED* workers to become *SKILD*

---

[20] This consequence of supply elasticity was explicitly stated by Ohlin (1933, 1967: 50, 79–81). But the introduction of elastic supply makes no fundamental difference to the pattern of trade. For as Ohlin noted (1967: 81–2), it makes *SKILD* labour even more relatively abundant in the North, and even more relatively scarce in the South. With a continuum of goods of varying skill intensity, the position of the break (between goods produced only in the North and goods produced only in the South) is determined by demand conditions in the two regions, not by the difference between their *SKILD/BAS-ED* wage ratios (cf. Jones and Neary 1984: 12–13, 18–19).

workers, which lessens the increase in the relative scarcity and wages of *SKILD* workers.

It is vital to distinguish between specific skills and skill in general. In the short and medium term, skills relevant only to particular products are 'specific factors', which may give a country a temporary comparative advantage in the products concerned (Jones and Neary 1984, sect. 2.4). Conversely, autonomous changes in trade may destroy the economic value of specialised skills in industries which are forced to contract. Such devaluation of specific skills has been one of the adverse side-effects of recent changes in North–South trade, but is not the principal concern of this book, which has a longer-run perspective. For in the long run the supply of specific skills is more or less infinitely elastic, at least among occupations requiring similar amounts of training. A rise in the demand for dentists relative to doctors, say, or for electricians relative to plumbers, should not have a permanent effect on their relative wages.

What is relevant in this book is something fundamentally different, namely the long-run elasticity of the aggregate supply of *SKILD* labour relative to *BAS-ED* labour (and in the South also of *BAS-ED* relative to *NO-ED* labour). This elasticity is undoubtedly greater than zero, and it is of interest to consider the extreme alternative assumption that it is infinite (as with specific skills). This assumption would be valid if all skills could be acquired through training that was equally available and beneficial to all workers. The wage differential between *SKILD* and *BAS-ED* workers would then depend simply on the cost of the training needed to become a *SKILD* worker and on the interest rate, which would determine the rate of return on this investment in human capital. The reduction in barriers to North–South trade would thus have no long-run effect on the relative wages of *SKILD* and *BAS-ED* workers in either region, but only on their relative numbers.

With such an infinitely elastic supply function, inequality of wages would exist only in a superficial sense, since after allowing for training costs the earnings of skilled and unskilled workers would be the same. Moreover, if unskilled labour could be so easily transformed into skilled labour, it would make little sense to treat either category as a scarce or an abundant factor. Differences among countries in the relative cost of skilled and unskilled labour might still in theory influence the pattern of trade, but this relationship, too, would be superficial. The underlying cause would have to be international differences in interest rates, which were argued above (in connection with physical capital) to be an inadequate basis for explaining the pattern of North–South trade.[21]

---

[21] Differences in the relative cost of skilled and unskilled labour might in principle also arise from differences in the efficiency of training institutions, e.g. in the amount of student or teacher time needed to acquire given skills. But such differences in efficiency would be hard to reconcile with the H–O idea that all countries have access to the same technology,

Limits on the skill supply

In short, infinitely elastic supply would undermine the central premiss of this book, which is that differences in the availability of skills are the main basis of North–South trade. It is thus essential to assume explicitly that the elasticity of the skilled-labour supply, though greater than zero, is far from infinite—so far, indeed, that such a supposition would be fundamentally misleading in the present context. This assumption, which would probably be widely accepted on the basis of casual observation alone, will be implicitly tested in subsequent chapters. But it is worth noting here the theoretical arguments against the 'unlimited supply' view—the general reasons why the skill supply function within each region is rather inelastic, and why there is also an enduring North–South difference in the relative availability of skilled labour.

Two familiar reasons for inelasticity are well explained by Willis (1986: 550–60). One is the *imperfection of capital markets*, compounded by the usual legal impossibility of securing loans on human beings, which means that different people have access to finance for investment in skill acquisition on widely varying terms. For some, such an investment would simply mean running down a saving deposit and forgoing the interest, while for others, stopping work in order to train would mean starvation. The second reason is that *people vary in their trainability*. In other words, there is variation among individuals in the degree of skill acquired for any given outlay on education and training, so that a higher wage premium is needed to induce a higher proportion of the labour force to acquire a given degree of skill. Variation in trainability arises basically from differences in innate ability and family background (Phelps Brown 1977).

A third relevant feature of skill formation is *increasing returns*.[22] Innate ability and preschool learning condition performance at school; success in basic schooling contributes to success at (and is necessary for access to) higher levels of schooling; capacity to benefit from (and access to) vocational training depends on success in prior general education; and better-educated workers learn more on the job (as evidenced by their more steeply rising age-earnings profiles). Such cumulative causation operates not only within the individual life cycle, but also inter-generationally:

and indeed seem inconsistent with the assumption that skills (including teaching skills) can be freely acquired by anyone. Findlay and Kierzkowski (1983) struggle with this issue, but eventually have to fall back on international differences in interest or discount rates.

[22] Increasing returns and externalities, discussed in the next paragraph, feature prominently in the 'new' growth theory literature (e.g. Romer 1986; Azariadis and Drazen 1990). But these two features of skill formation have deeper roots in the economics of education (surveyed by Freeman 1986; Psacharopoulos 1987, 1988; and Schultz 1988). See also Keesing (1966).

children with more educated parents acquire more skills, both in and out
of school. This strengthens the tendency for the dispersion of skills
among individuals to be wide and enduring, and contributes to the persistence of skill differences between North and South.

The fourth relevant feature of skill formation is *externalities*. The
amount of skill acquired by an individual in a learning context, formal or
informal, depends on the amount of skill possessed by the people with
whom he or she is interacting. The interaction may be with parents, as
already mentioned. The quality and qualifications of teachers likewise
affect how much students learn in school and college, and in specific
vocational training. The degree of skill acquired by on-the-job training
depends on the skills of colleagues and superiors, and of customers and
other contacts outside the workplace. By no means all skill acquisition
involves direct contact with other people; books and materials are also
vital. Nor, with phones and faxes, need personal contacts always be face
to face. But these sorts of externalities, in conjunction with limited mobility, contribute powerfully to the persistence of North–South skill
differences.

In a technical sense, these four analytical characteristics of the process
of skill formation apply equally to the North and the South. However,
this technical formulation fails to convey the appalling problems and
obstacles to skill acquisition in many developing countries (UNDP 1990,
1991; World Bank 1990). Children who never enter school or who drop
out after a couple of years, teachers with less than a primary education,
university libraries with few books, enforced cuts in already meagre education budgets—these are all too often the Southern reality of market
imperfection theory.

2.4.4 International labour mobility

Another assumption of the initial model was international immobility of
labour. This is a reasonably accurate assumption, especially in a
North–South context, where there are powerful political economy reasons
for immobility (Johnson 1968: 30–1; Minford 1989: 213). The wages of
most sorts of labour are higher in the North than in the South. Hence,
even abstracting from non-economic considerations, the coincidence of
people wishing to leave one country and being welcomed by the citizens
of another country (or their elected government) is relatively rare. Many
Southern workers might like to move to the North, but most Northern
residents would prefer to keep them out. Conversely, although many
skilled workers from the North might be welcome to move to the South,
few choose to do so.

Before considering some exceptions to this generalisation, it is worth returning to a point raised in Section 2.1.2 and enquiring *why*, in the present theoretical framework, the absolute wages of skilled as well as unskilled workers are generally higher in the North than in the South. This question is especially pertinent because earlier sections ruled out the two main answers that are usually offered: greater availability of most sorts of capital and superior technology in the North. The only possible explanation that has so far been mentioned is larger stocks of infrastructural capital in the North.

However, better infrastructure is probably only part of the reason why skilled workers earn absolutely more in the North, despite their greater relative abundance. The main reason seems to be that skilled workers are more productive when they are clustered together, in countries where they are relatively numerous, and in skill-intensive activities.[23] The causes of this phenomenon are closely related to some of the things mentioned in the preceding subsection, particularly externalities. The discussion in that subsection was about the *acquisition* rather than the *use* of skills, but for many *SKILD* workers the two activities are inextricably entwined.

International migration, though its relative scale is not great enough to warrant relaxation of the immobility assumption, does involve absolutely large numbers of people. In the present model of North–South trade in manufactures, where neither capital nor raw materials plays a fundamental role, the consequences of international labour mobility are simpler than in other models (Ruffin 1984). But the standard H–O proposition that trade and mobility have equivalent effects on factor prices has to be modified.

Consider first mobility from the South to the North, which at some times and in some places has been substantial (illegal migration into the USA being a current example). There are two reasons why movement of unskilled workers from the South tends to have a larger adverse effect (than imports of labour-intensive goods) on unskilled wages in the North. One is that trade leads to specialisation and incomplete factor price equalisation (Section 2.1.2), whereas immigration could in principle equalise wages. The other reason is that the impact of trade on Northern unskilled wages is muffled by the existence of nontraded final consumption sectors, especially services, which could be entered by immigrants.[24]

Mobility from the North to the South is almost entirely of skilled labour, is usually temporary, and in many cases occurs for non-economic

[23] See e.g. Reich (1991, chs. 18–19), Krugman (1991), and Romer (1992: V.2). The gains from clustering of skilled workers are reinforced by better infrastructure, especially communications. Thus skilled labour and infrastructure may be complements, as suggested to me by Christopher Bliss.

[24] By contrast, immigration of *skilled* workers from the South would tend to benefit unskilled workers in the North, by making them relatively more scarce. Its effects on skilled workers in the North are less clear: they would tend to gain from economies of clustering, but to lose from becoming more abundant relative to unskilled labour and infrastructure.

reasons, often as a gift, either from the workers concerned, who accept low wages, or from an overseas government or international organisation. However, other expatriate workers are in the South for economic reasons, usually because they have a specific skill which is of value in local production but rare or absent in the indigenous labour force. Its value in local production may arise from barriers to trade (in a protected industry or a nontraded service such as medicine), or from the need for such skills in producing for export goods in which the country has a comparative advantage for other reasons—in the past, usually primary products from mines or plantations, but now also labour-intensive manufactures.[25]

2.5 Wage Determination

Wages and the forces which govern them are at the heart of this book. Its theoretical approach to wage determination is for the most part extremely conventional. But it is worth mentioning a few non-standard features, and explaining how they relate to other recent theoretical contributions.

2.5.1 Relative wages

The impact of trade on the relative wages of skilled and unskilled workers is analysed in a standard supply and demand framework (set out in Section 5.2.1). Reduction of trade barriers shifts the relative demand function for skilled and unskilled labour, which initially causes excess demand for one type of worker and excess supply of the other. Competitive pressure then tends to alter the skilled–unskilled wage ratio, which, because the relative supply function is fairly inelastic, must change if demands and supplies in these two labour sub-markets are to be realigned.

Of course, labour markets are rarely perfectly competitive, and never in equilibrium. All sorts of imperfections and institutional influences are embedded in labour demand and supply functions. Moreover, many labour markets do not clear in textbook fashion, for various reasons. Unions, minimum wage laws, and similar institutional causes of wage inflexibility have long been recognised by economists. More recently, efficiency wages, implicit or incomplete contracts, and insider–outsider

---

[25] The use of expatriate labour is more often economic in setting up a production facility—in construction or training—than in operating it on a long-term basis. Expatriate labour, since it costs more than it would in the North (both relatively and absolutely), cannot give a Southern country a comparative advantage in a purely skill-intensive activity. Expatriates of this sort, incidentally, are also an exception to the rule that skilled workers earn more in the North than in the South.

conflicts have been identified as other possible reasons for the absence of clearing (see the surveys in Nickell 1990 and Layard, Nickell, and Jackman 1991).

Many of these special features of labour markets are not fundamentally incompatible with the idea that *shifts* in demand or supply functions move relative wages in the *directions* implied by elementary theory.[26] And the empirical evidence in later chapters suggests that in many countries the relative wages of skilled and unskilled workers have in fact been altered by trade-induced shifts in demand. However, in the North, and especially in Europe, the widening of wage differentials between skilled and unskilled workers has been resisted. As a result, the initial shortages of skilled labour and surpluses of unskilled labour have persisted, which has raised the equilibrium—and the actual—rate of unemployment, as is explained more fully in Chapter 8.

This resistance to wider wage differentials—or relative wage rigidity—appears to have arisen mainly from three institutional sources. One is unions, which have tended to use their bargaining power to enforce rather egalitarian wage structures, holding up the pay especially of unskilled workers against downward market pressures. The second source, in some countries, is laws which effectively fix the minimum wage as a proportion of the average wage. The third source has been minimum income provisions in social security systems, again often tied to the average wage, which tend to set the reservation wage for unskilled workers.

Although these three sources of relative wage rigidity involve different mechanisms, they all stem from moral principles of equity or fairness, and in particular from a common concern that wages or incomes should not be too unequal. The strength of this concern varies from country to country, and with it the degree of relative wage rigidity, but in some shape or form it appears to be almost universal. More generally, employers are often under pressure from their workers to set *fair relative wages*, even in the absence of unions or legislation (Wood 1978). This pressure can be integrated into efficiency wage theory (Summers 1988; Akerloff and Yellen 1990). Concern about fairness of relative wages—treated as an argument of worker utility functions—could be brought into other theoretical frameworks, too.[27]

Labour-market imperfections have been introduced into many other models of international trade (e.g. Ohlin 1933, 1967: 52–3; Brecher 1974; Krueger 1977, 1983, ch. 7; Leamer 1984: 28–31; Minford 1989). Most of

---

[26] e.g. this would still be true if efficiency wage (or other) considerations caused the wage to exceed its market-clearing level by some fixed proportionate amount.

[27] e.g. James Pemberton has suggested to me that ch. 5 of Wood (1978) could be reworked as an insider–outsider model. On the influence of ideas of fairness in labour markets, see also Solow (1990). In some cases, these ideas may refer to real wages, or to shares of monopoly profits. But it is notions of fair *relative* wages which appear to be most pervasive and enduring, though not unchanging (Wood 1978: 22–3, 32–6, 39, 212–15).

these models have been concerned with the ways in which wage distortions and other labour-market imperfections affect the pattern of trade. This issue is touched on in later chapters. But the main emphasis in this book, as outlined above, is on a different issue—the way in which labour-market imperfections and institutions affect the impact of trade on wages and employment.

2.5.2 Real wages

The average real wage (in contrast to relative wages, and to the average nominal wage) is assumed in this book to be determined largely outside the labour market. This should not be interpreted to mean that the real wage is institutionally determined.[28] It means simply that interactions between employers and workers concerning jobs and wage rates are not the principal influence on either of the two variables which determine the level of the average real wage (W) in a particular country at a particular time. These two variables are (a) average real output per worker, Y, and (b) the share of profits (and other non-wage income) in aggregate output, π. Thus, by accounting definition

$$W = (1 - \pi)Y \tag{2.1}$$

Because π varies only within a rather narrow range, Y, which may be loosely called average labour productivity, is by far the more important cause of international and intertemporal differences in real wages. Not least, there is a large North–South difference in average labour productivity, as well as huge differences within the South. There are many reasons for this gap in Y, but the most important one, it may reasonably be supposed, is the lower average level of skill in the Southern labour force.

The level of the real wage also depends to some degree on the share of profits. This share depends in turn fundamentally on the *rate* of profit, r, which determines π at any given aggregate capital–output ratio (c) by the accounting definition

$$\pi = rc \tag{2.2}$$

In addition, r may influence c. But the capital–output ratio is affected also by the state of knowledge and the sectoral composition of output.

In principle, π might be affected by foreign trade (which could alter r or c or both). But the discussion in Section 2.2 effectively rules out this possibility in the present context. For it was argued that r could reasonably be treated as exogenous with respect to the changes in North–South

---

[28] The present model thus diverges from certain other theories of North–South trade, which assume either an exogenous real wage in one or both regions (e.g. Evans 1989*b*, ch. 7) or a basic asymmetry between the two regions in the mechanism by which real wages are determined (Evans 1989*a*: 1275–6).

trade. It was also argued that North–South trade is not based on differences in capital intensity, implying that changes in the composition of output caused by this trade are unlikely to affect c. What is likely, however, is that expansion of Southern manufactured exports squeezed the profitability of installed capital in labour-intensive sectors in the North (a 'specific factor'). This probably caused a temporary reduction in the average profitability of all Northern manufacturing (see Section 5.4.1).

The conclusion that these changes in trade did not increase the share of profits in the North has an important bearing on the controversies discussed in the previous chapter (Section 1.1). For if correct, it refutes the 'pessimistic' view that trade with the South lowers average real wages in the North. In fact, the expansion of this trade is more likely to have had the opposite effect, partly by temporarily reducing π, but mainly by raising Y, in two ways. One is that greater specialisation through trade increases efficiency. The other, less benign way is that relative wage rigidity has caused this expansion of trade to emerge partly as higher unemployment among unskilled workers, raising the average skill level and productivity of the employed labour force. The pessimists are thus right to worry about distributional side-effects, but have missed the mark: the enduringly adverse effects of expanded trade with the South are confined to *unskilled* Northern workers.[29]

2.6 Summary

The labour-market effects of North–South trade in manufactures can be analysed in a simple Heckscher–Ohlin model, with North and South as the two countries, and skilled and unskilled labour as the two factors. In this model, reduction of trade barriers has opposite effects within the two regions. In the South, expansion of labour-intensive production for export boosts the wages of unskilled workers, while in the North such workers are hurt by reduced production of labour-intensive import substitutes. Skilled workers, conversely, lose in the South and gain in the North. Trade does not equalise factor prices, but it does cause convergence of Northern and Southern skilled–unskilled wage ratios.

Land is left out of the model for simplicity, but its inclusion would not make much difference here. Most of the raw materials used in manufacturing are internationally traded, and have little effect on comparative advantage within manufacturing. Abundant natural resources cause some countries to export fewer manufactured goods. But natural resource

---

[29] In the short and medium term (as noted in Sect. 2.4.3) workers with high levels of skill specific to particular industries may also be hurt.

abundance is not fundamentally what distinguishes the North from the South.

Capital is also left out of the model. Machines are traded, finance is internationally mobile, and buildings can be put up anywhere in a year or two. So, with the important exception of infrastructure, capital cannot generally be an enduring source of comparative advantage. Nor is it true that the North has a comparative advantage in capital-intensive goods *vis-à-vis* the South. Expansion of trade with the South is thus unlikely to have lowered the average real wage in the North.

An often-challenged assumption of H–O theory is that technology is the same in all countries. However, this assumption is a reasonable simplification in the present context, provided that technology is appropriately defined. It is defined here as *indirect skill*, i.e. skill which is embodied in capital and intermediate goods. Since most such goods are internationally traded, the same technology is usually available in all countries, although there are of course some exceptions. Those who argue that developing countries have 'inferior technology' are making an important point, but that point is expressed here by saying that the South has *a less-skilled labour force*.

The many facets of skill have to be roughly reduced to a single dimension, based for example on length of training. Along this dimension, the labour force must be divided for present purposes into a minimum of three groups. Two of these groups contain workers with at least a basic general education—those who have no more than this are called *BAS-EDs*, while workers with advanced education or training are labelled *SKILD*. In manufacturing, and in the North more generally, the workforce contains only these two groups. In the South, however, there is a third group, containing workers without schooling (*NO-EDs*), who are unemployable in manufacturing. Countries with many *NO-EDs* are unlikely to have a comparative advantage in manufacturing, making the distributional effects of lower trade barriers ambiguous.

Most labour is internationally immobile, and likely to remain so. Within countries, though, the supplies of skilled and unskilled workers may alter, partly in response to changes in wages. Supply elasticity thus lessens the impact of trade on relative wages. However, the supply of skilled labour is far from infinitely elastic, even in the long run, because of capital market imperfections, variations in trainability, increasing returns, and externalities. These characteristics of skill formation also explain why there is a large and enduring North–South difference in skill supplies.

Trade tends to alter the relative wages of skilled and unskilled workers through a simple demand and supply mechanism. But labour markets have many imperfections and idiosyncrasies. In parts of the North, the trade-induced widening of the wage differential between skilled and unskilled workers has encountered institutional resistance, because of a conflict with prevailing ideas of fairness. The underlying shift in relative demand has therefore emerged partly as a rise in the equilibrium rate of unemployment.

Introduction

Chapters 3 and 4 seek to test two broad hypotheses about the impact of North–South trade in manufactures on the labour markets of both regions. The first hypothesis concerns the *pattern* of the impact: it is that the principal effect of this trade is to alter the *skill composition* of the demand for labour. Put another way, the hypothesis is that this trade consists basically of the exchange of more skill-intensive products for less skill-intensive products. A corollary of this hypothesis is that North–South trade is *not* based, as often supposed, on differences in the availability of (physical) *capital*.

The second hypothesis is about *magnitudes*, and is perhaps better expressed as a question: *how large* is the impact on the skill composition of labour demand? This question is important, and more controversial than the first hypothesis. For it has often been argued that the impact of trade with the South on Northern labour markets is tiny, and hence of little concern. By contrast, this book is suggesting that the impact is substantial enough to merit serious attention by economists and governments.

Implicit in this formulation of the two hypotheses is a strong assumption about the direction of causation, namely that it flows simply from trade to labour markets. This is not generally true, since trade and labour-market outcomes in most cases are simultaneously determined. But in the present context, this assumption is a convenient simplification, which will not be questioned in the next two chapters. In other words, it will be taken for granted in Part A of this book that the changes in North–South trade were an exogenous cause of change in the composition of labour demand. In Part B, this assumption will be defended as a reasonable first approximation to the truth.

The first step in testing the hypotheses about pattern and magnitude is to look at the evidence provided by previous studies. That is the purpose of Chapter 3. In Chapter 4, new evidence will be provided to fill some holes in earlier work. The conclusion will be that the evidence, though limited and in some ways unsatisfactory, is consistent with both hypotheses.

The country coverage of the 'North' and the 'South' varies somewhat in the empirical chapters which follow, partly because different international organisations use varying definitions of 'developed' and 'developing'. But the variations are usually small. The only points to bear in mind are that (unless otherwise indicated) the North *excludes* the former Soviet Union and Eastern Europe, and the South *includes* China.[1] (Incidentally,

---

[1] More specifically, the 'North' in this book usually approximates most closely to what the World Bank calls 'high-income OECD-member' economies (before 1989 called 'indus-

'Germany' always refers to the former West Germany, and 'Korea' to South Korea.)

trial market economies'), but in some places it refers to all OECD countries, or to the UN's 'developed market economies'. The 'South' is usually the UN's 'developing market economies', plus China (which is what the World Bank now calls 'low and middle-income economies', minus a few East European countries, plus Hong Kong and Singapore).

3

Evidence from Previous Studies

This chapter starts with two sections on methodology, followed by three substantive sections, which review the findings of studies of developing countries, developed countries, and both sorts of countries together. The scope is limited to work on *North–South trade and labour markets*. Studies of North–South trade which have no bearing on its relationship with labour markets are omitted. So are studies which have looked at this relationship only for North–North or South–South trade, or for all trade, regardless of direction. (As Krueger (1977) explains, the characteristics of a country's trade may depend heavily on what group of trading partners is considered.)

3.1 Factor Content Methodology

Although the studies to be examined use a variety of methods, one recurs frequently, and is also used in some of the new work in this book. Its nature and limitations thus merit an introduction. The *factor content of trade* (FCT) method involves calculating the amounts of skill, labour, and capital embodied in trade flows. It is perhaps best known as an approach to testing H–O theory (Deardorff 1984*a*: 478–93; Leamer 1984, ch. 2), but has also been used, with some differences of emphasis, to estimate the impact of trade on factor demand.

In the context of North–South trade in manufactures, the impact on factor demand has typically been measured as follows. Factor content coefficients for the manufactured exports of the North (subscripted *N*) to the South (*S*) are calculated as

$$z_{xN} = A_N x_N \qquad (3.1)$$

where z_{xN} is a ($q \times 1$) vector of factor quantities per million dollars of exports. A_N is a ($q \times r$) matrix of coefficients specifying the quantity of each of the q factors used per million dollars of output in each of the r Northern manufacturing sectors. x_N is an ($r \times 1$) vector of sectoral shares of manufactured exports (which sum to unity). In short, z_{xN} is an export-weighted average of sectoral factor input coefficients.

Factor content coefficients for the North's manufactured imports from the South (which are the same thing as the South's manufactured exports to the North) are likewise calculated as

$$z_{mN} = A_N x_S \qquad (3.2)$$

or, in words, as an *import*-weighted average of sectoral factor input coefficients.

The South's manufactured exports to the North are assumed to finance an equal dollar value of Northern manufactured exports to the South. The impact of this trade on factor demand in the North is thus estimated as

$$Z_N = X_S (z_{xN} - z_{mN)} \qquad (3.3)$$

where Z_N is a vector of factor quantities, and X_S is the total (scalar) value of the South's manufactured exports to the North (in millions of dollars). Similarly, though using Southern input coefficients (A_S) to calculate the factor content coefficients, the impact on factor demand in the South is estimated as

$$Z_S = X_S (z_{xS} - z_{ms}). \qquad (3.4)$$

The meaning of equations 3.3 and 3.4 is straightforward. The demand for any factor, j, of which a larger quantity is used per dollar of exports than per dollar of imports $(z_{jx} > z_{jm})$ is *increased* by trade, while the demand for any factor used more in imports than in exports $(z_{jx} < z_{jm})$ is *reduced*. The *size* of the net impact on the demand for each factor depends also on the absolute amount of trade (X_S).

These equations resemble the standard factor content calculation used in tests of H–O theory, AT (where T is a vector of net exports), but there are three substantive differences. The present equations (*a*) are confined to trade in manufactures, (*b*) are limited to one group of trading partners, and (*c*) impose balanced trade. There are also some differences of form: the present equations distinguish exports from imports, and express each of these trade vectors as the product of a share vector and a scalar total.

Such FCT estimates of the impact of trade on domestic factor markets are recognised by everyone to be at best simplified approximations to proper general equilibrium calculations. For example, they take trade flows as given (rather than starting from, say, an exogenous reduction in tariffs), they assume that trade flows are an accurate measure of induced changes in domestic production, and they hold factor prices constant. However, it is also usually argued that these simplifications are reasonable, and that FCT estimates are of the right sign and roughly the right size (e.g. OECD 1989).

This book, too, broadly endorses and espouses the FCT approach as a good starting-point. Before moving on to the statistical results, however, it is worth mentioning a number of complications, limitations, and issues of interpretation that were glossed over in the preceding summary. Some are mere implementation problems, but others greatly affect the conclusions.

3.1.1 Balanced and unbalanced trade

The North has always had a large surplus in its manufactured trade with the South (offset by a deficit in oil and other primary products). So in some studies it has been argued (in effect) that equation 3.3 should be replaced by

$$Z_N = X_N z_{XN} - X_S z_{mN}. \tag{3.3a}$$

Because $X_N \gg X_S$, the impact of North–South trade in manufactures on the demand for labour and other factors in the North is thereby portrayed as strongly positive (Balassa 1986a, 1989, ch. 6; UNIDO 1986, ch. 3). That this line of argument is unsatisfactory becomes clear when the corresponding modification is made to equation 3.4:

$$Z_S = X_S z_{XS} - X_N z_{mS}. \tag{3.4a}$$

The implication that this trade greatly *reduces* the demand for labour and other factors in the South is hard to swallow—and conflicts sharply with the accepted view that exporting manufactures has generated a lot of jobs in developing countries.[2]

This curious result highlights the need, even in simple FCT calculations, explicitly to specify the *counterfactual* situation (or the 'without' case). In other words, any assessment of the impact of the South's manufactured exports on factor demand must, in principle, be conditional on assumptions about what would have happened in the *absence* of these exports. Implicit in equations 3.3a and 3.4a is the counterfactual assumption that, if the South did not export any manufactures to the North, then the North would not export *any* manufactures to the South. This is implausible, because it assumes that the South's primary trade surplus (which finances a large part of its imports of manufactures from the North) would somehow also vanish.

The conventional assumption (underlying equations 3.3 and 3.4) makes much more sense. It is that the absence of manufactured exports from the South would not alter this primary trade surplus (or the overall North–South balance of trade). So in the counterfactual case, the North's manufactured exports to the South would be reduced by exactly the amount of the South's manufactured exports to the North. (In this spirit, some FCT studies have examined the impact not of the South's *total* manufactured exports, X_S, but of a balanced *increment* in North–South trade in manufactures.)

It may be objected that the South's manufactured exports contain some primary products that would otherwise have been exported in raw or

---

[2] This implication of his calculations clearly troubled Balassa (1986a, 1989). However, Kunibert Raffer has pointed out to me that dependency theorists might accept this conclusion, because their assumptions about the counterfactual situation are 'unconventional'.

semi-processed form: thus if the South exported no manufactures, its primary trade surplus would tend to be larger. Cutting the other way, though, the extra manufactures which the South now imports from the North contain some primary products purchased from the South. The net effect on the South's primary trade surplus, as the calculations in Chapter 4 will show, is quite small, provided that manufactured exports are defined narrowly, to exclude 'processed primary' products such as refined oil and canned food. (This narrow definition is used in most trade statistics. But in production and employment data, manufacturing includes a lot of primary processing.)

Another possible objection to the conventional counterfactual assumption about trade flows is that it neglects the disappearance of the North's former labour-intensive manufactured exports to the South (Wolf 1979: 171; Beenstock 1984, table 3.7). The loss of these exports, because of import substitution in the South, amplified the effects of imports from the South on the skill composition of labour demand in the North. But this effect, too, will be shown in the next chapter to be of only moderate importance, at least for the North. The conventional assumption about trade flows is thus a reasonable first approximation in calculating the impact of North–South trade in manufactures on factor demand.

3.1.2 Alternative measures of factor content

Equations 3.3 and 3.4 do not specify the number or identity of the factors affected by trade. In practice, though, most North–South FCT calculations have been limited to one factor, labour, undifferentiated by skill level. Their z terms have simply measured the number of person-hours (or years) per unit of manufactured exports or imports. All studies of this type have found that $z_{xN} < z_{mN}$ and $z_{xS} > z_{mS}$, which they have interpreted as showing that the North's exports are less 'labour-intensive' than its imports, and vice versa for the South. The net effect of (balanced) North–South trade is thus to reduce the demand for labour in manufacturing in the North, and to increase it in the South, although in both regions, as these studies also show, some manufacturing subsectors gain and others lose.

How should these results be interpreted here, in relation to our hypotheses about the effects of trade on the relative demand for skilled and unskilled labour and capital? And how can their measure of 'labour intensity', based on a ratio of labour to *output*, be related to the usual theoretical concept based on the ratio of labour to some other *input*? These questions are most easily answered when output is defined as *value added*, since the ratio of labour to value added is the reciprocal of a more familiar variable—value added per worker, v. For a given sector (or basket of exports or imports), i, we can thus write the standard accounting identity

$$v_i = w_i + r_i k_i \qquad (3.5)$$

where w_i is the average wage in sector i, k is the value of physical capital per worker, and r is the rate of profit on capital. The w_i term can then be expanded to show the skill composition of employment

$$v_i = \sum_h w_{hi} n_{hi} + r_i k_i \qquad (3.6)$$

where w_{hi} is the wage rate of skill category h in sector i, and n_{hi} is the proportion of workers of skill category h in sector i's labour force.

It is also convenient to assume initially that, within countries, market forces equate profit rates and the wage rates of given skill categories across sectors. Then, for example, the Northern result that $z_{xN} < z_{mN}$ (meaning that value added per worker is higher in exporting than in import-competing sectors) must imply that exporting sectors on average have a higher ratio of skilled to unskilled workers, or more capital per worker, or both, than import-competing sectors.

Another point to emerge from equation 3.6 is that the results of labour-only FCT calculations are *factor-price-dependent*, in two senses—simply for accounting reasons, in addition to any economic effect of factor prices on factor input choices. First, the results may differ *among countries and over time* because of differences in the relative wages of different skill categories, or in the rate of profit. For, with given physical input coefficients in each sector, relative factor price differences would change the relative v_i of different sectors, and hence could alter the size of the gap between the 'labour intensity' of exports and of import substitutes.

Second, the size of this gap—and perhaps even its sign—is affected by differences in factor prices *among sectors*. For example, the higher value added per worker in exporting sectors might be wholly or partly the result of higher wage rates for given skill categories or higher profit rates than in import-competing sectors. Moreover, such inter-sectoral variations in factor prices might be *caused* by trade: for example, wage or profit rates might be lower in import-competing sectors precisely because of competition from imports. Labour-only FCT calculations must therefore be interpreted rather cautiously.

A related issue, in all FCT calculations, is whether the sectoral factor input coefficients in the A matrices should include the indirect use of factors embodied in intermediate inputs. In theory, everyone agrees that *some* indirect inputs should be included, but there is disagreement as to *which*, as well as variation in practice for reasons of data availability. Deardorff (1984a: 480) argues for the inclusion of *all* indirect inputs, on the grounds that they would affect autarky prices. By contrast, Krueger (1983: 94) argues that only *nontraded* indirect inputs should be included, since traded inputs do not shape a country's comparative advantage.

Whatever convention is adopted in this regard, the logic of equation 3.6 above is unaffected, provided that the numerator and denominator of v_i are consistent, and hence the value of the output is equal to the cost of the factor inputs. For example, Krueger works with the ratio of direct plus nontraded labour to direct plus nontraded value added. Things become more complicated, however, when factor input coefficients are measured per unit of *gross output*, rather than value added. For unless the whole of gross output is decomposed into domestic value added, as advocated by Deardorff, the relative 'labour intensity' of exports and import substitutes depends not only on the skill and capital intensity of the sectors concerned, but also on the varying shares of intermediate inputs in their gross output.

The use of gross output rather than value added coefficients need not make a large difference to the outcome, because the share of intermediate inputs is similar for most narrow manufacturing sectors. But it sometimes leads to odd results. This is because, with value added coefficients, if sector i uses more of one factor (per unit of output) than sector j, it must use less of at least one of the other factors, provided that the two sectors face the same factor prices. But with gross output coefficients, sector i might use more of *all* factors than sector j, because it had a higher ratio of value added to gross output, i.e. a lower intermediate input share.

This exposes an important dilemma that was finessed in the initial account of FCT methodology above, as it has been in many FCT studies. The results have most meaning when output is measured by value added. However, exports and imports are gross flows, and it is natural to interpret the assumption that the South's manufactured exports to the North finance an equal value of Northern exports to the South in gross terms. For the same reason, it is natural (and common) to base the A matrices on gross output. Hence the dilemma: if gross output is used, the effects on factor demand are blurred; but if value added is used, the linkage with trade flows is obscured.

A proper analysis of the impact of trade on factor markets must thus, at a minimum, keep track of both output measures, and of the traded intermediate input flows that make them diverge. This will be attempted in the new FCT estimates in the next chapter. Even so, there is no single best way to do the calculations. As is explained by Krueger (1983, sect. 5.1), it all depends on exactly what question is being asked, and on the specification of the counterfactual case.

3.1.3 Noncompeting manufactured imports

The most misleading assumption of the conventional application of the FCT approach (equations 3.1 to 3.4) is that all imports of narrowly defined manufactures are 'competing'. In principle, any FCT study has to calculate the *actual* factor content of exports, but the *counterfactual* factor content of imports—how much of each factor *would have been* employed to produce domestically the goods that are imported. The latter is conventionally estimated (see equation 3.2) from factor input coefficients in the domestic sectors which are in the same statistical categories as the imported goods.[3] For example, the counterfactual labour content of garment imports from the South is based on actual labour use in Northern garment production. The implicit assumption is that the imported goods are identical to those produced in the corresponding domestic sectors.

This assumption is not generally acceptable, for either the North or the South. As is well known, Northern firms have ceased to produce many manufactured items currently imported from the South. This is true both of finished products, especially when these are finely distinguished by type and quality, and of components and contributory services, the most labour-intensive of which have been delegated wherever possible to Southern suppliers. In the South, conversely, manufactured imports from the North are concentrated on types and specifications of goods that are not produced domestically, and which are typically more skill-intensive than the goods produced in the corresponding domestic sectors.

The manufactured imports of each country group from the other are thus largely 'noncompeting'.[4] This is not because it would be physically impossible to produce these goods at home (as with many noncompeting primary imports), but because it would be uneconomic to do so. The likelihood of, and theoretical reasons for, this outcome were pointed out by Krueger (1977). As explained in Section 2.1.2, she argued that the big differences in relative factor prices between developed and developing countries would tend to cause them to specialise in manufactured goods in different factor intensity ranges. But with the exception of some studies of the South which she directed (to be reviewed below), the implications of her insight for FCT analyses of North–South trade have been neglected.

When imports are noncompeting, the conventional method of calculation, using domestic input coefficients, is bound to *understate* the impact of trade on factor markets.[5] In the North, the usual method gives too low

[3] The conventional approach is criticised from a theoretical perspective by Deardorff (1982: 685-9), who argues instead that 'the factor content of imports is to be measured by the factors which produce them abroad'.

[4] The term 'noncompeting' has to be interpreted carefully. In one sense, almost all imports compete with domestic production, because there is scope for substitution in consumption. The point is really that noncompeting manufactured imports are *imperfect* substitutes for domestic goods (as with imported bananas and home-grown apples). In some models, this point is accommodated by the use of Armington elasticities (Dervis *et al.* 1982).

[5] If *all* imports were noncompeting, the expected value of the impact (wrongly) estimated by the conventional method would presumably be zero, since the factor intensities of the

an estimate of the counterfactual unskilled labour content of imports, since the 'corresponding' domestic sectors are producing more skill-intensive goods. Hence it must understate the net trade-induced reduction in the demand for unskilled manufacturing labour. In the South, by contrast, the usual method exaggerates the counterfactual unskilled labour content of manufactured imports from the North, and hence understates the net positive effect of trade with the North on the demand for unskilled labour.

The *degree* of understatement is not obvious, but is shown in the next chapter to be large—roughly one order of magnitude. What *is* obvious is that to ascertain the size of the error, we need an alternative and better method of estimating factor content coefficients for noncompeting imports. Moreover, since by definition such imports are not produced domestically, it is clear that any alternative method must rely on information from the economy of the trading partner—where the goods concerned are made. How this information should be used, though, is a difficult and potentially controversial issue, which will be touched on later in this chapter (in Section 3.3.2) and taken up at greater length in the following one.

Noncompeting imports give rise to a further problem for FCT calculations. Where imports are competing, their prices should in theory be the same as those of domestic substitutes. But the prices of noncompeting imports must be *lower* than those of their (counterfactual) domestic substitutes. This calls into question the conventional FCT assumption (implicit in equations 3.3 and 3.4) that trade flows are a good measure of induced changes in domestic production. For example, the labour-intensive goods imported from the South are cheaper than they would have been if produced in the North, so that Northern consumers buy more of them. The level of imports is thus greater than the trade-induced reduction of labour-intensive output in the North, and overstates the decline in the demand for unskilled labour. The alternative calculations in the next chapter will correct for this bias.

3.2 Disentangling Skill and Capital

One of the hypotheses under test is that North–South trade in manufactures is based on differences in the availability of skilled labour, but not

imports would be uncorrelated with those of the statistically 'corresponding' domestic sectors. The results of particular FCT studies would be randomly distributed around this zero mean. In practice, the results of conventional FCT calculations for North-South trade in manufactures generally have the 'right sign', because some imports are competing with domestic production, either temporarily or permanently (the specialised production structures of the two regions are likely to overlap at the margin, for reasons explained by Krueger 1977).

of capital, in developed and developing countries. By contrast, most of the empirical studies reviewed below treat both skill and capital as important influences. It is thus worth considering in advance how to interpret their results on this point, and in particular how to discriminate between the skill-only and the skill-plus-capital views of North–South trade.

The standard approach is to use FCT calculations to compare the skill and capital intensity of North–South and South–North manufactured trade flows. Some studies have found in this way that the North's exports to the South are both more skill-intensive and more capital-intensive than its imports from the South, and have concluded that this trade is based on differences in the availability of both skill and capital. This conclusion is unsound, partly because capital intensity is usually measured in an inappropriate way, and partly because of collinearity between capital intensity and skill intensity, but mainly because FCT calculations are not a sufficient test. These three limitations of the standard approach are elaborated below.

3.2.1 Measuring skill intensity and capital intensity

Before discussing how *capital* intensity should be measured, it is worth recalling how *skill* intensity is measured, and why. The natural way to compare the skill intensity of two goods (or baskets of goods) is in terms of the skill composition of employment required for their production. A more skill-intensive good is one that needs a higher ratio of skilled to unskilled workers. This is the natural measure of skill intensity in the present context, because it guarantees that a greater scarcity of skilled relative to unskilled labour—reflected in a higher ratio of skilled to unskilled wages—would increase the price of more skill-intensive goods relative to less skill-intensive goods. This measure is thus consistent with the H–O framework used here, and in particular with the proposition that the North's greater abundance of skilled relative to unskilled labour gives it a comparative advantage in skill-intensive manufactures.[6]

In practice, there is more than one way of measuring skill intensity. It can be done by splitting the labour force into two groups, and expressing the number of more skilled workers as a ratio of the number of less skilled workers, or as a share of the total. Or, if the wages of particular skill groups are reasonably uniform across industries, skill intensity can be measured by the average wage in each industry (see equations 3.5 and 3.6), or by some related measure of the average amount of human capital per worker. If the skill intensity of sector *i* is expressed as a ratio of that

---

[6] This measure is likewise consistent with the proposition that reduction of barriers to trade based on differences in skill intensity alters the demand for skilled relative to unskilled labour in the countries concerned.

of sector *j*, these related measures will all give the same answer in terms of direction (greater or less than unity), although the size of the ratio will vary, depending on the particular measure used.

The same is not true of another family of 'skill intensity' measures that is sometimes used in studies of trade, namely the ratio of skill input to the value of *output* (where skill input is measured either as the number of skilled workers, or as their wage bill, or as an amount of human capital). In some cases, the use of this family will produce results consistent with the 'natural' measures of skill intensity, but not invariably. The reason is that skilled and unskilled labour are not the only two inputs—a third is capital, whose cost is a substantial component of net output value. It would thus be quite possible for sector *i* to have a higher ratio of skill to output than sector *j*, but a lower ratio of skilled to unskilled labour, because the share of capital costs in sector *i* was much lower. The second family of measures is thus unsafe, implying (in this example) that sector *i* is more skill-intensive, when in fact a rise in the ratio of skilled to unskilled wages would make its products relatively cheaper.

The same logic that dictates the choice of a particular measure of skill intensity also identifies the appropriate measure of capital intensity in the present context, which is the capital–output ratio (and not, as most studies have assumed, the capital–labour ratio). It may seem curious to argue that capital intensity should be measured relative to output, when this sort of ratio was argued to be unsound for skill intensity. But the underlying reasoning is strictly analogous, namely that the choice of the intensity measure should be consistent with the theoretically postulated relationship between relative factor prices and relative goods prices.

In capital theory (discussed in Section 2.2), the basic measure of the relative price of capital and labour is the real interest rate—the nominal rate adjusted for changes over time in nominal wage levels. This rate, which in some models is labelled the rate of *profit*, determines the relative cost of using direct (or current or 'live') labour and indirect (or past or 'dead') labour. In H–O theory, a country in which capital is less abundant (or scarcer or more expensive) must thus be a country with a higher real interest rate, as Ohlin noted in his examples in 1933. Given this definition of the relative price of capital, the capital–output ratio is the natural measure of capital intensity, since it consistently ensures the truth of the proposition that more expensive capital raises the prices of more capital-intensive goods relative to less capital-intensive goods. This point is clearly explained by Pasinetti (1981: 180–8), who also notes that, if the rate of profit on capital is uniform across sectors, the share of profits in output is an equally good measure of capital intensity.

The capital–labour ratio, although it would give equivalent results in some circumstances, and although it is useful for some other purposes, is not a reliable measure of capital intensity. Pasinetti explains how and why the two measures are likely to conflict in comparisons across countries or over time, because of differences in wage levels. However, conflicts can arise even in a specific country at a specific time, when comparing one sector or good with another, because of inter-sectoral differences in skill intensity (which are excluded from Pasinetti's homogeneous-labour model). This point is important and simple, but unfamiliar, so it merits a fuller exposition.

If labour *were* homogeneous, the capital–labour ratio would tell the same story as the capital–output ratio about the relative capital intensity of different sectors. To see this, consider the accounting identity

$$c_i = \frac{k_i}{v_i} \tag{3.7}$$

where c_i is sector i's capital–output ratio, and k_i and v_i are, as before, its capital–labour ratio and value added (or net output) per worker.[7] By substituting for v_i from equation 3.5, the identity becomes

$$c_i = \frac{k_i}{w_i + r_i k_i} = \frac{1}{w_i/k_i + r_i}. \tag{3.8}$$

If labour is homogeneous, w_i is the same in all sectors (abstracting from differences in non-pecuniary advantages and labour-market imperfections), and so, by conventional assumption, is r_i. Hence

$$c_i = \frac{1}{w/k_i + r}. \tag{3.9}$$

It is clear from this expression that sectors with higher c_i must also have higher k_i, and vice versa.

But when labour is heterogeneous and products differ in skill intensity, the bond between these two indicators of capital intensity is broken. For w_i then varies across sectors, depending on the skill composition of their labour forces (see equation 3.6). It thus becomes possible for two sectors to have the same capital–output ratio, but different capital–labour ratios, or for one sector to have a higher c than the other, but a lower k, or vice versa. Among other things, inter-sectoral variations in k_i, for a given c_i, will be positively associated with variations in skill intensity. This can be shown by rearranging equation 3.8 as

$$k_i = \frac{w_i}{1/c_i - r_i} \tag{3.10}$$

and differentiating with respect to w_i. The derivative $1/(1/c_i - r_i)$ must be positive, because $r_i c_i$ is the share of profits in output, which must be less

[7] In most contexts, it would not be legitimate to ignore the influence of wages on the prices of capital goods, and hence on the size of k. But in this context it is acceptable to do so, since we are considering a specific country at a specific time, and hence wages and the profit rate are given.

than unity. Sectors with higher average wages (for whatever reason) tend to have higher capital–labour ratios, essentially because they tend to have fewer workers per (value) unit of output.

A simpler way to explain this point is to define the three factors not as capital, skilled labour, and unskilled labour, but as capital, (raw) labour, and skill (or human capital). It is then obvious that the capital–labour ratio, which depends on only two of these inputs, will not necessarily vary across sectors in the same way as the capital–output ratio, which depends on all three of the inputs (whose total cost is by definition the value of output). It is also clear that the relationship between these two capital-based measures depends on the relative importance of skill in the sectors concerned. For example, in a sector where the cost of skill was a large share of output, the capital–output ratio could be comparatively low, even though the capital–labour ratio was comparatively high.[8]

So when labour is differentiated by skill, the capital–labour ratio is an unsafe measure of the relative capital intensity of different sectors. A rise in the real interest rate, for instance, might lower rather than raise the relative price of the output of a sector with a higher capital–labour ratio, if the sector were also much more skill-intensive, and thus had a lower capital–output ratio. In analysing comparative advantage and trade, the capital–output ratio is thus a better measure of capital intensity.

This general point has particular relevance to previous studies of North–South trade in manufactures. For some of these studies, as will be shown below, have inferred differences in the capital intensity of exports and imports from differences in capital–labour ratios, whereas the use of the more appropriate measure—the capital–output ratio—would have revealed that there was no difference in capital intensity. What the difference in capital–labour ratios is showing, in such cases, is a difference in *skill* intensity, in the expected direction. In the North, the capital–labour ratio of exports exceeds that of import substitutes, implying (as shown in equation 3.10) that the former are more skill-intensive, and in the South this relationship is reversed.[9]

---

[8] From a *mathematical* point of view, with three factors, one needs two factor intensity ratios for a proper comparison of sectors, but there are many such pairs of ratios, all equally good. The reason for picking one particular pair in the present context (the skilled–unskilled labour ratio and the capital–output ratio) is their *economic* significance.

[9] This is not the only possible explanation of differences in k without differences in c. The algebra in the text suggests an alternative, based on differences in r between exports and import substitutes, although these ought to be temporary. For instance, in the South, the lower k in export sectors could arise from a lower r, due to less protection than in import-competing sectors, while in the North the higher k in export sectors could reflect a higher r, due to stiffer competition in import-competing sectors.

3.2.2 Collinearity of skill intensity and capital intensity

Although in some cases the alleged differences in capital intensity vanish when properly measured, in other cases, as will be seen, they remain. In some studies, more specifically, the North's exports of manufactures to the South are genuinely more capital-intensive as well as more skill-intensive than its imports of manufactures from the South. This finding, however, is harder to interpret than is usually recognised, because there is a positive correlation across manufacturing industries between capital intensity and skill intensity. Fig. 3.1 illustrates this with 1980 US data on 3–digit sectors, using the average wage in each sector as the measure of

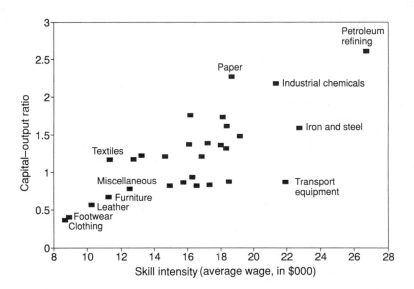

FIG. 3.1 Correlation between skill intensity and capital intensity (across three-digit manufacturing industries in the USA in 1980)
Notes and sources: Derived from data in Fischer and Spinanger (1986, table AII.2). The capital intensity data in the source refer to the capital–labour ratio (capital is measured as the value of fixed assets). The capital–output ratio in each industry was estimated from its capital–labour ratio and its average wage, using equation 3.8 in the present text, and assuming $r_i = 0.3$ in all sectors. (The use of other values for r_i would not much alter the appearance of the figure.)

To keep the figure readable, only the outlying industries are named.

its skill intensity. Forstner and Ballance (1990: 98) report similar results, using averages of data for forty-three countries in 1970–7 and 1978–85.[10]

The equations in the preceding subsection make it clear that there is no obvious *accounting* explanation for this cross-sectoral correlation between skill intensity and capital intensity. It appears to be simply a feature of industrial technology, related to the general complementarity between direct and indirect skill (Section 2.3.2), and to the empirically observed complementarity between skill and capital (Section 4.2.2).

The correlation in Fig. 3.1 is fairly strong ($R = 0.73$), but is heavily influenced by six industries—petroleum refining, in the top right-hand corner, and five others in the bottom left-hand corner. These five (with both low skill intensity and low capital intensity) are clothing, footwear, leather goods, furniture, and miscellaneous. Their products account for a substantial share of the South's narrow manufactured exports to the North, and have been especially prominent in the initial phase of each country's export growth, although by 1985 they were only about a third of the South's total narrow manufactured exports to the North (Wood 1991*c*, table 1).

The characteristics of these five industries are probably the main reason why some FCT studies have found that the manufactures which flow from the North to the South are on average more capital-intensive, as well as more skill-intensive, than those which flow the other way. On the face of it, this result is consistent with three alternative hypotheses. The present hypothesis is that North–South trade is based only on differences in skill availability, the association with capital intensity being a coincidence. The second hypothesis is that this trade is based solely on differences in capital availability, and only coincidentally linked with skill, while the third would be that both skill and capital availability are influential.

3.2.3 Factor content and factor endowments

To discriminate between these three alternative hypotheses, it is clearly necessary to introduce additional evidence, and in particular to compare directly the availability of skill and capital in the North and the South. This specific ambiguity in the results thus exposes a more general, and widely recognised, limitation of FCT calculations as a method of testing H–O theory, which is that they look at only half the picture. A proper

---

[10] Forstner and Ballance measure capital intensity by non-wage value added per worker, a close relative of the capital–labour ratio. Capital–output ratios cannot be derived from their data (as was done with the data used for Fig. 3.1), because they show only the ranking of sectors. However, comparisons with the data used for Fig. 3.1 strongly suggest that the positive correlation found by Forstner and Ballance would remain if their data were reworked using a more appropriate capital-intensity measure.

test needs to cover both factor *content* and factor *endowments* (Deardorff 1984*a*: 478–93; Leamer 1984, ch. 2). More precisely, to establish that trade is based on differences in factor availability, one must show (*a*) that countries are net exporters of certain factors (by FCT calculations) and (*b*) that these factors are comparatively abundant in these countries.

On these principles, all but the first of the hypotheses above can be rejected. The second hypothesis (that differences in the availability of capital are the sole basis of trade) is untenable because there is strong evidence of large North–South differences in the relative availability of skilled and unskilled labour, and hence good reason to expect differences in the skill intensity of trade flows between the two regions. Table 3.1 gives some indication of the magnitude of the difference in skill supplies, which would appear even larger if allowance could be made for the lower quality of most education in the South, and for skills acquired outside the formal educational system.

TABLE 3.1. *North–South comparison of skill availability* (selected indicators)

	Industrial countries	Developing countries
Scientists and technicians 1985–9 (per 1000 people)	81.0	8.9
Tertiary graduates 1986–8 (as % corresponding age group)	9.4	1.2
Mean years of schooling 1990 (in population over 24)	10.0	3.7
Adult literacy rate 1990 (% of population over 14)	[a]	64.0

[a] Not given, but approaching 100.

Source: UNDP *Human Development Report* 1992 (indicators table 5).

The third hypothesis—that both skill and capital are influential—is not persuasive because there is no evidence that capital is generally scarcer or more expensive in the South than in the North. As mentioned in Section 2.2.3, real rates of interest and rates of profit are similar in the two country groups, because financial capital is internationally mobile (and perhaps also for other reasons). Hence North–South trade should not be related in any fundamental way to differences in the capital intensity of the products involved, with the notable exception of one particular form of capital, namely infrastructure (Section 2.2.2).

The North–South similarity of interest and profit rates is well documented. For example, the World Bank (1989, fig. 4.2) compares the real interest rates in thirty-five developing countries during 1967–85 with that in the USA. The developing-country average is below the US rate in most years, and is never appreciably above it. In Asia, one of the four regions into which the developing countries are grouped, the real interest rate fluctuates around the US level. In the other regions it is usually much lower, although the difference is exaggerated, since these estimates are based on official interest rates, which are probably further below the average rates paid by borrowers in the South than in the North.

Essentially the same result emerges from a study by Harberger (1977), who used national accounts data to estimate real rates of return on capital in 1969–71 in eighteen countries. He found little difference between the developed and developing countries in his sample. Likewise, over the period 1965–85, rates of return on US overseas investment in manufacturing were generally similar in developed and developing countries (Evans 1989b, table A9.1.2, panel 3b; UNCTC 1983, annexe table II.5; UNCTC 1988, table V.3).

One possible objection to the present line of argument is that the rate of interest (or profit), r, is not the right measure of capital scarcity, and that the inverse of the wage–rental ratio (rp_K/w, where p_K is the price of capital goods) would be more appropriate. This objection, however, seems inconsistent with standard trade and capital theory, in which the interest rate is more fundamental (Section 2.2.4). Wage–rental ratios, which are higher in the North than in the South, influence the choice of technique, but do not govern a country's comparative advantage as between more and less capital-intensive goods. Nor, when capital is internationally mobile, should its scarcity be measured by the size of a country's capital stock, as has been done in some tests of H–O theory (reviewed in Section 3.5.2).

It may be recalled in this regard that empirical studies of trade which have treated capital as if it were a fixed factor, more abundant in richer countries, have generated a long series of peculiar results (summarised in Findlay and Kierzkowski 1983: 958–9; Deardorff 1984a: 478–93; Leamer 1984, ch. 2; Evans 1989b, sect. 9.2). Although most of these studies have not focused specifically on North–South trade in manufactures, the striking inconsistency of their results seems to support the present argument. The apparent influence of capital is sometimes 'right', sometimes 'wrong', and sometimes insignificant. A lot of effort has been put into trying to resolve these inconsistencies, without much success.

If the present line of argument is correct, though, there is no reason to expect consistency. Internationally mobile capital should not affect the pattern of trade. However, there are bound to be some exceptions to this rule, caused by sustained divergences between domestic and international interest rates, or by enduring differences in infrastructure. In addition, and perhaps more often, there will be spurious correlations. If the goods in which a country has a comparative advantage for other reasons happen to be of unusually high or low capital intensity, the country will appear to be exporting or importing capital. The association between skill intensity and capital intensity discussed above is one such example. Another well-known example concerns the exports of Canada to the USA, based on natural resources whose exploitation is capital-intensive (Niroomand 1991: 751).

To sum up, this book will include capital in its review of earlier studies of North–South trade and in its new FCT calculations, but the results will be interpreted in an unconventionally asymmetric way. Calculations of the capital content of North–South trade will be disregarded as evidence on the issue of whether or not this trade is based on the availability of capital, because there is no corroborating evidence of a North–South difference in the scarcity or cost of capital. However, because there is evidence of a North–South difference in the relative scarcity and cost of skilled labour, skill content calculations will be regarded as confirming or rejecting the hypothesis that this trade is based on differences in skill availability.

3.3 Studies of the South

The most important work in this field is the set of FCT studies by Krueger and others (1981, 1982, 1983). This covers twelve developing countries, using data mainly from the late 1960s and early 1970s. Although the evidence is rather old, these studies are outstanding in their scope and methodological sophistication. This section will look first at the Krueger results for competing imports, then at her results for non-competing imports, and lastly at some related studies. (Studies which consider the South and the North together are covered in Section 3.5, work on trade and income distribution in Chapter 6.)

3.3.1 Krueger results: competing imports

For each country, manufacturing sectors are split into three mutually exclusive categories: exportable, import-competing, and noncompeting. The distinction is based on their ratios of net exports to domestic use (the identification of noncompeting imports is discussed in more detail below). Weighted average factor content coefficients are then calculated for the exportable and import-competing categories, generally using sectoral shares of exports and imports as weights. Table 3.2 summarises the results. In this table (following Krueger 1983) each number is the *ratio* of the average in exportable sectors to that in import-competing sectors.

There are alternative estimates of factor content coefficients in most of

TABLE 3.2. *Factor intensity of trade in manufactures in selected developing countries*
(exportable sectors as ratio of import-competing sectors)

			Factor use per unit of domestic value added				Factor proportions		
			Labour (no. of workers)			Capital (see country notes)	Skilled/unskilled labour		Capital/ labour
			Total	Unskilled	Skilled		Numbers measure	Wages measure	
Argentina	1973		1.30+			0.59+			0.45+
Brazil	1971–2		1.54					0.92+	
Chile	1966–8	H	1.85*			2.00*		0.26*	1.08*
Colombia	1973		1.88+	2.17+	1.16+		0.53+	0.60	
Hong Kong	1973	H	1.21+		0.62+	0.81+	0.51+		0.67+
Indonesia	1971		1.72+	1.89+	1.03+	0.49*	0.55+		0.28*
Ivory Coast	1972	H	1.35+	1.50+	0.93+		0.62+	0.45*	
Pakistan	1969–70	H	1.45*						
Thailand	1973		2.00*						
Tunisia	1972		2.08+	2.69+			<1+	0.65+	
Uruguay	1968		1.85	1.99	0.98	0.79	0.49	0.58	0.42
Unweighted averages			1.66	2.05	0.94	0.93	0.54	0.58	0.58

Notes: The numbers refer to weighted averages of exportable and import-competing sectors, using either trade weights or (for import-competing sectors in some cases) output weights.

* = ratio based on trade with developed countries only.

+ = ratio based on trade with all partners.

Absence of * or + indicates ratio based on exports to developed countries only, imports from all partners.

H = includes home (nontraded) goods indirect factor use, otherwise direct use only.

Blank indicates data not available.

Unless otherwise indicated in the country notes, 'skilled' workers are white-collar (including managers) and 'unskilled' are blue-collar.

'Numbers' measure of skill ratio is number of skilled workers divided by number of unskilled workers.

'Wage' measure of skill is based in some way on the average wage per worker: the precise nature of the calculation varies among the country studies. For Chile and Indonesia the numbers were converted from a per-unit-of-value-added basis to a per-worker basis, for comparability with the other countries.

Capital–labour ratio derived by dividing capital–value added ratio by labour–value added ratio.

Country notes and sources ('81' refers to Krueger *et al.* 1981, '83' to Krueger 1983).

Argentina   Capital measured by cost of energy used. From 83, tables 5.1 and 6.3.

Brazil   From 81, table 2.18 (using average wage index); 83, table 6.2.

Chile   Capital measured by value of fixed assets. Pulp and paper excluded. From 81, table 3.15.

Colombia   Wage measure of skill excludes sugar, petrochemicals, and jewellery. From 81, tables 4.7, 4.16, 4.18.

Hong Kong   Capital measured by depreciation. 'Skilled' workers defined as professionals, and skilled/unskilled as professional/other. Value added in foreign trade rather than domestic value added. From 83, table 5.3.

Indonesia   Capital measured by horsepower. Excluding processed NRB sectors. From 81, tables 5.13 and 5.15.

Ivory Coast   Skilled workers include some blue-collar, unskilled include some white-collar, as well as 'artisans'. 'Modern' sector only. From 81, table 6.11.

Pakistan   Excluding PCB goods. From 81, table 7.12.

Thailand   Includes PCB goods. From 83, table 6.2.

Tunisia   Skilled workers include some blue-collar, but the number of skilled workers is not given, so the numbers measure of the skill ratio cannot be calculated. 'Manufactured' exports only (excluding NRB and traditional exports). From 81, table 10.11.

Uruguay   Capital measured by electricity used. Unskilled labour is 'blue-collar' plus 'unskilled'. From 81, table 11.12.

the country studies. The selection in Table 3.2 was made on the following principles: (*a*) the weights used in averaging should reflect trade with developed-country partners only; (*b*) exports whose existence depends on indigenous natural resources should be excluded (even so, it should be emphasised that for several of these countries in the years to which the calculations refer, their 'manufactured' exports were mainly processed primary products, rather than narrowly defined manufactures); and (*c*) the coefficients should include indirect factor use in nontraded sectors.

These three principles could not be applied in all cases, for lack of the necessary information in the country studies. In some cases, moreover, the principles conflicted, and were then applied in the stated sequence. As a result, the numbers in the table are not always strictly comparable across countries. However, this is unlikely to affect the conclusions, because in most cases the alternative estimates do not differ much. (An exception is that in some countries, if value added is measured at international rather than domestic prices, the factor content of import-competing sectors rises sharply relative to exportable sectors; Krueger 1983: 111–16.[11])

The ratios in the first column of Table 3.2 are based on labour-only coefficients. In every case, production for export uses more labour per unit of domestic value added than import-competing production (although in Argentina, Chile, Tunisia, and Uruguay the reverse is true when value added is measured at international prices). The ratios range from 1.21 in Hong Kong to 2.08 in Tunisia, and their unweighted average is 1.66. The other columns explain why these ratios exceed unity, by comparing the use of skill and capital in exportable and import-competing sectors.[12]

As regards skill, the right-hand (factor proportions) side of the table contains two columns which compare the skill intensity of exportable with that of import-competing manufactures. One column is based on the relative numbers of skilled and unskilled workers. The other column uses the average wage in each sector as a measure of the skill composition of its labour force. One or both measures are available for eight countries. In every case, the ratio is less than unity, implying that exportable sectors are less skill-intensive than import-competing sectors. The size of the ratios varies, but in both columns the average is between 0.5 and 0.6.

The two skill columns in the left-hand side of the table (from which the

[11] This occurs where import-competing sectors are heavily protected. The value added of these sectors is much lower at international prices than at domestic prices, and hence their factor content per unit of value added is much higher.

[12] Ratios in excess of unity, as explained earlier, could also be due partly to higher wage or profit rates in import-competing sectors, as the result of greater protection against imports. There is some evidence of this for Colombia in Krueger *et al.* (1982: 83–148). But the international value added calculations suggest that the main effect of protection is to permit the survival of inefficient activities.

'numbers' column in the right-hand side is derived) compare the number of skilled and unskilled workers *per unit of domestic value added* in the two sorts of sector. In all cases, unsurprisingly, the ratio for unskilled workers (usually defined as blue-collar workers) is greater than that for total labour—its average size is about 2—while the ratio for skilled workers is smaller. However, the average ratio for skilled labour is not far short of unity, implying that exportable sectors use nearly as many skilled workers per unit of output as import-competing sectors, despite their lower *ratios* of skilled to unskilled workers.

The closeness of this ratio to unity is most conspicuous for the three countries (Colombia, Indonesia, and Uruguay) where skilled labour is defined as white-collar workers. By contrast, in Hong Kong, where the definition is professional labour, the ratio is nearer to one-half. The number of observations is tiny, but they suggest that exportable activities employ at least as many *nonprofessional* white collar workers per unit of output as import-competing activities. This is true of managerial labour in two of the three countries for which there are data in Krueger (1983: 106), and is also consistent with some of the Northern evidence. The most likely reason is that a lot of managerial and clerical work consists of supervising, recruiting, and paying other workers. Hence industries with large numbers of blue-collar workers are bound also to need substantial numbers of white-collar workers.

Five of the countries have some data on capital, albeit measured in five different ways (by value of fixed assets, depreciation, horsepower, and use of electricity or energy). The last column of Table 3.2 compares *capital–labour* ratios. Exportable sectors in all countries apart from Chile use less capital per worker than import-competing sectors (on average about 40 per cent less). The comparison in the fourth column is based on capital per unit of domestic value added, a measure of the *capital–output* ratio, which was argued in Section 3.2.1 to be a more appropriate indicator of capital intensity. The capital–output ratios vary widely in size, from 0.5 in Indonesia (mainly because little capital is used in smoking and remilling rubber) to 2.0 in Chile (mainly because of the high capital intensity of fish canning and wine making).[13] Their average is 0.93, which is clearly not significantly different from unity, given their large variance.

3.3.2 Krueger results: noncompeting imports

An original feature of the Krueger studies is their attempt to deal with noncompeting manufactured imports (whose significance was explained

---

[13] Krueger *et al.* (1981, tables 3.12, 5.4, 5.14). Krueger (1983: 111) attributes the high level in Chile to pulp and paper exports to the Latin American Free Trade Area. But the number in the present table excludes pulp and paper, and is based on trade with developed countries only.

above, in Section 3.1.3). Such imports raise two problems: the first is how to identify them; the second is how to estimate their factor content.

Noncompeting imports are identified in the Krueger studies from sectoral ratios of net exports to domestic use. All the imports of a sector are classified as noncompeting if imports (net of exports) supply more than a specific proportion of its apparent domestic consumption (production plus imports minus exports). The proportions—or cut-off ratios— were left to the discretion of the individual country study authors, but were usually between 0.7 and 0.8 (Table 3.3). In almost all the countries, chemicals and machinery and equipment were the main noncompeting imports, and in several countries also basic metals, as well as various more minor items.

As can be seen from Table 3.3, the share of noncompeting items in total manufactured imports is sensitive to the cut-off ratio and to the level of sectoral disaggregation. In Pakistan, for example, a low cut-off (0.2) results in 89 per cent of manufactured imports being classified as noncompeting, while in the Ivory Coast, with approximately the same degree of sectoral disaggregation, a cut-off of 0.75 yields a 27 per cent noncompeting import share. Tunisia has a similar cut-off to the Ivory Coast, but much finer sectoral disaggregation, and hence a much higher (60 per cent) noncompeting import share. Some of the inter-country differences also reflect differences in trade policies. Thus although the apparently complete absence of noncompeting imports in Brazil is partly the misleading result of a high cut-off and a coarse sectoral breakdown, a similar cutoff and breakdown in Thailand yields a 44 per cent share of noncompeting imports, probably partly because of lesser tariff and quota incentives for import substitution.[14]

If data at a finer level of sectoral disaggregation were available, to which a high cut-off could be confidently applied, some of the imports classified with coarser data as noncompeting would turn out not to be so, but additional noncompeting imports would emerge from within the coarsely classified import-competing and exportable categories. The net effect, it may be inferred from Table 3.3, would probably be a substantial increase in the noncompeting import share, which in several of the countries is large even using coarser data. So, despite the inter-country variations, these calculations suggest that noncompeting items constitute a high proportion of total manufactured imports in most developing countries, which is what theory and casual empiricism would lead one to expect.

The second, and conceptually more difficult, issue is how to estimate what the factor input requirements for domestic production of

---

[14] Thailand is described as having moderate tariffs and quantitative restrictions, while Brazil, though by 1970 in an export-promoting phase, had long emphasised import-substituting industrialisation (Krueger *et al.* 1981: 33–7, 393; Krueger 1983, table 3.1).

TABLE 3.3. *Noncompeting manufactured imports in selected developing countries and years*

		Cut-off ratio	Importance of noncompeting imports		Nature of noncompeting imports			
			Share of manufactured imports (%)	No. of sectors/total no. of manufacturing sectors	Chemicals	Machinery and equipment	Basic metals	Other
Brazil	1970	0.75	0	0/56	[a]	[a]	[a]	[a]
Chile	1966–8	0.75	25	9/82	x	x		Wood and cork products n.e.c.; cutlery and hand tools; musical instruments; sporting goods.
Colombia	1973	0.40	—	20/80[b]	x	x	x	Watches; musical instruments; sporting goods.
Indonesia	1971	0.80	—	13/84	x	x	x	Watches; musical instruments.
Ivory Coast	1972	0.75	27	3/32	x	x		
Pakistan	1969–70	0.20	89	11/27	x	x	x	Paper; rubber; petroleum products; railroad ties; fabricated metal products
Thailand	1973	0.60–0.90	44	4/50	[c]	x	x	
Tunisia	1972	0.80	60	10/98	x	[d]	x	Toys; films; typewriter ribbons.
Uruguay	1968	0.70	69	—	[e]	x	[e]	[e]

Notes: The cut-off ratio is the ratio of net imports to apparent domestic consumption above which a sector's imports were classified as noncompeting. For Thailand, differing cut-off ratios were applied to data at differing levels of sectoral aggregation.

x indicates one or more sub-sectors within these sectors classified as noncompeting.

[a] Imports of chemicals, machinery and equipment, and basic metals acounted for 20%, 38%, and 14% respectively of total manufactured imports.

[b] Full list of noncompeting sectors not given, but there seem to have been about 20.

[c] Would have been included at a cut-off of 0.45.

[d] Some relevant sectors apparently omitted from table 10.A.1.

[e] Sectoral breakdown of noncompeting imports not provided.

Sources: Krueger *et al.* 1981: 53, table 2.A.3; 100, table 3.A.1; 149, 153, table 4.A.1; 209, table 5.A.1; 253–6, table 6.9; table 7.2; 414, table 9.5; 450–3, table 10.4, table 10.A.1; 517, table 11.9.

noncompeting imports would have been. The recommended method, applied to six countries, is to use information from a Northern trading partner (Krueger 1983: 100–3). More specifically, the counterfactual input coefficients in Southern noncompeting sector i are estimated with equations of the form

$$a_{is} = a_{cs} \left(\frac{a_{iN}}{a_{cN}} \right) \qquad (3.11)$$

where a_i is the input of the factor concerned per unit of sector i output, and C is a 'common' sector, whose output is currently produced both in the developing country and in its developed partner. In words, this involves calculating in the Northern partner the ratio of the input coefficient in the noncompeting sector to that in the common sector, and then applying the ratio to the input coefficient of the common sector in the developing country.

In providing a theoretical basis for this procedure, Krueger (1981: 24) assumes that the two countries have access to the same technology (as was argued in Section 2.3). She also assumes that the sectors involved all have the same elasticities of substitution among factors. International differences in factor input coefficients are thus caused solely by differences in relative factor prices, and are the same in all sectors. The assumption of identical elasticities is strong, but does not bias the outcome in any obvious way. A more serious weakness is probably the difficulty of identifying a genuinely common manufacturing sector from coarsely aggregated statistics. (The limitations of the Krueger approach are discussed further in the next chapter, Section 4.1.1.)

Table 3.4 summarises the results of applying this procedure in the Krueger country studies. Each number is the ratio of a factor input coefficient (or factor proportion) in exportable manufacturing to the estimated value of its counterpart in the hypothetical domestic production of noncompeting imports. For Argentina and Uruguay, contrary to theoretical expectations, these ratios are actually closer to unity than the corresponding ratios based on competing imports. But in the other countries, and especially in Hong Kong, Indonesia, and Korea, the ratios are (as they should be) farther from unity than those in Table 3.2 based on competing imports. None of the results in Table 3.4, unfortunately, refers to skill intensity. The three which refer to the capital–output ratio all suggest that exports are less capital-intensive than noncompeting imports.[15]

The objective of the Krueger studies is to consider the marginal impact of trade liberalisation, rather than the total effect of trade, on the demand for labour and other factors. Noncompeting imports are there-

---

[15] Two of the three relate to Korea. The third is the result for Uruguay: the wage share of value added is the complement of the profit share, which (with reasonably uniform r_i) is a proxy for the capital–output ratio.

TABLE 3.4. *Factor intensity of manufactured exports relative to noncompeting imports*

		Ratio	Comparator country		Measure of factor intensity
Argentina	1973	1.11	USA	1972	Labour per unit of domestic value added
Hong Kong	1973	0.32	USA	1947	Capital–labour ratio
Indonesia	1971	7.87	USA	1973	Labour per unit of domestic value added
South Korea	1970	0.31	Japan	1970	Capital–labour ratio
South Korea	1970	0.07	USA	1958	Capital–labour ratio
South Korea	1970	0.76	Japan	1970	Capital–gross output ratio
South Korea	1970	0.60	USA	1958	Capital–gross output ratio
Tunisia	1972	1.55	France	1972	Labour per unit of domestic value added
Uruguay	1968	1.44	USA	—	Wages per unit of domestic value added

Notes: Each ratio is calculated as the factor intensity of exportable manufacturing production divided by the estimated factor intensity of the counterfactual domestic production of noncompeting manufactured imports. The Indonesia ratio is based on trade with developed countries only, excluding processed NRB products. The Korea ratios include trade in primary products as well as manufactures, although some noncompeting primary imports are excluded. For Uruguay, year of USA data is not specified in the source.

Sources: Krueger *et al.* (1981: 212–3, 522, tables 5.15, 5.16, 8.10, 10.12, 11.12); Krueger (1983: 100–3).

fore excluded from their labour demand impact calculations, which concentrate instead on changes in exportable and import-competing production (Krueger 1983, ch. 8). The scope for increasing the demand for labour by modifying the composition of output *within* these two categories, mainly by making rates of effective protection more uniform across industries, is substantial in some countries (labour coefficients up by as much as 68 per cent). Labour coefficients could also be increased, by roughly the magnitudes shown in the first column of Table 3.2, by shifting resources from import-competing to exportable production.

3.3.3 Other studies

The FCT calculations of Lee and Liang (1982) for Taiwan and of Westphal and Kim (1982) for Korea help to fill a significant gap in the Krueger studies, although they use slightly different methods.[16] Table 3.5 summarises their results, which refer to much the same period as the Krueger studies. In both economies, as in all the countries in Table 3.2, manufactured exports contain more labour per unit of output than competing imports. There is no information on skill intensity for Korea, but

[16] Taiwan and Korea were both included in the Krueger project, but the work on Taiwan was not completed, and that on Korea was methodologically incompatible with the other country studies.

TABLE 3.5. *Factor intensity of trade in manufactures in Korea and Taiwan*
(exportable sectors as ratio of import-competing sectors)

		Labour per unit of output	Capital per unit of output	Skilled share of employment	Capital–labour ratio
Korea	1968	1.23	0.80		0.66
Taiwan	1966		1.07	0.71	0.67
	1969	1.60	0.82		
	1971		0.56	0.79	0.35

Notes and sources: Korea: Westphal and Kim (1982, table 8.22). 'Output' is gross output. Direct factor requirements only. Trade-weighted averages of sectoral coefficients. Imports apparently include all manufactures, not only competing items.

Taiwan: Lee and Liang (1982, table 10.20). 'Output' is value added at international prices, measured by the Balassa method. Capital–output ratios for 1966 and 1971 are derived from the capital–labour ratios in the years concerned and from the labour–output ratio in 1969. The capital–output ratio for 1969 is the mean of those for 1966 and 1971. Averages of coefficients within exportable and import-competing sector groups are based on output weights. Skilled workers are defined in the source as 'skilled workers, technicians and managerial personnel'.

in Taiwan exports are less skill-intensive than competing imports. However, the difference is not so pronounced as in most of the countries in Table 3.2, perhaps because there was generally less protection of import-competing activities in Taiwan, and hence a greater number of skill-intensive items were noncompeting imports.

The relative capital–output ratio of exports in Taiwan apparently almost halved in five years, from 1.07 to 0.56, mainly because of a sharp rise in the capital intensity of competing imports. However, the average of these two numbers (0.82) is similar to the estimated figure for Korea (0.80). A comparable estimate for Korea (0.86) can be derived from data in Krueger (1983: table 6.3). Both the Taiwan and Korea figures are thus close to that for Hong Kong (0.81) in Table 3.2. So in about 1970, in each of these three East Asian economies, which between them supplied the bulk of the South's exports of narrow manufactures to the North, exports were somewhat less capital-intensive (in the relevant sense) than competing imports.

Fischer and Spinanger (1986, table AII.4) compare the factor content of the manufactured exports of twenty-one developing countries (and of the UK, Japan, and Germany) with the factor content of US exports. They define manufactured exports broadly, including processed primary products except oil. Their factor content estimates, for 1965, 1973, and 1983, are North-bound export-weighted averages of 1980 US sectoral factor intensities (assuming that relative sectoral factor intensities are similar in all countries).

Table 3.6 is based on Fischer and Spinanger's results, but expresses the

TABLE 3.6. *Skill and capital intensity of developing-country North-bound manufactured exports*

(relative to developed-country manufactured exports)

	Skill intensity (average wage per worker)			Capital–labour ratio			Capital–output ratio (estimated)		
	1965	1973	1983	1965	1973	1983	1965	1973	1983
Taiwan	0.83	0.83	0.87	0.76	0.67	0.76	0.95	0.88	0.93
Korea	0.84	0.85	0.91	0.87	0.77	0.83	1.02	0.94	0.95
Brazil	0.88	0.88	0.95	1.02	1.07	1.24	1.10	1.13	1.18
Singapore	0.96	0.94	0.96	1.40	0.93	0.81	1.28	0.99	0.91
Hong Kong	0.82	0.83	0.85	0.65	0.64	0.63	0.88	0.87	0.85
China	0.87	0.80	0.84	0.94	0.82	0.91	1.05	1.02	1.05
Mexico	0.92	0.94	0.96	1.06	1.00	0.97	1.09	1.04	1.01
Malaysia	1.04	0.95	0.95	1.50	1.21	0.94	1.28	1.17	1.00
India	0.79	0.81	0.86	0.89	0.97	1.19	1.08	1.11	1.23
Thailand	0.92	0.90	0.88	1.27	1.09	1.01	1.23	1.12	1.09
Turkey	0.88	0.86	0.84	0.91	0.97	0.97	1.02	1.07	1.09
Indonesia	0.98	0.95	1.00	1.41	1.15	1.33	1.27	1.13	1.21
Argentina	0.86	0.87	0.90	0.90	0.90	1.05	1.03	1.03	1.10
Philippines	0.85	0.89	0.87	0.89	0.99	0.88	1.02	1.07	1.00
Pakistan	0.69	0.75	0.75	0.59	0.82	0.83	0.92	1.05	1.06
Colombia	0.85	0.85	0.87	0.81	0.92	0.93	0.97	1.05	1.04
Morocco	0.92	0.87	0.88	1.05	0.92	1.04	1.09	1.03	1.11
Ivory Coast	0.86	0.85	0.84	0.81	0.84	0.87	0.97	0.99	1.02
Tunisia	0.91	0.94	0.86	1.12	1.19	0.94	1.14	1.17	1.05
Egypt	0.76	0.75	0.83	0.78	0.86	1.09	1.02	1.08	1.18
Kenya	0.83	0.83	0.84	0.80	0.81	0.84	0.98	0.99	1.01
Unweighted averages	0.87	0.86	0.88	0.97	0.93	0.96	1.07	1.04	1.05

Notes: (1) Manufactures include processed primary products other than oil and coal products (ISIC 3, except 353 and 354).

(2) Countries ranked by value of manufactured exports in 1983.

(3) Factor intensities are North-bound export-weighted averages of 1980 US sectoral factor intensities.

(4) All figures derived from source by dividing by the unweighted mean of the figures for Germany, Japan, the UK, and the USA, in the year concerned.

(5) Capital refers to value of fixed assets

(6) Estimated capital–output ratio ($\tilde{c}$) is calculated from capital–labour ratio ($\tilde{k}$) and skill intensity or average wage ratio ($\tilde{w}$), using the following formula derived from equation 3.8 in the text:

$$\tilde{c} = (\tilde{k} + g)/(\tilde{w} + g),$$

where $g = r(k_x/w_m)$, k_x = average capital–labour ratio in exportable production, and w_m = average wage in production of import substitutes. The formula is derived by dividing equation 3.8 (with subscript $i = x$) by itself (with subscript $i = m$), and rearranging to express the result in terms of $\tilde{k}(= k_x/k_m)$ and $\tilde{w} (= w_x/w_m)$. The gross profit rate, r, is assumed to be a uniform 0.3 in all sectors ($r_x = r_m$) and countries; k_x/w_m is assumed to be 2 in all countries (on the basis of data in the source, table AII.2). Hence $g = 0.6$. The results are fairly insensitive to the value of g within a reasonable range.

Source: Fischer and Spinanger (1986, table AII.4).

factor intensity of each developing country's exports as a ratio of the average for the four developed countries, rather than for the USA alone. This average may be interpreted as a proxy for the manufactured imports (competing and noncompeting) of the developing countries concerned. The first three columns of the table show that the manufactured exports of these developing countries are less skill-intensive than their imports in sixty-one out of sixty-three cases (the exceptions are Malaysia in 1965 and Indonesia in 1983). This is consistent with all the evidence presented earlier.

The middle three columns of the table, which refer to the capital–labour ratio, are based directly on Fischer and Spinanger's results. The numbers in the last three columns, which refer to the capital–output ratio (the more appropriate indicator of capital intensity), are estimates derived from the data on skill intensity and the capital–labour ratio. For the four little East Asian tigers, ten of the twelve numbers in the capital–output ratio columns are below unity (which is consistent with the results noted above), but in most other cases the numbers are close to unity. Likewise, the developing-country case studies in Bourguignon and Morrisson (1989: 282) show that narrow manufactured exports are generally less skill-intensive than other manufactures, but in the two countries with relevant data, the capital–output ratio of exports is the same or higher.[17]

Regression analyses

Lee (1986) uses a method similar to FCT analysis to analyse the skill and capital intensity of the manufactured exports of Korea and Taiwan between 1965 and 1977.[18] He regresses the 'revealed comparative advantage' of each manufacturing subsector in each year (its relative share of world exports) on its skill intensity (measured by the average wage) and on its capital–labour ratio (proxied by nonwage value added per worker), using 1975 Korean sectoral input coefficients. In all cases, the estimated coefficients on the skill and capital variables have the expected negative signs. However, there is a striking difference in their significance levels. Taking the 5 per cent level as the cut-off, the skill intensity coefficient

[17] The two countries are Malawi (Bourguignon and Morrisson 1989: 147) and Peru (table VII-10, taking textiles to represent manufactured exports and 'those cited' as the import-substituting industries, and deriving the capital–output ratio by dividing the value of fixed assets per worker by value added per worker). In two other countries, Costa Rica and Morocco, exports had a lower *capital–labour* ratio. Bourguignon and Morrisson (1989: 282) also mention Malaysia and Taiwan, but without actual data on the use of capital. (Their statement that wages are lower in export sectors in Costa Rica is not consistent with the data in table III–12.) Kim and Vorasopontaviporn (1989) also examine the skill and capital intensity of trade, for Thailand, but unfortunately do not separate out manufactures.

[18] The family relationship between FCT calculations and cross-sectoral regressions is discussed by Leamer (1984: 56–7), who argues that the latter are theoretically unsound, although Clague (1991: 360) disagrees.

differs significantly from zero in every single case. The capital coefficient, by contrast, is insignificant in every year in Korea and in seven out of thirteen years in Taiwan.

Clague (1991) uses data on factor prices in five Asian developing countries and (an average of) seven developed countries to predict differences in the relative costs of producing different sorts of manufactured goods. He then uses the predicted relative costs (PRC) to explain the composition of trade in narrow manufactures between these Asian countries and the North in 1975. The factor prices used in his PRC calculations are the wages of skilled and less skilled workers, and the prices of machinery and buildings. The rate of return on capital, however, is taken to be the same in all countries.

In effect, then, Clague fits a model which corresponds closely with the present hypothesis, and his good results tend to support this hypothesis. Regressing sectoral net exports on a version of the PRC variable based only on differences in factor prices yields an R^2 of 0.51, better than in many other studies. However, Clague shows that additional influences shape the detailed pattern of North–South trade in manufactures. Allowing for scale economies in the PRC calculations raises the R^2 to 0.63. Adding variables reflecting some likely causes of North–South differences in the relative efficiency of different manufacturing sectors raises it further, to 0.71.

Education and gender

Some of the studies mentioned above note that the 'unskilled' workers who produce manufactures for export in developing countries usually have (and require) at least a basic education, defined as completing primary school or becoming literate (Krueger 1983: 27, 105). This is actually a feature of *all* manufacturing (e.g. World Bank 1980: 48, 1987: 63). But it is confirmed by other research on the characteristics of workers in export-oriented manufacturing activities in the South.

Lim (1980: 11) sums up several studies: in Mexico, workers in the border export industries had completed at least six years of school; electronics factories in Singapore required a primary education and preferred some secondary education, and in Malaysia their workers usually had at least nine years of formal schooling; in Korea, many of those working in foreign firms were high-school graduates; and more than two thirds of the factory workers in export–processing zones in the Philippines had a high-school or better education. In Sri Lanka in 1981, only 2 per cent of the production workers in the Katunayake export-processing zone had less than six years of schooling (Ramanayake 1984, table 7.24).[19]

[19] Ramanayake (1984: 82, 175) also contains data on the educational qualifications of workers in export-processing zones in Malaysia and the Philippines which corroborate the earlier studies surveyed by Lim.

The same studies document that a high proportion of the labour force in developing-country export-oriented manufacturing is female. In Mexico, women constituted 85 per cent of the workers in the border export industries, in Korea three-quarters of the workers in export industries, and in Malaysia and Mauritius more than 80 per cent of all workers in export-processing zones (Lim 1980: 6). In export-processing zones in the Philippines and Sri Lanka, the proportions of female workers were 74 per cent and 88 per cent respectively (Lee 1984: 173, 220). A similar conclusion emerges from comparisons of the male–female ratio in exportable and import-competing sectors in three of the Krueger country studies (Krueger *et al.* 1981: 155, 425, table 5.13). There is also a clear cross-country correlation between increases in the export orientation and female intensity of Southern manufacturing (Wood 1991*a*, fig. 1).

This evidence on the gender composition of employment constitutes, among other things, a reason for interpreting sectoral wage levels cautiously as an indicator of skill intensity. If there is wage discrimination against females, causing them to be paid less than males for any degree of skill, comparisons based simply on wages will exaggerate the difference between the skill intensity of exports and of import-substitutes. However, there is enough evidence based on other indicators of skill intensity to confirm that the wage data are generally pointing in the right direction.

3.4 Studies of the North

There are many empirical studies of the effects of trade in manufactures with the South on the demand for labour in the North.[20] Their results are summarised in this section under three headings, according to the methods used: import penetration ratios; factor content of trade; and sources of employment change. (Some studies of the effects of trade in general— not with the South in particular—on inter-sectoral wage relativities in the USA are reviewed later, in Section 5.4.1.)

3.4.1 Import penetration ratios

One sort of evidence that is sometimes cited in support of the view that trade with the South has little effect on the demand for labour in the North is the smallness of import penetration ratios. These ratios measure the share of imports of manufactures from the South in Northern con-

---

[20] So many that the review in this section cannot be comprehensive. But excellent surveys covering a wider range of studies are available in UNIDO (1978), OECD (1979, annexe II), Wolf (1979: 74–92), and OECD (1989).

TABLE 3.7. *Southern import penetration ratios* (%)

	1959–60	1969–70	1980–1	1984–5	1988–9
Primary products (UNCTAD)	11.6	12.9	26.5	20.5	16.7
Manufactures (including processed primary products)					
UNCTAD estimates	1.2	1.4	2.0	2.9	3.3
OECD estimates		1.7	3.2	3.7	
Hughes and Waelbroeck estimates		1.7	3.4		

Notes and sources: The Southern import penetration ratio is calculated as the share of imports from developing countries in total developed-country apparent consumption of the goods concerned. Apparent consumption is output plus imports minus exports. Definitions and coverage vary somewhat among the three sources: UNCTAD *Handbook of Trade and Development Statistics* (1972, 1984, 1990, 1991: table 7.1); OECD estimates are from Berthet-Bondet, Blades, and Pin (1988: 11–14), defining developing countries as non-OECD minus Comecon, and developed countries as all OECD; Hughes and Waelbroeck (1981, table 2, using their 1979 figure for 1980–1).

sumption of manufactures. In a few sectors—toys, clothing, jewellery, sports equipment, footwear, and leather products—this share is large (Hughes and Waelbroeck 1981; Berthet-Bondet *et al.* 1988). But for manufacturing in total, as Table 3.7 shows, the Southern import penetration ratio appears tiny. Even by the end of the 1980s, it was only 3 to 4 per cent for the North as a whole, although the ratio had tripled since the early 1960s.

Such figures are a valuable antidote to exaggerated claims and fears about manufactured imports from the South. But they do not shed much light on the magnitude of the effects of this trade on the demand for labour in the North, for three reasons. The first is that the import penetration ratios relate to output rather than employment. The distinction is vital, because Southern imports are concentrated on products and activities where output per worker is low, either actually (competing imports), or potentially or historically (noncompeting imports). These ratios are therefore bound to understate the impact of imports on the labour market.

The second limitation of these calculations (to be discussed further in Section 4.4.3) is that competition from imports can displace labour even where the import penetration ratio is low, since some Northern firms have responded to competition from the South by introducing new production methods that use less unskilled labour. The third limitation is that the import penetration ratio is a one-sided measure, which omits the positive impact of exports to the South on the demand for labour in the North.

3.4.2 Factor content of trade

FCT calculations are more informative than import penetration ratios in two of these three respects: they relate to labour content rather than output value, and to exports as well as imports. (The other limitation of import penetration ratios—their neglect of defensive labour-saving innovation—applies also to FCT calculations, however.) This review of the results of FCT studies of Northern trade in manufactures with the South looks first at labour-only calculations, then at estimates of skill and capital content.

Labour-only calculations

Table 3.8 contains a representative selection of results for a number of developed countries. In the first column, the labour content per dollar of

TABLE 3.8. *Factor content of Northern trade in manufactures with the South: labour-only calculations*

| | | Export–import labour content ratio | Estimated impact on employment | |
			Absolute impact (000 workers)	Share of total manufacturing employment (%)
All OECD	1975	0.65	−205	−0.28
All OECD	1983	0.80	−355	−0.48
USA	1983	0.74	−207	−0.99
Japan	1983	0.85	−20	−0.14
European Community	1983	0.76	−154	−0.60
Germany	1985	0.78	−54	−0.67
France	1985	0.80	−20	−0.41
Italy	1985	0.99	−1	−0.01
Netherlands	1985	0.80	−6	−0.62
Belgium	1985	0.85	−5	−0.63
UK	1985	0.78	−43	−0.74

Notes and sources: (1) Export–import labour content ratio; (*a*) this ratio is defined as labour input per dollar of Northern manufactured exports to the South divided by estimated labour input per dollar of Northern manufactured imports from the South; (*b*) the studies from which these ratios are derived are: OECD 1975 from Balassa (1979*a*, table 5); all the 1983 figures from Balassa (1989, table 6.5); all the 1985 figures from Schumacher (1989*a*, table A.10, last column); (*c*) all three of these sources: (i) use the narrow definition of manufactured exports; (ii) include only direct labour inputs; (iii) are based on gross output rather than value added.

(2) Estimated impact on employment; (*a*) method of calculation is described in the text (based on equation 3.3); (*b*) absolute impact calculations for 1975 and 1983 are based on data in the sources mentioned above, those for 1985 use OECD data on narrow manufactured imports from the South into the countries concerned; (*c*) total (broadly defined) manufacturing employment is obtained from OECD *Labour Force Statistics*, and refers to 1985 (all-OECD manufacturing employment was much the same in 1975 as in 1985).

manufactured exports *to* the South is expressed as a ratio of the estimated labour content per dollar of manufactured imports *from* the South. In each case the ratio is less than unity—though barely so in the case of Italy—and most of the ratios are between 0.7 and 0.9.[21] Similar results are to be found in other studies (see for example Schumacher 1983, 1984; Sapir and Schumacher 1985; and the surveys in UNIDO 1978 and OECD 1979, 1989).

All the results in Table 3.8 are based on the *direct* labour content of trade. As explained in Section 3.1.2, there is some debate about which indirect labour requirements should, in principle, be included. No study of the North has followed the Krueger principle of including only non-traded indirect inputs. A few studies include total indirect requirements (for example, Driver *et al.* 1984 and UNIDO 1986, ch. III): their export–import labour content ratios are usually somewhat higher, but still below unity.

Each of the results in Table 3.8 is also based on the narrow definition of manufactures. If all processed primary products were included, four of the six 1985 ratios in the table would be greater than unity (Schumacher 1989a: table A.10), implying that the North's exports were more labour-intensive than its imports. The reason is probably the low labour content of some of the processed primary imports, especially refined oil, which in turn is largely a reflection of the high share of intermediate inputs in the gross output of the sectors concerned.[22]

This anomaly draws attention to the fact that the results in this table, like most others for the North, are based on labour input per unit of gross output, rather than value added—as in the Krueger studies of the South. With narrow manufactures, however, the distinction appears less crucial, because the share of intermediate inputs in gross output is much the same for exports as for imports. In the few studies where results are available on both bases, they do not differ much: for example, in Balassa (1979a, summarised in Table 3.9), the gross-output-based ratio is 0.65, compared with 0.73 for the ratio based on value added.

In the context of this book, as explained earlier, traded services resemble narrow manufactures. However, trade in services is not well measured, and it is hard to match trade data with production and factor

---

[21] The ratio in the Balassa (1979a) study is unusually low, probably because he used an exceptionally disaggregated (184-sector) commodity breakdown. His ratio rises to 0.71 with an 18-sector breakdown, which conceals important variations in labour intensity within broad sectors.

[22] The all-merchandise-trade calculations in UNIDO (1986, ch. III) also imply that the exports of the North to the South are more labour-intensive than the North's imports from the South. The reason again is oil, which accounts for a large proportion of these imports and contains very little labour per value unit of output. The economic meaning of these UNIDO all-merchandise-trade calculations is questionable, partly because they treat all primary, as well as manufactured, imports as competing.

input data. Thus Sapir and Schumacher (1985, table 3) are the only authors to have attempted FCT calculations for North–South trade in services. Their estimates refer to labour content, without information on skill or capital, and cover three developed countries. In each case, the export–import ratio for trade with the South is less than unity, though not by much (the average is 0.94), and lower than (two cases) or the same as for trade in services with the North.

Employment impact calculations

Most of the studies that have calculated the unit labour content of the North's manufactured trade with the South have then proceeded to estimate the impact of this trade on manufacturing employment (or labour demand) in the North. However, as discussed in Section 3.1.1, different studies have made these estimates in different ways. Some studies have looked at the overall level of trade, others at increments to trade. Some studies have assumed balanced trade, others a Northern manufactured trade surplus. Many of their results thus cannot directly be compared with one another.

To overcome this problem, the employment impact estimates in Table 3.8 are standardised. In each case they are based on the principles summarised in equation 3.3, which refers to the overall level of trade, and assumes that the North's imports of narrow manufactures from the South finance an equal value of manufactured exports to the South. This assumption is not entirely satisfactory, as explained earlier, but it is a reasonable first approximation, and better than the assumptions that were actually made in some of the studies surveyed here.

The second column of Table 3.8 shows the estimated impact in absolute terms (thousands of workers). The impact is always negative, simply because the unit labour content of imports is greater than that of exports, which of course is why all the ratios in the first column are less than unity. The size of the impact depends on how far the ratio is below unity: in Italy, where the ratio is 0.99, the estimated employment impact is minute. The impact also depends on the absolute level of imports from the South, which tends to be larger in larger countries. To correct for this country-size effect, the third column of the table expresses the impact as a percentage of total (broadly defined) manufacturing employment.

The estimated employment impact in these countries and years would not be exactly the same if the calculations were based on other FCT studies, which contain somewhat different export–import labour content ratios. However, the numbers in the last column of Table 3.8 effectively convey one of the main conclusions of all these studies, namely that the impact of trade with the South on the total demand for labour in Northern manufacturing is tiny. In no case does the estimated reduction in employment exceed one per cent of all manufacturing employment, and in most cases it is much smaller.

This small figure is shown in most studies to conceal larger job losses in import-competing sectors, offset by employment gains in exporting sectors. The identity of these sectors is familiar, and similar in most Northern countries. In the six largest nations in 1983, the biggest gains were in metal products, machinery, electrical machinery, transport equipment, and chemicals, while the biggest losses were in textiles (including clothing), leather goods (including footwear), food products, and wood products (UNIDO 1986, figs. 3.15–20). The sectoral pattern was much the same for all OECD countries in 1976, except that the basic metals sector was at that time as large an employment gainer as chemicals (Balassa 1979*a*, table 4).

The principal problem caused by trade with the South, most FCT studies have thus concluded, is one of adjustment—moving workers among manufacturing sectors. There may be on balance a negative effect on the overall demand for labour in manufacturing, but it is too small to be of any consequence. None of these studies, however, has taken noncompeting manufactured imports into account: all of them have derived the labour content of imports from labour coefficients in 'corresponding' domestic sectors. As noted earlier (Section 3.1.3), there are theoretical and empirical reasons for believing that this approach is misleading, and in particular that it substantially understates the impact of trade on labour demand.

Skill content calculations

Labour-only FCT calculations conceal important variations not only among sectors but also among skill categories. Table 3.9 summarises a study by Balassa (1979*a*), which measures the skill content of the North's trade in manufactures with the South by applying 1975 all-OECD trade weights to US factor input coefficients.

Section A of the table uses an occupational breakdown of the labour force. The left-hand set of columns show the number of workers per million dollars of gross output. They reveal that the absolute difference in *total* labour requirements between exporting and import-competing sectors is roughly the same as the absolute difference in the number of *semiskilled and unskilled* manual workers (10 workers per million dollars, in both cases). Exporting industries employ 20 per cent more professional and technical workers, and 11 per cent more skilled manual workers, per unit of output.[23] But they have fewer managers and clerical workers,

[23] The proportional difference in skilled manual employment would perhaps be greater if the figures excluded foremen, of whom there are probably more in the more labour-intensive import-competing industries.

probably because, with fewer manual workers, there is less supervision and administration.[24] So total white-collar employment is lower than in import-competing industries.

The right-hand set of columns in section A of Table 3.9 show the *share* of each occupational category in total employment (a more appropriate measure of skill intensity). In exporting industries, the share of professional and technical workers is 86 per cent higher than in import-competing industries, and of skilled manual workers 73 per cent higher. The shares of managerial and clerical staff, and the overall share of white-collar workers, are also somewhat higher. The share of semiskilled and unskilled manual workers is 28 per cent lower, although they still constitute nearly half the work-force in exporting industries.

The greater skill intensity of exporting sectors is confirmed by the wage comparisons in section B of the table. The average wage per worker is 28 per cent greater than in import-competing industries, while human capital per worker (the present discounted value of the difference between the average wage and the unskilled wage) is 44 per cent greater. In another study, of Belgium, the excess of the average wage in exporting over import-competing sectors was 33 per cent, 20 per cent, and 16 per cent in 1965, 1970, and 1975 respectively (de Grauwe *et al.* 1979, table 2).

Table 3.10, based on occupational and educational measures of skill, shows the results of several other FCT studies of developed countries, together with Balassa's results for the USA. The data on labour-force shares in the first three columns reveal that in every case, the proportion of skilled workers is higher in sectors that export to the South than in those which compete with imports from the South. Some of the studies have more than two skill categories. Where workers are categorised by the amount of their education or training (The Netherlands and Germany), the ratio between the shares of exporting and import-competing sectors rises monotonically with the level of skill. The USA occupational data imply a similar relationship: the ratio is highest for professional and technical workers, with skilled manual workers second, and managers and clerical workers equal third.

The last two columns of Table 3.10 contain estimates of the net impact of trade with the South on workers in each skill category in the country and year concerned. The impact is calculated and presented in the same way as with the all-labour estimates in Table 3.8: the results are standardised across studies, and expressed both in absolute terms and as percentages of manufacturing employment in the relevant skill group. The absolute impact in all cases is largest for the lowest skill group, and except for Italy, the negative numbers in each country's bottom row dominate the numbers in the rows above. The latter are not always

---

[24] Consistently, exporting sectors in the South employ *more* managerial labour (Krueger 1983: 106).

TABLE 3.9. *Factor intensity of OECD trade in manufactures with the South in 1975*

	No. of workers per $ mill. of gross output			Share of labour force (%)		
	Exports to South	Imports from South	Exports/ imports	Exports to South	Imports from South	Exports/ imports
A. Skilled and unskilled workers						
Professional and technical	2.1	1.7	1.20	11.2	6.0	1.86
Managers and administrators	1.0	1.4	0.74	5.6	4.9	1.14
Clerical and sales	2.6	3.4	0.75	14.0	12.0	1.16
All white collar	5.7	6.6	0.87	30.8	23.0	1.34
Foremen and skilled manual	4.3	3.8	1.11	23.2	13.5	1.73
Semi- and unskilled manual	8.5	18.1	0.47	46.0	63.6	0.72
All manual	12.8	22.0	0.58	69.3	77.0	0.90
Total labour						
per $ million of gross output	18.4	28.5	0.65	100.0	100.0	1.00
per $ million of value added	54.9	75.2	0.73			
B. Wage-based measures of skill content ($000 per worker)						
Average wage	9.6	7.5	1.28			
Human capital	29.7	20.6	1.44			
C. Capital–labour ratio measures ($000 per worker)						
Fixed assets	16.6	10.5	1.58			
Non-wage value added	8.6	5.8	1.48			
D. Capital–output ratio measures						
Fixed assets/gross output	0.31	0.30	1.02			
Fixed assets/value added	0.91	0.79	1.16			
Non-wage share of value added	0.47	0.44	1.08			

Notes: Human capital is measured (in the source) as the discounted value of the difference between the average wage and the unskilled wage. Labour per unit of value added is derived from the sum of the average wage and non-wage value added per worker. Capital–output ratios are derived from capital–labour and labour–output ratios.

TABLE 3.10. *Skill intensity of Northern trade in manufactures with the South*
(occupational or educational skill categories)

	Shares of labour force (%)			Estimated impact of trade on employment (in manufacturing)	
	Exports to South	Imports from South	Exports/ imports	Absolute impact (000 workers)	Share of skill category (%)
USA 1975					
Professional and technical	13.3	6.8	1.96	3.5	0.2
Managers and administrators	6.0	5.0	1.18	−3.7	−0.4
Clerical and sales	14.8	12.3	1.20	−8.6	−0.3
Foremen and skilled manual	20.8	13.4	1.55	−1.8	−0.1
Semi- and unskilled manual	45.3	62.5	0.72	−91.2	−0.9
Netherlands 1973					
Semi-high and high	4.2	2.8	1.50	0.3	0.6
Medium	12.0	10.0	1.20	0.3	0.2
Broadened lower	41.9	40.6	1.03	−0.4	−0.1
Basic lower	40.7	45.6	0.89	−2.0	−0.4
Germany 1972–6					
University	2.6	2.0	1.29	0.8	0.4
Formal vocational/technical	9.4	7.9	1.19	1.7	0.2
On-the-job vocational	52.2	46.1	1.13	5.6	0.1
No vocational	35.8	43.9	0.81	−18.7	−0.5
Germany 1985					
Non-manual plus skilled manual	63.3	44.4	1.43	12.2	0.3
Semi- and unskilled manual	36.7	55.6	0.66	−66.1	−2.1
France 1985					
Non-manual plus skilled manual	68.6	54.5	1.26	0.4	0.0
Semi- and unskilled manual	31.4	45.5	0.69	−20.3	−1.2
Italy 1985					
Non-manual plus skilled manual	53.3	45.7	1.17	4.9	0.2
Semi- and unskilled manual	46.7	54.3	0.86	−5.6	−0.2
Netherlands 1985					
Non-manual plus skilled manual	57.3	42.4	1.35	1.0	0.2
Semi- and unskilled manual	42.6	57.6	0.74	−7.1	−1.7
Belgium 1985					
Non-manual plus skilled manual	57.1	47.0	1.21	0.5	0.1
Semi- and unskilled manual	42.9	53.0	0.81	−5.6	−1.4
UK 1985					
Non-manual plus skilled manual	58.7	48.4	1.21	−5.0	−0.2
Semi- and unskilled manual	41.3	51.6	0.80	−37.6	−1.5

Notes and sources: (1) Skill composition of labour force (and labour coefficients per unit of output) in exporting and import-competing sectors derived from the following studies: USA 1975: Balassa (1979*a*, table 5); Netherlands 1973: Kol and Mennes, as reported in UNIDO (1978, table 29); Germany 1972–6: Schumacher, as reported in UNIDO (1978, table 26); other countries: Schumacher (1989*a*, tables A.10–24), using the 'broad' export data in tables A.11–16 to proxy 'narrow' export data (compare Schumacher 1983, table 3).

(2) Estimated impact on employment. See notes to Table 3.8 for an outline of the methods and supplementary data sources used. All the estimates are approximate, those for the 1970s particularly so.

positive, even where the skill share ratio of exporting to import-competing sectors exceeds unity, since total labour requirements per unit of gross output may be proportionately even lower in exporting sectors. For example, in both the USA and the UK, trade appears to reduce non-manual plus skilled manual employment.

The percentages in the last column are interesting because they *quantify* the impact of trade on the relative demand for different skill categories (within manufacturing). In other words, although the skill shares in the first three columns are sufficient to show the *direction* of the impact (a rise in the relative demand for more skilled labour), they do not reveal its size. The numbers in the last column imply that the impact is small. The percentage decline in the least-skilled category tends to be larger than for labour in total, since the absolute decline is concentrated on this category, which accounts for no more than half of the manufacturing labour force. However, the difference between the proportional decline for unskilled workers and the proportional increase for skilled workers, which measures the change in relative demand, is in most of these cases only 1–2 percentage points.

The change in relative demand would seem even smaller if the denominators referred to *economy-wide* employment in each skill category, rather than to the 20–30 per cent of the labour force that is employed in manufacturing. Most FCT studies thus indicate that the impact of trade with the South on the skill composition of labour demand in the North is tiny, although Schumacher in all his articles emphasises that the decline in demand for unskilled labour is a significant problem, as do de Grauwe *et al.* (1979). As with the labour-only calculations, however, the trade-induced twist in the relative demand for skilled and unskilled labour must be underestimated in these studies, since they take no account of non-competing manufactured imports.

Capital content calculations

The only developed-country FCT study of North–South trade to have measured capital content explicitly appears to be that of Balassa (1979*a*). Table 3.9 contains his results, with all-OECD trade weights and US coefficients. Section C shows, using two alternative indicators, that the capital–labour ratio of exporting industries is on average about 50 per cent higher than that of import-competing sectors. The capital–output ratios in section D, which are better measures of capital intensity, show a much smaller difference: with each of the three indicators, the export/import-competing ratio is greater than unity, but on average by less than 10 per cent.

Similar results can be derived from the study of Belgium by de Grauwe *et al.* (1979). Using non-wage value added—one of Balassa's two indicators—as a measure of capital, the capital–labour ratio of sectors exporting to the South was 40 per cent, 41 per cent, and 18 per cent greater than for sectors competing with imports from the South in 1965, 1970, and 1975 respectively. Exporting sectors also had a higher average capital–output ratio, but by only 4 per cent, 11 per cent, and 1 per cent (in the same three years).

The results of Balassa and de Grauwe constitute a rather small sample of evidence, and in both cases are somewhat out of date. However, they are entirely consistent with the Southern FCT studies reviewed above. In the early 1970s, the capital intensity of the North's manufactured exports to the South was slightly greater than that of its imports from the South, matching the pattern observed in the East Asian economies which supplied the bulk of the South's manufactured exports.

A related regression study by Niroomand (1991) also supports the general impression which emerges from the FCT studies reviewed above. For the USA between 1963 and 1980, he regresses net exports on factor inputs across three-digit manufacturing industries, separately for different trading partners (most other Northern regression studies lump all trade together). He concludes that the comparative advantage of the USA *vis-à-vis* its main trading partners in the South is based on human (not physical) capital.

3.4.3 Sources of employment change

A number of studies measure the effects of trade on Northern labour markets with an accounting identity of the form

$$n_i = \frac{dd_i + x_i - m_i}{pv_i} \tag{3.12}$$

relating employment (n) in sector i to output, expressed as the sum of domestic demand (dd) and exports (x), less imports (m), and to average labour productivity (pv). The change in sectoral employment over a given period is then expressed as the sum of changes in each of the variables on the right-hand side, providing an indication of the relative importance of trade. Early applications of this technique are surveyed in UNIDO (1978) and OECD (1979); see also Krueger (1980) and Kol and Mennes (1983).

The most recent and most comprehensive calculations, summarised in Table 3.11, are by UNIDO (1986). They cover the six largest developed countries over the period 1975–80, and are based on input–output tables, changes in whose intermediate input coefficients appear as an additional source of employment change. Exports and imports are not shown separately, but the net effects of trade with different partners are distinguished. As in all other studies of this type, the change in employment is not disaggregated by level of skill.

TABLE 3.11. *Sources of change in industrial employment in six large developed countries, 1975–1980*

(thousand persons)

Domestic demand	9654
Foreign trade, of which:	−156[a]
Developed countries	−503
All developing countries	171
Nine selected developing countries[b]	−206
Input–output coefficients	165
Labour productivity	−10259
TOTAL	−830[c]

Notes: The six developed countries (and their period coverage if different from 1975–80) are: Germany, France, Italy (1975–8), Japan, UK (1975–9), and the USA (1973–80). Numbers in this table are totals for all six countries. Industry consists of manufacturing, mining, and utilities.
[a]Discrepancy between the total effect of foreign trade and the sum of the developed and developing country trade effects is 'due to service trade'.
[b]Argentina, Brazil, Hong Kong, Korea, Malaysia, Mexico, Philippines, Singapore, Thailand.
[c]Discrepancy between total and components may reflect interaction effects.
Source: UNIDO (1986, table 3.1).

The table suggests that trade is a minute source of change in total industrial employment. Changes in trade with all developing countries raised employment, but fifty times more jobs were added by increases in domestic demand. Similarly, although changes in trade with nine selected Southern exporters of manufactures reduced employment in these developed countries, the decline in employment attributed to rising productivity is fifty times greater. The effects of trade appear larger in particular industrial sectors than in these all-industry calculations, in which employment gains from exports in some sectors cancel out losses due to imports in other sectors. But even at the sectoral level, the UNIDO calculations suggest that changes in domestic demand and productivity usually have much more effect on employment than changes in trade.[25]

These results are consistent with those of earlier studies. For example, Cable (cited in OECD 1979, table 4) analysed employment changes in the UK during 1970–5 in thirty-four three-digit manufacturing industries in which imports from the South accounted for 2 per cent or more of domestic consumption. Total employment in these industries declined by

[25] The sectoral results in UNIDO (1986) show only the effects of trade with all partners, which are likely in general to be substantially larger than those of trade with developing countries alone. Out of approximately twenty manufacturing sectors in each country, the number in which foreign trade caused more job losses than productivity growth was four in Germany, two in France, none in Italy, three in Japan, seven in the UK, and none in the USA. The number of manufacturing sectors in which foreign trade created more jobs than domestic demand growth was three in Germany, two in France, nine in Italy, none in Japan, two in the UK, and none in the USA.

about 8 per cent, and trade with the South contributed to the decline, but productivity growth caused over thirty times more job losses. Even in clothing, the sector hardest hit by imports from the South, productivity growth caused four times as many job losses as trade (UNIDO 1978, table 12). A more recent study of the UK clothing industry in the 1970s, however, attributes about half its employment decline to Southern import penetration (OECD 1985: 117).

The main conclusion of these studies—that trade with the South has tiny effects on the demand for labour in the North—depends crucially on their assumption that labour productivity changes are exogenous and unrelated to foreign trade. Martin and Evans (1981), Beenstock (1984: 63–4), Baldwin (1984: 596), and others have pointed out that this assumption is misleading, since competition from low-cost imports is likely to prompt increases in labour productivity. These criticisms are supported by casual empiricism, including 'a prima-facie relationship at an industry level between import penetration and the scale of employment losses' (OECD 1985: 188), and by case studies of particular sectors.[26]

The critics mention various reasons why competition from imports may raise labour productivity: elimination of the least efficient firms in a sector, intensified pressure to cut costs and innovate, and induced substitution of capital for labour. In the context of Northern trade in manufactures with the South, two mechanisms seem especially important. The first is induced changes in product mix. Trade with the South causes firms in the North to abandon unskilled-labour-intensive activities, either by eliminating entire products, or by splitting up the production process and performing only the skill-intensive stages domestically. Such changes in activity mix increase average output per worker, both within particular sectors, and in Northern manufacturing as a whole. Their effect is in principle measured by labour-only FCT calculations, although in practice only imperfectly, due to coarse aggregation of activities and neglect of noncompeting imports.

The second important mechanism by which import competition from the South has raised labour productivity in the North is defensive unskilled-labour-saving innovation (discussed at greater length in Section 4.4.3). In order to survive Southern competition, that is, Northern manufacturers of labour-intensive goods have tried, often successfully, to find new ways of carrying out their production activities with less unskilled labour.

Because, by these two mechanisms, trade with the South has raised labour productivity in Northern manufacturing, the sources of employment change calculations summarised above must understate the impact

[26] See e.g. the summary in OECD (1985) on steel (esp. 102), textiles (122–5), clothing (125–8), and colour televisions (164).

of this trade on Northern labour markets. FCT estimates tend to be more accurate, because they capture the effects of changes in activity mix, but even they do not measure the effects of defensive innovation, since they take factor input coefficients as given.

3.5 Joint North–South Studies

The two previous sections reviewed empirical studies of North–South trade and labour markets in developing and in developed countries. This section considers work which looks simultaneously at both sorts of country. It starts with FCT analyses, then examines cross-country regression studies, and concludes with a review of some research on transnational companies.

3.5.1 Factor content of trade

A few FCT studies (Lydall 1975; Glismann and Spinanger 1982; Kol 1986; Balassa 1986*a*, 1989, ch. 6) explicitly estimate the effects of North–South trade in manufactures on employment in both groups of countries. All are labour-only calculations; none breaks down the effects by skill category, nor looks at capital content. However, in contrast to other labour-only FCT studies, they have an extra dimension. These studies not only compare the labour intensity of exporting and import-competing activities within the North and the South, but also compare labour-input coefficients between these two country groups.

Each of these studies finds, and emphasises, that labour requirements per unit of output are much greater in the South than in the North. But their authors offer differing interpretations of the significance of this large gap in labour productivity. The main message of Lydall, and of Glismann and Spinanger, is that the employment gains of the South from expansion of its manufactured exports to the North far exceed the associated losses of employment in the North. Lydall also stresses that these job losses are offset by induced increases in Northern exports to the South. He does not consider the possibility of these Northern exports reducing employment in the South. Indeed, he argues the opposite, on the grounds that Southern output is constrained by foreign exchange limitations on import capacity.

Kol, though, adopts a symmetrical approach, in which increases in imports displace employment both in the North and in the South. He calculates the effects of a balanced increase in trade in manufactures between the EC and four developing countries. His results, summarised in Table 3.12, imply that most of the Southern job gains from the increase

TABLE 3.12. *Employment effects of trade in manufactures between the European Community and four developing countries*
(thousand persons: balanced $10m. increase in trade)

	Indonesia	Korea	Mexico	Pakistan
Effects of developing-country exports (EC imports)				
In developing countries	+9.3	+2.6	+0.8	+8.9
In EC	–0.6	–0.6	–0.4	–0.7
Effects of EC exports (developing-country imports)				
In developing countries	–6.6	–2.1	–0.8	–5.6
In EC	+0.5	+0.5	+0.4	+0.4
Net effects of increased trade				
In developing countries	+2.7	+0.6	+0.0	+3.3
In EC	–0.1	–0.1	+0.0	–0.3

Notes: The trade data refer to 1983, but are expressed at 1975 prices to match the 1975 input–output data used. The anomalous employment effects for Mexico reflect the importance of pharmaceuticals in Mexico's exports to the EC.

Source: Kol (1986, tables 6 and 7).

in exports would be cancelled out by job losses caused by the accompanying increase in imports. However, the net effect on Southern employment is positive, because the exports are more labour-intensive than the imports. Moreover, although the net effect on Northern employment is correspondingly negative, it is (with the exception of Mexico) much smaller than the Southern employment gain, because of the large North–South difference in labour productivity.

Balassa too adopts a symmetrical approach, but, unlike Kol, considers the effects of unbalanced trade. He emphasises that the North has a large surplus in its trade in manufactures with the South, and hence concludes that the effect on employment in the North is positive. His calculations thus suggest that the effect on employment in the South is negative and large. Neither result is plausible (as explained in Section 3.1.1).

A weakness common to all four of these (as to most other) FCT studies is their neglect of noncompeting North–South trade in manufactures. In other words, they all use labour input coefficients in 'corresponding' domestic sectors to assess the employment effects of imports. As noted in Section 3.1.3, this causes the impact of trade on the demand for labour to be underestimated in both country groups. In the South, the labour content of imports is smaller (and hence the positive net effect of balanced trade on labour demand is greater) than these studies suggest. In the North, on the other hand, the labour content of imports is greater than these studies suggest, and so it is the negative net effect of trade on the demand for labour in manufacturing that is understated.

Factor intensity ranking of sectors

These joint North–South FCT studies cast some light on the issue of factor intensity reversal (see Section 2.3.1). In particular, they reveal that the ranking of manufacturing subsectors (usually at the three-digit level) by output per worker is fairly similar in the North and the South. This emerges both implicitly, because the estimated net employment effects of trade are of opposite sign in the two country groups, and from explicit comparisons (e.g. Lydall 1975: 70). Other studies have arrived at consistent results. Lary (1968, ch. 3) first documented the international similarity of industrial ranking by value added per worker, using data from the late 1950s and early 1960s.[27] Data for 1980 on value added per worker in three-digit manufacturing sectors yield a Spearman rank correlation coefficient of 0.82 between the North and the South (UNIDO 1986, fig. 4.1).

Forstner and Ballance (1990: 98–101), using data for forty-three countries in the mid-1970s and early 1980s, compare the ranking of three-digit industries not only by value added per worker, but also by average wages (a measure of skill intensity) and by non-wage value added per worker (a proxy for the capital–labour ratio).[28] They divide the twenty-three developing countries in their sample into three groups—newly industrialising economies (NIEs), second-generation NIEs, and other—and compare the average ranking of industries in each of these groups with the average ranking in developed countries. Seventeen of the eighteen Spearman coefficients—for three groups, three indicators, and two periods—are between 0.5 and 0.9 (ibid., table 6.2). Kendall's coefficient of concordance for the industry rankings *within* each of these groups is in all cases between 0.6 and 0.8 (ibid., table 6.4).

Forstner and Ballance emphasise the international *differences* revealed by their calculations. They conclude that factor intensity reversals, though the exception rather than the rule, are not uncommon. However, they too neglect noncompeting trade, and the associated tendency for the North and the South to specialise in producing different sorts of manufactured goods. Some of the inter-group variation in sectoral rankings must thus reflect not reversals in the relative factor intensities of the same products, but systematic variations in product mix within each sector. (Part of it also reflects deficiencies of the data, as Forstner and Ballance recognise.)

[27] Arrow *et al.* (1961: 241) had earlier arrived at a contrary view on the basis of comparisons between the USA and Japan, but this was subsequently shown to have been due largely to the inclusion of primary sectors (Lary 1968: 57–8).

[28] Fischer and Spinanger (1986, table AII.1) likewise compare the ranking of industries by capital–labour ratios in the USA with four Asian developing countries. Their results are similar to those of Forstner and Ballance.

In this light, what is surprising is not the differences between the North and the South, but the similarities. For if the North and the South were completely specialised producers of different sorts of manufactured goods within each sector, the ranking of sectors by skill and capital intensity in the two country groups might be totally different. In practice, though, there is a considerable degree of overlap in the composition of production. Some manufactured goods have high transport costs or artificial protection, and the economic boundary between Northern and Southern countries is fuzzy. The ranking of three-digit sectors by factor intensity may also be fairly robust with respect to systematic changes in the choice of products within each sector. For example, a ranking of sectors by skill intensity based on the most skill-intensive goods within each sector might be correlated with a ranking based on the least skill-intensive goods within each sector.[29]

3.5.2 Cross-country regression studies

Several empirical studies have tried to relate variations in trade patterns among countries to variations in their factor endowments. Recent examples include Leamer (1984), Bowen, Leamer, and Sveikauskas (1987), Balassa and Bauwens (1988), Minford (1989), and Forstner and Ballance (1990). Although these studies have not focused on North–South trade, their data span both developed and developing countries, and they implicitly test the hypothesis of this book that North–South trade is based on differences in skill (but not capital) availability. The results of these studies, moreover, are so mixed, and so often appear inconsistent with the present hypothesis, that they demand some explanation.

Specification

All these studies recognise that H–O theory postulates a particular set of relationships among three sorts of variables: trade flows (T), sectoral factor intensities (FI), and country factor endowments (FE). However, they specify their tests in different ways. The ideal specification is used by Bowen, Leamer, and Sveikauskas: they calculate the factor content (FC) of each country's trade from T and FI, and then compare variations in FC and FE across countries (by regression and in other ways).

Balassa and Bauwens approximate the ideal specification, first regressing T on FI across sectors for each country separately, then using the estimated T/FI coefficients as the dependent variables in a cross-country

---

[29] This could also explain why Yeats (1989: 125–7) finds little change in the labour-intensity ranking of coarsely defined manufacturing sectors in the USA during 1965–82, despite the large rise in labour-intensive imports from the South.

regression on *FE*. They also combine the two stages in a 'one-pass' procedure. In one of his tests, Minford uses the same two-step specification as Balassa and Bauwens. In another test, he treats export and import unit values as a proxy for *FC*, and regresses these on *FE* across countries within sectors.

Forstner and Ballance use various tests. Their two-stage method is first to regress *T* on *FE* across countries for each sector, then to regress the estimated *T/FE* coefficients across sectors on *FI*. Leamer (1984) regresses *T* on *FE* across countries within commodity clusters which were identified from trade data but turned out (within manufacturing) to have similar *FI* characteristics (ibid. 66).

Measurement of endowments

Leamer (with and without Bowen and Sveikauskas) considers trade in primary products as well as manufactures, and thus has to measure natural resources as well as endowments of skill and capital. The other studies (like this book) are confined to trade in manufactures, variously defined. Balassa and Bauwens, Leamer and Minford all consider narrow manufactures, while Forstner and Ballance include some processed primary products.[30]

The measures of sectoral skill and capital intensity (*FI*) used in these studies are much the same as those discussed in earlier sections of this chapter. Skill intensity is measured by the average wage or the relative numbers of workers in different skill categories. Capital intensity is measured by capital per worker (or, as a proxy, non-wage value added per worker). None of these studies uses the capital–output ratio (or its proxy the non-wage share of value added), which was argued in Section 3.2.1 to be the correct measure of capital intensity.

The measures of skill and capital endowments (*FE*) used in these studies vary. For skill endowments, Leamer (1984) and Forstner and Ballance break the labour force into three groups: illiterates, professional and technical workers, and the rest (literate workers not in professional and technical jobs). They note some of the limitations of this breakdown, including its neglect of manual craftsmen and skilled managers, and the widely varying skill levels of professional and technical workers in different countries. But they underestimate the seriousness of these limitations. Both studies also fail to recognise that the 'unskilled' labour force in manufacturing needs to be literate.

Bowen, Leamer, and Sveikauskas use the standard international break-

---

[30] Forstner and Ballance (1990, table B4) subdivide their manufactures into three groups, of which one ('Ricardian goods') consists mainly of processed primary products. The other two groups are 'H–O goods' and 'product-cycle goods', the latter being mainly chemicals and machinery.

down of the labour force into seven occupational categories. This is even less appropriate. Not only does it neglect the large cross-country (and in particular North–South) differences in the amount and quality of education and training of workers in each of these categories, but it also fails to recognise that, even within a given country at a given time, the standard occupational classification is not a categorisation of workers by level of skill. Skilled and unskilled 'production' workers are lumped together, and most of the categories are based on the type of work done (service, sales, clerical, agricultural) rather than on level of education or training.

Balassa and Bauwens (following unsuccessful experiments with occupational data, reported in Balassa 1979*b*: 262) measure a country's skill endowment by the average education level of its population, using the Harbison–Myers index, which is the secondary school enrolment rate plus five times the university enrolment rate, lagged six years. This is a more appropriate measure, but it suffers from being based on enrolment data rather than on direct information on the educational composition of the labour force (see Psacharopoulos and Arriagada 1986). Nor does it allow for cross-country differences in educational quality or in other forms of training.

Minford attempts to overcome these problems by measuring skill endowments simply by the national average wage level, converted into dollars at the official exchange rate. His assumption that variations in wages among countries are due mainly to variations in the average skill level of their labour forces is untested and unlikely to be exactly correct. However, it is a plausible first approximation. None of these authors uses data on the relative wages of skilled and unskilled workers, though Forstner and Ballance (1990: 74) mention this as a possibility for future research.

Endowments of capital are measured in all these studies (except that of Minford, who omits capital altogether) as the cumulated stock of past investment flows. This measure is highly inappropriate, for theoretical reasons discussed in Section 3.2.3. If capital were internationally immobile, and trade did not fully equalise factor prices, the appropriate indicator of its 'abundance' in a country would be the real interest rate. However, in a world in which financial capital is internationally mobile, tending to equalise interest rates, theory suggests that capital should simply be excluded from cross-country H–O analyses of trade, as in the present book and in Minford's study.[31]

The capital stock, as measured in the other studies, is closely correlated with GNP. This is because the main source of cross-country variation in absolute levels of investment, from which the capital stock estimates are

---

[31] Leamer (1984: 233–4) admits to 'discomfort' about his capital variable, on both conceptual and measurement grounds. Forstner and Ballance (1990: 13, 125) note at various points that the international mobility of capital could account for their odd results.

derived, is variation in GNP—the share of investment in GNP varies much less. The stock of capital per worker is thus strongly correlated across countries with GNP per worker (Leamer 1984: 275). GNP per worker in turn is bound to be correlated with the average wage, which is Minford's measure of skill endowment. The 'capital stock' variable is thus probably acting mainly as a proxy for skill endowments. This interpretation is supported by the collinearity which Balassa and Bauwens (1988: 31) discover between their measures of physical and human capital endowments.

Results

The preceding review of the variations and deficiencies of specification and measurement in these cross-country regression studies should make it easier to understand why their results have been mixed and in many cases peculiar, sometimes severely testing their authors' faith in H–O theory. A detailed evaluation of their results would go well beyond the scope of this chapter, but the main findings may be summarised as follows.

Leamer (1984) is able to show that the pattern of trade in primary products is governed largely by international differences in natural resources. But his regressions do not provide a clear, consistent, and credible explanation of the pattern of trade in manufactures (ibid. 115, 170–5, 187, 260–73). This is not really acknowledged in Leamer's book, but in his later paper with Bowen and Sveikauskas, using a better specification, he concedes that his results were presented in too positive a light (1987: 805). This joint paper comes to negative conclusions—its results give almost no support to H–O theory. However, its authors also note signs that this may be due to errors in the measurement of variables, which there certainly are, as explained above.

Forstner and Ballance, who measure their variables in much the same way as Leamer, have no more success than Leamer in relating trade in manufactures to differences in endowments of capital and skill, although, like Leamer, they take a positive view of their results. Their coefficients are often insignificant or have the wrong signs or contradict other information about the sectors concerned (Forstner and Ballance 1990: 85–6, 105, 120–5). However, when allowance is made for errors of measurement and interpretation, most of their results can be reconciled with the present hypothesis that North–South trade is based on differences in the availability of skill but not capital.

Balassa and Bauwens are much more successful in explaining the pattern of trade in manufactures, largely because they use a better measure of skill endowments.[32] Their misconceived measure of capital

---

[32] Their fine commodity disaggregation, and restriction of the country sample to substantial exporters of manufactures, probably also contribute to their greater statistical success.

endowments does not damage their results because (as mentioned above) it is so collinear with their skill endowment measure that for most purposes they combine the two into a single variable (Balassa and Bauwens 1988: 30–1). They also often combine their measures of skill and capital intensity into a single variable, which again does not much affect their results, since these two indicators are collinear across sectors (see Section 3.2.2).

The estimated coefficients in the cross-country regressions of Balassa and Bauwens are thus consistently significant, with the right signs. The only shortcoming is in the way the authors interpret their results. Balassa and Bauwens conclude that the pattern of trade in manufactures depends on skill and capital endowments. However, their results really only show dependence on *skill* endowments; as in the other studies, the influence of capital is not properly tested for.

Minford, whose theoretical framework is essentially the same as that of this book, makes various tests of the hypothesis that the pattern of trade in manufactures depends on international differences in skill endowments. First, he regresses export unit values (a proxy for skill content) against national wage levels (proxying skill endowments) across countries within each of eighteen selected three-digit manufacturing sectors (Minford 1989: table 8.1). In fifteen cases the estimated coefficient is positive, and in nine cases significantly so (at the 2.5 per cent level). Regressions using *import* unit values yield much the same results, with the signs of the coefficients reversed.

Minford then tries an alternative dependent variable: net exports in four-digit subsectors. He expects the sign of the coefficient on the wage level to be positive within two-digit sectors of (presumed) high skill intensity, and negative within sectors of low skill intensity. About one-third of the coefficients are significant with the right signs (ibid., table 8.3). Minford's final test, which is similar to that of Balassa and Bauwens, is to regress net exports on skill intensity across sectors in each country (using data on UK sectoral wage levels to measure skill intensity), and then to compare the signs of the estimated coefficients with national wage levels. As his hypothesis predicts, the signs are usually positive in high-wage countries and negative in low-wage countries (ibid., table 8.4).

Conclusions

Upon examination, the results of these cross-country regression studies seem consistent with the hypothesis of this book that North–South trade is based on differences in the availability of skill but not of capital. The consistency is most evident in the Minford study, but also emerges clearly from the results of Balassa and Bauwens. The other studies (Leamer 1984; Bowen, Leamer, and Sveikauskas; and Forstner and Ballance) do not actively support the present hypothesis, but the apparent inconsistencies—in some cases insignificant results, in others significant but conflicting results—can be explained by errors in the measurement of endowments. The Leamer and Forstner and Ballance studies also contain some other results which are worth noting here (and are independent of their factor endowment measures).

Leamer (1984) discovered a substantial change between 1958 and 1975 in the global pattern of trade in manufactures. 'Clustering' in the trade data revealed four distinct categories of manufactures, which (it then emerged) also had common factor intensity characteristics. Two of these categories were skill-intensive: 'chemicals' (capital-intensive) and 'machinery' (not capital-intensive). Of the third and fourth categories, both of low skill intensity, one was 'labour-intensive', the other 'capital-intensive'. In 1958, most countries were either net exporters of all four categories or net importers of all of them. But by 1975, the labour-intensive category had broken away from the other three. Most developed countries had reduced their net exports or increased their net imports of labour-intensive goods, and some had moved from being net exporters to being net importers, while several developing countries had moved the other way (ibid. 86–9, 96–9).

A similar but slighter tendency was evident for the capital-intensive category, e.g. iron and steel, metal products, textiles, rubber products. Several developed countries had reduced their net exports of capital-intensive manufactures, and one—the USA—had moved from being a net exporter to being a net importer, while two developing countries—Spain and Korea—had moved in the other direction. Moreover, the cross-country correlation between labour-intensive and capital-intensive net exports had remained positive, although much more weakly so, while the correlations between labour-intensive exports and both machinery and chemicals exports had switched from positive to negative between 1958 and 1975 (ibid. 85–6).[33]

These results confirm that a new pattern of North–South specialisation in different sorts of manufactures emerged after about 1960, and that it was based on differences in skill intensity, not capital intensity. The fact that the tendency was slighter and later for Leamer's capital-intensive goods than for his labour-intensive goods is not inconsistent with this conclusion, since the former are also somewhat more skill-intensive than the latter. On average, their share of professional and technical workers is about 70 per cent greater, and their wage level about 40 per cent higher

---

[33] There is strong evidence of reduced Southern reliance on imports of basic metals from the North during this period. See e.g. OECD 1985: 86–7, and the comparison in Sect. 3.4.2 between Balassa's 1976 and UNIDO's 1983 sectoral employment impact calculations, as well as Table 3.3, which shows that around 1970 basic metals were a major noncompeting import for most developing countries.

(Leamer 1984, table 3.4). This accords with the generally positive correlation across sectors between capital intensity and skill intensity, noted earlier.

Forstner and Ballance (1990: 30–1) also document the emergence of North–South specialisation within manufacturing, using data on production rather than trade. The sectors that grew relatively rapidly in the South during 1973–86 tended to be those that grew slowest or contracted in the North, and vice versa. Using a four-category breakdown of sectors, Forstner and Ballance also discover (ibid. 33–4) that expansion in the North was concentrated on skill-intensive, not on capital-intensive, industries, in accordance with the present hypothesis.[34] In the South, there was considerable expansion of capital-intensive sectors, but also of skill-intensive sectors. This last finding is consistent with earlier evidence that industrial growth in the South was more balanced across sectors than in the North (UNIDO 1985: 33). The main reason is probably the high levels of industrial protection in many developing countries during most of this period.

3.5.3 Transnational companies

Transnational companies play a big role in international trade (Kaplinsky 1991*a*: 29). Thus, although some direct investment flows are unrelated to trade, studies of such companies can shed light on the issues with which this book is concerned. Most foreign direct investment occurs within the North (Julius 1991). But employment in the Southern subsidiaries of TNCs is substantial—for manufacturing alone, in the mid-1980s, a lower-limit estimate of about 3 million workers (UNCTC 1988, table XIII.2).

The character of TNC activity in the South has changed over the past few decades. In earlier years, it was undertaken mainly to exploit natural resources or to get access to protected domestic markets for manufactures, notably in Latin America. The subsequent expansion, however, has been concentrated on export-oriented manufacturing activities, especially in export-processing zones (Fröbel *et al.* 1980, ch. 14). As the hypothesis of the present book would predict, the exports from these zones, whose main destination is the North, include some capital-intensive as well as non-capital-intensive items (ibid. 35–6, 328).

Most studies agree that, despite possible displacement of employment in national firms, direct foreign investment causes a net increase in the demand for labour in host countries (Dicken 1986: 372). There is more disagreement about the effects on the demand for labour in the country of origin. Some studies conclude that the effect is unambiguously nega-

---

[34] Forstner and Ballance's 'high-growth' and 'low-growth' categories are interpreted here as high-skill-intensity and low-skill-intensity groups.

tive, though of uncertain size (Fröbel 1980: 287). Others argue that the job losses caused by relocation of production could be more than offset by increased employment in supplying goods and services needed by overseas subsidiaries, e.g. the study by Hawkins summarised in Dicken (1986, table 11.3). Part of the disagreement arises from different assumptions about what would have happened in the absence of the overseas investment. Part is also due to confusion between investment in the North and the South.

All studies concur, though, on the effects of direct investment in the South on the *skill composition* of the demand for labour. TNC subsidiaries in developing countries mainly employ semi-skilled and unskilled production workers (Fröbel 1980: 344); and it is these categories that gain least or lose most in Northern parent companies (Dicken 1986: 383). The relative demand for higher-skilled white-collar workers in the parent companies is correspondingly increased, for example because research and development facilities are retained in the home country (ibid. 372). Lipsey *et al.* (1982) confirm this, and show also that TNCs employ smaller proportions of salaried workers in countries where salaries are higher relative to wages.

3.6 Summary

Two hypotheses are under test in this part of the book. One is that the main effect of North–South trade in manufactures on labour markets is to alter the relative demand for skilled and less-skilled workers, or (to put it another way) that this trade consists fundamentally of the exchange of more skill-intensive goods for less skill-intensive goods. A corollary of the first hypothesis is that this trade is not based on differences in the scarcity of physical capital. The second hypothesis is that the impact on the relative demand for skilled and unskilled labour is substantial.

The results of previous research strongly support the first hypothesis. Factor content of trade and related regression studies, both in developing and in developed countries, consistently find that the manufactured exports of the North to the South are concentrated on goods whose production needs a higher ratio of skilled to unskilled workers than the manufactured goods which the South exports to the North. This is confirmed by studies of the division of labour within transnational companies.

There is also strong evidence that this pattern of specialisation within manufacturing is based on a large North–South difference in the relative availability and cost of skilled and unskilled labour. A few cross-country regression studies have failed to detect this Heckscher–Ohlin relationship, but only because they have measured skill endowments in the wrong way.

The corollary of the first hypothesis, too, is consistent with the results of previous research, when these are correctly interpreted. Some factor content of trade studies have found that the North's exports to the South are more capital-intensive than its imports from the South. But this is often an illusion, caused by the use of an inappropriate measure of capital intensity (the capital–labour ratio, rather than the capital–output ratio).

In some cases, there is a genuine difference between the capital intensity of North–South and South–North manufactured trade flows. This difference, however, is coincidental; it exists because several sectors of low skill intensity also happen to be of low capital intensity. There is no evidence that capital is scarcer or more expensive in the North than in the South: real interest rates (and profit rates) are similar in the two regions, and capital is mobile between them. So there is no reason to attach any causal significance to differences in the capital intensity of trade flows.

The second hypothesis—that the impact of North–South trade on the relative demand for skilled and unskilled labour is substantial—is contradicted by the results of previous research on the North. However, the methods used in this research are biased in the direction of understatement.

One method estimates the impact from the difference between the factor content of exports and imports. Studies which use this method invariably find only a tiny effect on the skill composition of the demand for labour. These studies, though, miscalculate the factor content of imports, because they fail to recognise that a high proportion of North–South trade in manufactures is noncompeting: the goods which are imported are of types which are not produced in the countries concerned. The skill intensity of imports is overstated in the North and understated in the South, causing their impact on labour markets to be underestimated in both regions.

The other main method, which also suggests a tiny impact, is to estimate the effects of trade from an accounting decomposition of the sources of employment change. The weakness of this approach is its assumption that productivity growth is exogenous, since there are two mechanisms by which trade with the South raises manufacturing labour productivity in the North. One is changes in output mix: increased specialisation in more skill-intensive activities, with less skill-intensive activities moving to the South. The second is defensive unskilled-labour-saving innovation. The impact of trade with the South on the demand for labour in the North must thus have been larger than these studies imply.

The evidence available from previous empirical studies thus provides an adequate test of one of the two hypotheses, but an inadequate test of the other. The next chapter is therefore focused on filling this gap, by devising and applying a better method of estimating the size of the impact of North–South trade on the demand for skilled and unskilled labour.

4

Factor Content of Noncompeting Trade

This chapter develops and applies a modified version of the factor content method of estimating the impact of North–South trade in manufactures on the composition of the demand for labour in both country groups. Its principal objective is to obtain a more accurate indication of the *magnitude* of this impact, which is understated by conventional FCT calculations.

4.1 Methodology

The conventional FCT method of estimating the impact of North–South trade on factor demand was summarised in the previous chapter in two equations

$$Z_N = X_S (z_{XN} - z_{mN}) \qquad (3.3)$$

$$Z_S = X_S (z_{XS} - z_{mS}) \qquad (3.4)$$

where the Z terms are vectors of factor quantities, X_S is the total value of the manufactured exports of the South (S) to the North (N), and the z_X and z_m terms are export-weighted and import-weighted averages of sectoral factor input coefficients in the country group concerned.

The main shortcoming of the conventional method, Section 3.1.3 argued, is its neglect of noncompeting imports: its implicit assumption that imported manufactures are identical to those made in corresponding domestic sectors, and hence that the z_m terms can be estimated accurately from domestic input coefficients. Both theory and evidence suggest that this assumption is far from true of North–South trade. Most of the manufactures imported from the South are of types which are not produced in the North, because their high unskilled labour intensity would make them unprofitable. Conversely, the South's imports of manufactures from the North are concentrated on skill-intensive goods which it would not be economic to produce domestically.

4.1.1 Counterfactual import coefficients

Another method of estimating factor content coefficients for noncompeting imports is therefore needed. More precisely, we need a way of estimating the factor inputs that would have been required, counterfactually,
to make these goods domestically. Any such method clearly has to be
based in some way on information about factor input coefficients in the
trading partner, where the noncompeting imports concerned are produced.

One approach would be simply to use trading-partner export
coefficients, replacing each country group's z_m vector by the z_x vector of
the other group.[1] This approach is attractive, since the z_x vectors refer to
the relevant baskets of goods. But it is unacceptable as it stands, since it
assumes that domestic production of these goods would employ exactly
the same mix of factor inputs as in the trading partner. This is implausible, because of the large North–South difference in relative factor prices,
which would encourage firms to choose different techniques. For example, if unskilled-labour-intensive goods had to be made in the North,
rather than imported, this would be done using less unskilled labour, and
more skilled labour and capital, than in the South.

This flaw in the simple approach can be corrected, however, by making
an adjustment to allow for the factor price differences. More specifically,
the method applied in this chapter is to start from trading-partner export
coefficients, but to treat these as the outcome of a cost-minimising choice
among alternative techniques. One can then estimate, given information
on elasticities of substitution, how much of each factor would be used if
the noncompeting imports had to be produced domestically, at a different
set of relative factor prices (the details are explained in Section 4.2.3). So,
if all imports were noncompeting, the factor demand impact in the North
could be estimated as

$$Z_N = X_S\,(z_{XN} - z_{XS}^*)		\tag{4.1}$$

where z_{XS}^*, the counterfactual Northern import coefficient vector, is the
adjusted Southern export coefficient vector. The corresponding calculation for the South, using adjusted Northern export coefficients, would be

$$Z_S = X_S\,(z_{XS} - z_{XN}^*).		\tag{4.2}$$

This method invites comparison with that used in the pioneering work of
Krueger, described in Section 3.3.2. Her approach, applied to the South,
is to estimate counterfactual input coefficients in Southern noncompeting
sector i with equations such as

---

[1] This is the approach suggested by Deardorff (1982: 689) for imports in general, not
merely for noncompeting imports.

$$a_{is} = a_{CS} (a_{iN}/a_{CN}) \tag{3.11}$$

where a_i is the input of a given factor per unit of sector i output, and C is a sector common to the two country groups. The Krueger method resembles the present method not only in its use of trading-partner input coefficient data, but also in assuming that the North and the South have access to the same technology in each sector, and that factor inputs differ between the two country groups simply because of differences in relative factor prices. Moreover, both Krueger and the present chapter assume that elasticities of substitution do not vary across sectors.[2]

However, the Krueger method is not usable in the present context, because a_{is} does not measure the counterfactual factor content of a *dollar value unit of noncompeting imports*, which is what is needed in equations such as 4.1 and 4.2. Instead, it measures factor content *per value unit of output at the counterfactual domestic price* (the price that would be just enough to cover all costs if the noncompeting imports were produced domestically). This is clear from equation 3.11. The two partner-country coefficients, and their ratio a_{iN}/a_{CN}, are measured at partner-country prices. But the home-country common sector coefficient, a_{CS}, is measured at home-country prices, and hence so must be the counterfactual coefficient, a_{is}.

This matters mainly because the wages of most types of labour (expressed in a common currency) are much lower in the South than in the North, so that physical units of output tend to have a higher value when measured at the price that would be needed to cover production costs in the North than at the corresponding cost-covering price in the South, even allowing for the effects of factor price differences on the input mix. Thus, for example, the number of hours of labour embodied in a dollar's worth of manufactured imports from the South is much greater than the number of hours that would be embodied in a dollar's worth of output of the same items in the North, and it would be wrong to use the latter as an estimate of the former.[3]

---

[2] Or at least that cross-sectoral differences in elasticities are small. (Large differences, incidentally, would call into question the basic H–O assumption of no factor intensity reversal.) The present method differs from the Krueger method in that it needs more information—on the values of substitution elasticities and on factor prices—in exchange for which it provides more information about the counterfactual outcome.

[3] The Krueger method remains valid as a way of estimating counterfactual factor *proportions* (because the output denominators of the a_{is} coefficients cancel out when ratios between different such coefficients are calculated), provided that the factor inputs in the numerators are measured in physical units, such as hours of skilled and unskilled labour, or the labour content or horsepower of capital goods. This last condition is not fulfilled where the input of capital is measured by the value of the stock employed, since many capital goods are domestically produced, and so their value depends on the local wage level.

4.1.2 Counterfactual output levels

Some questions of a different kind about equations 3.3 and 3.4 were also raised in Section 3.1. They concern the accuracy of X_S as a measure of trade-induced changes in domestic production. One such problem is that noncompeting imports (unlike competing imports) ought to be cheaper than the same goods would be if produced domestically, and hence the demand for them should be greater. The level of imports thus tends to overstate the amount of domestic production displaced. Another problem of this kind concerns the primary exports that the South 'loses' when they are embodied in manufactured goods. A third concerns the labour-intensive manufactured exports that the North has 'lost' because of import substitution in the South. Finally, there are the ambiguities caused by fudging the distinction between gross output and value added.

To allow for these concerns, the conventional FCT approach will therefore be further modified in this chapter, although, as will be seen, the output-related modifications make less difference to the results than the change in import coefficients outlined above. The manufactured exports of the North and the South will be treated as two different goods, or baskets of goods, labelled *skill-intensive* (subscripted E for education) and *labour-intensive* (subscripted L, and meaning 'less skill-intensive'). The impact of trade on the output of each of the two goods in each of the two regions will then be examined separately. So, referring to the induced change in output as dQ (a scalar, which may be positive or negative), equations 4.1 and 4.2 become

$$Z_N = dQ_{EN}\, z_{XN} + dQ_{LN}\, z_{XS}^* \qquad (4.3)$$
$$Z_S = dQ_{LS}\, z_{XS} + dQ_{ES}\, z_{XN}^*. \qquad (4.4)$$

Clearly, the units in which the dQ terms are measured must be the same as those used in the output denominators of the corresponding z coefficients. Provided that this consistency is maintained, however, the units do not need to be the same for all the dQs. In this chapter, Q is always treated as physical (or constant-price) output, using different measurement units for the two goods, in order to disentangle price and quantity effects.

It should be emphasised that equations 4.3 and 4.4 involve only a fairly minor modification of the conventional FCT approach. Each of the four dQ terms, as will be explained in more detail later, is a function of X_S. The conventional approach thus becomes a special case in which these functions happen to be such that

$$X_S = dQ_{EN} = -dQ_{LN} = dQ_{LS} = -dQ_{ES}. \qquad (4.5)$$

The meaning of the operator d should also be clarified. It refers not to change over time, but to the difference between *actual* and *counterfactual* output levels, the latter being the level of output that would have been produced in the absence of North–South trade. (The difference is defined as actual *minus* counterfactual. Thus, for example, dQ_{LN} is negative, since the actual level of labour-intensive production in the North is less than the counterfactual level.) The need to consider counterfactual outcomes is implicit in the conventional approach, but there are advantages to making it explicit. One is as a reminder of the scope for disagreement about the results of these calculations simply because of differing views about what would have happened in the absence of the changes in North–South trade.

The scope for disagreement is widened by the fact that the conventional FCT approach neglects many general equilibrium interactions. The calculations in this chapter do not properly address this issue. What is offered is an improved version of the FCT approach, not a general equilibrium model as a replacement. Nor, for both theoretical and practical reasons, can there be any hope of the calculations arriving at precise answers. The object of the chapter is to assess the magnitude of the impact of trade on the demand for labour, and its emphasis will be placed on establishing, with the help of sensitivity analysis, the likely *range* within which the answer lies.

4.1.3 Identification of noncompeting imports

An immediate practical problem is that the extent of noncompeting imports cannot be measured accurately. To discover which imported manufactures are and are not produced domestically would require matched sets of data on trade and production of manufactures far more detailed than any currently available for developed countries, let alone developing countries.[4] Even within narrowly defined manufacturing subsectors, some types or qualities of product (or some stages in their production) are labour-intensive, while others are skill-intensive. Apart from the Krueger studies of the South (summarised in Section 3.3.2), the theoretical presumption that most North–South trade in manufactures is noncompeting is supported mainly by a mass of examples and anecdotes, with no firm basis for quantification.[5]

---

[4] The best source for developed countries is the OECD database (described in Berthet-Bondet *et al.* 1988), which goes down to the 4–digit level.

[5] It is particularly well documented that Northern firms have ceased to produce many of the manufactured goods currently imported from the South. Some specific examples are mentioned in OECD (1985), including offshore production of Japanese textiles (ibid. 122), product mix shifts by Japanese, German, Swiss, and Italian textile manufacturers (ibid. 122–5), shifts to lower-cost overseas sources of automobile components (ibid. 143), and offshore assembly of colour televisions (ibid. 164). Similar adjustments are documented for German firms in Fröbel *et al.* (1980), and for American and Swedish firms in Lipsey *et al.* (1982). In addition, there are countless newspaper articles based on interviews with business-

The initial assumption in this chapter (to which the sensitivity of the results will be tested) is that all North–South trade in *narrowly defined* manufactures is noncompeting. The narrow definition, it may be recalled, excludes 'processed primary' products such as food and refined petroleum (for details, see Wood 1991c, table 1). This assumption is a compromise: the processed primary category probably contains some items which in an economic sense are noncompeting manufactures; but some imports of narrow manufactures are competing with domestic production.[6] Ideally, separate calculations should be made for noncompeting and competing imports. But the present assumption about the scope of noncompeting trade makes it convenient (and not too inaccurate) to omit competing imports altogether, inverting the approach of conventional FCT calculations.

The rest of this chapter is arranged in the following way. Section 4.2 describes the estimation of the factor content coefficient vectors for exports and noncompeting imports, while Section 4.3 explains how the dQ terms are determined. Section 4.4 presents estimates of the impact on factor demand, obtained by combining the coefficient vectors and the dQ terms, subjects these estimates to sensitivity analysis, and discusses their limitations.

4.2 Factor Content Coefficients

The first step, described in Section 4.2.1, is to calculate actual factor content coefficients (z_{xN} and z_{xS}) for the narrow manufactured exports of, and factor prices in, both country groups. Section 4.2.2 discusses the choice of values for the elasticities of substitution, and Section 4.2.3 explains how the information on factor prices and elasticities is used to estimate the counterfactual factor content coefficients, z_{xN}^{*} and z_{xS}^{*}.

4.2.1 Actual coefficients and factor prices

The procedure followed is (*a*) to decompose the cost of exports among the different factors, (*b*) to estimate factor prices, and hence (*c*) to derive

men or assessments of specific firms or industries. For instance, on the day this note was originally drafted (7 Dec. 1987) the *Financial Times* contained three such articles. One reported that the UK woollen industry 'withdrew from the lower-value markets dominated by the Far East', and another that canvas and plastic shoes were 'a market British manufacturers left years ago'. The third article recounted how 'monochrome televisions are no longer made in Japan, while manufacture of some simpler videorecorder models has been moved to low-cost offshore sites', and cited other Japanese examples (air-conditioning units and paper-insulated copper cables). All this simply confirms what most consumers have noticed in the shops about the country origin of specific types of products.

[6] Either permanently (because there are costs and obstacles to trade, and because theory permits limited overlaps between countries—Krueger 1977), or temporarily (because of sunk costs in installed capacity).

factor content coefficients by dividing the cost components by the prices. This is not the standard FCT procedure, which is based on direct estimates of factor input coefficients in each sector (equation 3.1), but the mutual consistency of the numbers obtained by the present method facilitates the subsequent derivation of the counterfactual coefficients.

The coverage of the calculations is broad. The North is all developed market economies, and the South all developing countries (including China). The estimates thus involve a mixture of reliable and dubious data (and some assumptions). However, the sensitivity analysis suggests that the final results are not greatly affected by likely errors in the data.

TABLE 4.1. *Cost breakdown of manufactured exports, 1985*
(% of gross output at factor values)

	North's exports to South	South's exports to North
Delinked intermediate inputs:		
Primary and processed primary	18.1	28.0
Imported manufactures		19.6
Domestic nonprimary value added:		
Services	21.6	15.4
Manufactures, of which	60.3	37.0
Wages, of which	46.4	22.9
SKILD	31.3	7.4
BAS-ED	15.1	15.5
Gross profit	13.9	14.1
TOTAL COST	100.0	100.0

Source: Appendix A1.

Table 4.1 shows the estimated cost structure of the manufactured exports of each country group to the other group (the sources and methods used are described in Appendix A1). A basic distinction is made between 'delinked' intermediate inputs and all other inputs. Delinked intermediates are those whose production location is assumed to be fixed, that is, not to alter in the counterfactual case in which each group's manufactured imports from the other group are replaced by domestic production. Following Krueger, all primary and processed primary inputs are treated as delinked. So, in the South, are some manufactured intermediate inputs, namely skill-intensive components imported from the North.[7] All other costs are reduced (using input–output methods) to domestic value added: part of this arises in services, the rest in manufacturing, on

[7] In principle, imports of skill-intensive *capital* goods used in labour-intensive production should be treated in a similar way.

which the subsequent calculations focus. Manufacturing value added is split between wages and gross profits, with the wage bill further subdivided between *SKILD* and *BAS-ED* workers.

It can be seen from the table that the share of manufacturing value added in the gross value of manufactured exports is substantially lower in the South (37 per cent) than in the North (60 per cent), partly because of the higher primary product content, and partly because imported components make up about one fifth of total costs in the South. The share of manufacturing profits in the gross value of exports is similar in both country groups, and hence a higher share of manufacturing value added in the South. The share of *BAS-ED* (or unskilled) wages in the gross value of exports is also similar in the two groups. But the wages of *SKILD* workers (who, it may be recalled, include manual craftsmen as well as professional, technical, and managerial employees) account for a much larger share of total costs in the North.

Table 4.2 shows the estimated factor prices in the two country groups (the sources and methods are again explained in Appendix A1). The developing-country wage rates are open to some doubt, partly because of the problem of choosing a set of country weights that accurately reflects the distribution of labour-intensive manufacturing. On the basis of evidence suggesting (on average) much lower levels of education and training among *SKILD* workers in developing countries, a rough adjustment for labour quality is made, which puts the skill content of Southern *SKILD* labour at half that of the North. The cost of a standardised (Northern level) unit of skill in the South is thus twice the *SKILD* wage.

TABLE 4.2. *Factor prices in manufacturing, 1985*

	North	South
SKILD labour ($/hour)	14.99	2.34
BAS-ED labour ($/hour)	7.21	0.75
SKILD labour quality index	100	50
Skill ($/hour) of Northern quality	14.99	4.69
Gross profit rate (%)	23.9	33.2
Capital goods (price index)	100	60
Rental (%) at Northern prices	23.9	19.9

	North/South
Relative factor prices	
BAS-ED labour/capital	8.1
Skill/capital	2.7
BAS-ED labour/skill	3.0

Source: Appendix A1. The rental rate of capital is the gross (of depreciation) profit rate adjusted by the capital goods price index.

The estimated gross profit rate in the South is higher than in the North. As explained earlier (Section 3.2.3), most sources suggest that profit and interest rates are similar in the two country groups. These estimates are used here because they come from sources consistent with the cost data, and are, incidentally, less favourable to the present line of argument than the assumption of equal profit rates would be. The difference in profit rates is largely offset by the lower price of capital goods in the South (mainly because of lower wages in construction), and so the rental rate of capital is roughly the same in both country groups.

The bottom panel of Table 4.2 compares *relative* factor prices in the North and the South. The *SKILD* wage is about 50 per cent higher, relative to the wage of *BAS-ED* labour, in the South than in the North. (This is consistent with the independent estimates of Clague 1991: 366.)[8] However, because of the gap in labour quality, the cost of a standardised unit of skill, relative to the unskilled wage rate, is three times greater in the South than in the North. There is an even bigger difference between the two country groups in the cost of capital relative to unskilled labour: the *BAS-ED* wage–rental ratio is eight times greater in the North than in the South. (The reason is that there is a much smaller difference between the two country groups in the price of capital goods than in the wage rate, because machines are internationally traded. If all capital goods were produced domestically, as buildings are, there would be less of a gap in wage–rental ratios.)[9]

Table 4.3 shows the factor content coefficients, calculated by dividing some of the cost components in Table 4.1 by the relevant factor prices in Table 4.2. Comparing the two country groups, the most striking feature is the tenfold difference in *BAS-ED* labour requirements per dollar of gross exports. The gap in total labour requirements is smaller, because skill requirements are more similar, as are capital requirements.[10] The North's exports are thus produced with a much higher ratio of skill (and skilled labour) to unskilled labour. The difference in skill ratios reflects the greater skill intensity of Northern exports, but it is amplified by the lower relative cost of skill in the North, which induces firms to choose more skill-intensive techniques for all goods.

[8] Clague's wage data refer to six Asian countries, and are derived from Kravis *et al.* (1982). The unweighted average of his skilled blue-collar and professional wage ratios is almost exactly 50% greater than his unskilled blue-collar wage ratio. Clague also experiments with arbitrary increases in the relative cost of skilled labour in developing countries, similar to the present quality adjustment.

[9] See Sect. 2.2 (and esp. Sect. 2.2.4). Without trade, if profit rates were equal, technology identical, and labour homogeneous, there would be no difference in wage–rental ratios between economies with different wage levels (Pasinetti 1981: 194–7).

[10] To produce $1000 of manufactured exports in the South requires more of every factor except quality-adjusted skill than in the North. This does not necessarily indicate technological backwardness, however, since these are inputs into two physically different bundles of manufactured goods.

TABLE 4.3. *Factor content of manufactured exports, 1985*
(per $000 of exports at domestic factor values)

	North	South
Labour (hours)		
SKILD	21.0	31.7
BAS-ED	20.8	207.5
Total	41.7	239.2
Skill (hours of Northern quality)	21.0	15.8
Capital ($)		
At Northern prices	582	709
At domestic prices	582	426

Source: Derived from Tables 4.1 and 4.2, as follows. Manufacturing labour and capital costs per $1000 of exports are calculated by multiplying the last few lines of Table 4.1 by 10. These costs are then divided by the relevant factor prices in Table 4.2.

It is hard to check these coefficient estimates against those of previous FCT studies, which mostly refer to earlier years (when prices and factor productivities were lower, and so input coefficients per dollar of exports were higher), and to individual countries rather than country groups, and which treat intermediate inputs in various ways. However, the South–North total labour coefficient ratio, which is a vital ingredient of the present calculations, and is estimated here at 5.7 in 1985, can be compared with the 1983 ratio of 5.4 estimated in an entirely different way by Balassa (1989, table 6.4).[11] The disparity is encouragingly small (and well within the ± 22 per cent range of the sensitivity analysis reported in Table 4.11: B1).

Also vital to the present calculations are the *SKILD* shares of employment in the production of each country group's exports. The estimated share in the North (50 per cent) is based on reasonably reliable data, and is close to the shares estimated in other recent studies.[12] The estimated share for the South (13 per cent) is open to more doubt. As explained in Appendix A1, one can calculate quite accurately the share of white-collar workers in Southern export-oriented manufacturing, and also the share of *SKILD* workers within the white-collar group (professional, technical,

[11] The South–North ratio of Balassa's labour coefficients in manufacturing export production is 4.3, with labour measured in person-years. To achieve comparability with the present ratio, which refers to person-hours, the Balassa ratio has to be scaled up in proportion to the difference in hours worked per year between the two country groups (see Table 4.9).

[12] See esp. the 1985 estimates for 6 developed countries in Table 3.10. The share of non-manual and skilled manual workers in export production ranges from 53% to 69%, around an unweighted average of 60%. These figures include white-collar *BAS-ED* workers, and so overstate the *SKILD* share, but a corresponding figure can be obtained from the present estimates in Table A1.4—it is 62%, which is very similar.

and managerial employees). It is impossible, however, to make an accurate assessment of the share of *SKILD* workers (manual craftsmen) within the blue-collar group.[13]

Studies of export-processing zones and the Southern subsidiaries of TNCs are the main source of evidence on this last point: they suggest that the share of *SKILD* manual workers (those whose work requires an apprenticeship or other formal training of, say, two years or more) is negligibly small.[14] However, these studies understate the proportion of *SKILD* manual workers in the production of Southern manufactured exports as a whole. This is partly because the exports which require more manual craftsmen (for example, steel and ships) are rarely produced in these zones, and partly because the share of manual craftsmen is probably higher in Southern firms which manufacture intermediate inputs for export production.

The share of *SKILD* workers in the Southern blue-collar group is therefore set initially at 10 per cent (as compared with 45 per cent in the North). The sensitivity analysis varies the total *SKILD* labour share in Southern export production (initially 13 per cent) from 7 per cent to 25 per cent, the latter figure implying that about 24 per cent of blue-collar workers are *SKILD*.

4.2.2 Substitution elasticities

To derive the counterfactual coefficients z^*_{xN} and z^*_{xS} from the actual export coefficients z_{xN} and z_{xS} requires an assumption about the form of the production (or cost) function, and the specification of substitution elasticities. The functional form used in these calculations is two-level

[13] Only one of the Krueger studies summarised in Table 3.2 of the previous chapter includes manual craftsmen in its definition of skilled workers: in the Ivory Coast in 1972, the share of skilled workers in modern-sector HOS production is estimated at 17.5%, including skilled blue-collar workers and excluding semi-skilled white-collar workers (Krueger *et al.* 1981, tables 6.6 and 6.11). The study of Tunisia uses a similar breakdown, but relies on an assumption about the share of skilled blue-collar labour (ibid. 449–50 and n. 21). The study of Taiwan summarised in Table 3.5 of the present book puts the share of 'skilled workers, technicians, and managerial personnel' in total employment in manufacturing for export at 34% in 1966 and 43% in 1971 (Lee and Liang 1982, table 10.20 and n. 34). It seems likely that these figures are based on too broad a definition of skilled manual work: the corresponding percentage in Northern import-competing sectors in 1975 was only 24% (summing the professional, managerial, and foremen and skilled manual shares in Table 3.9 of the previous chapter; if clerical and sales workers are also included, the share was 37%).

[14] On export-processing zones, Lee (1984: 14) notes 'the low skill content of these jobs and the fact that the "learning curves" are typically very short—a matter of a few weeks at most'. Other studies in the same volume reinforce this point (ibid. 34, 56, 207), as does Fröbel (1980: 344). An apparent exception is one EPZ firm in Malaysia where 'half of the work-force was classified as skilled labourers': but the skill level of these workers cannot have been high, since they earned only 25% (females) and 33% (males) more than unskilled workers (Lee 1984: 89).

CES. The lower level aggregates capital and skill, which most evidence indicates are highly imperfect substitutes or complements (the elasticity of substitution is set at 0.1).[15] The upper level of the function combines capital-plus-skill with unskilled (*BAS-ED*) labour to produce net output (intermediate inputs are assumed to be separable). A less restrictive functional form would require more parameters to be specified, and would not affect the general magnitude of the results.

The results are more dependent on the specified values of the four substitution elasticities (two levels and two goods), and especially on that between capital-plus-skill and unskilled labour in the production of Southern exports. The larger (in absolute size) this elasticity, the more does the higher relative wage of unskilled labour in the North reduce the counterfactual labour content of imports, and hence the smaller is the estimated adverse impact of trade on the Northern demand for unskilled labour. To set a value for this elasticity, it is necessary to consider two families of econometric estimates, and some case-study evidence.

First, there are econometric studies of substitution between skilled and unskilled labour. Most recent estimates of (the absolute size of) this elasticity for highly educated versus less educated labour are between 1.0 and 2.0, although some are as low as 0.4 (Freeman 1986: 364–6). Recent best-practice estimates based on occupational skill categories range from zero to 3.7 around a mean close to unity (Hamermesh 1986, table 8.4).[16]

Second, there are the many econometric studies of substitution between capital and labour. A survey of recent work mainly on developed countries indicates that for labour undifferentiated by skill most elasticity estimates are between 0.5 and 1.5, with rather more of the outliers below than above this range (Hamermesh 1986: 451–5).[17] For blue-collar labour alone, best-practice estimates range from 0.14 to 2.10, with a mean close

[15] Relevant empirical studies are surveyed by Freeman (1986: 367) and Hamermesh (1986: 460–1), though Corbo and Meller (1982: 208) discover 'slight' evidence to the contrary. In the 11 studies summarised by Hamermesh, the estimated elasticities of substitution between skilled labour and capital range from –1.94 to 1.09, with a mean value of –0.33. The rather similar magnitude of most estimated elasticities of substitution between (*a*) capital and unskilled labour and (*b*) skilled and unskilled labour, to be documented below, gives additional support for aggregating capital and skill in this restrictive way (Corbo and Meller 1982: 194).

[16] The estimates in section IIa of the Hamermesh table are taken to be best-practice, because they are all translog, based on cost rather than production functions (ibid. 462), and include capital as well as skilled and unskilled labour (466).

[17] Most of the numbers tabulated by Hamermesh refer to the constant-output own-price elasticity of demand for labour. These have been converted into substitution elasticities using Hamermesh's (1986: 451) assumed ⅔ share of labour in value added, which is similar to the average of the North and South figures in Table 4.1. Estimates of the substitution elasticity between capital and labour based on time-series data, and on cross-country data (such as Behrman 1982), must be interpreted with great caution, since most of them fail to allow for the effect of differences in wage levels on the price of capital goods (see Pasinetti 1981: 180–8).

to unity (ibid. 460–2). Most econometric results for developing countries are rather similar, clustered between 0.5 and 1.2 (White 1978: 33).[18]

The econometric estimates, however, exaggerate the value of substitution elasticities in the specific sense required for the present calculations. For what is relevant is only the scope for factor substitution in the production of (a fixed-proportions bundle of) precisely specified manufactured goods, including intermediate components and semifinished products as well as finished items. Econometric estimates capture in addition other responses to differing factor prices, including variations in product quality and in product mix within more broadly defined sectors.[19] In some contexts, it would be important to include these other sorts of 'substitution', but the present calculations should exclude them.

Plant and product-specific case studies provide potentially better evidence on narrowly defined substitution elasticities. They confirm that there is usually scope for factor substitution, but that this is generally narrower when the product and its quality are precisely specified.[20] The most relevant case studies would seem to be those of the Southern subsidiaries of transnational companies. An econometric study of TNCs estimated elasticities mainly between 0.4 and 0.9, but these are biased upwards by the inability to control for variations in product mix (Lipsey *et al.* 1982). Interview studies tend to suggest that substitution elasticities are close to zero.[21] But they are biased downwards because of selective questioning and unrecognised scope for factor substitution in 'peripheral' operations such as materials movement and storage (White 1978: 43–4). There is sometimes even scope for varying the number of 'core' workers operating specific installed equipment (Pack 1987: 19–20, 24).

In light of this evidence and its shortcomings, the elasticity of substitution between capital-plus-skill and unskilled labour is set initially at 0.5, at the lower end of the econometric range. But the sensitivity analysis of the final results will use values between 0.1, as implied by some of the case-study evidence, and 0.9, in the middle of the econometric range (and

[18] More recent studies include Corbo and Meller (1982) and Battese and Malik (1987, 1988), which use cross-firm data and estimate elasticities to be close to unity in most manufacturing industries (at least for large firms). Earlier studies (e.g. Arrow *et al.* 1961) had concluded that substitution elasticities varied among manufacturing industries. However, Morawetz (1976) notes the lack of rank correlation of industry elasticities across different studies (of both developed and developing countries).

[19] As recognised e.g. by White (1978: 33), Lipsey *et al.* (1982: 219), and de Meza and Natale (1989: 1112, 1116).

[20] On the developing-country case-study evidence, see Stewart (1978: 196–204), White (1978: 34–9), Balasubramanyam (1983: 532–9), Bhalla (1985: 1–14), and Pack (1987: 29–32).

[21] Fröbel *et al.* (1980: 355–6) find that labour productivity in TNC subsidiaries in Southern export-processing zones is approximately equal to that achieved in the same activities in Northern parent companies, which suggests that the same production techniques are being used. Earlier interview studies suggesting little or no adaptation of techniques to local factor prices are summarised in Lipsey *et al.* (1982: 251–2), Balasubramanyam (1983, table 32.1), and de Meza and Natale (1989: 1113).

similar to the values used in many computable general equilibrium models).

The TNC and other case studies support another important assumption of the counterfactual coefficient calculations, namely that the South currently has access to the same technology for manufacturing labour-intensive goods as the North, and, in particular, that the production function for these goods has the same 'efficiency' parameter in both groups.[22] For if the high labour content of Southern production were largely due to backward technology, the labour content of counterfactual Northern production of the same goods would be much smaller, and hence so would be the adverse effect of trade on the demand for unskilled labour in the North. However, despite evidence of inefficiency in some parts of Southern manufacturing, there is little reason to suppose that the leading exporters of manufactures are using inferior technology.

4.2.3 Counterfactual coefficients and product prices

Using these values for the substitution elasticities, in conjunction with the estimated relative factor prices in the two country groups, the (cost-minimising) counterfactual factor content coefficients are calculated in two stages, as follows. (On the technical specification of CES production and cost functions, see for example Layard and Walters 1978: 272–6, and Varian 1978: 18–20.)

The *first stage* is to calculate the parameter values of the four CES functions involved, using the data on actual factor content coefficients, factor prices, and costs, together with the substitution elasticities. The unit-output production and aggregation functions are of the form

$$1 = \tau \left[\delta I^{-s} + (1 - \delta)J^{-s}\right]^{-1/s} \tag{4.6}$$

where τ is the efficiency parameter, δ the distribution parameter, s the substitution parameter, and I and J are factor input coefficients per unit of output (or per unit of skill-capital aggregate). First, the values of the substitution parameters are calculated as

---

[22] Much of the relevant evidence is reviewed by Pack (1988: 340, 358–65). For some products, proprietary information may be inaccessible. But most of the South's manufactured exports either use standard technology or are produced in collaboration with TNCs and other Northern firms (see the TNC case studies cited above, Westphal *et al.* 1981, and Rhee *et al.* 1984). Moreover, the scale of production in Southern exporters is economically efficient (in other cases, smaller scale has been shown to be an important cause of lower productivity; see Pack 1988: 360, Stewart 1978: 199–200, and Clague 1991: 368–71). From comparisons among textile plants in Kenya, the Philippines, and the UK, Pack (1987: 170–2) finds that the main reason for less-than-international-best-practice productivity in the two developing countries is excessive product diversification and hence short production runs.

$$s = \frac{1}{\sigma} - 1 \qquad (4.7)$$

using the estimated substitution elasticities, σ. Next, the values of the distribution parameters are calculated as

$$\delta = \frac{\mu}{1 + \mu}, \text{ where } \mu = \frac{\delta}{1 - \delta} \text{ and} \qquad (4.8)$$

$$\frac{\delta}{1 - \delta} = \left(\frac{w_i I}{w_j J} \right) \left(\frac{I}{J} \right)^s \qquad (4.9)$$

where w_i and w_j are the prices of factors i and j (and $w_i I$ and $w_j J$ are unit factor costs). Given s and δ, the efficiency parameter τ can then be calculated from equation 4.6 for each function.

The *second stage* is to use these parameter values to calculate what the input coefficients would be at trading-partner factor prices. The four cost-minimising input ratios can be calculated from a rearranged version of equation 4.9, namely

$$\beta = \frac{J}{I} = \left[\frac{w_i}{w_j} \frac{(1 - \delta)}{\delta} \right]^{\frac{1}{(1 + s)}} \qquad (4.9a)$$

Trading-partner factor prices can also be inserted into the four corresponding CES minimum-cost functions

$$\theta = \frac{1}{\tau} \left[\left(\frac{w_i}{\delta^{-1/s}} \right)^{\frac{s}{(1+s)}} + \left(\frac{w_j}{(1-\delta)^{-1/s}} \right)^{\frac{s}{(1+s)}} \right]^{\frac{(1+s)}{s}} \qquad (4.10)$$

to calculate for each of the two goods (*a*) the counterfactual cost, θ, of a unit of the skill-capital aggregate, and hence (*b*) the counterfactual cost of a unit of net output. Given θ and β, one of the counterfactual input coefficients in each of the four functions can be calculated by rearranging the cost accounting identity

$$\theta = w_i I + w_j J \text{ as} \qquad (4:11)$$

$$I = \frac{\theta}{w_i + w_j (J/I)} = \frac{\theta}{w_i + w_j \beta} \qquad (4.11a)$$

from which the other coefficient is calculated simply as $J = I\beta$.

The counterfactual input coefficients for noncompeting imports, z_{XN}^* and z_{XS}^*, estimated in this way, are presented in Table 4.4, and compared with the actual export coefficients z_{XN} and z_{XS}. The mix of factor inputs is substantially altered. For example, the number of *BAS-ED* hours required per unit of labour-intensive manufactured output, which is 208 in the South, would be reduced to 140 in the North. There would be compensating increases in the amounts of both capital and skill per unit of output, though more the former than the latter, since in the North skilled workers are more expensive relative to capital. Similarly, to produce one unit of the North's exports in the South would increase the number of *BAS-ED* hours required from 21 to 38, and would reduce the use of capital. The amount of skill used would also go down, but only slightly, since in the South it is cheaper relative to capital than in the North.

TABLE 4.4. *Actual and counterfactual factor content coefficients, 1985*

Actual coefficients	z_{XN}	z_{XS}
BAS-ED labour (hours)	20.8	207.5
Skill (hours of Northern quality)	21.0	15.8
Capital ($ at Northern prices)	582	709
Counterfactual coefficients	z^*_{XN}	z^*_{XS}
BAS-ED labour	38.3	139.7
Skill	18.9	23.0
Capital	477	1137
Substitution elasticities		
Capital/skill	0.1	
Capital-plus-skill/BAS-ED labour	0.5	

Source: Actual coefficients from Table 4.3; counterfactual coefficients derived from actual coefficients, as explained in text, using trading-partner factor prices from Table 4.2 and substitution elasticities shown above.

The information in Table 4.4 permits a proper comparison between the skill intensity of each country group's exports and its noncompeting imports from the other group. This is because the factor inputs into the two baskets of manufactures can now be compared at a common set of factor prices (actually at two common sets of prices, comparing z_{XN} with z^*_{XS}, and z^*_{XN} with z_{XS}). In terms of ratios of standardised skill to *BAS-ED* labour, the manufactures which the North exports to the South are about six times as skill-intensive as those which the South exports to the North. This difference in skill intensity would be only half as large without the skill quality adjustment, but would still (as expected) be larger than is implied by conventional FCT calculations, from which the exports of the North appear to be between 20 per cent and 100 per cent more skill-intensive than those of the South.[23]

Table 4.5 shows the estimated differences between the actual prices of imports and what these goods would cost if they were produced domestically. It suggests that labour-intensive manufactures would be counterfactually about three times more expensive to produce in the North than

[23] See Tables 3.2, 3.9 and 3.10. The estimates in Table 4.4 should be compared only with those conventional estimates which measure skill intensity by the relative *numbers* of skilled and unskilled workers, rather than by the average wage in different sectors. The wide margin of error surrounding the present estimate of skilled employment in Southern export production (Sect. 4.2.1) should also be borne in mind.

TABLE 4.5. *Counterfactual/actual product price ratios*

	Skill-intensive manufactures	Labour-intensive manufactures
Counterfactual/actual price	0.5	2.8
	Counterfactual cost breakdown (%)	
Delinked intermediate inputs:		
Primary and processed primary	36.7	10.8
Manufactures	0.0	6.5
Direct and linked intermediate value added:		
Services	16.7	24.2
Manufactures	46.6	58.4
TOTAL COST	100.0	100.0

Note: The counterfactual/actual price ratio is the estimated producer price of the goods concerned if they were manufactured in the economy of the trading partner, divided by their actual producer price.

Source: Counterfactual cost of value added in manufacturing is derived from counterfactual input coefficient calculations (see Sect. 4.2.3 of text). Linked intermediate value added in services is adjusted in proportion to manufacturing value added. Delinked intermediate costs remain the same as in the actual situation except for small adjustments to reflect differences in international transport costs.

they actually are to produce in the South. The reason is the large difference in wage levels, which is only partly offset by factor substitution. However, half the actual cost of these goods consists of delinked intermediate inputs and so is the same in the counterfactual case. The counterfactual nature of this threefold price difference makes it hard to check against any actual price data, although it receives some support from North–South comparisons of production costs in particular activities (OECD 1985: 71, 109).

Conversely, if skill-intensive manufactures were produced in the South, their price would apparently be only about one-half of what it costs to import them from the North. This result is not believable: it suggests that the South could produce *both* goods more cheaply than the North, and thus (among other things) conflicts with the theoretical presumption that noncompeting imports should be cheaper than domestic production.[24] The reason for this odd result is probably that the conventional production function used here greatly understates the potential costs of producing skill-intensive goods in the South, partly by failing to allow for the fact that *SKILD* workers are more productive when clustered together, as they are in the North (see Section 2.4.4).

A more realistic counterfactual price could be generated by setting the efficiency parameter in the production function for the skill-intensive

[24] Even at face value, though, this result does imply that the South has specialised according to comparative advantage in the goods for which its *relative* production costs are lower—and vice versa for the North.

good at a lower level in the South than in the North, in contrast to the labour-intensive good, where the efficiency parameter was argued above to be the same in both regions. However, the adjustment of the efficiency parameter would be arbitrary, and for the purposes of the counterfactual output calculations in the next section the same effect is achieved in a simpler way (see equation 4.21).

4.3 Output Effects

This section shows how the differences between actual and counterfactual output levels (the dQ terms in equations 4.3 and 4.4) are estimated. It starts, in Section 4.3.1, by trying to assess the extent of the North's lost labour-intensive exports. This assessment is used (in Section 4.3.2) to compare actual and counterfactual trade flows, from which (in Section 4.3.3) the effects of the changes in trade on output levels are derived.

4.3.1 Lost labour-intensive exports

As mentioned earlier (Section 3.1.1), the pattern of North–South trade has altered over the past few decades in two respects. Not only has the South become a major exporter of labour-intensive manufactures to the North, but there has also been a change in the composition of the North's exports of manufactures to the South. These Northern exports used to be a mixture of labour-intensive and skill-intensive goods, but are now almost entirely skill-intensive, because developing countries have learned how to make for themselves (and each other) the labour-intensive goods they formerly had to import from developed countries.[25] This process of import substitution must have affected the demand for labour in both country groups.

It would be impossible, for both conceptual and statistical reasons, to measure the North's lost labour-intensive exports precisely, but it seems important to make a rough estimate of their magnitude. A simple and quite plausible approach is to suppose: (*a*) that in the counterfactual situation the extent of the lost exports would have been determined by the capacity of developing countries to pay for them; and (*b*) that this capacity would have depended mainly on the value of developing-country primary exports.

In applying this approach, a convenient starting-point is Table 4.6, which summarises the composition of North–South merchandise trade flows in 1985. The South's primary (and processed primary) export sur-

---

[25] This change in the pattern of trade is best documented by Leamer (1984: 85–9, 96–9), whose results were discussed in Sect. 3.5.2.

TABLE 4.6. *North–South merchandise trade, 1985*
($bn. f.o.b.)

	From North to South	From South to North	Balance (+ means Southern surplus)
Primary	17.4	161.4	144.0
Processed primary	40.5	68.6	28.1
Narrow manufactures	236.1	120.2	–115.9
TOTAL	294.0	350.2	56.2

Source: Wood (1991*c*, table 1). The North is all OECD countries, the South (which includes China) is non-OECD countries excluding Comecon. Processed primary products are ISIC 3 manufactures with a high share of primary intermediate inputs in gross output value. Narrow manufactures are the rest of ISIC 3. The data underlying this table are from OECD sources and are not precisely comparable with those in Table 1.1.

plus was about $170 billion. This surplus would have been larger in the counterfactual case, because some of the primary products which are now embodied in the South's narrow manufactured exports would have been exported raw or processed, but only about $10 billion larger (as will be shown later). Otherwise, it will be assumed that the South's primary export surplus would have been of much the same size in the counterfactual case.[26]

It will also be assumed that the counterfactual primary export surplus (of about $180 billion) would have been equal to the value of the North's exports of manufactures to the South. This is based on the supposition that the South's exports of narrow manufactures to the North would have been negligible. It also supposes that total merchandise trade between the two country groups would have been in balance, with aid and net capital flows from the North being offset by a Northern surplus on trade in services. (In fact, as the table shows, there was a substantial Southern trade surplus in 1985, as a consequence of the debt crisis.)

The $180 billion of Northern manufactured exports would have consisted only partly of labour-intensive goods. The commodity composition of the South's manufactured imports from the North in 1955, prior to the changes in the pattern of trade between the two country groups, suggests that about half would have been skill-intensive even in the counterfactual case.[27] This gives an estimate of about $90 billion for the value of the North's lost exports of labour-intensive manufactures.

[26] This is a crude assumption. However, a more accurate assessment would not obviously be very different, and would be very hard to obtain, since it would require proper modelling of primary sector supply and demand (in both country groups) in the context of a full multisectoral general equilibrium analysis of production, prices, and trade.

[27] In 1955, the South's imports of manufactures (SITC 5 to 8 less 68) from the North consisted of machinery and equipment (42.5%), chemicals (12.5%), iron and steel (9.9%), and other (35.1%)—from the UNCTAD *Handbook of Trade and Development Statistics* 1976

This figure of $90 billion should not be compared directly with the $120 billion of Southern narrow manufactured exports in Table 4.6, because the North's lost labour-intensive exports would have been produced at a price well above that of similar goods manufactured in the South. To put them into comparable quantity units, the dollar value of the lost exports will therefore be divided by the counterfactual–actual price ratio of labour-intensive output in Table 4.5, which is about three.[28]

The estimated volume of lost labour-intensive exports is thus reduced to about $30 billion, or about one-quarter of the actual 1985 value of the South's manufactured exports to the North. This figure is much smaller than might be expected from the many specific Northern examples of lost exports.[29] But it would be hard to arrive at a figure that was both much larger and plausible. The severe constraint which Northern demand places on Southern primary export revenues precludes any much greater estimate of their counterfactual value, there is little reason to suppose that there would have been a large Southern merchandise trade deficit, and it seems unlikely that labour-intensive goods would have accounted for much more than half of the South's counterfactual manufactured imports.

4.3.2 Differences in trade flows

Table 4.7 shows the estimated differences between actual and counterfactual North–South trade flows in 1990 (expressed in 1985 dollars, for consistency with the factor input coefficients estimated earlier). The first line of the table refers to the South's exports of labour-intensive manufactures to the North. The $200 billion is a round number, obtained by extrapolating the 1985 figure in Table 4.6 (using the constant-price series in Fig. 1.1).[30] It assumes, as already mentioned, that there would have been virtually no such exports in the counterfactual case.

(table 3.4A). The first two categories are mainly skill-intensive, the other two mainly less-skill-intensive (as shown by Leamer 1984: 66–70, and discussed at the end of Sect. 3.5.2).

[28] This assumes that the lost labour-intensive exports are on average the same sorts of goods as the South's actual labour-intensive exports, with the same cost structure and the same mix of factor inputs. This convenient assumption is surely not strictly correct, but is probably not so wrong as to distort the results seriously.

[29] However, as Dieter Schumacher has pointed out to me, there seem to be more of these examples in the UK than in other developed countries such as Germany. This is consistent with other evidence that the UK depended to an unusual degree on labour-intensive manufacturing (Crafts and Thomas 1986).

[30] The exact number obtained by this method is $205bn. It must be regarded as an approximation, because the last two years of the constant-price series are only roughly estimated, and because the 1985 export figure and the constant-price series are from different sources. More generally, different international agencies provide significantly different estimates of the South's manufactured exports to the North, depending on how the two country groups are defined, and on how the data are obtained (see Ch. 1, n. 1). The 1985 figure

TABLE 4.7. *Actual minus counterfactual North–South trade flows, 1990: from the viewpoint of the South*
(estimated values in $bn. f.o.b. at 1985 prices)

Exports of labour-intensive manufactures	200.0
Exports of primary and processed primary products	–12.3
Imports of labour-intensive manufactures	–92.2
Imports of skill-intensive manufactured intermediates	46.5
Other imports of skill-intensive manufactures	177.2
Merchandise trade balance	56.2

Source: See text.

The second line of the table refers to the South's primary and processed primary exports to the North. It shows that these are smaller by $12.3 billion than in the counterfactual case. This is because of the North's lower output of labour-intensive manufactures, and hence lower demand for intermediate inputs of primary products, of which the South is assumed to be the marginal source of supply. Offsetting this, however, is the higher output of skill-intensive goods in the North, which raises the demand for primary intermediate inputs, and hence also the South's primary exports.

More precisely, the difference in these primary exports, dR, is

$$dR = a_{RL} dQ_{LN} + a_{RE} dQ_{EN} \qquad (4.12)$$

where, as before, d denotes an actual-minus-counterfactual value and Q_{LN} and Q_{EN} are Northern outputs of labour-intensive and skill-intensive goods. The coefficients a_{RL} and a_{RE}, based on the cost breakdown in Table 4.1, are primary intermediate input requirements per unit of labour-intensive and skill-intensive output respectively.[31] The net effect, dR, is much less than might be inferred simply from the 28 per cent primary product content of the South's $200 billion of manufactured exports. This is partly because dQ_{LN} is smaller than the value of the South's manufactured exports, as will be shown below, and partly because of the offsetting effect of higher Q_{EN}.

The third line of Table 4.7 refers to the North's lost labour-intensive exports, LX_N, whose extent is estimated in the way described above as

$$LX_N = \lambda(R - dR) \qquad (4.13)$$

in Table 4.6 is from OECD sources, and refers to the basket of exports used in calculating the factor input coefficients for labour-intensive goods. To combine the 1985 coefficients with a 1990 estimate of the South's total manufactured exports is inaccurate, because it neglects changes in the commodity composition of trade. But it would be even more inaccurate to neglect the large 1985–90 increase in the South's manufactured exports to the North.

[31] The coefficient a_{RL} is straight from Table 4.1, but a_{RE} is adjusted downward by a c.i.f./f.o.b. margin (of 7.4%), because the cost of primary inputs used in the North overstates what the South earns from exporting them.

where λ is the share of labour-intensive items and R is the South's actual primary export surplus, which is assumed to have been the same in 1990 as in 1985.[32] In this table of trade flows, the lost exports are expressed at Northern prices (because this is what they would have cost the South to import).

The fourth line of the table refers to Southern imports of skill-intensive components from the North for use in labour-intensive production. These imports of 'delinked' manufactured intermediates, dM_{EL}, are determined as

$$dM_{EL} = a_{EL}dQ_{LS} \qquad (4.14)$$

where dQ_{LS} is as before the difference between actual and counterfactual labour-intensive output in the South, and a_{EL} is a coefficient which shows skill-intensive intermediate input requirements per unit of output (derived again from the cost breakdown in Table 4.1).[33] These imports of components are larger than might be inferred from their 20 per cent share of the South's $200 billion of manufactured exports. The reason is that dQ_{LS} is greater than the value of these exports, because of import substitution in the South to replace the North's lost labour-intensive exports.

The gain in Southern foreign exchange earnings from increased exports and reduced imports of labour-intensive manufactures much more than outweighs the loss of primary export revenues and the extra cost of skill-intensive component imports. Part of the net gain is absorbed by the South's balance of trade surplus, which it was assumed above would not have existed in the counterfactual situation, and is assumed in Table 4.7 to have been the same size in 1990 as in 1985.[34] However, most of the net gain must have been spent on additional imports of skill-intensive manufactures from the North. The increase in these other imports, dM_{EO}, is shown in the penultimate line of the table. It is estimated as

$$dM_{EO} = X_S + LX_N + dR - dM_{EL} - dB \qquad (4.15)$$

where X_S is as before the South's manufactured exports, LX_N, dR, and dM_{EL} are as defined above, and dB is the difference in the South's balance of trade with the North (shown in the last line of the table).

The numbers in Table 4.7 are presented from the viewpoint of the South, but it is illuminating also to consider their meaning from the view-

[32] At the time these calculations were done, figures for 1990 were not available. More recent data with different country coverage show that the 1990 primary surplus in current dollars was slightly larger than in 1985: $174bn., compared with $152bn. (GATT *International Trade* 90–91, Vol. II, table A3).

[33] The coefficient a_{EL} is adjusted downwards by a c.i.f./f.o.b. margin (of 7.4%) because the cost of using these components in the South overstates what the North earns from exporting them.

[34] At the time these calculations were done, figures for 1990 were not available. More recent data with different country coverage show that the 1990 merchandise trade surplus in current dollars was somewhat smaller than in 1985: $36bn., compared with $48bn. (GATT *International Trade* 90–91, Vol. II, table A3).

point of the North. The North's balance of trade in labour-intensive manufactures has 'deteriorated' by \$292 billion (its loss of exports plus the increase in imports from the South). However, the North's balance of trade in skill-intensive manufactures has 'improved' by \$224 billion (dM_{EL} + dM_{EO}). The difference between these two numbers arises from the South's larger trade surplus and the drop in the North's primary imports, both of which reduce the South's capacity to purchase the North's skill-intensive exports.

The apparent precision of the numbers in Table 4.7 arises solely from the need for the arithmetic to be internally consistent, and should not beguile anyone into forgetting that they are only rough approximations, subject to challenge from two directions. First, there are the various limitations of the actual data. Second, there is scope for disagreement about the choice of counterfactual assumptions. For these reasons, the numbers will later be subjected to fairly drastic sensitivity analysis.

4.3.3 Differences in output levels

In assessing the effects of these differences in trade flows on domestic production levels, it is important, as explained earlier, to recognise that labour-intensive manufactures would be more expensive if they were made in the North. Fewer of them would therefore be bought in the counterfactual case, and so the change in labour-intensive manufactured output volume in the North would be smaller than the actual volume of imports. Conversely, the volume of the North's lost labour-intensive exports is smaller than the associated increase in Southern import-substituting production, for which there is a larger domestic demand because it is cheaper.

In estimating the size of these divergences between trade flows and output changes, the price elasticity of demand for labour-intensive manufactures is initially set at (minus) one-half. The average elasticity of consumer demand for manufactures appears to be between 0.5 and 1.0.[35] For clothing and footwear, two important components of the South's manufactured exports, the average elasticity is between 0.5 and 0.8, and for basic items such as underwear is well below 0.5.[36] The South's manu-

---

[35] The multi-country cross-section estimates for 33 nonfood manufactured items in Kravis *et al.* (1982, table 9.4), ignoring the two positive values, range from −0.11 to −2.49, with a mean of −0.97. The multi-country time-series estimates of Lluch *et al.* (1979, table 3.13) average −0.46 for clothing and −0.65 for durables. The single-country estimates of Blundell (1988, table 2) range from −0.71 to −0.85 for clothing, from −0.24 to −0.75 for food, fuel, and transport, and from −1.60 to −1.98 for alcohol.

[36] Kravis *et al.* (1982) estimate the price elasticity of demand for all clothing to be between −0.61 and −0.83 (tables 9.3 and 9.5), and for all footwear to be −0.52 (table 9.3). For men's and women's underwear, the estimated elasticities are −0.11 and −0.26 respectively (table 9.4). See also the estimates of Lluch and Blundell in the previous note.

facturing activities often involve only certain stages of the production of
final goods: there are no econometric estimates of price elasticities of
demand for such intermediate goods; but it seems likely that they would
also be below 0.5, and possibly close to zero.[37] One half is thus a compromise estimate, but the effects of choosing alternative values will be
explored below.[38]

To apply this elasticity, the counterfactual–actual *producer* price ratio
for labour-intensive goods (from Table 4.5) has to be adjusted to reflect
more accurately the difference in *purchasers'* prices, which depends also
on international transport costs and trade barriers. The direction of the
adjustment differs between the two country groups. In the North, labour-
intensive goods are imported in the actual situation, but would have been
produced domestically in the counterfactual situation, so that transport
costs and tariffs reduce the difference in prices. But in the South, the difference in purchasers' prices is larger than the difference in producer
prices because the labour-intensive goods in question are actually produced domestically, whereas in the counterfactual situation they would
have been imported from the North. Algebraically,

$$p_N = \frac{p}{(1 + t)(1 + b_N)} \tag{4.16}$$

$$p_S = p\,(1 + t)(1 + b_S) \tag{4.17}$$

where p is the ratio of the counterfactual to the actual producer price,
and p_N and p_S are the purchasers' price ratios. International transport
costs, t, measure the proportionate difference between c.i.f and f.o.b values (estimated at about 7 per cent), and b is the nominal tariff-equivalent
of trade barriers (applied to the c.i.f. price). The actual average value of
b_N is estimated at 0.14, while the counterfactual value of b_S is set at 1.0,
reflecting the generally much higher levels of industrial protection in the
South than in the North.[39]

---

[37] Some empirical support is provided by Goldsbrough's (1981) finding that price elasticities for intra-firm trade are unusually low.

[38] Econometric estimates of export and import price elasticities are an alternative source
of information. However, most studies of foreign demand for Southern exports relate not to
the South as a whole, but to individual countries, for whose exports the price elasticities of
demand are likely to be far higher (Riedel 1988, but for a contrary view, see Muscatelli *et
al.* 1992). Most studies of Northern import demand estimate elasticities of between -0.5 and
-1.0, but include imports from all sources (Goldstein and Khan 1985: 1076-9). A study of
11 manufactured goods in the US market by Grossman (quoted in Goldstein and Khan
1982: 15) does distinguish among imports by source: it estimates price elasticities of demand
(over one year) for imports from developing countries of between -0.52 and -3.69, with a
mean of –1.7.

[39] The value of t (7.4%) is an average of the 1985 figures for developed and developing
countries in the IMF *International Financial Statistics Yearbook*. The value of b_N is estimated from data on tariffs, and on the tariff-equivalents and coverage of non-tariff barriers,
in World Bank (1986, box 2.2), World Bank (1987, tables 8.1 and 8.4), and Hufbauer,
Berliner and Elliot (1986: 149 n. *a*). The value of b_S is roughly equal to a cross-country

One further adjustment is required in calculating differences in output levels from differences in trade flows, namely to strip out domestic trade and transport margins. This is because the factor content coefficients, z, are calculated per unit of output at 'factory-gate' prices, whereas the trade flows (measured f.o.b) also include the costs of getting the goods from the factory to the ship's hold. Failure to allow for these margins, which account for an estimated 9 per cent of the value of trade, would exaggerate the effect of the differences in trade flows on manufacturing output (and hence on factor demand).[40]

Table 4.8 shows the values of the four dQ terms corresponding to the trade flow estimates in the previous table. The differences between the actual and counterfactual values of labour-intensive output in each of the country groups are governed by the equations

$$dQ_{LN} = -(1 - tt) \left(\frac{LX_N}{p} + X_s \, e^{\alpha \hat{p}_N} \right) \qquad (4.18)$$

$$dQ_{LS} = (1 - tt) \left(\frac{LX_N}{p} e^{-\alpha \hat{p}_s} + X_S \right) \qquad (4.19)$$

where X_S and LX_N are as before the South's exports and the North's lost exports, tt is the domestic trade and transport margin, e is the base of natural logs, the operator $^\wedge$ denotes a natural log, and α (= $\hat{Q}/\hat{P}$ = –0.5)

TABLE 4.8. *Actual minus counterfactual gross output levels, 1990*
($bn. at 1985 factor values)

	North	South
Labour-intensive manufactures (valued at Southern prices)	–151	256
Skill-intensive manufactures (valued at Northern prices)	179	–81
Sum (valued at domestic prices)	–241	219
Sum as % of total actual gross manufacturing output	–5	24

Sources: Absolute differences in output: see text. Actual gross manufacturing output: actual manufacturing value added, multiplied by estimated gross output–value added ratios. Actual manufacturing value added data refer to 1985, and are derived from World Bank (1987, indicators table 3). Gross output–value added ratios: for the North, Chenery *et al.* (1986, table 3-6); for the South excluding China, Chenery *et al.* (1986, table 3-5); and for China, World Bank (1985a, annexe 5, table C.3).

average of the ratios of premium-inclusive import EERs to official parities in Krueger (1978, tables 5–1 and 6–2). It is similar to the figures for NICs and LDCs in Markusen and Wigle (1990, table 2).

[40] The weighted average transport and commerce margins on manufactured exports for the USA in 1967 were 2.3% and 7.7% respectively (from *Survey of Current Business* February 1974: 28–9). The 1983 Korea input-output table puts the share of commerce in total (mainly manufactured) exports at 6.6%, but the share of domestic transport cannot be calculated.

is the price elasticity of demand. The term LX_N (which is measured at Northern prices) has to be divided by the counterfactual–actual producer price ratio, p, to make it commensurate with Q_L and X_S, which are measured at Southern prices.

In both country groups, the difference in labour-intensive output depends mainly on the difference in the volume balance of trade in labour-intensive goods ($LX_N/p + X_S$), but is also affected by the difference in their price. In the North, the response of demand to the price difference makes dQ_L much smaller ($151 billion) than the difference in trade ($233 billion). In the South, the demand response pulls the other way, since domestic substitutes are cheaper than the North's lost exports would have been, and so dQ_L ($256 billion) is somewhat larger than the difference in trade. (In the special case in which $p_N = p_S = p$, $dQ_{LN}/dQ_{LS} = -e^{\alpha\hat{p}}$.)

If the price elasticity α were zero, dQ_{LN} and dQ_{LS} would be equal in size. If, in addition, tt were zero and the North's lost labour-intensive exports were ignored, $dQ_{LS} = -dQ_{LN} = X_S$, which is the conventional FCT assumption.

Turning now to skill-intensive production, the differences between actual and counterfactual levels are governed by the equations

$$dQ_{EN} = (1 - tt)(X_S + LX_N + dR - dB + a_{EL}dQ_{LN}) \qquad (4.20)$$

$$dQ_{ES} = -(1 - tt)\gamma(X_S + LX_N + dR - dB - a_{EL}dQ_{LS}). \qquad (4.21)$$

The sum of the four terms ($X_S + LX_N + dR - dB$), which are common to the two equations, is the increase in the North's exports of skill-intensive goods to the South, which is determined by the increase in Southern purchasing power. Each of the equations also contains an $a_{EL}dQ_L$ term, and in both of them this term is negative (recalling that $dQ_{LN} < 0$).[41]

The $a_{EL}dQ_L$ terms measure the changes within each country group in the demand for skill-intensive intermediates in labour-intensive production, which cause the change in skill-intensive *production* in each group to be smaller than the change in skill-intensive *trade* between the two groups. In the North, that is, the increase in sales of skill-intensive goods to the South is partly offset by lower demand from Northern labour-intensive manufacturing. In the South, the increase in skill-intensive imports is partly absorbed by the extra demand from labour-intensive manufacturing and to that extent does not tend to displace domestic skill-intensive production.

It would be unrealistic to assume that the South, in the counterfactual case, would substitute fully for the loss of skill-intensive imports from the North. Both theory and common sense suggest that the difficulty and cost of producing many skill-intensive goods in developing countries

---

[41] As mentioned in n. 33 above, the a_{EL} coefficient incorporates a c.i.f.-f.o.b. adjustment $(1 - t)$ to the relevant cost share in Table 4.1.

would cause the counterfactual change in the volume of domestic production to be less than the actual level of imports. These considerations are captured by the parameter γ, whose value is initially (and arbitrarily) set at one-half. This parameter is used, rather than a price-based adjustment of the sort applied in equation 4.18, because the estimated counterfactual–actual price ratio for skill-intensive goods is suspect, as noted earlier.[42]

As with the previous pair of equations, equations 4.20 and 4.21 contain the conventional FCT assumption, $dQ_{EN} = -dQ_{ES} = X_S$, as a special case. In this case, $\gamma = 1$ and $dB = tt = 0$. The conventional formulation also neglects the changes in intermediate demand for skill-intensive goods, the North's lost labour-intensive exports, and the effect on the South's primary exports.

The third row of Table 4.8 shows the net effect of these four differences in production on total gross manufacturing output in each of the country groups. Since the dQ_L and dQ_E terms are not measured in the same units, one of them in each group has been adjusted by the relevant counterfactual–actual producer price ratio from Table 4.5, so that both are measured at domestic prices. Expressed as percentages of actual gross manufacturing output in each group, these numbers suggest a net reduction in the North, but one which seems too small to be taken seriously, given the imprecision of the estimate. In the South, there is a larger proportionate increase, although this is exaggerated by the weakness of the skill-intensive price ratio, which undervalues the reduction in skill-intensive output.

The limitations of these production impact calculations must be reiterated. They are rough estimates, far less precise than their tabular presentation may suggest. Like conventional FCT calculations, moreover, they are of a partial equilibrium nature. For example, they neglect the possibility that trade might indirectly alter the demand for manufactured goods by changing aggregate output and incomes.

4.4 Impact on Factor Demand

In Section 4.4.1, the coefficient and output impact calculations from the two previous sections are combined to provide estimates of the effects of trade on factor demand. In Section 4.4.2, these estimates are subjected to sensitivity analysis. Section 4.4.3 considers two important reasons why the impact of trade is likely to be understated by these calculations.

---

[42] The value of γ affects only dQ_{ES}. It has no effect on the other three dQ terms. However, it is mainly because γ is less than unity that total world output of skill-intensive goods (like that of labour-intensive goods) is increased by the changes in trade.

4.4.1 Demand impact estimates

Table 4.9 presents the initial or 'base case' estimates of the impact of the changes in North–South trade on factor demand in each of the country groups. The table also compares the present results with those which would have been obtained using the conventional FCT method.

Panel A of the table, which for brevity is confined to total manufacturing labour, undifferentiated by skill, is based on the conventional equations

$$Z_N = X_S (z_{XN} - z_{mN}) \tag{3.3}$$

$$Z_S = X_S (z_{XS} - z_{ms}) \tag{3.4}$$

taking X_S, as above, to be \$200 billion, and using the z_X coefficients from Table 4.3. The z_m coefficients are not calculated properly (as in equation 3.2), but are simply derived from the z_X coefficients by applying ratios of a size typical of conventional FCT labour-only estimates: 0.8 in the North and 1.3 in the South (as in Balassa 1989, table 6.5).[43]

Panel B, which is also confined to total manufacturing labour, takes one step away from the conventional FCT method, by retaining the conventional assumption about the impact of trade on production levels, but using the present counterfactual import coefficients (from Table 4.4).[44] The semi-modified equations used in this panel were given earlier as

$$Z_N = X_S (z_{XN} - z_{XS}^*) \tag{4.1}$$

$$Z_S = X_S (z_{XS} - z_{XN}^*). \tag{4.2}$$

The difference between A and B is striking. In the North, the demand for labour in manufacturing is reduced with conventional coefficients by about one million person-years, but with the present coefficients by nearly 13 million person-years. (The whole of the difference arises, of course, in the import column.) In the South, the demand for labour in manufacturing is increased by about 14 million person-years on the basis of the present coefficients, compared to about 5 million using conventional coefficients. The difference again arises entirely in the import column, where the conventional approach suggests a larger offsetting reduction in demand.

Panel C of Table 4.9 takes the second step away from the conventional FCT method, by using the present output impact estimates as well as the present import coefficient estimates, and applying the equations

[43] The figure for the North also corresponds roughly with the average of the other estimates in Table 3.8. The figure for the South is closer to unity than most of those from the Krueger studies summarised in Table 3.2, but the Balassa estimate is used here because it refers (like X_S) to narrow manufactures, whereas the Krueger export data include many processed primary products.

[44] The calculation is done separately for *BAS-ED* labour and standardised skill units. The latter are then converted back into natural units, and added to the former.

TABLE 4.9. *Impact of North–South trade on factor demand in manufacturing (cumulative effect to 1990)*

	North			South		
	Exports	Imports	Net impact	Exports	Imports	Net impact
A. Conventional FCT method						
Total manufacturing labour (million person-years)	4.4	−5.5	−1.1	19.9	−15.3	4.6
B. Conventional output impact estimates and present coefficient estimates						
Total manufacturing labour (million person-years)	4.4	−17.1	−12.7	19.9	−6.4	13.6
C. Present method						
SKILD labour (million person-years)	2.0	−1.8	0.1	3.4	−1.3	2.1
BAS-ED labour (million person-years)	2.0	−11.1	−9.2	22.1	−1.3	20.8
Total manufacturing labour (million person-years)	3.9	−12.9	−9.0	25.5	−2.6	22.9
Capital ($bn. at domestic prices)	104.0	−171.6	−67.6	65.5	−13.9	51.6
D. Panel C results as percentage of actual employment of the factor concerned						
D1. In manufacturing						
Total labour			−12.1			11.2
Capital			−2.8			12.0
D2. Economy-wide						
SKILD labour			0.1			1.4
BAS-ED labour			−5.3			2.8
Total labour			−2.6			1.5
Capital			−0.5			1.6
Memorandum items						
Hours worked per year			1900			2400
Economy-wide employment:						
SKILD labour (million person-years)			174			154
BAS-ED labour (million person-years)			172			751
NO-ED labour (million person-years)			5			676
Total labour (million person-years)			351			1580
Capital ($bn. at domestic prices)			13040			3240

Notes and sources: (1) Panels A–C: see text. In this table, the results have been converted into 'natural' units: labour demand is measured in person-years rather than hours (see memorandum items for number of hours per year); skill is measured in hours or years of *SKILD* labour (by reversing the quality adjustment in Table 4.2); and capital is measured at domestic rather than Northern prices (by reversing the price adjustment in Table 4.2).

(2) Hours worked per year: averages estimated from UN *Industrial Statistics Yearbook* 1985, ILO *Yearbook of Labour Statistics* (1987, table 12A), and Roy (1987, table 6).

(3) Manufacturing and economy-wide employment for North from OECD *Labour Force Statistics* (total OECD minus Turkey, refers to 1989), and for South from sources cited in Table 5.2 (including China, refers to 1990). The economy-wide skill breakdown is based on data from Psacharopoulos and Arriagada (1986, tables 1 and A-1). Workers with tertiary and completed upper-secondary education are classified as *SKILD*, those with incomplete secondary or (complete or incomplete) primary schooling as *BAS-ED*, and those with 'no education' as *NO-ED*.

(4) Capital stock. Rough estimates, referring to 1985, based on data from OECD *Stocks and Flows of Fixed Capital*, World Bank (1985a, annexe 5, tables 2.2, E.1 and C.3), and Chenery et al. (1986, table 8-1).

$$Z_N = dQ_{EN}z_{XN} + dQ_{LN}z_{XS}^* \tag{4.3}$$

$$Z_S = dQ_{LS}z_{XS} + dQ_{ES}z_{XN}^*. \tag{4.4}$$

Comparing the total manufacturing labour row in panel C with the numbers in panels A and B, it is clear that the present departure from the usual way of estimating the output impact of trade has much less of an effect on the results than the new approach to estimating import coefficients.

However, the differences between panels B and C are not trivial. In the North, the present method of estimating the output impact makes the effect on factor demand about 30 per cent smaller than the conventional method, mainly because it allows for the fact that the demand for labour-intensive imports is greater than it would have been for higher-priced domestic substitutes. In the South, the divergence is in the opposite direction, and larger (nearly 70 per cent). The reason is again mainly the lower price of Southern-made labour-intensive goods, which makes the demand for domestic substitutes greater than it would have been for the North's lost labour-intensive exports.

It remains to look more closely at the results in panel C, which show the estimated impact of trade on skilled and unskilled labour separately (and also the impact on the demand for capital). These absolute numbers are put into perspective in panel D by expressing the net impact as a percentage of total employment of the factor concerned, both in manufacturing and in all sectors of the economy.

In the North, the biggest change is in the demand for *BAS-ED* labour, which is about 9 million person-years lower. The lower level of labour-intensive manufacturing activity reduces demand by about 11 million person-years, but this is partly offset by an additional 2 million person-years of demand for *BAS-ED* workers in skill-intensive activities. The net effect on the demand for *SKILD* labour is positive but tiny, mainly because there is only a small difference between exports and import substitutes in skill requirements per unit of output, despite the big difference in the ratio of *SKILD* to *BAS-ED* labour. The estimated net impact on the demand for capital is also tiny, again mainly because exporting and import-substituting activities do not differ much in terms of capital requirements per unit of output.

The reduction in the overall demand for labour in Northern manufacturing is equivalent to about 12 per cent of actual manufacturing employment. In proportion to total employment in all sectors in the North, it is much smaller (under 3 per cent). However, the proportionate reduction in the demand for *BAS-ED* labour is larger (more than 5 per cent of economy-wide *BAS-ED* employment), because such workers account for only about half of the labour force. So although the rise in demand for *SKILD* workers is only about 1 per 1000, it represents an increase of about 5½ per cent *relative* to the demand for *BAS-ED* workers.[45]

In the South, too, the biggest effect is on *BAS-ED* labour, for which the demand is increased by about 21 million person-years. This is about twice as large, in absolute terms, as the counterpart reduction in the North, partly because *BAS-ED* labour coefficients are higher (as a result of the difference in relative factor prices), and partly because labour-intensive production rises by much more in the South than it declines in the North (due to the reduction in the output price).

The estimated impact on the demand for *SKILD* labour in the South is also positive, and larger than in the North. This is because trade raises the overall level of Southern manufacturing output, which increases the demand for both *SKILD* and *BAS-ED* labour (relative to the *NO-EDs* who still make up about 40 per cent of the South's labour force). Trade also reduces the share of skill-intensive products in Southern manufacturing output, but the effect of this on the demand for skilled labour is smaller, because of the modest absolute difference between exporting and import-substituting activities in skill requirements per unit of output. Similarly, the net effect of trade is to increase the demand for capital in Southern manufacturing.

The absolute change in the demand for all labour in Southern manufacturing (plus 23 million person-years) is more than twice as large as in the North (minus 9 million), but in relation to economy-wide employment only three-fifths as large (1½ per cent), because the South's total labour force is over four times the size of the North's. In both country groups, however, the impact is about the same proportion (11–12 per cent) of employment in manufacturing, which accounts for a substantially higher share (about 21 per cent) of total employment in the North than on average in the South (about 13 per cent).[46]

---

[45] The relative increase, which is 5.4%, is calculated as

$$\frac{n_E/n_L}{(n_E - dn_E)/(n_L - dn_L)} - 1$$

where n_E and n_L are actual employment of *SKILD* and *BAS-ED* workers, and dn_E and dn_L are the (actual minus counterfactual) effects of trade on the demand for each type of worker, and hence $(n_E - dn_E)$ and $(n_L - dn_L)$ are the counterfactual levels of demand. To compare this result with the standard FCT estimates of the relative demand shift in Table 3.10, it must be converted from an economy-wide to a manufacturing-only basis. *SKILD* workers make up 50–60% (Schumacher 1989a, table A.9) of a total Northern manufacturing work-force of about 75 million workers. The figures in panel C of Table 4.9 thus imply a change in the relative demand for *SKILD* and *BAS-ED* labour within manufacturing of 20–30%, as compared with 1–2% for most of the conventional FCT estimates.

[46] It may be noted that the increase in Southern manufacturing *employment* (11%) is proportionally smaller than in Southern manufacturing *output* (24%, from Table 4.8). This rise in labour productivity may seem odd, given that the South has become more specialised in labour-intensive goods. It occurs partly because the rise in output is overstated (see the text accompanying Table 4.8). A further reason is that the South's manufactured exports are concentrated on middle-income countries, where output per worker is higher than the

Similarly, the increase in *BAS-ED* demand in the South, though absolutely much larger than the corresponding reduction in the North, is a smaller proportion (about 3 per cent) of economy-wide *BAS-ED* employment, since there are four times as many *BAS-ED* workers in the South as in the North. But the rise in Southern demand for *SKILD* labour is proportionally greater than in the North, since there is little difference between the two regions in the absolute number of *SKILD* workers. The estimated effect of trade on the economy-wide demand for *BAS-ED* relative to *SKILD* workers in the South (an increase of about 1½ per cent) is thus much smaller than in the North.[47] It must be stressed that this result refers to the South as a whole: the effect on the skill structure of labour demand in those developing countries which specialised in exporting manufactures was undoubtedly more substantial.

4.4.2 Sensitivity analysis

The apparent precision of the demand impact estimates in panels C and D of Table 4.9 is misleading. They are in fact rough approximations, and some of the data and assumptions which underly them are open to serious doubt. In this section, the consequences of varying the more questionable data and assumptions within plausible ranges will be examined, to obtain an idea of the likely margins of error and uncertainty surrounding the numbers in the table.

Before starting on the sensitivity analysis of the demand impact estimates in panel C of the table, it should be mentioned that there is an additional source of uncertainty about the proportionate effects in panel D, namely that the actual skill composition of employment in the two country groups cannot be precisely measured. There is room for disagreement in principle about where to draw the line between *SKILD* and *BAS-ED* workers. Nor do the available educational and occupational data permit an accurate drawing of the particular line proposed in this book (Section 2.4.2), mainly because they do not distinguish between skilled and unskilled manual workers.

The skill breakdown of the labour force shown at the bottom of Table 4.9 is based on educational data. It identifies *SKILD* workers with those who have a tertiary or completed upper secondary education, while *BAS-*

Southern average. The changes in trade have made production in these countries more labour-intensive, but have also increased their share of Southern manufacturing (pulling up its average labour productivity).

[47] The relative increase, which is 1.4%, is calculated as

$$\frac{n_L/n_E}{(n_L - dn_L)/(n_E - dn_E)} - 1$$

which is simply a variant of the expression in n. 45 above.

ED workers are those with primary or incomplete secondary schooling. On this basis, *SKILD* workers account for about 50 per cent of the whole Northern labour force (the same percentage as in export-oriented manufacturing), while in the South, *SKILD* workers account for 17 per cent of the non-*NO-ED* labour force (as compared with 13 per cent in export-oriented manufacturing), and *BAS-ED* workers for 83 per cent.

One simple sensitivity test is thus to vary these breakdowns of the total labour force. Plausible ranges for the share of *SKILD* workers in the non-*NO-ED* labour force are from 40 per cent to 60 per cent in the North, and from 10 per cent to 30 per cent in the South. The resulting variation in the estimated economy-wide increase in the demand for *SKILD* relative to *BAS-ED* labour in the North is from 4.5 per cent to 6.7 per cent, around the initial estimate of 5.4 per cent. The corresponding range for the increase in the relative demand for *BAS-ED* labour in the South is from 0.2 per cent to 2.6 per cent, as compared with the initial estimate of 1.4 per cent.

Production-related experiments

The first group of experiments on the demand impact estimates themselves, whose results are summarised in Table 4.10, focuses on variations which affect only the *dQ* terms, leaving all the *z* coefficients unaltered. Only two indicators are shown for each country group in this and the following table: the absolute impact on the demand for all labour in manufacturing, and the proportionate change in the economy-wide relative demand for *SKILD* and *BAS-ED* labour. (It should be pointed out that the latter indicator is calculated differently for the two country groups: for the North, it shows the rise in the relative demand for *SKILD* labour, for the South the rise in the relative demand for *BAS-ED* labour. This convention minimises the need to calculate percentage decreases, which are less easy to interpret.)[48]

The first sub-group of experiments in Table 4.10 addresses the uncertainty about the share of noncompeting items in North–South trade in manufactures (discussed in Section 4.1.3). The initial assumption was that all trade in narrowly defined manufactures is noncompeting. The table shows the effects of two downward variations, setting the South's noncompeting exports at 80 per cent and 60 per cent of its narrow manufactured exports. The larger of these variations diminishes the increase in the relative demand for *SKILD* labour in the North from 5.4 per cent to 3.6

---

[48] More specifically, the problem with percentage decreases in ratios is that (as conventionally calculated) the absolute value of the decrease is not equal to the absolute value of the increase in the reciprocal of the ratio. This may be seen from the formulae in nn. 45 and 47 above. To give a concrete example based on Table 4.9, the increase in the relative demand for *SKILD* labour in the North is 5.4%, while the decrease in the relative demand for *BAS-ED* labour is 5.1%.

TABLE 4.10. *Sensitivity analysis: production-related experiments*

	North estimated impact of trade on		South estimated impact of trade on	
	Total demand for labour in manufacturing (million person-years)	Economy-wide demand for *SKILD* labour relative to *BAS-ED* (%)	Total demand for labour in manufacturing (million person-years)	Economy-wide demand for *BAS-ED* labour relative to *SKILD* (%)
Initial results (Table 4.9, Panel C)	−9.0	5.4	22.9	1.4
A1. Level of South's noncompeting manufactured exports (initial value $200bn.)				
$160bn.	−7.6	4.5	19.7	1.2
$120bn.	−6.2	3.6	16.5	1.0
A2. Demand for labour-intensive manufactures (initial price elasticity [minus] 0.5)				
Price elasticity = 0.2	−12.3	6.6	20.2	1.4
Price elasticity = 0.8	−6.4	4.4	27.6	1.6
A3. Labour-intensive share of South's counterfactual manufactured imports (initial value 0.5)				
Labour-intensive share = 0.25	−8.7	4.9	19.9	1.2
Labour-intensive share = 0.75	−9.4	5.9	25.9	1.7
A4. Difference between actual and counterfactual Southern trade surplus (initial value $56bn.)				
$25bn.	−8.1	5.2	21.2	1.5
Zero	−7.4	5.0	19.8	1.5
A5. Southern skill-intensive import substitution parameter (initial value = 0.5)				
Parameter = 0.2	−9.0	5.4	24.5	1.0
Parameter = 1.0	−9.0	5.4	20.4	2.1

Note: On the calculation of the economy-wide relative demand impact see nn. 45 and 47 of the text.
Source: See text.

per cent, and the increase in the relative demand for *BAS-ED* labour in the South from 1.4 per cent to 1.0 per cent.[49] An upward variation would also be possible, since some of the South's processed primary exports are noncompeting manufactures, but a proper estimate of its effects would require different z coefficients.[50]

The next pair of experiments vary the price elasticity of demand for labour-intensive manufactures, initially set at (minus) 0.5, from 0.2 to 0.8. These variations have opposite effects on the outcome in the North and the South, and a larger effect in the North, for reasons that are clear from equations 4.18 and 4.19. The lower price elasticity amplifies the increase in the relative demand for *SKILD* labour in the North, from 5.4 per cent to 6.6 per cent, while the higher elasticity reduces it, to 4.4 per cent. The corresponding variation in the impact on the total demand for

[49] These reductions in impact are somewhat overstated because no allowance is made for competing exports, whose extent becomes greater as the share of noncompeting items is reduced.

[50] Processed primary products differ from narrow manufactures in their delinked intermediate input requirements (more raw materials and fewer manufactures) and may also have different skill and capital requirements.

manufacturing labour in the North is from –12 to –6 million person-years.

The third pair of experiments in Table 4.10 vary the parameter λ (equation 4.13) from 0.25 to 0.75, which has the effect of halving the North's lost labour-intensive exports and increasing them by 50 per cent, respectively. This makes little difference to the estimated demand impact in the North, and only a moderate difference in the South. Nor is the outcome much affected by the reduction in the Southern trade surplus (in experiment A4). Varying the size of the Southern import substitution parameter (experiment A5) does not affect the North, but it considerably alters the impact on the relative demand for *BAS-ED* labour in the South, which ranges from 1.0 per cent with $\gamma = 0.2$ to 2.1 per cent with $\gamma = 1.$[51]

Coefficient-related experiments

Table 4.11 summarises the results of a second group of experiments, which focus on variations in data and assumptions whose main effect is on the z coefficients, though they also indirectly affect the dQ terms, by altering the counterfactual price of labour-intensive goods. The first pair vary the blue-collar (skilled and unskilled) wage rate in Southern manufactured export production, which is subject to problems both with the country data and with the choice of country weights (see Appendix A1.4). Setting this wage rate at a higher level diminishes the impact of trade in both country groups, by reducing the estimated labour content of Southern exports, and vice versa for a lower level.[52] The largest effect is on the total demand for manufacturing labour in the South.

Experiment B2 varies the share of *SKILD* workers in Southern manufactured export production, which is also subject to considerable uncertainty (for reasons explained at the end of Section 4.2.1). This variation has little effect on the demand for manufacturing labour in total, but it does substantially alter the impact on the relative demand for *SKILD* and *BAS-ED* labour, because it alters the difference in skill intensity between the goods exported by the two country groups. Reducing this *SKILD* share from 13 per cent to 7 per cent boosts the increase in the relative demand for *SKILD* labour in the North from 5.4 per cent to 6.7 per cent,

---

[51] This is the only experiment in Table 4.10 in which the two indicators move in opposite directions—the impact in the South on the total demand for manufacturing labour is *smaller* with the higher value of γ. This is because a higher value of γ reduces the positive impact on the demand for both sorts of labour, but by proportionately more for *SKILD* labour.

[52] This is because the labour content of exports is estimated by dividing their wage cost by the wage rate (Sect. 4.2.1). However, this effect of varying the wage rate on the results for the North is damped by offsetting variation in the size of the gap between actual and counterfactual labour coefficients, because the amount of substitution between capital and labour depends on the size of the gap between Northern and Southern wage levels.

TABLE 4.11. *Sensitivity analysis: coefficient-related experiments*

	North estimated impact of trade on		South estimated impact of trade on	
	Total demand for labour in manufacturing (million person-years)	Economy-wide demand for *SKILD* labour relative to *BAS-ED* (%)	Total demand for labour in manufacturing (million person-years)	Economy-wide demand for *BAS-ED* labour relative to *SKILD* (%)
Initial results (Table 4.9, Panel C)	−9.0	5.4	22.9	1.4
B1. Blue collar wage in Southern manufactured export production (initial value $0.86 per hour)				
$1.05 per hour	−7.9	4.9	19.0	1.3
$0.67 per hour	−10.6	6.0	29.0	1.7
B2. Proportion of *SKILD* workers in Southern manufactured export production (initial value 13%)				
Proportion = 7%	−9.7	6.7	22.9	2.7
Proportion = 25%	−7.9	3.3	22.9	−1.0
B3. Southern skilled labour quality index (initial value 50)				
Parity with North (100)	−9.9	4.7	22.9	1.1
Index = 25	−8.4	5.8	22.1	2.2
B4. Substitution between skill and capital (initial elasticity [minus] 0.1)				
Elasticity = 0.5	−8.7	5.6	22.8	1.6
Elasticity = −0.5	−9.5	5.1	23.1	1.2
B5. Substitution between capital-skill and unskilled labour (initial elasticity [minus] 0.5)				
Elasticity = 0.1	−11.7	7.7	22.7	1.6
Elasticity = 0.9	−6.3	3.0	23.1	1.2

Variations in data or assumptions which made only a small difference to the initial results.
C1. Level of blue-collar wage in Northern manufactured export production (± 25%: initial value $9.41)
C2. Proportion of *SKILD* workers in Northern export production (40% to 60%: initial value 50%)
C3. *SKILD/BAS-ED* wage: North (± 25%: initial value 2.1); and South (−20% to +30%: initial value 3.2)
C4. Price index of capital goods in the South relative to the North (30 to 100: initial value 60)
C5. Profit rate in South (24% to 50%: initial value 33%)

Source: See text.

and the increase in the relative demand for *BAS-ED* labour in the South from 1.4 per cent to 2.7 per cent. Raising this *SKILD* share to 25 per cent cuts the increase in the North to 3.3 per cent, and reverses the direction of the impact on relative demand in the South.[53]

Experiment B3, which varies the quality adjustment applied to Southern *SKILD* labour, also has the effect of altering the estimated difference in skill intensity between the goods exported by the two groups. The more drastic the adjustment, the larger is the difference in skill intensity, and hence the larger is the impact of trade on the relative demand for *SKILD* and *BAS-ED* labour. This effect is muted, however, because a more drastic quality adjustment also generates a larger North–South gap

[53] The *absolute* demand for Southern *SKILD* labour is increased in all the experiments reported here, as in the initial case, for reasons explained in the text. But so long as $dn_E/dn_L < n_E/n_L$ the relative demand for *SKILD* labour is reduced (see the formulae in nn. 45 and 47 above). This experiment expands dn_E and shrinks dn_L to the point where this inequality is reversed.

in the cost of skill relative to *BAS-ED* labour, and thus causes more substitution between the two types of labour in the counterfactual case.

Experiments B4 and B5 vary the substitution elasticities. The results are fairly insensitive to variations in the elasticity of substitution between skill and capital (which is used in aggregating the two factors). Varying the elasticity of substitution between capital-plus-skill and *BAS-ED* labour over the widest plausible range (from 0.1 to 0.9, as explained in Section 4.2.2) makes more of a difference, at least in the North. The impact on the demand for all labour in manufacturing ranges from –6 to –12 million person-years (around its initial value of –9 million). The impact on the economy-wide relative demand for *SKILD* labour is increased from 5.4 per cent to 7.7 per cent by the low elasticity, and reduced to 3.0 per cent by the high elasticity.

The lower part of Table 4.11 mentions some other experiments, which have little effect on the results. Experiments C1 to C3 vary the blue-collar wage and the share of *SKILD* workers in Northern export production, and the *SKILD/BAS-ED* wage ratio in both country groups: they cause the increase in the relative demand for *SKILD* labour in the North to vary between 4.7 per cent and 6.1 per cent, and the increase in the relative demand for *BAS-ED* labour in the South to vary between 1.2 per cent and 1.7 per cent. Experiments C4 and C5 vary the cost of capital, which has even less effect on the results.

More extreme variations

All these experiments are intended to give an idea of the likely ranges of error around the initial point estimates of the impact of trade on factor demand. In the North, they suggest a range of plus or minus 2 percentage points around the initial estimate of 5½ per cent for the increase in the economy-wide demand for *SKILD* relative to *BAS-ED* labour. As regards the impact on the total demand for labour in Northern manufacturing, the corresponding range around the initial estimate of –9 million person-years is plus or minus 3 million. In the South, the likely range for the relative demand impact is rather more than plus or minus 1 percentage point around the initial estimate of 1½ per cent (say from 0.2 per cent to 2.6 per cent), while for the impact on the total demand for manufacturing labour, the range around the initial estimate of 23 million person-years is roughly plus or minus 5 million.

These ranges could evidently be enlarged by additional experiments using combinations of the variations reported above. However, if the errors in data and assumptions underlying the initial estimates are independent of one another, as is to be hoped, the likelihood of results outside these ranges should be low.

The range of outcomes could clearly also be widened by the choice of more extreme values for some of the variables and parameters. For example, the true values of the substitution and price elasticities could conceivably be much higher than most evidence suggests. The results would be especially affected in the North, where a high substitution elasticity between *BAS-ED* labour and capital-plus-skill would slash the counterfactual labour content of imports, while a high price elasticity for labour-intensive goods would greatly diminish the estimated adverse effect on domestic production of the goods concerned. Raising this substitution elasticity to 2, for instance, would shrink the reduction in Northern demand for manufacturing labour to –1.5 million person-years, and would cause the relative demand for *SKILD* labour in the North to be *reduced*, rather than increased.

The implausibility of a substitution elasticity of this magnitude in the present context arises not only from the difficulty of reconciling it with the empirical studies reviewed in Section 4.2.2, but also because *it would make the exports of the South more skill-intensive than those of the North*, when compared at a common set of factor prices.[54] (This is why the sign of the impact of trade on the relative demand for *SKILD* labour in the North changes.) The reason is simple. Because of the North–South difference in the relative cost of skilled and unskilled labour, 'moving' the production of the exports of one country group to the other group changes its skilled-unskilled labour ratio. If the substitution elasticity were 2 (or more), this change would be bigger than the actual difference in the skill ratios of the two sets of exports (at the actual factor prices in each group).

The notion that the South's manufactured exports are more skill-intensive than those of the North is strongly contradicted by the evidence reviewed in the previous chapter. More generally, theory suggests that trade based on differing factor proportions (of which North–South trade in manufactures is an example) is more likely when elasticities are relatively low. For if different factors, and goods of differing factor intensities, were readily substitutable for one another, there would be less to be gained from trade among partners with differing factor endowments. Moreover, the size of the gains from trade is intimately related to the size of the impact of trade on domestic factor markets. With high elasticities, the impact on factor markets would be small, but the arguments against protection in the North (and for export-orientation in the South) would lose much of their force.

4.4.3 Two sources of understatement

The sensitivity analysis in the previous section stressed the imprecision of this chapter's factor demand impact estimates. It is also important, how-

---

[54] This is not factor intensity reversal in the usual sense, since the ranking is consistent at different sets of factor prices.

ever, to note some of their more fundamental limitations. One of these is failure to disaggregate the country groups. Both the North and South—but especially the latter—are clearly internally heterogeneous.

The modified FCT method used here also shares some of the limitations of the conventional FCT method. Both are partial equilibrium approaches, which attempt to measure the first-round impact of changes in trade on factor demand. The subsequent effects on factor prices and employment are not overlooked in this book—they form the subject of Part B—but in principle one should also take account of feedback effects on factor demand through induced changes in aggregate output, in nontraded activities, and in trade flows themselves. Neglect of these second-round repercussions is a further reason for regarding the present estimates as imprecise.

The most serious limitation of the modified FCT estimates, though, is not their imprecision. It is that, in principle, they are bound to understate the impact of North–South trade on the skill composition of labour demand, for two reasons. The first is that these estimates make no allowance for defensive innovation. The second is that they refer only to manufacturing, omitting the effects of trade on other sectors. In neither case, as will be explained below, can the degree of understatement be measured properly, but in both cases it seems likely to be substantial.

Defensive labour-saving innovation

Neither the conventional nor the modified FCT method allows for the effects of trade on technical progress: the former takes factor input coefficients as given; the latter takes production function parameters as given. This omission is of limited significance in the South, which is usually a taker rather than a maker of new technology. Since most of the world's research capability, most of its advanced equipment manufacturers, and most of their customers, are located in the North, it is unlikely that the special needs and requirements of Southern firms have much influence on the direction of research and development activity.

In the North, by contrast, the exclusion of trade-induced technical change probably has a large effect on the accuracy of the demand impact estimates. Most Northern manufacturers of labour-intensive goods seem to have reacted to Southern competition by seeking new production techniques that use less unskilled labour.[55] Their search has been spurred by the most powerful of all instincts—the urge to survive—and they have been able to mobilise not only their own (initially often limited) research

[55] Given relative factor prices, cost-minimising firms cannot gain from switching among *existing* techniques. However, the line between finding new techniques and splitting up existing ones (to shed their labour-intensive ingredients) is blurred.

resources, but also those of their equipment suppliers, in some cases with government support.

In some lines of activity, this innovative effort has failed. Either no new techniques have emerged, or they have been too expensive (labour-saving machines which cost more than the wages they would save—see UNIDO 1987: 17). Or the new techniques have economised on skilled as well as unskilled labour, and have thus been readily transferable to the South, providing only temporary relief to firms in the North. In such cases—exemplified by many sorts of clothing and footwear—production in the North has been gradually extinguished by imports from the South.

In other lines of activity, however, defensive innovation has succeeded in keeping Southern imports at bay. New techniques have been found that are much more efficient than the old techniques, and also more skill-intensive and hence uneconomic for Southern producers. This has some-times involved only process innovation, with no change in the nature of the product. But in other cases a similar effect has been achieved or rein-forced by *product* innovation: introducing new and better goods whose production requires a more skilled labour force. Either way, successful defensive innovation has moved some products along the skill intensity continuum. Production in the North has continued—as for example with many sorts of textiles—but at higher levels of output per worker.

In principle, it should be possible to estimate the extent to which defen-sive innovation has reduced the relative demand for unskilled labour in the North. In practice, however, the difficulties of doing so seem insur-mountable at present. An ideal approach would start by measuring the bias of technical progress in Northern manufacturing (as between skilled and unskilled labour), and would then isolate the causal contribution of trade with the South by regression methods. Existing studies of technical progress (discussed in Section 7.3.4) unfortunately shed almost no sub-stantive light even on the direction or strength of its biases in the skilled–unskilled labour dimension, let alone on its causes. Moreover, these studies suggest that any new attempt along these lines would be a major undertaking, and would not necessarily yield clear-cut results.

A less direct, but in the present context adequate, approach would be to estimate the impact of defensive innovation jointly with the impact of the trade-induced reallocation of labour among manufacturing sectors on which the FCT method focuses. A simple method of this kind is described and used in Appendix A2. It is based on the principle that trade with the South should have increased the skill intensity of Northern manufacturing relative to the skill intensity of nontraded sectors, and that it should thus be possible to estimate the impact of this trade from the change in relative sectoral skill intensities.

As explained in the appendix, the application of this method is afflicted by shortages (and other deficiencies) of time-series data on labour force skills. The results obtained confirm that the relative skill intensity of Northern manufacturing has increased in recent decades, and are consistent with the view that expansion of trade with the South contributed to this trend. However, none of the calculations provides an acceptably precise and reliable estimate of the *size* of the impact of trade, which is what would be needed to measure the degree of understatement caused by omitting defensive innovation from the FCT calculations.

The only other basis for an estimate of the magnitude of the effects of defensive innovation is case studies and newspaper articles on particular firms, industries, and countries.[56] This body of evidence has the vice of being scattered without the virtue of being random. It is mixed in type and quality, and only in part quantitative. A reasonable inference from this assortment of material, however, would probably be that the effect of defensive innovation on the level and skill composition of the demand for labour in Northern manufacturing has been at least as large as the effect of relocating labour-intensive activities to the South (and expanding the production of skill-intensive exports). In other words, the case studies tend to suggest that the inclusion of defensive innovation would require the impact estimated by the FCT method to be doubled, at a minimum.[57]

This inference, based on second-hand casual observation, receives some support from the calculations in Appendix A2. At the least, movements in relative sectoral skill intensities do not contradict this informed guess, and some of the results can be viewed as providing positive confirmation, although their accuracy is open to serious doubt. In any event, the case-study evidence seems too strong for defensive innovation to be overlooked, and thus it seems preferable to offer some quantitative assessment of its impact, however tentative, rather than none. No great weight will be put on the doubling estimate in the rest of this book, but it will be checked against—and found to be consistent with—other evidence on the size of changes in employment, unemployment, and relative wages (Sections 5.4.2, 7.2.2, 8.2.4).

It remains to consider the second source of understatement in the

---

[56] The following works are both relevant in themselves and contain many references to other studies: Fröbel *et al.* (1980), OECD (1985), Hufbauer, Berliner, and Elliot (1986), Renshaw (1986, esp. ch. 5), UNIDO (1986: 136–9; 1987: 15–22), Hoffman and Kaplinsky (1988), Hamilton (1989), North-South Institute (1989), Best (1990), Kaplinsky (1991*a*), Reich (1991, esp. ch. 7).

[57] The impact of trade actually has two distinct aspects: on the relative demand for skilled and unskilled labour, and on the total demand for labour in manufacturing. A doubling of one of these aspects does not necessarily imply a doubling of the other, e.g. defensive innovation might need a greater number of skilled workers, and hence reduce the relative demand for unskilled labour by more than it reduced the total demand for labour in manufacturing. However, the reduction in total manufacturing labour demand would certainly still be substantial, because *SKILD* labour is roughly twice as expensive as *BAS-ED* labour. To achieve the objective of cutting labour costs, the use of *BAS-ED* labour would thus have to be reduced by more than twice as much as the use of *SKILD* labour was increased.

modified FCT estimates presented in this chapter, which is that they are restricted to manufacturing, and take no account of the impact of changes in North–South trade on factor demand in other sectors. The omitted effects are of two different sorts, which will be considered separately below. There are (*a*) the direct effects of trade in items other than manufactured goods, and (*b*) the indirect effects of changes in all traded sectors on factor demand in nontraded sectors.

Non-manufacturing trade

What is relevant in the present context is not simply the extent of other sorts of trade, but the extent to which non-manufacturing trade between the North and the South has been subject over the past few decades to the same sorts of changes as trade in narrowly defined manufactures. These changes were caused mainly by the lowering of several sorts of barriers to trade in both outputs and inputs (as mentioned in Chapter 1 and discussed further in Chapter 5). They caused the South to become a major exporter of unskilled-labour-intensive manufactures, while the North became specialised in skill-intensive manufactures.

In this light, it seems unlikely that extending the analysis to include trade in primary and processed primary products would greatly alter its results. This trade is large—narrow manufactures are still only about half of the South's merchandise exports to the North (Table 1.1)—and it has benefited from reductions in transport costs. Artificial barriers to trade, however, are high in the North for temperate agricultural products, and have increased since the 1950s (World Bank 1986, box 1.3, fig. 1.5). Moreover, where artificial barriers are low, as for tropical agricultural products and for minerals, the overwhelming impression is of continuity, not change, in the pattern of North–South trade. Finally, of course, most trade in primary and processed primary products is based on international differences in the availability not of skilled and unskilled labour, but of natural resources.

There are a significant number of exceptions to all these generalisations. Within the processed primary category, as defined statistically (ISIC 3 manufactures with a high share of primary intermediates in gross output value), there are many items whose raw materials have low transport costs, so that the location of the processing activity is determined by its skill intensity.[58] Even within the primary category, there are some items, such as coal and temperate agricultural products, for which the relevant natural resources are available in (parts of) both the North and the

---

[58] See Krueger *et al.* (1981: 15), and their results (summarised in Table 3.2), which include many processed primary products, as do the results of Fischer and Spinanger (1986), summarised in Table 3.6. See also Schumacher (1989*a*, Table A.10), who provides results both including and excluding processed primary products.

South, and hence the pattern of comparative advantage between the two country groups is governed by the relative cost of skilled and unskilled labour.

Nor have barriers to trade in primary and processed primary goods become uniformly higher—for many items, the reductions in transport costs have been important. A detailed investigation would thus probably reveal some shift towards greater North–South specialisation in accordance with skill availability, even for primary and processed primary products. It seems unlikely, however, that this would increase the estimated impact of trade on the skill composition of labour demand in either country group by more than (say) 10 per cent, bearing in mind that labour is only a small share of the cost of petroleum products, which account for about half of the South's primary and processed primary exports (Table 1.1).

Changes in trade in *services* have probably had a more substantial impact. The statistics in this field are inadequate, and generally understated, but it appears that the South's exports of services are equivalent to about 50 per cent of its exports of narrow manufactures.[59] These service exports also appear to have grown fast. Moreover, there is a substantial amount of evidence, albeit of a fragmentary nature, that in services, as in manufactures, the pattern of North–South trade has changed. Developing countries have become exporters of unskilled-labour-intensive services to the North, while the developed countries have specialised in skill-intensive activities.

One of the South's major service exports is international shipping, both openly and through fleets registered under flags of convenience and crewed by low-paid developing-country nationals.[60] Tourism—provision of hotel, restaurant, and entertainment services to visitors from the North—has also become a big Southern export. Many developing countries contribute to the international construction business, some by providing complete packages, others supplying only unskilled labour services. Offshore data-processing—using lower-paid workers to copy written records into computers—is also expanding rapidly.[61] There are many other examples of low-skill-intensive Southern service exports, including various forms of temporary migration.[62] The North, by contrast, exports

[59] GATT (*International Trade 88–89*, Vol. I: 27–43) estimates that in 1987 services were slightly less than 20% of the total exports (merchandise plus services) of developing countries. Narrowly defined manufactures are about half of developing-country merchandise exports (see Table 1.1). The GATT estimate refers to exports in all directions, not only to the North.

[60] GATT *International Trade 88–89* Vol. I: 33–5. See also John Lloyd, 'The threat of the museum', *Financial Times*, 26 Apr. 1988.

[61] See Canute James, 'Caribbean seeks role as world's paperless tiger', *Financial Times*, 9 Apr. 1992.

[62] See UNCTAD *Trade and Development Report* 1988: 216. Not all the South's service exports are of low skill intensity; e.g. India is building up exports of computer software, see

skill-intensive services such as insurance, engineering, design, higher education, and medical care to the South.

There are many barriers to international trade in services, some natural, some artificial. The natural barriers have been falling, as with trade in manufactures, because of improvements in transport and telecommunications facilities. The artificial barriers remain substantial in many areas, but they have not prevented the growth of trade in services (and their gradual reduction was a major objective of the Uruguay round of GATT negotiations).

It is not possible, with the data now available, to make a proper estimate of the impact of the changes in North–South trade in services on the skill composition of labour demand.[63] The most plausible assessment would seem to be that including traded services in the calculation would increase the estimated impact on factor demand in proportion to the ratio of the South's service exports to its exports of narrow manufactures, that is, by about one-half.

Indirect effects in nontraded sectors

The factor demand impact estimates in this chapter also omit the indirect effects of trade in manufactures on workers in nontraded sectors, through the purchase of intermediate services. In theory, these effects should be included (as explained in Sections 2.1.3, 2.2.2, and 3.1.2). Moreover, the first steps towards doing so were taken in the cost breakdown calculations reported in Table 4.1, which shows the share of value added in services in the total cost of each country group's manufactured exports. However, it was not possible to obtain adequate estimates of the skilled and unskilled labour content of intermediate services, especially for the South, and so the later stages of the calculations were confined to manufacturing.

The initial cost breakdown, though, gives an indication of the likely size of the indirect impact on factor demand in nontraded sectors. It shows that value added in services is 36 per cent of value added in manufacturing in the North, and 42 per cent in the South.[64] It may thus be inferred that the estimated impact of trade in manufactures on the skill composition of labour demand would be increased by roughly 40 per cent if its indirect effects could be included in the calculations. This assumes

Jenny Mill, 'High tech flourishes amid the sacred cows', *Independent on Sunday*, 29 Apr. 1990.

[63] The initial attempt of Sapir and Schumacher (1985, table 3), discussed in Sect. 3.4.2, is limited to total labour content, and considers only competing imports.

[64] These percentages are smaller than standard estimates of the ratio of indirect to direct effects, which are usually of the order of 100% (see e.g. UNIDO 1986, ch. 3). This is because the present estimates already include indirect effects within manufacturing.

that more skill-intensive manufacturing needs proportionately more skill-intensive intermediate services than less skill-intensive manufacturing, which seems fairly plausible.[65] A similar assumption seems reasonable for traded services, to which the 40 per cent increase to allow for these indirect effects will also be applied (for want of any better estimate).

Together, the assessments that the inclusion of traded services would add about 50 per cent to the estimated impact on factor demand, and that the inclusion of nontraded intermediate services would add 40 per cent, imply that the estimates for manufacturing alone should be roughly doubled. The highly approximate nature of this figure must be emphasised. It gives no more than a general indication of the likely magnitude of the results of extending the present calculations to include sectors other than narrowly defined manufacturing.

Combining the two sources of understatement

How would the modified factor content estimates presented earlier in this chapter be altered by the combination of the two sources of understatement discussed separately above—neglect of the effects of trade on technical progress, and restriction to manufacturing? Neither of these shortcomings affects the estimated impact on the overall demand for manufacturing labour in the South. In the North, however, the tentatively suggested allowance for defensive innovation would raise the central estimate of the reduction in manufacturing labour demand from about 9 million to about 18 million.

The estimated impact on the economy-wide demand for unskilled relative to skilled labour in the South is likewise subject to only the second source of understatement. The central estimate of the increase in this relative demand would be raised from about 1½ per cent to about 3 per cent by the inclusion of non-manufacturing sectors. In the North, both sources of understatement are relevant: in conjunction, the adjustments suggested above (a doubling for both defensive innovation and the inclusion of non-manufacturing sectors) would roughly quadruple the estimated increase in the economy-wide demand for skilled relative to unskilled labour, boosting the central estimate from about 5½ per cent to about 22 per cent.

---

[65] Theory suggests that there should be some such relationship, since the skill intensity of a product encompasses that of its nontraded intermediate inputs (see Sect. 2.1.3). Whether the relationship is proportional is more questionable. In three of the four cases in which the Krueger studies compare the skill intensities of exports and competing imports on the basis of both direct and direct-plus-home-goods-indirect inputs, the difference is more muted on the latter basis (Krueger *et al.* 1981, tables 2.18, 3.14–15, 10.13; Krueger 1983, table 5.3).

4.5 Summary

Conventional factor content calculations underestimate the impact of North–South trade in manufactures on the composition of the demand for labour in both country groups, because they fail to recognise that most of this trade is noncompeting. The conventional calculations thus understate both the amount of unskilled labour embodied in the North's imports from the South, and the amount of skill embodied in the South's imports from the North.

To obtain better estimates of the skill and labour content of noncompeting imports, one must start by measuring the inputs used to produce the goods concerned in the economy of the trading partner. These actual inputs must then be adjusted, to allow for the large North–South difference in wages, which would cause different amounts of skill and labour to be used if the goods concerned were produced at home, rather than imported. For example, if the North were to replace its labour-intensive imports from the South with domestic production, firms would use more skill and capital, and less unskilled labour, than are actually used to make these goods in the South. The unadjusted inputs would thus exaggerate the adverse effect of these imports on the demand for unskilled labour in the North.

If noncompeting imports were produced domestically, they would cost more, and so people would buy fewer of them. This difference in price also has to be allowed for in calculating the impact of trade on the composition of labour demand. For example, the volume of labour-intensive imports from the South is greater than the volume by which Northern production of these goods would rise if the imports were to disappear. The usual practice of equating the trade-induced change in production with the level of imports would thus again exaggerate the adverse impact on the demand for Northern unskilled labour.

Even after correction for these two possible sources of exaggeration, the modified factor content method, which treats most manufactured imports as noncompeting, suggests that trade has much more of an effect on the demand for labour than the conventional method implies. The estimated impact in the South is roughly five times larger, and in the North roughly ten times larger, than standard calculations would suggest. The modified estimates are subject to fairly wide margins of error, however, because of the poor quality of some of the data, and uncertainty about the values of some of the parameters used in the calculations.

In the South, the cumulative effect up to 1990 of the recent changes in the pattern of trade with the North was to increase the total demand for labour in manufacturing by about 23 million (plus or minus 5 million) person-years—equal to about 11 per cent of actual employment in

Southern manufacturing. This was associated with a rise of about 1½ per cent (plus or minus rather more than 1 per cent) in the demand for unskilled but educated labour, relative to more skilled labour, in the economy of the South as a whole. In individual developing countries which specialised in exporting manufactures, the proportionate effect on the skill structure of labour demand was probably much larger.

In the North, the cumulative effect up to 1990 of the changes in trade with the South was to reduce the demand for labour in manufacturing by about 9 million (plus or minus 3 million) person-years—or by about 12 per cent of actual employment in Northern manufacturing. There was an accompanying increase of about 5½ per cent (plus or minus 2 per cent) in the economy-wide demand for skilled, relative to unskilled, labour.

These estimates are subject to two sources of understatement. One is that they ignore the effects of trade on technical progress. This exclusion is probably unimportant in the South, but in the North many firms have reacted to Southern competition by devising new production techniques that use less unskilled labour. The extent and consequences of this defensive innovation cannot be measured properly, but fragmentary evidence suggests that it has been at least as important as the relocation and reallocation effects that are captured by the modified factor content method. The impact of trade on the demand for labour in Northern manufacturing is thus likely to have been at least twice as large as the modified factor content estimates imply.

The other source of understatement is that these factor content estimates are confined to manufacturing. The shifts in the economy-wide relative demand for skilled and unskilled labour must have been amplified by other sorts of trade, especially by trade in services, and by indirect effects in nontraded sectors which supply intermediate inputs to manufacturing and traded services. The degree of amplification cannot be assessed properly, but the limited data available suggest that including traded and nontraded services in the calculations would approximately double the direct impact of trade in manufactures alone.

Only the second source of understatement applies to the South: it would raise the central estimate of the trade-induced increase in the economy-wide demand for unskilled relative to skilled labour from about 1½ per cent to about 3 per cent. In the North, both sources of understatement are relevant: in combination, they would quadruple the central estimate of the increase in the relative demand for skilled labour from about 5½ per cent to about 22 per cent.

PART B
Causes and Consequences

Introduction

The main conclusion of Part A of this book is that the recent changes in North–South trade have shifted the relative demand for skilled and less-skilled workers, in both country groups. Part A also concludes, contrary to earlier studies, that this shift in the skill composition of labour demand has been quite substantial. Part B focuses on two related issues which the analysis in Part A leaves open, both of which are vital to the discussion of the future and of policy implications in Part C.

One of these issues is the *causes* of the change in North–South trade. In Part A, the changes in trade flows were taken for granted: treated simply as an exogenous determinant of the alterations in the skill composition of labour demand. This assumption is at best unsatisfactory, because it begs the obvious question of what caused the changes in trade; and it could even be misleading, because causation might flow the other way. The changes in trade, that is to say, might have been caused by shifts in labour demand (or supply) conditions internal to one or both of the country groups.

The other issue is the *consequences* of trade-induced alterations in the skill composition of labour demand. If indeed the changes in trade were exogenous, how much did the resulting alterations in labour demand affect the wages of skilled and less-skilled workers, and what was the impact on levels of employment? Were the consequences symmetrical as between North and South? How did they vary among the different countries within these two large groups?

Chapter 5 examines the likely causes of the changes in North–South trade, and their effects on the sectoral structure of employment. The next two chapters analyse the consequences of the changes in trade for the relative wages of skilled and less-skilled workers in the South (Chapter 6) and in the North (Chapter 7). The fourth and final chapter of Part B considers the consequences for unemployment in the North.

5

Trade Shifts and Sectoral Side-Effects

Section 5.1 seeks an explanation for the changes in the pattern of North–South trade in recent decades. Section 5.2 sets out the theoretical framework within which evidence on the consequences of these changes in trade will be interpreted. The last two sections focus on the effects of shifts in the sectoral (as opposed to skill) composition of labour demand. Section 5.3 examines the contribution of the changes in trade to growth of manufacturing employment in the South, while Section 5.4 considers their role in the deindustrialisation of the North.

5.1 Causes of Change in North–South Trade

The changes in trade that require an explanation were described earlier. The most obvious one is the growth of the South's North-bound manufactured exports from virtually nothing in the 1950s to about $250 billion in 1990. Also noteworthy, however, is the elimination during the same period of the South's labour-intensive manufactured imports from the North. As a result, the North, which initially exported all sorts of manufactures to the South, became a net importer of labour-intensive items and a specialised exporter of skill-intensive items. A similar transition seems to have occurred in traded services.

The underlying cause of the pattern of North–South trade that has emerged was argued in Part A to be differences in the relative supplies of skilled and unskilled labour in the two country groups. But why did these changes in trade occur when they did? Theory suggests three main possible reasons: lower trade barriers; shifts in domestic labour supply or demand functions; and transfer of technology. The following subsections will examine each of these possibilities in turn. A final subsection sums up.

5.1.1 Lower barriers to trade

The most commonly suggested reason for the altered pattern of North–South trade in recent decades is reductions in trade barriers, either 'natural' (transport and communications costs) or 'artificial' (tariffs, quotas and other policy obstacles to importing or exporting).[1] Lower barriers have not only made it easier and cheaper to move outputs from the South to the North, but have also facilitated the flow of inputs in the other direction—components, machinery, finance, and information, including visits from technical and marketing experts. As a result, many of the costs and obstacles that previously inhibited the full participation of developing countries in the international division of labour have been lessened.

Natural barriers to trade, though not well documented, have undoubtedly declined substantially over the past few decades, partly because of more investment in infrastructure and partly because of advances in technology. In addition to the construction of more ports, there have been important technical improvements in sea freight (the main means of international transport of manufactures), most notably containerisation, which has cut both handling costs and the risk of damage to goods in transit. The unit costs of all forms of transport have been further diminished by reductions in the weight and volume of many manufactured goods.[2] The expansion of the South's exports of manufactures (and services) to the North has also been aided by the remarkable cost reductions and technical improvements in air transport and telecommunications.[3] Quality and cost control in the distant sourcing of finished goods, and the co-ordination of different stages of the manufacturing process in widely dispersed locations, have been made much easier and cheaper by instant phone calls, faxes, and the ability to fly buyers and engineers almost anywhere in the world within a day.

These reductions in natural barriers, which have made the world smaller in an economic sense, provide a plausible explanation for the overall growth of the South's manufactured exports, and for the increases in some primary exports, such as cut flowers and out-of-season vegetables. They are less obviously able to explain the precise timing of these trade changes, and the concentration of the South's manufactured exports on a few developing countries. As regards timing, the limited data in Fig. 5.1 suggest that the growth of these exports accelerated in the early 1960s, but there is no reason to suppose that there was a discontinuity in the rate of decline in transport and communications costs at that time.

Nor can the country concentration of the South's manufactured exports be explained simply by autonomous differences in transport and communications facilities. Of course, it was easier for Hong Kong and Singapore to export manufactures because of their well-developed ports,

---

[1] See e.g. Ballance *et al.* (1982: 48–50, 65–6), Wolf (1983: 4–5), Fröbel (1984: 74–5), Godfrey (1985: 222), and Reich (1991: 70, 210, 221–2).
[2] Reich (1991: 70); GATT *International Trade* 88–89, Vol. I: 35.
[3] See e.g. GATT *International Trade* 89–90, Vol. I: 36–40.

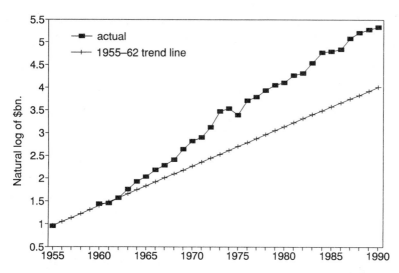

FIG. 5.1 Manufactured exports of the South to the North (constant 1980 dollars: logarithmic scale)
Notes and sources: As for Fig. 1.1, of which this is simply a logarithmic transformation. The 1955–62 trend is calculated by OLS regression.

while some developing countries have been effectively excluded from export-oriented manufacturing by grossly inadequate infrastructure. But it would be hard to argue, for example, that Korea and Taiwan inherently possessed any greater transport and communications advantages than dozens of other developing countries which made no headway in exporting manufactures.

Changes in *artificial* barriers to trade in the North also affected the pattern of North–South trade. Successive rounds of GATT negotiations reduced developed-country tariffs on manufactures from an average of 40 per cent in the late 1940s to 5–6 per cent in the late 1970s (World Bank 1987: 134–5). These cuts, and the elimination of import and exchange controls, created a more liberal world trading environment which greatly, albeit unintentionally, facilitated the growth of developing-country manufactured exports to the North (Wolf 1983: 5, 14).

In the 1970s, moreover, most Northern countries introduced schemes under the Generalised System of Preferences (GSP), intended to provide better access to their markets for manufactured exports from the South. However, because these schemes were limited in various ways, the GSP did not give much help to most Southern countries.[4] Northern tariffs on

[4] See the survey in Brown (1988: 347–55), the comments of Bhagwati (1990: 13), and Frances Williams, 'Developing countries look for better deal on trade', *Financial Times*, 21 May 1992.

manufactured imports from developing countries remained somewhat higher (7–9 per cent) than average, and were increasingly supplemented by other sorts of barriers, epitomised by the Multi-Fibre Arrangement (World Bank 1987: 136–40).

Changes in artificial trade barriers in the South have been in different directions in different countries and sub-periods. Import-substituting industrialisation was widely practised in the 1950s, and extended in the 1960s to many newly politically independent countries. A few countries, however, adopted export-oriented industrialisation strategies, and their economic success subsequently caused other developing countries to shift their policies increasingly in the direction of export orientation.

The simultaneous adoption of export-oriented policies by Korea and Taiwan provides the most plausible explanation for the acceleration of Southern manufactured exports in the early 1960s. In 1959, Korea introduced new export incentives, unified and devalued its exchange rate between 1961 and 1964, and from 1962 tied import licences to export performance (Westphal and Kim 1982: 214–16). Taiwan introduced comparable measures from 1958 onwards, completing its exchange rate reform by 1961, liberalising import restrictions for exporters, and providing tax incentives and low-interest loans for export production (Lee and Liang 1982: 315–17). Similar policies were adopted by Singapore a few years later, in 1967–9 (Tan and Hock 1982: 282–3), while Hong Kong already had an open trade regime.

These export-oriented policy shifts in the little East Asian tigers thus appear to explain not only the timing of the South's manufactured export take-off, but also its country concentration. However, policies promoting import substitution in other developing countries (and earlier in three of the four tigers) also helped to change the pattern of North–South trade, by reducing the North's exports of labour-intensive manufactures to the South. Imports of textiles and simple consumer goods were obvious initial targets for protection aimed at stimulating domestic production, and the resulting barriers were often an effective, albeit theoretically suboptimal, way of encouraging the investment and learning needed to realise a potential comparative advantage in such manufactured products.

5.1.2 Labour-market pressures

In a Heckscher–Ohlin framework, such as that set out in Chapter 2, changes in the pattern of trade can be caused by changes in relative factor supplies—or domestic demands. The best-known proposition of this sort is the Rybczynski theorem, which states that an increase in the supply of a factor causes greater production of commodities which use that factor intensively, and reduces the output of other commodities. The movement of labour-intensive manufacturing from the North to the South might thus have been precipitated by increased abundance of unskilled labour in the South, and/or by increased scarcity of unskilled labour in the North.

These possibilities require special attention in the present book, which has thus far assumed that causation flows mainly in the other direction, with autonomous changes in North–South trade affecting the labour markets of both country groups. To assume, instead, that labour-market pressures caused the changes in trade would transform some of the conclusions of the book and their implications for policy. In particular, it is vital to determine whether the rapid increase in imports of manufactures from the South represents, for the North, an unskilled-labour-displacing intrusion (as so far supposed), or an unskilled-labour-saving response.

Relative wage movements as evidence

Movements in the relative wages of skilled and unskilled workers are an important source of evidence on the direction of causation. In the context of North–South trade, where the factor price equalisation assumed in formal Heckscher–Ohlin theory does not occur (Section 2.1.2), it is particularly relevant to look at such movements in both trading partners simultaneously. Using the 'textbook' assumption that relative wages are determined by the intersection of imperfectly elastic demand and supply curves, Fig. 5.2 summarises the logical implications of the four possible combinations of movements in the wages of *BAS-ED* relative to *SKILD* workers that might be observed. Let us consider each of its quadrants in turn.

(1) Increases in the relative wage of *BAS-ED* labour in both country groups would be consistent with the hypothesis that the changes in trade were caused by an autonomous increase in the scarcity of *BAS-ED* workers in the North. This would have reduced the economic attractiveness of labour-intensive production in the North, and hence sucked more *BAS-ED* workers in the South into labour-intensive manufacturing for export, pulling up their relative wages, too. These wage trends would not rule out the possibility that the changes in trade were autonomous, since a trade-induced reduction in the relative demand for *BAS-ED* labour in the North might have been more than offset by autonomous supply or domestic demand shifts. But it would be impossible to argue that the changes in trade were caused by increased abundance of *BAS-ED* labour in the South.

(2) Decreases in the relative wage of *BAS-ED* labour in both country groups would be consistent with the hypothesis that the changes in trade were caused by increased relative abundance of *BAS-ED* labour in the

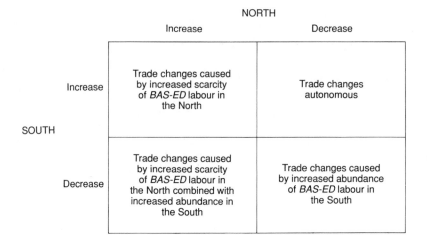

FIG. 5.2 What relative wage movements suggest about causation (changes in *BAS-ED/SKILD* wage ratio)

South. This would have enhanced the economic attractiveness of labour-intensive manufacturing for export in the South, and hence pushed *BAS-ED* workers out of the corresponding sectors in the North, depressing their wages. Again, the expansion of trade might have been autonomous, and might have lessened a domestically driven decline of *BAS-ED* wages in the South. But it would not be possible to argue that the changes in trade were caused by *BAS-ED* labour shortages in the North.

(3) An increase in the relative wage of *BAS-ED* labour in the North and a decrease in its relative wage in the South would be consistent with the hypothesis that the changes in trade were caused by some combination of increased scarcity of *BAS-ED* labour in the North and increased abundance in the South. These wage movements could also in principle be consistent with an autonomous change in trade, but only if its effects on labour demand had been more than offset by autonomous labour supply and demand shifts within both country groups.

(4) A decrease in the relative wage of *BAS-ED* labour in the North and an increase in its relative wage in the South would be consistent with the hypothesis that the changes in trade were autonomous, boosting the relative demand for *BAS-ED* labour in the South, and reducing it in the North. This combination of wage movements would rule out the possibility that the changes in trade were caused *either* by increased scarcity of *BAS-ED* labour in the North *or* by increased abundance of *BAS-ED* labour in the South. It is thus the combination that would be expected if this book's initial assumption about the direction of causation were correct.

Relaxation of the 'textbook' assumption about wage determination requires some qualifications to this line of argument. Non-clearing markets make little difference so long as movements in excess demands and supplies point in the same direction as movements in relative wages. However, if these quantity and price indicators were to conflict with one another, implying that there had been institutionally determined changes in relative wages, which might have contributed to the changes in trade, the analysis would become more complicated. In addition, the simple categorisation in Fig. 5.2 has to be extended to recognise the possibility of different relative wage movements in different sub-periods, and of inter-country differences within the North and South groups.

Chapters 6 and 7 examine changes in the relative wages of skilled and less-skilled workers in the South and the North. So although the focus of these chapters is on the *consequences* of the change in North–South trade, they also shed light on its *causes*. The next few paragraphs anticipate the findings of these chapters, as well as reviewing some other evidence on the question of whether or not the change in the pattern of trade was caused by domestic labour-market pressures.

Evidence from the South

There is only a small amount of information on relative wage trends in the South. However, the case studies of the four little tigers in Chapter 6 support the conventional view that adoption of export-oriented policies in these economies narrowed the wage differential between *SKILD* and *BAS-ED* workers, thereby making the distribution of personal incomes less unequal. Across a wider sample of Southern countries, there is also a weak inverse correlation between growth of North-bound manufactured exports and changes in income inequality. These results suggest that causation flowed from trade to labour markets, rather than the other way around.

None the less, it is likely that supply-side changes in developing-country labour markets did contribute to the shifts in the pattern of trade with the North. Of particular importance has been the rise in literacy rates since about 1950 (see Table 5.1). This trend may not have increased the supply of *BAS-ED* relative to *SKILD* labour, because higher education also expanded. But it made both these types of educated labour more abundant relative to *NO-ED* workers, and so tended to move the comparative advantage of the South away from primary production towards manufacturing (sections 2.1.4 and 2.4.2; see also Beenstock 1984: 71).

Table 5.1 also shows that the four little tigers had unusually educated populations, with adult literacy rates of around 70 per cent by 1960 in three of the four cases. These high levels of literacy, which enabled the

TABLE 5.1. *Literacy in the South, 1950–1990*
(adult literacy rates, %)

	1950	1960	1970	1990
All developing countries	31	39	46	64
Hong Kong		70	77	88
Korea		71	88	96
Singapore	46	50	74	86
Taiwan	47	67	79	92

Sources: All developing countries. 1950: World Bank (1980, fig. 4.1); 1960: World Bank (1983, indicators table 25); 1950 and 1960 figures for low-income and middle-income countries averaged using population weights for 1960 from World Bank (1983, indicators table 1); 1970 and 1990: UNDP *Human Development Report* (1992, indicators table 4).

Hong Kong. 1950: no data; 1960: as for all developing countries; 1970 and 1990 (actually 1985): UNDP *Human Development Report* (1991, indicators table 4).

Korea. 1950: conflicting data (see n. 30, Ch. 6); otherwise, as for all developing countries.

Singapore. 1950 and 1960: UNESCO *Yearbook* (1976, table 1.3, data refer to 1947 and 1957); 1970 and 1990 (actually 1985): UNDP *Human Development Report* (1991, indicators table 4).

Taiwan. 1950: over-15 literacy rate calculated from 1956 *Census Summary Report*, extrapolated backwards to 1950 on the basis of the change in the 'over free school age' literacy rate from the *Statistical Yearbook of the Republic of China* (SYROC) 1978; 1960: backward extrapolation of the 1963 adult literacy rate on the basis of the change in the 'over free school age' literacy rate (both from SYROC 1986); 1970, 1990: SYROC 1991.

little tigers to become successful exporters of manufactures, were in part the result of ancient traditions of education, but also reflected large-scale expansion of primary schooling and adult literacy campaigns in the 1950s, especially in Korea and Taiwan.[5] Subsequently, the little tigers expanded higher education, which raised the ratio of *SKILD* to *BAS-ED* workers, and helped to shift their comparative advantage in manufacturing towards more skill-intensive products (see Sections 6.3.5 and 9.3.2).

Evidence from the North

Faster accumulation of skills in the North than in the South over a period of two centuries raised the wages of Northern unskilled workers relative to skilled workers, thereby providing the basis for the contemporary division of labour between the two country groups (cf. Krueger 1980; Wolf 1983). It has also been argued that it was a sudden increase in the relative cost of unskilled labour in the North in the 1950s and early 1960s which triggered the shift of labour-intensive manufacturing to the South (e.g. Godfrey 1985: 221–2). In this view, post-war full-employment policies and expansion of higher education caused unprecedented shortages of unskilled labour, which boosted wages and undermined labour

[5] The remarkable increase in literacy during the 1950s in Taiwan is clear from Table 5.1. On Korea, see n. 30, Ch. 6.

discipline, stimulating Northern firms to transfer production to lower-wage developing countries.

The evidence on this point is mixed. In the 1950s and 1960s, unemployment rates did fall to remarkably low levels. Moreover, immigration of *BAS-ED* labour from the South was welcomed, which is consistent with the view that there were shortages of unskilled labour. In particular, 4.5 million guest workers entered continental Western Europe during the 1960s, most of them literate but with no specialised skills, and many of them coming to work in manufacturing industries (Swamy 1985). However, there was no clear trend in the relative wages of skilled and unskilled workers during these decades—differentials narrowed in some Northern countries, but widened in others (OECD-EO 1987: 93; Goldin and Margo 1992: 4).

In the 1970s, by contrast, most skill differentials in wages did tend to narrow (as detailed in Chapter 7 and Appendices 3–5). The fall in relative wages was especially marked for college graduates and higher-level white-collar workers, and is usually attributed to rapid expansion of tertiary education, reinforced in some European countries by wage controls which discriminated in favour of lower-paid workers. In some countries, though, some skill differentials were widened by increases in the relative supply of younger workers. Moreover, unemployment rose during the 1970s, and controls on immigration were tightened, particularly for workers without specialised skills (Appleyard 1977), suggesting reversal of the previous shortages of unskilled labour.

Through the 1970s, then, conditions in Northern labour markets could be argued to be consistent with the hypothesis that the changing pattern of trade with the South was a response to unskilled labour shortages arising from domestic demand and supply pressures. However, not all the evidence suggests this direction of causation. Almost all the subsequent evidence, moreover, points in the opposite direction. In the 1980s, most sorts of skill differentials widened in most Northern countries, clearly indicating a growing relative surplus of unskilled labour. It would thus be impossible to argue that the massive increase in the volume of manufactured imports from the South during this decade (see Fig. 1.1) was sucked in by a shortage of unskilled labour.

What could be argued, though, is that the earlier shortages of unskilled labour precipitated an irreversible process of learning about overseas sourcing. Unskilled labour scarcity in the 1960s may well have prompted some Northern manufacturers to relocate to low-wage countries. This was initially hard, since it required new techniques of managing procurement, and of decomposing and co-ordinating dispersed production.[6] Once learned, however, these techniques proved so profitable for their pioneers

[6] On the nature and significance of these organisational innovations, see e.g. OECD (1979) and Fröbel (1984).

that a growing number of other firms followed. Thus within a decade or two, Far Eastern sourcing of labour-intensive manufactures ceased to be a novelty, and became a standard ingredient of business strategy. In this way, what started as a response to unskilled-labour scarcity may subsequently have contributed to the emergence of an unskilled-labour surplus.

5.1.3 Transfer of technology

The recent changes in the pattern of North–South trade might alternatively be explained as the result of transfer of manufacturing technology from the North to the South. This explanation has obvious affinities with the neo-Ricardian view that international differences in technology constitute the main basis of trade, as well as with product cycle theories (discussed in Section 2.3.3).

A simple version of this explanation might emphasise that the transfer of technology was sectorally uneven. The South was initially backward in all sectors, and acquired Northern technology mainly in manufacturing, rather than in agriculture. This uneven transfer reduced the cost of production in manufacturing relative to agriculture, and thus shifted the comparative advantage of the South towards manufacturing. Such a hypothesis would be consistent with the observed changes in trade: the South's rising share of world manufactured exports, and its declining share of world agricultural exports (World Bank 1986, table 1.7). It also appears to be confirmed by casual observation—photographs of modern factories springing up beside traditional peasant agriculture.

However, this sort of explanation is not easily fitted into the Heckscher–Ohlin framework of the present book. North–South trade in manufactures is argued here to be based fundamentally on differences in relative supplies of skilled and unskilled labour. More specifically, Section 2.3 defended the standard Heckscher–Ohlin assumption that technology is the same in all countries as an acceptable theoretical simplification in this context, and Chapters 3 and 4 presented empirical evidence which supports this claim.

The gap between these two approaches can be minimised by recognising that some of the things which were classified in Section 5.1.1 as reductions in trade barriers—easier movement of components, machinery, and information from North to South—could also be classified as transfers of technology. But there may still be an underlying disagreement over the extent to which such transfers of technology should be regarded as endogenous rather than exogenous, or perhaps over the precise nature of the endogeneity.

The view that technology transfers are strictly exogenous is difficult to defend. It is much more plausible to argue that they depend on the scope for economic gains, as for example where there are minerals in the ground or a literate low-wage labour force that could be engaged in manufacturing for export. In effect, the Heckscher–Ohlin view is that the technology of particular activities tends to be transferred to wherever relative factor prices would make production for export profitable. This is an incomplete view of endogenous technology transfer (cf. Grossman and Helpman 1991, chs. 11–12), but it seems to be consistent with case-study evidence on the role of transnational companies and Northern customers in the acquisition of manufacturing technology by developing countries (Pack 1988: 340, 358–65).

5.1.4 Conclusions

The initial assumption, it may be recalled, was that the changes in North–South trade were an autonomous cause of shifts in the skill composition of the demand for labour in both country groups. The discussion in the three preceding subsections suggests that this assumption is a reasonable first approximation to the truth. Reductions in natural and artificial barriers to trade were probably the main cause of the changing North–South division of labour in manufacturing. Improvements in transport and communications, trade liberalisation in the North, and export-oriented industrialisation policies in the South, were all important in this regard. As a result of these reductions in trade barriers, the relative demand for *BAS-ED* labour appears to have been increased in the South and reduced in the North.

However, the preceding discussion also suggests that the initial assumption has to be qualified in various ways. Trade and labour-market outcomes are in general determined simultaneously: to suppose that one causes the other is at best a simplification. Moreover, the direction of causation was not uniform in all sub-periods and countries. For example, growth of primary education in the South made it possible to expand manufacturing employment. Likewise, shortages of unskilled workers in the North in the earlier part of the period may well have stimulated the interest of Northern firms in overseas sourcing of labour-intensive manufactures.

In addition, it should be recognised that reductions in trade barriers, which are conventionally regarded as exogenous causes of changes in trade, must be to some extent endogenous. Alterations in trade policies, such as liberalisation or the adoption of an export-oriented strategy, are likely to be shaped by potential economic gains, and hence influenced by changing economic circumstances (Ranis 1991). The same may apply to reductions in natural barriers. Investment in transport and communications is motivated by potential gains from trade, which also provide a stimulus to devise and apply new world-shrinking technologies.

5.2 Wage and Employment Effects

This section provides a simple theoretical introduction to the employment and wage effects of trade-induced shifts in the composition of the demand for labour. It emphasises the distinction between the *sectoral* dimension of such shifts (textiles versus machinery, for example) and the *factoral* dimension (skilled versus less-skilled labour).

5.2.1 Theoretical considerations

The possible consequences of changes in the composition of labour demand (along either of these dimensions) can be outlined with supply and demand curves. The only special feature of the diagrams in Fig. 5.3 is that their axes measure relative rather than absolute prices and quantities. The vertical axis shows the wage of labour category i relative to that of labour category j, while the horizontal axis measures the i/j employment ratio. The downward slope of the demand curve reflects substitution by producers and consumers in response to changes in relative wages, and the upward slope of the supply curve (in panel (a)) implies that relative wages also affect the relative availability of the two categories of labour.

The immediate impact of a change in trade is represented in Fig. 5.3 as a horizontal shift in the demand curve (from D to D'). It raises the demand for labour category i, relative to that for category j, at all wage ratios. The effects of this shift in the composition of demand depend in familiar fashion on the elasticities of the two curves, and on whether or not the relative wage adjusts to equate demand and supply.

Panel (a) of the figure is the textbook case of imperfectly elastic demand and supply. The shift in demand causes an increase in both the relative employment (from n to n') and the relative wage (from w to w') of category i, with category j becoming correspondingly worse off on both counts. In panel (b), the relative supply curve is perfectly elastic at the prevailing wage ratio, implying that workers move freely between the two categories. In this case, the trade-induced shift in the composition of labour demand causes only a shift in relative employment, without changing the relative wage.

By contrast, in panel (c) the relative supply curve is completely inelastic, implying that there is no mobility between the two categories. To maintain the initial employment ratio in the face of the trade-induced demand shift, there has to be a larger (than in panel (a)) change in the wage ratio. As in panel (*a*), though, the size of the relative wage change depends both on the extent of the trade-induced shift in the relative demand curve, and on the elasticity of this curve. The more imperfect the substitutability between the two categories of labour, the larger the decline in the relative wage of category *j*.

Panel (*d*) depicts the case in which, with an imperfectly elastic relative supply curve, institutional or other rigidities prevent the relative wage (w^*) from adjusting in response to the shift in demand. This results in excess relative demand ($n^* - n$) for category *i*, or equivalently an excess relative supply of category *j*. The ultimate consequences of this sort of imbalance depend on how employers and the government respond (as explained in Section 8.1.1), but one obvious possibility is that some of the workers in category *j* become unemployed.

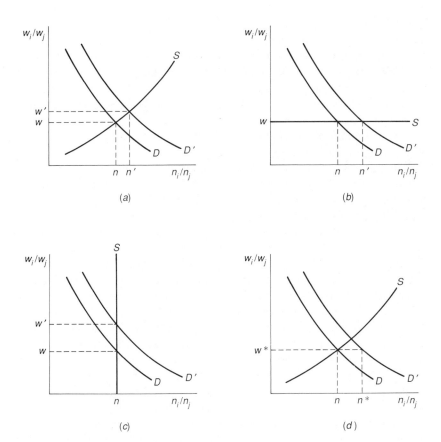

FIG. 5.3 Possible effects of a trade-induced shift in demand on relative wages and employment

5.2.2 Factoral versus sectoral outcomes

The empirical results in Chapters 3 and 4 show that the changes in North–South trade have altered the composition of the demand for labour in two dimensions. First, they have twisted the relative demand for skilled and unskilled labour. Second, they have raised the demand for labour in some sectors relative to other sectors: in particular, the demand for labour in manufacturing has been increased in the South and reduced in the North.

The alteration in skill composition, which may be labelled the 'factoral' dimension, is the more fundamental of the two, since it is a direct result (in the present Heckscher–Ohlin framework) of North–South trade being based on differences between the two country groups in the relative availability of skilled and unskilled labour. The shift in the sectoral composition of labour demand is in a theoretical sense incidental—a side-effect, as the title of this chapter puts it. It arises partly from restructuring within the traded sectors (for example, a rise in the share of skill-intensive industries in Northern manufacturing), and partly from concomitant changes in the demand for labour in traded sectors relative to nontraded sectors (for example, net displacement of labour from Northern manufacturing).

In its depiction of the effects of shifts in the composition of demand on wages and employment, Fig. 5.3 does not distinguish between the factoral and the sectoral dimensions. At such a general level, it does not matter whether labour categories i and j are identified by the nature of their contributions to production or by the sectors in which they are employed. In practice, however, this distinction is important.

To begin with, supply elasticities are likely to differ between the two dimensions. The difference is particularly stark in standard Heckscher–Ohlin theory, which assumes both that factor supplies are fixed and that factors are perfectly mobile among sectors. However, much other economic reasoning is based on similar, though less extreme, assumptions: supplies of factors such as skilled and unskilled labour are commonly taken to be rather unresponsive to their prices; and it is also widely supposed that mobility of labour tends to eliminate inter-sectoral differences in skill-specific wage rates, other than those which compensate for variations in working conditions. To the extent that these assumptions are realistic, the factoral consequences of trade-induced demand shifts will approximate to the model in panel (c) of Fig. 5.3 (with changes in the relative wages of skilled and unskilled workers, but not in their relative employment), while the sectoral consequences will approximate to panel (b) (changes in relative employment levels, but not in relative wages).

These strong assumptions about differences between sectoral and factoral supply elasticities must be qualified. As noted in Section 2.4.3, relative supplies of skilled and unskilled labour surely respond in some degree to changes in relative wages (and there are theoretical models in which this relative supply elasticity is infinite). Inter-sectoral supply elasticities, conversely, are bound to be less than infinite in the short run. This may also be the case in the medium run for categories of workers with high levels of skill specific to one industry, and more generally if there are artificial barriers to entry into certain sectors. Despite all these qualifications, however, the conventional assumptions about factoral and sectoral supply elasticities do appear to capture an important aspect of reality.

Another important difference between the factoral and sectoral effects of trade-induced demand shifts concerns their impact on income inequality, and relatedly the likelihood of institutional impediments to market-clearing wage adjustments (as in panel (*d*) of Fig. 5.3). In particular, changes in the relative wages of skilled and unskilled workers generally have larger, more persistent, and more conspicuous distributional effects than changes in the relative wages of workers in different sectors. An increase in the ratio of skilled to unskilled wages, for instance, tends to aggravate the overall inequality of personal incomes. Such an increase would also tend to be noticed and collectively resisted by unskilled workers.

By contrast, changes in the relative wages of particular skill groups in different sectors have little effect on overall income inequality. They are also less likely to be resented, because people assess the fairness of their own incomes mainly through 'local' comparisons (Wood 1978: 23–4). In addition, such wage changes are harder for workers to resist, because few unions are cross-sectoral. These differences should not be exaggerated. The collapse of a sector concentrated in one region can cause serious and conspicuous deprivation. Workers in particular sectors have also often battled collectively to achieve or maintain parity of wages with those in other sectors. Even so, the social significance of changes in sectoral wage relativities seems generally smaller than that of changes in skill differentials.

These two differences (in supply elasticities and in social significance) between the factoral and sectoral dimensions of shifts in the composition of the demand for labour are particularly striking in combination. In the sectoral dimension, trade-induced changes in relative wages are likely both to be smaller and to provoke less concern and resistance. In the factoral dimension, more of the effect of demand shifts tends to emerge in relative wage changes, which in turn have more of an effect on inequality, and are more likely to be resisted. This asymmetry between the two dimensions is reflected in the balance and organisation of this book. The discussion of sectoral consequences is confined to the remainder of the present chapter, whereas the analysis of the consequences for skilled and unskilled workers is spread over the following three chapters.

5.3 Sectoral Consequences in the South

The changes in the pattern of trade with the North increased the overall demand for labour in Southern manufacturing and traded services. Within manufacturing, there were increases in the relative demand for labour in low-skill-intensity industries, such as clothing and footwear. There must thus have been corresponding reductions in the relative demand for labour in other industries, as well as in agriculture and non-traded services.

There is almost no evidence regarding the effects of these shifts in the composition of demand on inter-sectoral wage ratios in the South. In a competitive labour market, such effects should be small in the medium-to-long term, and Krueger (1983), Fields (1984), and others have argued that the labour markets of the successful East Asian exporters were unusually competitive, with wages virtually unaffected by unions, minimum wage laws, and other 'distortions'.[7] What may have happened in other countries is less clear. Different theories of wage determination in uncompetitive markets suggest different possible outcomes.[8] However, it appears that most Southern labour markets are more competitive than theorists have tended to suppose (Berry and Sabot 1978; Gregory 1986).

5.3.1 Manufacturing employment

The main sectoral effect of the changes in trade was thus probably on the composition of employment, with, in particular, an increase in the share of manufacturing. Table 5.2 presents estimates of both the absolute level of employment in manufacturing and its share of total employment for the South as a whole (including and excluding China) between 1950 and 1990. These estimates are extremely rough.[9] However, they provide a con-

[7] Addison and Demery (1989) present time-series for Malaysia and Singapore which suggest that wages in export industries increased relative to those in other industries, but by very little in the latter economy.

[8] e.g. rents earned by *BAS-ED* workers in manufacturing, relative to *BAS-ED* workers in agriculture, might be enhanced by increased bargaining power, or eroded by increased shortages of agricultural labour.

[9] They combine two different sources of information: ILO data on the economically active population (in agriculture, industry, and services); and data on manufacturing employment from the UN *Industrial Statistics Yearbook*. These two sources agree closely on trends in manufacturing employment. However, the absolute level of manufacturing employment is open to much more doubt. The ILO data, based on population censuses and labour

TABLE 5.2. *Manufacturing employment in the South, 1950–1990*

	Including China		Excluding China	
	Number of workers (millions)	Percentage of total employment	Number of workers (millions)	Percentage of total employment
1950	42	6.4	29	6.4
1960	60	7.6	42	8.0
1970	88	8.9	58	9.2
1980	155	12.7	98	12.2
1990	205	13.0	121	12.0
Increase	% p.a.	% point p.a.	% p.a.	% point p.a.
50–70	3.8	0.13	3.6	0.14
70–80	5.9	0.38	5.3	0.30
80–90	2.8	0.03	2.2	–0.02
70–90	4.3	0.20	3.7	0.14

Sources: (1) South excluding China. Benchmark estimates for 1985 are extrapolated forward and backward using indices of manufacturing employment from the UN *Industrial Statistics Yearbook*, and ILO total economically active population estimates. The benchmark estimates for 1985 are derived from labour force data in the UNCTAD *Handbook of Trade and Development Statistics* 1987, data on the share of industry in total employment from World Bank (1987, indicators table 32), and population census data on the average share of manufacturing in industrial employment in a sample of large countries.

(2) China. From data on industrial employment in various issues of the *Statistical Yearbook of China*, assuming the share of manufacturing in industrial employment to have been the same as in the 1982 population census, and adjusted to include village industry in all years.

text in which to consider the Southern sectoral demand impact estimates from the previous chapter.

In relation to the numbers in this table, the central estimate of the trade-induced increase in the demand for manufacturing labour, namely 23 million person-years in 1990 (Table 4.9), seems rather modest.[10] In that year, total manufacturing employment in the South was around 200 million (out of a total labour force of about 1.6 billion). Even the increase in manufacturing employment between 1970 and 1990, at nearly

force surveys, have suitably wide coverage, but are disaggregated only down to the broad industry level. Industrial census data, on which the UN *Industrial Statistics Yearbook* and UNIDO manufacturing employment series are based, are suitably disaggregated but have undesirably narrow country and enterprise size coverage. For example, the UNIDO figure for total manufacturing employment in developing countries excluding China in 1981 is 30.9 million workers, while for India alone the 1981 population-census-based figure is 26.6 million.

[10] However, part of manufacturing employment, as defined in population census data, consists of small-scale traditional handicrafts. The effect of trade on large-scale factory employment must have been proportionally greater than the numbers in this table suggest.

120 million, is five times the size of the estimated impact of the changes in trade with the North. If this increase had been 23 million smaller, manufacturing employment would have grown over the period at an average annual rate of 3.7 per cent rather than 4.3 per cent, and its 1990 share of total employment would have been 11.5 per cent rather than 13.0 per cent—noticeable but not large differences.

If China is included, manufacturing employment in the South grew faster during 1970–90 than during the preceding two decades, both in absolute terms and as a share of total employment. Moreover, if the 1990 level of manufacturing employment had been 23 million lower (as in the absence of the changes in trade), there would have been no such acceleration. With China's huge manufacturing work-force excluded, however, the acceleration disappears. Table 5.2 also suggests that manufacturing employment grew much faster in the 1970s than in the 1980s, which is the opposite of what might be expected from the relative size of the increases in the South's manufactured exports during these two decades (Fig. 1.1). One likely reason for this slowdown in manufacturing employment growth is the debt crises and other global shocks that afflicted many developing countries during the latter decade.

Evidence from other studies confirms that the changes in trade with the North did not greatly accelerate manufacturing employment growth for the South as a whole. As mentioned in Section 3.5.2, work by UNIDO and by Forstner and Ballance shows that expansion of industry in the South was by no means confined to sectors of low skill intensity. In addition, the results of Chenery and Syrquin suggest that the share of industry in total employment did not rise unusually fast during 1950–83. On average, both for middle-income and for low-income developing countries, but especially for the latter group, the rate of increase was less than would have been predicted from the Chenery–Syrquin cross-country regression.[11]

5.3.2 Cross-country variation

An altogether different impression of the impact of the changes in trade with the North on manufacturing employment emerges from comparisons among individual developing countries differentiated by their trade performance. Fig. 5.4 is a scatter diagram of the cross-country relationship between changes in the share of manufacturing in total employment over

---

[11] Syrquin (1988, table 7.2) gives the results of time-series regressions of the share of industrial employment against the log of per capita income for low-income, lower-middle-income, and upper-middle-income countries: the mean values of the slopes for these three groups are 0.05, 0.07, and 0.08 respectively. The corresponding cross-country slope is 0.09 (estimated from table 4 of Syrquin and Chenery 1989 over the range $300–$4000).

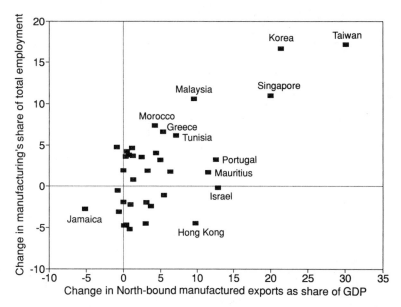

F IG. 5.4   Changes in manufactured export and employment shares in the South, 1960–1985 (percentage points)

Notes and sources: Change in both variables defined as difference between early and recent levels (measured in percentage points).

Manufacturing employment measured as share of total economically active population. Data, from the ILO *Yearbook of Labour Statistics* and national population censuses and labour force surveys, refer to various years in or close to the periods 1960–5 and 1980–5. Manufacturing employment data for Hong Kong include construction, and for Israel include mining.

Data on manufactured exports and GDP, from World Bank (1987, indicators tables 3 and 14), in general refer to 1965 and 1985. Manufactured exports (unlike manufacturing employment) exclude processed primary products.

For clarity, only the outlying countries are labelled. The unlabelled countries are Argentina, Chile, Costa Rica, Dominican Republic, Ecuador, Egypt, Ghana, India, Indonesia, Liberia, Mexico, Pakistan, Panama, Paraguay, Peru, Philippines, South Africa, Sri Lanka, Syria, Thailand, Trinidad, Turkey, Uruguay, and Venezuela.

the period from the early 1960s to the early 1980s (Y) and changes over much the same period in the ratio of North-bound manufactured exports to GDP (X). The diagram reveals a clear positive relationship between these two variables. Countries whose manufactured exports to the North expanded relative to GDP tended also to experience increases in the share of manufacturing in total employment.

Fitting an OLS regression to the observations in Fig. 5.4 yields

$$Y = -0.37 + 0.53X \qquad R^2 = 0.47 \qquad (5.1)$$
$$(5.50)$$

(*t*-statistic in parentheses). Nearly half the cross-country variance of changes in the manufacturing employment share is explained. The intercept is close to zero, implying that countries which did not raise their North-bound manufactured export–GDP ratios did not, on average, achieve any increase in their manufacturing employment shares. The slope coefficient, which differs from zero at any conventional level of significance, implies that a one percentage point increase in the export–GDP ratio is associated with about half a percentage point increase in the manufacturing employment share. (If exports were measured, like GDP, in terms of domestic value added content, rather than gross value, this coefficient would be close to unity, since, as shown in Table 4.1, the average share of value added in the South's narrow manufactured exports is about one-half.)

The appearance of the diagram and the fit of the regression are heavily dependent on three unsurprising outliers—Korea, Singapore, and Taiwan, which all substantially increased both their export–GDP ratios and their manufacturing employment shares. In Hong Kong, though, the manufacturing employment share, which was unusually high at the beginning of the period, declined somewhat, despite a rise in the manufactured export ratio, which, like that of Singapore, is roughly adjusted to exclude re-exports.[12] If these four observations are excluded, the regression fits much less well ($R^2 = 0.13$), and the slope coefficient differs from zero only at the 5 per cent level of significance. For the remaining thirty-two countries in the sample, the relationship between trade performance and sectoral employment change is presumably muffled by a combination of errors in the data and changes in other determinants of manufacturing employment.

In summary, the evidence on the consequences of trade-induced changes in the sectoral composition of labour demand in the South is limited, but suggests some reasonably clear and uncontroversial conclusions. The main sectoral effect of the changes in North–South trade during 1960–90 was to make the share of manufacturing in total employment larger than it would otherwise have been. For most developing countries,

---

[12] The data on the total re-exports of Hong Kong and Singapore in GATT *International Trade* are not broken down by commodity and destination, and hence one cannot determine accurately what proportions of their exports of narrowly defined manufactures to the North consist of re-exports. But to make no adjustment would be misleading. So for both economies, the North-bound export–GDP ratio is simply halved (which also halves the change over the period). The effect of this adjustment on Fig. 5.4 is to shift the two points concerned leftwards, making the regression line steeper. The accuracy of the Hong Kong observation is also reduced by the unavoidable inclusion of construction in manufacturing employment.

and for the South in aggregate, trade seems to have been only one of a number of influences on the evolution of the sectoral structure of employment, with other forces collectively being of greater importance. But for a few export-oriented economies, the changing pattern of trade with the North was the dominant cause of alterations in the sectoral composition of employment.

5.4 Sectoral Consequences in the North

The effects of the changes in trade on the sectoral pattern of demand in the North were largely a mirror-image of the effects in the South. Within manufacturing, the relative demand for labour increased in skill-intensive industries and declined in other industries. The overall demand for labour in manufacturing and other traded sectors was also reduced relative to nontraded sectors. This section looks at the consequences of these shifts in demand, first for the sectoral structure of profits and wages, then for the sectoral structure of employment.

5.4.1 Profits and wages

The conventional assumption of high inter-sectoral supply elasticities, as explained in Section 5.2.2, implies that demand shifts have little effect on relative earnings in different sectors. However, the exceptions that are admitted for specific factors and uncompetitive markets appear to have been of some significance in the North, even though the principal enduring effect has been to change the sectoral composition of employment.

Relative profitability of manufacturing

It is likely that the immediate effect of more competition from the South was to reduce the profitability of low-skill-intensive industries. New investment in these industries was either discouraged or concentrated on defensive innovation, while installed plant and machinery went on producing for a while with lower-than-expected profits.[13] This reduction of profits in labour-intensive industries may well also have pulled down the average profitability of the whole manufacturing sector, since there was probably less of an offsetting rise in the profits of the expanding skill-

---

[13] The effects of import competition on relative sectoral profitability are documented by Grossman and Levinsohn (1989), but for trade in general rather than for trade with the South in particular.

intensive industries.[14] However, the decline in average manufacturing profitability should later have been reversed, when the inherited capital stock of the labour-intensive industries was eventually scrapped.

The profit rate series in Fig. 5.5, which are weighted averages for the seven largest Northern countries, seem consistent with this interpretation. From the mid-1960s to the early 1980s, the profitability of manufacturing

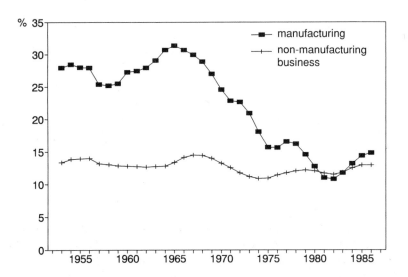

FIG. 5.5 Sectoral profit rates in the North (weighted average of seven largest countries)

Notes and sources: The series are three-year moving averages of profit rates on capital, averaged across countries (Canada, France, Germany, Italy, Japan, UK, USA) using 1985 dollar GDP weights. The series are derived from unpublished data used by Armstrong *et al.* (1984, 1991), kindly supplied by Andrew Glyn.

Profits are net of depreciation as calculated by national accountants, and also net of inventory valuation adjustment (or stock appreciation), but are gross of taxes and interest payments. Income from self-employment is either omitted (by including only incorporated businesses) or its estimated wage content is subtracted from profits.

The capital stock, which includes only fixed assets, is measured net of depreciation, and at current (rather than historic) cost.

Non-manufacturing business excludes sectors in which profits cannot meaningfully be identified, such as government, housing, and finance. Its capital stock is roughly twice as large as that of manufacturing.

---

[14] Beenstock (1984: 74–5, 107–8) also argues that more trade with the South reduced profitability in the North, but for a different reason (and one which is inconsistent with the theory and evidence in Chs. 2 and 3 of this book), namely that it caused a relatively capital-intensive sector, manufacturing, to contract.

declined substantially, relative to the profitability of non-manufacturing business (which fluctuated within a much narrower range), but recovered to some degree during the rest of the 1980s. Although the data underlying the figure are open to various doubts, this pattern of movement is confirmed by other studies.[15]

It is improbable, however, that expansion of trade with the South alone could have caused such a large decline in the profitability of Northern manufacturing. Several other downward influences on profit rates during this period have been identified, though not all of them seem capable of explaining the deterioration in the relative position of manufacturing.

First, acceleration of inflation during 1960–80 was associated with a decline in real interest rates, and vice versa in the 1980s (World Bank 1990, fig. 1.6). These variations in inflation also increased, and later reduced, the inventory valuation adjustment (or stock appreciation) that national accountants deduct from profits.[16] Second, the average tax rate on profits was reduced, and hence the net-of-tax profit rate fell by less than the gross-of-tax rate shown in the figure (Chan-Lee and Sutch 1985: 33; Weisskopf 1988, figs. 1–4). Third, the ratio of inventories to fixed assets declined, so that the fall in the rate of profit on fixed assets—which is what the figure shows—overstates the decline in the rate of profit on the total capital stock (Chan-Lee 1986, table I.1).

More specifically unfavourable to manufacturing were the increases in the price of oil in the 1970s, which reduced the profitability of installed energy-intensive plant. Intensified competition in manufacturing among developed countries, associated with more North–North trade, could also have contributed to the reduction in profitability. Some studies argue that profits declined in the late 1960s and 1970s because of labour force militancy (for example, Sachs 1979), and others that the cessation of this decline in the 1980s was caused by repression of unions (Armstrong *et al.* 1984, 1991; Bowles *et al.* 1986; Reati 1986), though in neither phase were these labour-market developments confined to manufacturing.

How much expansion of trade with the South contributed to the decline and later recovery of the relative profitability of manufacturing is thus hard to determine. Some additional evidence is provided by Fig. 5.6, which reveals wide variation among the seven countries averaged in the previous figure. The change from 1963–7 to 1978–82 in the relative profitability of manufacturing (measured by subtraction of the

---

[15] See e.g. Hill (1979), Holland (1984: 25), Chan-Lee and Sutch (1985: 31 and chart B), and Weisskopf (1988).

[16] See Hill (1979, ch. 5, esp. table 5.1). However, changes in depreciation rates apparently did not contribute to the trends in net (of depreciation) profit rates shown in the present Fig. 5.5 (Holland and Myers 1984, app. 2C; King and Mairesse 1984: 244–7). Nor do the trends appear very different when allowance is made for changes in net interest payments by firms (Lovell 1978: 776–7; Chan-Lee 1986, table 4).

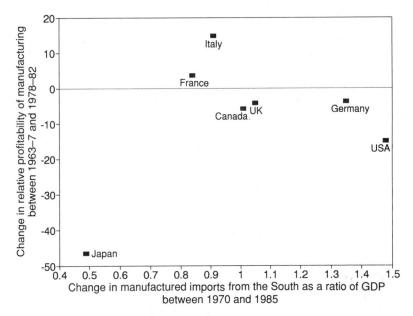

FIG. 5.6 Changes in relative profitability of manufacturing and Southern import penetration (percentage points)
Notes and sources: On profitability data, see notes to Fig. 5.5. Relative profitability of manufacturing measured by subtracting profit rate of non-manufacturing business. Change measured as difference between 5-year-average end-points.

Southern import penetration measured by expressing manufactured imports from the South as a percentage of GDP in the country concerned. Change in import penetration is the difference between the 1970 and 1985 percentages.

Import data from OECD trade statistics. South defined as non-OECD non-Comecon plus Greece, Portugal, Turkey, and Yugoslavia. Manufactured imports defined as SITC 5 to 9 less 68. GDP data from OECD *National Accounts*.

non-manufacturing profit rate) ranged from a rise of 15 percentage points in Italy to a fall of 46 percentage points in Japan, most of which occurred between 1970 and 1975. However, if the Japanese observation is disregarded as unbelievable, the figure suggests that the relative profitability of manufacturing declined more, the larger was the increase in Southern import penetration.[17]

[17] The import penetration ratio used here is discussed further below, in connection with Fig. 5.10. If its denominator were manufacturing value added (as in Appendix A2), rather than GDP, the correlation in Fig. 5.6 would be partly spurious, since profits are part of value added, and hence a decline in profits would tend to raise the import penetration ratio for accounting reasons. As explained in Sect. 5.4.2, changes in Southern import penetration are generally collinear with changes in Northern import penetration. However, the changes

Inter-sectoral wage ratios

The initial decline in the profitability of installed capital in labour-intensive industries probably acted as a cushion, delaying the impact of the changes in trade on the sectoral composition of labour demand. The full force of these changes was not felt by workers until existing plants were closed down, a process which was spread over a fairly long period, partly because some labour-intensive plants were initially newer (or for some other reason more profitable) than others. However, alterations in the sectoral pattern of new investment acted more promptly to raise the relative demand for labour in skill-intensive industries, as did attempts at defensive labour-saving innovation in labour-intensive industries.

The theoretical presumption that inter-sectoral labour supply elasticities are high is supported empirically by the inter-spatial and inter-temporal similarity of sectoral wage structures (Wood 1978: 175–9; Katz and Summers 1989). Although there are some variations among countries and over time, the overwhelming impression is of stability in inter-sectoral wage ratios, despite large changes in relative employment levels. None the less, shifts in demand should in theory affect the sectoral wage structure where there are costs or obstacles to labour mobility, as is generally the case in the short run, and may also do so if wages are determined by bargaining rather than by competition.[18] For example, lower profits reduce union power (by making strikes less costly to employers), while lower product demand may—or may not—induce unions to offer wage concessions to preserve jobs.

Immobility is a particularly serious problem for workers with high levels of skill specific to individual industries. Skilled workers in Northern labour-intensive industries, though a minority, have thus often been even harder hit than their less-skilled colleagues by the changes in trade with the South. The wages of unskilled workers in declining sectors must stay competitive with other sectors, whereas most skilled workers cannot move laterally, even if reduced demand drives their wages well below those of workers with equally long and costly training in other sectors. Skilled wages can be maintained by union action, but this increases the risk of skills being devalued completely by loss of jobs.

Several studies of US manufacturing have found statistically significant reductions in the wages of manual workers in industries subject to strong competition from imports, although none of these studies looks at

in relative manufacturing profitability do not appear to be inversely correlated with increases in Northern import penetration unless the observation for the USA (as well as that for Japan) is disregarded.

[18] The response of wages to demand shifts in unionised labour markets is theoretically ambiguous (Wood 1978: 9–14; Brauer 1991: 17–18; Revenga 1992: 258). There are also conflicting empirical results, e.g. Brauer (ibid. 25) finds the effects of import competition on wages to be smaller in unionised labour markets, while Revenga (1990) finds the opposite.

imports from the South in particular (Grossman 1982; Galbraith and Calmon 1990; Brauer 1991; Freeman and Katz 1991; Revenga 1992). In all these studies, however, the effect of imports on wages is quite small, and in the three where a comparison can be made (Grossman, Freeman and Katz, and Revenga) is much smaller than the effect on employment in the industries concerned. Thus the elasticities with respect to import prices estimated by Revenga range from 0.06 to 0.09 for wages and from 0.24 to 0.39 for employment.

5.4.2 Deindustrialisation of employment

There is some disagreement among these US studies concerning the absolute size of the effect of imports on employment. Grossman found a substantial employment effect in only one of his nine 'trade-impacted' sectors (radios and televisions), and no employment effect in two sectors with big imports from the South (footwear, and toys and games). However, these results are open to doubt. For example, the lack of impact in footwear conflicts with case-study evidence that Southern competition has much reduced the number of Northern jobs in this sector (Hamilton 1989). The employment reduction is clear in Grossman's data, but his model attributes it to other causes.

The case studies could be wrong about causation, but there could also be something wrong with Grossman's model. Among other things, the lags seem suspiciously short: the employment-reducing effects of lower import prices are compressed into eighteen months, rather than spread over several years (as existing plant is gradually eliminated or replaced).[19] Revenga (1992) concludes that the problem lies in Grossman's estimation technique. Like him, she uses a price measure of import competition, but discovers larger and more consistent effects with instrumental variables than with ordinary least squares. Freeman and Katz, who measure competition by the quantity rather than the price of imports, also find more substantial effects on employment than Grossman.

These studies, it should be recalled, refer to the impact of imports from all trading partners on employment in specific manufacturing industries in one country. By contrast, the estimates in the previous chapter refer to

[19] Thus the effect of import competition may be captured mainly in the time trend term, which is the only sector-specific independent variable other than the import price index. In a subsequent paper applying the same methodology to the US steel industry, Grossman (1986) tested lags of up to 24 months, but his model suggested full adjustment within 18 months. The results in this paper imply that 'import competition' substantially reduced employment, accounting for about a quarter of the actual decline in steel employment during 1976–83 and about a half during 1979–83. However, this intensified competition was mainly the result of the dollar's appreciation. And over the full period, an unexplained time trend accounted for more of the employment decline.

changes in both sides of the trade account with one trading partner—the South—and to the impact of these changes on the demand for labour in the manufacturing sector as a whole and in the North as a whole. The factor content calculations in that chapter suggest that the cumulative impact up to 1990 was to reduce the net demand for labour in Northern manufacturing by between 6 and 12 million person-years. It was also suggested, though more tentatively, that allowance for the effects of defensive innovation would require these estimates to be approximately doubled.

So if, as seems likely from the preceding discussion, the effects of this shift in the sectoral composition of demand on relative wages were quite small, the changes in trade with the South should have had a large effect on the sectoral structure of employment. As is well known, moreover, the share of manufacturing in Northern employment did in fact decline during 1960–90. The next few pages will look more closely at this decline, at other possible reasons for its occurrence, and at evidence which might discriminate among the competing explanations of deindustrialisation.

Trends and explanations

Fig. 5.7 shows what happened to manufacturing's share of total employment in the seven largest Northern economies (added together) between the early 1950s and the late 1980s. It rose gradually from about 27 per cent to about 29 per cent at the end of the 1960s, then declined steadily to about 21 per cent at the end of the period. The absolute number of manufacturing workers did not decline much (from 66 million in 1969 to 62 million in 1989); but there was a large rise in total employment (from 230 to 290 million), and an even larger increase in the total labour force, because unemployment rose (by 12 million).

Although the relative decline of manufacturing employment in the North has been widely recognised, its causes are still debated (Singh 1987). Even at an accounting level, controversy continues to surround the identity

$$n_i = \frac{q_i}{v_i/v} \qquad (5.2)$$

where n_i is manufacturing's share of total employment, q_i is its share of total output, and v_i and v refer to output per worker in manufacturing and in the whole economy respectively. The controversy is about how much the decline in n_i reflects a decline in q_i, as opposed to a rise in v_i/v (the relative productivity of manufacturing workers).

Some people argue that there has been little change in manufacturing's share of *real* output, and that most or all of its relative employment decline reflects a rise in the relative productivity of manufacturing

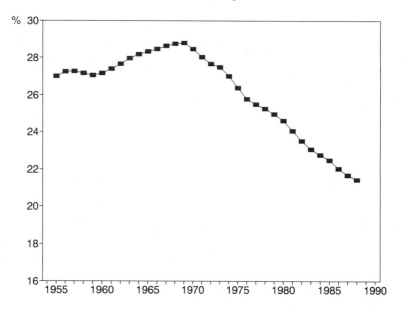

F IG. 5.7 Share of manufacturing in Northern employment (sum of seven largest countries)
Notes and sources: Three-year moving average of the sum of manufacturing employment in Canada, France, Germany, Italy, Japan, UK, and USA, divided by the sum of total employment in these countries.

Data from OECD *Manpower Statistics* 1950–62 and *Labour Force Statistics* 1960–71 and 1969–89. Gaps in manufacturing employment series were filled by linear interpolation for Germany 1980–6, Italy 1971–6, and USA 1963–8, and by extrapolation on the basis of movements in all-industry employment for Germany 1954–61 and Italy 1954–9.

workers (measured in terms of real output per worker). This rise in relative productivity, these people also argue, has caused the relative price of manufactured goods to decline, which explains why the share of manufacturing in *nominal* GDP has fallen. Other people, however, contend that manufacturing's share of real output has fallen, too, and there has been a lively debate about the accuracy of official real manufacturing output statistics (de Leeuw 1988).

The economic (as opposed to the accounting) causes of deindustrialisation are subject to even more dispute. The hypothesis of this book— which is that expansion of trade with the South has been the main cause—is by no means original, being perhaps the most widely held view among the general public (and propounded also by a few economists, such as Beenstock 1984: 105–7). Most economists, however, have rejected this hypothesis, citing the earlier empirical studies reviewed in Section 3.4, which found the net employment effect of trade with the South to be tiny (Singh 1987: 305–6). This reason for rejection is undermined by the new estimates in Chapter 4, which suggest a far larger effect. But there are, of course, other possible reasons for the deindustrialisation of employment, which might supplement or supplant the present hypothesis.

Rowthorn and Wells (1987, app. 2) argue that deindustrialisation is a natural consequence of economic 'maturity', which is defined as the share of agriculture in total employment falling below a critical level. They assume that labour productivity consistently grows faster in manufacturing than in services, but that the demand for (and hence the output of) these two sectors grows at roughly the same rate. As a result, throughout the process of development, the ratio of manufacturing to service employment steadily falls. The share of agriculture in total employment also falls throughout, because agricultural labour productivity rises and the demand for agricultural output is income-inelastic. Prior to maturity, when the share of agriculture in total employment is large, its shrinkage provides room for both other sectors to expand, so that the share of manufacturing in total employment rises. After the agricultural employment share has become small, however, manufacturing employment is bound to decline not only relative to services, but also as a share of total employment.

This neat explanation of the observed curvilinear path of manufacturing's share of employment is based on fairly realistic assumptions.[20] However, these assumptions can be modified in ways that allow the economic maturity model to be combined with other explanations of deindustrialisation. In particular, within the Rowthorn–Wells framework, expansion of trade with the South could have accelerated the decline of manufacturing's employment share by widening the gap in productivity growth between manufacturing and services. Moreover, it was argued earlier (Section 3.4.3) that trade with the South has indeed raised labour productivity in Northern manufacturing, both through changes in activity mix (abandoning labour-intensive products and stages of production) and through defensive innovation.[21]

Other forces that may have contributed to deindustrialisation can also be blended into the economic maturity framework. For instance, expansion of *North–North* trade, too, could have widened the gap in labour

[20] The outline of the economic maturity model in the preceding paragraph is less precise than in Rowthorn and Wells (1987, app. 2), although the latter includes some assumptions made simply for expository convenience.

[21] It might be argued (e.g. on the basis of Table 4.8) that the recent changes in trade with the South have also reduced manufacturing output in the North (by lowering net foreign demand). This argument must be treated cautiously, however. The net Southern demand for manufactures from the North depends on other components of the overall balance of trade (not least, the size of the South's primary trade surplus). Moreover, the estimates in Ch. 4 do not allow for general equilibrium interactions, including the positive effect of trade on aggregate Northern output.

productivity growth between manufacturing and services, by causing more specialisation in manufacturing and hence greater realisation of scale economies.[22] Such a widening of the productivity growth gap could also have been the result of an autonomous surge of technical progress concentrated on manufacturing. It would also be possible to modify the assumption that Rowthorn and Wells make about the evolving structure of demand, to accommodate the suggestion that consumption of services tends to rise more rapidly than consumption of manufactures (but see Kravis *et al.* 1983 and Singh 1987: 302–3).

These explanations all refer to the deindustrialisation of employment in the North as a whole. Other, more specific, forces may have been relevant to individual Northern countries. For example, Rowthorn and Wells suggest that 'late-comers' such as Japan experienced faster growth of productivity in manufacturing, and thus smaller rises (and smaller subsequent falls) in the share of manufacturing employment. They also argue, in the case of the UK, that the decline in manufacturing employment partly reflects a reduced need to earn a trade surplus in manufactures, because of a falling primary trade deficit (due to agricultural subsidies and the discovery of oil in the North Sea), and a rising surplus in traded services.

Timing and magnitude

One sort of evidence which is helpful in judging the relative correctness of these alternative explanations is the *timing* of the deindustrialisation of employment in the North. Fig. 5.7 suggests that the change in trend was quite abrupt. This impression is reinforced by the regression results of Syrquin and Chenery (1989: 68–9), who find that after 1973 there was a downward shift, confined to high-income countries, in their cross-country relationship between the industrial employment share and the level of per capita income. It is thus hard to believe that the decline in the share of manufacturing employment was simply the result of longstanding trends in sectoral productivity growth or in the composition of demand.

The timing of the change in trend—around 1969—also casts doubt on the contribution of North–North trade, which grew faster in the 1950s and 1960s (when the share of manufacturing employment was rising) than in the two following decades (when this share was falling).[23] Nor does the timing of the change in trend favour the view that deindustrialisation was caused by an autonomous surge of new labour-saving technology in manufacturing. As is well known, productivity growth in most sectors slowed

---

[22] This possibility was suggested to me by Bob Rowthorn.

[23] The average real growth rate of North–North manufactured exports was 10.2% during 1955–70, and 6.1% during 1970–88. These growth rates are estimated from nominal trade data in the UNCTAD *Handbook of Trade and Development Statistics*, deflated by the GATT index of the unit value of world manufactured exports.

down during the 1970s, and so did growth of civilian R & D expenditure (see for example Lindbeck 1983; Patel and Pavitt 1991, figs. 1 and 2; and the other studies cited in Section 7.3.3).

The hypothesis that changes in trade with the South were the main cause is clearly more consistent with the time-path of the manufacturing employment share, because these changes occurred during the latter part of the period. However, the correspondence with the time-path of the South's manufactured exports to the North is far from exact. The growth rate of these exports accelerated in the early 1960s (Fig. 5.1), while deindustrialisation did not begin until the end of the 1960s. Moreover, these exports rose less in absolute terms in the 1970s than in the 1980s (Fig. 1.1), while the fall in the manufacturing employment share was similar in both decades. These discrepancies require some explanation.

The lag at the beginning could have occurred, as explained above, because the impact of Southern competition on Northern workers was delayed by an initial decline in the profitability of labour-intensive manufacturing (which started in the mid-1960s: Fig. 5.5). The lack of acceleration of deindustrialisation, despite the increasing absolute size of the increments in Southern exports, has two possible explanations. One is that Southern import substitution (which reduced the North's labour-intensive exports, as discussed in Section 4.3.1) was concentrated in the earlier part of the period. The other is that the elimination of manufacturing activities in the North proceeded in diminishing order of labour-intensity, so that each unit of the earlier increments in Southern exports displaced more labour than the more recent increments.

Another approach to the evidence is to ask how accurately the alternative hypotheses explain the *magnitude* of the deindustrialisation of employment in the North. Table 5.3, which refers to all OECD countries, compares the actual change in the manufacturing employment share with simulations based on the economic maturity model. These simulations show what would have happened if the actual rates of productivity growth in manufacturing and services during the 1950s and early 1960s had been maintained during the next two decades. It is assumed that real output would have grown at the same rate in both sectors, and that employment in agriculture and mining would have followed its actual path of decline.

The results of the simulations vary somewhat, depending on their starting-points and on the sources of data on productivity growth, but in three of the four cases in the table the share of manufacturing employment does decline, as predicted by the economic maturity model.[24] Even in these cases, however, the simulated decline is considerably smaller than the actual decline. The lowest of the simulated values in 1989 is about 25

[24] In the fourth, the estimated gap between the productivity growth rates of manufacturing and services in the 1950s is only 0.6 percentage points.

TABLE 5.3. *Actual and simulated changes in sectoral shares of OECD employment*

	Agriculture and mining	Manufacturing	Services	Total
Actual shares (%)				
1960	22.8	26.1	51.1	100.0
1969	15.1	27.6	57.3	100.0
1989	8.1	20.8	71.1	100.0
Simulated shares in 1989 (%)				
1	Assumed	24.9	67.1	100.0
2	same as	28.1	63.8	100.0
3	actual	24.8	67.1	100.0
4	share	26.7	65.2	100.0
Discrepancies in 1989 (million person-years)				
1	0	–14.9	14.9	0
2	0	–26.9	26.9	0
3	0	–14.6	14.6	0
4	0	–21.7	21.7	0

Notes and sources: (1) Actual shares, calculated from OECD *Labour Force Statistics*, are based on totals for all OECD countries.

(2) Simulated shares in 1989. Loosely based on the economic maturity model of Rowthorn and Wells (1987, app. 2). In each year, given the actual share of agricultural (plus mining) employment, the simulated shares of manufacturing and services are calculated by assuming (*a*) that the real output of these two sectors rises by an equal proportion, and (*b*) that labour productivity growth rates in these two sectors are the same as in the 1950s and early 1960s. Simulations 1 and 2 start from actual 1960 shares, and use the 1950–60 productivity growth rates from Table A2.4 (1 is based on the UNISY series, 2 on the UNNAY series, in which manufacturing productivity grows more slowly). Simulations 3 and 4 start from actual 1969 shares, and use the 1950–65 productivity growth rates from Table A2.4 (3 is based on the UNISY series, 4 on the UNNAY series).

(3) Discrepancies in 1989. Calculated by applying the differences between the actual and simulated 1989 shares to total OECD employment in 1989.

per cent, as compared with the actual value of 21 per cent (and the 1969 figure of 28 per cent).[25] In absolute terms, the actual number of manufacturing workers in 1989 is between 15 million and 27 million less than the simulated numbers.

Although the results of the simulations are spread over a considerable range, these discrepancies between the simulated and actual numbers of manufacturing workers are similar in magnitude to the previous chapter's estimates of the impact of the changes in trade with the South on the demand for manufacturing labour in the North (12 million to 24 million, including the allowance for defensive innovation). Even the smallest discrepancy (15 million in 1989) might be viewed as consistent with the central demand impact estimate (18 million in 1990), since part of the

[25] These percentages, which refer to all OECD countries, differ slightly from those in Fig. 5.7, which refers only to the seven largest countries (which account for about 80% of total OECD employment).

demand shift was probably absorbed by a change in inter-sectoral wage relativities (see Section 5.4.1).

The magnitude of deindustrialisation could thus be fully explained by the combination of two hypotheses. Up to 3 of the 7 percentage points by which the all-OECD manufacturing employment share fell between 1969 and 1989 could be attributed to economic maturity, and the rest to changes in trade with the South. These calculations, of course, do not prove that this explanation is correct or complete. The other influences mentioned earlier (North–North trade, a technical surge in manufacturing, and shifts in domestic demand) may also have contributed, but their impact cannot readily be quantified.[26]

Cross-country variation

The extent of deindustrialisation varied greatly among Northern countries. Fig. 5.8, which refers to all OECD members except Turkey (a lower-middle-income developing country), shows that during 1969–89 manufacturing's share of employment fell by more than 12 percentage points in Belgium, the UK, and Switzerland, but by less than 3 points in Japan and Austria, while in Greece and Portugal the employment share of manufacturing actually increased.

The figure also reveals an inverse relationship between the fall in the manufacturing share and its initial level. Countries with larger shares of employment in manufacturing in 1969 tended to experience larger declines in this share over the following two decades. So in proportion to the initial shares, these declines varied less among countries. This pattern suggests that some common shrinking force was at work, but is consistent with more than one of the possible reasons for deindustrialisation discussed above.

To begin with, this pattern conforms with the economic maturity hypothesis of Rowthorn and Wells in two respects. First, the inverse relationship in the figure is what would be expected if 'late-comers' experienced both smaller rises and smaller subsequent declines in manufacturing employment than early industrialisers (Rowthorn and Wells 1987: 329–32). Second, the cross-country variations in the initial employment share of manufacturing are inversely related to variations in

---

[26] The difference between the actual and simulated values in Table 5.3 more or less disappears if the actual rates of productivity growth during 1960–85 and 1965–85 (from Table A2.4) are substituted for the 1950–60 and 1950–65 rates used in the simulations. The discrepancies thus seem to be due mainly to a widening of the gap in labour productivity growth between manufacturing and services (not to slower output growth in manufacturing). However, this conclusion is open to the objection that the growth of real output, and hence of productivity, in manufacturing has been mis-measured. Even if correct, this conclusion is neutral as between North-South trade, North–North trade, and an autonomous acceleration of technical advance in manufacturing as causes of the widening of the productivity growth gap.

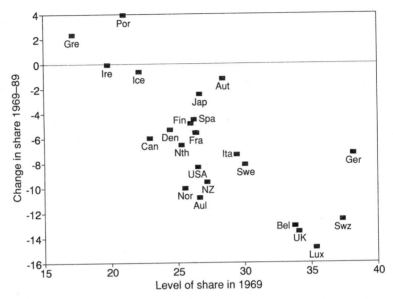

F_{IG}. 5.8 Changes and initial levels of manufacturing employment shares
(percentage points)
Notes and sources: 'Share' refers to manufacturing employment as a percentage of
total employment. The change in this share is the absolute difference between its
1969 and 1989 levels.

Data from OECD *Labour Force Statistics* 1960–71 and 1969–89. The data for
1969 for Denmark refer to 1972, and for Finland and Greece to 1971.

Among the less obvious abbreviations, Aul is Australia, Aut is Austria, Nth is
The Netherlands, and Spa is Spain.

the initial share of employment in agriculture. Initial agricultural employment shares are thus strongly and positively related to subsequent
changes in the share of manufacturing, as shown in Fig. 5.9 (an update of
Rowthorn and Wells's fig. 10.3). This relationship clearly supports the
view that deindustrialisation is caused by the share of employment in
agriculture falling to a low level.

The pattern in Fig. 5.8 is also consistent with the influence of more
trade with the South, which, it may be recalled, caused labour-intensive
activities to contract (and to shed labour through defensive innovation),
and skill-intensive activities to expand. This would have resulted in an
equi-proportional contraction of manufacturing employment in all
Northern countries if (*a*) all these countries had started with identical
ratios of labour-intensive to skill-intensive activities within their manufacturing sectors, and (*b*) they had all experienced equal increases in exposure to trade with the South. The absolute size of these contractions

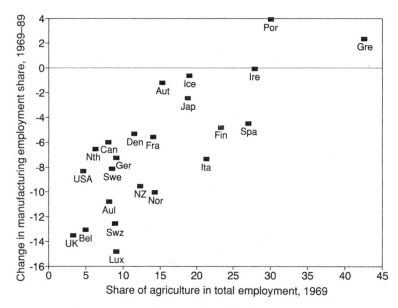

FIG. 5.9 Changes in manufacturing employment shares and initial levels of agricultural employment shares (percentage points)
Notes and sources: See Fig. 5.8.

would have varied from country to country, though, depending on the initial share of employment in manufacturing (which varied for several reasons, including differing balances of trade in primary products and services, as emphasised by Rowthorn and Wells 1987: 31–6, 62–75).

Assumption (*a*) is unlikely to be strictly accurate. Although the skill endowments of Northern countries appear fairly similar by comparison with those of the South, there is some intra-North variation, which provides a theoretical reason to expect differences in the initial ratio of labour-intensive to skill-intensive activities within their manufacturing sectors. For example, factor content of trade studies show that Belgium has tended to specialise in manufactures of relatively low skill intensity.[27] Such a country should have started with a larger-than-average share of employment in manufacturing (as Belgium did), and experienced a larger-than-average proportional decline in this share (as it also did).[28] There

[27] See Koekkoek and Mennes (1984: 42–3) and Schumacher (1992). Another country which has long specialised in manufactures of relatively low skill intensity is the UK (Crafts and Thomas 1986).
[28] In 1969, manufacturing's share of employment in Belgium was 33.8%, as compared with 27.6% for the OECD as a whole. Between 1969 and 1989, this share declined by 39% in Belgium, and by 25% in the OECD as a whole.

should thus be some downward curvature, rather than strict equi-proportionality, in the relationship in Fig. 5.8 between the initial share of manufacturing employment and its subsequent decline.[29]

Nor is assumption (*b*) likely to be strictly accurate. The increases over this period in the exposure of Northern countries to trade with the South varied, depending on the height of their initial barriers (artificial and nat-ural) to this trade, and on the degree to which they lowered or raised these barriers during the period. Countries whose exposure to trade with the South increased more than average should thus have experienced larger-than-average reductions in manufacturing employment, as appears to have been the case.

Fig. 5.10 relates the change in manufacturing employment shares dur-ing 1969–89 to the change in imports of manufactures from the South (expressed as a percentage of GDP) over much the same period. Five of

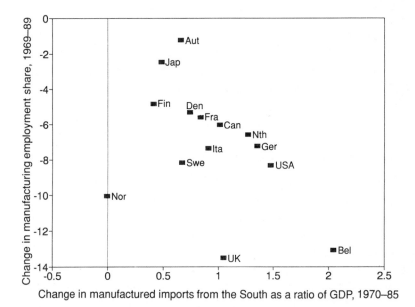

Fig. 5.10 Changes in manufacturing employment shares and Southern import penetration (percentage points)
Notes and sources: Employment data as in Fig. 5.8. Import penetration data as in Fig. 5.6.

[29] The data in Fig. 5.8 are too scattered (due to other influences) to assess reliably whether or not there is actually downward curvature. The coefficient of variation of the manufacturing employment share was slightly smaller in 1989 than in 1969, suggesting greater proportionate reductions in countries with larger initial shares, but the opposite is true if the poorer OECD countries are excluded (as in Fig. 5.10).

the countries in the previous figure are excluded for lack of the necessary trade data (Australia, Iceland, Luxemburg, New Zealand, and Switzerland). Also left out are four more of the poorer OECD countries—Greece, Spain, Portugal, and Ireland—which lie in the intermediate zone between North and South. (In 1969, all four had more than 25 per cent of their employment in agriculture, and in 1989 their per capita incomes were all below those of Israel, Hong Kong, and Singapore.)

It seems more appropriate to measure the change in import penetration by the absolute than by the proportional increase in the ratio to GDP, since doubling a large ratio would have more of an effect on the domestic labour market than quadrupling a tiny ratio.[30] However, this import penetration variable is by no means ideal. It does not directly measure changes in the height of barriers to trade with the South: the ratio of imports from the South to GDP could alter for reasons other than changes in these barriers, including movements in the real exchange rate (which affect this ratio by altering the prices of traded goods relative to nontraded goods). This variable also neglects changes in exports. In particular, some Northern countries, such as Belgium and the UK, lost more manufacturing jobs than others because they were initially more dependent on exports of labour-intensive goods, either to the South or to other Northern countries.

None the less, Fig. 5.10 suggests a strong inverse relationship between changes in the Southern import penetration ratio and changes in the share of manufacturing in total employment, with the exception of two countries (Norway and the UK) which lie well below the others. These two countries, however, were the main beneficiaries of the exploitation of North Sea oil during this period, which caused their manufacturing sectors to shrink.[31] Allowing for this influence with a dummy variable (*OIL*, with a value of 1 for Norway and the UK, and zero for other countries) yields the following OLS regression

---

[30] It is also more appropriate in this context to make the denominator of the ratio GDP, rather than manufacturing value added (as in Table A2.5). This is because the share of manufacturing in total employment is related by an accounting identity to the share of manufacturing value added in GDP. The correlation between changes in the manufacturing employment share and changes in the ratio of imports to manufacturing value added would thus be partly a reflection of this accounting identity.

[31] Rowthorn and Wells (1987: 64–5, 165) show that the non-manufacturing trade balances of Norway and the UK improved by far more than in any other Northern country, and explain why this adversely affected manufacturing. Their explanation is related to 'Dutch disease' (although they argue in app. 13 that this disease was in fact not serious in The Netherlands). The associated reduction in manufacturing output ought to have increased imports of manufactures as well as reducing manufacturing employment, thus tending to move the observations for Norway and the UK in Fig. 5.10 to the right as well as downwards. However, this movement to the right was offset by the oil-induced appreciation of these countries' real exchange rates, which tended to reduce the measured ratio of imports to GDP.

$$EMPCH = -1.57 - 4.83 \; IMPCH - 7.68 \; OIL \qquad R^2 = 0.77 \qquad (5.3)$$
$$(4.66) (5.27)$$

(with t-statistics in parentheses). Both coefficients are significant at the 1 per cent level, and a lot of variance is explained.[32] If Belgium (which is an outlier) is omitted, R^2 remains high (0.74), but the downward slope of the line is less steep (the coefficient on $IMPCH$ is –3.78, significant at the 2 per cent level), perhaps because of the neglect of exports mentioned above.

Between them, Figs. 5.9 and 5.10 are consistent with what was suggested by the evidence on timing and magnitude, namely that deindustrialisation was caused by a combination of economic maturity and expansion of trade with the South. However, the cross-country data do not permit these two influences to be disentangled, because of collinearity ($R = 0.66$) between the initial agricultural employment share and changes in Southern import penetration. If the 1969 share of agricultural employment is added to equation 5.3, its coefficient is far from significant ($t = 0.19$), and R^2 remains at 0.77, but if it is substituted for $IMPCH$, its coefficient is significant at the 5 per cent level (with R^2 falling to 0.58).[33]

Collinearity likewise precludes a satisfactory test of the hypothesis that expansion of North–North trade contributed to the deindustrialisation of employment. $IMPCH$ is strongly correlated across countries with the change in the ratio of manufactured imports from the North to GDP over the same period ($R = 0.86$).[34] If the Northern import variable is added to equation 5.3, its coefficient is insignificant ($t = 0.35$), and R^2 remains almost the same, while if it is substituted for $IMPCH$, the Northern import variable is significant at the 1 per cent level (with $R^2 = 0.68$). However, excluding Belgium (which is an outlier also with respect to imports from the North) renders the coefficient on the Northern import variable insignificant ($t = 1.53$).

Although the Southern import variable thus has somewhat more explanatory power than its Northern counterpart, it is worth considering why these two variables are so strongly collinear. Part of the explanation must be that they share the same denominator (GDP): real exchange rate appreciation, for example, makes all trade flows seem smaller relative to

---

[32] These results are consistent with the strong cross-country correlation reported in Sect. A2.6 between rises in Southern import penetration and acceleration of productivity growth in manufacturing.

[33] The fit in this last case is better if the full sample of countries in Fig. 5.8 is used (the coefficient on the initial agricultural employment share is significant at the 1% level, and $R^2 = 0.65$).

[34] The Northern import data for 1970 and 1985 are derived from Berthet-Bondet *et al.* (1988), and in two respects are not strictly comparable with the Southern import data. First, they refer to broad (ISIC 3) rather than narrow (SITC 5–9) manufactured imports, and thus include processed primary products. Second, they refer to imports from all OECD partners, and thus treat Greece, Portugal, Turkey, and Yugoslavia as part of the North.

GDP. In addition, the numerators of both variables have been influenced by some of the same changes in barriers to trade. Countries which have remained relatively impenetrable to imports of manufactures from the South, whether because of deliberate protectionism or because of inadvertent institutional barriers, are likely also to have been harder for their Northern trading partners to penetrate, Japan being a familiar example.

Another possible explanation for the collinearity between the Southern and Northern import variables, and for their mutual correlation with changes in the manufacturing employment share, is that cross-country differences in all three of these variables are governed by some other influence. If, to take an extreme example, a country simply stopped producing manufactures, its ratio of manufactured imports (from both the North and the South) to GDP would rise, and its manufacturing employment share would fall. It is harder, though, to think of any cause of this type which could plausibly account for all the facts of deindustrialisation.

An autonomous wave of labour-saving technical progress in manufacturing, for instance, could explain both the average decline in manufacturing's share of employment in the North, and the tendency for the declines to be of a similar proportionate size in different countries. But it does not seem able to explain why the countries with larger absolute declines in employment also experienced larger rises in import penetration, since the rises in productivity should not have reduced their manufacturing output. Differing national capabilities in product innovation, by contrast, could explain the cross-country correlation between rises in import penetration and falls in the manufacturing employment share, but not why the share of employment in manufacturing declined for the North as a whole.

Overview of the evidence on deindustrialisation

To conclude, the evidence on the causes of deindustrialisation—on its timing, magnitude, and cross-country variation—seems to give most support to the view that it was the result partly of economic maturity and partly of changes in trade with the South. The economic maturity hypothesis (that manufacturing's share of employment declines after the share of employment in agriculture falls below a certain level) is supported both by the cross-country evidence, and by the direction of the time-series simulations. But this hypothesis cannot explain why deindustrialisation started so abruptly, and it leaves at least three-fifths of the decline in manufacturing's share of employment unaccounted for.

The changes in trade with the South had a large enough effect to fill this gap. The timing of these changes also coincided reasonably well with that of deindustrialisation. Moreover, this explanation is consistent with the pattern of cross-country variation, including a strong correlation between reductions in the manufacturing employment share and increases in Southern import penetration.

Other possible explanations of deindustrialisation are less well supported by the evidence. The hypothesis that it was caused by expansion of North–North trade is consistent with the pattern of cross-country variation, but not with the evidence on the timing of deindustrialisation. The hypothesis that an autonomous surge of new labour-saving technology was responsible is likewise inconsistent with the evidence on timing, and is hard to reconcile with some of the cross-country evidence. Finally, none of this evidence suggests that the sudden slide in manufacturing's share of employment was caused by a shift of the pattern of domestic demand towards services.

The evidence on the causes of deindustrialisation, however, is by no means complete or clear-cut. In particular, one cannot rule out the possibility that North–North trade, or a surge of new technology, or shifts in domestic demand, made a significant contribution to the decline in the manufacturing employment share. With more data and more powerful techniques of analysis, clearer—and perhaps different—conclusions might be obtained.

5.5 Summary

The main cause of the recent changes in the pattern of North–South trade seems to have been reductions in natural and artificial barriers to trade, which enabled developing countries to realise their comparative advantage in unskilled-labour-intensive manufacturing. Improvements in sea and air transport, and in telecommunications, made it easier and cheaper not only to move outputs from the South to the North, but also to convey essential inputs (including information) in the other direction. Liberalisation of trade policies in the North, and the adoption of export-oriented policies by an increasing number of developing countries, also contributed to the changes in trade, although it was protection which provided the initial impetus to labour-intensive manufacturing in many parts of the South.

This conclusion about the reasons for the changes in North–South trade makes it possible to argue, as this book does, that these changes were an exogenous cause of shifts in the skill structure of the demand for labour in both country groups. In principle, causation could have flowed in the opposite direction, with shifts in domestic demand and supply conditions in labour markets as the main reason for the changes in trade. Moreover, there was some reverse causation of this kind. In the South, educational expansion created the literate labour force needed for manufacturing. In the North, shortages of unskilled labour in the 1960s stimulated firms to start learning how to manage remote sourcing of labour-intensive items.

None the less, the assumption that causation has flowed mainly from trade to labour markets seems to be a reasonable first approximation, especially in the latter part of the period. The resulting shifts in the composition of the demand for labour have tended to alter wage and employment levels in two distinct dimensions. The more fundamental dimension (explored in the next three chapters) concerns the relative economic position of skilled and unskilled workers. The other dimension involves the relative position of labour in different sectors. In particular, these changes in trade raised the demand for labour in manufacturing—relative to other sectors—in the South, and reduced it in the North. The main consequence in both country groups has been changes in manufacturing's share of total employment.

Although the changes in trade created more than 20 million extra jobs in manufacturing, the effect on the structure of employment in the South as a whole was modest—an increase of 1–2 percentage points in the share of manufacturing in 1990—simply because the total labour force is so vast. However, the additional jobs were concentrated in a few countries, where changes in the sectoral structure of employment were far bigger. Between about 1960 and the early 1980s, the share of manufacturing in employment increased by 17 percentage points in both Korea and Taiwan. During this period, moreover, developing countries that did not raise their ratios of North-bound manufactured exports to GDP did not, on average, achieve any increase in their manufacturing employment shares.

In the North, the immediate effect of more competition from the South was to reduce the profitability of labour-intensive manufacturing, and of the manufacturing sector as a whole, relative to other sectors. This fall in the relative profitability of manufacturing was eventually reversed, when existing capacity in labour-intensive sectors was scrapped, but initially it acted as a cushion, insulating the labour market from the full effects of the changes in trade.

The trade-induced shift in the sectoral composition of labour demand had some effects on inter-sectoral wage relativities in the North. In general, these effects were small, because labour tends to be mobile among sectors, except in the short run. However, skilled workers with industry-specific training in labour-intensive sectors were hit particularly hard, because their skills and earning power were not transferable to other sectors.

The shift in the sectoral composition of demand in the North thus emerged mainly as a fall in the share of manufacturing in total employment. From 1969 to 1989, this share dropped by 7 percentage points in the North as a whole. Not all of this decline was caused by trade with the South: up to 3 percentage points was probably the natural result of 'economic maturity'. The manufacturing employment share declined by widely varying amounts in different Northern countries. The falls tended to be bigger in countries which experienced greater increases in Southern import penetration.

6

Skill Differentials and Inequality in the South

This chapter investigates the effects of trade with the North on the relative wages of skilled and unskilled workers, and on income inequality, in the South. Section 6.1 elaborates the theoretical framework. Section 6.2 reviews evidence concerning the impact of trade on income inequality. Section 6.3 examines the experience of some specific countries, focusing on the four little East Asian tigers.

6.1 Theoretical Considerations

The basic theory underlying the discussion in this chapter was set out in Chapter 2 (especially Sections 2.1.1 and 2.4.2), and in Section 5.2.1 of the preceding chapter (which used supply and demand curves to illustrate how changes in trade affect relative wages and employment). This section recapitulates and elaborates some of that earlier material, with special reference to conditions in the South.

6.1.1 Demand shifts

To analyse the effects of trade on skill differentials in the South, it is necessary to consider not the usual two categories of labour—skilled and unskilled—but three. These categories are *NO-ED* workers (little or no education), *BAS-ED* workers (primary or general lower-secondary schooling), and *SKILD* workers (substantial post-basic education or training). *NO-EDs* are not generally employable in manufacturing and other modern activities. Thus although both *NO-EDs* and *BAS-EDs* are often described as 'unskilled', the distinction between them is crucial in the context of the changes in North–South trade, which have mainly involved manufactures and services.

Overall income inequality depends also on the prices of other factors of production—capital and land (or natural resources)—relative to wages. However, the changes in North–South trade have probably had little effect on these other factor price ratios (for reasons set out in Sections 2.1.4 and 2.2). What probably *has* been altered by the changes in trade, though, and would be important in a fuller treatment of the effects on inequality than this chapter can provide, is the balance of demand within the *BAS-ED* category between male and female workers. Women are over-represented in the South's export-oriented industries, making it likely that expansion of manufactured exports has improved their relative economic position (see Wood 1991*a* and the studies cited at the end of Section 3.3.3).

In analysing movements in skill differentials, one must consider how the changes in trade affected the skill composition of the demand for labour in the economy as a whole. However, the demand impact estimates in Part A of this book are largely confined to a single sector, manufacturing. Within that sector, it was established that expansion of exports to the North had increased the demand for *BAS-ED* labour relative to *SKILD* labour. It also emerged that these changes in trade, by boosting the South's manufacturing output, had caused a net increase in the absolute demand for *SKILD* as well as *BAS-ED* labour in manufacturing.

Without proper estimates for other sectors—let alone a model of the economy as a whole—caution is needed in generalising from these results for manufacturing. It is highly likely, though, that the changes in trade increased the economy-wide demand for *BAS-ED* labour relative to both *SKILD* and *NO-ED* labour. Indeed, it was argued in Section 4.4.3 that extending the estimates to include other traded sectors (particularly services), and the indirect demand for labour in nontraded services, would substantially increase—perhaps double—the economy-wide impact on the demand for *BAS-ED* relative to *SKILD* labour. Moreover, since these changes in trade had little direct effect on agriculture—the main activity of Southern *NO-ED* labour—they probably raised the demand for both *BAS-ED* and to a lesser extent *SKILD* workers relative to *NO-ED* workers.[1]

6.1.2 Elasticities

How much relative wages alter in response to trade-induced shifts in the skill composition of the demand for labour depends on demand and supply elasticities. On the demand side, evidence concerning elasticities of substitution among labour of different skill levels was reviewed earlier (Section 4.2.2), in calculating the factor content of noncompeting trade.

---

[1] The changes in trade must have had some indirect effects on the demand for *NO-ED* labour (e.g. through more expenditure on food by workers in manufacturing), but not all these effects would have been positive, and it is unlikely that they would have been sufficiently large to reverse the direct effects. For an important qualification of principle on this point, see the last two paragraphs of Sect. 6.1.3.

In considering the elasticity of economy-wide demand, however, a broader concept of substitution is relevant, embracing not only variation of skill mix in the production of specific goods, but also variation of product mix (substitution among goods of differing skill intensities). Conventional econometric elasticity estimates are therefore more useful in this chapter than in Chapter 4, for whose purposes they are biased upwards because of their lack of control for variation in product mix. These estimates vary around an average close to unity.

There appear to be no econometric estimates for developing countries of the relevant supply elasticities—the responsiveness of the relative supplies of the three skill categories of labour to changes in their relative wages (discussed in Section 2.4.3). However, it seems probable that these elasticities are generally rather low, and in particular lower than in the North, because capital markets are more imperfect, and because government expenditure on education is more severely rationed.

Even in the South, though, it would be misleading to suppose that skill supplies are completely inelastic. Enrolment in primary education is limited in some countries by the perception of parents that the economic benefits of schooling are low in relation to its costs (Colclough 1993). In such circumstances, a rise in the relative wage of *BAS-ED* labour would increase its supply, relative to both *NO-ED* and *SKILD* labour. Moreover, this supply response would probably raise the average education level of the labour force, since the absolute number of *NO-ED* workers would fall, but tertiary enrolment (which is usually rationed) would be maintained. However, employers might cut back their training of *SKILD* labour.

The two preceding paragraphs may be contrasted with the often-expressed view (stemming from Lewis 1954) that in developing countries the supply of unskilled labour is infinitely elastic.[2] However, there is not necessarily a contradiction. As explained in Chapter 5, the elasticity of the supply of labour to particular sectors tends to be close to infinite: thus demand-driven flows of labour between (say) agriculture and manufacturing usually take place without sustained or substantial changes in *inter-sectoral* wage relativities. But it is mobility and wage relativities between *skill categories* that are relevant here. For example, the economy-wide wage of *BAS-ED* labour could increase relative to that of *NO-ED* labour without any change in the wages of *BAS-ED* workers in manufacturing relative to *BAS-ED* workers in agriculture.

As explained in Section 2.4.3, there are good reasons why long-run skill

---

[2] It has also been shown that in the early phase of industrialisation in the now-developed countries the real wage of unskilled labour rose very slowly (Williamson 1985; World Bank 1990, box 3.4). However, the reason for this seems to have been not a highly elastic supply curve but (*a*) a shifting supply curve, because of population growth, and (*b*) slow growth of demand, since industrial development was initially skill-intensive.

supply elasticities are far from infinite. None the less, it is possible that in some countries and periods, the short-term economy-wide supply of *BAS-ED* labour has been almost infinitely elastic, and hence increases in the relative demand for *BAS-ED* workers have not pulled up their relative wage. This could happen if some *BAS-ED* labour were initially unemployed, or underemployed in land-scarce agriculture or the informal sector. It is more likely where a high proportion of workers in all sectors is literate. In many developing countries, this is not the case: *NO-ED* underemployment in agriculture coexists with a scarcity of the *BAS-ED* labour needed for factory and other modern sector employment.

Institutional obstacles to wider wage differentials between skilled and unskilled workers are important in the North (see especially Chapter 8). In the South, these particular obstacles are less relevant, because the trade-induced shift in demand has tended to *narrow* the wage differential between *SKILD* and *BAS-ED* workers. It is possible that *SKILD* workers as a group might be able to resist this narrowing, but this seems likely only where the public sector is the main employer of both *SKILD* and *BAS-ED* labour, as in some African countries in the 1960s. Nor is it plausible, in the circumstances of most developing countries, to suppose that *NO-ED* workers could prevent a trade-induced widening of the gap between their wages and those of *BAS-ED* workers. What is possible, though, is that *BAS-ED* workers as a group might previously have been able to widen this gap artificially, so that the shift in demand would not make it any wider.

6.1.3 Causal variations

Even in the absence of institutional counter-pressures, relative wages might not move in the ways implied by the trade-induced shifts in demand, simply because of other shifts in relative demand and supply functions. This outcome is more likely in comparatively closed economies, but could have occurred also in countries heavily involved in the changes in North–South trade, which must also have been subject to other sources of change in the skill composition of the demand for labour, and to shifts in skill supply functions.

Of particular importance are autonomous changes in the size and shape of the education system. Increased enrolment rates in primary and general secondary education reduce the proportion of *NO-EDs* in the labour force, and tend to lower the relative wage of *BAS-ED* labour (World Bank 1980, table 5.4; Schultz 1988, fig. 13.3). Increased enrolment in post-basic education adds to the supply of *SKILD* workers, and tends to reduce their relative wage (Knight and Sabot 1983; Mohan and Sabot 1988). Thus, for example, a high tertiary-education enrolment rate in a country with few *NO-ED*s would amplify the effects of the trade-induced shift in demand, raising the relative wage of *BAS-ED* workers. Faster expansion of basic than of post-basic education, by contrast, would offset the effects of trade, and could widen the wage gap between *SKILD* and *BAS-ED* workers.

Such autonomous changes in the relative supplies of labour in different skill categories, moreover, would tend to alter the country's comparative advantage and hence its pattern of trade. The discussion in this section (as in most of the rest of this book) has concentrated on one direction of causation: the effects of more exposure to trade on the labour market. In a country that was already exposed to trade, though, causation from labour markets to trade would also be important. Expansion of higher education, for example, by increasing the supply of *SKILD* relative to *BAS-ED* labour, would tend gradually to upgrade the composition of a country's exports of manufactures, goods of low skill intensity being replaced by more skill-intensive items. This sort of progress up the 'ladder of development' is discussed at greater length in a later chapter (Section 9.3.2).

Reverting here, however, to the effects of more exposure to trade on the labour market, it is important to assess the *longevity* of these effects, which depends partly on the causes of the increase in exposure. Consider, for instance, one of the causes of change in North–South trade identified in Chapter 5, namely Southern countries switching from inward-oriented to export-oriented industrialisation strategies, and suppose (conveniently but inaccurately) that such switches simply involved removing all policy-created barriers to trade. Theory implies that this removal of barriers, other things being equal, would have caused a *once-and-for-all* change in relative wages in the countries concerned. The movement from the old to the new wage structure might have been spread over a considerable period, as the existing stock of sector-specific skills and capital was replaced. After this transitional period, however, there should have been no further tendency for (say) the wage gap between *SKILD* and *BAS-ED* workers to narrow.

In reality, barriers to trade in these countries were not simply removed, but lowered, modified, and supplemented with export incentives (White 1988; Wade 1990). The process, moreover, was prolonged: implemented in stages in each country, and at different times in different countries, extending the period during which relative wages were altered. In addi-tion, there are the other causes of change in North–South trade. Some of these, too, were essentially once-and-for-all changes: reduction of trade barriers in the North, and learning how to manage far-flung manu-facturing operations. Again, however, the changes were spread over a considerable period, either gradually or in discrete steps. Other causal changes were more continuous, such as reductions in transport and communications costs. So although the changes in North–South trade are mainly of a one-step nature, the step has been protracted and is not yet complete (Section 9.2.1).

Finally, it should be emphasised that the preceding discussion of the effects of reductions in Southern trade barriers implicitly assumed that the countries concerned have a comparative advantage in labour-intensive manufacturing. This assumption is by no means correct for all developing countries, since it depends on their factor endowments, and in particular on the balance between their human and natural resources (as explained in Sections 2.1.4 and 2.4.2). For example, all four of the little East Asian tigers lack natural resources, and all had high literacy rates when their manufactured exports took off.[3] By contrast, the comparative advantage of developing countries with abundant natural resources and/or low literacy rates lies in exporting primary and processed primary products. (For further discussion of this point, see Section 9.1.2.)

The experiences of primary exporting countries lie outside the scope of this book, which is concerned with North–South trade in manufactures and services. However, it is worth recalling that trade in primary products continues to be of overwhelming importance for many developing countries, especially the poorest ones. It is also worth remembering that trade in primary products, as in manufactures, can affect domestic relative factor prices and income inequality (for some evidence on its impact, studied by economists from Ricardo onwards, see the end of Section 6.3.6).

6.2 Changes in Income Inequality

Much discussion of the internal effects of trade changes in the South has focused not on relative wages as such, but on the distribution of income. In particular, proponents of export-oriented industrialisation have often argued that this strategy reduces income inequality (e.g. Balassa 1988: 35), though some have taken a more equivocal view (Keesing 1974, 1979; Krueger 1983: 266–8). Moreover, because there are few statistics on relative wage movements in developing countries, most empirical investigations of the effects of trade have relied instead on data on the size distribution of personal incomes, though these too are scarce and often unreliable.

---

[3] Table 5.1 shows their literacy rates. Korea and Taiwan had literacy rates of about 70% in the early 1960s, as did Singapore by the late 1960s. However, there is no readily available information on the literacy rate of Hong Kong in the 1950s, when its manufactured exports started to grow.

6.2.1 Predictions

Before addressing the data, however, it is worth considering further the predicted effects of trade on income inequality. In the previous section, it was argued that expansion of manufactured exports, other things being equal, would narrow the wage differential between *BAS-ED* workers and (more highly paid) *SKILD* workers, tending to reduce income inequality. Cutting the other way, however, would be a fall in the wages of *NO-ED* workers, the worst-paid category of labour, relative to both *BAS-ED* and *SKILD* workers.

These opposite movements in relative wages make the net effect on income inequality potentially ambiguous. In practice, however, the chances that expansion of manufactured exports would be associated with more inequality are reduced by the fact that this trade pattern is unlikely in a country with a high proportion of *NO-EDs* in its labour force (as noted at the end of the previous section).[4] Thus in the typical exporter of manufactures, because there are comparatively few *NO-EDs*, the relative deterioration in their position tends to be dominated by the improvement in the position of the more numerous *BAS-EDs* relative to *SKILD* workers.

A further potential source of ambiguity is that most statistical measures of inequality depend not only on the relative incomes of different groups but also on the relative numbers in those groups.[5] This is relevant here because skill supply functions have some elasticity, so that trade-induced demand shifts tend to alter the relative numbers in each skill category as well as their relative wages. It seems likely, however, that in this case the changes in numbers would reinforce rather than offset the tendency for inequality to decline, since the middle-income *BAS-ED* group would tend to expand relative to both the other (richer and poorer) groups.[6]

All this assumes that manufactured export expansion is the sole source of change in income distribution. Once it is admitted that other forces are likely to be at work simultaneously, the outcome becomes much less clear-cut. As mentioned in the previous section, there are many other possible influences on the relative wages and numbers of workers in different skill categories. In addition, there are other forces which may alter measured income inequality even if skill differentials remain constant,

[4] The discussion here, it should be reiterated, refers to the effects on inequality of (*a*) expansion of manufactured exports, not of (*b*) increased exposure to trade in general. For reasons noted in the previous section, (*b*) does not necessarily lead to (*a*).

[5] On the influence of changes in relative numbers on movements in income inequality, see Kuznets (1955), Robinson (1976), and Mohan and Sabot (1988). It should be recalled, too, that different measures of inequality sometimes conflict with one another.

[6] However, a trade-induced rise in the participation rate of (lower-paid) female *BAS-ED* labour might tend to increase measured inequality.

including changes in the distribution of physical and financial assets, in household size and composition, and in taxes and transfer payments.

6.2.2 Cross-country comparisons

The relationship between increased exports of manufactures and reductions in income inequality is thus somewhat ambiguous in theory, and liable in practice to be distorted or concealed by the influence of other variables (not to mention deficiencies in the data). These complications affect all approaches to the evidence, but are particularly relevant to cross-country statistical comparisons. For the relationship between exports and income distribution is likely to vary among countries, as are other influences on inequality. Moreover, the data that would be needed to control properly for these variations are largely unavailable, which may explain why many previous cross-country analyses of income distribution have yielded 'mixed and sometimes contradictory' results (Adelman and Robinson 1989: 958).

Most of these other studies focus on testing the Kuznets-curve hypothesis that inequality first increases and then decreases as income levels rise, or sometimes the related hypothesis that rapid growth increases inequality (Adelman and Morris 1973; Chenery *et al.* 1974, ch. 1; World Bank 1990: 46–9; Fields and Jakubson 1990). Many of these studies include other explanatory variables, but only a few consider trade. Moreover, all of the latter try to explain levels of, rather than changes in, inequality, and their results vary. Papanek and Kyn (1987) find no association between inequality and manufactured exports. Berger and Webb (1988) find a correlation between inequality and foreign exchange restrictions, proxied by the black market exchange rate premium, but it is inverse (tighter restrictions reduce the income share of the richest quintile).

By contrast, Bourguignon and Morrisson (1989, ch. II) find a significant relationship in the more commonly predicted direction. They use a more homogeneous set of income distribution data than Berger and Webb, though from much the same period (around 1970), and a careful specification of independent variables. In particular, they distinguish between primary exports and manufactured exports, and within the primary category between mineral exports and agricultural exports, including a further distinction between the products of small-scale and of large-scale agriculture. They establish that higher ratios of both mineral and agricultural exports to GDP are strongly associated with greater income inequality, except where the agricultural exports are produced by small-scale farmers.[7]

---

[7] This tends to confirm the conclusion of Adelman and Morris (1973) that concentrated ownership of natural resources is the main source of extreme income inequality in developing countries.

When primary exports are controlled for, Bourguignon and Morrisson find that higher levels of protection of manufacturing are associated with greater income inequality. They also find that countries where a high share of manufacturing output is exported tend to have lower levels of inequality. These findings clearly support the usual view that export-oriented industrialisation improves the distribution of income. However, they should be regarded cautiously, partly because of various limitations of the data used (including their age), but mainly because the estimated relationship concerns *levels* of inequality. The reasons why inequality varies among countries are both numerous and ill-documented, so that one cannot be sure that the apparent association with manufactured exports is genuine, rather than the result of both variables being correlated with some other excluded variable.[8]

In principle, a cross-country relationship between *changes* in manufactured exports and *changes* in inequality would be more convincing.[9] This is because many of the undocumented country-specific influences on income inequality (such as the distribution of land ownership) probably change only slowly. Their unmeasurable contribution to inter-country differences in inequality is thus probably larger for levels than for changes. An immediate practical problem, though, is the shortage of acceptable data on changes in income distribution over time in developing countries. Even in particular years, the quality of the estimates is often poor, for example because of limited coverage and understatement of income, while strict comparability of sources and methods in different years is rare.[10]

Fields (1989, 1990) has produced an extremely useful compendium of the available data, excluding those which did not meet minimal standards of reliability. To be included, the data have to be derived from an actual household survey or census, rather than being patched together from other sources, and have to be national in coverage, rather than for particular cities or for urban or rural areas. Moreover, for comparisons over time, the income concept and the recipient units in successive surveys must be consistent. Applying these criteria, Fields identified twenty-six developing countries with usable income distribution data for more than one year.

[8] e.g. Bourguignon and Morrisson (1989: 48 and n. 11) discover that their education variable (the secondary school enrolment rate ten years earlier) is collinear with the share of manufacturing output exported, though not with the level of protection of manufacturing. This finding calls into question the causal connection between manufactured exports and inequality, but tends to confirm that manufactured exports depend on the availability of educated labour (as mentioned in Sect. 6.1.3).

[9] The same is true of the many studies that have used cross-country data on *levels* of inequality (and income) to test the Kuznets-curve hypothesis, which is a proposition about *changes*. Most studies conclude in favour of the hypothesis. However, Fields and Jakubson (1990) demonstrate that the available data on changes over time clearly refute the hypothesis.

[10] On these problems, see e.g. Moll (1992: 690–1 and nn. 1–3).

For present purposes, some of these countries have to be excluded, either because the period covered by their data is too short (less than a decade), or because too much of the data precedes the period (from the early 1960s) during which the South's manufactured exports have been expanding rapidly. Table 6.1 thus shows changes in inequality over time in only seventeen developing countries. In most cases the data are drawn directly from Fields, but in a few instances they have been extended or supplemented with information from other sources, and two countries not treated as developing by Fields have been added (Israel and Yugoslavia). In all cases, for want of any readily available alternative, inequality is measured by the Gini coefficient.

Fig. 6.1 shows the cross-country relationship between these changes in inequality and changes in the ratio of North-bound manufactured exports to GDP between 1965 and 1985. The apparent inverse correlation is con-

TABLE 6.1. *Changes in income inequality in the South*

	Time-period	Gini coefficients		
		Early	Late	Change
Bangladesh	1968/9–81/2	0.29	0.39	0.10
Brazil	1960–83	0.53	0.57	0.04
Colombia	1971–88	0.54	0.48	−0.06
Costa Rica	1961–86	0.50	0.42	−0.08
Hong Kong	1966–86	0.47	0.45	−0.01
Indonesia	1964–84	0.33	0.31	−0.03
Israel	1963/4–79/80	0.33	0.32	−0.01
Jamaica	1968–80	0.63	0.66	0.03
Korea	1965–82	0.34	0.36	0.01
Malaysia	1970–84	0.50	0.48	−0.02
Pakistan	1963/4–84	0.36	0.38	0.02
Philippines	1965–85	0.47	0.45	−0.02
Singapore	1966–82/3	0.50	0.47	−0.03
Sri Lanka	1963–81/2	0.45	0.45	0.00
Taiwan	1964–86	0.36	0.32	−0.04
Thailand	1962/3–81	0.41	0.44	0.03
Yugoslavia	1963–79	0.35	0.30	−0.04

Notes and sources: (1) Bangladesh, Indonesia, Jamaica, Korea, Malaysia, Pakistan (spliced at 1979), Philippines, Sri Lanka: Fields (1989). Brazil, Colombia, Costa Rica: Fields (1990).

(2) Israel, Yugoslavia: Jain (1975) for early date, Mahler (1989, table 1) for later date. Hong Kong: Lin (1985), extrapolated to 1986 on the basis of Terasaki (1991, table 1, col. 1). Singapore: Rao and Ramakrishnan (1980, table 4) for 1966–73, spliced to Fields (1989) for 1972/3–1982/3. Taiwan: Kuo (1989, table VIII-1) for early date, DGBAS (1986, table 9) for later date. Thailand: Ikemoto and Limskul (1987, table 1).

(3) Distributions refer to pre-tax household income, except Colombia (individual income), Indonesia (per capita expenditure), Jamaica (wage income), Pakistan (per capita household income after 1979), Sri Lanka (spending unit income).

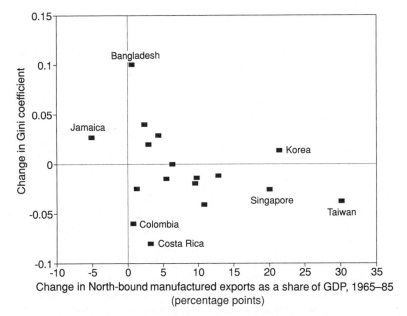

Fig. 6.1 Changes in income inequality and manufactured exports
Notes and sources: Income distribution: see Table 6.1. Manufactured export share: as for Fig. 5.4. Hong Kong and Singapore data adjusted for re-exports. Pakistan figure used for Bangladesh in 1965.

sistent with the view that expansion of manufactured exports reduces inequality, and with the relationship in levels reported by Bourguignon and Morrisson, although their results could not be reproduced with the present data.[11]

The correlation is statistically insignificant, but it becomes significant at the 5 per cent level if the three countries with large changes (greater than 0.05) in their Gini coefficients are excluded. The justification for this exclusion is that both deterministic and stochastic models of the size distribution of income imply a high degree of stability, which suggests that

[11] There is a simple inverse correlation between the terminal level of the Gini coefficient and the terminal level of the manufactured export–GDP ratio. However, this correlation is not statistically significant, and (unlike the correlation in changes) cannot be rendered significant by the exclusion of a few suspect observations. The scatter diagram exhibits a triangular pattern: there are countries with low levels of inequality at all levels of the export variable; but the upper limit of the inequality range declines as the export variable increases. Nor is the export ratio significant when combined with other influences on inequality in multiple regressions (using the levels counterparts of the independent variables described in the text). These other variables, though, are not identical to those of Bourguignon and Morrisson, who also had a much larger sample, and excluded countries with total-export-to-GDP ratios under 10%.

large changes may be due to weaknesses in the data.[12] Moreover, the correlation remains significant at the 10 per cent level even if the four little East Asian tigers (three of which are clearly outliers) are also excluded.

To investigate further, this simple inverse correlation was analysed by multiple regression, introducing several other independent variables.[13]

(1) The level of the adult literacy rate proxied the proportion of *NO-EDs* in the labour force. Theory suggests that a high proportion of *NO-EDs* would weaken the relationship between changes in manufactured exports and in inequality (and might even make it positive rather than inverse).

(2) The level and change of the tertiary education enrolment rate served as (unsatisfactory) proxies for increases in the relative supply of *SKILD* labour, which should tend to reduce income inequality.[14] Levels and changes of secondary and primary school enrolment rates and the change in the adult literacy rate were also included.

(3) The average ratio of investment to GDP over the period could be relevant because of the apparent complementarity between capital and skills (mentioned in Sections 2.3.2 and 4.2.2). A higher rate of investment might thus increase inequality by raising the relative demand for *SKILD* labour.

(4) The change in the ratio of primary exports to GDP was included because of the important role of the corresponding variable in the levels analysis of Bourguignon and Morrisson.[15]

(5) The growth rate of per capita GNP was also introduced, mainly because it (or the level of income) is used as an explanatory variable in most other cross-country studies of income distribution.

The results of this regression analysis were inconclusive.[16] Various subsets of the independent variables were tried (the small size of the sample precluded the use of all of them together), both including and excluding the three countries with suspiciously large Gini coefficient changes. In no

[12] On the insensitivity of the size distribution to exogenous and policy shocks in deterministic models, see e.g. Adelman and Robinson (1989: 981), and on stochastic models, Champernowne (1973).

[13] Most of the data were drawn or derived from the indicators tables of World Bank (1987), supplemented by data on literacy from UNDP (1990) and national sources for Taiwan.

[14] These proxies are inadequate because there is no simple relationship between enrolment rates and changes in the relative shares of different education groups in the labour force. However, prior to Barro and Lee (1993), data on changes in these shares were available for only a few countries. (In principle, moreover, expansion of higher education need not reduce income inequality, although in practice it usually does, because the compression of wage differentials dominates the increase in the proportion of relatively highly paid workers. See e.g. Mohan and Sabot 1988.)

[15] A priori, *changes* in this variable seem less likely to be important, except possibly for the effects of the increased oil price. The apparent primary exports of Hong Kong and Singapore were omitted.

[16] Details of the results are available from the author on request.

case did the addition of other independent variables strengthen the association between changes in manufactured exports and changes in inequality.[17] Moreover, some of the additional independent variables are collinear with the change in manufactured exports, and so weaken or eliminate this association. This collinearity is particularly evident with the growth rate of per capita GNP, the investment rate, and the level and change of the secondary enrolment rate (all of which are positively correlated with the change in manufactured exports).

The unsatisfactory nature of the results could be due to shortcomings of the income distribution data, or to deficiencies of the variables proxying for non-trade influences on inequality, or to the smallness of the sample. But, in the absence of better data, the conclusion from this analysis, as from the other studies summarised above, appears to be that cross-country comparisons provide only rather limited support for the proposition that exporting manufactures tends to reduce income inequality.

6.2.3 Simulations

A better approach to the evidence is to use structural models of particular economies, in which the effects of changes in trade on income distribution can be investigated through simulations. This approach is vulnerable to inaccuracies and disagreements concerning the economic assumptions and data on which the model is based. In principle, however, it permits controlled experiments to be undertaken, in which the effects of trade, and the way in which these depend on other features of the economy and on other policies, can be definitively disentangled.

There are various sorts of models and simulations (surveyed by Adelman and Robinson 1989: 973–82). One class of models sticks closely to input–output tables and other accounting relationships, with few assumptions about economic behaviour other than the constancy of certain ratios. With such a model, one can calculate how changes in the level or composition of trade would alter the sectoral structure of production. This information is combined with data on the differing proportions in which the incomes arising in different sectors accrue to particular factors of production and household income categories (for example, sector-specific income means and variances). The effects of trade-induced changes in the pattern of production on the overall distribution of income can then be estimated.

Applying the input–output method to data for Brazil, Clements and Kim (1988) show that on average exporting generates less income

---

[17] Except for the change in tertiary enrolment in the reduced sample, whose coefficient, however, had the wrong sign.

inequality than import substitution. However, the difference is small, especially when the comparison is restricted to industrial exports.[18] Similarly, Kim and Vorasopontaviporn (1989) conclude that a shift from import substitution to exporting would improve the distribution of income in Thailand, because it would increase the demand for low-wage agricultural labour. Bourguignon and Morrisson (1989, ch. XI) simulate the effects of increasing exports on income inequality in Costa Rica, Malawi, Morocco, and Peru. They discover that in all cases the effects are 'practically negligible' (ibid. 291), largely because the effects of increased demand in export sectors are widely diffused among other sectors through backward linkages and induced increases in consumption. However, Bourguignon and Morrisson emphasise the limitations of their calculations, including the assumption that prices, including wages and other factor prices, do not alter.

By contrast, in computable general equilibrium models most prices and quantities are simultaneously determined by the interaction of supply and demand (Dervis, de Melo, and Robinson 1982, especially chs. 12–13). Such models have been used on a number of occasions to assess the effects of trade on income inequality (e.g. de Melo and Robinson 1980; Adelman 1984). But the most thorough study of this type remains that of Adelman and Robinson (1978), which is based on Korean data, though some of its conclusions are of wider relevance. One of these, which is confirmed by other studies (Adelman and Robinson 1989: 981), is that the inequality of the overall size distribution of personal incomes exhibits great stability, even if changes in economic policies substantially alter the relative incomes of different socio-economic groups.

Comparing alternative simulations over a nine-year period, Adelman and Robinson conclude that rapid growth of labour-intensive manufactured exports caused Korea's income distribution to be less unequal than it would have been under a strategy of import substitution (1978: 119–27). This is largely because of improved internal terms of trade between agriculture and industry: with an import substitution strategy, manufactured goods would have been more expensive, and agricultural goods cheaper due to lower demand. As a result, the real incomes of farmers and agricultural workers would have been lower, relative to those of the urban population. Within the urban population, the wages of 'unskilled' workers would also have been somewhat lower relative to 'skilled' workers, though virtually unchanged relative to engineers, technicians, and other white-collar workers (ibid., table 41). Surprisingly, however, the simulations suggest higher, rather than lower, total employment in manufacturing with an import substitution strategy, and agricultural

---

[18] This is because the distribution of income in export-oriented industry is more unequal than in export-oriented agriculture.

employment and rural–urban migration much the same as with rapid export growth (ibid., table 42).[19]

Even with an export-oriented strategy, moreover, the simulations suggest a tendency for income inequality to increase over time (ibid. 111–16). This again occurs mainly because of a deterioration in the internal terms of trade in the latter years of the simulation, which causes the real incomes of the agricultural population to fall (ibid., tables 28, 35). The reason is declining demand for agricultural goods, due both to their low income elasticity and to reductions in the relative income and size of groups that spend a lot on agricultural goods (ibid. 116). There are also widening wage differentials within the urban population between unskilled workers on the one hand and technicians, skilled, and white-collar workers (but not engineers) on the other (ibid., table 35). These relative wage movements partly reflect assumptions about the supply of labour, whose growth is exogenously specified for some categories (including engineers, technicians, and white-collar workers) and responsive to wages in others (ibid. 210–11, 255).

Finally, although they conclude that export-oriented industrialisation caused income inequality to be less than it would have been with a strategy of import substitution, Adelman and Robinson argue that this beneficial outcome was dependent on Korea's initially rather egalitarian distribution of productive assets, including education and land (1978: 192–3, 199). Without widespread literacy, it would not have been possible for rural workers to be drawn into industrial jobs, and without widely dispersed land ownership the gains from improved internal terms of trade would have been concentrated on an affluent minority of farmers.

6.3 Time-Series Case Studies

Most of the empirical evidence in this area is methodologically much simpler, consisting of case studies of particular countries in which causal linkages are more informally assessed. The usual approach in such a study is to assemble time-series data on relative factor prices or income distribution, and to look for a relationship between movements in these series and changes in trade policies or performance, taking into account also changes in other likely influences on inequality. In principle, this sort of investigation could use formal econometric methods, but in practice there are usually too few observations. The conclusions thus tend to rely heavily on judgement and general knowledge of the economy concerned.

---

[19] These conclusions from the comparison of the basic dynamic run and the import substitution counterfactual in ch. 6 of Adelman and Robinson (1978) are all confirmed by a further simulation comparing the basic run with an even more export-oriented counterfactual in ch. 8 (Experiment B-5, whose detailed results are presented in their annexe F).

This section (which occupies the rest of the chapter) examines some case study evidence, focusing on the experience of the little East Asian tigers. These four economies are not representative of the South as a whole, but their experience is invariably cited in support of the view that export-oriented industrialisation promotes distributional equity (e.g. World Bank 1987: 87). In addition, the informal methodology seems more defensible where—as in these four instances—changes in manufactured exports have been large relative to total output, making it more likely that simple correlations will reveal economic relationships between trade and relative wages. By contrast, in more closed economies, or in primary exporters, or in countries whose trade pattern had changed less, these relationships might be completely obscured by other influences.

The section is laid out as follows. There are separate subsections on Taiwan, South Korea, Hong Kong, and Singapore, each of which examines the available evidence on movements in relative wages and income inequality, and on the causes of these movements, including possible influences other than trade. A fifth subsection summarises and evaluates the findings of the first four. The final subsection reviews evidence from some other countries.

6.3.1 Taiwan

Information on changes in the relative wages of workers in different skill categories in Taiwan is rather limited. There are few relevant statistics prior to the mid-1960s. Moreover, the longest available series refer only to the average differential between 'staff' (white-collar employees) and 'workers' (blue-collar employees), a breakdown which conceals important intra-group variations in skill levels (see Sections A1.3 and A1.5).

The ratio of staff to worker wages in manufacturing seems to have narrowed somewhat during the 1950s.[20] It was apparently compressed much more during the next two decades, especially in the 1960s.[21] This narrowing of skill differentials is also observed in more detailed, though fragmentary, data on wages by occupation. For instance, between 1964 and 1972 the earnings of professionals declined from 2.0 to 1.6 times those of labourers (Fields 1980, table 6.23). However, the proportional income gap

---

[20] This assessment is based on the 1952–72 wage series for all employees and for workers in DGBAS (1977: 404, 408). The ratio between these two series is not a satisfactory indicator of the staff–worker wage ratio, because it is also affected by changes in the relative numbers of employees in these categories. This ratio also behaves peculiarly, remaining virtually constant within the periods 1952–6 and 1957–68.

[21] Kuo (1989: 247). However, the specific numbers she mentions, which refer to real wage rises for staff and workers during 1961–71 and 1971–81, are puzzling. If used to extrapolate the staff–worker wage ratio backwards from 1981, they imply an unbelievably large value for this ratio in 1961. The explanation could be differences in the consumption baskets (and hence price indices) of these two groups.

between the top 10 per cent of wage-earners and the bottom 10 per cent appears to have widened between 1964 and 1968, although it too narrowed between 1968 and 1972 (Fei *et al.* 1979, fig. 3.8).

During the 1980s, the ratio of staff to worker earnings in manufacturing apparently ceased to narrow: though there were fluctuations from year to year, the 1980–2 and 1987–9 averages are virtually the same (DGBAS 1990: 184). There are also some data for the 1980s on another skill differential indicator, namely household income classified by the education level of the head of the household. This is an imperfect indicator, since it includes sources of income other than the earnings of the household head, but it suggests a slight widening of skill differentials. Between 1978 and 1990, the proportional income differences between primary and secondary school graduates were compressed a little, but the university/primary-educated income ratio increased from 1.6 to 1.8, and the illiterate/primary ratio fell from 0.8 to 0.6 (DGBAS 1979: 480–1; 1991, table 66).

The income distribution data for Taiwan are critically reviewed by Moll (1992). A consistent series is available only from 1964. There are some estimates for the 1950s, which suggest a rapid decline in inequality prior to 1964, but their reliability and comparability with the later numbers are extremely doubtful (ibid. 694–5). Between 1964 and 1968, there was little change in inequality, but thereafter the Gini coefficient tended to fall until 1980, with most of the decline occurring between 1968 and 1974.[22] During the 1980s, though, this trend was reversed: for example, the Gini coefficient of the official income distribution series rose from 0.28 in 1980 to 0.30 in 1989 (ibid., table 1).

This information is broadly consistent with the hypothesis that Taiwan's shift to export-oriented industrialisation around 1960 altered relative wages in ways that reduced inequality. Particularly noteworthy in this regard are the decline in the staff–worker wage ratio during the 1960s and the narrowing occupational differentials and declining Gini coefficient in the late 1960s and early 1970s. The smaller movements in the late 1970s, and their cessation or reversal in the 1980s, are likewise consistent with the theoretical expectation that changes in trade policy cause once-and-for-all changes in relative wages. The concentration of the reductions in inequality at the end rather than the beginning of the 1960s also suggests that the relative supply of unskilled labour was initially highly elastic.

It is possible, though, that these movements in relative wages were caused (in whole or in part) by forces other than foreign trade. The supply of educated labour was also expanding, especially at the upper levels: between 1966 and 1980, the initially high percentage of literate workers

---

[22] Much faster decline during 1968–74 than during 1974–80 is suggested by sources (1) and (4), but not by source (8), in Moll (1992, table 1).

rose only modestly, but the proportions of college and senior high-school graduates in the labour force more than doubled.[23] This must have acted in the same direction as the expansion of manufactured exports, tending to narrow skill differentials. The apparently greater compression of these differentials during the 1960s than in the previous and subsequent decades suggests that the change in trade policy did have an independent influence. But the simultaneous expansion of the educational system makes it hard to assess the size or duration of the influence of trade (or the elasticity of the supply of skilled labour).

Why skill differentials and income inequality ceased to decline in the 1980s is also hard to establish. Educational expansion continued, which should have caused a further narrowing of skill differentials. However, the pattern of Taiwan's trade also changed, with the transfer of its most unskilled-labour-intensive export products to neighbouring countries with lower wages.[24] This change in trade was probably partly a consequence of the rising relative wage of unskilled labour in Taiwan (and so should not have caused a widening of skill differentials). But this relocation was also partly autonomous, undertaken to circumvent Northern import quotas and in response to trade policy changes in lower-wage countries, and so could have reduced the relative wages of less-skilled workers in Taiwan. (The theoretical reasons for this are explained in Section 9.2.3.)

6.3.2 Korea

Information on relative wage movements in Korea begins in the early 1960s. The longest available series refer to the average ratio between salaries and wages—the earnings of white-collar and blue-collar workers. This ratio declined from 1.9 in 1963–4 to 1.4 in 1971–2, rose to 1.8 in 1976–7, then fell again to 1.6 in 1979–80.[25] Almost as long is the series on the average wage increases for professional, technical, and managerial workers, compared with the average for production workers (Amsden 1989, table 8.3). This more precise skill differential narrowed continuously between 1965 and 1984, but the rate of narrowing varied: there was substantial compression during 1965–70, little change during 1971–4, and only slightly more during 1975–8. These differences among sub-periods parallel the fluctuations in the average salary-wage ratio.

---

[23] The proportion of college graduates rose from 5.0% to 11.7%, and of senior high-school graduates from 9.6% to 22.2% (*Extract Report of the Population and Housing Census*, 1966 and 1980, table 18).

[24] See e.g. Bob King, 'Taiwan's shoemakers seek foothold abroad', *Financial Times*, 1 Sept. 1988, and surveys of Taiwan in the *Financial Times* of 10 Oct. 1988 and 9 Oct. 1992 (esp. p. 3).

[25] These two-year averages are calculated from data in the annual reports of Korea's *Family Income and Expenditure Survey*.

More data on wages by occupation are available from the early 1970s (Lee.1986–7, table 4).[26] The earnings of professional and technical workers, managers, and clerical workers all increased, relative to the earnings of production workers, between 1971–2 and 1975–6. These three relativities then declined (to 1985). Also available since the late 1960s are data on wages by level of education. The earnings of college graduates, relative to primary graduates, fell somewhat between 1967 and 1970, but rose sharply in the first half of the 1970s (Choo 1985, table 10; Kwack 1987: 131). By contrast, the relative wages of lower secondary school graduates increased slightly during the late 1960s, and fell during the early 1970s, while the earnings of high-school graduates remained more or less constant, relative to those of primary graduates.[27]

From the late 1970s to the late 1980s, differences in wages by level of education narrowed considerably (Amsden 1989, table 9.6; Lee 1991, table 9; Davis 1992, fig. 6E). The wages of college graduates, as a ratio of the wages of workers with lower secondary education or less, fell from 3.9 in 1976 to 2.5 in 1988, while the wages of high-school graduates, relative to these less-educated workers, declined from 1.7 to 1.2 (Lee). There was thus a more modest narrowing of the wage differential between college and high-school graduates: controlling for changes in age distribution, this ratio declined from 1.9 in 1979 to 1.7 in 1988, though wage differentials by age widened in both groups, especially among college graduates (Davis, figs. 5E and 6E). The overall distribution of wage income also became less unequal over this period: the Gini coefficient, which was 0.40 in both 1972 and 1976, had declined to 0.31 by 1988 (Lee 1991, table 3).[28]

Income distribution data are available from the mid-1960s, but have some weaknesses which were overlooked in early studies of inequality in Korea. These shortcomings are noted by Choo (1985), who adjusts the data to arrive at a more defensible series for benchmark years, which is cited in many other studies (including Fields 1989). This series suggests that income inequality declined slightly between 1965 and 1970 (the Gini coefficient falls from 0.34 to 0.33), but increased sharply during the first half of the 1970s (raising the Gini coefficient to 0.39 in 1976). Subsequently, inequality declined again (to the end of Choo's series in

---

[26] The data in Amsden (1989, table 9.5) are identical except for 1971, in which the differentials are all wider (and less consistent than those of Lee with the other evidence).

[27] These relative wage movements for lower secondary school graduates are roughly consistent with the rates of return in Schultz (1988, fig. 13.3).

[28] The results of Lee (1986–7) confirm that the inequality of the wage distribution declined between 1975 and 1985. They also suggest that there was a reduction in wage inequality during 1970–5—which contradicts all the other evidence—but Lee notes (1986–7: 84) that this might be due to deficiencies in the wage distribution data. Davis (1992: 5 and fig. 2), who also notes possible problems with the data, has observations on wage inequality only in 1971, 1983, and 1986, which suggest a declining trend.

1982). A more recent series, based on a different survey, shows that income inequality declined steadily between 1980 and 1988.[29]

Any attempt to explain these movements in skill differentials must take account not only of trade policy, but also of rapid educational expansion. Between the mid-1940s and the early 1960s, primary schooling was extended to all children, and the proportion of illiterate workers declined sharply (Adelman and Robinson 1978: 41; Amsden 1989, table 9.3).[30] Secondary and higher education also expanded rapidly. The appearance of some educated unemployment caused the government to restrain further increases in higher (but not secondary) enrolment rates in the 1960s and early 1970s (Adelman and Robinson: 41–2; Amsden: 221). None the less, between 1966 and 1980 the proportion of college graduates in the labour force doubled (to about 8 per cent), while the proportion of high-school graduates rose to about a quarter.[31] By 1989, Korea's tertiary enrolment rate was 38 per cent, not far below the 43 per cent average for OECD countries (World Bank 1992, indicators table 29).

The compression of skill differentials that occurred during the 1960s is consistent with the expected effects of Korea's change of trade policy in the early years of that decade.[32] (The associated reduction in overall income inequality appears to have been only slight.) It is possible that this compression of differentials was also partly or wholly caused by the initial excess supply of highly educated workers. However, the problem of unemployment in the early 1960s was by no means confined to these workers (23 per cent of the labour force in Seoul is estimated to have

[29] This series is published in the Economic Planning Board's annual *Social Indicators in Korea*. The Gini coefficient for 1980 is 0.389; that for 1985 is given as 0.363 in the 1987 issue of the *Indicators* (quoted in Lee 1989), and as 0.345 in the 1989 issue, which also provides a Gini coefficient of 0.336 for 1988.

[30] However, the 1963 figure of 5.5% for the proportion of workers with no schooling quoted by Amsden is unbelievably low: the census data referred to in the next note suggest figures of 31% for 1966 and 15% for 1980. More generally, although the rapid expansion of Korean education since the end of the Second World War is not disputed, there is conflicting information about the initial educational attainments of the population. Adelman and Robinson (1978: 37, 41) cite a 1944 primary school enrolment rate of about 50%, and literacy rates for 1944, 1953, and 1963 of 22%, 30%, and over 80% respectively. Park (1988) also mentions a literacy rate of 22% for 1945, and 90% for the early 1960s. By contrast, the data cited in Amsden (1989, table 9.3) suggest that in 1946 about 60% of the labour force had primary schooling or above. The 1976 UNESCO *Yearbook* (table 1.3) implies a 1955 literacy rate of 77%, as compared with the 1960 rate of 71% in World Bank (1980, indicators table 25).

[31] The proportion of the employed population over 13 years of age with a college education was 4.3% in 1966 and 7.9% in 1980 (*Population Census of Korea 1966*, 12–1 Whole Country, table 5; and *Population and Housing Census 1980*, Vol. 2, 15% Sample Survey, 3–1 Economic Activity, table 10). From the same source, Psacharopoulos and Arriagada (1986, table 1) estimate the college-educated share in 1980 to have been 9.1% (perhaps using a different age cut-off), and a share of 23.4% with completed secondary school.

[32] By contrast, Adelman and Robinson's simulations (described in Sect. 6.2.3) suggest an increase in income inequality in Korea during the 1960s, even with an export-oriented strategy. But in the 1970s there was such a rise in inequality, and their simulations expose one of the reasons for it, namely relatively slow growth in the supply of high-level manpower.

been out of work in 1965—Kuznets 1988: 59). In any event, the timing of the narrowing of differentials, which appears to have begun soon after the change in trade policy, does not suggest that the relative supply of less-skilled labour was initially almost infinitely elastic.[33]

That skill differentials ceased to narrow in the early 1970s, ten years after the trade policy shift, is also in accordance with the theoretical expectation that such a shift would have a once-and-for-all impact on relative wages. Nor is it difficult to find a consistent and plausible explanation for the widening of skill differentials during much of the 1970s (Kuznets 1988: 62; Mizoguchi 1985a: 319). On the supply side, the expansion of tertiary education had been restricted, while lower-level enrolment rates had continued to rise, making college-educated labour relatively scarcer. On the demand side, in the mid-1970s the Korean government embarked on a major effort to develop heavy and chemical industries, which use skilled labour intensively.

The resumption of rapid expansion of higher education in Korea after the mid-1970s likewise provides a plausible explanation for the narrowing of skill differentials (and the reduction in income inequality) between the late 1970s and the late 1980s. This interpretation is particularly well supported by the widening of age–earnings differentials among high-school and (especially) college graduates, since educational expansion causes a disproportionate increase in the supply of younger graduates.

From the late 1970s, as was happening also in Taiwan, production of some labour-intensive exports moved away from Korea to lower-wage countries.[34] In so far as this transfer was autonomous—caused by quota avoidance or by the adoption of export-oriented policies in these other countries—it must have tended to widen skill differentials, as it apparently did in Taiwan. The fact that these differentials narrowed in Korea could be attributable to the higher rates of enrolment in tertiary education during the 1980s in Korea than in Taiwan, which caused faster growth of the relative supply of skilled labour.[35]

---

[33] However, Kuznets (1988) and others have argued that until about 1975 Korea was a labour-surplus economy.

[34] See e.g. the survey of Korea in the *Financial Times* of 9 May 1988, esp. p. VI.

[35] Faster growth of the skilled labour supply would not only offset any decline in the relative demand for unskilled labour, but would probably also mean that less of the transfer of production to poorer countries was autonomous (rather than being due to the rising relative cost of domestic unskilled labour). In 1984, the Korean tertiary enrolment rate was 26%, compared with 21% in Taiwan, and in 1989 the Korean rate was 38%, compared with 28% in Taiwan. These are gross enrolment rates, with the 20–24 age group as the denominator. The Korean rates are from the indicators tables of World Bank (1987, 1992). The rates for Taiwan are calculated from data in tables 4 and 107 of DGBAS (1991), whose table 109 also gives tertiary enrolment rates using an 18–21 denominator (22% in 1984 and 31% in 1989).

6.3.3 Hong Kong

Movements of skill differentials in wages are fairly well documented for Hong Kong, thanks to Chow and Papanek (1981), who compiled 1948–77 series for the average earnings of skilled, semi-skilled, and unskilled workers—though the occupational coverage of these groups is unspecified. Fig. 6.2 charts the skilled/unskilled and semi-skilled/unskilled wage ratios. From 1977 to 1982 there is unfortunately a gap. After that, the figure includes information (to 1990) from another source, which refers to wage relativities among three groups: managers and professionals; supervisory, technical, and clerical workers; and craftsmen and operatives.

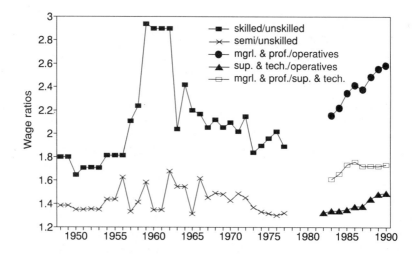

FIG. 6.2 Skill differentials in Hong Kong, 1948–1990
Notes and sources: Skilled, semi-skilled, and unskilled wage rates from Chow and Papanek (1981, table 6).

Earnings of managers and professionals; supervisory, technical, and clerical workers; and craftsmen and operatives, from Hong Kong *Annual Digest of Statistics* (1989, table 3.18; 1991, tables 3.17, 3.19, using the all-sector indices). In converting these data into ratios, 1988 average daily earnings of managers and professionals were assumed to be $HK350.

In the late 1940s, skill differentials seem to have narrowed. During the 1950s, though, they widened, with a large increase in the wage gap between skilled and unskilled workers, and a smaller and more volatile increase in the semi-skilled/unskilled ratio. From the early 1960s to the late 1970s, both these differentials narrowed again, returning to roughly their 1950 levels. Some of the movements in these series appear odd, particularly the abrupt rise and fall of the skilled/unskilled ratio in the late 1950s and early 1960s. However, the widening of skill differentials during the 1950s and their narrowing during the 1960s are confirmed by detailed data on the pay of government employees by occupation (Chau 1984, table 4).

Between the late 1970s and the early 1980s, all that is known is that skill differentials widened among manual construction workers.[36] During the rest of the 1980s, the new series in the figure suggest that there was a general increase in skill differentials, with the wages of craftsmen and operatives falling relative to those of both other groups, particularly managers and professionals. Wage differentials by level of education also became wider between 1981 and 1986, having narrowed in the previous five years (Terasaki 1991, table 10). The distribution of income among the working population became more unequal during both 1976–81 and 1981–6 (ibid., table 1).

Longer-term trends in overall income inequality are less well documented (Chow and Papanek 1981, app.). There are three different sources of data—housing surveys (for 1957), expenditure surveys (from 1963–4), and quinquennial censuses (starting in 1966)—and different authors calculate varying Gini coefficients from the same sources of data (Lin 1985, tables I and II; Terasaki 1991, table 1). Between 1957 and 1966, there appears to have been little change in inequality (although the path in the intervening years is unclear). During 1966–76, most indices of inequality decline.[37] Between 1976 and 1981, income inequality among households increased, while from 1981 to 1986 it remained roughly constant (Terasaki 1991, table 1).

In trying to explain these movements in relative wages and inequality, it should be noted that Hong Kong became a major exporter of labour-intensive manufactures because of changing external circumstances in the early 1950s (and not, like Korea and Taiwan, because of a change of trade strategy in the early 1960s). Many industrialists and some skilled workers fled from Shanghai to Hong Kong in the late 1940s and early 1950s. An international embargo on trade with China demolished Hong Kong's entrepôt business, but access to world markets was improved by

[36] This view is based on a comparison between the wages of plasterers and labourers during 1979–82 (Hong Kong *Annual Digest of Statistics* 1989: 47); and on comparisons among the wages of bricklayers, plasterers, bricklayers' and plasterers' labourers, and unskilled labourers, from the March issues of *Employment, Wages and Material Prices in the Construction Industry* (Census and Statistics Department of Hong Kong) between 1978 and 1982.

[37] Chow and Papanek (1981, table 4), Chau (1984, tables 5 and 6), Lin (1985, tables I and II). The main exception concerns the Gini coefficients estimated by Lin (1985, table I) from census data, which imply increased inequality both between 1966 and 1971 and between 1966 and 1976. However, Lin himself (ibid. 396) describes the 1966–79 period as one of declining inequality.

trade liberalisation in the North, although this was soon partially reversed in response to the 'disruption' caused by Hong Kong's textile exports (Wolf 1983: 14).

Hong Kong's trade transition—and the impact of this transition on the skill composition of the demand for labour—thus occurred mainly during the 1950s. The share of manufacturing in total employment, which provides a reasonable measure of the trade-induced change in the demand for labour (as Fig. 5.4 confirms), greatly increased during that decade, reaching 43 per cent in 1961.[38] After 1960, however, although Hong Kong's manufactured exports continued to expand rapidly, manufacturing's share of total employment rose more slowly, to a peak of just under 48 per cent in 1971, and then declined. In the 1980s, the absolute number of workers in manufacturing also started to fall.

On the face of it, then, the correlation in Hong Kong between changes in trade flows and movements of relative wages and inequality is the opposite of what might be expected.[39] During the transition to export-oriented industrialisation in the 1950s, skill differentials widened markedly, and only after the transition was more or less over, in the 1960s, did these differentials start to narrow and inequality to decline. However, there is a plausible explanation for this apparent incongruity, which is that the observed movements in skill differentials were caused mainly by other forces, especially changes in labour supply conditions.

In the 1950s, the most important such influence was the huge influx of refugees from China, most of whom were unskilled (or had skills for which there was insufficient local demand).[40] The supply of suitably skilled workers probably increased much more slowly, while the demand for them was pulled up by the rapid expansion of manufacturing production, even though this was concentrated on unskilled-labour-intensive activities. However, if the production of manufactures for export had not expanded so rapidly, the plight of unskilled workers would have been far worse. Not least, the fall in the unemployment rate, from 16 per cent in 1954 to 2 per cent in 1961 (Chau 1984: 3–4), made these workers much better off than they would otherwise have been. So although no one has simulated the likely counterfactual course of relative wages, the experi-

[38] There are no comprehensive employment statistics prior to 1961, but other evidence suggests a large rise in the share of manufacturing (Chau 1984: 3–5 and table 1; Lin 1985: 396–7). The information on manufacturing employment after 1961 is from Chow and Papanek (1981, table 8) and the 1986 Hong Kong By-Census (*Main Report*, Vol. 1, table 33).

[39] This is not usually recognised. Most studies confidently assert that the decline in inequality in Hong Kong in the 1960s and 1970s was due to its outward-oriented trade strategy (e.g. World Bank 1987: 87). But such an inference seems contrary to both theory and evidence.

[40] An estimated 1.4 million refugees arrived between 1945 and 1956, and although some of these moved on, the influx continued on a substantial scale until 1962, causing average real wages to stagnate during the 1950s (Chow and Papanek 1981: 466, 474, and table 6).

ence of Hong Kong during the 1950s does not in fact cast doubt on the proposition that export-oriented industrialisation disproportionately benefits less-skilled workers.

The narrowing of skill differentials that occurred between the early 1960s and the late 1970s was probably partly due to changes in trade: there were further reductions in natural and artificial barriers, for example, more learning by Northern firms about remote sourcing. The share of employment in manufacturing continued to rise for a while, and there was an increase in the relative weight of less skill-intensive sectors (Chow and Papanek, table 10). But because the ratio of skilled to unskilled employment was rising within most sectors, the share of unskilled workers in the total manufacturing labour force rose by only 2 percentage points between 1964 and 1974 (ibid., tables 9 and 11). A more important cause of the narrowing of skill differentials is thus likely to have been the declining relative supply of unskilled labour, partly because of the slowdown in immigration, and partly because of the expansion of post-basic education, which doubled the proportion of both college and upper secondary graduates in the labour force between 1961 and 1981.[41]

Changes in labour supply conditions were also probably part of the reason why skill differentials started widening again in the 1980s. Hong Kong did not sustain rapid growth of post-basic education, especially by comparison with Taiwan and Korea. In 1984, for example, the gross tertiary enrolment rates in these two other economies were 21 per cent and 26 per cent respectively, but only 13 per cent in Hong Kong.[42] For secondary education, the enrolment rates were 87 per cent and 91 per cent in Taiwan and Korea, as compared with 69 per cent in Hong Kong. Population movements also increased the relative supply of unskilled labour during the 1980s—renewed immigration of unskilled workers from China, and emigration of skilled workers in anticipation of China's resumption of sovereignty.[43]

However, trade-related shifts in the composition of demand also tended to widen skill differentials in Hong Kong after the late 1970s. Changes in global and regional circumstances enhanced the importance of Hong Kong as an international financial and business services centre, which boosted the relative demand for skilled labour.[44] In addition, as a result of China's economic reforms and open door policy, Hong Kong

[41] In 1961, 3.0% of the labour force had a university education, and 14.0% a senior secondary education or above (OECD 1969*a*); and in 1981, 5.6% had a polytechnic or university education, and 33.0% an upper secondary education or above (1981 *Census of Hong Kong*, table C6).

[42] For the sources of these numbers, see n. 35.

[43] On immigration, see Terasaki (1991: 106–7). On emigration, see the survey of Hong Kong in the *Financial Times* of 10 May 1991.

[44] Between 1983 and 1990 the salary index for managers and professionals in financial institutions rose from 100 to 245.3, as compared with a rise to 216.2 for managers and professionals in all sectors (Hong Kong *Annual Digest of Statistics* 1991, table 3.19).

businessmen set up many joint ventures and subcontracting operations in nearby Guangdong province, mainly in unskilled-labour-intensive manufacturing activities. By 1990, some 2 million Chinese workers were employed in these operations.[45] This opportunity for access to China's huge supply of low-wage labour may well have reduced the relative demand for unskilled workers in Hong Kong, even though the unemployment rate in Hong Kong has remained very low.[46]

6.3.4 Singapore

The longest available relative wage series in Singapore refer to three broad occupational groups: professional and managerial workers; clerical, sales, and service workers; and production, transport, and other manual workers. Fig. 6.3 traces the wage ratios among these skill categories between the mid-1960s and the late 1980s. All three differentials were compressed between 1966 and 1972, though the data for these years are not strictly comparable. Thereafter, their paths diverge. The professional–clerical wage ratio fluctuates, with no clear trend. The clerical–manual wage differential narrows more or less continuously. The professional–manual wage ratio declines until 1981, then rises somewhat, and declines again during 1986–90. Data for 1972–80 on income by level of education show a general narrowing of differentials, except for the tertiary/upper-secondary ratio and the completed primary/less-than-primary ratio.[47]

Reliable income distribution data for Singapore also begin only in the mid-1960s (Mizoguchi *et al.* 1980: 333–4). The best study of movements during the early part of the period is that of Rao and Ramakrishnan (1980), which refers to the distribution among individuals of income from employment and self-employment. This study shows a reduction in inequality between 1966 and 1972, with the Gini coefficient falling from 0.50 to 0.44, but no clear trend during 1972–5.[48] More recent data from a different source suggest that income inequality among households

[45] Survey of Hong Kong, *Financial Times*, 10 May 1991. On the size of the trade flows involved, see also GATT *International Trade* 90–1, Vol. II, table III.63.

[46] Under 2% during 1987–90 (Hong Kong *Annual Digest of Statistics* 1991, table 3.2).

[47] This assessment combines information from two sources. The 1972–7 data, which refer to average income per working person of both sexes, are from table 12 of the *Report on Survey of Households* April 1977 (Dept. of Statistics, Singapore, 1978). The 1980 data are from table 11 of Release No. 7 of the *Census of Population 1980* (Dept. of Statistics, Singapore, 1981). Because the educational categories in the latter source are more aggregated, the statement about the tertiary/upper-secondary ratio refers only to 1972–7.

[48] Rao and Ramakrishnan (1980: 173) note a conflict of evidence for 1966 concerning the mean income in the open-ended upper-income class. In their calculations they use the higher of the two alternatives. With the lower alternative, the Gini coefficient for 1966 would be 0.48, implying a smaller (but still quite marked) reduction in inequality during 1966–72.

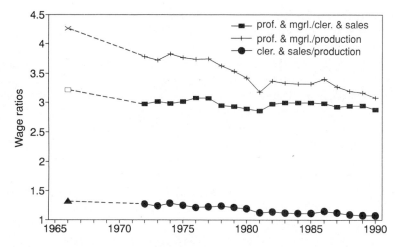

FIG. 6.3 Skill differentials in Singapore, 1966–1990

Notes and sources: Data for 1972–89 from table 3.7 of *Economic and Social Statistics Singapore 1960–82* (Dept. of Statistics, Singapore, 1983) and from table 3.10 of *Yearbook of Statistics Singapore 1990* (Dept. of Statistics, Singapore). 'Wages' are average weekly earnings in earlier years, average monthly earnings in later years. The data refer to employees and are averages across all sectors.

The full descriptions of the three occupational groups in the sources for 1972–89 are: professional, administrative, managerial, executive, and related workers; clerical, sales, service, and related workers; and production, transport, and other manual workers.

Between 1984 and 1985, the lower size limit of the establishments covered by the underlying surveys was raised from 10 to 25 workers. The marked compression of skill differentials between these two years implied by the data is thus probably illusory and has been suppressed by splicing (using the 1985–9 data to extrapolate movements from 1984 levels).

The wage ratios for 1966 were calculated from table H85 of Report No. 1 of the *Singapore Sample Household Survey 1966* (Government Printing Office, 1967). The occupational classification is probably not strictly comparable with that of the later data. Moreover, because the frequency distribution in the table has an open-ended upper income class ($1000 plus), the derived wage ratios depend on the assumption made about the mean income within this class. The ratios shown in the figure are based on the assumption that the mean was $2000, which is consistent with the evidence from income tax data cited by Rao and Ramakrishnan (1980: 173), and more conservative than the assumption they actually use. With an assumed mean of $1750, all three differentials would still narrow between 1966 and 1972; but with a mean of $1500, the two larger ratios would widen somewhat.

declined between 1972–3 and 1977–8, and then increased to 1982–3 (Fields 1989: 39). The Gini coefficients in these years were 0.40, 0.37, and 0.42 respectively.

These movements in relative wages and income distribution are broadly consistent with the hypothesis that Singapore's switch to a strategy of export-oriented industrialisation, which occurred in 1967–9 (Tan and Hock 1982: 282–3), caused a reduction in inequality during the following decade. This inference is strengthened, because it is unlikely that educational expansion contributed to the compression of skill differentials during the 1970s. For in response to concern about educated unemployment, Singapore decided in the late 1960s not to expand higher education: between 1965 and 1980, the enrolment rate at this level declined, and the proportion of the labour force with a university degree barely increased.[49] The percentage of secondary school graduates in the labour force almost doubled, though. Primary school enrolment was universal throughout this period, reducing the share of the labour force with less than a complete primary education from (a surprisingly high) 54 per cent in 1966 to 22 per cent in 1980.[50]

This relative contraction of higher education probably explains why the wage differentials between professional and clerical workers, and between tertiary and upper secondary graduates, did not narrow during the 1970s. But it clearly cannot explain the compression of professional–manual and tertiary–primary wage differentials. Nor can the relative decline in the supply of workers with less than a complete primary education explain the widening gap between their incomes and those of primary-school graduates. These movements must have been due to an increase in the relative demand for manual workers with primary education, which is exactly what is to be expected from expansion of export-oriented manufacturing.

What happened subsequently is less straightforward. In the late 1970s, the government decided to force up wages as a way of encouraging movement into higher-productivity activities. During 1979–81, nominal wage

---

[49] As a ministerial quotation on the front cover of the *Annual Report of the Ministry of Labour* 1967 put it: 'We will cease making the mistakes which nearly all developing countries are now making—over-producing unemployable numbers of educated white-collar workers.' Enrolment rates are from World Bank (1983, indicators table 25; 1988, indicators table 30). Breakdowns of the labour force by educational qualifications can be calculated from table P78 of Report No. 1 of the *Singapore Sample Household Survey 1966* (Government Printing Office, 1967) and from table 46 of Release No. 4 of the *Census of Population 1980* (Dept. of Statistics, Singapore, 1981). Between 1966 and 1980, the share of the labour force with a university degree rose from 3.3% to 3.6%, while the share with completed lower or upper-secondary schooling rose from 13.4% to 23.9%.

[50] For sources, see n. 49. In 1966, 19% of the labour force (37% for females) lacked even an incomplete primary education. There is no information on illiteracy in 1966, but nine years earlier about 40% of the labour force had been illiterate (*Report on the 1957 Census of Population*). The illiteracy rate in 1957 among the adult population as a whole was 50% (see Table 5.1).

rates were therefore increased by about 20 per cent per year (Lim and Fong 1982: 34). Since the wage rates concerned were mainly those of lower-paid workers, these increases compressed skill differentials, particularly between professional and manual workers (as can be seen in Fig. 6.3).

However, the forced wage increases also reduced Singapore's international competitiveness, which caused manufacturing employment to shrink during the first half of the 1980s, both absolutely and as a share of total employment (by 5 percentage points, compared with an increase of 8 points during the 1970s).[51] The resulting excess supply of less-skilled labour, reflected in a rising unemployment rate, probably caused the widening during 1981–6 of the professional–manual wage differential (and cessation of decline in the clerical–manual differential). In 1985, though, the government abandoned its longstanding system of wage guidelines, and during 1986–90 employment in manufacturing rose rapidly, unemployment fell, and skill differentials narrowed again.

The fluctuations associated with this attempt to push Singapore up the ladder of development make it hard to disentangle the effects of longer-term influences on relative wages in the 1980s. The resumed narrowing of skill differentials in the second half of the decade was probably partly caused, as in the 1970s, by expansion of export-oriented manufacturing. However, this renewed expansion was not triggered by a reduction in trade barriers, but (apparently) by the government's decision to stop trying to force up wage rates, and to try other ways of raising the skill intensity of Singapore's manufactured exports.[52] Moreover, the narrowing of skill differentials may have been caused partly by changes in relative supply: the policy of restraining higher education was reversed, tripling the enrolment rate at this level between 1979 and 1989.[53]

6.3.5 Four little tigers: overview

The time-series case-study evidence on the four little tigers is by no means so clear-cut as is commonly supposed. There are many gaps and deficiencies in the data on relative wages and income inequality. More importantly, the shortage of information on other determinants of these variables, and the paucity of proper modelling (either econometric or simulation), makes it hard to disentangle the effects of trade in a logically rigorous or quantitatively precise way.

---

[51] On the decline in competitiveness, see the survey of Singapore in the *Economist*, 22 Nov. 1986, pp. 6–7. Data on manufacturing employment are from table 3.4 of *Yearbook of Statistics Singapore 1989* (Dept. of Statistics, Singapore).

[52] On these more recent attempts, see e.g. the survey of Singapore in the *Financial Times* of 30 Apr. 1991 (esp. p. IV).

[53] Calculated from tables 2.4, 2.5, and 15.1 of *Yearbook of Statistics Singapore 1989* (Dept. of Statistics, Singapore), using the 20–24 age group as the denominator.

Nevertheless, most of this evidence is in accordance with theoretical expectations. In particular, all of these cases are consistent with the hypothesis that expansion of export-oriented manufacturing increases the demand for *BAS-ED* labour relative to *SKILD* labour. They all also tend to confirm that such a switch of trade strategy causes a step change in the composition of demand, whose effects on skill differentials in wages are spread over a period of about ten years. In three of the four cases, the wage differential between *BAS-ED* and *SKILD* labour actually declined during the relevant decade. In the fourth case, Hong Kong, the wage differential widened, but this was probably caused by a simultaneous and more-than-offsetting increase in the relative supply of unskilled labour.

Relative expansion of post-basic education is an alternative possible explanation of narrowing skill differentials. But in all three of the cases in which differentials narrowed, the change in trade orientation appears to have been at least partly responsible, either because the narrowing was faster than in adjacent decades, or because expansion of higher education was deliberately constrained during the period concerned. The fact that wage differentials narrowed also supports the view that the relative supply of *BAS-ED* labour is less than infinitely elastic, although some of the evidence could be construed as indicating that this elasticity was higher in the earlier than in the later years of the relevant decade.

Movements in income distribution in these four economies are also broadly consistent with the view that a switch to export-oriented industrialisation tends to reduce inequality. In the three cases in which the *SKILD/BAS-ED* wage differential narrowed following such a switch, there was a decline in income inequality, too. In theory, such a change of trade strategy should also tend to widen the wage differential between *BAS-ED* and *NO-ED* workers, and in the one case (Singapore) where data on this relativity is available during the relevant decade, it did indeed widen. However, in all four of these economies there were comparatively few *NO-ED* workers, which explains not only why (on balance) exporting manufactures reduced inequality, but also why these economies had a comparative advantage in manufacturing.

What happened in these four cases after their initial decades of export-oriented industrialisation was more varied. In general, there was further narrowing of skill differentials, whose main cause was expansion of higher levels of the education system. This rise in the relative supply of more highly educated labour seems (as expected) to have contributed to changing the pattern of trade, pulling these economies up the ladder of development. By the mid-1980s, all four were starting to abandon some of the unskilled-labour-intensive manufactures in which they had initially specialised, and their governments—apart perhaps from that of Hong Kong—were trying to accelerate this process in various ways.

Korea's heavy and chemical industry drive in the mid-1970s widened skill differentials. Moreover, in the other three economies, the reduction in inequality seems to have ceased or been reversed during at least part of the 1980s. There are plausible country-specific reasons for this in two cases: in Hong Kong, growth of financial service exports, combined with migration and slow expansion of higher education; and in Singapore, the reversal of an earlier artificial compression of differentials. However, there was also a more general tendency in this direction, caused by the adoption of export-oriented policies by countries with lower wages (and under-utilised Northern import quotas): Malaysia, Thailand, Indonesia, and China. Only in Korea (and perhaps in Singapore at the end of the decade) did higher education expand fast enough to offset the resulting downward pressure on the relative wages of unskilled workers in the four tigers.

6.3.6 Other countries

There are many other studies of income distribution and (to a lesser extent) relative wages in developing countries.[54] Few of them, however, cast any light on the issue with which the present chapter is concerned, namely the effects of recent changes in trade with the North. Most of these studies focus on *describing* inequality, since their data and methods rarely permit satisfactory analysis of causation. Furthermore, in most of the countries and periods studied there have not been substantial changes in trade. The findings of some studies that are exceptional in these respects were summarised in earlier sections (Fields 1984; Clements and Kim 1988; Kim and Vorasopontaviporn 1989). Davis (1992) argues that reductions in wage inequality during the 1980s in Brazil, Colombia, and Venezuela may have been partly a result of expansion of trade with the North, but he does not establish this linkage empirically.

A recent set of case studies that specifically addresses the relationship between trade and income distribution is Bourguignon and Morrisson (1989). The countries covered, in addition to Taiwan, are Costa Rica, Malaysia, Malawi, Morocco, and Peru. The authors of some of the individual country studies conclude either that trade has not had much effect on distribution, or that its effects cannot be disentangled from those of other influences on income distribution.[55] However, the editors of the

---

[54] For references, see the surveys of Fields (1980, 1988, 1989), Bigsten (1983, 1987, sect. 4.4), Lecaillon *et al.* (1984), Mizoguchi (1985*a*, 1991), Adelman and Robinson (1989), Sundrum (1990), and World Bank (1990: 46–51).

[55] 'All in all, the preceding partial analyses suggest that the relationship between income distribution and external trade is relatively weak in Costa Rica' (Bourguignon and Morrisson 1989: 81). 'The few effects we have been able to identify point to a restricted influence of export structure on income inequality' in Malawi (ibid. 148). 'It is evident that much work remains to be done before strong conclusions can be advanced on the trade-distribution relationship in Peru' (ibid. 231).

volume arrive at some more definite conclusions, by assembling a patch-work of insights and evidence from the country studies.

Some of these conclusions (ibid. 282–5) relate to trade in manufactures, and are similar to those of the other studies referred to in Sections 3.3 and 6.2.3. Bourguignon and Morrisson distinguish processed primary products from manufactured exports proper, and show that the latter have a number of characteristics which imply that their expansion tends to reduce income inequality. Particularly important is the relatively higher demand for unskilled labour in sectors which produce manufactured exports than in primary processing and import substituting sectors.[56] In addition, wage dispersion within these sectors is similar to other manufacturing sectors, while their average wage is usually close to the national average (above agriculture but below other manufacturing and service sectors), so that an increase in their relative weight in the economy tends to reduce overall income dispersion.

Also valuable, as a way of putting manufactured exports into perspective, is Bourguignon and Morrisson's analysis (1989: 273–81) of the effects on income distribution of exporting primary products.[57] Mineral exports tend to increase inequality, because their production requires relatively little unskilled labour, and because the ownership of mineral resources is usually highly concentrated. Only where the government captures a large share of the rent, and then spends it in ways that disproportionately benefit lower-income groups, are mineral exports likely to reduce inequality. The effect of agricultural exports on distribution depends crucially on the pattern of land ownership. Where such exports are produced mainly on plantations or large farms, their expansion tends to increase inequality, unless the land is publicly owned, or workers are highly unionised (for example, rubber in Malaysia). By contrast, increased exports of the agricultural products of small and medium-sized farms (such as coffee in Costa Rica), and of fish, tend to reduce inequality.

6.4 Summary

In the South, theory suggests that expansion of North-bound manufactured exports tends to raise the demand for—and hence the wages of—workers with a basic general education (*BAS-EDs*), relative to *SKILD* workers (who have more education and training). This narrowing of skill differentials tends to make the distribution of income less unequal. The

---

[56] Primary processing is actually a heterogeneous category, whose skill intensity varies widely, depending on the nature of the product and the stage of processing (see e.g. World Bank 1981: 23).

[57] However, Bourguignon and Morrisson neglect the distributional effects of primary product import substitution, as do most other studies, with the exception of Moore's analysis (1990: 17–18) of the expansion of Dry Zone paddy production in Sri Lanka.

demand shift also raises the wages of *BAS-EDs* relative to those of workers with little or no education (*NO-EDs*), which tends to make the distribution of income more unequal. However, because countries with a lot of *NO-EDs* usually do not have a comparative advantage in manufacturing, the net effect of more exports of manufactures is likely to be a reduction in inequality.

This theoretical prediction is supported, though not strongly, by cross-country comparisons. Developing countries which export a higher share of their manufactured output, or have lower levels of industrial protection, also tend to have less unequal income distributions. Moreover, countries whose manufactured exports expanded faster between the mid-1960s and the mid-1980s experienced greater reductions (or smaller increases) in income inequality over this period. The latter test (in changes) is in principle more convincing than the former (in levels), but yields less significant statistical results.

The proposition that exporting manufactures tends to reduce inequality is also supported by a small number of simulations using structural models of particular developing countries. The effect of trade on distribution seems small in simple input–output models, but it is larger in computable general equilibrium models which allow prices and wages to alter. All such tests, however, are vulnerable to disagreements about model specification and assumptions.

Another sort of evidence consists of case studies of particular countries, in which movements over time in relative wages and income distribution are examined, and their causes more informally assessed. Although a few other countries have also been studied, most of this material refers to the four little East Asian tigers (Korea, Taiwan, Hong Kong, and Singapore). The time-series evidence for these economies is much flimsier than is usually supposed, especially in its limited power to discriminate among alternative possible explanations of observed trends, but most of it is consistent with the hypothesis that exporting manufactures tends to reduce inequality.

In three of these four economies, the wage differential between *SKILD* and *BAS-ED* workers did narrow after they shifted to export-oriented strategies, and overall income inequality declined. The exception was Hong Kong, where skill differentials widened during the 1950s, despite massive expansion of manufactured exports, because the relative supply of unskilled labour was boosted by immigration from China. The experience of these four economies also supports the theoretical prediction that adopting an export-oriented strategy tends to cause a step (or once-and-for-all) change in relative wages, which is spread over a period of about ten years.

After this initial decade, skill differentials in the four little tigers generally narrowed further, but this was mainly due to expansion of higher education, which increased the relative supply of *SKILD* labour. It also helped to propel these economies into more skill-intensive activities, by increasing the relative cost of their *BAS-ED* labour. Their movement away from labour-intensive manufacturing was accelerated when other East Asian countries, with lower wages, also adopted export-oriented policies. This competition, however, tended to reduce the wages of unskilled workers in the four tigers, which all showed some signs of increasing inequality in the 1980s, apart from Korea, where the supply of highly educated labour was expanding at a phenomenal rate.

Each of the types of evidence reviewed above is not wholly satisfactory on its own, but in combination they strongly support the view that exporting manufactures tends to narrow the wage gap between *SKILD* and *BAS-ED* workers, and hence to reduce income inequality. What this evidence does not show, however, is that *export-oriented policies* necessarily lead to expansion of manufactured exports and reductions in inequality. In countries with high proportions of *NO-EDs* and/or abundant natural resources, liberalisation of trade policies could cause manufacturing to contract, and primary exports to expand, with uncertain effects on the distribution of income.

7

Skill Differentials and Inequality
in the North

This chapter is the first of two which do for the North what the previous chapter did for the South, namely to assess the 'factoral' consequences of changing trade relationships with countries on the other side of the North–South divide (the 'sectoral' consequences were considered in Chapter 5). Section 7.1 describes trends in the relative wages and unemployment rates of skilled and less-skilled workers. Section 7.2 examines the consistency of these trends with the expected effects of more trade with the South. Section 7.3 discusses other possible explanations of these trends, with special reference to new technology. The following chapter considers the effects of trade with the South on aggregate unemployment in the North.

7.1 Trends in Skill Differentials

The effects of trade on skill differentials in the North are not entirely symmetrical with those in the South. This is because the North has few *NO-ED* workers, so that there are in effect only two broad skill categories (*SKILD* and *BAS-ED*), rather than three, as in the South. In other words, the 'unskilled' labour force of the North consists mainly of people with a primary or general lower-secondary education. The North also has a much higher proportion of workers with substantial post-basic education or training (which makes the crudity of the *SKILD* category more apparent).

The evidence in Part A of this book suggests that, within manufacturing, changes in trade with the South have reduced the demand for *BAS-ED* labour relative to *SKILD* labour. There are no proper estimates for other sectors, but it is highly likely that this result for manufacturing also applies to the economy as a whole (which is the context in which skill differentials are determined). Fragmentary evidence suggests that in traded services, as in manufacturing, trade with the South has reduced the relative demand for unskilled labour. Moreover, these intrasectoral changes are unlikely to have been offset by trade-induced changes in sectoral weights: the main such change has been a reduction in the employment share of manufacturing relative to services; and the ratio of *SKILD* to *BAS-ED* labour is not on average higher in manufacturing than in services.[1]

This shift in demand must have tended to raise the wages of *SKILD* relative to *BAS-ED* workers, to an extent dependent on the elasticities of demand and supply (both of which appear to be far from infinite—sections 2.4.3 and 6.1.2). However, in so far as institutional forces restrained this widening of wage differentials, the demand shift should have emerged instead in the form of shortages of *SKILD* workers and surpluses of *BAS-ED* workers, or more precisely as a widening of skill differentials in unemployment and vacancy rates. In addition, forces other than North–South trade may have altered the relative demand for *SKILD* and *BAS-ED* labour, and there must have been autonomous shifts in relative supply, both of which could have either muffled or amplified the effects of trade on skill differentials.

The next three subsections review recent trends in skill differentials in the North, using three indicators of skill, namely education, occupation, and wage levels. This evidence strongly suggests that skill differentials have in fact widened in most Northern countries since about 1980, and that the cause has been a shift in the skill composition of labour demand. A fourth subsection reviews parallel trends in overall income inequality.

This review of trends can be brief, because its conclusions are now widely accepted. (What remains controversial is the underlying cause of the shift in the skill composition of demand, with which the rest of the chapter is concerned.) The review thus consists simply of a summary of Appendices A3 to A5, which contain a detailed survey of the evidence, including a fuller set of skill differential indicators for a larger number of countries than is available at the time of writing in any other source.

7.1.1 Returns to education and experience

The wages of college graduates, relative to those of workers with only a secondary education, declined in the 1970s, but rose in the 1980s. This pattern is best documented for the USA, but it is apparent also in virtually all the other Northern countries for which data are available. The rise in the relative earnings of college graduates in the 1980s appears to have been large in the USA, the UK, and Germany, and slight in Australia, France, Italy, Sweden, and Japan, with Canada and probably The Netherlands in between.

---

[1] Different indicators give different impressions of the relative skill intensity of these two broad sectors. Educational and occupational data suggest that on average services are far more skill-intensive (Tables A2.1 and A2.2). Average wages in manufacturing were slightly higher than in services even in the early 1970s (Table A2.3), but this is probably more a reflection of the lower share of female workers (see Sect. 7.2.4), and perhaps of less attractive working conditions, than of higher skill.

Unemployment rates among more-educated workers, relative to less-educated workers, generally followed a path consistent with that of wages. In the 1970s, joblessness among college graduates rose faster than average. In the 1980s, by contrast, it was the least-educated workers—particularly people with no more than a basic secondary education—who suffered the largest rise in unemployment. Moreover, official unemployment statistics understate the deterioration in the relative position of less-educated workers, many of whom have withdrawn from the labour force.

The wages and employment prospects of younger, less-experienced, workers also deteriorated, relative to those of more-experienced workers, in many Northern countries during part or all of the 1970s and 1980s. The widening of wage differentials by age is evident in almost all countries during the 1980s, and in some countries during the 1970s. It was particularly marked among less-educated workers. Unemployment differentials by age widened in most countries in the 1970s, although this trend was reversed in the early 1980s. Unemployment among younger workers appears to have risen less in countries and periods where their relative wages declined.

Some of these movements in the relative wages and unemployment rates of different education and age groups can be explained by supply-side shifts. The deterioration in the relative position of college-educated labour in the 1970s was caused mainly by a large increase in the number of college graduates, and in most countries for part of the period the deterioration in the relative position of younger workers was aggravated by generational crowding (baby booms). Lower spending on education and slower growth of the number of young people may also have amplified the widening of skill differentials during the 1980s.

However, most of the widening of education and age differentials in wages and unemployment rates during the 1980s appears to have been caused by a shift in the skill composition of the demand for labour. Above all, the relative numbers of more-educated workers, as well as their relative wages and chances of employment, have been rising, a combination which could not have been caused by shifts in supply. This conclusion is based mainly on studies of the USA, but almost certainly applies also to other developed countries. Moreover, generational crowding is not sufficient to explain the sustained deterioration in the relative position of younger workers.

Movements in education and age differentials thus strongly suggest that there was a decline in the relative demand for less-skilled workers during the 1980s. The skill composition of the demand for labour was probably shifting in this direction also during the 1970s, even though changes in relative wages and unemployment rates during that decade were dominated by supply-side shifts. However, the shift in the skill composition of demand appears to have accelerated in the 1980s.

7.1.2 Occupational relativities

The average wages of white-collar (or non-manual) workers rose, relative to those of blue-collar (or manual) workers, in many Northern countries after about 1980, reversing a general narrowing of this coarsely defined skill differential during the 1970s. In five of the fifteen countries for which data are available (Austria, Germany, Italy, the UK, and the USA), there was a clear and sustained rise in the white–blue wage differential. In seven other countries, there was a less clear uptrend or cessation of a previous downtrend. Only in three countries (Belgium, France, and Sweden) did the white–blue wage differential apparently continue to decline in the 1980s. Moreover, for reasons explained in Appendix A4, the indices concerned are often biased downwards (thus tending to suggest, for example, that skill differentials are constant even though they may actually be widening).

Because lower-level white-collar workers are paid roughly the same as the average blue-collar worker, movements in the white–blue wage differential largely reflect changes in the relative pay of higher-level (professional, technical, and managerial) and lower-level (clerical) white-collar workers. In most of the Northern countries for which data are available, the wage gap between higher and lower white-collar workers did indeed widen during the 1980s, having narrowed in the 1970s. The widening was particularly marked in the UK and the USA, but occurred to some extent also in Austria, Canada, Germany, Italy, and Sweden, although not in France or Norway. In most countries, these data understate the widening of skill differentials, because professional workers have become relatively younger.

By contrast, movements in the relative wages of skilled and less-skilled blue-collar workers varied widely among countries. Both in the USA and in the UK, there was a steep rise in the skilled–unskilled manual wage ratio in the 1980s, but in the USA this was continuing a trend that began in the early 1970s, whereas in the UK it simply cancelled out a decline in this ratio during the previous decade. In France and Italy, also, there was compression of skill differentials among manual workers during the 1970s, but little or no movement in the opposite direction in the 1980s. And in Austria, Denmark, and Germany, there was not much change in either decade. An obvious possible explanation for this more varied pattern is that wage differentials among blue-collar workers are more strongly influenced than other relativities by institutional forces, particularly in Europe.

Occupation-specific unemployment rates are poor indicators of movements in skill differentials. Unemployed people literally have no occupation, and (especially where their skills are narrow) may be unable to return to their former occupations, or even to other occupations requiring similar amounts of training. In most countries, the unemployment rate among white-collar workers, as a ratio of that among blue-collar workers, declined between the early 1970s and the late 1980s, suggesting an improvement in the relative position of skilled labour. But there was no general trend in the relative unemployment rates of higher and lower white-collar workers. Among blue-collar workers, movements in the relative unemployment rates of the skilled and the less-skilled varied among countries and sub-periods, with little change in North America, and even deterioration in the relative position of skilled manual workers in some European countries in the 1970s and early 1980s, although this seems to have been reversed by the late 1980s. (This set of evidence is considered further in Section 8.2.)

Data on occupation-specific vacancy rates suffer from a different set of problems, and are rarely available. However, in France, Germany, and the UK, trends in vacancies for professional and managerial, clerical, white-collar, blue-collar, and skilled and unskilled manual workers generally suggest increasing relative scarcity of skilled labour in the late 1970s and early 1980s. There is even less data on vacancies for workers with different qualification levels, but in both Germany and The Netherlands, the relative scarcity of workers with more education and training clearly increased in the 1980s. Since the early 1970s, moreover, firms in the UK have felt increasingly constrained by shortages of skilled rather than of unskilled labour.

To assess whether movements in occupation-based skill differentials have been caused by shifts in demand or in supply, it is not possible, as with the education and age-based differentials, to compare them with movements in shares of the *labour force*. This is because the labour force cannot be divided exhaustively among a set of mutually exclusive occupational groups, since some of its members currently have no occupation, and most of its members could work in more than one occupation. Instead, however, one can look at contemporaneous changes in occupational shares of total *employment*. Movements of relative wages and employment in the same direction tend to imply predominance of demand shifts, and in opposite directions of supply shifts, provided that the changes in relative scarcity implied by the wage movements are not contradicted by movements in relative unemployment and vacancy rates, as might happen if wages were institutionally determined.

In this framework, the proximate causes of the observed movements in the relative pay of higher- and lower-level white-collar workers, and of the associated movements in the ratio of white- to blue-collar pay, are clear. The shares of professional and other higher-level white-collar workers in total employment, and indeed of white-collar workers as a whole, have been rising in most Northern countries for a long time. The concurrent rise in their relative wages during the 1980s must thus have been principally due to a shift in the composition of demand towards these more-skilled groups. Conversely, the decline in their relative wages in the 1970s (and in most earlier decades) was caused mainly by expansion of the supply of highly educated labour. However, in several European countries this decline was accelerated by institutional forces, such as the UK's incomes policies.

The movements in skill differentials among blue-collar workers are harder to interpret, partly because there is less information, and partly because (as mentioned above) the outcome seems to have varied widely from country to country. But most of the evidence is consistent with the hypothesis of a general upward shift in the demand for skilled, relative to unskilled, manual labour, combined with differing degrees of institutional pressure on the relative wages of these two groups. Hence in the USA, where wages are determined largely by market forces, most of the demand shift appears to have emerged as a widening of the wage differential between skilled and less-skilled manual workers, with little change in their relative numbers. (The alternative view that the skill structure of employment in the USA has been 'hollowed out' is discussed—and rejected—in the next subsection.)

By contrast, in most European countries, where institutional pressures on blue-collar wages are more powerful, the demand shift has emerged mainly as a rise in the ratio of skilled to less-skilled manual employment. In these countries, that is, the relative wages of less-skilled manual workers have been propped up by unions, minimum wage laws, and social security income floors, but fewer and fewer of these workers have been able to find jobs. The UK appears to be an intermediate case: strong institutional constraints on relative wage movements were deliberately weakened during the 1980s, but by no means eliminated, so that among blue-collar workers there was both a widening of skill differentials and a decline in less-skilled employment.

7.1.3 Wage dispersion

The distribution of wages and salaries among full-time workers became more dispersed during at least part of the 1980s in all the Northern countries for which data are available. This trend was apparent both for males and for females, though its timing and strength varied from country to country (as is set out in more detail in Appendix A5). The increase in dispersion was most conspicuous in the USA, with sustained increases also in Canada and the UK, and sharp increases in shorter series for Australia and Germany. In Sweden, there was also a sharp rise in dispersion, but only after 1983. In France, the rise dates from 1984, and was slight, although increasing dispersion in the upper half of the wage distribution started much earlier. There were small increases in wage dispersion during the 1980s also in Austria, Denmark, The Netherlands, and New Zealand.

Before the 1980s, the direction as well as the strength of trends in wage dispersion varied among countries as well as between males and females. In the USA, wage dispersion among males started to rise in the late 1960s, but the trend was milder in the 1970s than after 1980, and there may have been a decline among females in the early 1970s. In Canada, too, wage dispersion among males increased in the 1970s (but again less than in the 1980s, and only in the lower half of the distribution), and there was also increasing dispersion among females. In the UK, however, the rise in dispersion began only in the late 1970s, with prior declines among both males and females. Wage dispersion declined during the 1970s also in France (in the lower half of the distribution), Germany, Italy, and Sweden, and perhaps in Denmark.

The widespread increases in wage dispersion during the 1980s are in part explicable by the widening of wage differentials among education, age, and occupational groups discussed in the two previous subsections. However, increasing dispersion of wages *within* such groups also made an important contribution.[2] Because intra-group differences in wages among (full-time) workers largely reflect 'unobservable' differences in levels of skill, it can plausibly be argued that the increases in intra-group dispersion, and hence the whole of the overall increase in wage dispersion, were the result of wider wage differentials between skilled and less-skilled workers. It is also plausible to suppose that the increases in intra-group dispersion, like the widening wage gaps between skill groups, were caused mainly by a rise in the relative demand for skilled labour.

In some European countries, the increases in wage dispersion in the 1980s were permitted or amplified by relaxation of institutional pressures that had compressed skill differentials, and hence reduced wage dispersion, in the 1970s. Incomes policies which discriminated in favour of lower-paid workers were dropped in the UK, the wage indexation system was amended in Italy, and centralised wage bargaining collapsed in Sweden. In France, by contrast, the legal minimum wage was reinforced in the 1980s (see Section 8.3.3), which probably explains why the rise in wage dispersion was so slight.

Another possible explanation for the increase in wage dispersion is that it was mainly due not to wider skill differentials in wages, but to 'hollowing out' (or disappearance of the middle) of the skill distribution of workers or of jobs. Both in the USA and in the UK, there is some evidence that the proportion of jobs with middling *wages* has fallen, because of the

---

[2] Intra-group dispersion increased also during the 1970s in the USA and in Canada, but not in France, Sweden, or the UK.

decline in manufacturing employment. However, there does not appear to have been a rise in the proportion of jobs with low, as compared to middling, *skill requirements*. On the contrary, the limited evidence available shows that the number of jobs requiring low levels of skill has been expanding more slowly than the number of jobs requiring higher levels of skill.

7.1.4 Income inequality

In several Northern countries, the distribution of income among households became more unequal during the 1980s, in contrast to the general trend in the two preceding decades. In none of the nine countries for which data are available (see Table A5.2 of Appendix A5) did income inequality rise during the 1960s or early 1970s, and in seven of them inequality declined. In the 1980s, though, inequality rose in six out of eleven countries, and in only three (France, Germany, and Italy) did it continue to decline. The rise in inequality started around 1980 in Japan and The Netherlands, and at some point in the 1970s in the USA and the UK. There was no trend during these three decades in Canada (and for Sweden, Australia, and New Zealand the series are too short to permit an assessment of longer-term trends).

Although the evidence is inadequate, it seems likely that the widening of skill differentials (in wages and unemployment) discussed in the three previous subsections was the main cause of these changes in the trend of household income distribution. Of course, the size of skill differentials is but one of many influences on household income inequality. Also vital, for example, are variations in the number of workers (and dependents) per household, and in income from sources other than wages. The relationship between movements in wage dispersion among full-time workers of each sex (discussed in the previous subsection) and in the distribution of income among households likewise depends also on trends in the relative earnings and numbers of males and females, and of full-time and part-time workers.

In most Northern countries, it is thus also likely that other forces have acted to amplify or to muffle the effects of wider skill differentials on household income inequality. In the UK, for instance, the sharp increase in inequality during the 1980s was exacerbated by regressive changes in the tax and social security systems. In France, by contrast, increased social security benefits and tax progressivity, in conjunction with the smallness of the increase in wage dispersion, reduced income inequality. In Germany, the adverse effects of wider skill differentials on income inequality were more than offset by a rise in the proportion of households with more than one wage-earner.

It is worth noting, however, that changes in household income inequality are not necessarily a good or sufficient measure of the undesirable social effects of a deterioration in the relative economic position of unskilled workers. The widening of skill differentials appears to have raised the proportion of poor households in most Northern countries, which is to be deplored. But even if offsetting demographic forces were to cause a net *reduction* in household income inequality, lower pay and more unemployment among young under-educated males would still be likely, for example, to aggravate drug abuse and crime.

7.2 Consistency of the Trade Explanation

The preceding section (a summary of Appendices A3–A5), described recent trends in skill differentials in the North, using a variety of indicators. This section asks whether the available evidence fits the hypothesis that these trends were generated by changes in trade with the South. (The next section will examine alternative possible explanations of these trends.)

Although the underlying data are not entirely satisfactory, two apparently robust conclusions emerge from the previous section. One is that there was a general tendency for skill differentials to widen in the North during the 1980s. This can be seen from the overview in Table 7.1, which covers eight indicators and seventeen countries, and shows the directions of change with pluses and minuses.[3] (The format is taken from Marsden 1989b, table 2.1.) All but one of the indicators suggest that skill differentials widened, the exception being wage relativities among blue-collar workers, for which the pattern is mixed. This trend, moreover, was evidently pervasive: in every country, at least one indicator suggests widening skill differentials, and in no country are there more signs of narrowing than of widening. In four countries, though, at least one indicator suggests narrowing.

The other main conclusion is that this widening of skill differentials was caused predominantly by a shift in demand—more specifically, by increased demand for skilled relative to less-skilled workers.[4] For the widening of skill differentials in wages was associated with increases in the relative numbers of skilled workers. In several countries, trends in relative wages were also affected by institutional forces: in a few cases, the relaxation of earlier constraints allowed wage differentials to widen; in

[3] The table omits the less reliable data on unemployment by occupation, most of which also suggests widening skill differentials (see Table 8.1). Also omitted are the limited data on unemployment by age group, which suggest that skill differentials narrowed in the early 1980s, after widening in the 1970s (for reasons explained in Sect. 7.2.1).

[4] Katz and Loveman (1990) draw the same conclusion from a comparative study of France, the UK, and the USA.

TABLE 7.1. *Trends in skill differentials in the North during the 1980s*

	Education		Age	Occupational wages			Vacancy data	Wage dispersion	Overall score**
	Wages	Unempt.	Wages	White/ blue*	Intra- white	Intra- blue			
Australia	+		++					++	4.0
Austria				+	+	0		+	1.5
Belgium		++		−					2.5
Canada	+	++	++	+	+			+	3.0
Denmark				+		0		+	1.3
Finland				+					2.0
France	?		++	−	0	−	++	(+)	1.6
Germany	++	++	++	+	+	−	++	++	3.6
Italy	+	++		(+)	(+)	?			1.8
Japan	+		+	0					1.3
Netherlands	?	++	++	0			++	+	2.8
New Zealand								+	2.0
Norway		?		+	?				0.7
Sweden	+	?	+	−	+			(++)	1.5
Switzerland				+					2.0
UK	++	++	+	++	++	+	++	+	3.9
USA	++	+	++	+	++	+		++	3.7

Key to symbols:
+   = widening skill differential
++ = strongly widening skill differential (increase of 15% or more on a 10-year basis)
( ) = widening only for latter part of 1980s
−   = narrowing skill differential throughout 1980s
0   = no trend
?   = unclear trend or conflicting evidence
    = no information on this indicator for this country
*   = where this indicator is based on the ratio of monthly salaries to hourly wages, cessation of narrowing is interpreted as equivalent to widening for other indicators, for reasons explained in Sect. A4.1.
** = each country's 'overall score' (rounded to one decimal place) is calculated by averaging across all the available indicators, assigning the following values (alternative values are discussed in the text):
      ++   = 5
      (++) = 3
      +   = 2
      (+) = 1
      0   = 0
      ?   = 0
      −   = 0

Sources (see also notes to Table 7.2): Education indicators: App. A3; wages by age: Davis (1992, table 2B and, for Japan, fig. 4B); occupational wages, vacancies: App. A4; wage dispersion: App. A5. Note that the unemployment and vacancy results for Germany are both based on Franz (1991), in preference to other sources, for reasons given in Apps. A3 and A4.

rather more cases, these forces apparently continued to constrain the widening of wage differentials, especially among blue-collar workers. As a result, there was also a general (though not universal) widening of skill differentials in unemployment and vacancy rates.

On the face of it, then, the evidence on movements in skill differentials in the North is clearly consistent with the expected effects of changes in trade with the South, which were shown in earlier chapters to have reduced the demand for less-skilled labour. Of course, these movements might also be consistent with other explanations, which will be considered later. An essential preliminary step, though, is to look more closely at the apparent consistency of the evidence with the North–South trade hypothesis. Does this explanation really stand up to scrutiny, or are there discrepancies which cannot readily be accounted for? The examination of consistency in the following five subsections considers timing, magnitude, inter-country variations, differences between males and females, and tests of related hypotheses in other studies.

7.2.1 Timing

The first issue is whether and to what extent the observed movements in skill differentials in the North coincided in time with the changes in trade (or more precisely with the predicted effects of these changes).

Prediction

As explained in Section 6.1.3, the removal of barriers to trade in theory causes a once-and-for-all change in relative factor prices, but in reality this change may be protracted. The case of most relevance in the previous chapter was of a Southern country switching from an import-substituting to an export-oriented trade strategy. The effects of such a switch on skill differentials appear to be spread over a period of about ten years. The same theoretical point applies to the North. In practice, moreover, the timing of the skill differential changes in the North must in some way be related to the timing of the counterpart changes in its Southern trading partners. This step change in the North, however, is likely to have been spread over much more than a ten-year period.

One reason for this, discussed in Section 5.4.1, is that the impact of changes in trade with the South on Northern labour markets was initially cushioned by changes in profitability in Northern product markets. More specifically, the North initially had a large amount of installed capacity in low-skill-intensive activities. The ultimate effect of the reduction in trade barriers was to eliminate this capacity, but the immediate effect was simply to reduce its profitability. This decline in profits soon deterred new investment in such activities, and hence reduced the incremental demand for unskilled labour. However, it was economically rational to continue using the existing capacity, and to go on employing its workers, so long as prices covered marginal costs. Only as Southern competition intensified, and existing Northern plants had to be shut down (a process which was quite protracted), were the full effects transmitted into the labour market.

The other reason why the effects of this trade on skill differentials in the North were spread out over a longer period than in the South is that the reduction in trade barriers was more protracted. For the developing countries concerned, the most important element of barrier reduction may well have been the (quite rapid) changes in their own trade policies. But from the viewpoint of developed countries, these policy switches were only one of several causes of change in North–South trade (discussed in Section 5.1), and not necessarily the most important. Most of the other causes were more gradual, particularly the fall in transport and communications costs, and the process of learning how to manage and co-ordinate globally dispersed manufacturing activities. Finally, the switches of trade policy in the South did not all occur simultaneously: Hong Kong started to export labour-intensive manufactures in the 1950s, Taiwan and Korea in the early 1960s, Singapore in the late 1960s, and a series of other countries in the 1970s and 1980s.

During the three decades 1960–1990, the trend growth rate of the South's manufactured exports to the North did not change much, though there were year-to-year variations (see Fig. 5.1). What did change, however, is that the absolute increments in export volume became larger and larger. In particular, the absolute increase in the South's manufactured exports during the 1980s was about 2.5 times as large (at constant prices) as the absolute increase over the two previous decades combined (see Fig. 1.1). Manufacturing production in the North also expanded during these decades, but not nearly so rapidly as manufactured imports from the South, and hence the absolute increments in Southern import penetration ratios also became larger and larger.

This point is highly relevant to the timing of the trade-induced changes in skill differentials in the North, because the magnitude of these changes clearly depends on the absolute rather than the proportional increase in the volume of trade. Doubling a large volume of manufactured imports, for instance, would displace far more domestic production than quintupling a tiny volume of imports. The phasing of Southern export expansion and the initial cushioning effect of the profitability decline thus both predict that the trade-induced widening of skill differentials would have occurred largely in the latter part of the period.

The prediction, however, has to be qualified in three ways. One is that the skill composition of labour demand in the North was also affected (though to a lesser extent) by labour-intensive import substitution in the South, which was probably concentrated in the earlier part of the period. A second is that the displacement of manufacturing activities in the North probably proceeded approximately in diminishing order of unskilled labour intensity, so that the adverse impact of a given increase in the volume of imports from the South on the demand for *BAS-ED* labour became smaller over time.[5] The third qualification is that the timing of defensive innovation, which also affected the skill composition of labour demand, may not have paralleled that of the changes in Southern import penetration.

Out-turn

If these qualifications are set aside, the prediction appears consistent with the timing of the change in skill differentials. For it was in the 1980s, rather than in earlier decades, that widening of these differentials became common in the North, both in its spread across countries and in its spread across different statistical indicators of skill. Moreover, what seem upon more detailed examination to be discrepancies in timing can fairly easily be reconciled with the North–South trade explanation.

One such apparent discrepancy concerns the 1970s, when trade should also have been tending to widen skill differentials, but most of them narrowed. The reasons for this narrowing, though, are not controversial, and were mentioned earlier. The most important and widespread was rapid expansion of higher education, which shifted the relative supply of skilled labour faster than the relative demand. This squeezed not only education-related differentials, but also the associated gaps between higher and lower white-collar workers and between all white-collar and blue-collar workers. In addition, in some countries, skill differentials in wages were compressed during the 1970s by incomes policies and union wage bargaining strategies. However, the relative demand for less-skilled labour does appear to have been declining in this decade, albeit more slowly than in the 1980s.[6]

Another apparent discrepancy concerns the youth unemployment rate in the 1980s, which declined relative to the rate among adults (at least during the first half of the decade). This improvement in the relative position of a less-skilled group is at variance with all the other indications of widening skill differentials. Over the longer period between the early 1970s and the mid-1980s, though, the relative youth unemployment rate had risen, which is in accordance with the expected effects of a fall in the relative demand for less-skilled labour. The widening of this particular skill differential occurred earlier than for the education-related and occupational indicators because the effects of the demand shift were not offset by a supply shift. Indeed, in most Northern countries for part of the

---

[5] Autonomous growth of labour productivity should have a similar effect: because each unit of output embodies progressively less labour, the impact of a given volume of trade on labour demand declines.

[6] See Katz and Murphy (1992) and Murphy and Welch (1992), discussed at the end of Sect. A3.3, as well as Bound and Johnson (1992: 385–6).

period 1960–90, a supply shift in the form of a rise in the relative size of the youth cohort reinforced the demand shift.

The partial reversal during the 1980s of the rise in the relative youth unemployment rate probably had different causes in different countries. The general decline in the relative wages of young workers, which priced some of them back into employment, may have been the main cause in the USA and Canada (Myles, Picot, and Wannell 1988: 90–5). In Europe, the change appears to have been mainly the result of government actions—spurred by public concern about large-scale youth unemployment—involving a mixture of training, public work programmes, and subsidies to employers (EC 1987; Marsden 1989*a*: 2.9). Part of the reversal of the uptrend in the relative youth unemployment rate may also have been a statistical illusion, caused by increasing withdrawal of young people from the labour force.[7]

7.2.2 Magnitude

The second issue of consistency is whether the *size* of the movements in skill differentials accords with the North–South trade explanation.

Prediction

Chapter 4 of this book tried to estimate, for the North as a whole, the general magnitude of the trade-induced shift in the relative demand for skilled and unskilled labour. The most precise calculations are of the factor content of noncompeting trade in manufactures, which suggest that the cumulative effect up to 1990 was to raise the economy-wide demand for *SKILD* relative to *BAS-ED* labour by about 5½ per cent, plus or minus roughly 2 percentage points. These calculations do not allow for trade-induced unskilled-labour-saving innovation, nor for effects in non-manufacturing sectors, each of which (it was argued in Section 4.4.3, on the basis of much less information) would approximately double the estimated impact. The total increase in the demand for *SKILD* relative to *BAS-ED* labour was thus probably between 14 per cent and 30 per cent (around a central value of 22 per cent).

How much this demand shift would tend to widen skill differentials depends on demand and supply elasticities. The relevant substitution (or demand) elasticity appears to be in the region of unity (Section 6.1.2). Thus to induce the continued employment of the same numbers of *SKILD* and *BAS-ED* workers, in the face of a 14–30 per cent increase in

---

[7] See e.g. Edward Balls, 'Youth "non-employment" in Britain and France', *Financial Times*, 30 Sept. 1991.

relative demand, the relative wage of *SKILD* workers would also have to rise by 14–30 per cent.

In practice, the required wage change would be smaller than this, because the elasticity of relative supply must be greater than zero (Section 2.4.3). The only evidence on the size of this elasticity appears to be from studies of the choice by high-school graduates of whether to go to college, which depends on the wage premium earned by college graduates. These studies (summarised by Freeman 1986: 372) put the supply elasticity for this age group between 1 and 2, both in the USA and in the UK. It is presumably lower for the labour force as a whole in the short and medium run, since changes in the educational qualifications of new entrants have only a small immediate impact on the total supply of college graduates.

Even without information on the exact size of the supply elasticity, the *upper limit* of the relative wage change can be predicted, as is true also if institutional forces constrain the widening of wage differentials. In the latter case, skill differentials in vacancy and unemployment rates should have widened instead, but not necessarily to the same extent.[8] Moreover, the information on these quantity indicators is patchier, which favours limiting this consistency test to relative wage movements. The prediction would thus be that the changes in trade tended to widen skill differentials in wages by *up to* 14–30 per cent.

Testing the trade hypothesis on the basis of this prediction is of course complicated by the likelihood that wage differentials were also affected by other shifts in demand and supply, for which it is not possible to control accurately. However, this problem can be alleviated by confining the test to the 1980s, since supply shifts were particularly important in the 1970s, and since about 70 per cent of the trade-induced demand shift probably occurred in the 1980s (judging, as before, from the increases in Southern manufactured exports). This figure of 70 per cent can also be used to scale down the predicted upper limit range of the relative wage change, from 14–30 per cent to 10–21 per cent.

Out-turn

This prediction is based on a coarse breakdown between *SKILD* and *BAS-ED* labour, and refers to the North as a whole, whereas the available data on changes in relative wages (summarised in Table 7.2) use assorted measures of skill, and refer to particular countries. The best estimates of the *SKILD/BAS-ED* relativity are perhaps provided by the third/first quartile ratios in the wage dispersion column, since the

[8] This depends on the responsiveness (if any) of relative demand and supply to shortages and surpluses of labour, and on the accuracy with which shortages and surpluses are reflected in unemployment and vacancy rates.

TABLE 7.2. *Standardised magnitudes of increases in skill differentials in wages in the North, 1970–1990* (percentage increase over period shown – where symbol instead of number, see key below)

| | Education university/secondary | | Age 40s/late 20s | | Occupational differentials | | | | | | Wage dispersion Q75/Q25 ratios | |
| | | | | | White/blue* | | Intra-white | | Intra-blue | | | |
	1970–90	1980–90	Trough-87	1980–90	1970–90	1980–90	1970–90	1980–90	1970–90	1980–90	1970–90	1980–90
Australia	–	6		19	5	8		9		0		44**
Austria						–						6
Belgium												
Canada	–	4	7	26	–	3	–	1			14	11
Denmark					–	+			–	0		+**
Finland					–	+						
France		5	34	25	–	–	–	0	–	–		0**
Germany		15		94	17	8	6	7	–	?		58**
Italy	–	4			–	(+)	–	(+)	–			
Japan	3	5	15	13	–	0			–			
Netherlands		?		20		0						9
New Zealand												3**
Norway						+	–	?				
Sweden		5	7	3	–	–	2	13			–	29**
Switzerland						+						
UK	–	29	10	12	16	15	14	17	3	8	13	13
USA	10	15	22	21	8	10	11	15	15	11	34	17

Key to symbols:

+ = widening skill differential whose magnitude cannot be comparably measured
(+) = as above, but widening only in latter part of 1980s
− = narrowing skill differential over the period
0 = no trend
? = unclear trend or conflicting evidence
* = no information on this indicator for this country
** = where this indicator is based on the ratio of monthly salaries to hourly wages, calculation of magnitude of change is not possible
** = dispersion measure other than Q75/Q25.

Note: Increases shown are standardised for the differing lengths of the periods covered by the data. The standardisation procedure, which is applied separately within each decade (1970–80 and 1980–90), assumes that the annual proportional rate of increase in the indicator was constant throughout the decade. The result for 1970–90 is then obtained by combining the results for the two decades. Wherever possible, three-year averages are used as starting and end-points.

Sources and specific notes: Education indicators: App. A3. Australia, Canada, Germany, and Sweden numbers based on Davis (1992, table 3). Japan numbers refer to starting salaries. USA numbers refer to all experience levels and to the decades 1969–79 and 1979–89.

Wages by age: Davis (1992, tables 2A and 2B, and fig. 4B). 'Trough-87' refers to the change between the lowest value of this indicator during 1960–90 and its value in 1987. The data in the two age columns are from different sources, and are not comparable.

Occupational differentials: App. A4. For the intra-white collar series, the German numbers are adjusted to eliminate the effect of the 1982–3 discontinuity, and the Swedish numbers for the two decades are from different sources.

Wage dispersion: App. A5 and Davis (1992, fig. 1B, Australia and Germany). Canada, UK, and USA data are from the same sources as in Fig. A5.1, but refer to different quantiles (Q75/Q25 rather than Q90/Q10), for reasons explained in text. For some countries, only non-quantile measures of dispersion are available.

Northern labour force is divided more or less equally between these two skill groups (Table 4.9). The other measures of wage dispersion in that column, and the education, age, and occupational wage ratios, are worse approximations, but may give some guide to the size of changes in the overall *SKILD/BAS-ED* wage ratio. For ease of reading, the table provides numerical estimates only for differentials that have widened—narrowing is noted symbolically. Although the main emphasis is on the 1980s, the table also wherever possible shows the combined change over the two decades 1970–90.

Although many of the numbers in Table 7.2 are rather inaccurate, the size of most of them is consistent with the predicted upper limit effect of the change in trade. Ten of the sixty-one observations for the 1980s are cases where the increase cannot be quantified or the trend is unclear. Of the other fifty-one cases, sixteen are between 10 per cent and 21 per cent (the predicted upper limit range), and twenty-eight lie below this range, including five cases in which differentials narrowed (presumably because of institutional pressures). In only seven cases is the increase in the 1980s above the predicted range.

One of these cases is the education relativity in the UK: its sharp rise might be the result of mismeasurement (Davis 1992, table 3 estimates the increase at about 10 per cent), but could also partly reflect relaxation of the institutional compression of wage differentials that had occurred during the 1970s. Three other anomalous cases are in the wage dispersion column: each is based on a measure of dispersion which is more sensitive than the third/first quartile ratio to the extremes of the wage distribution, which seem to have diverged by more than the overall *SKILD/BAS-ED* relativity.[9] The remaining three anomalous cases are in the age column, and may have been caused by simultaneous supply-side shifts.[10]

Another suspiciously large number in Table 7.2 is the increase in wage dispersion in the USA over the longer period 1970–90. The third/first quartile ratio rose by 34 per cent, which is somewhat greater than the 30 per cent upper limit of the estimated range of the trade-induced demand shift during the full period 1960–90. The discrepancy arises not during the 1980s, but in the 1970s, a decade for which different studies of wage dispersion in the USA have reached markedly different conclusions (Section A5.1). However, the estimates in the source used for this table are similar to those of Davis (1992, fig. 1A). The unusually large increase in wage dispersion in the USA is thus probably genuine, and requires some explanation.

[9] For Australia and Germany, the measure is the standard deviation of logs, and for Sweden the ratio of the top to the bottom decile. In the three countries in which a comparison is possible (Canada, the UK, and the USA), the proportional increase in Q90/Q10 was greater than in Q75/Q25.
[10] Although there are probably also measurement errors (esp. with the huge German increase, which is calculated from two different household surveys: Davis 1992, table 1).

In principle, this anomaly might reflect the unusually large increase in Southern import penetration in the USA (see Fig. 7.1), or the effects of illegal unskilled immigration. However, it could also indicate that the rise in the relative demand for skilled labour caused by more trade with the South was amplified by some other force (the most plausible being new technology, discussed in the next section). This interpretation has the virtue of being able to explain why, despite a large rise in the relative supply of skilled (or at least college-educated) labour during 1970–90, wage dispersion widened by more than the trade-induced shift in demand.

This line of reasoning also requires some qualifications to the results of all these magnitude comparisons, including the great majority in the 1980s which appear to support the trade hypothesis by being below the predicted upper limit. It is established for the USA (Bound and Johnson 1992, table 6), and likely for other Northern countries, that the shift increase in the relative supply of most sorts of skilled labour continued during the 1980s, albeit more slowly than in the 1970s. The upper limit of the widening of skill differentials in wages should therefore have been *smaller* than the trade-induced shift in demand, which means that the sixteen cases in Table 7.2 which lie in the 10–21 per cent range could be interpreted as implying that some other force, such as new technology was amplifying the demand shift.

7.2.3 Cross-country variation

Although there is some evidence of widening skill differentials during the 1980s in all the Northern countries for which data are available, Tables 7.1 and 7.2 suggest that there was considerable variation among countries in the size and even the direction of the changes in particular indicators. Some of this variation surely arises from noncomparability or inaccuracy of the underlying data. Moreover, the quantity of information on movements in skill differentials seems too limited to permit a proper explanation of the inter-country differences. However, it is worth considering whether these variations are consistent with the hypothesis that the general widening of skill differentials was caused by changes in North–South trade.

The mere existence of variations in the outcome does not cast doubt on the hypothesis. There are three sorts of reason why the impact of changes in trade with the South on skill differentials should differ from country to country within the North. One (discussed earlier, in the 'cross-country variation' subsection of 5.4.2) is that the extent and character of the changes in trade varied, partly because of differences in natural barriers and artificial trade restrictions, and partly because of differences among Northern countries in the supply of skilled relative to less-skilled labour (which shapes their comparative advantage *vis-à-vis* the South). The second reason is the varying influence of other forces causing simultaneous shifts in the relative demand for, and supply of, skilled and unskilled labour. The third is differences in institutional pressures on relative wages.

Within this framework, a more specific test of consistency is to examine the cross-country correlation between movements in skill differentials and changes in trade with the South. If other influences are controlled for, the correlation should be positive—more widening of skill differentials in countries with greater increases in exposure to trade with the South. The measure of trade exposure to be used for this purpose is the ratio of (narrowly defined) manufactured imports from the South to GDP, with the change in exposure being measured by the absolute increase in this ratio between 1970 and 1985. The reasons for choosing this specification, and some of the limitations of this measure, were discussed in Chapter 5 (in connection with its use in Fig. 5.10).

It is harder to control for influences on skill differential movements other than trade. The evidence reviewed earlier (Section 7.1) suggests that some skill differentials were affected by changes in the supply of highly educated labour. In principle, it should be simple to control for this supply shift, but in practice data on the educational composition of the labour force over time were available for only a few countries until very recently.[11] All that was generally available was the tertiary education enrolment ratio, which is a seriously defective proxy. So to reduce the need for a control, the analysis was restricted to skill differential changes during the 1980s, when shifts in educational supply appear to have been less important than in the 1970s. (However, this restriction worsens the correspondence of time periods with the trade variable, which refers to 1970–85.)

Constructing a suitable dependent variable from the mixture of information on changes in skill differentials in Tables 7.1 and 7.2 is even more of a problem. It seems vital in some way to combine the data on wage movements with that on changes in relative unemployment (and vacancy) rates, since the impact of the demand shift depended on the strength of institutional pressures on wage differentials. It also seems appropriate, in order to offset some of the noncomparabilities between indicators and countries, not to pay too much attention to differences in the exact sizes of particular indicators. Finally, in order to keep up the number of countries in the sample, and the number of indicators for each country, it is desirable to make use of information on the direction of change even where its size cannot be calculated (as in about a dozen of the cases in Table 7.1).

[11] Only after the completion of this book did the availability of time-series educational data greatly improve, thanks to the work of Barro and Lee (1993).

With these principles in mind, a composite measure of the change in skill differentials was derived for each country from the information in Table 7.1 (shown in the 'overall score' column). The score is arrived at by assigning a particular numerical value to each of the symbols, and then averaging these values across all the available indicators. For example, a double plus counts for 5 and a single plus for 2, while minuses and queries as well as actual zeros count for zero. (The notes to the table contain the full list of values.) The maximum possible score for a country is 5, and the minimum zero: in practice, the range is from 0.7 in Norway to 4.0 in Australia.

This summary measure of the extent of the change in skill differentials is plotted in Fig. 7.1 as a scatter against the import penetration change variable. Visual inspection suggests a strong positive correlation. This is confirmed by an OLS regression, whose slope coefficient is significantly different from zero (at the 1 per cent level on a two-tailed t-test). It explains about half the cross-country variation in skill differential movements ($R^2 = 0.49$). Moreover, much of the unexplained variance is clearly due to only one country—Belgium, which lies well below the line, perhaps because the summary score does not give enough weight to its massive rise in unskilled unemployment (Tables A3.5, 8.2).

If Belgium is excluded from the regression, not only does R^2 rise to 0.72, but the slope of the line becomes steeper (as shown in the figure), causing it to pass virtually through the origin, which is what would be expected if the changes in trade with the South were the main cause of the widening of skill differentials in the North. The second largest deviation is the UK, which lies well above the line, perhaps because the sharp widening of wage differentials in the 1980s was in part simply a reversal of their forcible compression in the 1970s.

The sensitivity of the results to variations in the scoring system can be investigated. Alternative positive scores for the plus signs make little difference. Assigning a value of –2 to the minus signs makes the positive association much less significant (only at the 10 per cent level). Dropping the unemployment and vacancy indicators from the overall scores renders the correlation insignificant, because it leaves Belgium, the country with the largest increase in import penetration, with a single negative indicator of skill differential change. Even if Belgium is excluded, the association is weaker ($R^2 = 0.46$, compared with 0.72 if unemployment and vacancies are included), mainly because the scores for France, Italy, and The Netherlands are pulled down, away from the regression line. This experiment tends to confirm that the widening of wage differentials has been institutionally constrained in Europe, and has therefore emerged largely as a widening of skill differentials in unemployment and vacancy rates.

The limitations of the data, which preclude the application of more powerful statistical methods, should be reiterated. It would be wrong to

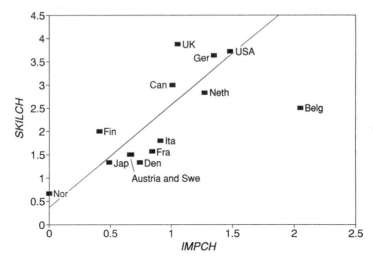

F<small>IG</small>. 7.1 Changes in skill differentials and trade with the South
Notes and sources: The regression line shown was estimated excluding Belgium. The equation of the line (*t*-statistic in parentheses) is

$$SKILCH = 0.37 + 2.20 IMPCH \qquad R^2 = 0.72$$
$$(5.29)$$

Had Belgium been included, the equation would have been

$$SKILCH = 0.93 + 1.41 IMPCH \qquad R^2 = 0.49$$
$$(3.40)$$

SKILCH is composite measure of skill differential widening, including wage, unemployment, and vacancy indicators (overall score column of Table 7.1).

IMPCH is absolute increase between 1970 and 1985 in import penetration ratio (narrowly defined manufactured imports from the South as percentage of GDP in the Northern country concerned). For sources, see notes to Fig. 5.6. This variable is not available for Australia, New Zealand, and Switzerland.

rely solely or heavily on this sort of correlation, either as evidence that trade with the South has been the cause of widening skill differentials in the North, or as a description of the way in which the effects of this trade have varied among countries. But it can be asserted with much more confidence that the cross-country variations in the skill differential data are not inconsistent with the North–South trade explanation. There are clear signs of a positive association, and none of a negative association. This is important, among other reasons, because it reinforces the argument (in Section 5.1.2) that expansion of trade with the South was autonomous, not caused by a growing scarcity of less-skilled labour in the North.[12]

7.2.4 Males and females

Several studies of the USA have noted that the widening of skill differentials in wages during the 1980s coincided with a narrowing of the gap in wages between male and female workers (for example, Murphy and Welch 1989, and Bound and Johnson 1992). The ratio of female to male employment also rose, which implies that the narrowing of the wage gap was caused mainly by an increase in the relative demand for female labour. In other Northern countries, too, there is evidence of a similar shift: the share of females in total employment has risen almost everywhere; and in most countries the female–male wage ratio has also increased during the past two or three decades, albeit at varying times and to varying degrees (Chiplin and Sloane 1988: 833; Katz and Loveman 1990).[13]

These trends, and their variation among countries, were surely influenced by many forces, including legislative efforts to reduce gender differences in pay and employment opportunities. It is beyond the scope of this book to examine them properly. However, it seems important to ask whether the general and more or less simultaneous increase in the relative demand for female labour is or is not consistent with the hypothesis that the widening of skill differentials was caused by changes in North–South trade.

On the face of it, there would appear to be an inconsistency. Women are over-represented in the sectors on which manufactured imports from the South have been concentrated, and under-represented in the manufacturing sectors which export to the South (Schumacher 1984, table 1; 1989, tables A.8, A.10). Women are also over-represented among trade-displaced workers (Baldwin 1984: 593). This evidence suggests that trade with developing countries has tended to reduce, rather than increase, the relative demand for female labour in manufacturing.

[12] For if a growing scarcity of unskilled labour had been the cause, one would expect a *negative* association (more import penetration in countries where skill differentials had widened least or narrowed most). However, this evidence is not conclusive, because the time-periods of the dependent and independent variables in Fig. 7.1 are poorly matched. In particular, the import penetration change variable spans the 1970s, when many skill differentials narrowed, as well as the first half of the 1980s.

[13] Japan may be an exception: the data on wages by education and age underlying Table A3.4 do not show a clear and general narrowing of the male–female wage gap, either for university graduates or at lower levels of schooling. This exception would not necessarily contradict the argument (in the last paragraph of this subsection) that trade with the South has tended to benefit female workers. For although the female intensity of Japanese manufacturing is unusually high, especially among blue-collar workers (Wood 1991a, tables 2, 4), Japan has experienced a comparatively small increase in Southern import penetration and a comparatively small decline in the share of manufacturing in total employment (Fig. 5.10).

Close examination of the data, however, gives a different impression (Wood 1991a). The female intensity of Northern manufacturing did not generally decline between the early 1960s and the mid-1980s, either absolutely or relative to nontraded sectors. There were declines in some countries and increases in others, but these cross-country variations seem uncorrelated with the extent of Southern import penetration. Further work is needed on reconciling this finding with those of the other studies mentioned in the previous paragraph, but one possible explanation is that displaced female workers are more easily reabsorbed into other manufacturing sectors than displaced males, because they have fewer sector-specific skills.[14]

In any event, the relative demand for female labour within manufacturing does not generally appear to have declined. Moreover, manufacturing is a comparatively male-intensive sector: on average across Northern countries the female–male employment ratio in manufacturing is less than three-fifths of the corresponding ratio in nontraded sectors (Wood 1991a, table 2). Thus if, as argued in Section 5.4.2, trade with the South has reduced the share of manufacturing in total Northern employment, it must also have tended to reduce the relative economy-wide demand for male labour.[15] In this way, the simultaneous improvements in the economic position of women and of skilled workers may be reconciled with the trade explanation.

7.2.5 Related tests in other studies

In the USA, a number of studies have argued that the widening of skill differentials in wages in the 1980s was caused by changes in foreign trade. Reich (1989; 1991, especially chs. 16–17) concludes from various sorts of evidence that this trend reflects the increased integration of the USA into the world labour market. Workers who provide 'routine production services' have suffered from competition with foreign workers, but skilled 'symbolic analysts' have gained because 'the services they have to offer are quite scarce in the context of the whole world' (1989: 27).

Murphy and Welch (1989, 1992) suggest more specifically that the emergence of a large trade deficit, particularly in durable manufactures, may have been the main cause. They support their argument with calculations based on three traded sectors (durables, nondurables, and services) and a single nontraded sector (1989: 23–9). Actual changes in the distrib-

---

[14] Bean and Pissarides (1991, table 7.2) note that the duration of unemployment is shorter for females than for males in the UK.

[15] Booroah and Lee (1988) show that changes in the sectoral structure of employment in the UK have increased the economy-wide relative demand for female workers, as do some of the studies of the USA discussed in Sect. 7.2.5 (though these are criticised by Bound and Johnson 1992: 381).

ution of total employment among these four sectors correspond reasonably well with those predicted from changes in trade flows. Moreover,
using information on the education, sex, and racial composition of
employment within each of these sectors, Murphy and Welch discover
that the changes in the sectoral structure of employment (both the actual
changes and those predicted from trade flows) imply shifts in the education, sex, and racial composition of total employment which correspond
reasonably well with observed movements in relative wages.

Bound and Johnson (1992), by contrast, conclude that shifts in sectoral
structure cannot explain the changing pattern of US relative wages in the
1980s. They argue that the effects of these shifts may not even have been
in the right direction, and were certainly too small to have offset supply
shifts in the opposite direction. The difference in results arises partly from
a different method of estimating product demand shifts (to counter a possible bias in the method used by Murphy and Welch), and partly because
Bound and Johnson work with seventeen rather than four sectors, expos-
ing conflicting pressures on the skill composition of labour demand. Thus
the share of manufacturing, a large employer of less-educated males,
declined, but so did the share of two sectors which employ a lot of
college-educated labour—education and public administration.

Katz and Murphy (1992) use an even larger number of sectors. They
find that shifts in employment among fifty industries (and three occupations) explain 'a large minority' of the rise in the relative demand for
skilled workers during 1963–87, but that most of this rise occurred *within*
industries and occupations (ibid. 76). Katz and Murphy also find that
changes in trade, by altering the industrial structure of employment, contributed to this shift in the skill composition of demand (ibid. 63–6). The
trade effect seems small, especially prior to the 1980s, but is larger if
imports and exports are treated asymmetrically (as, in a different way,
they are in Chapter 4 of the present book). Katz and Murphy also note
that trade, in the form of 'shifts of portions of industry production out of
the United States', is among the 'important sources of within-industry
shifts' in the skill composition of labour demand (ibid. 54).

Other North American studies have examined the contribution of
changes in industrial structure to increased wage dispersion. In the USA,
Bluestone (1990: 305–6) and Harrison and Bluestone (1990: 361–2) maintain that the rise in dispersion was partly caused by the shift of employment towards services, away from goods in general and manufacturing in
particular. However, Lawrence (1984) argued earlier that the effect of the
decline in manufacturing must have been small, since the dispersion of
wages within manufacturing does not differ much from the average in
other sectors. The calculations of Juhn, Murphy, and Pierce (1989, table
6) confirm this view: changes in the industrial structure of employment
contributed only 11 per cent of the increase in overall wage variance

between 1979 and 1987, and not much more (16 per cent) during 1967–87. Similarly, Picot, Myles, and Wannell (1990: 21) calculate that in Canada changes in the industrial structure of employment explain only 13 per cent of the 1981–6 change in the overall wage distribution.

Few of the studies which propose or test the hypothesis that trade caused the widening of skill differentials distinguish clearly between trade with the South and trade with all partners. An exception is Davis (1992), who puts forward essentially the same line of argument as in the present book, namely that reduction of trade barriers has caused skill differentials to converge, becoming narrower in the South and wider in the North. He shows that skill differentials did narrow in four Southern countries during the 1980s. However, he does not establish empirically that this narrowing was associated with expansion of trade with the North, and he recognises that it could have had other causes. (In one of his four countries— Korea—the narrowing of skill differentials during the 1980s is much more likely to have been caused by educational expansion: see Section 6.3.2.)

Davis also notes that, in theory, the convergence of skill differentials should be associated with convergence of inter-industry wage differentials. He tests this latter hypothesis, using data on wages in manufacturing in about twenty countries (of which one-third are Southern) from the mid-1970s to the late 1980s. The simple version of the hypothesis is strongly rejected by the data: inter-industry wage relativities appear to have. become less rather than more similar (within the Northern sub-group as well as in the full country sample). However, there was a significant but small tendency for these relativities to converge more (or diverge less) in Northern countries which had become more open to trade (as measured by the ratio of trade, particularly imports, to GDP).

The results of these various studies seem reasonably consistent with the hypothesis that the widening of skill differentials was caused by changes in trade with the South. One effect of this trade has been to reduce the employment share of manufacturing and other traded sectors. There should thus be some association (as most of these studies have found) between the widening of skill differentials and changes in the sectoral structure of employment. However, the essence of the hypothesis is that the reduction of employment in traded sectors is a by-product of changes in their internal skill structure (more specialisation in skill-intensive prod-ucts and activities, and elimination of labour-intensive ones). Thus it also seems consistent that the widening of skill differentials has apparently arisen more from intra-sectoral than from inter-sectoral pressures.[16]

---

[16] Similarly, Jackman, Layard, and Savouri (1991: 60) note that the rate of inter-industry structural change (or 'turbulence') has been lower in recent decades than in the inter-war period, while Abraham (1991: 457) emphasises that the skill composition of demand within industries could have changed without much affecting their shares of total employment.

7.3 Another Explanation: New Technology

The preceding section established the consistency of the North–South trade explanation of widening skill differentials with several sorts of evidence (on timing, magnitude, cross-country variation, males and females, and from other studies). The main purpose of this section is to examine a plausible alternative explanation: the diffusion of new technology with an autonomous unskilled-labour-saving bias.

7.3.1 Competing interpretations

Before turning to new technology, however, it is convenient to look briefly at a number of other possible (but less plausible) explanations of widening skill differentials, some of which were considered in Section 7.1 (and are discussed at more length in Appendices A3–A5).

Political pressures and supply-side shifts

It has sometimes been argued that the widening of skill differentials was caused mainly by political and ideological changes which made institutional influences on wages less egalitarian. Such changes undoubtedly occurred. There was a general political shift in the 1980s, away from regulation of markets and reduction of income inequality. In some countries, this shift included measures to weaken unions and minimum wage laws, and to reduce the level and availability of unemployment benefits. There can be little doubt that these policy changes helped to widen wage differentials, especially in the USA and the UK.[17]

At the same time, it is impossible to believe that these political changes in institutional mechanisms fully explain the general widening of skill differentials in the 1980s. Even as regards wages, this tendency was too persistent and too pervasive across countries, apparently regardless of their political complexion and specific labour-market policy changes. It also seems to have started in the USA well before the election of President Reagan, and in the UK somewhat before Mrs Thatcher. More crucially, skill differentials in unemployment and vacancy rates generally appear to have widened even where wage differentials did not, which strongly implies the presence of some more fundamental shift in the balance between relative demand and relative supply.

---

[17] However, other inegalitarian policy changes, such as reducing the progressivity of taxation and government expenditure, probably had little or no effect on pre-tax relative wages. If anything, to the extent that taxes are shifted, diminished progressivity should have tended to narrow rather than widen wage differentials.

The evidence summarised in Sections 7.1.1 and 7.1.2 suggests that this shift did not occur mainly on the supply side. The slower expansion of higher education in the 1980s in some countries probably made the widening of skill differentials larger than it would otherwise have been, and in the USA this tendency may have been amplified by illegal unskilled immigration. It might even be argued that higher real interest rates in the 1980s caused an upward shift in the supply curve of skilled labour by raising the cost of education and training. But in no country does the relative supply of skilled workers actually appear to have declined.

Another sort of supply-side explanation focuses on the rising non-wage costs of employing labour (fringe benefits and social insurance). In so far as these costs are the same in absolute terms for all workers, they raise the relative cost of unskilled labour. In principle, this could explain the widening of skill differentials in unemployment rates (to the extent that relative wages are rigid), and in wages (to the extent that they are flexible and non-wage costs are shifted).[18] Moreover, in Belgium, Germany, and the UK, non-wage costs as a proportion of total labour costs did rise faster for manual than for non-manual workers between 1966 and 1981 (OECD-EO 1986, table 30). In France and Italy, however, there was little change, and there is no evidence of further general movement in this direction in the 1980s, when most of the widening of skill differentials occurred.

In short, explanations which do not include declining relative demand for unskilled labour seem unable to account satisfactorily for the widening of skill differentials. Expansion of trade with the South, moreover, has been presented above as a theoretically and empirically well-grounded reason for such a shift in relative demand. But it is not the only possible reason. In principle, that is, one might accept that the widening of differentials was the result of a decline in the relative demand for unskilled workers, while attributing this decline to some completely different cause. (Nor, of course, are the consistency tests of the North–South trade hypothesis in the previous section sufficient to establish its correctness, since some other explanation of the demand shift might be even more consistent with a wider range of evidence.)

---

[18] This point was made to me by Michael Lipton, who notes that it could also explain the expansion of labour-intensive imports from the South, and unskilled-labour-saving innovation. Non-wage labour costs are discussed at length in OECD-EO (1986, ch. IV). Their effects can be analysed using the diagrams in Ch. 10. If proportionally higher for unskilled than for skilled workers, such costs tend to widen wage differentials for two reasons: (*a*) they increase the relative demand for skilled labour, and (*b*) they reduce the relative supply of skilled labour (higher benefits for unskilled workers make it less attractive to become a skilled worker). The net effect on the ratio of skilled to unskilled employment is ambiguous if relative wages are flexible.

Other influences on relative demand

Economic theory permits an exhaustive taxonomy of reasons for a decline in the relative demand for unskilled labour. The possibilities are: (*a*) a shift in the structure of demand in product markets towards more skill-intensive goods, due to changes either in domestic demand or in the pattern of foreign trade; (*b*) an increase in the supply of some other factor of production complementary to skill (or substitutable for unskilled labour); and (*c*) a general skill-using change in production technology. It is the third of these categories which will receive most attention below, but a few hypotheses in the other two categories also deserve mention.

In category (*b*), faster growth of the stock of physical capital, to which skilled labour is believed to be complementary, might in principle have widened skill differentials during the 1980s. However, this explanation seems inconsistent with the evidence on the share of investment in GDP, which in each of the seven largest Northern countries was lower during 1980–9 than during 1970–9 and, except for Italy, 1960–9.[19]

Within category (*a*), where the North–South trade explanation is located, there are two other candidates. One is changes in the composition of domestic final demand in the North: consumer tastes might have shifted spontaneously towards relatively skill-intensive goods and services; or there might have been a similar movement in the structure of government consumption or of investment expenditures. Casual observation sheds little light on this hypothesis, since many conflicting instances spring to mind, and it does not appear to have been empirically tested (though in principle it could be, given sufficiently detailed data on the composition of final output, and on the prices and factor content of all the items involved).

The other candidate in category (*a*) is North–North trade. In value terms, this trade is far larger than North–South trade. From a theoretical point of view, however, it is not nearly such an obvious explanation of widening skill differentials. This is because most North–North trade appears to be based on increasing returns to scale and product differentiation, rather than on differences in relative factor endowments (as in the case of North–South trade). If correct, this assessment rules out the usual (Heckscher–Ohlin) theoretical reason, expounded in Chapter 2, for supposing that trade affects skill differentials.

Factor content of trade studies support this conclusion. They show that differences between the skill intensity of exports and imports are small for

---

[19] IMF *International Financial Statistics Yearbook* (1990: 170–1). The rate of growth of the capital stock need not move in the same direction as the share of investment in GDP, but to reconcile the decline in the latter with an increase in the former it would be necessary to suppose that the capital–output ratio and/or the depreciation rate had declined, neither of which seems likely.

trade with other Northern countries (and smaller than for trade with the South: Sapir and Schumacher 1985, tables 1 and 2; Schumacher 1989*a*, table A.10; Schumacher 1992). There are some slight differences in the skill content of intra-North trade flows, which is to be expected, since all developed countries clearly do not have identical relative supplies of skilled and less-skilled labour. For this reason, changes in North–North trade could alter skill differentials within the countries concerned, and might even explain some of the observed intra-North differences in skill differential movements. But the movements would tend to be in *opposite* directions in the countries concerned, and thus cannot explain why skill differentials in most developed countries moved in the *same* direction.[20]

There might be some other theoretical reason why expansion of North–North trade should raise the relative demand for skilled labour in all countries. This would happen, for example, if traded sectors were less skill-intensive than nontraded sectors, and greater realisation of scale economies reduced the share of total employment in traded sectors. It could also happen if North–North competition were based mainly on product quality, and skilled workers were needed to produce high quality goods. This view is supported by Gasiorek, Smith, and Venables (1991: 28), who predict that the effect of European integration from 1992 will be to increase the relative demand for skilled labour in manufacturing. However, Schumacher (1989*b*: 267) arrives at the opposite conclusion.

As explained earlier (in the cross-country variation Section of 5.4.2), there is a strong positive correlation across Northern countries between the rise in manufactured import penetration from the South and from the North. In other words, developed countries which have become relatively more open to trade with the South have also tended to become more open to trade with the rest of the North. As a result, there is a positive cross-country correlation (analogous to that in Fig. 7.1 for Southern imports) between the extent of the widening of skill differentials and rises in the ratio of Northern manufactured imports to GDP.[21] However, the correlation with Northern imports is not so close as with Southern imports ($R^2 = 0.20$ as compared with 0.49, or, with Belgium excluded, 0.57 as compared with 0.72), and if both import variables are included in the regression, the Northern one is insignificant.

This sort of test does not have much discriminatory power, but it tends to reinforce the preceding argument that expansion of North–North trade is a less plausible explanation of widening skill differentials than expansion of North–South trade. The argument is further reinforced by the

[20] Though in opposite directions, the movements would not necessarily cancel out exactly (esp. if the changes in trade were unbalanced, as was the case among developed countries in the 1980s), so that there might be some change in the all-North average of skill differentials.

[21] Using the same dependent variable and country sample as in Fig. 7.1, the change in the Northern import ratio between 1970 and 1985 is derived from the source (and subject to the limitations) mentioned in Ch. 5, n. 34.

lack of correlation between the *timing* of the widening of skill differentials and expansion of North–North trade, which (as reported in Section 5.4.2) grew more slowly after 1970 than in the two previous decades (and no faster in the 1980s than in the 1970s).

7.3.2 Biased technical change

The last (and most plausible) alternative explanation of the increase in the relative demand for skilled labour is autonomous technical progress with an unskilled-labour-saving bias. More specifically, the hypothesis is that the relative demand for *BAS-ED* labour was reduced, not by expansion of trade with the South, but by the widespread introduction of microprocessor-based technologies. Leontief (1982) was perhaps the first to suggest that the ensuing automation of the mental functions of workers would increase wage inequality. In a recent review of explanations of widening US skill differentials, Bound and Johnson (1992) likewise conclude, albeit largely by default, that skill-biased technical change was the principal cause.

Plausibility

Several things make this explanation plausible. First and foremost is the mass of casual evidence of remarkable technological change in virtually every home, office, and factory. The scale of this change is surely large enough to have significantly altered the skill structure of labour demand. Its timing also appears to coincide broadly with the widening of skill differentials, becoming significant in the 1970s and gaining rapidly in importance thereafter. Moreover, the pervasiveness of these changes, which have affected all Northern countries, is consistent with the similarly pervasive widening of skill differentials. Finally, it is clear that microprocessor-based equipment can replace routine and repetitive human work, and that this is the sort of work which *BAS-ED* labour usually does.

This possible explanation of the shift in the relative demand for skilled and less-skilled labour needs to be related to the discussion of technology in Section 2.3.2. Technology was defined there as knowledge embodied in capital goods and intermediate goods (as contrasted with skill, which is knowledge embodied in people). Since microprocessors are material objects, this definition is compatible with the general statement that the relative demand for skilled labour has been increased by changes in technology, and with the popular vision of unskilled workers being displaced by production-line robots. Moreover, because technology can also be regarded as indirect skill, because microprocessors embody a lot of indirect skill, and because indirect and direct skill are often complementary, there is a theoretical basis for supposing that greater use of computers and other microprocessor-based equipment would raise the demand for skilled labour.

Care is also needed with the concept of bias, since on some theoretical definitions, technical progress which is biased against unskilled workers need not reduce the relative demand for them. Such a decline in relative demand necessarily occurs if unskilled-labour-saving bias is defined relative to Hicks-neutrality (as a reduction in the marginal product of unskilled labour relative to the marginal products of other inputs at any given input ratio).[22] But if bias is defined in the spirit of Harrod, and hence better described as unskilled-labour-augmenting than as unskilled-labour-saving, it may either reduce or increase the relative demand for unskilled labour, depending on substitution elasticities.[23] In the present context, this issue will be side-stepped by defining the 'technological explanation' more generally as the hypothesis that new production processes have reduced the relative demand for unskilled labour, regardless of the nature or direction of their bias in any particular strict sense.

Reservations

Despite the immediate plausibility of the technological explanation, three important reservations should be noted. One is that a large part of the effect of the microprocessor revolution has been not on producer goods (and hence on production processes), but on the quality and variety of consumer goods, private and public. Many of the new consumer goods, moreover, are produced by processes involving a high ratio of unskilled to skilled direct labour—for example, the assembly of CD players and electronic toys—even though some of the intermediate goods used in production embody advanced technology. For (as mentioned in Section 2.3.2) there are many exceptions to the rule about complementarity between direct and indirect skill. Thus the overall effect of consumer goods innovations on the demand for skilled relative to unskilled labour need not have been positive.

---

[22] On alternative conceptions of neutrality and bias, see e.g. Hahn and Matthews (1965: 47–53) and Pasinetti (1981: 206–13). However, these and most other discussions of bias focus on capital and labour, neglecting the distinction between skilled and unskilled workers.

[23] As is emphasised by Bean and Pissarides (1991). This is because unskilled-labour-augmenting technical change not only reduces the number of unskilled workers needed per unit of output, but also reduces the relative cost of unskilled labour at any given wage, since each worker becomes more productive, which encourages employers to substitute unskilled labour for other inputs. If the elasticity of substitution between unskilled labour and other inputs is less than unity, the net effect is a decline in the relative demand for unskilled workers; if it is unity there is no change in relative demand; and if it exceeds unity the relative demand for unskilled workers actually increases.

A second reservation is that microprocessors, to the (large and growing) extent that they are embodied in producer goods and thus affect production processes, have had a wide variety of effects on the demand for specific sorts of skilled and less-skilled workers, whose net result may not have been a general increase in the relative demand for skilled labour. Many less-skilled manual and clerical workers clearly have been replaced by intelligent machines, and the associated increase in the relative demand for skilled labour sometimes reinforced by the creation of new skilled jobs, or by the need to upgrade the skills of existing jobs. On the other hand, many skilled occupations have also been displaced by microprocessor-based equipment, including a range of white-collar jobs, both technical (draftsmen) and professional (some sorts of engineers and accountants), as well as manual crafts (such as those of compositors and typesetters).

In some occupations, moreover, the required number of skilled people has been reduced because new equipment increases their productivity. This is accomplished in some cases by automating routine aspects of the work and delegating their implementation to less-skilled subordinates, thereby reducing the proportion of skilled workers. The new technology also often reduces the need for indirect labour by making it possible to operate with less working capital, due to improved inventory control, or with less fixed capital, because of the higher utilisation rates achieved with more versatile machines (Wilson 1984, ch. 2). Because much of the indirect labour embodied in capital goods is skilled, fewer machines per direct worker may increase the relative demand for less-skilled labour.

The third reservation, in so far as process innovations have reduced the relative demand for less-skilled labour, is that this bias need not have been *autonomous*, in the sense of being unrelated to the expansion of trade with the South, but could have been *induced* by trade. In particular, as explained in Section 4.4.3, defensive innovation to reduce reliance on unskilled labour has enabled some manufacturing sectors threatened by competition from low-wage Southern suppliers to maintain or expand their output, though with reduced employment. Of course, it would be absurd to suggest that trade with the South precipitated the invention or diffusion of microprocessors, but it seems rather likely that competition from the South influenced the ways in which microprocessors were introduced into production processes.

7.3.3 Circumstantial evidence

There are thus reasons for doubting, as well as for believing, that it was principally new technology which increased the relative demand for skilled labour. Anecdotal and case-study evidence cannot resolve the issue, since different bits of information point in different directions. Moreover, as will emerge below, there is little direct evidence of a more powerful kind. It is possible, however, to look more closely at the consistency of the technological explanation with circumstantial evidence. Not least, it seems appropriate to ask, as with the North–South trade explanation, about timing and inter-country variations, although in this case consistency of magnitudes cannot be examined, since there are no independent quantitative estimates of the impact of new technology on relative demand.

Timing

As already mentioned, casual evidence regarding the timing of the diffusion of microprocessors is consistent with the technological explanation of the widening of skill differentials, since both occurred largely in the 1980s. Data on research and development expenditures also suggest acceleration of technical advance in this decade, after a slowdown in the 1970s (Patel and Pavitt, 1991, fig. 2). Less favourable to the technological explanation, however, is the fact that the increase in the relative demand for skilled labour—which appears to have started in the 1970s, although the widening of most skill differentials was postponed to the 1980s—coincided with a slowdown in aggregate productivity growth. (Harrison and Bluestone (1990, table 3) document the correlation for wage dispersion in the USA.) For if the driving force were indeed the economy-wide displacement of unskilled workers by intelligent machines, it seems more reasonable to suppose that aggregate productivity growth would have speeded up.

The scope and causes of the productivity slowdown are still matters of controversy, despite extensive investigation. It may have been due partly to other countries catching up with US technology, but this cannot have been the sole cause, since there was a slowdown also in the USA (Chan-Lee and Sutch 1985: 56). Nor did it simply reflect the shift of employment from manufacturing to lower-productivity services, since the growth of productivity slowed down also (indeed more) in the service sectors.[24] Most studies agree that the decline in labour productivity growth was due partly to less new investment per worker, but there is disagreement about the possible unrecorded scrapping of existing capital goods.[25] There is

---

[24] See e.g. Lindbeck (1983), Baily (1984), and Sect. A2.6 of the present book. The slowdown of productivity growth in services disposes of the accounting possibility that the aggregate slowdown was caused simply by a shift of labour from manufacturing into sectors with a lower level or growth rate of productivity. It leaves open the economic possibility that this shift somehow reduced productivity in services by more than it raised productivity in manufacturing, and so pulled down the economy-wide average, but even this argument is not easy to sustain (Baily 1981: 24–5).

[25] See esp. Baily (1981, 1984) and Baily and Gordon (1989).

also disagreement about the contribution of higher energy prices, lower research and development expenditures (in the 1970s), more female participation in the labour force, and more environmental and safety regulations.[26]

In any event, the slowdown of productivity growth in the North does not necessarily disprove the hypothesis that the widening of wage differentials was caused by an autonomous wave of labour-saving technical progress. It could be argued, for example, that the microprocessor revolution cut the relative demand for unskilled labour, but increased the absolute demand for skilled (and hence total) labour to produce new and better products, whose improved quality was not reflected in output statistics.[27] Alternatively, the contribution of the new technology to raising labour productivity might be subject to long lags, or simply outweighed by one or more of the other negative influences noted in the previous paragraph. At a minimum, though, the slowdown of productivity growth raises questions and doubts about the technological explanation of the decline in the relative demand for less-skilled labour. (It appears to shed no light one way or the other on the correctness of the North–South trade explanation.[28])

Cross-country variation

If the microprocessor revolution were the cause, it would be logical to expect (holding other influences constant) that skill differentials would have widened more in countries where the revolution was more advanced. But the limited evidence available in this regard is clearly inconsistent with the technological explanation. On the basis of the number of robots per worker, Japan and Sweden are leaders in applying the new technology, while the USA and the UK are laggards.[29] Yet skill differentials widened much more in the USA and the UK than in Japan and Sweden

[26] In addition to the works cited in the previous note, see e.g. Griliches (1980), Denison (1983), and Lindbeck (1983).

[27] Baily and Gordon (1989) conclude that such under-recording of output growth explains part of the slowdown. Ironically, however, attempts by US national accountants to improve matters by allowing for improvements in the performance of computers have been widely criticised (de Leeuw 1988).

[28] There are several possible linkages between expansion of trade with the South and aggregate productivity growth. Productivity would tend to be raised by the efficiency gains from specialisation, and also, if relative wages were rigid, by reduced employment of unskilled workers (see Sect. 8.1.1). On the other hand, productivity growth might be reduced by contraction of manufacturing (but see n. 24). However, the timing of events casts doubt on any such connection: the productivity slowdown in most Northern countries appears to have started rather abruptly, in 1972–4, whereas the increase in their trade with the South occurred gradually, and in absolute terms was larger in the 1980s.

[29] 'Sweden', *The Economist*, 3 March 1990: 17. The *Financial Times* of 14 May 1991 ('Computers in Manufacturing': VI) quotes the UN Economic Commission for Europe as stating that of a world population of 388,000 industrial robots at the end of 1989, 220,000 were in Japan, 56,000 in Western Europe, and 37,000 in the USA.

(see Table 7.1). Other indicators of technological activity likewise suggest either an inverse association or none at all.[30] Civilian R & D as a proportion of GDP in the 1980s was higher in Japan and Sweden than in the USA and the UK (Patel and Pavitt 1991, table 1). Within Europe, Germany greatly outperformed the UK in terms of patenting in the USA during the 1980s (ibid., table 4), but skill differentials widened to a similar degree in the two countries.

These apparent inconsistencies with the technological explanation are not conclusive. For example, use of personal computers might be more relevant than use of industrial robots as an indicator of the effects of innovation on the skill structure of labour demand, and might provide more supportive results. Alternatively, the consequences of differing rates of innovation could have been masked by other differences among countries. For instance, skill differentials might have been prevented from widening in Sweden by institutional wage rigidities, combined with unusual efforts to train and re-employ displaced unskilled workers. Skill differentials might likewise have failed to widen in Japan, despite strong demand pressure from the new technology, because of unusually rapid growth of the skilled labour supply. However, it would be more plausible to argue that the high skill level of Japan's work force was the *cause* of the more rapid spread of new production processes. And again, at the least, the simple cross-country comparisons above raise questions and doubts about the technological explanation.

Relocation

A further piece of circumstantial counter-evidence, which weighs actively in favour of the North–South trade explanation, is the movement of most tradeable unskilled-labour-intensive activities to developing countries in which unskilled labour is relatively cheap. This movement started in the North, and was reinforced in the 1980s by a second generation of transfers from countries such as Korea and Taiwan to their poorer neighbours. If the world had truly experienced a wave of autonomous technical progress with an unskilled-labour-saving bias, as the technological explanation of widening skill differentials implies, it would be harder to explain why this pattern of relocation occurred and persisted. For this new technology would have eroded the incentive to reduce unskilled labour costs by moving production abroad. Some people argue that there has in fact been such an erosion, citing instances where companies have

[30] There is no discernible cross-country correlation between the overall index of skill differential widening in Table 7.1 and (*a*) the share of industry R & D in GDP (Patel and Pavitt 1991, table 1) or (*b*) per capita patenting in the USA (Pavitt and Patel 1988, table 4, excluding the USA for the reason stated in the notes to that table). The limitations of these technological indicators are clearly explained by Pavitt and Patel.

moved activities back from the South to the North, but these seem so far to have been exceptional.[31]

The relocation of labour-intensive activities does not logically preclude the possibility that the relative demand for unskilled labour in the North was simultaneously being reduced by new technology. An autonomous decline of domestic unskilled labour costs might have been outpaced by reduction of trade barriers, to which microprocessor technology contributed, especially in telecommunications. At a minimum, however, this pattern of relocation implies that expansion of trade with the South must have caused part of the increase in the relative demand for skilled labour in the North.

7.3.4 Direct investigations

Biases in technical progress have been exhaustively discussed in the theoretical literature, but there have been comparatively few attempts at empirical estimation, and even fewer attempts to distinguish autonomous from induced biases (Jorgenson 1985: 1876–82; Slade 1989). Moreover, most estimates use only a single category of labour, sometimes adjusted for quality, with capital and sometimes energy and materials as the other inputs, and are thus not directly relevant in the present context.[32]

One recent econometric study of technological bias as between skilled and unskilled labour is Bean and Pissarides (1991), which refers to manual and non-manual workers in fifteen manufacturing industries in the UK between the early 1970s and the late 1980s. Its estimates suggest that, on average across these industries, technical change neither reduced nor increased the relative demand for unskilled labour.[33] The authors note the general widening of the wage differential between manual and non-manual workers, and the likelihood that this was due to a decline in the relative demand for manual labour. However, they conclude that this

[31] Among the proponents of the view that a general reversal of this kind is occurring is Kaplinsky (1984: 83–4). However, UNIDO (1987: 15–17) and Winters (1987: 13–17) take a more cautious view of the evidence. That reversals in the location of production of particular items are not a new phenomenon is suggested by the discussion in Kindleberger (1963: 126–7).

[32] e.g. Berndt and Khaled (1979) conclude that technical change in US manufacturing was capital- and energy-using, and labour- and materials-saving. Their data stop in 1971. Many of the econometric studies surveyed by Wilson (1984) are even older, and often contradictory. They suggest that technical change is generally biased, but not always labour-saving. Wilson's survey of case studies of the impact of information technology on the engineering industry concludes that there is no clear evidence of bias for or against labour. A similarly agnostic conclusion emerges from the survey by Kaplinsky (1987) of studies of the employment effects of the new technology.

[33] Bean and Pissarides discover that technical progress was mainly non-manual-labour-augmenting, but did not affect relative demand because the relevant elasticity of substitution was close to unity.

demand shift was probably the result of changes in the sectoral structure of the economy, towards relatively skill-intensive industries.

The findings of Bean and Pissarides do not support the technological explanation, but neither are they entirely consistent with the North–South trade explanation. In particular, the lack of evidence in this study of unskilled-labour-saving technical progress in manufacturing seems hard to reconcile with the argument in Section 4.4.3 that expansion of trade with the South induced defensive technical change of this type. Indeed, since the manufacturing industries in the Bean and Pissarides study are coarsely defined, some such statistical effect would be expected merely from trade-induced movement within industries towards a less unskilled-labour-intensive product and activity mix. Its absence may be a result of the unsatisfactory nature of the manual/non-manual division of the labour force (see Section A1.5). Especially in manufacturing, the most important trade-induced changes in the skill composition of labour demand seem to have occurred within rather than between these coarse groupings.

The Bean and Pissarides inference that the shift in the skill composition of labour demand was caused mainly by changes in the sectoral structure of the economy also conflicts with the North American studies summarised in section 7.2.5, most of which use education and age-based indicators of skill, rather than occupational groupings. Especially notable is the conflict with Bound and Johnson (1992), who conclude that almost all the demand shift occurred within, not between, industries. Bound and Johnson also argue that the main cause of this shift was technical change biased against less-skilled labour. However, they note that this interpretation cannot be verified by direct observation, and mention some other possible interpretations, particularly changes in unmeasured labour quality.

Though not included among Bound and Johnson's alternative interpretations, changes in trade with the South, too, could have generated intra-sectoral shifts in the skill composition of demand, through alterations in product mix and defensive innovation. Such trade-induced shifts, moreover, need not have been confined to sectors producing traded goods, since services are increasingly traded, and because the effects of trade percolate back into nontraded sectors supplying intermediate inputs (see Section 4.4.3). However, the shifts would presumably be larger in sectors directly engaged in trade. It is thus unfavourable to the trade hypothesis that Bound and Johnson can explain much of the change in relative wages by assuming that intra-sectoral shifts in the skill composition of demand were common to all sectors. They do find an additional effect in four sectors which employ a lot of blue-collar workers, but it is small, and two of these sectors are nontraded (the other two cover manufacturing).

Bound and Johnson buttress their conclusion that technical change is the main cause of widening skill differentials by referring to two studies which provide more direct evidence. One, by Berndt and Morrison, finds a large increase in the ratio of 'high-tech' to total capital stock in US manufacturing from 1976 to 1986, and that 'within two-digit manufacturing industries, increases in the high-tech intensity of capital are associated with both shifts in labour demand from production toward nonproduction workers and increases in the average educational attainment of production workers' (Bound and Johnson 1992: 388). This finding reinforces the view mentioned above that direct and indirect skill are often complementary, but leaves open the question of whether the movement of US manufacturing into more (directly and indirectly) skill-intensive activities was propelled by the availability of new technology or by pressure from foreign trade.

The other study, by Krueger (1991), relates wage changes to increased use of computers. Controlling for other influences on wages, it finds that workers who use computers tend to be paid more. It also finds that the rise in computer usage between 1984 and 1989 was particularly great among more-educated workers and females, two groups whose relative wages rose in the 1980s. On this basis, Krueger estimates that between one-third and two-thirds of the 1984–9 widening of the wage differential between more-educated and less-educated workers was due to increased use of computers. This evidence is clearly consistent with the new technology explanation of widening skill differentials, but there is room for doubt about causation. Both the correlation between computer usage and individual wages, and the concentration of increased computer usage on more-educated workers, could be seen simply as further examples of complementarity between direct and indirect skill (and the concentration of computers on females as a result of their over-representation in secretarial and clerical jobs).

7.3.5 Weighing the evidence

What does the assortment of evidence reviewed in previous sections suggest about the relative correctness of the more-trade-with-the-South explanation of widening skill differentials and the new technology explanation, both of which are well grounded in theory and seem plausible on the basis of casual observation? In summing up, it is worth reiterating that both explanations involve skill-biased technical change: the issue is whether this bias is induced (by competition from the South), or autonomous. Nor, in principle, does acceptance of one of these explanations necessarily require rejection of the other: both trade with the South and an autonomous bias in technical change may have contributed to the widening of skill differentials in the North, the issue then being their relative importance.

The evidence presented in Part A appears to establish beyond reasonable doubt that expansion of trade with the South has caused a large reduction in the relative demand for unskilled labour in the North. There remains considerable room for doubt, however, about exactly how large this effect was. As explained in Section 7.2.2, the estimates in Chapter 4 of the trade-induced demand shift seem large enough in most cases to account for the whole of the observed widening of skill differentials, but could leave some room for the new technology explanation, in two respects. One is that the estimates of the trade-induced demand shift may be too large, especially as regards the rough allowances made for defensive innovation and the impact on the service sectors. The other is that supply has been shifting in the contrary direction, so that the estimated effect of trade on demand may not be large enough to explain the whole of the widening of skill differentials.

The studies surveyed in Section 7.3.4 contain some formal evidence which is highly consistent with the new technology explanation. Most of it can be reconciled with the North–South trade explanation, too, but the fit is not always a comfortable one. This is especially true of those aspects of the evidence (and of casual observation) which suggest new-technology-related reductions in the relative demand for less-skilled labour in sectors whose exposure to foreign trade (directly or indirectly) is small. For this and other reasons, it is hard to believe that new technology could have had *no* autonomous effects on the skill composition of the demand for labour.

Two sorts of circumstantial evidence appear to favour the North–South trade explanation over the new technology explanation. One concerns timing: the widening of skill differentials in the 1980s seems consistent with the big rise in imports from the South during that decade, while the credibility of the new technology explanation is reduced by the simultaneous slowing down of aggregate productivity growth. However, the time-path of imports from the South may not be an accurate reflection of their impact on the labour market (for reasons mentioned in Section 7.2.1). It may be possible, too, to reconcile the productivity slowdown with the new technology explanation of widening skill differentials (as noted in Section 7.3.3).

The other sort of evidence which favours the North–South trade explanation concerns variations among Northern countries in the extent of the widening of skill differentials in the 1980s. These variations appear positively correlated with variations in Southern import penetration, but negatively correlated or uncorrelated with variations in technology indicators. The contrast is suggestive, but should be regarded with caution. The index of skill differential widening is crude, the technology indicators may be inappropriate, and other influences are not properly controlled for.

In conclusion, it would be hard to reject a general synthetic hypothesis that both trade with the South and autonomous changes in technology made some contribution to the shift in the skill composition of the demand for labour in the North. A more specific version of this synthetic hypothesis that seems particularly consistent with the limited evidence available is that the main effect of trade and trade-induced changes in technology was on workers in the lower half of the skill distribution (cutting the demand for unskilled labour), while the main effect of the autonomous changes in technology was on the upper half of the skill distribution (increasing the demand for skilled labour). This dichotomous interpretation should not be pushed too far, though: both sorts of influence must have had some effects on both halves of the skill distribution (and from some points of view the distinction does not matter anyway).

What seems impossible, pending further research, is to arrive at any firm conclusion about the relative sizes of the contributions which these two forces made during 1960–90 to the overall shift in the relative demand for skilled and unskilled labour in Northern countries. The evidence reviewed above is consistent with the view that most of this demand shift was caused by expansion of trade with the South, but it does not permit one to reject with any confidence the alternative view that autonomous technical change played the larger role. The agnosticism of this conclusion needs to be recognised in exploring policy implications (in Chapter 10).

7.4 Summary

Theory and the evidence presented in earlier chapters suggest that trade with the South has increased the demand for skilled labour, relative to less-skilled labour, in the North. This demand shift must have tended to widen skill differentials in wages, or, in so far as such wage changes are restrained by institutional forces, in unemployment and vacancy rates.

Skill differentials clearly did widen in most Northern countries during the 1980s. The wages of workers who were better educated and more experienced rose, relative to those of less-educated and younger workers. So did the wages of higher-level white-collar occupations, relative to those of other white-collar and blue-collar workers, although skill differentials within the blue-collar group moved in different ways in different countries. The overall distribution of wages (and in most countries of household income) also became more unequal. Skill differentials in unemployment and vacancy rates widened, too, though more clearly among education groups than among age groups and occupational categories.

Moreover, the widening of skill differentials is generally agreed to have been caused mainly by rising relative demand for skilled labour. Supply shifts could not have generated the observed combination of widening skill differentials and rising relative numbers of skilled workers. The skill structure of labour demand appears to have been moving in this direction also during the 1970s, albeit more slowly. However, skill differentials narrowed in that decade, largely because of rapid expansion of the supply of college graduates. The compression of wage differentials during the 1970s was reinforced in some countries by institutional pressures, whose relaxation in the 1980s amplified the widening of wage differentials.

These trends are in accordance with the expected effects of expansion of trade with the South. Closer examination tends to confirm this impression of consistency. The absolute increase in imports of manufactures from the South during the 1980s was much larger than in the two previous decades, which could explain why the relative demand shift speeded up, and why the widening of skill differentials occurred mainly towards the end of the period. The magnitude of the widening of wage differentials also seems consistent in most cases with the estimated size of the impact of trade on the relative demand for skilled and unskilled labour. In addition, skill differentials appear to have widened more in countries which experienced larger increases in Southern import penetration.

An apparent inconsistency is that the economic situation of females has improved in most Northern countries, despite the fact that industries with many women workers have been particularly hard hit by Southern imports. A likely explanation is that displaced females are more successful in finding other jobs than displaced males, and that females as a group have been less affected by the relative decline of employment in manufacturing (a male-dominated sector). Only a small part of the rise in the relative demand for skilled workers, however, is directly attributable to the decline of manufacturing. This finding seems consistent with the North–South trade explanation, in which the reduction of employment in manufacturing occurs essentially as a by-product of changes in its internal skill structure.

Of the alternative possible explanations of the rising relative demand for skilled labour, by far the most plausible is autonomous technical progress with an unskilled-labour-saving bias—more specifically, the diffusion of microprocessor-based equipment. This technology explanation is consistent with much casual observation and some formal evidence. However, skilled as well as unskilled workers have been replaced by microprocessors, and even where new technology has clearly been associated with a reduction in the relative demand for unskilled labour, this bias has sometimes been induced by competitive pressure from the South. The new technology explanation is also hard to reconcile with the slowdown of aggregate productivity growth, and with evidence that skill differentials have widened less in countries where the microprocessor revolution seems more advanced.

Although the evidence falls far short of what would be needed for a proper comparative appraisal of the trade and technology explanations, it suggests that both these forces have made some contribution to the widening of skill differentials in the North. A more specific but more tentative conclusion would be that the main contribution of trade with the South was to reduce the demand for unskilled workers, while the main effect of the autonomous spread of microprocessors has been to boost the demand for skilled workers. As regards the relative size of the contributions of these two forces, the evidence is consistent with the view that trade with the South played the larger role, but does not rule out the possibility that new technology was more important. This residual uncertainty has to be borne in mind in considering policy responses to widening skill differentials.

8

Unemployment in the North

This chapter continues the investigation of the effects on the North of changes in trade with the South. The discussion in the preceding chapter concentrated on changes in skill differentials and inequality. However, it was also hypothesised in Chapter 2 that the changes in trade would make it harder to reconcile low inflation with low unemployment. This chapter tests that hypothesis. Section 8.1 considers alternative explanations of recent macroeconomic trends, Section 8.2 examines the evidence on mismatch unemployment, and Section 8.3 analyses variations in unemployment among Northern countries.

8.1 Alternative Explanations

The first part of this section describes the mechanism by which expansion of trade with the South could have raised unemployment in the North. The second part outlines the main competing hypotheses that have been advanced to explain the rise and persistence of unemployment in recent decades.

8.1.1 Present hypothesis

In many Northern countries, for reasons to be elaborated below, there is institutional resistance to wider skill differentials in wages. The rise in the relative demand for skilled labour caused by expansion of trade with the South thus tends to generate shortages of skilled labour and surpluses of unskilled labour (as illustrated in Fig. 5.3(d)). The shortages cause the money wages of skilled workers to rise, because of competition among employers. However, the money wages of unskilled workers are pulled up, too, because of the institutional pressures that prevent widening of the wage relativity between the two groups. The average money wage level thus tends to rise, pushing up costs and the price level. Simultaneously, the unskilled labour surpluses tend to raise aggregate unemployment.

The outcome of this deterioration in the macroeconomic trade-off between inflation and unemployment (defined more precisely below) depends on how the government reacts. If its main concern were to restrain inflation, as with most Northern governments during the 1980s, a likely response would be tighter fiscal and monetary policies, which, by lowering the overall level of economic activity, could eliminate the excess demand for skilled labour, and thus the inflationary pressure. However, this strategy would also reduce the demand for unskilled labour, resulting in an even larger rise in unemployment. Hence if the government reacted in this way, the deterioration of the macroeconomic trade-off would emerge purely as higher unemployment, with no enduring increase in skilled labour shortages.

Various other sorts of government reaction are clearly also possible. In the 1960s and 1970s, a more typical response would have been to accept the rise in inflation, avoiding deflation because of the rise in unemployment, and perhaps even easing fiscal and monetary policy in order to restore the previous level of employment. This strategy would cause the deterioration in the macroeconomic trade-off to emerge partly or mainly as a rise in the rate of inflation. Another typical response in the 1960s and 1970s would have been to try to contain the rise in nominal wages through an incomes policy (or in some countries by agreement among employers to refrain from wage competition for skilled labour). In the 1980s, though, deflation was often accompanied by efforts to reduce labour market 'rigidities'.

The present hypothesis is compatible with most macroeconomic theory. It can be simply and precisely articulated in the framework of a NAIRU model, which provides a reasonably accurate description of past trends (Nickell 1990: 427). In such a model, expectations tend to generate a constant rate of inflation, and shortages of skilled labour would tend to make inflation accelerate (Wood 1988). The deterioration of the macroeconomic trade-off could thus be expressed as an increase in the rate of unemployment needed to maintain a constant rate of inflation. The nature of the trade-off would be different if expectations were formed in some other way, but the core of the present hypothesis would survive. Even if expectations were 'rational' (or model-consistent), precluding a trade-off with inflation, a shift in the skill structure of labour demand combined with inflexible relative wages would raise the equilibrium or 'natural' rate of unemployment.[1]

To arrive at a result of this kind it is not necessary to suppose that the wage differential between skilled and unskilled workers is totally rigid, but merely that it is not fully flexible—unable to widen sufficiently to restore the balance between the relative demand and supply of skilled and unskilled workers. Thus a trade-induced rise in the relative demand for skilled labour might emerge partly as a widening of skill differentials in wages, and partly as a deterioration of the macroeconomic trade-off. And if relative wages were completely flexible, the shift in demand would

---

[1] In Nickell's (1990) terminology and notation, it would increase mismatch and hence raise z_w.

emerge purely as a widening of skill differentials, with no macro side-effects. In this sense, the macroeconomic trade-off has a third dimension: between greater wage inequality and a higher equilibrium rate of unemployment.[2]

It is worth noting in passing that this deterioration in the macroeconomic trade-off would tend to be associated with an *improvement* in other economic indicators, particularly aggregate productivity and the average real wage. The reason is that the rise in unemployment would be heavily concentrated on unskilled workers—the least productive part of the labour force—and would thus raise the average skill level of employed workers. This might help to explain, for example, why average real wages rose during the 1970s and 1980s in Europe, but not in the USA (where relative wages are less rigid and hence there was less of a rise in unemployment).

Sources of relative wage rigidity

As discussed in Section 2.5.1, wages may fail to clear labour markets for many reasons, some long familiar, others much better understood as a result of recent research (for example, on incomplete or implicit contracts). In the context of this book, however, it is one specific type of rigidity that matters (and one that has been comparatively neglected in economic theory), namely resistance to wider wage gaps between higher- and lower-paid workers. All such resistance arises fundamentally from an ethical principle, that people's incomes should not be 'too unequal'. There are variations in the strength and interpretation of this idea of fairness (see Section 10.2.2), but as a general principle it appears to command wide support.

In practice, there are three main institutional mechanisms by which this idea of fairness restrains economic pressures for wider wage differentials between skilled and unskilled workers. One is unions and other forms of collective bargaining, in which an important objective is often to protect the interests of (actually or potentially) low-paid workers. A second is minimum wage legislation, particularly because the minimum is usually set and/or adjusted in relation to average wages. The third is income support provided through the social security system to people who are not working, which is again usually (explicitly or implicitly) related to actual wages, and which (if available on a long-term basis, with few conditions)

---

[2] In an open economy, there is also a fourth dimension, involving the trade balance (Layard, Nickell, and Jackman 1991: 384–90). In the context of the present hypothesis, for example, the shortages of skilled labour might be eased by importing additional skill-intensive goods. But this dimension is in principle temporary, because of the difficulty of running protracted large trade deficits. It is also of less relevance for the North as a whole (or on average) than for individual countries.

sets an effective lower limit to the unskilled wage.[3] An occasional fourth mechanism is statutory wage controls favouring lower-paid workers.

The nature and scope of these institutional rigidities vary widely among countries, and have also changed over time (for a valuable summary, see Layard, Nickell, and Jackman 1991, annexes 1.3 and 1.4). In the USA, for example, relatively few workers are unionised, and in most Northern countries the proportion of workers in unions has fallen since 1980. In Germany, there is no legal minimum wage, and in the USA the minimum declined in relative terms during the 1980s. The coverage, level, and duration of social security benefits for unemployed people all differ widely from country to country: Sweden for instance offers generous but temporary support, while the United Kingdom provides more meagre benefits over an indefinite period, and Italy virtually none.

But in most Northern countries, and especially in Europe, at least one of the three mechanisms appears to be powerful and pervasive. The present hypothesis thus seems broadly consistent with two major features of recent trends in unemployment rates (both actual and estimated equilibrium rates—Layard, Nickell, and Jackman 1991: 1, 436–7). One is that the macroeconomic trade-off deteriorated in 'most Northern countries between the 1960s and the 1980s, a period over which their imports of manufactures from the South greatly increased. The other is that the deterioration was much worse in Europe than in the USA. That this was due to greater rigidity of relative wages in Europe is suggested also by the evidence (summarised in section 7.1) that skill differentials in wages widened more in the USA.[4]

The hypothesis that expansion of trade with the South, in conjunction with relative wage rigidity, has had adverse macroeconomic consequences in the North therefore seems rather plausible. The rest of this chapter will be devoted to a more detailed assessment of its consistency with the facts, both absolutely and in comparison with competing hypotheses.

8.1.2 Other hypotheses

A considerable part of the vast literature on unemployment has sought to explain its general rise in the North during the three decades 1960–90, as well as the wide variation among countries in the extent of this rise. The

[3] Formal mechanisms of this kind are not the only possible reasons for a floor under the relative wage of unskilled workers in conventional forms of employment. Support from family and private charity, and opportunities for income from other sorts of activity, including crime, make people unwilling to devote time and effort to formal employment at very low wages.
[4] e.g. if the overall scores in Table 7.1 are calculated without the unemployment and vacancy indicators, the USA score is 4.0, matched only by Australia. The average score for the twelve European countries is 1.7, with the UK score highest (3.5).

suggested explanations, and the research on which they are based, are well summarised and elucidated in Nickell (1990) and Layard, Nickell, and Jackman (1991), henceforward for brevity cited as LNJ. The views of these authors will be taken as representative of the current state of thinking on these issues, although they are careful to note differences of view and areas of uncertainty, and provide numerous references to the work of others.

Their explanation of the trend increase in unemployment distinguishes two phases. During the first phase (from the 1960s to about 1980), a number of forces could have caused the macroeconomic trade-off to deteriorate in many or all Northern countries. These include greater union militancy, more extensive and generous unemployment benefits, increased taxation, and the two oil price rises, coupled with worker resistance to real wage cuts (Nickell 1990: 427). Differences among countries in the response of unemployment to these forces can be explained by differences in the size of the import price shocks (which were larger in countries with fewer natural resources), in conjunction with measurable differences in the degree of real wage resistance and nominal wage rigidity, resulting from differences in labour-market institutions and social security systems (LNJ: 409).

The second phase, which covers the 1980s, is more problematic. It started with deliberate severe restriction of aggregate demand and a large increase in unemployment, reflecting a shift of political priorities towards control of inflation. However, the shocks that apparently raised the equilibrium unemployment rate during the first phase were generally reversed: oil and commodity prices fell, taxes were cut, unions weakened, and unemployment benefits restricted. In the second half of the decade, aggregate demand restrictions were eased and unemployment rates declined. But these rates did not fall back to their 1960s levels, and remained high in many European countries, mainly because of increases in the duration of unemployment, and especially in the extent of long-term unemployment (LNJ: 4, 218–25).

This stimulated a hunt for reasons why high unemployment, once established, might persist. Hysteresis, as this persistence is labelled, has two main suggested causes. One is that 'insider' workers bargain with employers over wages without reference to the interests and existence of unemployed outsiders (Lindbeck and Snower 1989). The other, emphasised by LNJ, is that long-term unemployment demotivates and deskills people, making them unsuitable for re-employment—or at least that employers believe this to be so. The extent of long-term (and hence total) unemployment depends on the duration of unemployment benefits—long in most European countries, but short in the USA and Japan (as well as in Sweden). Unemployment also varies among countries, LNJ suggest, because of differences in the extent of active labour-market policies (provision of jobs and training) and co-ordination of wage bargaining.

These explanations of persistent high unemployment, especially the long-term unemployment variant, are consistent with macroeconomic statistical evidence (LNJ: 55–6, 408–37). But there is also plenty of room for doubt. Although the greater influence of insiders on wage bargains is plausible, this model is not particularly well supported by microeconomic evidence (Blanchflower 1990). More crucially in the present context, it is hard to understand why the influence of insiders should have become greater during a decade when the power of unions was clearly reduced.

The long-term unemployment explanation of hysteresis seems more consistent with microeconomic evidence, but may well be mistaking the symptom for the cause. The long-term unemployed do not appear to be a random sample of the labour force (or even of the unemployed), whose skills and motivation are low merely because they happen to have been out of work. A high proportion of them lacked marketable skills when they entered unemployment, usually because they had little education or training, but in some cases because specific skills they had acquired were no longer in demand (due to the shrinkage or disappearance of the sectors concerned).[5]

The present hypothesis thus provides an alternative explanation of the rise of long-term unemployment which at first sight seems both simpler and more consistent with the evidence. It is that the combination of a decline in the relative demand for less-skilled workers and downward inflexibility of their relative wages has caused an increasing proportion of them to become permanently unemployable. In some respects, it should be emphasised, this explanation overlaps with the other two. For example, the view that ideas of fairness inhibit the widening of skill differentials in wages could be treated in an insider–outsider framework as a specific form of the insider utility function.[6] Similarly, unemployment

---

[5] All studies show that the long-term unemployed are less well educated than the short-term unemployed (and even less so than the employed): e.g. in the UK in 1986, among men aged between 25 and 54, 66% of those out of work for more than a year had no qualifications, as compared with 46% of shorter-term unemployed and 27% of those in work (*The Economist*, 4 Apr. 1987: 25). Similar results for various countries are reported by OECD-EO (1983: 58–63), Jackman (1986, table 2.2), and Paqué (1990, table 4). The incidence of long-term unemployment is also higher among people who are older, and hence potentially more experienced, but this does not necessarily contradict the view that the long-term unemployed are less skilled, since older workers tend to have less opportunity and incentive to retrain if they become de-skilled by shifts in demand. There is strong evidence that employers discriminate in hiring against the long-term unemployed (Nickell 1990: 420). The evidence is mixed on the question of 'state dependence': whether and to what extent the poor re-employment prospects of the long-term unemployed are aggravated purely by the length of their unemployment. Johnson and Layard (1986: 933) report two studies that found no strong evidence of true state dependence. Franz (1991: 123) cites two studies that suggest state dependence. But Nickell (1990: 431) notes that what had seemed to be irreversible unemployment in the 1930s swiftly disappeared with the revival of demand during the war.

[6] This was pointed out to me by James Pemberton, who also suggested the general point made in the following paragraph.

benefits of long duration play a role both in the LNJ model and in the present hypothesis (as a cause of relative wage rigidity).

More generally, one could also 'unbundle' the present explanation, and combine each of its two constituents with other ingredients to produce hybrid explanations of the deterioration in the macroeconomic trade-off. For instance, more trade with the South, in the role of a shock to the economic system, could be amalgamated with other reasons for hysteresis. Conversely, ethical constraints on widening wage differentials between skilled and unskilled workers could be combined with other reasons for a rise in the relative demand for skilled labour, the most likely being autonomous diffusion of new technology (discussed in Section 7.3). However, for most of the rest of this chapter, it will be convenient to keep the present hypothesis in its initial bundle, and to treat other hypotheses as distinct alternatives.

8.2 Evidence on Mismatch

The possibility that expansion of trade with the South contributed to the rise of unemployment in the North is not mentioned by Nickell (1990) or LNJ.[7] However, they do consider the general class of explanations to which the present hypothesis belongs, namely *mismatch* between the structure of labour demand and supply. In principle, in most models, an increase in the degree of mismatch would cause a rise in the aggregate unemployment rate. In practice, moreover, casual observation and anecdotal evidence has led most politicians, journalists, and members of the public to believe that this is indeed a major cause: that 'the unemployed either do not have the right skills or attitudes or live in the wrong parts of the country'.[8]

More formal empirical evidence consistent with the view that increased mismatch explains the secular rise in unemployment is the associated outward shift of the Beveridge curve—the inverse relationship between the aggregate unemployment rate and the aggregate vacancy rate. Between the 1960s and the 1980s, in almost every Northern country, this relationship clearly deteriorated, in the sense that there was a marked rise in the unemployment rate at any given vacancy rate (LNJ: 36–7; Schioppa 1991: 9; Abraham 1991: 457–60). It is likely, moreover, that the deterioration is understated by the use of official unemployment statistics, which fail to capture withdrawal of discouraged workers from the labour force.[9] This

---

[7] Although it was dismissed earlier by Layard (1986: 81–2).

[8] Samuel Brittan, 'A fresh look at pay and work', *Financial Times*, 24 July 1986.

[9] Edward Balls ('Exploding some 1980s "unemployment" myths', *Financial Times*, 17 Feb. 1992) shows that using non-employment rates rather than unemployment rates reverses the slight improvement in the US Beveridge curve between 1980 and 1990, and eliminates most of the large improvement in the UK curve between 1986 and 1990.

omission might explain why the US Beveridge curve moved outward but then back. (In Sweden, the curve did not shift, perhaps because of the active labour-market policy, but other evidence suggests increased difficulty in matching job applicants with vacancies—Edin and Holmlund 1991: 419.)

8.2.1 Disagreement

Although increased mismatch between the distributions of skills possessed by workers and required by employers is an obvious explanation for this general rise in the aggregate ratio of unemployment to vacancies, it is not the only possibility. Among other suggested explanations is an increase in mismatch on some other dimension, most notably location. However, the available evidence, which is quite robust, is not consistent with the hypothesis of a general increase in geographical mismatch (Abraham 1991: 420). Alternative explanations, unrelated to mismatch, include the two possible causes of hysteresis discussed above, especially the hypothesis that long-term unemployment reduces the effectiveness of job search (LNJ: 39). Worker search intensity could also have fallen because of improved unemployment benefits, while greater choosiness of employers about hiring might be due to more legal restrictions on firing. But these alternative explanations are neither self-evidently more plausible than increased skill mismatch, nor supported by much direct evidence (Abraham 1991: 459).

More evidence consistent with the hypothesis that skill mismatching was a major cause of high unemployment in the 1980s is the well-documented and heavy over-representation of less-skilled workers among the unemployed. Recent data for a range of Northern countries are summarised by Jackman, Layard, and Savouri (1991: 45–51). For example, the unemployment rate among university graduates is consistently lower—usually far lower—than the average for the whole labour force.[10] The same is true of professional, technical, and managerial workers. The unemployment rate among all white-collar workers is everywhere lower than among blue-collar workers. And within the blue-collar group, craftsmen are less afflicted by unemployment than the semi-skilled and unskilled. The range from the top to the bottom of the skill hierarchy is large: in the UK and the USA in the mid-1980s, the unemployment rate among semi-skilled and unskilled workers was more than four times that among professional and managerial workers (ibid. 45).

The present hypothesis of a decline in the relative demand for unskilled

[10] The two exceptions to this generalisation in table 2.6 of Jackman, Layard, and Savouri (1991) are females in Greece and Spain, countries which are not classified as Northern in the present book.

labour with rigid relative wages is not the only possible explanation for this pattern. To begin with, this sort of wage rigidity could account for higher unemployment rates among unskilled workers, even without a decline in relative demand (cf. Akerloff and Yellen 1990). There are also several quite different reasons why one would expect this pattern, at least in the North.[11] The first is that skilled workers are qualified for unskilled jobs, but not vice versa (Bean and Pissarides 1991: 334). Another is that unemployment is a less attractive option for workers, the more their wages exceed the social security benefit level. A third is reluctance among employers and employees to waste investment in training.[12] Hence in the UK in the 1930s, just as in the 1980s, unemployment rates were much higher among unskilled than among skilled manual workers (Pilgrim Trust 1938: 25–6).

However, the present hypothesis (like other skill-mismatch explanations) also predicts that the rise in aggregate unemployment during 1960–90 should have been accompanied by a trend *increase* in the degree of concentration of unemployment on less-skilled workers. To establish whether or not such an increase has occurred is thus a crucial test of the hypothesis. Moreover, the issue is a controversial one. A number of studies have concluded that there is no evidence of a general increase in skill—or other forms of—mismatch (Jackman and Roper 1987; and most of the papers in Schioppa 1991). Their negative conclusions are endorsed by LNJ, who accept that the *level* of mismatch unemployment is substantial, but reject increased mismatch as an explanation of the *rise* in unemployment, with the possible exception of the UK in the 1980s (LNJ: 38, 44–8, 446–7).

Others have contended, though, that the data and methods used in these skill-mismatch studies are open to serious doubt (Wood 1988; Paque 1989; Abraham 1991). Indeed, it will be argued below that most of the evidence currently available suggests an increase in skill mismatch. The argument will be developed in three stages, first clarifying the *prediction* of the present hypothesis, then examining data on the *direction* of recent trends in skill mismatch, and finally evaluating alternative measures of the *magnitude* of the contribution of mismatch to aggregate unemployment.

---

[11] In some developing countries, in the absence of a social security system, unemployment is higher among the educated, whose families tend to be richer and better able to support them while they seek work.

[12] This last consideration could in principle have the opposite effect. The expected return to an extended period of job search might be greater for skilled than for unskilled workers (Bean and Pissarides 1991: 327). Two other possible reasons for lower unemployment rates among skilled workers are suggested by Jackman, Layard, and Savouri (1991: 65–7).

8.2.2 Prediction

With only two skill categories, and a rigid relative wage, a reduction in the relative demand for unskilled labour would clearly tend initially to increase the unemployment rate among unskilled workers as a ratio of that among skilled workers, and vice versa for vacancy rates.[13] It was further assumed in Section 8.1.1 that inflationary pressure on wages would depend on the balance between unemployment and vacancies among skilled workers alone. So if the objective of the government's aggregate demand management policy were to maintain a constant degree of inflationary pressure, the pre-existing levels of unemployment and vacancy rates among skilled workers would tend to be restored, and the eventual outcome would differ only in respect of the unemployment rate (higher) and vacancy rate (lower) among unskilled workers. But the *relative* unemployment rate of skilled workers would still have declined, and their relative vacancy rate increased.

However, the opposite could happen, at least temporarily, if tighter aggregate demand restraint raised the unemployment rate also among skilled workers. This might occur because the government sought to reverse the initial surge of inflationary pressure, or simply wished to shift to a lower inflation trajectory, as in the North in the early 1980s. It could raise the relative unemployment rate among skilled workers, simply (though somewhat paradoxically) because there is generally more unemployment among unskilled workers. More precisely, a skill-neutral reduction in aggregate demand would raise the unemployment rates of both skilled and unskilled workers by (approximately) the same number of percentage points, and thus by a larger proportion for skilled than for unskilled workers, causing the ratio (< 1) of the skilled to the unskilled rate to rise.[14] Similarly, the combination of a relative demand shift and general deflation could leave the skilled–unskilled ratio unchanged.

[13] In principle, if the rigid skill differential in wages were initially too *wide*, and the associated excess supply of skilled workers were working in unskilled jobs, the net effect might be a reduction in unemployment among unskilled workers, who would be drawn into jobs vacated by skilled workers. In this case, the market-clearing wage differential would move towards rather than away from the institutionally determined differential. In practice, institutional rigidities usually make skill differentials too narrow rather than too wide, but there are exceptions, e.g. craft unions in printing used to obtain substantial rents for their members.

[14] I owe this point to OECD-EO (1987, ch. 3, n. 30). More formally, let the unemployment rate among skilled workers be $u_E = U_E/N_E$, where U_E is the absolute number of unemployed skilled workers and N_E is the total supply of skilled workers, and hence $(N_E - U_E)$ is skilled employment. Similarly, the unemployment rate among unskilled workers is u_L ($= U_L/N_L$). Let employment among both types of worker be reduced by the same proportion, ϕ. Absolute unemployment among skilled workers rises to $U_E + \phi (N_E - U_E)$, which causes their unemployment rate to become $u_E^* = (u_E + \phi (1 - u_E)) = u_E(1 - \phi) + \phi$. The rate for unskilled workers likewise becomes $u_L^* = u_L(1 - \phi) + \phi$. Given that $u_E/u_L < 1$ and that $\phi > 0$, u_E^*/u_L^* must be greater than u_E/u_L.

Temporary movement of relative unemployment rates in the 'wrong' direction might also be observed if skill differentials in wages were to some extent flexible, but with a lag. In other words, the initial rise in the relative unemployment rate among unskilled workers might subsequently drive down their relative wage, causing a decline in their relative unemployment rate, though this would not completely reverse the initial increase unless the relative wage were fully flexible. Finally, relative unemployment rates could move in the 'wrong' direction if the reduction in the relative demand for unskilled labour coincided with a similar shift in relative supply.

8.2.3 Direction

The available evidence on trends in skill differentials in unemployment and vacancy rates is assembled and evaluated in two appendices (Sections A3.2 and A4.3), whose contents are simply summarised here. The data are based on two different sorts of indicator of skill: personal attributes, such as education and experience; and job attributes, as reflected in occupational classifications. In practice, neither indicator is ideal—education and experience, for example, being roughly proxied by years of schooling and age—but the occupation-based data are particularly problematic. One reason for this is that occupational classifications are designed primarily to distinguish types of work (sales workers versus service workers, for instance), rather than levels of skill. Differences in skill levels can be inferred only for some coarse occupational aggregations (professional and manual, for example). In addition, unemployed people are hard to classify by occupation, since in principle they could work in a range of occupations and may not resume the occupation they had prior to becoming unemployed.

The most reliable information is thus probably that on unemployment rates by education and age (reviewed in Section A3.2). Of the nine countries for which data on the educational dimension are available, six show a strong trend increase in the relative unemployment rate of less-educated workers (Belgium, Canada, Germany, Italy, The Netherlands, the UK), one country a smaller increase (the USA), and two countries no clear trend (Norway and Sweden). In most cases, the upward trends would probably be stronger if allowance could be made for the disappearance of growing numbers of less-educated workers from official labour force and unemployment statistics.

The widening of skill differentials in unemployment on the educational dimension is apparent in data spanning both the 1970s and the 1980s, but was concentrated in the latter decade. In the former decade, the supply of college graduates increased faster than the demand for them, causing their relative wages to decline and (probably) their relative unemployment rate to rise, which, where skill differentials in wages were too narrow, must have *reduced* the degree of mismatch. Increases in skill mismatch during the 1970s are therefore likely to have occurred only *within* the college-educated and non-college-educated groups (for example, between skilled and unskilled blue-collar workers).

The relative unemployment rate of younger, less experienced, workers also rose in most Northern countries between the early 1970s and the mid-1980s. This increase was partly reversed after 1980. As explained at the end of Section 7.2.1, some of the reversal was probably an illusion, caused by young people vanishing from the official statistics; but some of it was probably real, in the USA and Canada mainly because of the steep decline in youth relative wages, in Europe mainly because of government action to provide more training and jobs for young people.

A second type of information is on relative vacancy rates by skill level (reviewed in Section A4.3). Only two countries appear to have such data classified according to educational qualifications—Germany and The Netherlands—and in both of them there is a strong trend increase in the relative vacancy rate for skilled workers. There are also data for France and the UK based on a coarse skill-related aggregation of occupational vacancies—and in the UK also on an employer-defined distinction between skilled and other labour shortages—which in both countries also suggest a trend increase in the relative vacancy rate for skilled workers.

Jackman and Roper (1987, table 7) use occupational vacancy data for eight countries in compiling skill-mismatch indices. These indices do not show any general tendency to rise, at least up to 1982 or 1983, when the series end. However, this evidence is open to more doubt, for two reasons. One is that these vacancy (and unemployment) data are based on more detailed classifications of (up to forty) occupations, which are not specifically related to skill level. The other is that the vacancy data, except in the UK, are not corrected for changes over time in their coverage, which have been important in some countries (Abraham 1991: 458–9).

The third type of information, which has to be interpreted with particular caution, concerns unemployment rates by occupation. The available data are summarised in Table 8.1, the first four columns of which refer to ratios between the unemployment rates of pairs of skill-related aggregations of occupations, while the final column refers to the relative dispersion of unemployment rates among some more detailed classification of occupations not specifically related to skill. The best data are probably those in the first column, which run to 1985 or later for all countries: in all six cases, they show a trend increase in the unemployment rate of blue-collar workers relative to white-collar workers, though the trend is barely significant in Australia and Canada.

TABLE 8.1. *Trends in relative occupational unemployment rates during the 1970s and 1980s*

	Coarse skill-related aggregations of occupations (ratio of less- to more-skilled unemployment rates)			Relative dispersion of unemployment rates (based on more detailed occupational classifications)
	Blue-collar/ white-collar JLS	Clerical/ professional and managerial	Unskilled/ skilled manual	JLS
Australia	+	+	0		+
Austria					
Belgium					
Canada	+	0	0	0	0
Denmark					
Finland					
France		+	+	+	
Germany	+	[?]	[0]	[–]	+
Italy		[–]	[–]	[+]	
Japan					
Netherlands					
New Zealand					
Norway					
Sweden	+	0	0		+
Switzerland					
UK	+	?	?	?	0
USA	+	+	0	?	+

Key to symbols:
+　= widening skill differential
–　= narrowing skill differential
0　= no trend
?　= unclear trend or conflicting evidence
　　= no information on this indicator for this country
[ ]　= assessment based on absolute numbers unemployed rather than on unemployment rates

Notes and sources: (1) The general source is Sect. A4.3.

(2) The two columns headed JLS are based on Table A4.2, which in turn is based on the data of Jackman, Layard, and Savouri (1991). The criterion for + in these columns is significance at the 10% level on a one-tailed *t*-test.

(3) The other columns are based mainly on visual inspection of OECD-EO (1987, chart 3.5). However, the entry for France in the unskilled/skilled manual column is based on the OECD *Economic Survey* of France (1990–1: 56), which uses more recent data and refers to unemployment rates rather than absolute levels (although the denominator of the ratio is the average unemployment rate rather than the skilled manual unemployment rate). The ? entries for the UK also reflect the conflicting evidence of Micklewright (1984) and Moll (1991).

The next three columns (the first of which again refers to blue- and white-collar workers) give a much more mixed impression. In thirteen out of twenty-two cases there is no clear trend, and in three cases the relative unemployment rate among unskilled workers appears to have fallen. But the data may well be less reliable. This is partly because some of them (including all the minus signs) are based on absolute unemployment numbers rather than rates, which inevitably makes the trend seem less favourable to skilled workers.[15] It is also partly because most of the series stop sooner, and so are more dominated by the deflation of the early 1980s, which, as explained above, could have caused relative unemployment rates to move temporarily in the 'wrong' direction. The last column also shows more mixed results, but the relative dispersion of unemployment rates rose in four out of six cases.

Another likely reason why the earlier data on unemployment rates by occupation (and the related indices of Jackman and Roper) do not consistently suggest an increase in skill mismatch is the supply-driven decline in the relative economic position of college graduates during the 1970s, which was associated with a similar decline for the higher-level occupations in which many of these graduates are employed, particularly the professions. There may have been a simultaneous increase in other sorts of skill mismatch, but much of this would have been concealed by the standard international occupational classification, which does not distinguish skilled from less-skilled blue-collar workers. In general, moreover, unemployment rates by occupation (like those by education and age) tend to understate the widening of skill differentials by neglecting the disappearance of less-skilled workers from the statistics.

8.2.4 Magnitude

The evidence on trends in relative unemployment and vacancy rates by skill is clearly rather limited, of uneven quality, and not entirely consistent. However, most of it, including almost all of the more reliable evidence, tends to suggest that the relative position of unskilled workers worsened in most Northern countries during the 1970s and 1980s. In some countries and some periods there were movements in the opposite direction, but these do not necessarily contradict the present hypothesis.

Conventional measures

It remains to consider whether the increases in mismatch have been large enough to account for the rise in aggregate unemployment. In principle, this can be assessed only in the context of a more fully specified model, including additional assumptions or information about economic behaviour. Two different measures of the proportional contribution of mismatch to aggregate unemployment are proposed by Jackman, Layard, and Savouri (1991). The first, due originally to Jackman and Roper (1987), is

---

[15] This is because the share of skilled workers in the labour force is rising, which tends to push up the denominator of (and hence reduce) their unemployment rate.

$$mm = 1 - \Sigma (u_i f_i)^{1/2} \tag{8.1}$$

where u_i and f_i are the shares of aggregate unemployment and vacancies in each sub-market. The second measure is

$$MM = \tfrac{1}{2}\mathrm{var}(u_i^*) \tag{8.2}$$

where u_i^* is the unemployment rate in each sub-market expressed as a ratio of the aggregate unemployment rate.

A characteristic of both measures is that they suggest that skill mismatch makes only a small contribution to aggregate unemployment. For example, in the UK, mismatch across occupations is estimated by the first measure to have accounted for 12 per cent of total unemployment in 1982 (Jackman and Roper 1987, table 2), and by the second measure for 11 per cent of total unemployment in 1985 (Jackman, Layard, and Savouri 1991: 70). Even with other dimensions of mismatch added on, the share is only about one-third (ibid. 71). If these measures were accurate, it would evidently be hard to believe that the increases in skill mismatch documented above could explain much of the rise in unemployment in the 1970s and 1980s.

The smallness of the contribution suggested by these measures has prompted both their creators and other authors (Wood 1988; Paqué 1989; Abraham 1991) to consider whether the measures themselves are biased or otherwise defective. One area of doubt concerns the hiring function assumed by the first measure—its form and elasticity, and how it varies across the sub-markets for different skill categories of labour. However, errors in this regard would not necessarily bias the measure downward. Moreover, there is sufficient empirical support for the assumed form of the hiring function to make it seem unlikely that these errors are large. The results are also quite insensitive to the curvatures of the price and wage functions assumed in the second measure (Jackman, Layard, and Savouri 1991: 71–2).

By contrast, the accuracy of both measures is much more sensitive to their assumptions about other aspects of wage determination, which differ from those of the present model. As explained earlier, it is assumed here that in many Northern countries, particularly European ones, institutional pressures make the wage relativity between skilled and unskilled workers rather rigid. The degree of upward pressure on nominal wages therefore depends on the demand–supply balance only in the skilled sub-market, in which labour is generally scarcer, and is 'copied' in the unskilled sub-market. If and where this model of wage determination is correct, it can be shown that the first of the two measures greatly understates the true contribution of mismatch to aggregate unemployment (Wood 1988). The creators of the second measure likewise note that such a 'leading sector' model of wage determination would cause the contribution of mismatch to be 'grossly underestimated' (Jackman, Layard, and Savouri 1991: 73).

The empirical evidence on this crucial issue is strong, though not entirely clear-cut.[16] On the basis of casual observation and formal studies (Wood 1978, ch. 6; Akerloff and Yellen 1990), it seems almost impossible to doubt that institutional pressures of various kinds make the relative wages of different skill categories of labour much less than fully flexible in many countries. Absolute rigidity is rare, but is not required by the present model, which simply predicts less mismatch unemployment where relative wages are more flexible. It also appears to be generally accepted, though not so well documented, that excess demand for skilled labour can pull up average nominal wages even when there is an excess supply of unskilled labour. Skill shortages are of course not the only source or determinant of the degree of upward pressure on nominal wages (other influences are discussed in Wood 1978, chs. 5–6 and LNJ, chs. 2–4). But other things being equal, variations in the extent of skilled labour shortages are likely to be an important cause of variations in the degree of wage pressure.

Alternative measures

The present model suggests a different measure of the contribution of mismatch to aggregate unemployment. In its simplest version, it is

$$Mm = 1 - \frac{u_E}{u} \tag{8.3}$$

where u_E is the skilled unemployment rate, and u is the aggregate unemployment rate. (Paqué 1989 arrives at a similar measure by a different route.) The contribution of mismatch is thus straightforwardly the excess of actual unemployment over what it would be if the unemployment rate among unskilled workers were as low as that among skilled workers.

A refined version of *Mm* would include vacancy rates. It should perhaps also recognise the possibility of skilled people working involuntarily in unskilled jobs, which might cause the simple version to overstate the share of mismatch unemployment (as open unemployment among skilled workers would understate their degree of excess supply). However, disguised unemployment exists also among unskilled workers, either because they genuinely withdraw from the labour force, since their prospects of jobs at acceptable wages are so poor, or because they are excluded from

---

[16] Jackman, Layard, and Savouri (1991: 74–9) demonstrate the apparent absence of *regional* wage leadership in the UK and the USA, but are less confident about the *skill* dimension, which is what is relevant here. They note the widening of occupational wage differentials in the UK in the 1980s, but also the apparent inflexibility of these differentials in other European countries, and the possibility that this could be 'a partial clue to high European unemployment' (ibid. 79).

the official unemployment statistics by ineligibility for unemployment benefits. Mm would probably be more accurate—and higher—if calculated with data on non-employment (rather than unemployment) rates.[17]

Other practical difficulties with this measure concern the identification of the relevant skilled sub-market. For example, even categories such as professional workers or people with a university degree are heterogeneous in terms of skill, although much less so than coarser groupings such as white-collar and blue-collar workers. Using their average unemployment rate as the skilled rate may thus tend to understate the contribution of mismatch at any point in time. It may also tend to understate the absolute (though not necessarily the proportional) increase in mismatch over time.

Ignoring these problems, and applying equation 8.3 with the unemployment rate of professional and managerial workers as the proxy for u_E, mismatch appears to account for a large share of total unemployment. For instance, for males in the UK, Mm was 74 per cent in 1985, up from 49 per cent in 1973–4, and higher than in the USA in 1987 (65 per cent).[18] The increase over time in the UK as well as the high share in 1985 are clearly consistent with the present hypothesis. (However, the initial share was also quite high, so that the proportional increase was only about one half.) The gap between the UK and the USA is also in the expected direction, but it is small, perhaps partly because of the rise in relative wage flexibility in the UK in the 1980s. (Moreover, if the calculation is done for 1988 with unemployment among degree-holders as the proxy for u_E, the estimated share of mismatch for males is slightly higher in the USA than in the UK.)

These calculations suggest that the rise in skill mismatch documented in the previous subsection could have been large enough to account for most of the trend rise in aggregate unemployment. However, they also expose a feature of the data which in principle cannot be explained by the present hypothesis, namely variations in the skilled unemployment rate, both over time and among countries. In the UK, for example, the unemployment rate among male professional and managerial workers rose from 1.3 per cent in 1973–4 to 2.9 per cent in 1985, whereas in the USA in 1987 this rate was only 2.2 per cent.

Such variations probably arise partly from errors and inconsistencies of measurement, but they also have two genuine causes. One is differences in macroeconomic policy. Northern governments gave much higher priority to controlling inflation in the 1980s than in the 1970s, and so pursued

---

[17] See esp. the article by Balls cited in n. 9.

[18] These calculations are based on data in Micklewright (1984, table 3, which refers only to males) and Jackman, Layard, and Savouri (1991, tables 2.1 and 2.2; the educational calculation mentioned later in this paragraph draws on their table 2.6). The years 1973–74 were chosen for comparison with 1985 because they were at a similar phase of the cycle.

more restrictive demand management policies, which raised the actual rate of unemployment relative to the equilibrium rate (LNJ: 436–7). In terms of the present model, the strategy was to reduce upward pressure on nominal wages by raising the unemployment rate among skilled workers.

The other likely cause is variations in the relationship between nominal wage pressure and the skilled unemployment rate. These might be due to forces internal to the skilled-labour sub-market, such as differences among countries in the degree of unionisation among professional workers, or in the extent of agreement among employers not to compete for skilled workers by offering higher wages (Soskice 1991: 395), or changes over time in the duration of earnings-related unemployment benefits. They might also arise from economy-wide forces, for instance, a rise in import prices which caused skilled (and other) workers to press for compensation through higher wages. Both sorts of forces, moreover, are clearly related to some of the determinants of wage pressure emphasised by Nickell (1990) and LNJ.

There is thus no logical difficulty in combining the present hypothesis with other ingredients. This is just as well, because it would be absurd to suggest that increasing skill mismatch could provide a comprehensive explanation of the behaviour of unemployment in Northern countries during 1960–90. Even if the explicandum is limited to the trend of equilibrium unemployment rates (neglecting shorter-term changes and the influence of macroeconomic policy on actual rates), other forces surely exerted some influence, especially in particular countries. However, the statistical evidence reviewed above, though limited and in some ways unsatisfactory, does seem reasonably consistent with the view that the rise in aggregate unemployment during 1960–90, especially in Europe, was caused *largely* by increased skill mismatch.

Impact of trade

The present hypothesis, of course, is more specific, because it maintains that expansion of trade with the South was what caused the decline in the relative demand for unskilled labour underlying the rise in skill mismatch. It is thus vital to ask whether the magnitude of the impact of this trade is consistent with the magnitude of the rise in aggregate unemployment.

As explained in Section 7.2.2, the cumulative impact of more trade with the South during 1960–90 was estimated in Part A to have been a rise in the demand for *SKILD* labour, relative to *BAS-ED* labour, of between 14 per cent and 30 per cent, around a central value of 22 per cent. The reduction in the demand for *BAS-ED* labour, relative to *SKILD* labour, would appear slightly smaller than this (because convention requires percentage increases and decreases to be calculated in an asymmetric way), with the central value being close to –20 per cent.[19]

It was further suggested in Section 8.1.1 that governments would be unwilling, because of the need to restrain wage inflation, to allow the absolute demand for *SKILD* labour to exceed its absolute supply. Thus if the wage relativity between the two groups were inflexible, the absolute trade-induced decline in the demand for *BAS-ED* labour would be similar in size to the relative decline: –20 per cent, or –10 per cent of the total labour force, of which *BAS-ED* workers make up about one-half (Table 4.9).

In principle, this figure of 10 per cent is an upper bound on the amount of unemployment that could be caused by such a shift in relative demand. In practice, wage differentials between skilled and less-skilled workers widened, and hence the rise in unemployment must have been smaller than this. The degree of widening varied among countries and indicators (Table 7.2), and the coverage of the data is limited, but the average change was probably 10 per cent or so during the 1980s, when the bulk of the demand shift occurred. So if (as argued in Section 6.1.2) the relevant elasticity of substitution is in the region of unity, this change in the relative wage should have offset about half of the relative demand shift, reducing the expected rise in unemployment to about 5 per cent of the labour force.

This estimate is clearly a crude one, which makes no allowance for other demand and supply shifts. But it is of the same general magnitude as the actual trend increase in unemployment: in the late 1980s, the weighted average unemployment rate in OECD countries was about 4 percentage points higher than in the mid-1960s (LNJ: 399). So in this respect, too, the present hypothesis seems reasonably consistent with the evidence.

This statement must be qualified in light of the discussion in Section 7.3.5, which weighed the view that more trade with the South was the main cause of the reduction in the relative demand for unskilled labour against the competing view that this trend was due mainly to autonomous diffusion of new technology. There is persuasive evidence that new technology caused part of the demand shift. Furthermore, the estimates of the impact of trade on relative demand are rough, and may be too large. The specific conclusion that the trend rise in unemployment was caused mainly by expansion of trade with the South is thus more open to doubt than the general conclusion that this trend was caused mainly by rising skill mismatch.

---

[19] See n. 48 of Ch. 4.

8.3 Cross-Country Variation

The extent of the trend increase in unemployment in specific countries varied widely, and an obvious further test of the present hypothesis concerns its ability to explain these variations. As already mentioned, the greater rise of unemployment in Europe than in the USA is an important feature of the evidence consistent with this hypothesis. But as Table 8.2 shows, there were large variations within Europe (from zero to more than 7 percentage points), and in Japan the increase was also small. These differences have attracted much attention, and there have been many attempts to explain them (Nickell 1990: 428–30; LNJ: 48–61, ch. 9).

TABLE 8.2. *Unemployment rates and explanatory variables in the North*

	Unemployment rate (%)			Explanatory variables (defined below)				
	Level		Change					
			UNCH	IMPCH	UNION	ALMP	BENDUR	EMCD
	1969–73	1986–90						
Australia	2.0	7.2	5.2	n.a.	3	3	48	1
Austria	1.1	3.4	2.3	0.7	3	11	48	3
Belgium	2.4	9.5	7.1	2.1	3	7	48	2
Canada	5.6	8.3	2.7	1.0	2	4	6	1
Denmark	1.4	8.6	7.2	0.7	3	8	30	3
Finland	2.3	4.3	2.0	0.4	3	13	48	3
France	2.6	9.8	7.2	0.8	3	4	45	2
Germany	0.8	5.9	5.1	1.4	3	10	48	3
Italy	4.2	7.7	3.5	0.9	3	1	6	1
Japan	1.2	2.5	1.3	0.5	2	6	6	2
Netherlands	2.0	8.8	6.8	1.3	3	3	48	2
New Zealand	0.3	5.6	5.3	n.a.	2	13	48	1
Norway	1.7	3.5	1.8	0.0	3	10	18	3
Sweden	1.8	1.7	–0.1	0.7	3	35	14	3
Switzerland	0.0	1.9	1.9	n.a.	2	4	12	3
UK	3.4	8.8	5.4	1.1	3	5	48	1
USA	4.9	5.8	0.9	1.5	1	2	6	1

Definitions and sources: Unemployment rate: in most cases OECD standardised rates (from LNJ: 398).

IMPCH: 1970–85 absolute change in ratio of (narrowly defined) manufactured imports from the South to GDP (for further details and sources, see notes to Fig. 5.6).

UNION: index of the proportion of workers whose wages are determined by collective bargaining (from LNJ: 50 and annexe 1.4). 3 = over 75%, 2 = 25–75%, 1 = under 25%.

ALMP: expenditure in 1987 on active labour-market programmes per unemployed person as a percentage of output per person (LNJ: 423).

BENDUR: length of time for which unemployment benefits continue at a reasonable level, in months, with indefinite duration represented as 48 months (LNJ: 418).

EMCD: index of co-ordination among employers, formal and informal, in the process of wage bargaining (LNJ: 419).

8.3.1 Explanatory variables

The sources of cross-country variation suggested by the present hypothesis, which overlap with some of the explanations suggested by other people, are implicit in the discussion of earlier sections. But it is convenient to elucidate them further, and to consider the availability of relevant data, before proceeding to some statistical analysis.

The objective is to explain inter-country differences in the trend of the unemployment rate, which will be measured as the absolute change between 1969–73 and 1986–90 (the variable *UNCH* in Table 8.2). It would be better to base the dependent variable on *non*-employment rates, thus allowing, as explained earlier, for the omission of workers from official labour force statistics. However, suitable data on non-employment rates are not readily available. It is also likely that discrepancies between unemployment and non-employment rates are a less serious problem in comparisons of *changes* across countries (as here) than in comparisons of levels.

Changes in the actual rate of unemployment (measured by *UNCH*) may deviate from changes in the *equilibrium* rate of unemployment, which are what the present hypothesis purports to explain. In the framework of a NAIRU model, the most likely cause of deviations is changes in macroeconomic policy, reflected in the acceleration or deceleration of inflation.[20] However, changes in macroeconomic policy are not likely to explain much of the trend of unemployment, and even less of inter-country variations in trend, since the reduction in tolerance of inflation has been common to most countries.

Another possible cause of variations in *UNCH* among Northern countries is differences in the extent of their (non-primary) trade with the South, and more specifically differences in the *change* in this trade over the period concerned. Such differences could be due to variations in barriers to trade (for example, more protection against imports from the South in some Northern countries than in others). They could also arise from differences in the skill structure of the labour force—the potential gain from trade with the South being greater, the larger the ratio of skilled to unskilled workers in the Northern trading partner. As before, trade with the South is measured by the ratio of narrowly defined manufactured imports to GDP, and its change by the absolute difference in this ratio between 1970 and 1985 (*IMPCH* in Table 8.2). *IMPCH* is not an ideal variable, for reasons explained earlier (Section 5.4.2), but the period over which it is measured and its absolute difference form make it reasonably comparable with *UNCH*.

The amount of unemployment caused by a given change in trade

---

[20] As Nickell (1990, n. 21) says, what is accelerating or decelerating in a NAIRU model is actually not the inflation rate, but the price level.

depends on the degree of relative wage rigidity. One measurable determinant of downward inflexibility in the relative wage of unskilled workers is the duration of unemployment benefits (*BENDUR* in Table 8.2). Changes over time in the coverage, availability, and level of unemployment benefits may also affect the flexibility of this wage differential, which for example would tend to be narrowed by a rise in the replacement ratio (benefits as a proportion of the average wage). Comprehensive data on such changes are not available, but benefit systems are known to have become more generous until about 1980 in Europe, though not in the USA, and less generous in the 1980s (LNJ: 3, 447–8). Another measurable determinant of wage rigidity is the coverage of collective wage bargaining (*UNION* in Table 8.2). This too increased in many countries, though not in the USA, until about 1980, but subsequently declined.

A third potential determinant of wage rigidity is the existence, level, and coverage of legal minimum wages.[21] In several European countries, the law reinforces collective bargaining by making some or all industry-level wage bargains legally binding on employers (Belgium, France, Germany, Italy, The Netherlands, the UK). Legal minimum wages independent of union–employer bargaining exist in five of the countries in Table 8.2 (Canada, Denmark, France, The Netherlands, the USA), but their impact on wage flexibility is likely to have varied widely. In the USA, for example, the minimum declined between 1981 and 1987 from 44 per cent to 34 per cent of average non-farm wages. It also declined in The Netherlands, from a remarkable 77 per cent of the average wage in 1978 to 68 per cent in 1987. By contrast, in France (to be discussed further below) the minimum wage was raised in both the 1970s and the 1980s.

The adverse effect on the equilibrium unemployment rate of a trade-induced shift in relative demand coupled with rigid skill differentials in wages could be reduced if employers agreed not to compete for skilled workers by offering higher wages. The variable *EMCD* in Table 8.2 is the LNJ index of employer co-ordination in wage determination. Unemployment among unskilled workers can also be reduced by government action to create jobs and provide training. *ALMP* in Table 8.2 is the LNJ active labour-market policy index. It shows wide variation among countries, with Sweden far above all others. Autonomous shifts in the relative supply of, and other sources of change in demand for, skilled and unskilled workers are also likely to have modified the impact of changes in trade on unemployment, but are hard to measure (see Chapter 7, n. 11).

---

[21] The sources of information for this paragraph are LNJ (annexe 1.4), Marsden (1989*b*: 3.6–7), and Peter Norman, 'The poor cousin of poverty fighters', *Financial Times*, 25 June 1991.

TABLE 8.3. *Results of preliminary cross-country unemployment change regressions* (size and significance of estimated coefficients on independent variables)

Regression no.	IMPCH	UNION	ALMP	BENDUR	EMCD	R^2	$\bar{R}^2$
1	2.41 *					0.22	0.16
2	2.95 ***	2.40 **				0.53	0.44
3	2.32 ***	2.94 ****	−0.16 ***			0.76	0.69
4	2.05 *	2.47 **	−0.16 ***	0.21		0.77	0.67
5	2.59 ***	2.62 ****	−0.19 ***		0.65	0.78	0.69
6		2.72 ****	−0.20 ***			0.58	0.50

Definitions, notes, and sources: (1) The dependent variable is the trend change in the unemployment rate (*UNCH*).
   (2) Definitions, values, and sources of all variables are given in Table 8.2. In brief, the independent variables are:
   IMPCH: increase in Southern import penetration
   UNION: extent of collective bargaining of wages
   ALMP: expenditure on active labour-market policies
   BENDUR: duration of unemployment benefits
   EMCD: degree of co-ordination among employers in wage bargaining
   (3) The regressions were all estimated by OLS, on 14 observations. $\bar{R}^2$ is R^2 adjusted for degrees of freedom. The significance levels of the estimated coefficients, on a two-tailed t-test, are indicated as follows: **** = 1%; *** = 2%; ** = 5%; * = 10%.

8.3.2 Preliminary regressions

In order to explore the relationships in the dataset, an initial set of OLS regressions was run, whose results are summarised in Table 8.3. It should be emphasised that the number of observations is very small—only one per country, with three of the seventeen countries in Table 8.2 lost for lack of trade data—which puts a premium on conserving degrees of freedom by using as few independent variables as possible.

The coefficient on *IMPCH* always has the hypothesised sign and does not vary much in size. On its own (regression 1), it is barely significant, which is unsurprising, since the effect of trade on unemployment is contingent on the response of relative wages.[22] This is confirmed by regression 2, in which *IMPCH* becomes highly significant when combined with

---

[22] The 'dual' of this result, in Sect. 7.2.3, is that the cross-country association between import penetration and relative wage changes is much clearer when changes in relative unemployment and vacancy rates are also included.

UNION, a measure of wage rigidity, which also enters significantly and with the right sign. The explanatory power of the equation is substantially increased by adding *ALMP* as a third independent variable. All the coefficients in regression 3 are highly significant and have the expected signs, and 76 per cent of the variance in the trend change in unemployment is explained. If *IMPCH* is omitted (as in regression 6), the other two variables remain significant, but the adjusted R^2 is about 20 percentage points lower.

It seems likely that the variable *UNION*, based on the extent of collective bargaining, is also acting more generally as a proxy for differences in national sentiment concerning the degree to which wages and incomes should be governed by market forces, and is thus picking up other institutional sources of wage rigidity. For example, *UNION* is positively correlated ($R = 0.62$) with the duration of unemployment benefits (*BENDUR*), although using *BENDUR* as an additional or alternative variable did not appreciably improve the results (regression 4). Moreover, *UNION* is almost equivalent, as may be seen from Table 8.2, to a dummy variable for Europe. It may thus also be picking up the influence of increases in the generosity of unemployment benefits and union power in European countries in the 1970s, which probably increased the rigidity of their wage systems relative to the USA.

Experiments with several other likely explanatory variables did not improve the results. The degree of co-ordination in wage bargaining among employers (*EMCD*) has an insignificant coefficient of the wrong sign (regression 5), though this is partly because *EMCD* is mildly collinear with *ALMP* ($R = 0.62$). Neither did co-ordination among unions appear significant, nor the change in acceleration of inflation, which in principle should explain some of the difference between movements in actual and equilibrium unemployment rates. The results were also much worse when *UNCH* was replaced as the dependent variable by the change in equilibrium unemployment rates (as estimated by LNJ: 436).[23]

8.3.3 Improved specification

Although the results of these regressions are consistent with the present hypothesis, their (standard) functional form is clearly inappropriate. It implies that the explanatory variables act additively and independently of one another, whereas the hypothesis predicts that they should interact in a particular way. A conventional way of dealing with this shortcoming

---

[23] *IMPCH* calculated on the broad, rather than the narrow, definition of manufactured imports also performed less well, as would be expected, since it includes refined petroleum and other processed primary products.

would be to add, and estimate, interaction variables. However, there are so few degrees of freedom that this seems impractical. In principle, too, it is more desirable to impose the functional form suggested by theory.

A plausible and simple form, including only the three variables with most explanatory power in the preliminary regressions, is

$$UNCH = \psi IMPCH \times (UNION') \times (1 - ALMP') \qquad (8.4)$$

where $UNION'$ is a transformation of $UNION$ that makes it lie between 0 (complete flexibility of relative wages) and 1 (complete rigidity). $ALMP'$ is a similar transformation of $ALMP$, with 1 indicating commitment to spend enough on training and job creation to eliminate mismatch unemployment. The coefficient ψ reflects the size of the impact that $IMPCH$ would have on $UNCH$ if wages were completely rigid ($UNION' = 1$) and there were no active labour-market policy ($ALMP' = 0$). This simple proportional relationship between $UNCH$ and $IMPCH$ seems reasonable, since both variables are absolute differences in ratios of national totals.

One important and appropriate characteristic of this form is that if $IMPCH$ is zero, so will be $UNCH$, regardless of the values of the other variables. Similarly, if wages were fully flexible ($UNION' = 0$), changes in trade would have no effect on $UNCH$. And even if $IMPCH$ were large and wages completely rigid, a strong enough commitment to active labour-market policies ($ALMP' = 1$) could prevent any increase in unemployment. The transformations underlying $UNION'$ and $ALMP'$ must evidently be such that they act proportionally between their extreme values. (For example, if $UNION' = 0.5$, the effect on $UNCH$ should be midway between the effects of complete wage rigidity and complete flexibility.)

To make maximum use of available information, quantitative and qualitative, the specific forms for the transformations were chosen by a combination of a priori reasoning and experimentation. The wage rigidity transformation that seemed most plausible was

$$UNION' = (UNION - 0.8)/2.5. \qquad (8.5)$$

This implies that skill differentials in the USA are highly—but not fully—flexible (a value of 0.08), whereas in Europe there is a high degree of—but not complete—relative wage rigidity (a value of 0.88). The other chosen transformation was

$$ALMP' = ALMP/34.6 \qquad (8.6)$$

which gives Sweden a value of unity, Austria and Germany values of about 0.3, and Italy and the USA values of almost zero. These equations were then used to calculate for each country the value of the composite variable

$$COMP = IMPCH \times (UNION') \times (1 - ALMP') \qquad (8.7)$$

(which is simply the right-hand side of equation 8.4 without the ψ term).

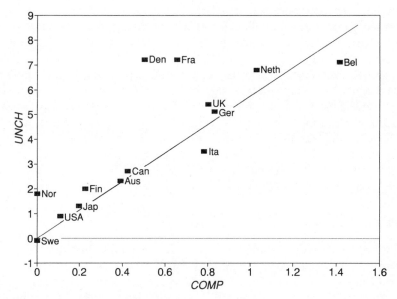

FIG. 8.1 Explanation of trend change in unemployment
Notes and sources: For definitions and sources of *UNCH* and *COMP*, see text and Table 8.2. The OLS regression line shown here was estimated excluding Denmark and France, and forcing the intercept to zero. The equation of the line (with the *t*-statistic in parentheses) is

$$UNCH = 5.73COMP \qquad R^2 = 0.88$$
$$(16.2)$$

See text for a discussion of the results of regressions using alternative specifications.

Fig. 8.1 is a scatter plot of *UNCH* against *COMP*. It strongly suggests that the relationship between the two variables is positive, linear, and passes through the origin, as predicted by the present hypothesis. And with two obvious exceptions (France and Denmark), the relationship appears to fit the data remarkably closely, given the fewness and other limitations of the explanatory variables. If the intercept is forced to zero, as the hypothesis implies, an OLS regression explains 60 per cent of the variance, or 88 per cent if France and Denmark are excluded (this being the line shown in the figure).

If the intercept is unconstrained, R^2 is 0.67 with France and Denmark included, and 0.91 if they are excluded. The unconventional method of estimating the transformations in equations 8.5 and 8.6 above probably makes standard tests inapplicable, but it is impossible to doubt that the estimated slope coefficient is significantly greater than zero. With the intercept unconstrained, the t-statistics are 5.0 (including France and Denmark) and 10.1 (excluding them). If the intercept is forced to zero, the t-statistics are larger, because the line is steeper (9.8 and 16.2 respectively).

The R^2 of 60 per cent with a zero intercept and all observations included may be compared with that of 76 per cent obtained in regression 3 in Table 8.3. That it is lower is to be expected, because a particular functional form has been imposed, but the decline in explanatory power is fairly small. Nor does this decline necessarily imply that the imposed form of the relationship between *UNCH* and *IMPCH* is inappropriate: it could merely be preventing the explanatory variables from picking up other influences on *UNCH*.

A closer look at the deviations

Most of the observations are so close to the regression line shown in the figure that it seems worth asking whether there is some obvious reason why Denmark and France (and to a lesser extent Norway) deviate from the line. It is obviously necessary to be cautious about attempting to rationalise deviations, especially with few observations, since there might also be *ad hoc* reasons for moving countries *away* from the line. The best approach is clearly to introduce additional variables covering all countries: where *ad hoc* explanations (or dummy variables) are introduced, it is likewise vital to check that these explanations are not relevant (in either direction) to other countries.

Some of the deviations might be reduced if better measures of exposure to trade and wage rigidity were available. For example, the evidence in Appendices A3–A4 suggests that relative wages in France were more rigid than in other European countries. Denmark, too, has legal minimum wages (and an unusually high replacement ratio—LNJ: 49). However, even the assumption of complete wage rigidity (*UNION* = 3.3) would leave *UNCH* in France nearly 3 percentage points, and in Denmark nearly 4 percentage points, above its predicted value. Nor in principle, since *IMPCH* was zero in Norway, can errors in the measurement of *UNION'* or *ALMP'* explain why this country lies nearly 2 percentage points above its predicted value. Moreover, it seems unlikely that these three deviations are attributable to errors in the measurement of *IMPCH* or to unusual defects in its capacity to proxy the true effects of changes in exposure to trade with the South.

As emphasised earlier, trade with the South cannot have been the sole influence on the trend of unemployment rates. The deviations from the regression line in Fig. 8.1 are thus probably mainly a reflection of other influences. The residuals are not significantly correlated with any of the explanatory variables mentioned in Section 8.3.1, except for a positive association ($R = 0.47$) with the replacement ratio, which reflects its unusually high level in Denmark. But there are plausible country-specific explanations for the three largest deviations.

In both Denmark and Norway, the late 1980s (which are the end-point for *UNCH*) were a period of severe restraint of domestic demand in order to eliminate structural trade deficits, which in Norway had arisen from the oil price collapse, and in Denmark had persisted for the previous 25 years.[24] Unemployment in these two countries therefore rose sharply towards the end of the 1980s, whereas in almost all other Northern countries it declined (LNJ, annexe 1.6).

For France, the single most plausible explanation of the unusually large trend increase in unemployment is the trend increase in the relative level of its legal minimum wage (the SMIC).[25] This was pushed up in 1973 and 1981, rising from just under 40 per cent of the average wage in the late 1960s to about 50 per cent in the 1980s. During the 1980s, moreover, the government made a strong effort to increase the degree of compliance with the legal minimum wage among private-sector employers. These policy shifts appear to have been unique to France (at least within the North). Their contribution to the rise of unemployment in France is disputed, but many observers believe it to have been substantial. In the context of the present hypothesis, this forced compression of wage differentials was clearly additional to the influence of increased exposure to trade with the South. However, it had much the same effect, namely to increase skill-mismatch unemployment.

A closer look at the non-deviations

The other eleven countries in Fig. 8.1 all lie close to the regression line, and it is of interest to consider what this figure (in conjunction with Table 8.2) suggests about the reasons for the wide variation in their unemployment trends. There was no single common cause for the unusually *small* increases in unemployment rates. In both Finland and Japan, the increase in trade with the South was small and its effect on unemployment was muted, in Finland by active labour-market policies and in Japan by a moderate degree of wage flexibility.[26] In Austria and Sweden,

---

[24] This assessment is based on the OECD *Economic Surveys* of these two countries (the 1986–7 and 1990–1 surveys for Denmark, and the 1987–8 and 1990–1 surveys for Norway). It is supported by the data on constant-price GDP growth rates for Northern countries in the IMF *International Financial Statistics Yearbook* (1990: 162–3).

[25] The sources of information for this paragraph are Marsden (1989*b*: 3.7); Katz and Loveman (1990, fig. 16); the OECD *Economic Survey* of France (1990–1: 54–6); Peter Norman, 'The poor cousin of poverty fighters', *Financial Times*, 25 June 1991; and Edward Balls, 'Youth "non-employment" in Britain and France', *Financial Times*, 30 Sept. 1991.

[26] The *UNION* score of 2 for Japan in effect reflects an average between the rigid relative wages of large firms and the flexible relative wages of the extensive small-firm sector (LNJ: 427 and annexe 1.4).

IMPCH was larger, and relative wages were rigid, but unemployment was prevented (partially in Austria and totally in Sweden) by active labour-market policies. And in the USA, where *IMPCH* was large and *ALMP* negligible, the smallness of the rise in unemployment was due entirely to the high degree of wage flexibility. At the other end of the line, however, the unusually *large* rises in unemployment all had the same cause—above-average *IMPCH* in conjunction with rigid relative wages (muted somewhat in Germany by *ALMP*).

To isolate the contribution of trade and wage rigidity to cross-country differences in *UNCH*, the value of *ALMP* was set to zero for all countries. The R^2 of the zero-intercept regression excluding Denmark and France fell moderately, from 0.88 to 0.72 (mainly because the Swedish deviation was larger). With Denmark and France included, it fell by a similar amount (from 0.60 to 0.46). One can also ascertain how much of the variation of *UNCH* was due to variation in *IMPCH* alone, by setting the value of *IMPCH* in each country equal to the all-country mean. The R^2 of the zero-intercept regression declines from 0.88 to 0.57 (including *ALMP*), which implies that 31 per cent of the cross-country variation in *UNCH* was due to variation in *IMPCH* and 57 per cent to variation in *UNION* and *ALMP*. This result assumes the validity of the suggested country-specific reasons for excluding Denmark and France. If these two countries were included, the contribution of variation in *IMPCH* would appear much smaller (4 per cent in the zero-intercept regression).[27]

Finally, the slope of the regression line in Fig. 8.1 is of interest. The value of ψ is about 5.7, although it is sensitive to the form of the transformation functions.[28] This implies that a one percentage point increase in *IMPCH* would cause a 5.7 percentage point increase in *UNCH*, if relative wages were completely rigid and *ALMP* were zero. It thus measures the impact of trade with the South on the skill composition of the demand for labour, and invites comparison with the estimates in Part A. The factor content of trade calculations in Chapter 4 imply a value for ψ of about 1.5.[29] If, as suggested in Section 4.4.3, this estimate should be

[27] With a common value for *IMPCH*, the Danish and French observations lie closer to the regression line, although most of the other observations are farther away from it. This is because both countries have high values of *UNION* and low values of *ALMP*, and hence, for a given value of *IMPCH*, a high predicted value of *UNCH*.

[28] e.g. if the denominator of equation 8.5 were 2.2 rather than 2.5 (implying that European wages were completely rigid) or if the form of equation 8.6 were quadratic—$ALMP' = (ALMP/34.6)^2$—ψ would fall to 4.9, and if both these changes were made ψ would be 4.2. However, these changes would somewhat worsen the fit of the regression of *UNCH* on *IMPCH*: excluding Denmark and France, the two changes together would reduce R^2 from 0.88 to 0.85; the Danish deviation would be smaller, but the French one larger.

[29] If macroeconomic policies kept the absolute demand for *SKILD* labour constant (for reasons noted in Sect. 8.1.1), the calculations reported in Table 4.9 imply that the absolute demand for *BAS-ED* labour would be reduced by about 2.7% of total employment (2.6% plus the 0.1% deflation needed to offset the rise in the demand for *SKILD* labour). This

doubled to allow for induced technical progress, and redoubled to allow for similar effects in non-manufacturing sectors, the predicted value of ψ would be 6, close to the slope of the regression line.

This last conclusion should be interpreted cautiously. As noted earlier, the estimates of the impact of trade on the skill composition of the demand for labour are rough, and the double doubling may be too large. Moreover, these estimates refer to the North as a whole, so that it is necessary here to assume also that in each country induced technical progress and effects in other sectors had an impact that was more or less the same in proportion to the increase in manufactured imports (on which *IMPCH* is based). This additional assumption is plausible, but not verifiable.[30]

8.3.4 Complementary and competing explanations

The results of the cross-country statistical analysis are consistent with the hypothesis that expansion of trade with the South, in conjunction with rigidity of relative wages, raised unemployment in the North. Regardless of specification, there is a positive association between *IMPCH* and *UNCH*. Indeed, the combination of variations in *IMPCH* and wage rigidity explains about half of the variation among countries in the unemployment trend, and most of the remaining variation can be explained by other forces which do not conflict with the present hypothesis. Moreover, it was shown earlier that the magnitudes are such that this hypothesis could account for the whole of the average trend increase in Northern unemployment.

It should be emphasised that the hypothesis purports to explain only the trend of unemployment rates between the 1960s and the 1980s. The dependent variable (*UNCH*) excludes not only short-term cycles of unemployment, but also the oil shocks of the 1970s and the exceptional demand shock imposed by the change in macroeconomic priorities in the early 1980s, which caused major fluctuations in unemployment, whose magnitude varied systematically from country to country. A complete history of

includes the reduction in demand caused by the loss of labour-intensive Northern exports to the South: if these were excluded, as might be more appropriate for the comparison with the effects of *IMPCH*, the reduction in demand would be 2.1% of total employment. This is based on $200bn. of manufactured imports from the South in 1985 prices, or about $280bn. in 1990 prices, which is 1.75% of total Northern GDP in 1990 (World Bank 1992, indicators table 3, taking the North to be high-income OECD-member economies). The implied value of ψ is thus 1.54 (= 2.7/1.75), or 1.20 (= 2.1/1.75) excluding lost labour-intensive exports.

[30] The extent of the innovative response to import competition is likely to have been related to the change in import penetration. Moreover, the change in import penetration is likely to have been determined mainly by two forces common to all traded sectors, namely the skill structure of the national labour force and national attitudes towards protection against imports from the South.

unemployment during 1960–90 would obviously have to introduce these other dimensions. But this would not necessarily cause any conflict with the present hypothesis about the general trend and the reasons for its variation among countries, which are the two aspects of this history that are acknowledged to be least well understood (Nickell 1990: 431).

There are, of course, other explanations of the trend of unemployment and its cross-country variation, including statistical models which also fit the data well (Nickell: 427–30). Some of these, too, complement rather than compete with the present hypothesis, which does not need (or claim) to be an exhaustive explanation, as witness the supplementary role of active labour-market policy in the preceding analysis. Moreover, even where there is a fundamental conflict about causation and behaviour, there may be an overlap of variables, with different interpretations being placed on the same statistical relationships. Collective bargaining and social security institutions, for example, are ingredients of many models of unemployment.

It would be misleading, however, to overlook the genuine and substantial disagreements between the present hypothesis and other explanations. Most economists (exemplified by LNJ) maintain that increases in skill mismatch were not at the root of the general trend increase in unemployment. Some economists do see skill mismatch as an important cause, but usually argue that new technology was the underlying reason for the shift in the skill structure of demand, rejecting the popular view that more trade with the South played a major role. The disagreements are thus on two levels: one concerns *whether* trade with the South contributed to the trend rise in unemployment in some or all Northern countries; the other concerns *how much* it contributed.

On the first issue, the evidence already presented makes it hard to doubt that trade with the South had at least some influence. But the case may be strengthened by a further test, using the LNJ (ch. 9) multi-country model. This is a structural model, fitted to annual data for nineteen OECD countries over the period 1956–88. It explains unemployment rates with four time series variables (real import prices, replacement ratios, a wage explosion dummy, and the stock of money), several variables which are different among countries but constant over time (benefit duration, co-ordination of wage bargaining, the proportion of workers with job tenure of less than two years, and the length, indexation, and synchronisation of wage contracts), and a set of country dummies.

LNJ use the model to generate estimates of the average equilibrium rate of unemployment in each country in the 1960s and the 1980s, from which the predicted actual average rates, and hence a prediction of the trend in each country, can be derived.[31] Since the model fits the data

---

[31] The equilibrium rate estimates are on p. 436 of LNJ, where the theoretical relationship between the equilibrium and actual rates is also stated. This relationship was used (by the

closely, these predictions are quite accurate: in an OLS regression they explain 76 per cent of the actual variation in the trend of unemployment among the countries in Fig. 8.1.[32] However, if *IMPCH* is brought into the regression as a second independent variable, its coefficient is positive and significant, and the proportion of explained variance rises to 91 per cent, although much of the improvement is due to a single country (Belgium).[33]

The second issue, concerning the *size* of the contribution of trade with the South to the trend rise in unemployment in Northern countries, is harder to resolve. This is largely because the statistical results depend on the way in which the model is specified—what other variables are used and how they are combined with *IMPCH*. If the specification 'locks out' trade with the South, as in the LNJ multi-country model, the ability of *IMPCH* to explain residual variance is likely to underestimate its true contribution. However, if the model is tailored to the trade hypothesis (as in equation 8.4), its true contribution may be overstated. Moreover, it seems unlikely that all such disagreements about specification can be resolved simply by goodness-of-fit tests, given (for instance) the small number of countries and the collinearity among some of the explanatory variables. The relative plausibility of different macroeconomic specifications may thus ultimately turn more on their consistency with microeconomic evidence.

8.4 Summary

Unemployment rates in the North rose between the 1960s and the late 1980s. The hypothesis of this book is that the rise in unemployment was caused by expansion of trade with the South (which reduced the relative demand for unskilled labour), in conjunction with rigidity of relative wages (which meant that the shift in demand emerged partly in the form of shortages of skilled workers and surpluses of unskilled workers, rather

present author) to predict the actual rates, using LNJ's data on d^2p (p. 437) and *NWR* (p. 407).

[32] Over all the nineteen countries covered by LNJ, the proportion of variance explained is 87%, but this drops to 80% without Spain (an outlier, and a country which is not included in the North in this book), and to 76% if the sample is restricted to the 14 countries with data on *IMPCH*. The actual trend in unemployment is based for this purpose on the 1960–8 and 1980–8 averages used by LNJ (p. 436), whereas *UNCH* refers to 1969–73 and 1986–90.

[33] The estimated coefficient on *IMPCH* is 2.39 (t = 4.2), which is similar to the corresponding coefficients in Table 8.3. When *IMPCH* is introduced, the coefficient on the predicted trend variable becomes more significant (t rises from 6.1 to 7.5) and closer to its expected value of unity (from 1.25 to 1.06). If Belgium is excluded, the t-statistic (2.0) on *IMPCH* is barely significant, mainly because the size of the coefficient is halved, and the increase in explained variance is much smaller (from 91% to 94%).

than simply as wider skill differentials in wages). The underlying reason for relative wage rigidity is the widespread view that people's incomes should not be too unequal, which is translated into practice, especially in Europe, by unions, minimum wage laws, and social security income floors.

An alternative hypothesis is that unemployment increased during the 1960s and 1970s as a result of other shocks, such as the oil price rises, and persisted during the 1980s. The persistence (or hysteresis) is argued to have occurred either because of insider power in wage setting, or because of the erosion of skills and motivation among those who remain unemployed for a long time (due to the long duration of unemployment benefits). The hysteresis view is not wholly convincing: for example, it cannot explain why so many of the long-term unemployed have little education.

If this book's hypothesis is correct, skill differentials in unemployment and vacancy rates should have widened. In other words, there should have been a rise in skill mismatch unemployment. Earlier studies maintain that this was not the case. However, most of the evidence now available shows that these skill differentials did widen. The minority of evidence which still suggests the contrary is based on unsatisfactory data, or reflects short-term movements which do not conflict with the present hypothesis.

Another necessary condition for the correctness of this book's hypothesis is that skill mismatch should be *large* enough to account for the increase in Northern unemployment. The formal measures proposed in earlier studies make this appear doubtful, because they suggest that mismatch accounts for only a small part of aggregate unemployment. But these measures are based on a theory of wage determination which does not allow for relative wage rigidity. When more appropriately measured, skill mismatch accounts for a high proportion of all unemployment. Moreover, the estimated size of the impact of trade with the South on the skill structure of labour demand is consistent with the size of the increase in Northern unemployment.

The hypothesis of this book explains why unemployment rose more in Europe, where relative wages are less flexible, than in the USA. More generally, differences among individual Northern countries in the extent of Southern import penetration and in relative wage rigidity account for about half the cross-country variation in the trend of unemployment. Most of the remaining variation, too, can be explained in ways which do not contradict the present hypothesis, such as the differing degree to which governments pursued active labour-market policies to combat the rise in unemployment.

In short, the evidence seems consistent with the hypothesis that expansion of trade with the South, combined with relative wage rigidity, caused most of the trend increase in unemployment in the North. It should be stressed, however, that this hypothesis does not claim to provide a complete account of the behaviour of unemployment during 1960–90, and could thus be combined with other explanations. For instance, the rise in skill mismatch was probably amplified by the autonomous spread of new technology. Moreover, there were major fluctuations around the rising unemployment trend, caused by other sorts of shocks and by variations in macroeconomic policies.

PART C
Prospects and Policies

Introduction

Part A of this book concluded that the recent changes in North–South trade have caused fairly large shifts—in opposite directions—in the relative demand for skilled and unskilled workers in the two country groups. Part B examined the consequences of these demand shifts, both in the South, where wage inequality has been reduced by the changes in trade, and in the North, which has experienced rising wage inequality and growing unemployment among unskilled workers.

Parts A and B were thus *backward-looking* and, as economists use the term, *positive*. In other words, the main purpose of the book so far has been to explain some important trends in the world economy during 1960–90. Part C, by contrast, is *forward-looking* and *normative*. Chapter 9 attempts to peer into the future, asking whether past trends will continue, or whether they will cease or change. Chapter 10 offers some policy advice to governments in the North, concerning possible responses to the decline in the relative demand for unskilled labour caused by expansion of trade with the South.

Why is there no chapter offering policy advice to governments in the South? This book, if its arguments are correct, has important implications for the choice of policies in developing countries, which are summarised in general terms in Section 10 of the first chapter. But to provide a proper account of these implications, appropriately tailored to the enormous diversity of economic circumstances within the South, would overburden an already long book. More importantly, a proper statement of policy implications for the South could not be written without substantial further research.

It should also be stressed that the benefits of the policies suggested to Northern governments in Chapter 10 would not be confined to the citizens of developed countries. On the contrary, a central objective of that chapter is to encourage Northern governments to adopt policies which would lessen the political pressure for protection against imports from the South, and so help to remove a major obstacle to the efforts of hundreds of millions of people in the South to work their way out of poverty through trade.

9

Past and Future

This chapter looks at possible future changes in the pattern of North–South trade, and at their impact on skilled and unskilled workers in both country groups, and in different Southern sub-groups. The first section outlines the general approach of the chapter, the second analyses the likely effects of changes in barriers to trade, and the third examines the consequences of alterations in skilled and unskilled labour supplies.

9.1 General Approach

Predictions of the future course of events are always inaccurate, and often spectacularly wrong. None the less, in considering policy responses to the trends in trade and labour markets explored in earlier chapters, the need to attempt such predictions cannot be avoided. In particular, it is vital to ask whether these trends will continue, or whether their direction will alter, or whether their causes were merely temporary.

Ideally, an exploration of the future would involve numerical projections with a formal model. What is offered in this chapter is much simpler, and entirely qualitative. It is based on the theoretical framework set out in Chapter 2, informed by the empirical evidence presented in later chapters. This framework provides a means not only of understanding what happened in the past, but also of assessing whether past trends are likely to continue, and of predicting the consequences of future changes in key parameters and exogenous variables.

9.1.1 The basic model recalled

It may thus be helpful to begin with a brief recapitulation of the theory. In its simplest form, it is a Heckscher–Ohlin (H–O) model with: (*a*) two factors, namely *SKILD* and *BAS-ED* labour; (*b*) two countries, of which one—the North—has a higher *SKILD/BAS-ED* labour supply ratio than the other—the South; and (*c*) two manufactured goods of differing skill intensity, as measured by their *SKILD/BAS-ED* labour input requirements (at any given relative wage).

What happened during 1960–90, in terms of this model, was that barriers to North–South trade in manufactures declined. This caused an increase in trade, with the North becoming a specialised exporter of the skill-intensive good, and the South of the labour-intensive good. The resulting shifts in the structure of production raised the relative demand for *SKILD* labour in the North, and reduced it in the South, with opposite effects on the *SKILD/BAS-ED* wage ratio in the two country groups.

This encapsulation suggests that the past trends on which this book has focused had two key determinants. One was the reduction in trade barriers (both natural and artificial). The other was the difference between the North and the South in the relative supply of *SKILD* and *BAS-ED* labour, which is the basic source of comparative advantage in North–South trade in manufactures (and services).

This simplified vision of the past in turn suggests a way of organising the discussion of the future. Section 9.2 will consider the first of the two key determinants, asking about the scope for further reductions in trade barriers, and their likely consequences. Section 9.3 will deal with the other key determinant, examining the consequences of possible changes in the relative supply of *SKILD* and *BAS-ED* labour in the two country groups.

9.1.2 Additions and refinements

Before embarking on this two-stage exploration of the future, it is worth giving advance warning of a few ways in which the model will be elaborated in the course of the discussion. One is to acknowledge that there are not simply two sorts of manufactures (or traded services), but a continuum of goods of differing skill intensity. Similarly, it will be illuminating to go beyond the coarse division of the world into North and South, with high and low *SKILD/BAS-ED* labour supply ratios, and to recognise that this skill supply ratio, too, defines a continuum along which several country groups may be distinguished.

In describing and using the basic model in earlier chapters, it was argued that the North–South difference in the skill supply ratio is so large that the two country groups tend to become completely specialised in goods of differing skill intensity. Partly for this reason, factor prices (i.e. the wages of *SKILD* and *BAS-ED* workers) are not, as in the textbook H–O model, *equalised* between the two country groups. Instead, the lowering of trade barriers causes relative factor prices to *converge*, with, in particular, a narrowing of the skill differential in wages in the South and a widening of this differential in the North.

This tendency towards complete specialisation in trade will be assumed to exist also in the more elaborate version of the model with many goods and several country groups. In other words, it will be supposed that there is a rough matching between the skill hierarchy of *goods* (defined by their *SKILD/BAS-ED* labour input requirements), and the skill hierarchy of *countries* (defined by their *SKILD/BAS-ED* labour supply ratios). For example, countries with middling skill supply ratios tend to specialise in goods of medium skill intensity.

There is, it may be recalled, a third type of labour (*NO-ED*), which is rare in the North, but all too abundant in many developing countries. This type of labour is omitted from the model as so far described, because *NO-EDs* are assumed to be unemployable in modern manufacturing and services. The basic model also omits land (or natural resources), which plays only a minor role in shaping the pattern of international trade in manufactures and services. From other points of view, though, *NO-ED* labour and land are important, and must be drawn into the discussion below. In particular, these two omitted factors have a major influence on the pattern of trade in primary products, exports of which are still crucial for many developing countries.

Trade in primary products is handled by adding a second dimension to the basic H–O model outlined above. The essential distinction between primary goods and manufactures is assumed to be that producing the former requires a higher ratio of land to educated labour (*SKILD* plus *BAS-ED* workers). In other words, primary production needs a higher ratio of natural-resource to human-resource inputs than manufacturing. The *allocation of a country's exports between primary goods and manufactures* thus tends to be determined by its ratio of natural resources to human resources (this ratio being positively related to the share of *NO-EDs* in its labour force), while the *skill intensity of its manufactured exports* tends to be determined by its ratio of *SKILD* to *BAS-ED* workers.

For example, at various points below it will be convenient to distinguish a sub-group of Southern countries whose factor endowments tend to restrict their exports to primary (and processed primary) goods. More specifically, P countries, as this sub-group will be labelled, are those which have high ratios of natural to human resources, because they have a lot of land per worker, or a high proportion of *NO-ED* workers, or both.[1] Some P countries are rich, such as the Gulf oil states. However, most are poor, with few natural resources, but even less education, such as Somalia.

It may also be worth recalling that physical capital plays no active part in the theoretical framework to be deployed in this chapter. As explained

[1] Thus not all countries whose current exports consist only of primary products belong in the P group. Some such countries are prevented from exporting manufactures and services by the biases of their trade regimes, or by lack of the necessary institutions or infrastructure. Conversely, some P countries, particularly richer ones, may export manufactures and services, by restraining consumption of natural resources or subsidising other sorts of activities (Botswana being a possible example).

in Section 2.2 (and confirmed by the evidence in Part A), the international mobility of finance and machines means that the pattern of North–South trade is not much influenced by differences in the availability of capital, except perhaps for infrastructure, which is not internationally mobile, and whose extent and quality differs greatly between the North and the South.

9.2 Trade Barrier Reductions

If (as argued in Section 5.1) reduction of barriers to trade was the main reason for the emergence during 1960–90 of a North–South division of labour based on differences in skill availability, an obvious first question about the future concerns the scope for further reductions in these barriers.

9.2.1 Scope

It is conceivable that this source of change in North–South trade has been exhausted. Transport and communications costs may have been reduced to minimal levels by an unrepeatable technological revolution, and protective tariffs and other artificial barriers may now be as low as they will ever be, in both the North and the South. But this does not seem likely.

As regards *natural barriers*, much scope clearly remains for bringing transport and communications networks up to what is now the technological frontier. This is particularly true of the networks within developing countries, whose often rudimentary or dilapidated condition is a major obstacle to the participation of hundreds of millions of their inhabitants in domestic (let alone international) trade. And even where transport and communications facilities are at the frontier, there are probably still many new opportunities for using them to increase trade, especially in services. Finally, it is unlikely that the current technological frontier is terminal. Historically, people have tended to see each stage of the astonishing improvement in transport and communications facilities over the past few centuries as the last—and they have always been wrong.

As regards *artificial barriers*, there are two respects in which further reductions seem assured. In the South, an increasing number of countries, often under pressure from their creditors, are liberalising their trade regimes. And in the East, the countries of Eastern Europe and the former Soviet Union, as part of the transformation of their economic systems, are seeking integration into the world economy.

What will happen to artificial barriers in the North is much less certain. The Uruguay Round of GATT negotiations, at the time of writing, is not yet complete, but should reduce barriers to trade in agriculture, manufactures, and services. Regional trade groupings—enlargement of the EC, the North American Free Trade Agreement, and ideas for an Asian equivalent—are becoming more prominent, and will have mixed effects on the level and pattern of North–South trade. In addition, outside the GATT rules, Northern countries maintain numerous unilateral and bilateral barriers to trade, including dubious anti-dumping penalties, 'voluntary' restraints, and other non-tariff measures.

Some of these unilateral and bilateral barriers to trade in the North are directed against Japan and other Northern countries, but most of them are intended to restrict imports from the South, as are some features of the formal tariff structure. The main reason for these barriers, the argument of this book suggests, is the harm that expansion of trade with the South inflicts on unskilled workers in the North, which provides protectionism with its most potent and durable political fuel. Substantial reduction of these barriers will remain difficult, if not impossible, unless and until other measures (discussed in Chapter 10) are actively used to counteract the adverse side-effects of more trade on Northern unskilled workers.

In addition to barriers to trade as conventionally measured (by transport costs and tariff rates or their equivalents), it is necessary to consider possible future changes in *distance penalties*. With products where the tastes or needs of customers are volatile and require frequent changes in specification, the time-lags involved in low-cost transport modes such as sea freight are a serious problem. Just-in-time production methods, too, require proximity of component suppliers. Greater affluence, and changes in technology and organisation, might therefore erode the cost advantages of manufacturing labour-intensive goods for Northern markets in the South.[2] There are already enough examples of this happening with specific products for it to deserve serious consideration as a possible general future trend. So far, however, there is no sign of a slowdown in the growth of Southern manufactured exports in aggregate.

9.2.2 Consequences

In summary, many barriers to trade will persist into the future, and some may even increase. In general, however, it seems likely that both natural and artificial barriers to North–South trade will continue to decline. In considering the consequences of this decline (in the rest of Section 9.2), it will be convenient to abstract temporarily from changes in skilled

[2] Hoffman and Kaplinsky (1988), Kaplinsky (1991*a*). For a contrary view, see Yeats (1989).

and unskilled labour supplies within countries (to be examined in Section 9.3).

Future reductions in trade barriers will extend the range of goods and services which can be traded profitably between the North and the South. In particular, better transport and communications facilities and further splitting up of production processes will expose more Northern unskilled-labour-intensive activities to competition from the South. In so far as this occurs, the past trends described above will evidently continue: trade will expand, specialisation will increase, and the skill composition of labour demand will shift in opposite directions in the North and the South. The process may slow down, but will not necessarily do so.[3]

There will also be movement towards greater uniformity of trade barriers among countries within the South, largely because more of them will adopt export-oriented trade regimes, but perhaps also through upgrading some of the worst transport and communications infrastructure. The consequences of more uniformity will vary according to the resources of the developing countries concerned. In P countries, which were defined earlier as those with high ratios of natural to human resources, trade liberalisation will not cause greater exports of (narrowly defined) manufactures and services. On the contrary, these countries should in principle export more primary goods, and *import* more manufactures (skill-intensive items from the North and labour-intensive items from other parts of the South). In practice, however, they may be unable to increase their primary export earnings, because of inelastic demand or Northern protection of agriculture.

In other Southern countries, with higher human–natural resource ratios, the levelling down of trade barriers will tend to increase exports of labour-intensive manufactures and services. Within these countries, the relative demand for *BAS-ED* labour will rise, with effects on inequality described earlier. However, their entry into the market will intensify competition among Southern exporters of manufactures, tending to drive down the world price of labour-intensive relative to skill-intensive items. The terms of trade of Southern manufacturers as a group will thus tend to deteriorate, with a corresponding improvement for the North (the results of Sarkar and Singer 1989 imply that this is already happening). The new entrants may still gain from the reduction of barriers, but less than they would have done if the terms of trade had been unaffected.

The consequences of this induced shift in the terms of trade for the skill

---

[3] This depends partly on the general speed of barrier reductions, and partly on their commodity bias. Among other things, barriers probably tend to decline faster where the gains from expansion of trade would be greater. Thus the past reductions in barriers to North–South trade might have been concentrated on items at the low-skill end of the commodity spectrum, and might have exhausted more of the potential for such reductions at this end than nearer the middle of the spectrum. If so, the shifts in the skill composition of labour demand will tend to occur more slowly in the future.

structure of labour demand within the *established* Southern exporters, and within the North, are not straightforward. The outcome depends on various elasticities, on linkages between traded and nontraded goods, and on the skill supply ratios of the new entrants, relative to those of established Southern exporters. However, to the extent that the established Southern exporters are already specialised in labour-intensive production, and the North in skill-intensive production, the terms of trade shift cannot have much effect on the output mix of their traded sectors, so that its effect on the relative demand for *SKILD* and *BAS-ED* labour within the established Southern exporters and within the North may be quite small.

9.2.3 More country groups

Additional insights into the consequences of lower trade barriers can be obtained by introducing a larger number of country groups. The first step is to isolate the P countries, whose export potential is limited to primary products. All remaining countries may then be ranked according to their skill supply ratios, or more precisely, their ratios of *SKILD* to *BAS-ED* labour, bearing in mind that *NO-ED* labour is not used in the production of manufactures and services. This ranking can then be split into country groups. H–O trade theory offers a criterion for assessing the number of economically distinct groups, each of which consists of countries which tend to specialise in the same set of traded goods.[4] In principle, the country groups defined below are all assumed to be distinct in this sense, although in practice their number is dictated by ease of exposition.

So far in this book, only two groups have been distinguished. The North (with a high *SKILD/BAS-ED* labour ratio) has generally been defined rather narrowly, including most of Europe, North America, and Japan, but excluding the poorer OECD countries such as Spain. The South (with a low *SKILD/BAS-ED* ratio) has correspondingly been defined rather broadly, and includes a much more diverse collection of countries, even after the P group has been separated off. An obvious next step thus appears to be to divide the rest of the South into two groups, labelled M for middle and L for low (which, with N for North, yields the alphabetical hierarchy L-M-N).[5]

[4] See e.g. Krueger (1977: 2–9) and Leamer (1984: 19–20). If the set contains only one good, the countries are said to lie in the same 'region of complete specialisation'. If the set contains two or more goods, the countries are in the same 'cone of diversification', and tend to experience mutual factor price equalisation through trade, even though their factor endowments may vary somewhat. But the factor prices within each group do not tend to be equalised with those in other groups, which specialise in different sets of goods. The sets may overlap, but not by much: with zero trade barriers, the maximum permissible overlap between groups is one good.

[5] It may be worth noting that the M and L groups do not correspond with the middle-income and low-income categories of developing countries used by the World Bank, partly

These two groups are hypothetical, in the sense that more empirical work would be needed to specify their exact country composition. However, the M group clearly includes a few countries classified as 'developed' by the UN (Spain, Portugal, and Greece, for instance), as well as the four little East Asian tigers and other more advanced 'developing' countries. In the future, it should also include most of the countries of Eastern Europe and the former Soviet Union, which have quite high ratios of *SKILD* to *BAS-ED* labour (Wang and Winters 1991).

It is instructive to suppose initially that there are only two sorts of good (skill-intensive and labour-intensive) and that M is a straddle group, which produces both sorts, while N and L each specialise completely in one sort. This situation is illustrated diagrammatically in panel (*b*) of Fig. 9.1, while panel (*a*) shows the original two-country-group case. (The figure, incidentally, is a variant of one in Krueger 1977, the essential modification here being that the hierarchy of countries and goods is based on differences in skill ratios rather than in capital–labour ratios.)

In this stylised situation, new entry into the L group, caused by wider adoption of more open trade policies, will have distinctive consequences for the M group. The increased supply of labour-intensive goods, which pulls down their world price relative to skill-intensive goods, and thus worsens terms of trade for L countries and improves them for N countries, will have little effect on the terms of trade of M countries, because they produce both sorts of goods. However, this change in world prices, which (it was suggested above) has little effect on the relative wages of *SKILD* and *BAS-ED* workers within the L and N groups, will tend to widen the *SKILD/BAS-ED* wage differential within the M group.

The widening of the wage differential follows from a standard proposition of H–O trade theory, which is that in a small country producing more than one traded good, the relative prices of its (two) factors of production are governed by the world prices of the goods concerned.[6] (The N and L groups, by contrast, are completely specialised in one good, and so their internal factor prices are independent of world prices.) Moreover, the proposition that new entry into the L group tends to widen skill differentials in the M group is of more than theoretical interest. As noted

because P countries are excluded, and partly because the L–M distinction is based on the skill structure of the labour force, rather than on per capita income.

[6] See e.g. Krueger (1977). Intuitively, what happens is that the change in world prices initially alters the relative profitability of the two sectors in M countries. The production of labour-intensive goods thus tends to contract, and of skill-intensive goods to expand, creating excess demand for *SKILD* labour and excess supply of *BAS-ED* labour. The resulting change in relative wages restores equality between the profit rates of the two sectors. But the eventual output share of the labour-intensive sector in M countries will be smaller than it was before the world price change. This is because the increase in the relative wage of *SKILD* labour induces all sectors to use less skill-intensive techniques: full employment of the given supplies of *SKILD* and *BAS-ED* labour therefore requires the share of skill-intensive goods in aggregate output to be larger.

Commodities

(a)

Countries	Skill intensive	Labour intensive
North	x	
South		x

(b)

	Skill intensive	Labour intensive
North	x	
Middle	x	x
Low		x

(c)

Commodities ranked by skill intensity

	1	2	3	4	5
North	x	x			
Middle		x	x	x	
Low				x	x

(d)

	High skill intensive	Middle skill intensive	Low skill intensive
North	x		
Middle		x	
Low			x

FIG. 9.1 Country groups and commodity categories
Note: x indicates production of (or, more precisely, comparative advantage in) these commodities in the countries concerned.

in Section 6.3, such a widening did occur during at least part of the 1980s in three of the four little tigers, and in Korea was apparently prevented only by unusually rapid growth in the supply of tertiary-educated labour.[7]

---

[7] Under strict theoretical assumptions, this statement about Korea could not be correct: the rise in its *SKILD/BAS-ED* supply ratio should merely have increased the share of skill-intensive items in its output, with no effect on relative wages (which should be determined simply by world prices). In practice, though, changes in the skill composition of the labour supply are likely to affect both output composition and relative wages (Krueger 1977: 16).

9.2.4 More goods

In reality, as mentioned earlier, there is a continuum or chain of goods (manufactures and services) of varying *SKILD/BAS-ED* intensity. Cutting it arbitrarily in two (as in panels (*a*) and (*b*) of Fig. 9.1) is illuminating in some respects, but conceals the important possibility that the M group may have its own area of specialisation. This situation is illustrated in the lower two panels of the figure. In panel (*c*), where the chain is assumed to have five distinct segments, M is still a straddle group, but is also the sole producer of commodity 3.

In panel (*d*), more simply, the overlaps between groups are supposed to be negligibly small, so that the chain has only three segments, in which each of the groups is completely specialised.[8] M-countries thus export items of middling skill intensity to N countries and L countries, from whom they import goods of high and low skill intensity respectively. For instance, Korea might sell ships and steel both to Indonesia, in exchange for shoes and shirts, and to Germany, in exchange for chemicals and machine tools.

Introducing more than two sorts of good permits, among other things, a simple analysis of the consequences of falling barriers to trade between Eastern Europe and the former USSR (the East) and the rest of the world.[9] This change may be viewed as an enlargement of the M group, whose effects can be explored along much the same lines as in the earlier discussion of new entry into the L group.

Consider first the stylised situation depicted in panel (*d*), with a unique correspondence between the skill intensities of commodity groups and the skill endowments of country groups. The entry of the East into the M group will tend to increase the relative supply of middling-skill-intensive items on world markets, and thus to reduce their prices relative to those of high and low skill-intensive items. As a consequence, the terms of trade of M countries will deteriorate, and those of N countries and L countries will improve.

The impact of this terms-of-trade change on the relative demand for *SKILD* and *BAS-ED* labour within the N and L groups, and within the countries that already belonged to the M group, is not easy to predict (but may be small, as explained earlier, if the groups are highly specialised). Nor, in this case, is it easy to predict the impact on the skill

---

[8] The extent of the overlap between segments depends on transport costs. As mentioned earlier (n. 4), if there were no transport costs or other barriers to trade, the overlap could contain no more than one good without melting the economic boundaries between groups. With positive transport costs, the overlaps can contain more goods, including those which are not tradable. See esp. Krueger (1977: 4–5, 16–19).

[9] See also Wang and Winters (1991), Hamilton and Winters (1992), and Stevens and Kennan (1992, ch. 2).

composition of labour demand within the countries of the East, since greater specialisation in middling-skill-intensive goods will cause them to reduce production at both the high end and the low end of the skill-intensity chain.

Next, consider the situation depicted in panel (*c*), where M countries are a straddle group, and the entry of the East thus increases the world market supply of all three of the goods produced by the M group. As in the panel (*d*) case, this will tend to worsen the terms of trade of M countries, and to improve those of L and N countries. And again, the impact on the relative wages of *SKILD* and *BAS-ED* workers within the M group (both its old and its new members) is not easy to predict.

In panel (*c*), however, the impact on skill differentials within the L and N groups is much clearer. Each of these groups produces one good in common with the M group, and one other good. The world price of the common good will decline, relative to the price of the other good, because of the rise in the supply of the common good caused by the entry of the East; and this change in relative world prices will alter relative wages within the group concerned (for the standard H–O reason mentioned earlier).

In the L group, the common good (number 4) is the more skill-intensive of its pair of goods, and thus the relative wage of *SKILD* labour will tend to decline. In the N group, by contrast, the common good (number 2) is the less skill-intensive of the two, and so the relative wage of *SKILD* labour will tend to rise. Thus in both the L group and the N group, the entry of the East will amplify the changes in the skill structure of labour demand that have occurred—and are likely to continue to occur—as a result of more general reductions in barriers to North–South trade.

9.3 Skill Supply Changes

Changes in natural and artificial barriers were identified above as one of the two key influences on future trends in North–South trade. The other is changes in relative supplies of skilled and unskilled labour, which in the present theoretical framework govern each country's comparative advantage. Some changes in relative skill supplies may be *induced* by trade, but it is appropriate here to focus on *autonomous* changes. It is also convenient to assume that barriers to trade remain constant, as do other possible sources of change in trade, and to go on using the same three categories of labour (*NO-ED*, *BAS-ED*, and *SKILD*), and four groups of countries (L, M, N, and P).

9.3.1 Patterns

'Autonomous' changes in the skill composition of a country's work-force are always caused by the interaction of several forces. Government policies and expenditures are extremely important, but are often shaped as much by economic and social pressures as by political preferences. Demography is a powerful influence: for example, larger cohorts of young people provide more opportunity to upgrade the educational level of the labour force, but may also make it financially impossible to maintain or improve enrolment rates and school quality. The actions of individual people, families, and firms with respect to education and training likewise depend partly on autonomous preferences, and partly on external incentives and constraints. In many cases, decisions and outcomes depend on existing, inherited, stocks of skills, with vicious and virtuous circles of cumulative causation.

The direction of movement in the average skill level of a country's labour force is thus not necessarily always upwards—primary school enrolment rates fell in many developing countries in the 1980s. Moreover, increases in the *average* level of skill, which in the present theoretical framework are the main determinant of long-term economic growth, may be associated with more than one pattern of change in the *relative sizes* of different skill categories (which govern the composition of trade and the internal distribution of income). In a backward country, for example, expansion of tertiary education would raise the *SKILD/BAS-ED* ratio, while expansion of primary education would lower this ratio, although it would cut the share of *NO-EDs* in the labour force.

To simplify the exposition, however, the discussion below will concentrate on cases in which neither the *SKILD/BAS-ED* ratio nor the *BAS-ED/NO-ED* ratio declines. Particular attention will be given to the case, often apparently associated with successful development, in which educational resources are initially concentrated on reducing the share of *NO-EDs* in the labour force to an inconsequentially low level, followed by a second phase in which the ratio of *SKILD* to *BAS-ED* workers steadily increases.

9.3.2 Ladders of development

Let us consider first the consequences of rising skill supplies in a single country too small to have a perceptible effect on other countries or on the world market. Within this sphere, it is necessary to distinguish between two fundamentally different sorts of movement: out of the P group; and up the L-M-N ladder.

Out of the P group

As explained earlier, P countries are those whose exports are limited to primary products by high ratios of natural to human resources. Increases in the supply of educated labour in such a country will tend to lower the natural–human resource ratio, and could thus propel it out of the P group. The difficulty of leaving the P group should not be underestimated, though, since comparative advantage in a H–O model depends on resource endowments *relative* to those of other countries. In other words, to exit from the P group a country must not merely raise the average educational level of its labour force, but do so more rapidly than the rest of the world, which for a poor nation is a formidable task.

Which group a country would enter upon leaving the P group depends on its *SKILD/BAS-ED* labour supply ratio. A poor country with a low per capita natural resource endowment, which had concentrated initially on reducing illiteracy, would move into the L group. But a rich P country, with a lot of natural wealth per person, might move into the M group or the N group, even if it too had concentrated initially on basic education. For in such a rich country, the natural–human resource ratio would not fall to a low enough level until a much higher level of education had been attained (and might never fall to such a level). By this point, the stage at which *NO-EDs* become an insignificant share of the labour force would probably be long past, and the *SKILD/BAS-ED* ratio already quite high.[10]

Whichever group it enters, the ex-P country will not stop exporting primary products (and its natural resources will always cause it to have a higher per capita income than other countries with similar human resources). But as it continues to accumulate skills, the share of primary products in its exports is likely to become smaller. How fast this share declines depends on several things, including the scope for using increased skill supplies to raise primary export earnings (which varies among primary commodities). And in practice the share might sometimes rise, if the world price of the primary export rose, or new domestic natural resources were discovered or harnessed. New mineral finds might even move a country back into the P group (this being a version of 'Dutch disease').

Up the L-M-N ladder

For a non-P country, what matters in the present framework is changes in its *SKILD/BAS-ED* labour supply ratio, which was assumed above to

---

[10] The point made in this paragraph may be compared with the proposition of Krueger (1977: 11–16) that countries with more natural resources tend to export more *capital-intensive* manufactures. This specific proposition was discussed and rejected in Chapter 2 (Sects. 2.1.4 and 2.2.4 and n. 15), but it is similar in spirit to the present point that countries with more natural resources tend to export more *skill-intensive* manufactures.

have an upward trend. The rise in this skill ratio will tend to have three long-term effects: (*a*) the income level of the country will increase, as the accumulation of skills raises average labour productivity; (*b*) relative wage differentials between skilled and less-skilled workers will narrow, because the latter category will become scarcer; and (*c*) the composition of the country's exports (and production) of manufactures and services will tend to become increasingly skill-intensive, in the sense of including a higher proportion of items with relatively high *SKILD/BAS-ED* labour input requirements.

The third of these tendencies depends crucially on the present assumption that the supply of skilled labour is rising only in this one country. For, as mentioned above, comparative advantage in a H–O model depends on skill supply ratios *relative* to those of other countries. So if the *SKILD/BAS-ED* labour supply ratio in the country concerned were rising, but more slowly than in most other countries, the skill intensity of its exports would tend to decline. In this case, moreover, the second tendency (narrowing wage differentials) would tend to be more pronounced, because the effect of the larger relative supply of *SKILD* labour would be reinforced by the decline in the relative demand for its services in the production of exports.

Even if the analysis is restricted to a rising skill supply ratio in one country in isolation, theory suggests that the second and third tendencies may not occur continuously or steadily, especially if (as assumed earlier) countries or country groups specialise in goods and services in particular segments of the skill intensity chain. In principle, indeed, it would be possible for a country to move up the commodity chain in an alternating two-phase sequence: one phase having narrowing wage differentials but no change in export structure, the other having constant relative wages but rising skill intensity of exports.[11] In reality, though, the distinction between such phases is likely to be blurred.

The process by which a rising relative supply of *SKILD* labour may take a country from the L group into the M group, and from there eventually into the N group, is clearly movement up a 'ladder of development'. However, the nature of this ladder is somewhat different from that envisaged by other economists who have used this terminology. For example, Krueger (1977) depicts the process mainly in terms of accumulation of physical capital raising capital–labour ratios and the capital intensity of exports. Similarly, many accounts of the upward progress of the four little tigers suggest that rising real wages and wage–rental ratios have

---

[11] See Krueger (1977: 9–11, 16–19) and Leamer (1984: 19–20), although in both these studies the two factors are capital and labour rather than (as here) two skill categories of labour. What blurs the distinction between such phases in practice is the fact that countries always produce (far) more than two sorts of goods, mainly because of transport costs and other barriers to trade, which partially insulate domestic product prices from world markets.

caused shifts from a labour-intensive to a more capital-intensive export and production structure. Even Balassa (e.g. 1979b, 1981), who also stresses accumulation of human capital, aggregates it with physical capital.

This physical-capital-based interpretation does not seem plausible, for reasons given in Section 2.2 (and empirically documented in Chapters 3 and 4). Capital intensity in the sense relevant to trade should refer to the capital–*output* ratio rather than the capital–*labour* ratio, and should depend on the rate of profit or interest rather than on the wage–rental ratio. Furthermore, there are no general theoretical or empirical grounds for expecting a decline in the rate of profit as a country develops, and hence for supposing that its comparative advantage will move towards more capital-intensive commodities.

By contrast, there is much reason to suppose that development involves a rise in the relative supply of skilled labour, and a shift of comparative advantage towards more skill-intensive exports. Average real wages thus rise mainly because the average worker becomes more skilled. This is not to deny the importance of physical investment, both in infrastructure and in directly productive assets, to economic development. Without it, the gains in productive potential that come with increases in skills could not be realised. And the process of investment and production itself makes a vital contribution to skill acquisition. But physical investment should be seen as the equipment which the climber uses to get up the ladder, not as the driving force which propels his or her ascent.[12]

9.3.3 Cross-country effects

The consequences of changing skill supplies have thus far been confined to the country concerned by the assumption that it was small. But since some countries are large, and since parallel changes may occur in more than one country, it is necessary to consider the consequences for other countries, too. In practice, these are likely to be complicated, partly because many different sorts of skill supply changes will be occurring at the same time. However, various tendencies can be disentangled, using analysis similar to that applied earlier to reductions in trade barriers.

The simplest case to consider is that in which each of the country groups is completely specialised in a particular (non-overlapping) segment of the manufactures and services chain (as in panels (a) and (d) of Fig. 9.1), and the skill supply changes are not so large as to move the country concerned into a different group. A rising supply of skilled labour in one country will raise that country's productive capacity, and so increase the

---

[12] The climbing metaphor is similar to that of Scott (1989), although his interpretation of causality is fundamentally different.

global output of its group's good, which (because the country is large) will tend to reduce the relative price of that good on world markets. The countries in its group will thus experience a terms-of-trade loss, and countries in other groups will gain. In this case, there will be little effect on the relative wages of *SKILD* and *BAS-ED* workers within other countries, since the composition of their traded-goods production does not alter.

Where there are overlaps between the segments of the chain in which each group specialises, as in panels (*b*) and (*c*) of Fig. 9.1, such changes in world relative prices will also affect skill differentials in wages within groups (for the standard H–O reason referred to earlier). In panel (*b*), for example, expansion of the *SKILD* labour supply in an N country, which raised the global output of skill-intensive goods and thus reduced their relative world price, would tend to narrow the wage differential between *SKILD* and *BAS-ED* workers in the M group. This narrowing occurs because the M group produces both of the two goods, and because the fall in the relative world price of the skill-intensive good induces a shift in the composition of M-group output towards the labour-intensive good.[13]

In panel (*c*), where each of the country groups produces more than one good, it is of particular interest to consider an increase in the *SKILD/BAS-ED* labour supply ratio in a large M country. This supply shift should raise the country's output of its most skill-intensive good (number 2) and lower the output of its least skill-intensive good (number 4), in the spirit of the Rybczynski theorem.[14] As a result, the relative world price of good 2 should fall, while that of good 4 should rise. This change in relative world prices would tend to narrow skill differentials in wages in other M countries (for the same reasons as in the previous paragraph), but to widen them in the other two groups.[15]

The widening of wage differentials in the L group occurs because the price of its *more* skill-intensive good *rises*, which induces a shift in output mix towards that good (and away from good 5), thus raising the relative demand for *SKILD* labour. By contrast, the widening in the N group occurs because the price of its *less* skill-intensive good *falls*, shifting the composition of output towards its more skill-intensive good (number 1), and hence also raising the relative demand for *SKILD* labour.

---

[13] The mechanism is explained (with reference to a change in the opposite direction) in n. 6.

[14] This theorem, which is one of the basic propositions of the H–O model, is briefly explained at the beginning of Sect. 5.1.2.

[15] It may seem paradoxical that an increase in the relative supply of *SKILD* labour can *increase* its relative wage, albeit only in other country groups. This happens because the world is supposed to be divided up into a hierarchy of specialised country groups. If, as in most formulations of H–O theory, all countries were supposed to be a single group within which factor prices were equalised, an increase in the relative supply of *SKILD* labour in any large country would tend to reduce its relative wage in all countries. Even in the present framework, the narrowing of differentials in the M group is likely to outweigh the widening in the other two groups (and hence a 'world average' of wage differentials would narrow).

This effect on the N group constitutes a further reason why the past shift in the structure of the demand for labour in the North against unskilled workers could continue in the future. In other words, rising *SKILD/BAS-ED* labour supply ratios in M countries will intensify competitive pressure on the least skill-intensive parts of Northern traded-goods production (much as the entry of the East into the M group will do—Section 9.2.4).[16] The mechanism differs, however, from that by which most reductions in barriers to trade lower the relative demand for unskilled labour in the North. For goods which are produced in both M countries and N countries (e.g. number 2) are 'competing', while the most important effect of barrier reductions is probably to move the production of less skill-intensive goods (e.g. numbers 3–5) out of N countries altogether, making them into noncompeting imports.

9.3.4 Further investigation

This chapter has studied some possible future tendencies in a simplified analytical framework. It should be seen as a preliminary investigation—the beginning rather than the end of a research agenda. A fuller account would admit more forces and more complications, as well as attempting to assess the magnitude of the tendencies concerned.

One obvious issue that deserves further investigation concerns interactions between changes in trade barriers and changes in skill supplies, which were considered separately above. Another set of issues would arise from the relaxation of the assumption that there are only three skill categories of labour, each internally homogeneous. The *SKILD* category is a particularly crude amalgam of different skill levels—from manual craftsmen to research scientists—but there are also substantial variations (among countries and people) in knowledge and ability within the *BAS-ED* category. Thus, for example, a country may increase its effective skill supply without altering the relative numbers of workers in these categories. Likewise, increased education and training which made *SKILD* workers more skilled rather than more numerous might widen rather than narrow wage differentials.

Introducing technical change would open up further possibilities. The analysis might not be fundamentally altered, since 'skill' and 'technology' are related concepts (see Section 2.3.2). But it is important to recognise that the skill-intensity chain of commodities is continually changing, in two respects. New specifications or production techniques may make

[16] This last statement refers only to the N group. In the L group, the rising skill supply ratio in the M group and the entry of the East will exert *conflicting* pressures on skill differentials, because the former *reduces* world production of good number 4, while the latter *increases* it.

particular items more or less skill-intensive, moving them up or down the chain, and into or out of the specialised segments of particular country groups. The chain may also become longer at the top, as new products and techniques of unprecedented skill intensity are introduced, partly in response to increased supplies of highly skilled labour.[17]

Finally, it would be instructive to introduce other sorts of trade. Like earlier chapters, this one has focused on trade based on differences in resource endowments, particularly skill supplies. This Heckscher–Ohlin approach (if appropriately specified) provides a convenient and reasonably accurate description of North–South trade, with which the present book is concerned. But a fuller account of future prospects should also consider trade based on economies of scale, product differentiation, and innovation (as for instance in Grossman and Helpman 1991). It should probably also look more closely at the issue of international migration.

9.4 Summary

Will the past trends in North–South trade, and their effects on skilled and unskilled workers, continue in the future, or will they cease or change? To answer this question, it is essential to look at the likely future course of the two key determinants of these past trends: (*a*) reductions in barriers to trade; and (*b*) the North–South difference in relative supplies of skilled and unskilled labour.

It is also essential to split the South into at least three sub-groups. One such sub-group contains the P-countries, which are those with a high ratio of natural resources to human resources, and thus with a comparative advantage in primary rather than manufactured exports. The two other sub-groups are L (low) and M (middle) countries. The distinction between L and M countries, and between them and Northern (or N) countries, is based on their supplies of *SKILD* relative to *BAS-ED* labour, which govern the skill intensity of their exports of manufactures and services.

Barriers to trade, both natural and artificial, will probably continue to decline, bringing an ever-widening range of goods and services within the scope of the skill-based North–South division of labour. Growth of trade will thus probably go on raising the relative demand for *BAS-ED* labour in the South, and reducing it in the North. However, this process will continue to be impeded by protection in the North, unless better ways of helping Northern unskilled workers are more actively pursued.

An increasing number of Southern countries are likely to liberalise

---

[17] Some recent research on 'flexible specialisation' and 'new competition' might be formalised in terms of these sorts of changes in the commodity chain. See e.g. Hoffman and Kaplinsky (1988), Best (1990), Murray (1992), and Kaplinsky (1991*a*, 1991*b*).

their trade policy regimes. Such changes cannot make P countries into industrial exporters, but will cause more L countries to start exporting labour-intensive manufactures. The consequent rise in the supply of these goods on world markets will drive down their price, worsening the terms of trade of L countries. This will not much affect the relative position of *SKILD* and *BAS-ED* workers in the North, where the most labour-intensive goods are no longer produced. But it will widen skill differentials in wages in M countries, which produce both labour-intensive and more skill-intensive goods.

The integration of the countries of Eastern Europe and the former Soviet Union into world markets will enlarge the M group. The resulting increase in the global supply of goods of middling skill intensity will cause this group's terms of trade to deteriorate. It will also tend to widen skill differentials in the North, and to narrow them in the South, reinforcing the effects of other sorts of reductions in trade barriers.

Some countries will progress up the ladder of development by raising their supplies of skilled labour, which involves first reducing the share of *NO-EDs* in the work-force, then increasing the ratio of *SKILD* to *BAS-ED* labour. Rising skill supplies will thus propel some countries out of the P group, and move others from the L to the M group, and from the M to the N group. Within countries, increases in the relative supply of skilled labour will tend to narrow skill differentials, as well as raise average real wages. However, rising skill supplies in M countries will intensify competitive pressure on the least skill-intensive traded sectors in the North, which will tend to widen skill differentials there.

The preceding assessment of the future pattern and effects of North–South trade should be treated with caution. Its assumptions may turn out to be wrong, the magnitudes of the tendencies that have been identified are not known, and the underlying theory provides only a partial view of reality.

10

Policy Options for the North

This last chapter explores the implications of earlier chapters for policy in the North (on policies for the South, see Section 1.10). Section 10.1 introduces the issues. Section 10.2 reviews motives for government action. Possible policy instruments are considered separately in Section 10.3 and in combination in Section 10.4, while Section 10.5 discusses the costs of mistaken policy choices.

10.1 Problems and Possibilities

The massive expansion of trade with the South during the past few decades has had mixed effects on the North. On average, people in the North have gained, probably substantially, from the greater specialisation permitted by the increase in trade. This conclusion is in accordance with economic theory, with casual observation of the abundance of inexpensive Southern manufactured goods in Northern shops, and with the calculations in Chapter 4, which suggest that these goods would typically cost about three times as much if they were made in the North.

However, the expansion of trade with the South has caused two sorts of problems for particular groups of people in the North. One such problem, which is well recognised, arises from the imperfect mobility of labour and capital among products and sectors. Trade-induced shrinkage of particular industries imposes costs on workers with industry-specific skills and on the owners of industry-specific capital goods. Considerations of equity, and the need to reduce political pressure for protection against imports, argue powerfully for compensation and assistance, which can help blighted localities to revive and displaced workers to retrain (Wolf 1979, chs. IV and V; Hufbauer and Rosen 1986, ch. 5).

The second sort of problem, on which this book focuses, is less widely recognised, but more pervasive and enduring. It is that more trade with the South has hurt *less-skilled workers in all sectors of the economy* by permanently reducing the relative demand for their labour, and is likely to cause further shifts in this direction in the future. In countries where wages are flexible, such as the USA, this problem has emerged mainly in the form of wider skill differentials—lower incomes for the working poor. Where the widening of wage differentials is inhibited by institutional forces, as in Europe, the relative demand shift has emerged as higher unskilled unemployment—larger numbers of non-working poor.

The policy interventions which are needed to deal with the first sort of problem (easing the pains of structural adjustment) are clearly inadequate for the second sort of problem. The purpose of this chapter is therefore to ask what other measures could and should be added. In principle, the answer might be 'none'. Thus, although the chapter will in fact suggest several sorts of action, it is essential, in the course of the discussion, to look closely at the grounds for regarding the reduction in the relative demand for unskilled labour as a problem for society at large (as distinct from the workers concerned), and to consider the possible difficulties and disadvantages of government intervention to alleviate the problem.

A convenient way to begin the discussion is simply to list the four types of intervention which might be used to 'solve' (in some sense of the word) the problem of more trade with the South reducing the relative demand for unskilled labour in the North. These are:

(*a*) raising barriers against manufactured imports from the South;
(*b*) reducing the relative supply of unskilled labour by education and training (to offset the reduction in relative demand);
(*c*) boosting the relative demand for unskilled labour by public works programmes or employment subsidies; and
(*d*) using taxes and transfers to redistribute income from skilled to unskilled workers.

Each of these interventions would benefit unskilled workers. Each of them, however, has costs and shortcomings—some obvious, some more subtle—and each of them could be implemented in more than one way. Moreover, although the differing strengths and weaknesses of these interventions favour policy packages which contain more than one of them, the choice of such a package is complicated by interactions and conflicts among its elements. A fuller analysis is therefore needed before any conclusions can be drawn.

The limitations of this chapter should be emphasised. It deals only with general principles and directions. To get these basic points straightened out is the first step in policy design, but leaves much of the task undone. Even within the realm of economic analysis, more quantification is needed than this chapter can provide (including probably some general equilibrium modelling). Technical, administrative, and legal aspects of policy design are also vital, but beyond the scope of this book. Finally, although some space is devoted to ways in which policy choices might vary among Northern countries, more attention to specific circumstances and institutions would be needed to get to the stage of having policies ready to implement in any particular country.

10.2 Motives for Intervention

The first question to ask, from a logical point of view, is *why* it might be appropriate for governments to take action in response to a decline in the relative demand for unskilled labour. The answer to this question clearly determines *whether* there should be any intervention, but is also important in deciding *how much* to intervene, and in *what ways*. The question will be approached below in the standard manner of economists, looking initially at efficiency arguments, and then at equity arguments. It will be necessary, though, to go a little beyond the standard economic framework, and to look also at some political and social arguments.

10.2.1 Efficiency

Policy intervention is conventionally held to be justified on 'efficiency' grounds only if it would improve resource allocation by counteracting some sort of market failure, such as an externality, or a missing or imperfect market. This conventional line of reasoning is often criticised for using too narrow a definition of efficiency. There is also a lot of disagreement about the extent to which markets actually do fail, and about the extent to which the failures can be cured by government action. However, for present purposes, the conventional logic will simply be accepted.

On the face of it, there may appear to be no efficiency justification for policy intervention in the circumstances under consideration here. For a change in the pattern of factor demand caused by reduction of barriers to trade in no sense constitutes a market failure. Moreover, the efficiency argument cuts *against* many sorts of intervention to help unskilled workers, which would involve raising taxes or introducing other kinds of distortion into the economy. Such interventions might be justified on other grounds, as will be explained below, but this would be despite, rather than because of, their effects on economic efficiency.

However, it is possible in principle that a shift in the pattern of factor demand might exacerbate the economic cost of genuine market failures, and hence provide an efficiency justification for government intervention (or for an increase in the level of existing intervention). The clearest and most general possibility of this kind here arises from the capital-market imperfections and externalities which tend to restrict the skilled labour supply (see Sections 2.4.3 and 10.3.2). This is because the trade-induced shift in the pattern of demand for labour increases the relative economic value of skilled workers, and hence raises the cost (in terms of forgone output) of having too small a supply of them. Government intervention to expand the supply of skilled labour could thus increase efficiency.

The other important possibility of this kind in the present context arises from the existence of relative wage rigidity. In most Northern countries, and particularly in Europe, the widening of the wage differential between skilled and unskilled workers in response to the trade-induced shift in the relative demand for their services has been restricted by unions, minimum wage legislation, and social security income floors (discussed in Sections 2.5.1 and 8.1.1). The demand shift has thus emerged partly in the form of greater unemployment among unskilled workers.

In these circumstances, where institutional pressures constrain relative wage movements, more interventions can be defended on efficiency grounds than where relative wages are completely flexible. This is because the rigidity causes the actual wage of unskilled labour to exceed the shadow wage, so that the economic benefit from additional employment of unskilled workers is understated, and the economic cost of training them overstated. Standard economic reasoning thus suggests that the unskilled unemployment caused by a shift in relative demand with relative wage rigidity could be tackled efficiently by subsidies to unskilled employment, or to training.

In theory, it would be even more efficient to remove the sources of wage rigidity. In reality, moreover, most Northern governments (and above all those of the USA and the UK) did indeed try during the 1980s to make wages more flexible, by weakening unions and minimum wage laws, and by lowering, and limiting entitlements to, social security benefits. But the political drive for greater wage flexibility was inhibited, especially in Europe, by the unwillingness of the public to accept that further hardship should be inflicted on workers and families whose incomes were already low. Whether more efforts to increase wage flexibility would be appropriate if coupled with other measures to tackle inequity, will be considered later (Section 10.4.3). For the time being, though, the existence of some relative wage rigidity will be taken for granted.

10.2.2 Equity

In outline, the equity argument for government intervention to counter the effects of the decline in demand for unskilled labour is obvious. Because unskilled workers and their families are already poor (by comparison with others in the North), it seems unfair that their relative economic position should deteriorate as a result of economic changes which benefit the people of the North as a whole. However, to assess the policy implications of the equity argument, it is necessary to examine ideas of fairness more closely.

Fairness is something on which opinions vary widely, among people and from country to country. Moreover, disagreements specifically about what would constitute fair relative wages underlie many labour-market conflicts (and tend to drive up the average money wage level: Wood 1978). But in a given country at a given time, there are usually some widely accepted principles of fairness, and it is these that matter most in the context of policy choice. In other words, in the sort of democratic political system that exists in most Northern countries, ideas of fairness are likely to affect policies, but only to the extent that they are shared and regarded as important by a majority of the electorate.[1] Such ideas, which may change over time, will be referred to below as 'politically effective'.

It is also essential to recognise that politically effective ideas of relative income fairness are usually the basic reason why the skilled–unskilled wage ratio is inflexible. This is clearest where the rigidity arises from a minimum wage law, or from unemployment benefits. But it is also true to a considerable extent where rigidity reflects the action of unions, whose coverage of the labour force and powers are much influenced by laws and government actions, which in turn depend ultimately on public opinion. In making an equity case for possible new policies, it is thus vital to take account of the ethical principles behind the policies that are already in place.

Existing policies and institutions are an imperfect guide to politically effective ideas of fairness in the country concerned. Where government policies are now a major cause of relative wage rigidity, as in Europe, proposals for change which ignore relative income equity arguments are unlikely to be accepted. But the absence of wage rigidity is potentially more ambiguous. A society with no concern about the fairness of relative incomes would allow wages to be flexible. However, the converse is not necessarily true, since in principle social concern for fairness could be reconciled with wage flexibility by redistributive taxes and transfers.

In practice, though, greater enthusiasm for wage flexibility is usually associated with lesser concern about the fairness of relative incomes, and vice versa. This is clear from comparison of the USA and Europe. It can also be seen from the trends in most Northern countries in the 1980s, when attacks on the institutional foundations of wage rigidity were accompanied by reductions in the progressivity of tax and transfer systems. This past association, moreover, has undoubtedly affected future policy options, by prejudicing many people who care about fairness against any solution that would involve more wage flexibility.

It should be emphasised that fairness is a *multidimensional* concept, of which concern about relative incomes is only one aspect. Other aspects of fairness are also relevant in the present context, for example, equality of

---

[1] This simplified formulation skips over some difficult political science issues—coalitions, electoral systems, voting paradoxes, and so on.

opportunity, and the belief that only those who are unable to work are entitled to income without working. Views about the fairness of relative incomes are also *multi-layered*: specific opinions in this regard arise from deeper moral beliefs, some of which provide justification for *in*equality, such as the principle that hard or unpleasant work deserves higher pay (Wood 1978: 26–32). Thus for many people, whether—and how—policies should assist workers and families with relatively low incomes depends at least partly on *why* their incomes are low.

Of particular importance in the present context are the reasons why some workers are skilled and others unskilled. The more this is a result of well-informed individual choice, effort, and expense, the harder is it to make an equity case for policies to help unskilled workers. For similar reasons, almost everyone believes that it is fair for skilled workers to get somewhat higher wages.

However, most people also accept that the children of unskilled workers should not suffer poverty as a result of the decisions of their parents, and recognise, too, that the higher wages of skilled workers are partly a matter of luck, or, in economic language, rent. Some workers were born with more abilities than others, into families with more resources than others. Moreover, today's unskilled workers could not have foreseen the decline in the relative demand for unskilled labour. It is these sorts of considerations which give force to the equity argument for intervention.

10.2.3 Social corrosion

The arguments for government action set out in the two previous sections are incomplete. More specifically, the conventional efficiency and equity framework of analysis does not fully capture the problems which the trade-induced decline in the relative demand for unskilled labour has caused in the North, because it touches only incidentally on something that will be called here *social corrosion*.

Falling relative wages and rising unemployment for unskilled workers have apparently aggravated a number of serious social problems in most Northern countries. The most obvious is crime, which has become a more attractive means of making a living as the opportunities for, and pay in, legitimate unskilled work have declined.[2] Another, related, problem is drug abuse, which offers not only opportunities for illegal earnings, but also an escape from the demoralisation of enforced idleness. Deprivation, insecurity, and alienation among ill-paid and unemployed people contribute to racial tension and periodic riots. Increasing numbers of beggars and homeless people provide an everyday spectacle of degradation in

---

[2] Some evidence for the USA is provided by Freeman (1991*b*).

the richer parts of cities, while the poorer parts decay into dangerous slums.

With sufficient intellectual ingenuity, these sorts of social corrosion could be dragged into the efficiency and equity framework.[3] But it seems doubtful whether this would add much to the case for doing something about them. There can be few citizens of the North who do not already want their governments to tackle these problems, albeit for a variety of reasons, and in a variety of ways. Moreover, most citizens are clearly willing to contribute to the fiscal cost of appropriate policy measures, partly from narrow economic self-interest, but also because of a broader and longer-term concern for the social environment in which they, their fellow-citizens, and later generations must live.

It should, of course, be emphasised that these social problems have many causes, some of which long pre-date the recent shifts in the structure of the demand for labour, and that even now these problems are confined to a minority of unskilled people. It would thus be absurd to suggest that all these problems could be solved by the sorts of policy measures outlined in this chapter, or that solving these problems should be the main objective of these measures. But it would be hard to deny that recent labour-market trends have exacerbated these problems. It therefore seems essential to add the social corrosion argument to the efficiency and equity arguments for government intervention to assist unskilled workers.

10.3 Policy Instruments

This section examines the four possible types of policy response mentioned at the outset (trade barriers, education and training, boosting the demand for unskilled labour, and redistribution of income). The merits of each of them are evaluated separately, in relation to the motives for intervention discussed in the previous section and from other points of view. How they might be combined into policy packages is explored in the next section.

10.3.1 Protection

Imposing tariffs, setting quotas, and raising other sorts of barriers to manufactured imports from the South undoubtedly has more immediate popular appeal than any of the other types of policy intervention to be

---

[3] Crime and riots, and measures to combat them, have economic costs and are thus 'inefficient'. Violence and homelessness are 'inequitable'. The presence of beggars reduces the 'utility' of passers-by.

discussed below. Yet, upon closer analysis, this protectionist approach is clearly the least desirable of the possible alternatives. There is thus a sharp conflict between instinct and reason on this point, which poses a serious political problem for democratically elected governments.

The popular appeal of protectionism is easy to understand. This approach would be effective, in the sense that higher barriers to labour-intensive imports from the South would unquestionably improve the economic position of unskilled workers in the North. Protection also satisfies the common desire for solutions which are simple, appear to strike at the root of problems, and lay the blame for problems on outsiders. People who are directly hurt by trade are therefore often able to attract wider political support in their campaigns for trade restrictions.[4]

The standard economic argument against raising barriers to trade is that they would reduce efficiency. As is well known, 'old' trade theory shows that protection is inefficient. This conclusion is supported empirically by several studies which have calculated that the costs of trade barriers to Northern society at large far outweigh the gains to those in protected sectors (OECD 1985; de Melo and Tarr 1988). More generally, this approach to solving the problems which expansion of trade with the South causes for unskilled workers in the North would mean also abandoning all the economic gains which this trade confers on everyone in the North.

If the costs which Northern trade barriers inflict on Southern countries are included, the efficiency case against protection becomes even stronger. For protection in the North denies the South the opportunity to specialise, and thus prevents its resources from being used in the most productive way. The inclusion of the South also disposes of the optimal tariff exception to the 'old' trade theory case against trade barriers. (The North might gain from protection by improving its terms of trade, but the loss to the South would exceed the gain to the North.)

'New' trade theory, based on increasing returns to scale, innovation, and imperfectly competitive markets, can be used to justify protection in some instances (Helpman 1984*a*, 1989; Venables 1985; Grossman and Helpman 1991). Its arguments, however, do not seem applicable to most North–South trade, which, as argued in earlier chapters of this book, is quite well described by the Heckscher–Ohlin model. In particular, although there may be strong infant industry arguments for protection in Southern countries seeking to catch up, it would be hard to argue that barriers against imports from the South would realise scale economies in the North (which is a huge economy), or that this would stimulate innovation in the North (or in the world as a whole), since the manufactures

---

[4] Governments themselves have often found protection attractive, because tariffs are an easy source of tax revenue. However, most Northern trade barriers are now of other types, which channel the rents elsewhere.

imported from the South are produced with knowledge borrowed from the North.

Most of the people who advocate barriers to trade, of course, do not rely on new trade theory, but make their case on grounds of equity. They argue that considerations of fairness should take precedence over considerations of efficiency. This argument, in its most general form, is important and logically defensible, but fails to recognise that there may be other, less inefficient, ways of achieving an equitable outcome. For instance, taxes and transfers that redistributed income from skilled to unskilled workers would usually reduce allocative efficiency, but by less than an equivalent (in terms of narrowing the skilled–unskilled income gap) increase in trade barriers. This is because the taxes and transfers would be more precisely targeted. In a global sense, moreover, protection is highly *in*equitable, because of its adverse effects on people in the South, most of whom are much poorer than unskilled workers in the North.

It would be wrong, however, simply to forget about the equity arguments for protection. There are indeed better policy alternatives. But unless those alternatives are actually implemented, the problem of inequity will remain, and so will the political pressures to solve it by raising trade barriers. If Northern governments, that is to say, fail to help unskilled workers in comparatively efficient ways, they are more likely to be forced to maintain and raise barriers to trade.[5] So whether one is concerned with efficiency in the North or with damage to the South, the best way to fight protection is not to deny—as some well-intentioned economists have done—that trade with the South hurts workers in the North, but to acknowledge the problem and promote better ways of dealing with it.

10.3.2 Education and training

In many ways, the most attractive solution to the problems caused by the decline in the relative demand for unskilled labour would be to engineer a matching reduction in the relative *supply* of unskilled labour, or, to put it another way, for the government to take action to *increase* the relative supply of *skilled* labour. This would move some unskilled workers into the higher-paid skilled category, while workers who remained unskilled would benefit because their sort of labour would become relatively scarcer. The wage and unemployment differentials between skilled and

---

[5] That such an outcome is likely is suggested both by casual observation and by serious research. Baldwin (1984: 579–82) summarises the results of many empirical studies, in a range of Northern countries, that have tried to explain inter-industry variations in levels of protection in terms of other industry characteristics. Barriers to imports tend to be highest in industries with high labour-input coefficients, with high proportions of unskilled workers, and with low average wages (which again indicate that most of their workers are unskilled). Barriers also tend to be higher where imports from developing countries are substantial.

unskilled workers would thus tend to shrink, improving equity and reducing social corrosion. Moreover, this approach could increase economic efficiency, since market failures tend to cause underinvestment in skill acquisition.

This approach would also be consistent with the emphasis put by Northern governments in recent years on better education and training. During the 1980s, there was rising public concern about deficiencies in the school system. The OECD, in its annual *Employment Outlook*, urged governments to upgrade worker skills, in order to assist labour-market adjustment and to promote economic growth. Particular countries responded with reforms and innovations. In the UK, for instance, there was expansion of university student numbers, introduction of a national school curriculum, and more training for the unemployed. In the USA, education and training became a central ingredient of economic strategy with the election of President Clinton (much influenced by Reich 1991).

One of the main conclusions of this chapter will be that government action to raise the supply of skilled labour is, indeed, essential to solving the problems posed by the decline in demand for unskilled labour. Nothing that is said in the next few pages should detract from this central point. But it is also essential to recognise the limitations and difficulties of this approach. To proceed on the assumption that improvements in education and training are a simple or sufficient solution would be a costly mistake.

Behaviour and incentives

A fundamental consideration is that the supply of skilled labour (unlike, say, the supply of roads) is not something over which any government has direct control. The size of the skilled-labour supply depends, rather, on the behaviour of a large number of individuals, families, and institutions, which in each case is to some extent a matter of choice and to some extent shaped by constraints and opportunities. Governments must thus intervene indirectly, by trying to alter the choices, constraints, and opportunities of the people and organisations who make up the economy and society.

In this context, it is clearly also important to bear in mind the need for *incentives* to encourage people to acquire skills. For although some skills are innate, and learning others is a costless and pleasurable process, the acquisition of most skills involves costs—cash outlays, forgone earnings, sacrifice of leisure time, and the sheer effort of diligent study. To induce people to acquire skills, there must be economic rewards large enough to compensate for these costs. These rewards consist mainly of the difference in wages and unemployment rates (and thus in living standards) between skilled and unskilled workers.

One way of increasing the supply of skilled labour would thus be for the government to widen this gap in living standards, for example by heavier taxation of unskilled workers, so creating stronger incentives to acquire skills. However, this approach would not make sense here, since it would intensify rather than alleviate the problems caused by falling demand for unskilled labour. What is needed, on the contrary, is a narrowing of the gap in living standards, to achieve which the government must increase the relative supply of skilled workers *at any given gap* in living standards.

These points are illustrated in a simple way in Fig. 10.1, which shows the relative numbers of *SKILD* and *BAS-ED* workers demanded and supplied as functions of their relative wage, which is taken in this instance to be flexible. In this figure (and in later figures in this chapter), the demand curve is that which prevails *after* the expansion of trade with the South. Moreover, it will be assumed for simplicity that the proportional tax burden on skilled and unskilled workers is initially equal, making the net-of-tax wage ratio (which governs relative living standards) equal to the gross-of-tax wage ratio, and hence removing the need for an initial distinction between gross and net supply and demand curves.

Panel (*a*) shows the effect of raising the tax rate on unskilled workers, which pushes the gross supply curve below the net supply curve, because, given any gross wage differential, the net differential is now larger. The result is *movement up* the net supply curve, which raises the relative number of skilled workers supplied, and narrows the gross wage differential, but not by enough to offset the disequalising change in relative tax rates. The net-of-tax wage differential is therefore widened, making unskilled workers worse off. By contrast, panel (*b*) depicts an *outward shift* of the supply curve, which makes unskilled workers better off by reducing both the gross and the net wage differential. It is this second sort of change that the government must seek to achieve through improved education and training.

Fiscal constraints

To contrive such an outward shift of the skill supply function may seem easy. For there is almost limitless scope for greater public expenditure on making many forms of education and training cheaper, of better quality, and more accessible. Nor can it be doubted that such improvements, other things being equal, would motivate and enable many more people to acquire economically useful skills. However, it is also necessary to consider the more difficult question of how this additional public expenditure would be financed. There might be some room for compensating cuts in other public expenditure, or for more borrowing. But for the most part extra spending on education and training would have to be matched by higher taxes.

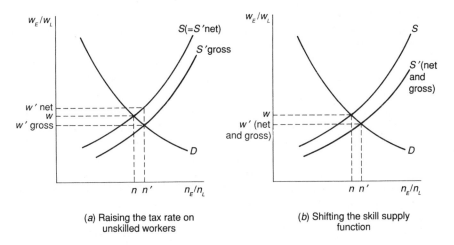

(a) Raising the tax rate on
unskilled workers

(b) Shifting the skill supply
function

FIG. 10.1 Two ways of increasing the skilled labour supply
Notes (relevant also to later figures in this chapter): For an introduction to these
relative supply and demand diagrams, see Sect. 5.2.1 (and Fig. 5.3).

w_E and w_L are the wage rates of *SKILD* and *BAS-ED* (that is, skilled and
unskilled) workers respectively, and thus w_E/w_L is the ratio of skilled to unskilled
wages. Likewise, n_E and n_L are the numbers of *SKILD* and *BAS-ED* workers.

Labels without prime superscripts (e.g. w, S) refer to the situation *without* government intervention, those with primes (e.g. n', $S'gross$) to the situation *with* government intervention.

'Gross' refers to the wage ratio (w_E/w_L) gross of income taxes paid by workers,
which in this diagram is also the ratio paid by employers (so that the new equilibrium in panel (a) is determined by the intersection of D with $S'gross$). 'Net' refers
to the ratio of wages net of income taxes, which determines the relative living
standards of the two groups of workers.

The extra taxes might fall partly on people whose incomes come mainly
from capital, but most would inevitably have to be paid (directly or indirectly) by *workers*, whose earnings account for the bulk of national
income. In the present context, moreover, raising taxes either on unskilled
or on skilled workers would have some rather obvious disadvantages.
(The argument which follows owes much to Jackman, Layard, and
Savouri 1991: 81–7, though it has a somewhat different orientation.)

Raising taxes on *unskilled* workers would cause an immediate reduction
in their living standards, and thus aggravate the problems caused by the
fall in demand for their labour. This reduction might be only temporary,
since in theory the relative position of unskilled workers could be
improved by taxing them more heavily and using the proceeds to improve

education and training, provided that the extra spending caused a large enough shift in the skill supply function. (This possibility could be shown in panel (*a*) of Fig. 10.1 by shifting *S'gross* and *S'net* substantially to the right.) Even in this case, however, the skill supply shift would occur slowly, and in the intervening period unskilled workers would still be worse off.

For the time being, it thus seems appropriate to rule out any increase in taxes on unskilled workers, and to assume that extra spending on education and training would have to be financed by higher taxes on *skilled* workers. This approach, though, would have the disadvantage of narrowing the net-of-tax difference in wages between skilled and unskilled workers, which would diminish the incentive to acquire skills, and so tend to *reduce* the skilled labour supply, offsetting the extra spending on education and training.

Fig. 10.2 illustrates the interaction of these two conflicting pressures. The extra spending on education and training shifts the net supply curve to the right (from *S* to *S'net*). The higher taxes on skilled workers lift the gross supply curve (*S'gross*) above the net supply curve (a wider gross wage differential is now needed to attain any given net differential), causing movement down the net supply curve. In panel (*a*), the final outcome is an increase in the relative supply of skilled labour, but a smaller one than would have been anticipated simply by considering the effects of the extra spending on education and training.

Panel (*b*) is a simplified close-up of part of panel (*a*), labelled to show the forces at work in more detail. The degree to which the positive direct effect on the skill supply of a given improvement in education and training (AB) is offset by the indirect disincentive effect depends on two things. One is how much the improvement *costs*, which determines the increase in taxes on skilled workers (BC). The other is the *elasticity* of the supply curve, which determines how much this increase in taxes reduces the number of skilled workers (CF). Thus the cheaper the improvement, and the lower the elasticity, the closer will be the final outcome (FG) to the positive direct effect.

It is then easy (though rather sobering) to see something which was not obvious at the outset, namely that the final outcome of efforts to improve education and training could be a *reduction* in the skilled-labour supply, as is illustrated in panel (*c*). This would occur if the improvements had only a small direct effect, or if they were expensive to implement, or if the skill supply function were highly elastic. It can also be seen that for the final outcome to be an increase in the skill supply, the new gross supply curve (*S'gross*) must lie below the old (gross and net) supply curve *S*, which makes more precise the sense in which the supply curve has to be shifted if this approach is to be effective.

Inadvertently to generate an inward shift of the skill supply function,

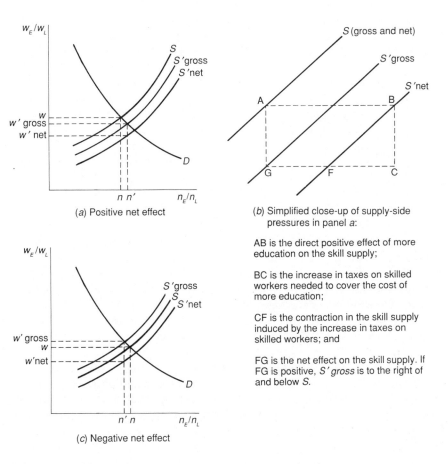

FIG. 10.2 Conflicting pressures on the skilled labour supply

while striving to move it outward, would be most unfortunate. The result would be inefficient. It would also tend to amplify, rather than diminish, the problems of inequity and social corrosion caused by falling demand for unskilled workers, since shifting the supply function the wrong way would make their labour relatively more abundant, rather than scarcer. The net-of-tax skill differential in wages would be narrowed, as can be seen from panel (c), but only because of the rise in taxes on skilled workers. This improvement in the *relative* position of unskilled workers would be little consolation for the *absolute* decline in their living standards.[6]

---

[6] Changes in the absolute wages of unskilled workers cannot be shown in the sort of diagram used here. However, the net unskilled wage must tend to fall, because the supply of unskilled workers rises, driving down their gross wage, while the tax rate on unskilled workers is unchanged.

Scope for intervention

The implication is not, of course, that all government action to improve education and training would be unhelpful. What the analysis does imply, though, is that this approach is more limited and more complicated than is commonly supposed, and that there is a risk of this approach backfiring if overdone or poorly planned. It is thus worth looking more carefully at the scope for its use, and at the principles which should guide policy design.

It is helpful to start by considering a limiting case in which government intervention, however well designed, could not bring about the appropriate sort of shift in the skill supply function. This would be the case in a 'perfect' world, as imagined in much economic theory, where everyone was optimising with full information (including about the future), and where all relevant markets were present, free from all sources of imperfection and failure, and in equilibrium. In such a world, the skill supply could not be shifted by taxing and spending, because everything on which public money might fruitfully be expended would already have been undertaken by private agents—households, firms, or schools. At best, in such a world, government action would have no impact, since it would amount to taxing skilled workers with one hand and subsidising them with the other.

Needless to say, the perfect world is not a realistic case. However, it illustrates some important truths, and is worth keeping in mind because it forces clear thought about when, why, and how government intervention might in reality be able to shift the skilled-labour supply function. To put it another way, the perfect world case should not be taken literally, but it should be taken seriously.

To begin with, this limiting case shows that the reasons why, in practice, government intervention often *can* shift the skill supply are more or less the same as the well-known reasons why markets tend to fail in this area (Section 2.4.3). The main problems are externalities, imperfect capital markets, and lack of information. Thus many firms underinvest in training because their skilled workers can be poached. Many people and families likewise underinvest in education and training because they cannot borrow for this purpose on market terms, or because they know too little about the opportunities and means involved. Knowledge is also subject to increasing returns—the less one has, the harder it is to get more— so that people can be trapped by their own ignorance.

This rather obvious conclusion, that the area for government action is fundamentally the same as the area of market failure, confirms that the scope for intervention to shift the skill supply function in the desired direction is limited. It should be recalled, moreover, that governments are already spending huge sums on education and training. The scope for *further* intervention is thus bound to be even more limited than a simple assessment of the extent of market failure would suggest.

The positive implication of this conclusion, however, is that in so far as there *is* scope for further intervention to shift the skill supply function outward, such action will usually also increase economic efficiency. This is why the education and training solution to the problem of falling demand for unskilled labour is so attractive: it could in principle improve equity and reduce social corrosion at no (indeed, negative) economic cost.

Implications of relative wage rigidity

The efficiency case for government intervention to increase the supply of skilled labour may be reinforced (as mentioned earlier) by the rigidity of skill differentials in wages in many Northern countries. This is because artificially narrow wage differentials tend to understate the benefits and to overstate the opportunity costs of skill acquisition. However, it must be recognised that the higher unemployment among unskilled workers caused by relative wage rigidity is, to some extent, a substitute for wider wage differentials, since they both increase the incentive to acquire skills. Indeed, if these two sorts of incentive both had the same-sized impact on the skill supply, wage rigidity would not create an efficiency case for government action to expand the skill supply.

In practice, wider skill differentials in unemployment rates have less of an effect on incentives than wider wage differentials would have done, and so the case for intervention is weakened rather than annulled.[7] The main reason is the existence of unemployment benefits, which reduce the cost of being without a job. Moreover, where (as in many European countries) the principal cause of relative wage rigidity is not union action or a minimum wage law, but rather unemployment benefits (or some other social security income floor) tied to the average wage, this case for intervention retains most of its force. For in such circumstances, many unskilled workers are likely to be more or less indifferent between unemployment and working, so that the risk of unemployment provides little incentive to acquire skills.

The choice of interventions in the rigid-wage case is constrained, as in the flexible-wage case, by the need not to do anything that would further

[7] For a given degree of shift in the relative demand function for skilled and unskilled labour, the resulting increase in the skilled labour supply would be the same with rigid as with flexible wages only if (a) there were no unemployment benefits and leisure had no value, (b) workers responded simply to the expected unskilled wage (the actual wage multiplied by the probability of employment), and (c) the relative wage elasticity of demand were unity. The last two assumptions are reasonable, but the first is not, and hence the increase in the skilled-labour supply would usually be smaller with rigid than with flexible relative wages. However, if the demand elasticity were much larger than unity, it would be possible for the skill-supply increase to be larger with rigid than with flexible wages.

reduce the living standards of unskilled workers. This constraint rules out one otherwise obvious response to an unduly narrow wage differential—using taxes to widen the skill differential in living standards. However, in countries where the government provides the unemployed with a perma-nent income, another obvious way of sharpening the incentive to acquire skills is to make this income support conditional on participation in training. This has long been the practice in Sweden, and is now being applied and advocated elsewhere (Layard, Nickell, and Jackman 1991: 62–3). A serious limitation of this approach, though, is that most unskilled workers lack the potential for advanced training (as will be dis-cussed further below).

The efficacy of general improvements in education and training in the rigid-wage case is also subject to much the same constraints as in the flexible-wage case. Such improvements can be financed only by increased taxes on skilled workers, and will reduce unskilled unemployment only if their positive direct effects are greater than the indirect disincentive effect of the tax increase. Fig. 10.3 illustrates this: panel (*a*) is a case where the excess relative supply of unskilled labour (or demand for skilled labour)

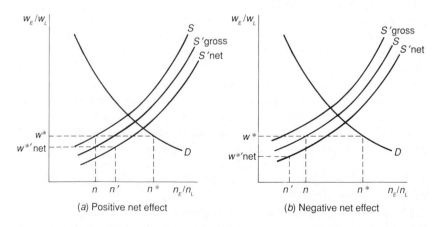

(*a*) Positive net effect   (*b*) Negative net effect

F IG. 10.3 Supply-side intervention with relative wage rigidity

Notes: In the initial situation, the degree of excess relative demand for skilled labour is determined by where w^*, the fixed wage ratio, intersects D (which deter-mines n^*) and S (which determines n). Following the supply-side intervention, n' is determined by where $w^{*'}net$ intersects $S'net$. The relative number of workers demanded, n^*, does not alter, because the gross wage ratio is unchanged.

Whether the gap between n^* and n (or n') actually emerges in the form of shortages of skilled labour, or as surpluses of unskilled labour, cannot be inferred from this diagram, but depends on macroeconomic policies (see Sect. 8.1.1).

is reduced, from $(n^* - n)$ to $(n^* - n')$, because the new gross supply curve is below the old supply curve; panel (*b*), by contrast, is a case where education and training interventions enlarge the excess supply of unskilled labour. In both panels, although it cannot be shown explicitly in the diagram, the induced change in excess supply is muted by the effect of the associated change in the unskilled unemployment rate on the incentive to acquire skills.[8]

Both panels of Fig. 10.3 assume that it is feasible to narrow the net wage differential by higher taxation of skilled workers, which moves the wage ratio down from w^* to $w^{*'}net$. In this sense, the wage differential is not completely rigid—though movement in the opposite direction might be infeasible.[9] If the net wage differential *were* completely rigid, there would be much less room for manœuvre, since government spending could be increased only by an equi-proportional tax rise for both sorts of workers, which would breach the constraint that unskilled workers must not be made absolutely worse off.

Principles of policy choice

There are many possible specific ways in which governments might try to shift the skill supply function: spending more on education and training in traditional ways, introducing new technology for learning, managerial reform in schools and colleges, spreading information about education and training opportunities. It is beyond the scope of this book even to list them all, let alone to say which should or should not be pursued.

However, some general principles emerge from the preceding discussion. The most basic is that each prospective intervention should undergo one common test, comparing (*a*) its direct positive effect on the skilled-labour supply with (*b*) the disincentive effect of the rise in taxes on skilled workers that would be entailed by its cost. Desirable interventions are those for which (*a*) exceeds (*b*), and vice versa.

To put it another way, all prospective interventions can be ranked by the direct increase in the number of skilled workers they would generate per dollar of public money spent. The cut-off point in this ranking, below which lie the interventions that are not worth pursuing, depends on the elasticity of the skilled-labour supply function with respect to the net-of-tax wage differential between skilled and unskilled workers. The lower is

---

[8] In panel (*a*), the reduction in excess supply causes the supply curve to shift to the left, because it reduces the incentive to acquire skills, and vice versa in panel (*b*). These shifts could not be so large as to reverse the direction of the final outcome, since e.g. the induced shift to the left in panel (*a*) would not occur unless the final outcome were a reduction in excess supply.

[9] This would be so if the initial level of the net wage differential were generally regarded as fair, since a disequalising change in tax rates would then tend to be cancelled out by institutional pressure to narrow the gross wage differential.

this elasticity, the larger is the number of worthwhile education and training interventions. This is because a low supply elasticity would imply that the wages of skilled workers were partly a *rent*, which could be taxed away without reducing the number of skilled workers available.

The size of the skill supply elasticity in theoretical models varies from zero to infinity (see Section 2.4.3), but the few empirical estimates available put it between 1 and 2 (Section 7.2.2). If there were no market failures, the size of this elasticity would depend only on the distribution of 'trainability' in the population: in other words, the supply curve would rise simply because some people are inherently harder to educate and train than others, or find the process of skill acquisition less attractive or less interesting. In reality, market failures are an additional reason for supply inelasticity, because they affect some people more than others. And as ever, the elasticity of supply tends to be lower, the shorter the period considered, because the main effect of any change in incentives would be on the skill composition of new entrants to the labour force.

Speed and direction

In weighing the benefits and costs of possible sorts of intervention, one hard issue is the extent to which it is worth trying to transform people who are now unskilled workers into skilled workers. For if the share of skilled workers were raised only among new entrants to the labour force (by educating young people better in school or college), the share of skilled workers in the labour force as a whole would inevitably rise only slowly. The problems of inequity and social corrosion caused by the fall in demand for unskilled labour would thus go on festering for much longer than if large numbers of existing unskilled workers could be turned into skilled workers.

There must be serious doubt, however, about the cost-effectiveness of upgrading unskilled workers, not only because many of them are old (and thus would not continue working for long enough to pay off the investment in training), but also because many of them were initially poorly educated, making it harder and more costly to teach them higher-level skills later.[10] So although it is often economic to give *skilled* workers further training in mid-career, most potential interventions to transform existing unskilled workers into skilled workers would probably lie below the cut-off point defined above.

Other choices which are hard, both analytically and politically, concern the priorities for additional intervention in skill acquisition prior to

---

[10] This could explain e.g. why recent UK efforts to train the unemployed have had a low success rate. Of those completing the Employment Training scheme, only 36% went into jobs, self-employment, or full-time training (Lisa Wood, 'Hour of reckoning for training schemes', *Financial Times*, 4 Sept. 1992).

labour-force entry. The aim of raising the proportion of skilled workers might suggest that what is needed is more government expenditure on *post-basic* education and training. However, it might be more cost-effective to spend public money on improving the quality of basic education, so as to increase the proportion of people who could economically acquire advanced skills at a later stage, perhaps at their own expense.[11] More generally, subsidies to education and training in all Northern countries are already enormous. What is needed may thus be not an overall increase in spending, but some reallocation of the total among alternative uses.

In considering educational priorities, it is also important to be aware of the limited perspective of the present model, in which the North has simply two homogeneous categories of workers (*SKILD* and *BAS-ED*), implying that the only scope for intervention lies in moving workers from one category to the other. In reality, there are other worthwhile educational objectives. One is to improve the quality of *BAS-ED* labour for its own sake: the example of Japan suggests that good basic education of ordinary production workers has considerable economic value, while substantial numbers of secondary school graduates in other Northern countries are still remarkably badly educated.

Another objective might be to raise the quality of *SKILD* workers. In general, though, this seems less likely to be the domain in which markets are failing. Most *SKILD* workers (and their families of origin) are well informed about education and training opportunities, financially able to pursue them, and well placed for informal learning from people with whom they associate. By contrast, it is unskilled workers and their children who are most seriously affected by imperfect capital markets, ignorance, and the negative externality of ill-educated parents, fellow-pupils, and workmates. Indeed, the situation of many people from poorer backgrounds makes the 'perfect world' model of skill acquisition referred to earlier seem like a bad joke.

In summary, government intervention to increase the skilled-labour supply is the most attractive policy response to the problems caused by declining demand for unskilled labour, because it is potentially both equitable and efficient. However, the scope for additional intervention of this kind is more limited than usually recognised, and to go beyond these limits would be counterproductive. Moreover, cost-effective interventions in education and training will improve the economic position of unskilled workers only slowly. For these reasons, it is important also to consider (in the next two subsections) other possible types of policy response.

---

[11] e.g. US firms have found that workers sometimes need remedial teaching in basic literacy and numeracy before they can be trained (John Gapper, 'Redefining the three Rs', *Financial Times*, 24 Aug. 1992).

10.3.3 Boosting demand for unskilled labour

One such response would be to tackle the problems of unskilled workers
from the demand side of the labour market, rather than from the supply
side. In particular, the government might use taxes and public expenditure to boost the relative demand for unskilled labour. Alternative ways
in which this could be done will be compared below, but to begin with it
is simplest to suppose that employers would receive a periodic subsidy for
each unskilled worker on their payrolls, while paying a tax for each
skilled worker. The subsidy and tax are assumed to be self-financing—set
at rates that would cause this scheme to have no net effect on the government budget.

Flexible relative wages

The impact of such a scheme is illustrated in panel (*a*) of Fig. 10.4, which
refers to a case in which relative wages are flexible. The demand curve *D*,
which shows how the ratio of skilled to unskilled workers hired depends

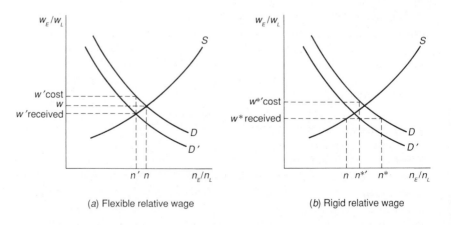

(*a*) Flexible relative wage   (*b*) Rigid relative wage

Fig. 10.4 Demand-shifting intervention
Note: In panel (*a*), the new equilibrium is determined by the intersection of *D'*
and *S*, both of which refer to the wage *received* by workers. In panel (*b*), the relative number of (skilled) workers demanded is reduced from *n** to *n*'*, because the
relative wage *cost* of skilled workers increases. The relative number of skilled
workers supplied appears to remain unchanged in panel (*b*), because the relative
wage received does not alter. In reality, though, the skill supply would be
reduced, because the change in relative unemployment rates would shift *S* to the
left (as explained in the text).

on their relative *cost to employers* (their relative wage plus any tax or minus any subsidy), is unchanged. However, for any given relative cost to employers, the skill differential in wages *received by workers* is now narrower, as shown by the lower curve D'. Equivalently, the demand curve could be said to have moved inwards, from D to D', in the sense that, for any given skill differential in wages received, employers want to hire a lower ratio of skilled to unskilled workers. The outcome, as the figure shows, is that the skill differential in wages received is narrowed, though the narrowing is partly offset by a supply response.

It is worth noting that, if and where the relative wages of skilled and unskilled workers are flexible (as is assumed in this diagram, and fairly close to the truth in the USA), there would be no efficiency justification for this sort of intervention, because there would be no market failure on the demand side to correct. The widening of the wage differential caused by expansion of trade with the South would be signalling, correctly, that the opportunity cost of unskilled labour had fallen, and would already be giving employers an appropriate incentive to hire more unskilled workers.

Correspondingly, although this sort of intervention could be justified on grounds of equity or reduced social corrosion, there would be some cost in terms of reduced efficiency. This cost would arise from the reduction in the relative supply of skilled labour, shown in the diagram, as the result of the narrowing of the skill differential in wages received. The extent of the cost depends on the elasticity of the skill supply: the higher this elasticity, the greater the cost. Only in the limiting (and unrealistic) case of a completely inelastic supply curve would there be no cost, since there would be no change in the availability of skilled labour, nor in the relative cost to employers (and indirectly to consumers) of the two sorts of labour, because the tax/subsidy would be fully shifted on to workers.

Rigid relative wages

Where institutional forces cause skill differentials in wages to be inflexible, the case for this sort of demand-side intervention need not be based solely on improving equity and reducing social corrosion, since it could also increase efficiency. This is because institutional compression of the skill differential in wages, as in most European countries, makes it attractive for employers to hire an inefficiently high ratio of skilled to unskilled labour. The inefficiency is visible as high unemployment among unskilled workers—underutilisation of human resources. A tax on skilled employment and a subsidy on unskilled employment could therefore increase efficiency by reducing the ratio of skilled to unskilled workers hired.

Panel (*b*) of Fig. 10.4 shows the impact of a tax-and-subsidy scheme with a rigid skill differential in the wages received by workers, and an

initial excess relative supply of unskilled labour. The effect on the
demand side is the same as in panel (*a*), but in this case there is no
change in the relative wage received, simply a reduction in the excess relative demand for skilled labour, from $(n^* - n)$ to $(n^{*\prime} - n)$. What this figure
cannot show, however, is that the reduction in excess demand is partly
offset by a leftward shift of the supply curve (a decline in n), because the
incentive to acquire skills created by high unskilled unemployment is
reduced.[12]

The offsetting shift in the skill supply is likely to be small in most of
the countries where wage differentials are rigid, since in such countries (as
explained earlier) this sort of incentive to acquire skills is usually blunted
by income support for the unemployed. However, to the extent that such
a shift occurred, the net gain in efficiency from implementing such a tax-
and-subsidy scheme would be reduced. In other words, some part of the
increase in aggregate output permitted by fuller utilisation of unskilled
labour would be lost through reduced availability of skilled labour. And
in theory, the net effect could be to *reduce* efficiency, if the marginal productivity of skilled labour greatly exceeded that of unskilled labour,
and/or the skill supply were highly sensitive to unemployment rates.

Alternative instruments

The simple tax-and-subsidy scheme outlined above would not be feasible
in reality, since there are not two homogeneous categories of labour
(skilled and unskilled, or *SKILD* and *BAS-ED*), but many different types
and levels of skill. However, its basic objective could still be achieved.
The closest approximation to the simple scheme would be a *progressive
payroll tax*: this tax, paid by employers, would be a proportion of the
wage of each of their employees, the proportion (or tax rate) being
greater, the higher the wage of the worker concerned. The rates of tax for
lower-paid workers would be negative (that is, subsidies), and at some
intermediate wage level the tax rate would be zero.

Administratively, the cheapest way to implement such a scheme (originally proposed by Layard 1985) would be to alter the rate structure of
the social security (or national insurance) contributions that employers
already make on behalf of their workers in most Northern countries.
These contributions have traditionally been a fixed sum or a fixed pro-

---

[12] With either flexible wages or rigid wages, this sort of demand-side intervention would
tend partially to reverse the expansion of trade with the South, because it would raise the
cost to employers of skilled relative to unskilled labour, and thus make it relatively cheaper
to produce labour-intensive goods in the North. However, this shrinkage of trade would be
small, for two reasons: (*a*) these demand-side interventions would affect the whole economy,
not only traded sectors, some of which, moreover, are engaged mainly in North–North
trade; and (*b*) trade with the South would be altered by the change in relative labour costs
only to the limited extent that Southern imports are competing or close to competing.

portion of the wage, but the proportion could be made to rise with the average hourly wage.[13] The contributions at low-wage levels would not necessarily have to be negative: the lowest rate could be zero, with the desired impact on the relative cost to employers of more- and less-skilled workers being achieved by the higher rates at higher wage levels. The choice would depend on the current social security contribution structure, and on other tax and spending plans, which would determine how much net revenue had to be generated by the scheme.[14]

This sort of progressive payroll tax has some disadvantages, because the correspondence between relative wage levels and relative skill levels is imperfect. For example, such a tax causes an inefficient contraction of activities where high pay reflects unpleasant working conditions. And in jobs where high pay is due to bargaining power or artificial restrictions on entry, the existing distortion may be aggravated. At the lower end of the skill spectrum, moreover, such a subsidy would be a crude instrument, especially if there were a single effective wage floor, as with a legal minimum wage. This is because the workers who are unemployed at this wage vary in their skill levels: a common subsidy rate would be unnecessarily high for some, but for others not high enough, to price them into jobs.

An alternative way of achieving the basic objective of the simple tax-and-subsidy scheme would be for the government and public agencies directly to provide more unskilled jobs, financing this perhaps by a general increase in taxation, for example, a rise in indirect tax rates. The traditional model of public works, used for instance in the USA in the 1930s, involves labour-intensive investment projects to improve infrastructure and public amenities. The same approach could be used, though, to increase unskilled employment in recurrent activities, such as better maintenance of public buildings and facilities. In principle, direct provision of public jobs would be less efficient than a progressive payroll tax (which would give *all* employers an automatic and uniform incentive to hire more unskilled workers), but its greater transparency could be a political advantage.

10.3.4 Redistribution

Another possible policy response to the problems caused by the decline in demand for unskilled labour would be to redistribute income from skilled

[13] The generally regressive rate structures in Northern countries in 1975 and 1983 are summarised in OECD-EO (1986, chart 13). Since then, there have been some changes. Most notably, the UK has introduced a structure which is progressive below (roughly) the average wage—the rates rise in four steps from zero to 10.4%, after which they remain constant.

[14] At present, employers' social security contributions are a big source of government revenue, and would presumably be expected to remain so. This makes it more likely that the lowest rate of a progressive structure would be zero, but is not necessarily incompatible with subsidies at the bottom.

to unskilled workers through personal income taxes and transfers. The type of transfer that would be most appropriate would vary, depending on the degree of wage flexibility. In other words, the choice of instrument would depend on whether, in the country concerned, unskilled workers had suffered mainly a decline in relative wages, or mainly an increase in unemployment.

It is also worth bearing in mind that most Northern countries already practise redistribution through taxes and transfers of various sorts on a massive scale, that this process is subject to some well-known problems, and that low skills are not the only cause of low income. Additions or changes to existing transfer programmes in any particular country would thus have to be consistent with the other objectives and administrative mechanisms of these programmes, which are barely touched on below.

Flexible relative wages

If and where the skill differential in wages is flexible, the appropriate type of transfer would be an income supplement for low-wage workers. Thus the relative *wage paid by employers* to unskilled labour would be allowed to decline, which would have the benefit of maintaining unskilled employment, but the relative *living standards* of unskilled workers and their families would be kept up by cash transfers. In so far as unskilled workers now pay personal income tax and social security contributions, an initial step in the direction of transfers could be to lower or eliminate these levies. The transfers to, or tax reductions for, unskilled workers would be financed by higher rates of personal income tax on skilled workers.

From an analytical point of view, the effects of this sort of scheme would be similar to those of the employment taxes and subsidies discussed in the previous section. This is because relative wages are assumed here to be flexibly determined by supply and demand. In these circumstances, one of the fundamental propositions of economic theory is that the incidence of a tax or subsidy depends simply on the elasticities of the supply and demand functions, and not on whether it is the buyer or the seller who nominally pays the tax or receives the subsidy. So, for instance, a payroll tax and subsidy scheme, and a personal income tax and transfer scheme, if applied at identical rates, would tend to cause an identical narrowing of the net wage gap between skilled and unskilled workers, though the gross wage gap would behave differently.

From a practical point of view, however, the two sorts of schemes may not be interchangeable. There are some substantive differences: for example, it would be easier to tailor income supplements than payroll subsidies to the varying family circumstances of individual low-wage workers, and thus to make these supplements consistent with other income support programmes. There are also some presentational differences: people and politicians are not often familiar with the theory of tax incidence, and so would tend to be averse to giving subsidies to 'rich employers', preferring instead to make transfers directly to poor workers.

Schemes which provide financial assistance to the working poor already exist on a small scale in some countries.[15] For instance, the UK since 1970 has had a formal system of low-wage supplements, called (in recent years) Family Credit. As its name suggests, it is limited to workers with children. More importantly, the amounts of money available through Family Credit are small, and (not unrelatedly) many families who would be eligible for it fail to apply. In the USA in the 1970s, too, the rules for Aid to Families with Dependent Children were such that it acted as a low-wage supplement (Watts 1987).

The political appeal of confining low-wage supplements to workers with children is obvious, but should be resisted if such a scheme were to be implemented on a larger scale. This is because, for single people and couples without dependent children, as for families with children, low wages cause hardship, discourage work, and encourage crime. To provide nothing to workers without children, while enlarging the supplements to those with children, would clearly also increase the incentive to have children. This last problem, however, cannot entirely be avoided. For even if low-wage supplements were extended to workers without children, moral and political considerations would surely dictate that the *amount paid* should increase with the number of dependent children.

How the size of the supplement should vary with the level of the wage is also a difficult issue, since (as with all transfer schemes) there is an unavoidable three-way trade-off between greater generosity, lower fiscal cost, and stronger incentives to earn more.[16] For example, supplements which were concentrated on the lowest-paid workers would cost less, and would give more help to the poorest, but would deter the lower-paid from trying to earn more, since the supplement would be withdrawn rapidly as their wages rose. The disincentive to earning more could be reduced by making the supplements taper off gradually, but this would require either less to be given to the poorest or an increase in the overall fiscal cost of the scheme, and hence higher marginal tax rates on other groups.

Rigid relative wages

Where the relative wages of skilled and unskilled workers are inflexible, so that the demand shift emerges mainly as additional unemployment

---

[15] In addition, on a larger scale and in many countries, other sorts of social security benefits narrow the proportional gap in living standards between low-wage and high-wage workers, including *allocations familiales* in France, child benefit in the UK, and food stamps in the USA.

[16] See e.g. Dilnot, Kay, and Morris (1984).

among unskilled workers, the policy options are quite different. For a start, payroll taxes and subsidies are no longer even analytically equivalent to personal taxes and low-wage supplements. As was shown in Fig. 10.4(b), the former sort of intervention would reduce unskilled unemployment, but not affect the net wage differential, while the main effect of the latter sort of intervention would be to narrow the net wage differential (which would tend to *increase* unskilled unemployment).[17]

More fundamentally, to the extent that relative wages are rigid, there is less *need* for supplements to low wages, but more need for transfers to people out of work. Indeed, if the wage rigidity were based strictly on politically effective notions of fairness, and so unskilled workers were already being paid at what society regarded as an equitable rate, there would be no case at all for low-wage supplements.

State income support for the unemployed, commonly in the form of social insurance, is a familiar and long-established institution. Its problems are also well recognised, particularly the conflict between alleviating hardship and maintaining financial incentives to work, especially in low-paid jobs. Changing political attitudes towards this conflict in recent years have led some Northern governments to reduce or restrict access to unemployment benefits. However, the basic principle that the government should transfer income to the unemployed continues to command widespread public support in most Northern countries.

In the context of this book, income transfers to the unemployed play a double role, because they are one of the *causes* of relative wage rigidity, as well as a *solution* to the problems caused by other sources of relative wage rigidity (unions and minimum wage laws). Wage flexibility would not be reduced by temporary transfers to the unemployed, or even by permanent transfers which were limited to people who are physically unable to work, as in the USA. At the other extreme, where permanent state income support is provided to able-bodied adults on demand, as in much of Europe, it is bound to set a floor under unskilled wages. In between, eligibility for support can be made conditional on availability-for-work tests of varying stringency: the less stringent the tests, the greater the rigidifying effect on relative wages.

The effects of permanent income transfers on relative wages are not an accident or anomaly. Like other causes of wage rigidity, they reflect politically effective views of fairness. Thus social limits to inequality of living standards not only dictate that there should be permanent income support for the unemployed, but also help to explain why work tests are weak. For with an excess supply of labour, if the tests were stringent,

---

[17] Unskilled unemployment would tend to increase because the narrower net wage differential would reduce the supply and employment of skilled labour, while the ratio of skilled to unskilled workers hired by employers would be unchanged, since there would be no change in the gross wage differential.

people would be forced to work for wages too low to provide them with the socially acceptable minimum standard of living. 'Solutions' which ignore prevailing ideas of fairness, by merely reducing unemployment benefits or by making work tests more stringent, are thus unlikely to be politically acceptable in countries where relative wages are inflexible.

Negative income tax

However, there is another class of solutions which try to reconcile this apparently strong conflict between equity and efficiency considerations. Its best-known representative is the negative income tax, but there are several other closely related schemes: basic income, guaranteed income, minimum income, and social dividend (Wolfson 1986*b*, 1987; Watts 1987; Brittan and Webb 1990). In the simplest version of such a scheme, each household would be guaranteed a minimum income, related to the number and ages of its members. This minimum would be provided either as a grant or as a tax credit that would be refunded if the household's tax liability were negative. All other income would be taxed, initially at a constant proportional rate, though with some progressivity in the upper ranges.

This sort of scheme has some very attractive features, both in the context of the present book and more generally. It addresses social concern about inequality of living standards, by establishing a minimum household income. At the same time, it avoids some problems associated with permanent income support to the unemployed. More specifically, because entitlement to the minimum income would be unaffected by other income, it would be much less likely to discourage work or to set a reservation wage for unskilled work. Moreover, such a scheme would be effective both where relative wages were rigid (for other reasons) and where they were flexible: a negative income tax, that is, could achieve the objectives of *both* income support for the unemployed *and* low-wage supplements.

Despite the enthusiasm of a wide range of economists, no country has yet introduced a comprehensive negative income tax. There is disagreement about the extent to which existing transfer programmes could or should be replaced by such a scheme, and general concern about its fiscal cost. In the context of the present argument, much of this criticism can be summed up by saying that a negative income tax would conflict—in one of two different ways—with politically effective ideas of fairness.

Thus in the USA, where relative wages are flexible, and the able-bodied are denied permanent income support, the main objection is that such a scheme would give money to people who chose not to work. In Europe, by contrast, where relative wages are rigid, and permanent income support is readily available to the able-bodied, the objection is that a negative income tax would make some people worse off, including unemployed unskilled workers. This is because it would be too costly, in terms of the overall burden of taxation, to set the guaranteed minimum income for all households at the existing level of unemployment benefits.[18]

At both ends of the spectrum of politically effective ideas of fairness, then, a comprehensive negative income tax tends to be regarded as inferior to the arrangements currently in place. So although in some ways such a tax would be an ideal solution to the problems caused by a decline in the relative demand for unskilled labour, the best that can realistically be expected is piecemeal movement in this general direction.

10.4 Alternative Policy Packages

The previous section examined four possible types of policy response to the trade-induced decline in the relative demand for Northern unskilled labour: higher trade barriers, more education and training, unskilled job creation, and income redistribution. The purpose of this section is to choose among these four approaches, and in particular to identify some promising policy *combinations*. The first subsection examines issues of policy design that are common to all countries, while the next two subsections identify some elements that would need to differ between America and Europe. It may be worth reiterating that the discussion is limited to the general principles and directions of policy: more quantification and attention to technical issues would be needed to make the suggested approach operational.

10.4.1 General considerations

The least attractive of these four types of policy response would be to raise barriers to imports from the South. Protection would help Northern unskilled workers, but it would be more costly (to Northern society as a whole) than other ways of achieving this goal, and would hurt much poorer workers in the South. However, the fact that there is political pressure to maintain and increase trade barriers makes it all the more

---

[18] For the UK, Brittan and Webb (1990) show that a 'no losers' scheme, which would set the guaranteed minimum at the current level of Income Support, and withdraw benefits at the standard income tax rate, would require the standard income tax rate to rise from 34% to 49% (including employee social security contributions). However, Wolfson (1986b, 1987) proposes a guaranteed income scheme for Canada that would not reduce the incomes of the poor *and* would not require a general increase in marginal tax rates. This is achievable because (*a*) the duration of unemployment benefits is shorter than in Europe, and would be further reduced by the Wolfson proposal, (*b*) the federal guaranteed income would be a supplement to provincial support targeted on people who are unable to work, and (*c*) the tax base would be broadened.

important to seek and implement better policies. Failure to implement some other type of intervention could thus be to choose protection by default.

Supply-side measures

In choosing among and combining the three other types of policy response, the analysis in the previous section suggests a possible logical sequence. The *first step* would be to review education and training options, in order to assess the scope for shifting the skill supply function. This involves asking how many (and which) interventions of this sort would pass the cost-effectiveness test described earlier, which requires their direct positive impact on the supply of skilled labour to be greater than the disincentive effect due to the associated increase in taxes on skilled workers.

Education and training interventions which pass this test should certainly be implemented, since they would increase efficiency as well as improving equity and reducing social corrosion. Conversely, education and training interventions which fail this test should definitely not be implemented, since, in addition to reducing efficiency, they would worsen the inequity and social corrosion caused by falling demand for unskilled labour.

It is impossible, without more research, to be more definite about the scope for, and specific means of, shifting the skill supply function. In principle, this is determined by the extent to which the market is failing in ways that have not already been corrected by government intervention. It thus seems likely that there is *some* scope for further action in most Northern countries, especially in reducing obstacles to skill acquisition among people from poorer backgrounds, but not a lot. It is also likely that this approach would yield results slowly, since it would need to be concentrated on new entrants to the labour force.

Demand-side and redistributive measures

Having thus first chosen some measures to improve education and training, the *second step* would be to ask how far short these measures would fall of a satisfactory solution to the problems caused by the drop in demand for unskilled labour. In particular, the smaller the number of education and training measures that passed the cost-effectiveness test, and the greater the urgency of tackling inequity and social corrosion, the stronger would be the case for supplementary use of the other two kinds of intervention: boosting the demand for unskilled labour, and redistributing income from skilled to unskilled workers.

Although the choice between (and specific design of) these two kinds of intervention still needs to be considered, one or other would undoubtedly be effective in narrowing the gap in wages or unemployment rates between skilled and unskilled workers. However, by the same token, both kinds of intervention would have the disadvantage of reducing the skilled labour supply, since they would dilute the incentive to skill acquisition that is provided by these gaps between the two sorts of workers. This reduction in the skill supply would have an economic cost.

Demand-shifting and redistributive interventions thus generally involve a trade-off between objectives: greater efficiency on the one hand, and less inequity and social corrosion on the other. In consequence, the choice of whether and how much to intervene in these ways is bound to be affected by social and political preferences. This is in contrast to the choice among education and training measures, where there is no trade-off (a particular measure either contributes to the attainment of all objectives or to none of them), and hence decisions can be based, at least in principle, simply on technical assessment.

There is one important exception to the proposition that demand-shifting measures entail a trade-off between objectives. This arises when relative wages are rigid, and demand-shifting measures would reduce unemployment of unskilled workers. The reduction in unemployment, by causing labour to be more fully utilised, would increase efficiency. Even in this case, though, there would also be an efficiency-reducing contraction of the skill supply, because the decline in unskilled unemployment would reduce the incentive to acquire skills. The net gain in efficiency would therefore be less, and could even be negative.

Supply responsiveness

The trade-off depends on the responsiveness of the skill supply to the gap in living standards between skilled and unskilled workers. In the case of flexible relative wages, this is simply the usual elasticity of the supply function with respect to the relative wage. In the case of rigid relative wages, what matters more is the sensitivity of the skill supply to the gap in unemployment rates between skilled and unskilled workers (which depends on, among other things, the generosity of unemployment benefits).

Responsiveness of both sorts was argued earlier to be quite low. It is worth noting, though, that a more responsive skill supply might not imply that policy-makers faced a worse dilemma. Clearly, the trade-off would be sharper, since any given narrowing of the gap in living standards between skilled and unskilled workers would induce a larger reduction of the skill supply. On the other hand, however, with a more responsive skill supply, the problems caused by the decline in demand for unskilled labour would be less severe, and thus there would be *less need* to narrow the gap in living standards. In other words, if the skill supply were more responsive, the shift in demand would not have caused so much of a widening of the gap in wages and unemployment rates between skilled and unskilled workers.[19]

More generally, the amount of intervention needed to tackle the problems caused by expansion of trade with the South for unskilled workers in the North must depend fundamentally on the *size of the relative demand shift* generated by the change in trade. For instance, the evidence in earlier chapters implies that, for the North as a whole, the relative demand for unskilled labour was shifted downwards by about 20 per cent.[20] In the flexible-wage case, to restore the relative wage to its previous level would thus clearly require a tax-plus-subsidy of about 20 per cent, e.g. a 10 per cent tax on skilled employment and a 10 per cent subsidy on unskilled employment. Likewise, in the rigid-wage case, these rates of payroll tax and subsidy would be required to restore unskilled unemployment to its original level.

However, this conclusion needs to be qualified in several ways. One is that, although in a technical sense the elasticity (or responsiveness) of supply does not affect the amount of intervention required to restore the previous situation, it is bound to affect whether or not any intervention is undertaken. For if the skill supply were highly responsive, and hence the shift in demand had little effect on the relative living standards of skilled and unskilled workers, the problem would not be serious enough to merit political attention. In other words, it is the unresponsiveness of the skill supply which has translated the changes in trade with the South into pressing problems of inequity and social corrosion for the North.

Another qualification is that the tax-and-subsidy rates needed to restore the previous gap in living standards will be smaller than the demand shift to the extent that education and training interventions can shift the skill supply function outwards. Similarly, the analysis above assumes that other things remain equal: the demand and supply functions are likely to have shifted for other reasons (such as expansion of higher education or the autonomous diffusion of new technology), so that intervention to offset the demand-shifting effects of trade with the South

[19] In the flexible-wage case, this is just the elementary point that the size of the price change induced by a demand shift is inversely related to the elasticity of supply. In the rigid-wage case, the more responsive the relative supply of skilled labour to the relative unemployment rate among unskilled workers, the smaller will be the final impact of a demand shift on the relative unemployment rate.

[20] See the summaries in Sects. 7.2.2 and 8.2.4, based on Ch. 4. More specifically, the earlier estimates suggest that the relative demand for unskilled workers was shifted *inwards* (in the quantity dimension) by about 20%. However, the elasticity of demand appears to be close to unity, so that the *downward* shift (in the wage dimension) would also have been about 20%. The crudeness of this estimate should be recalled: it is the central point of a wide range, an average for all Northern countries, and distinguishes only two skill categories of labour.

would not restore the relative positions of skilled and unskilled workers prior to the expansion of trade. Finally, the notion of 'restoring' the skill differentials that existed at some earlier point in time is itself somewhat arbitrary.

Combining policies

In summary, it is suggested here that governments should pursue a *mixture* of supply-side (education and training) and demand-side or redistributive interventions. Such a mixture would be in line with conventional economic thinking on labour market policy, e.g. Johnson and Layard (1986: 949–58), but may appear to conflict with the more recent conclusions of Jackman, Layard, and Savouri (1991: 81–7) and Layard, Nickell, and Jackman (1991: 482). The two sets of authors argue strongly that governments must operate either on the demand side or on the supply side of the labour market, and that it is illogical to operate on both sides simultaneously.

The Jackman–Layard–Nickell–Savouri (JLNS) analysis is extremely important, particularly in its attention to the fiscal constraints on policy options, and to the responsiveness of the skill supply. These considerations rule out many otherwise attractive policy mixtures, to an extent which earlier studies did not recognise. However, these considerations have been taken into account in the present chapter, whose conclusions are actually quite consistent with the JLNS logic. The apparent inconsistency arises merely from differences of emphasis, in three main respects.

One difference is that the present chapter places more emphasis on market failures in the area of skill supply, in the absence of which there would be no case for intervention on the supply side as well as the demand side. A second difference is that the present argument assumes the skill supply to be rather unresponsive to changes in wage and unemployment differentials between skilled and unskilled workers, while JLNS tend to assume that the skill supply is highly elastic. The third difference is that the present chapter strongly emphasises the objectives of reducing inequity and social corrosion, as well as the objective of greater efficiency, while JLNS (in these particular works) are entirely concerned with increasing efficiency, and mention equity arguments only in passing.

Cross-country variation

Northern countries differ in many ways that are relevant to the choice of policies to address the problems caused by more trade with the South. To begin with, the expansion of this trade has occurred to different degrees in different countries, and so there are differences in the extent of the problems caused for unskilled workers (see Sections 7.2.3 and 8.3.3).

Underlying these differences in trade are variations in relative supplies of skilled and unskilled labour, and in barriers to trade. There are also many differences in laws and institutions that would affect the details of policy design, and in some cases the overall shape of policy packages.

However, there is one sort of difference among Northern countries to which special attention has been given in this book, and which has an especially important bearing on policy choice. It is the degree of flexibility in the relative wages of their skilled and unskilled workers, which has determined the form of the problem caused by more trade with the South. In countries where wages are rather flexible, the fall in relative demand for unskilled labour has emerged mainly in the form of wider wage differentials, whereas in countries where wages are rather rigid, it has emerged mainly as a rise in unskilled unemployment.

Moreover, such inter-country differences in wage flexibility are largely a symptom of more basic differences in the degree of social and political concern about income inequality. These differences in social outlook are bound to have a strong influence on the choice of policy responses, and it would be futile to offer suggestions which ignored them. The rest of this section is thus divided, offering two alternative policy packages for two different sorts of country. One is for 'America', where there is assumed to be little concern about inequality, and wages are flexible. The other is for 'Europe', where low relative incomes are regarded as inequitable, and relative wages are rigid.

Although most Northern countries approximate to one or other of these two stylised types, some countries lie in between, and thus both packages may be of relevance to them. For example, in Canada there has long been more concern about inequality than in the USA, while the UK during the 1980s was pushed away from Europe in the direction of America. Japan is an unusual mixture, with a large-firm sector which in some ways resembles the Europe model and a small-firm sector more like the American model.

The supply-side aspects of the suggested package are essentially the same in the two country types. Needless to say, there is much variation among Northern countries in education and training systems, and in the strengths and weaknesses of these systems. The scope for shifting the skill supply function outward must thus also vary, as must the extent and nature of the specific policy measures needed to achieve this shift. However, the basic principles that such a shift (to the extent that it is feasible) would be highly desirable, and that consideration of the supply-side possibilities should be the first step in policy design, are common to all countries.

What differs more fundamentally is the second step in policy design: the choice of demand-side and redistributive measures. The two issues, which are the focus of the next few pages, are *how much* to do in these respects, and *in what ways*.

10.4.2 America

In a country where there is little social concern about income inequality, there must be some question about whether to implement *any* demand-side or redistributive measures. With flexible relative wages, there would be no efficiency justification for doing so. Indeed, such measures would reduce economic efficiency, by diminishing the incentive to acquire skills. The preferred approach might thus be simply to improve education and training, and then quit.

Motives

One obvious possible reason for going further would be to reduce social corrosion. Declining wages and employment opportunities for the unskilled have aggravated crime, violence, racial tension, urban decay, begging, and homelessness. To a greater or lesser extent, all members of society have suffered from this process of deterioration, and all would correspondingly gain from economic measures to reverse it. The argument is partly one of self-interest: skilled workers could raise their own living standards by financing public action to improve the economic position of the unskilled. (For example, it is preferable to be taxed than to be mugged.) But many people may also be moved by a sense of civic or national pride—a common desire to create a safe and civilised social environment.

In addition, there is unquestionably *some* ethical concern about poverty in this type of country, some limits on the degree of income inequality that is socially acceptable, even though these limits are wider than in Europe. However, the American attitude to poverty also involves a clear distinction between the deserving and the undeserving poor, and a deep determination to deny help to the undeserving, even if this penalises the deserving, too.[21] The moral *case* for demand-side or redistributive measures must thus be that what has happened to unskilled workers is not their fault: that the fall in demand for their labour was exogenous and unanticipated, and that it is now too late for most of them to become skilled. The *mode* of intervention must also respect these attitudes, by being linked to effort on the part of the beneficiaries, though with concessions for their dependent children.

---

[21] The fundamental difference between American and European attitudes to the relief of poverty appears to be (in statistical language) a different weighting of Type I and Type II errors. Americans are willing to accept a lot of Type I errors (failing to help the deserving) in order to avoid Type II errors (helping the undeserving), whereas Europeans want to avoid Type I errors and are thus willing to accept a lot of Type II errors. (Up to a point, by careful screening, it is possible to reduce the number of both Type I and Type II errors, but this is administratively expensive.)

These concerns to reduce social corrosion and achieve a minimal level of equity are not in themselves sufficient justification for demand-side or redistributive measures. For in principle, these non-economic objectives might be achieved to the desired extent simply by improving education and training. In practice, however, the scope for shifting the skill supply function is probably rather limited, and would yield results only slowly, which makes the case for some supplementary demand-side or redistributive measures much more persuasive.

Instruments

As regards the choice *between* demand-side and redistributive measures, it was explained earlier (Section 10.3.4) that, with flexible wages, the two approaches are analytically equivalent. That is to say, if one wishes to raise the living standards of unskilled workers it makes little difference from a narrowly economic point of view whether one does so by subsidising their employment or by supplementing their wages, or by a mixture of the two approaches. However it is done, the outcome will be essentially that illustrated in Fig. 10.5, which shows the effect of a package of supply-side and demand-side measures to narrow the net wage differential (from w to $w'received-net$).[22]

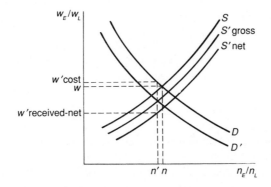

FIG. 10.5 Policy package with flexible relative wage
Note: The initial equilibrium is determined by the intersection of D and S, the new equilibrium by the intersection of D' and $S'gross$ (both of which refer to the gross-of-tax relative wage received by workers).

---

[22] In this diagram, the net effect of the package on the relative number of skilled workers is negative. In principle, it could be positive if the supply-side shift were large relative to the demand-side impact, but the latter outcome is less plausible, for if there were so much scope for shifting the supply function, there might be no political desire to add demand-side or redistributive measures.

However, it was also explained that the two sorts of measures are usually not equivalent from an administrative or political point of view, and
so it is on these grounds that the choice must be made. In particular,
these non-economic considerations appear to rule out one of the possible
demand-side approaches, namely general subsidies to unskilled employment financed by payroll taxes on skilled workers. One problem is that it
would be hard with such a system to provide greater help to workers
with more dependants, since employers would usually be unable or
unwilling to monitor the family circumstances of their employees. In
addition, politicians and the public might be inclined to doubt that subsidies paid to employers would end up in the pockets of their employees.

Direct public provision of jobs is an alternative method of boosting the
demand for unskilled labour that would be less open to these objections.
Indeed, there is already widespread enthusiasm in America for 'workfare',
which requires able-bodied recipients of government income support to
take some form of public sector employment. The main objective of
workfare has been to reduce disincentives to work, not to help unskilled
workers. But most of the employment involved is low-skilled, and so has
the incidental effect of boosting the relative demand for unskilled labour.

There is only limited scope for giving a greater boost to the demand
for unskilled labour by expanding workfare in its present form, simply
because most able-bodied people in America are not eligible for government income support. However, workfare could in principle be supplemented by greater public employment of unskilled workers in general,
and this approach might command political support, whether in the traditional public works form of investment projects or in recurrent maintenance or community work. Even here, though, there may be quite tight
political limits, associated with reluctance to expand the size of the public
sector.

The most generally attractive of the various possible approaches is thus
probably income supplements for low-wage workers ('low-wage supplements', for short). As explained in Section 10.3.4, these would be a mixture of tax relief and cash grants for unskilled workers, financed by a rise
in personal income tax rates on skilled workers, thus narrowing the gap
in living standards between the two groups. For the scheme to be
effective, all low-wage workers should be eligible to receive the supplements, but more would be provided to those with children and other
dependants. The scheme would probably best be administered, in terms
of both convenience and image, as an extension of the tax (rather than
the welfare) system.

Low-wage supplements are an attractive option in the American context for several reasons. One is that they benefit only those who are willing to work—in the same spirit as workfare. Another attraction is that
these supplements leave the labour market to function freely, without

direct intervention in wage-setting or employment decisions. These supplements are also in principle neutral as between the public and private sectors, although they would probably not often be paid to workers in the public sector, where unions usually keep unskilled wages above market-clearing levels. Finally, they satisfy the political need for transparency, in that the money is paid directly to the intended beneficiaries.

A worry

A likely source of concern is that the provision of low-wage supplements would enable employers to set wages even lower, thereby failing to raise the living standards of unskilled workers and benefiting their employers instead. This concern is largely misplaced, but it needs to be addressed carefully, because it could reduce the political appeal of the scheme.

In so far as the aggregate supply of skilled (relative to unskilled) labour is elastic, and wages are determined in competitive labour markets, there would indeed be some shifting of the wage supplements, as may be inferred for example from Figs. 10.4(a) and 10.5. In other words, the gross wage differential between skilled and unskilled workers would inevitably widen somewhat, since the supply of skilled workers would shrink, so that the net wage differential would narrow by less than the rates of tax and supplement would imply. However, this is simply something that has to be taken into account in setting the tax and supplement rates to achieve any desired narrowing of the net wage gap. The shifting is associated with a real problem, but a different one, which is shared by all demand-side and redistributive measures—the efficiency cost of the induced shrinkage in the skilled labour supply.

In the competitive case, the partial shifting of the low-wage supplements would not benefit employers. However, the supply of labour to individual employers is sometimes less than infinitely elastic, giving the employers some monopsony power over their workers, which enables the employers to increase their profits by paying lower wages and employing fewer workers. This too is a real problem—of inequity and inefficiency—and is often used to justify union action and minimum wage laws.[23] However, low-wage supplements should not make this problem any worse: the employer's degree of monopsony power depends fundamentally on the elasticity of his labour supply, and there is no general reason why this should be reduced by the payment of low-wage supplements. In other words, these supplements would usually help low-paid workers even where their low pay was partly due to the monopsony power of their employers.

[23] For recent evidence of the existence of monopsony power on both sides of the Atlantic, see Katz and Krueger (1992) and Machin and Manning (1992).

10.4.3 Europe

The reasons for going beyond supply-side measures in Europe are different from, and less open to dispute than, those in America. Concern about income inequality, though generally much greater than in America, is not the main reason. This is because the wages of the unskilled workers who have jobs are in most cases held up by institutional pressures, while most of those who are unemployed receive income support from the government.

The high rates of unemployment among unskilled workers do provide the main motive for action, but for two other reasons. One is the *inefficiency* of not using a substantial part of the labour force. The other reason is the contribution of persistent unemployment to *social corrosion*. For it is not merely the low incomes of the unemployed, but also their enforced idleness and sense of rejection, that generate more robbery, violence, rioting, and racial hatred.

Moreover, there are even fewer grounds than in America for supposing that supply-side measures would be enough to solve these problems. To improve education and training would be highly desirable in both sorts of country, but only up to a point (beyond which it would be counter-productive), and would be slow. In addition, in Europe, supply-side measures would fail to correct the bias of incentives towards hiring too low a ratio of unskilled to skilled workers that is created for employers by narrow and inflexible skill differentials in wages.

Instruments

There is also little scope for choice in Europe, unlike America, between demand-shifting and redistributive measures. With relative wage rigidity, these two sorts of measures are not equivalent, even in theory. Moreover, because problems of income inequality are already being addressed in other ways in Europe, the decline in demand for unskilled labour does not create much need for additional redistributive action. What is mainly needed is more intervention to boost the relative demand for unskilled labour. This is illustrated in Fig. 10.6, again showing a package of supply-side and demand-side measures, which between them reduce the relative excess demand for skilled labour from $(n^* - n)$ to $(n^{*\prime} - n')$.[24]

Where there is a choice in Europe is among different *methods* of boosting the relative demand for unskilled labour. The two main methods dis-

---

[24] In this diagram, the net effect of the package is to increase the relative supply of skilled labour. However, it might have the opposite effect, if there were little scope for shifting the skill-supply function by more education and training. For then the dominant effect on the skill supply would be the reduction of incentives to acquire skills created by high unskilled unemployment.

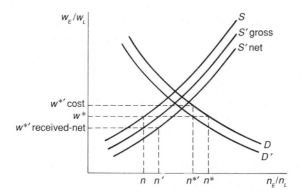

FIG. 10.6 Policy package with rigid relative wage
Note: The initial degree of excess relative demand for skilled labour is determined by the intersection of w^* with D and S. The final degree of excess relative demand ($n^{*\prime} - n'$) is determined by where $w^{*\prime}cost$ intersects D and where $w^{*\prime}$ *received-net* intersects $S'net$.

cussed in Section 10.3.3 were direct provision of public employment, and payroll tax and subsidy schemes. Public employment projects involving a high proportion of unskilled workers would be effective in creating jobs, and could usefully contribute to more (and better maintained) infrastructure and amenities. However, there are limits—economic and political— to enlargement of the public sector, so that to achieve a big enough impact, in a reasonably efficient way, it would be better to apply a progressive payroll tax to all employers. The simplest way to do this, as explained earlier, would be to modify the structure of employers' social security contributions, perhaps with subsidies for the lowest-paid workers.

Other measures

Although skill mismatch accounts for a large share of total unemployment (Section 8.2.4), it is not the sole cause of unemployment, and hence this sort of scheme should not be expected to eliminate *all* unemployment. In particular, beyond the point at which pure skill-mismatch unemployment had vanished, it would be ineffective merely to boost the relative demand for unskilled labour, because no more workers would be willing to take jobs at the current unskilled wage. Those who remained unemployed, that is, would be people for whom unskilled work was less attractive than unemployment. To get them back into jobs, the expansion of demand for unskilled labour would have to be coupled with tighter conditions on the availability of unemployment benefits (Layard, Nickell, and Jackman 1991: 62–3).

It should also be remembered that trade with the South has had a double effect on labour in the North. In addition to reducing the economy-wide demand for unskilled workers, it has displaced many workers (skilled as well as unskilled) from specific sectors, particularly in manufacturing. Progressive payroll taxes and public employment schemes would not bring back most of the specific jobs that have disappeared, which is a problem because some of the people, particularly males, who formerly worked in manufacturing are reluctant to move into other sectors. In consequence, there may be some *sectoral* mismatch unemployment which can be eliminated only by the passage of time.

The general point, then, is that in so far as unemployment has causes other than skill mismatch, as emphasised in Section 8.3.4, it requires solutions other than (or in addition to) those suggested above. Not all these other causes, moreover, are structural or microeconomic. The recession which is afflicting the world at the time of writing is an unwelcome reminder of the extent to which macroeconomic mismanagement can contribute to unemployment of workers in all skill categories.

In some circumstances, reducing unemployment might require a reduction in the average real wage, either to induce firms to use more labour relative to other factors of production, or, for an individual country, to reduce production costs relative to other countries (and so avoid the increase in the foreign trade deficit that would otherwise be caused by a higher level of domestic economic activity).[25] This downward pressure might be offset by other forces which tend to raise real wages, such as technical progress. However, if an absolute reduction in real wages *were* required, it would be important to persuade unions not to react by demanding higher money wages, for example, by introducing a temporary incomes policy.[26] Moreover, to the extent that the unskilled wage is propped up by unemployment benefits, these too would need to fall in real terms.

---

[25] In the theoretical framework set out in Ch. 2 of the present book, the most likely other factors of production for the North as a whole would be infrastructure and land, though it is usually capital that is mentioned in this context, as e.g. in Layard (1985: annexe 1). How the balance of payments constraint might give rise to an inverse relationship between total employment and the average real wage is explained in Layard, Nickell, and Jackman (1991: 384–90). Incidentally, *average* labour productivity is bound to be lowered by a reduction in skill-mismatch unemployment, which raises the ratio of unskilled to skilled workers, but this need not entail a reduction in the productivity or real wage of either group of workers.

[26] A temporary incomes policy could also be an efficient way of shifting to a lower equilibrium inflation rate (Layard, Nickell, and Jackman 1991: 68). Permanent administrative restraint of the wages of skilled workers could in principle reduce skill-mismatch unemployment, by decreasing the inflationary pressure which arises from shortages of skilled labour (see Sect. 8.1.1), but would be hard to enforce, although employers in some countries voluntarily agree not to poach skilled workers from one another. There may be scope, too, for permanent changes in wage bargaining systems to reduce the inflationary effect of other conflicts over relative wages (Wood 1978, ch. 7).

A radical alternative

The general policy approach suggested here for Europe, which is to accept relative wage rigidity and to concentrate on boosting the relative demand for unskilled labour, could be criticised as fundamentally second-best in terms of efficiency. An alternative would be to make relative wages more flexible, thus letting the market price unskilled workers back into jobs, and to provide low-wage supplements to offset the decline in their living standards. However, this approach seems much less attractive.

The main reason is that implementing this strategy would involve profound political conflict. It would entail abolishing or lowering legal minimum wages, weakening unions, and introducing severe work tests on the payment of unemployment benefits, all of which would be anathema to many European citizens. The divisiveness and bitterness that would be created by making these major institutional changes would surely amplify, rather than reduce, the problem of social corrosion.

Even in theory, moreover, the gains in efficiency from implementing this approach would be small or non-existent, unless basic European attitudes towards income inequality changed. Suppose, for instance, that the net wage differential between skilled and unskilled workers were to be held constant, by providing low-wage supplements generous enough to compensate fully for the widening of the gross wage differential that would be the result of making wages flexible. The outcome would be fundamentally the same as if the wage differential stayed rigid, and a progressive payroll tax were used to eliminate the excess supply of unskilled labour.[27]

Both outcomes would be inefficient, in the sense that the relative supply of skilled labour would be smaller than it would have been with the wider net wage differential that would have arisen with wage flexibility and no intervention. However, the only way to reduce this inefficiency—after taking all feasible supply-side measures—would be to make the net wage differential wider, for example by providing smaller low-wage supplements. Thus so long as the European standard of what constitutes an unacceptably low relative income is maintained, the demand-shifting approach proposed here would be just as efficient as, and far less conflictual than, the flexible-wage strategy.[28]

---

[27] Indeed, if relative wages were made flexible, this sort of demand-side intervention would in principle be an alternative (to low-wage supplements) means of achieving any desired net wage differential.

[28] What happened in the UK in the 1980s was fundamentally an attempt to move away from European standards of equity, towards those of the USA, and not simply an attempt to change the institutional mechanisms for achieving a given standard of equity. The result was a sharp rise in inequality (as documented in Apps. A3–A5), and worse social corrosion. Whether there was also an increase in efficiency is more open to dispute.

10.5 Costs of Being Wrong

The policy suggestions in this chapter stem from the analysis in earlier parts of the book, which described and explained the effects of expanded North–South trade on labour markets in both sorts of countries. But what if the analysis is wrong? Some of it is controversial: open to criticism and disagreement, from several angles. Some of the conclusions, moreover, are much better supported by empirical evidence than others, on which at present there is simply not enough information. The conclusions represent the author's best current judgement, but there is much scope for further research in the vast field which this book covers, some of which is bound to lead to different conclusions, perhaps radically different ones.

But policy makers cannot wait. Things have to be done (or not done) now, in response to immediate problems, and in the light of the current state of knowledge. None the less, choices among alternative courses of action may be improved by sensitivity analysis—exploring the consequences of possible errors of information about how the world works. That is the purpose of this section. It focuses on four key points which are either subject to strong disagreement or on which the evidence is unsatisfactory, and in each case briefly considers the relative costs of (in statistical jargon) Type I and Type II errors. In plain English, the question is whether it would be worse to act on the assumption that this book is right, when in fact it is wrong, than to act on the assumption that the book is wrong, when in fact it is right.

10.5.1 Size of the impact on the North

The policy suggestions are based on the conclusion that expansion of trade with the South has caused a substantial decline in the relative demand for unskilled labour in the North—by about 20 per cent up to 1990. The quality of the evidence supporting this conclusion is mixed. There can be no doubt that trade with the South has caused *some* reduction in the relative demand for unskilled labour, and little doubt that this reduction is at least one order of magnitude greater than the tiny estimates made in earlier studies. However, the figure of 20 per cent involves two further doublings on the basis of much shakier evidence regarding induced technical change and effects in sectors other than manufacturing. It is possible that this is a great overstatement, and that the true figure is not much more than 5 per cent, spread, it should be recalled, over a couple of decades.

Suppose, then, that the present policy recommendations for the North were implemented, but that the trade-induced demand shift were much smaller than has been assumed in formulating them. The money spent on education and training would not be wasted, since its rationale is to combat market failures. However, in Europe too much public money would be spent on the creation of unskilled jobs, causing inefficiency (for example, because of the distortions induced by higher marginal tax rates), and thus lowering average incomes. In America, there would be too much redistribution from the skilled to the unskilled, in relation to prevailing ideas of equity, and in relation to the efficiency costs involved (including the reduction of incentives to acquire skills). The South might also lose, since its exports could be hit by excessive subsidies to unskilled work in Europe, and by lower aggregate demand arising from reduced efficiency throughout the North.

Now suppose, by contrast, that nothing were done in response to the trade-induced reduction in the relative demand for unskilled labour in the North, on the grounds that the impact was tiny, but that the impact was actually substantial. The outcome would be more inequality and poverty in America, and more unemployment in Europe, than if the policies suggested above were implemented. Greater hardship would be inflicted on unskilled workers and their families. More human resources would be wasted in Europe. Life in the North would be less agreeable for all its citizens, with more beggars, crime, urban decay, and racial conflict. Finally, there would be stronger political pressure for protection against imports from the South, reducing the opportunities for many millions of people in developing countries to work their way out of poverty.

Which is the lesser of these two sorts of error? The answer depends partly on numbers—how much loss of efficiency, how much more protection—and partly on personal and political preferences. However, many people would probably agree, even on the basis of the preceding qualitative assessment, that the consequences of underestimating the trade-induced reduction in the demand for unskilled labour in the North are likely to be worse than those of overestimating it. This strengthens the case for implementing the present policy suggestions.

10.5.2 Trade versus technology

The evidence on wages and unemployment presented in Chapters 7 and 8 makes it hard to doubt that the relative demand for unskilled labour in the North declined during the 1980s. There is more room for question about the cause of this decline. This book has concluded that expansion of trade with the South was the main cause, but there is a plausible alternative explanation, which is the autonomous spread of new technology with an unskilled-labour-saving bias. The limited evidence available does not permit a satisfactory comparative appraisal of these two explanations, but was argued in Section 7.3.5 to be consistent with the view that trade played the larger role.

Suppose that this book were wrong, and that technology rather than trade were the main cause of the demand shift in the North. Would the book's policy recommendations also be wrong? As it happens, the error would make little difference. This is because the suggested policies in the North do not involve interference or linkage with trade flows (unlike, for example, protection or trade-related adjustment assistance).[29] They are designed to respond efficiently and equitably to an autonomous decline in the relative demand for unskilled labour, regardless of the cause of that decline.

10.5.3 Mismatch versus hysteresis

The trend increase in aggregate unemployment·in the North, especially in Europe, between the 1960s and the 1980s is argued in this book to be the result of expansion of trade with the South, in conjunction with relative wage rigidity, thus aggravating skill mismatch. An altogether different view is taken by Layard, Nickell, and Jackman (1991), who attribute the rise in unemployment to other causes, and interpret its continuing high level as a manifestation of hysteresis. In particular, they argue that people who have been unemployed for a long time lose skills and motivation (or that this is believed by employers), making it increasingly difficult for them to find work. The evidence presented in Chapters 7 and 8 gives more support to the mismatch than to the hysteresis explanation, but there is not enough information to be confident about this conclusion.

There are important overlaps between the policies suggested in this book and those advocated by Layard, Nickell, and Jackman, who agree that there is also some mismatch unemployment, and that many of the long-term unemployed lack skills. Training, job subsidies, and public provision of employment appear on both lists. But there is also an important difference, which is that the measures needed to reduce hysteresis unemployment are temporary, whereas those needed to reduce mismatch unemployment are permanent. This is the distinction, for example, between a one-shot *recruitment* subsidy and a continuing unskilled

---

[29] Linking policies to trade flows is not always a bad idea. Hufbauer and Rosen (1986: 67) argue that this may be needed to make compensatory measures affordable. However, their focus is on the losses inflicted on people with industry-specific skills, which are large but concentrated on a small number of workers. The present focus, by contrast, is on the losses experienced by unskilled workers throughout the economy, which are smaller (per worker) but affect a much larger number of people, most of whom never worked in the specific sectors affected by trade. In this context it would be impossible to link compensation and other measures to trade flows.

employment subsidy; or between retraining those who are currently unemployed and permanently raising the proportion of skilled workers in the labour force.[30]

The two possible sorts of error in this regard are thus, in essence, taking temporary measures when permanent ones are needed, and taking permanent measures when only temporary ones are needed. Policies aimed at mismatch unemployment would probably be quite effective even if unemployment were mainly a matter of hysteresis, but they would be unnecessarily costly, both fiscally and in terms of the loss of efficiency caused by higher taxes and redundant subsidies. By contrast, temporary measures aimed at hysteresis unemployment would be cheaper, but would not be effective if mismatch were the main problem. For example, recruitment subsidies would be 'churned'—employers hiring and firing unskilled workers to get repeated subsidies.

In the long run, the second sort of error would clearly be worse, since a considerable amount of public money would be spent, and the unemployment problem would not be solved. However, the second sort of error is also more likely to be detected than the first sort: as usual, it is easier to see when one is paying too little for something than when one is paying too much. A case could thus be made, in the face of uncertainty about the true nature of the problem, for starting with temporary measures, and moving to permanent ones only if the temporary ones were ineffective. There are also possible compromises. Sweden, for example, long succeeded in keeping down unemployment by active manpower policies which were a mixture of temporary and permanent measures (Layard, Nickell, and Jackman 1991: 63–4).

10.5.4 Chance versus choice in skill acquisition

A fundamental premiss of this book is that skill acquisition is only in part a matter of individual choice. People do and should choose how much time and money to invest in education and training—their own or their children's—and their choices are influenced by the wage premia which skilled workers command. Yet the options which people face in this regard are heavily constrained by forces over which they, as individuals, have no control. They inherit different sets of genes, they are born into families with differing financial and intellectual resources, and they have access to schools of differing quality. In these senses, chance (or luck) also greatly affects what skills people acquire.

---

[30] However, some of the policies needed to deal with mismatch unemployment would be more permanent than others. The gradual rise in the proportion of skilled workers caused by more education and training of new entrants would reduce the need for measures to stimulate unskilled employment.

Few economists deny that chance plays some role in skill acquisition, but many treat it as a minor influence, reasoning as if the difference between skilled and unskilled workers were simply the result of individual choice. The disagreement emerges in assumptions about the elasticity of the skilled labour supply. In this book, the elasticity is assumed to be positive but small. The opposing view is that this elasticity is more or less infinite, at least in the medium-to-long term, so that there is an unlimited supply of skilled labour, provided that the wage premium over unskilled labour is sufficient to provide a normal rate of return on investment in education. The evidence supports this book's assumption, but is rather limited, which makes it worth considering the policy implications of error on this point.

If the policy suggestions in earlier sections were implemented, but the skill-supply elasticity were actually close to infinity, the outcome would be inefficient. Wage supplements to unskilled workers, and unskilled job creation, would tend to make the supply of skilled labour too small, by reducing incentives to train. They would also be inequitable, since they would discriminate against people who had put time and money into education and training, and in favour of people who had chosen to remain unskilled. In so far as relative wages were flexible, these problems would be offset by an automatic widening of gross skill differentials—the wage supplements would in effect be shifted. Both problems would be diminished, too, by the recommended improvements in education and training. But there would still be a loss of efficiency, because of the administrative and tax distortion costs of replacing private with public expenditure, and of reducing some incentives to train while increasing others.

Suppose instead that the policy suggestions of the present book were not implemented, on the grounds that infinitely elastic supply makes shifts in the relative demand for skilled and unskilled labour unimportant, but that this elasticity were actually quite small. Efficiency would be lower than if the policies were implemented, especially in so far as relative wages were rigid, and in so far as the supply of skills was subject to market failures. There would also be more inequity: those favoured neither by nature nor by nurture would have standards of living even further below the average, and to this injury would be added the insult of being wrongly blamed for being poor. Their reactions, as explained earlier, would blight Northern society as a whole, and would also hurt people in the South by increasing political pressure for protection against imports.

As in the other cases, there is room for disagreement about which of these two errors would be worse, especially in the absence of information on the magnitudes involved. However, it seems to the present author—and it is hoped to most readers—that the consequences of wrongly assuming the skill supply elasticity to be very high would be more adverse than the costs of wrongly assuming it to be rather low.

10.6 Summary

Expansion of trade with the South has, on average, benefited people in
the North, but has hurt unskilled workers, by reducing their wages or,
where wages have not been allowed to fall, by making them unemployed.
It seems inequitable that the poorer members of Northern society should
suffer as a result of these generally beneficial changes in trade—and the
resulting unemployment is a waste of resources. In addition, the decline
in demand for unskilled labour has aggravated crime, violence, and racial
conflict in most Northern countries.

These problems would justify government action to assist unskilled
workers. But a choice needs to be made among four types of policy
response: raising barriers to imports from the South; reducing the supply
of unskilled labour by more education and training; boosting the relative
demand for unskilled labour; and redistributing income from skilled to
unskilled workers.

More protection against Southern imports is the worst of the four
options. It would help unskilled workers in the North, but would be
more costly (to Northern society as a whole) than other ways of doing
so, and would inflict serious harm on much poorer workers in the South.
However, the need to reduce political pressure for higher trade barriers
makes it all the more important to assist unskilled workers in better
ways.

In principle, the best option would be to expand the skilled labour
supply by improvements in education and training, since this could raise
economic efficiency, as well as narrowing the gap in wages and unemployment between skilled and unskilled workers. Government action in this
area should thus be an important part of any solution. However, the
scope for raising the skilled labour supply is more limited than usually
recognised, because the additional taxes on skilled workers that would be
needed to finance better public education and training would have an
offsetting effect, by making it less attractive for people to acquire skills.
Excessive or ill-planned efforts to increase the skill supply would therefore be counter-productive. Moreover, education and training improvements should probably be focused on new entrants to the labour force,
and hence would improve the economic position of unskilled workers
only slowly.

Action to increase the skilled labour supply is thus unlikely, on its
own, to be able to solve the problems caused by declining demand for
unskilled labour. However, improvements in education and training could
be combined with the two other sorts of response: creating more demand
for unskilled labour, and redistributing income from skilled to unskilled
workers. The appropriate combination of policies would vary between

America, where the relative wages of skilled and unskilled workers are flexible, and Europe, where relative wages are more rigid, mainly because there is more concern about income inequality.

In America, the best approach would be to combine improved education and training, greater public employment of unskilled workers, and a system of income supplements for low-wage workers. These supplements would consist of tax relief and cash grants for all people in low-paying jobs, but would be larger for workers with dependent children. They would be financed by raising personal income taxes on higher-paid workers. The outcome would be a narrower gap in living standards between the skilled and the unskilled, without reducing labour market flexibility or incentives to work.

In Europe, what is required, in addition to better education and training, is measures to raise the relative demand for unskilled workers. Although public employment projects would be useful, the best approach would be to introduce a progressive payroll tax, which could be achieved by modifying the existing system of employers' social security contributions. The tax rate on the employer would be greater, the higher the wage of the worker concerned, perhaps with subsidies for the lowest-paid workers. This tax would reduce unemployment by offsetting the bias against hiring unskilled labour which is now created by narrow and inflexible wage differentials.

This book's diagnosis of the problems caused in the North by the expansion of trade with the South may be wrong. If so, there would be various costs to implementing these policy suggestions. But failing to implement these or similar policies, on the grounds that the diagnosis was wrong, when in fact it was right, would be an even more costly mistake.

Appendix A1
Cost Breakdown and Factor Prices

This appendix to Chapter 4 provides the sources of the cost breakdown of manufactured exports in Table 4.1 and of the factor prices in Table 4.2.

A1.1 Delinked Intermediates and Value Added

The first step is to split the cost of each country group's manufactured exports between delinked intermediate inputs and domestic nonprimary value added. Delinked intermediates are subdivided between primary (including processed primary) inputs and, in the South, imports of manufactures. Nonprimary value added is subdivided between (narrow) manufacturing and services (defined to include all sectors other than primary, processed primary and manufacturing). The data and methods used are explained in detail in Wood (1991c), and may be summarised as follows.

The data on the manufactured exports of the South to the North, and vice versa, broken down by ISIC categories, are from OECD sources (the totals are shown in Table 4.6). The cost of these exports is decomposed into the components mentioned above using the input–output tables of Korea (for the South) and the USA (for the North). The possible biases arising from the use of the Korean table to represent the whole of the South are discussed in Wood (1991c), but are unlikely to be a serious problem.

The calculations for the North do not require intermediate manufactured imports to be disentangled. The matrix of direct (domestic plus imported) intermediate input coefficients, A, is rearranged and partitioned, grouping the primary and processed primary sectors in the upper rows and left-hand-side columns, with the (narrow) manufacturing and service sectors below and to the right. The lower right submatrix A_l (l for linked), which describes intermediate transactions among the manufacturing and service sectors, is extracted and inverted. The resulting inverse matrix, $(I - A_l)^{-1}$, is then postmultiplied by the Northern vector of manufactured exports, X (extended with zeros in the service sector cells). This yields an 'export-oriented' gross output vector, Q_{xl}, showing the levels of gross output in each of the linked sectors directly and indirectly required to produce these exports.

The vector Q_{xl} is then used to generate the required cost breakdown. The delinked intermediate content of exports is derived by multiplication of Q_{xl} and the upper right submatrix of A, which specifies the direct primary and processed primary input requirements of the linked sectors. The value added content of the export basket is derived by multiplication of Q_{xl} and the (diagonalised) vector of value added coefficients, V_l, which specifies the share of value added in gross output for each of the linked sectors. The manufacturing and service elements of the resulting value added vector are then totalled separately. When added up, the value of the primary and processed primary inputs and the manufacturing and service value added exactly equals the total value of manufactured exports.

The cost breakdown calculations for the South extend the same basic procedure, using two separate direct coefficient matrices, A_h and A_m, referring respectively to domestically supplied and imported intermediates $(A_h + A_m = A)$. Each matrix is rearranged and partitioned as described above, and the submatrix A_{hl} is extracted and inverted. Multiplication of $(I - A_{hl})^{-1}$ by the extended vector of Southern manufactured exports, X, again yields the export-oriented gross output vector Q_{xl}. Multiplication of Q_{xl} with the upper right submatrices of A_h and A_m yields, respectively, the domestically supplied and the imported primary and processed primary intermediate inputs required to produce X. Similarly, multiplication with the lower right submatrix of A_m yields the requirements for intermediate imports of manufactures and services, while the linked value added content of X is calculated just as before.

The reader is cautioned that A, the conventional notation for the matrix of *intermediate* input coefficients, is used in Section 3.1 of this book with a different (but also conventional) meaning, namely as the matrix of *factor* input coefficients.

A1.2 Wages and Profits

The second step is to subdivide manufacturing value added between wages (actually 'employee compensation') and gross profit (net operating surplus plus capital consumption). For the South, this subdivision is again based on the (1983) Korea input–output table, which for each sector specifies the constituent elements of value added (including indirect taxes, which were stripped from both value added and gross output during the first step, see Wood 1991c: 18 and n. 4). The export-weighted average share of wages in value added is calculated using sectoral shares in the manufacturing segment of Q_{xl} as weights. Part of the net operating surplus—the labour component of self-employment income—is transferred to wages, using data on self-employment from the ILO *Yearbook of Labour Statistics*, and making the usual assumption that this labour component equals the average wage.

For the North, similar calculations are performed with US data, although the absence of a value added breakdown in the input–output table requires the use of more coarsely aggregated national accounts statistics.[1] The results are adjusted to allow for the fact that the US share of wages in total manufacturing value added in 1985 was higher than in other large developed countries (in all cases corrected for self-employment).[2]

---

[1] To attain the maximum possible degree of disaggregation for 1985, data from OECD *National Accounts* 1973–85 (Detailed Tables, Vol. II) are combined with those in *Survey of Current Business* July 1987. Only at this stage of the calculation is it possible to strip out indirect taxes, which, however, amount to only 3.4% of value added.

[2] Adjusted for self-employment and excluding indirect taxes, the wage share of manufacturing value added in 1985 was 75% in the USA, as compared with a value-added-weighted average of 72% for the USA, Germany, the UK, and Japan (OECD *National Accounts* 1973–85).

A1.3 White-collar and Blue-collar Workers

The next step is to separate out the wages and employment of blue-collar and white-collar workers. For each three-digit manufacturing sector in the USA (1985) and Korea (1984), the average blue-collar wage and the average white-collar wage can be calculated, as well as the numbers of blue-collar and white-collar workers employed per unit of gross output.[3] From these figures, suitably weighted averages for export-oriented manufacturing can be derived and compared with averages for the whole of manufacturing.

For both the North and the South, the weights for the export-oriented averages are based on the Q_{xl} vectors. For the North, the weights for the all-manufacturing averages are based on the sectoral distribution of US gross manufacturing output, which is reasonably representative. For the South, by contrast, the all-manufacturing averages are based not on Korean weights (since these would be unrepresentative), but on UNIDO data which describe the output mix of all developing-country manufacturing.[4]

The resulting averages, summarised in Table A1.1, will be drawn upon at various points below. But the differences between export-oriented and all manufacturing merit immediate comment. Perhaps the most striking feature is how *small* these differences are—much smaller, for example, than would be suggested by looking at an individual export-oriented sector such as (in the South) clothing.

TABLE A1.1. *Wages and employment of blue-collar and white-collar workers in manufacturing*

	USA 1985		Korea 1984	
	Export-oriented manufacturing	All manufacturing	Export-oriented manufacturing	All manufacturing*
Average pay ($000/year)	23.80	22.68	3.23	3.47
Blue-collar pay ($000/year)	20.17	19.38	2.90	3.07
White-collar pay ($000/year)	31.78	30.21	4.92	5.08
White/blue-collar pay	1.58	1.56	1.70	1.65
White-collar share of employment (%)	31.28	30.50	16.12	19.76
Employment per $million of gross output (person-years)	8.60	7.70	35.30	24.20

Notes: * Based on output weights for all developing countries, not for Korea alone: see text. Pay refers to wages and salaries rather than employee compensation (i.e. it excludes 'supplements'); blue-collar workers are 'production workers' as defined in industrial census data; white-collar workers are total employees less production workers.

Sources: See text.

[3] This information was derived mainly from industrial census data summarised in the UN *Industrial Statistics Yearbook*, which are not fully consistent with the national accounts and input–output data used above.
[4] These (three-digit-level) data are from the UNIDO database, and exclude China. They refer to value added, and were converted to a gross output basis using the Korean 1984 sectoral gross-output-to-value-added ratios from the UN *Industrial Statistics Yearbook*.

The smallness of the differences reflects partly the sectoral dispersion of manufactured exports, and partly the (even wider) dispersion of the intermediate manufactured inputs indirectly required to produce these exports.[5] It is consistent with the basic assumption of the modified FCT calculations in Chapter 4 that both the North and the South have become specialised in the production and export (to one another) of manufactured goods within particular ranges of skill intensity.

All the indicators for the North confirm that export-oriented manufacturing is more skill-intensive than manufacturing in general. The average pay of blue-collar workers is higher, suggesting a larger proportion of skilled manual workers. So is the average pay of white-collar workers, who also constitute a slightly bigger share of the labour force. Export-oriented manufacturing employs somewhat more workers (blue- and white-collar) per unit of gross output than manufacturing as a whole. This is probably because the present definition of manufactured exports excludes processed primary products, which have a high ratio of gross output to value added.

For the South, all the indicators correspondingly confirm that export-oriented manufacturing is *less* skill-intensive than manufacturing in general. Both blue-collar and white-collar average wages are lower, suggesting lower proportions of skilled workers within these categories, and the share of white-collar workers in the labour force is smaller. The difference in labour requirements per unit of gross output is in the same direction as (though much more pronounced than) in the North, with export-oriented production employing far more than the all-manufacturing average number of workers. This again probably partly reflects the exclusion of primary processing, but also reflects the fact that Southern exports of narrow manufactures are concentrated on labour-intensive items.

A1.4 Blue-collar Wage Levels

The next step is to estimate average hourly blue-collar compensation in export-oriented manufacturing in the North and the South. ('Compensation' includes social insurance contributions and other employer supplements to wages and salaries, so matching the national accounts definition of wages.) For the North, comprehensive data of good quality are available from the US Bureau of Labour Statistics (unpublished data were kindly supplied by John Rhee). The 1985 numbers, reproduced in Table A1.2, range from under $5 in New Zealand to nearly $13 in the USA. They were averaged across countries using manufacturing employment weights. The resulting figure, which refers to the whole of manufacturing, was adjusted by the ratio of the US export-oriented to all-manufacturing blue-collar wage averages from Table A1.1.

For the South, manufacturing wage data are much scarcer and frequently of uncertain coverage and quality, as well as being more often affected (when expressed in US dollars) by large and irregular alterations in exchange rates. The BLS data cover only a few developing countries, and have to be supplemented from other sources detailed in the notes to Table A1.3, which summarises the

---

[5] Intermediate inputs account for 36% of (the sum of the elements of) Q_{xl} in the North, and for 38% in the South.

TABLE A1.2. *Wage rates in Northern manufacturing, 1985*
(hourly compensation of production workers)

	Hourly compensation ($US)	Manufacturing employment (millions)
Australia	8.14	1.14
Austria	7.25	0.93
Belgium	8.92	0.81
Canada	10.81	1.98
Denmark	8.13	0.53
Finland	8.08	0.53
France	7.52	4.84
Germany	9.56	8.15
Ireland	5.80	0.20
Italy	7.40	5.01
Japan	6.47	14.91
Netherlands	8.97	0.88
New Zealand	4.45	0.32
Norway	10.60	0.33
Spain	4.79	2.41
Sweden	9.66	0.89
UK	6.19	5.73
USA	12.96	19.87
Employment-weighted all-manufacturing average	9.04	
Export-oriented manufacturing average	9.41	

Notes: Export-oriented manufacturing average derived from employment-weighted all-manufacturing average by applying relevant US blue-collar wage ratio (1.0408) from Table A1.1. Wages in local currency are converted to dollars at official exchange rates.

Sources: Wages: US Dept. of Labor, Bureau of Labor Statistics, 'Hourly Compensation Costs for Production Workers, 40 Manufacturing Industries, 34 Countries, 1975 and 1977–87', Aug. 1988. Employment: OECD *National Accounts* 1973–85, Vol. 2, Detailed Tables, except for Austria, Canada, France, Ireland, and New Zealand whose data come from ILO *Yearbook of Labour Statistics* 1987.

results for export-oriented manufacturing. Some of the numbers are reliable and confirmed by other sources, some are more dubious, and some are rather puzzling, not least those for India and Turkey, whose ranking is the opposite of what one would expect. But none is suppressed, partly because it would be hard to know where to stop, and partly because the errors appear to vary in direction and thus tend to cancel one another out in the process of constructing an average for the South.

In constructing this Southern average, the choice of country weights is more important than in the North, because the proportionate range of wage variation is much wider (from $0.2 in China to $3.5 in Greece). In the present context, one

Appendix 1

TABLE A1.3. *Wage rates in Southern manufacturing, 1985*
(hourly compensation of production workers in export-oriented sectors)

	Source	Hourly compensation ($US)	Manufactured exports ($bn.)	Manufacturing employment (millions)
Argentina	B	1.62	1.42	2.16
Brazil	A	1.15	8.91	8.54
Chile	B	0.95	0.26	0.57
China	E	0.22	13.38	106.37
Colombia	D (1983)	1.25	0.61	2.36
Costa Rica	B	1.13	0.32	0.12
Dominican Republic	D (1983)	1.10	0.16	0.22
Ecuador	B (1984)	1.30	0.02	0.35
Egypt	D (1983)	0.72	0.38	1.77
Greece	A	3.45	2.24	0.70
Guatemala	B	1.01	0.28	0.24
Hong Kong	A	1.65	13.77	1.03
India	A	0.49	5.89	30.20
Korea	A	1.28	27.67	3.78
Malaysia	D (1983)	0.90	4.40	0.75
Mauritius	D (1983)	0.54	0.12	0.09
Mexico	A	1.97	7.13	3.18
Morocco	D (1983)	1.80	0.88	1.04
Pakistan	A	0.47	1.73	3.93
Peru	B	0.35	0.24	0.65
Philippines	C (1984)	0.42	2.53	1.77
Portugal	A	1.42	4.41	1.00
Singapore	A	2.33	6.66	0.29
Sri Lanka	A	0.26	0.40	0.49
Taiwan	A	1.38	30.35	2.49
Thailand	D (1983)	0.60	2.58	1.97
Tunisia	D (1983)	1.30	0.76	0.37
Turkey	A (1984)	0.39	3.85	2.20
Export-weighted average		1.24		
Employment-weighted average		0.48		
Midpoint between these averages		0.86		

Sources: (1) Wage data (in the order of preference applied when more than one source was available).

A. US Bureau of Labour Statistics (same source as for Table A1.2). Estimates for India and Pakistan in 1985 derived by assuming same ratio to Sri Lanka as in earlier years. Export-oriented manufacturing averages derived from BLS all-manufacturing averages by applying relevant Korean blue-collar wage ratio (0.9437) from Table A1.1.

B. ILO *Yearbook of Labour Statistics* 1987, tables 12A and 17A. Wage data adjusted where necessary from a monthly or daily basis, using data on hours of work, and converted to a compensation basis by adding 20% (based on information in source D). Export-oriented manufacturing estimates then derived as in note A above.

C. UN *Yearbook of Industrial Statistics* 1985. Hourly wage rates for all manufacturing derived by dividing annual operatives wages and salaries by number of hours worked. Conversion to hourly compensation estimates for export-oriented industries as in note B.

TABLE A1.3. *Notes continued*

D. Fröbel, Heinrichs, and Kreye (forthcoming, table IV-10). 'Labour cost' assumed equivalent to compensation (in some cases wages had to be adjusted to a compensation basis, by adding 20%). Data in present table taken from upper limit of range given in source, which refers to pay in export processing zones. Choice of upper limit was based on comparisons with other sources (in countries where these were available), which suggested that average EPZ wages are usually lower than in export-oriented manufacturing in general, probably because of EPZ concentration on clothing and electronics, in which most workers are female.

E. *Statistical Yearbook of China* 1986. Average annual wage of staff and workers in industry (p. 565) adjusted to compensation basis by adding 28% for labour insurance and welfare funds (pp. 562, 575), plus an additional arbitrary 25% to reflect large subsidies to housing. Result assumed to approximate blue-collar compensation (because white/blue wage differentials are small), converted to hourly basis assuming 48-hour week and 51-week year, adjusted to export-oriented basis as in note A above, and expressed in dollars using exchange rate on p. 498 of SYC.

(2) Other data. Manufactured exports: World Bank (1987, indicators table 14). For Taiwan, from *Statistical Yearbook of the Republic of China* 1987: 391. Most data are for 1985, though some refer to other (unspecified) years. Hong Kong and Singapore numbers arbitrarily halved to allow for re-exports.

Manufacturing employment: total labour force for 1985 (from UNCTAD *Handbook of Trade and Development Statistics* 1987, table 6.10A) multiplied by most recent available estimate of manufacturing share in total labour force from ILO *Yearbook of Labour Statistics*. For Taiwan, from *Yearbook of Labour Statistics*, Republic of China, 1987: 14. For China, from the *Statistical Yearbook of China* 1986: 84, 92 (census share of manufacturing in industry applied to 1985 industry total).

obvious possibility is to weight the wage rates for individual countries by the level of their manufactured exports. The resulting average wage ($1.2) is—unsurprisingly—close to that of Korea. This average, however, has an upward bias of unknown but substantial size, because it should in principle be based on employment in export production rather than on the value of exports, and because employment per dollar of exports is likely to be greater in lower-wage countries.

Moreover, the modified FCT method in Chapter 4 allows for displacement of some Northern exports by labour-intensive import substitution in the South (see Section 4.3.1). This import substitution has undoubtedly been more widely diffused among developing countries than the growth of manufactured exports, which suggests the alternative possibility of weighting the wage rates for individual countries by their manufacturing employment. Two poor countries, China and India, between them account for three-quarters of all Southern manufacturing employment. Thus the weighted average on this basis is much lower ($0.5) than with export weights. But the employment-weighted average is biased downwards as an estimate of the average wage in Southern *labour-intensive* manufacturing, because labour-intensive sectors constitute an unusually low proportion of China's manufacturing industry.

For the purposes of the present calculations, the right wage rate lies somewhere in the range between the export-weighted and employment-weighted averages, which would be much narrower if their respective biases could be corrected. Initially, it is assumed to lie midway between them, with the sensitivity of the results to this assumption tested in Section 4.4.2. The choice of the midpoint is based on three considerations: (*a*) the South's labour-intensive exports appear much larger than the import substitution corresponding to the North's lost labour-intensive exports (as explained in Section 4.3.1), which argues for a wage well above the midpoint; (*b*) the upward bias of the export-weighted average is probably larger in absolute terms than the downward bias of the employment-weighted average, favouring a wage below the midpoint;[6] and (c) the choice of a wage below the midpoint is favoured also by the upward bias of the underlying manufacturing wage data, which are mostly derived from surveys that exclude small firms, in which wages are much lower, even for workers with similar qualifications (Little *et al.* 1987: 251–9, 274, 310).

A1.5 *SKILD* and *BAS-ED* Workers

The next step is to estimate the wages and employment of *SKILD* and *BAS-ED* workers in export-oriented manufacturing in each country group. This is difficult, because these two skill categories (defined in Section 2.4.2) cannot be identified simply from education-related data, since these omit all forms of skill acquisition other than formal schooling, nor from most occupational data, in which manual workers are not differentiated by skill level. Moreover, neither educational nor detailed occupational data for finely disaggregated manufacturing sectors are readily available, which precludes a direct extension of the input–output methods applied above.

The approach used here is thus to start from the ratios of white- to blue-collar wages and employment (from Table A1.1), and to combine these with data on employment and wages from several other sources (and some assumptions), within an accounting framework that divides both white- and blue-collar workers between *SKILD* and *BAS-ED*.[7] This framework is helpful not only in synthesising information from various sources, but also in assessing the plausibility of the assumptions needed to fill gaps in the data, which can be chosen iteratively, with an eye on their implications for derived variables (including similarities and differences between the North and the South). Table A1.4 presents the results.

Within the white-collar group, information on professional and technical and managerial employment is the main basis for distinguishing *SKILD* from *BAS-ED* workers, but an assumption is required about the *SKILD* share of the clerical and sales category.[8] The wages of *SKILD* relative to *BAS-ED* white-collar workers are based on earnings by education level, identifying *SKILD* with tertiary education and *BAS-ED* with primary education in both country groups. For the North, this

---

[6] A maximum estimate of the upward bias of the export-weighted average can be obtained by using as an alternative weight for each country its export value divided by its wage rate—this being a crude measure of employment in export production. The resulting weighted average is $0.80, which is $0.44 lower than the simple export-weighted average. This correction seems too extreme: a more reasonable reduction would be half this ($0.22), giving a corrected export-weighted average of $1.02. As regards the downward bias of the employment-weighted average, a reasonable adjustment might be to halve the weight of China, giving a corrected average of $0.59.

[7] The ratio of white-collar to blue-collar wages for the North in Tables A1.1 and A1.4 (1.56 for all manufacturing, 1.58 for export-oriented manufacturing) is close to the 1985 average of 1.50 for the five large countries in App. 4, Fig. A4.1 (allowing for the scaling factors in that figure).

[8] In the North, professional and technical workers constitute almost half of all white-collar *SKILD* workers, as compared to one-fifth in the South, where the dominant white-collar *SKILD* group is managers.

TABLE A1.4. *Skilled and unskilled employment and wages in export-oriented manufacturing*

	North	South	Notes and sources
A. Composition of employment (%)			
White-collar workers	31.28	16.12	a
SKILD	19.31	4.86	
Professional and technical	9.27	1.10	b
Managerial	7.05	3.76	c
Other	2.99	0.00	d
BAS-ED	11.97	11.26	
Blue-collar workers	68.72	83.88	a
SKILD	30.92	8.39	e
BAS-ED	37.80	75.49	
All *SKILD*	50.24	13.25	
Total employment	100.00	100.00	
B. Wage ratios			
White-collar/blue-collar	1.58	1.70	a
White *SKILD*/white *BAS-ED*	2.72	4.19	f
Blue *SKILD*/blue *BAS-ED*	1.68	2.54	g
White *SKILD*/blue *SKILD*	1.62	1.65	
Average *SKILD*/*BAS-ED*	2.08	3.15	h
C. Hourly compensation ($)			
Average blue-collar	9.41	0.86	i
Average employee	11.12	0.96	
Average *SKILD*	14.99	2.34	
BAS-ED workers	7.21	0.75	

Notes and sources: Absence of a note indicates derived arithmetically from other numbers shown.
[a]Table A1.1.
[b]In the North, the proportion of professional and technical workers in export-oriented manufacturing is assumed to be equal to the proportion in manufacturing as a whole (manufacturing-employment-weighted average of developed countries calculated from data in the ILO *Yearbook of Labour Statistics*). For the South, the starting point is a weighted average (2.7%) of the professional and technical shares of all manufacturing employment in Hong Kong, Korea, and Taiwan, again using data from ILO *Yearbooks*. This is adjusted downwards to allow for the likely lower professional intensity of export-oriented manufacturing, especially in the South as a whole. The adjusted figure (1.1%) may be compared with Krueger (1983, table 5.3), which shows the professional share of employment in export-oriented manufacturing in Hong Kong in 1973 to have been 0.8%. The adjusted figure yields plausible values for the various wage ratios in the present table.
[c]For the North, assumed equal to that in all manufacturing (see n. b above). For the South, assumed equal to weighted average of all-manufacturing shares for Hong Kong, Korea, and Taiwan (see n. b).
[d]Based on assumption that *SKILD* workers constitute 20% of non-professional non-managerial white-collar employment in the North, and 0% in the South.
[e]*SKILD* workers taken to be 45% of blue-collar employment in the North and 10% in the South: see text.
[f]Average pay of higher-educated workers relative to primary-educated workers. Calculated from private rate of return data in Psacharopoulos (1980, table 2), using the formula in equation 8 of the same source, and basing average years of schooling at each level on the data in Kaneko (1986, table A.4).
[g]See text.
[h]Derivation assumes white-collar *BAS-ED* wage equals blue-collar *BAS-ED* wage: see text.
[i]For the North, from Table A1.2. For the South, from Table A1.3.

wage ratio (2.7) can be checked against data on wages in higher and lower white-collar occupations (Figs. A4.4(*a*) and (*b*)): it is at the top of the observed range. It is also assumed that white-collar *BAS-ED* workers earn the same as blue-collar *BAS-ED* workers, which seems consistent with the evidence for the North in Table A4.1.

Within the blue-collar group, the *SKILD/BAS-ED* division has to be made on the basis of the few occupational statistics that distinguish skilled from unskilled manual workers. For the North, the estimates appear reasonably sound. The share of skilled workers in manual employment in manufacturing varies among developed countries, probably partly because of differences in definition (see the data and sources cited in Section A4.4). But the present estimate of the share of *SKILD* workers (white- plus blue-collar) in export-oriented manufacturing in the North is in line with other recent estimates (Schumacher 1989*a*, table A.9). The *SKILD/BAS-ED* blue-collar wage ratio in the North (1.7) is at the top of the observed range of skilled–unskilled manual wage ratios (Fig. A4.3).

The breakdown of the Southern blue-collar group is the least well-grounded aspect of these calculations. The limitations of the available employment data are explained at the end of Section 4.2.1 of the text. The 10 per·cent share of *SKILD* blue-collar workers in Table A1.4 is thus a rough estimate, and is varied (between 7 per cent and 25 per cent) in the sensitivity analysis in Section 4.4.2 of the text. The blue-collar *SKILD/BAS-ED* wage ratio (2.5) is based on the assumption that this ratio is larger than in the North by roughly the same proportion as the corresponding white-collar wage ratio. The proportional difference between the overall *SKILD/BAS-ED* wage ratio in the South (3.2) and the North (2.1), which is especially important in the present context, is similar to that estimated by Clague 1991 (see Chapter 4, n. 8).

Panel B of Table A1.4 illustrates the limitations of the white–blue collar ratio as an indicator of skill differentials in wages. This ratio is rather small, because both the white-collar and the blue-collar categories are mixtures of *SKILD* and *BAS-ED* workers. Moreover, the white–blue wage ratio is only slightly larger in the South than in the North, because the proportion of *SKILD* workers is lower in the South in the white-collar as well as in the blue-collar category. In other words, the table confirms that the most important skill differences are to be found within, rather than between, the white-collar and blue-collar categories.

Panel C of Table A1.4 combines the skill ratios from the upper two panels with the blue-collar wage rate averages from Tables A1.2 and A1.3 to obtain estimates of the absolute hourly compensation of *SKILD* and *BAS-ED* workers in the North and the South.

A1.6 Labour Quality Adjustment

For the modified FCT calculations in Chapter 4 to be accurate, labour in each of these two skill categories should be of identical quality in the North and the South. This assumption seems reasonable enough for *BAS-ED* workers. International comparative tests do reveal substantially lower subject-specific achievement levels in primary and secondary schools in developing countries.[9] But such test scores seem unlikely to have much bearing on the proficiency of *BAS-ED* workers in unskilled and semi-skilled factory work. The differences in achievement levels are of much greater economic relevance in the case of post-basic education and training. It thus seems essential to make explicit allowance for a North–South gap in the average knowledge of *SKILD* workers.

The only simple way of doing this is to divide the *SKILD* wage by a quality index whose value is lower in the South than in the North, which increases the effective cost of skill in the South relative to its cost in the North. The implicit assumption that 'skill' is a homogeneous ingredient, of which each Southern *SKILD* worker contains less than his Northern counterpart, does not fully capture the truth. It would be absurd, for instance, to suggest that two poorly trained computer programmers could simply replace one well-trained programmer. But there is no feasible alternative to the quality index approach, and it seems preferable to make some quality adjustment rather than none, provided that its limitations are recognised.

Calculating an appropriate value for the *SKILD* quality index in the South (in the North it is set at 100) is also problematic, because there is so little hard evidence. The test scores mentioned above cover only four developing countries—though a reasonably representative sample—and are rather old. They also refer only to formal education, do not go beyond secondary school, and vary somewhat from subject to subject. The most relevant available subject in the present context is science, in which the average developing-country test score in the last year of pre-university education in 1971 was 45 per cent of the developed-country average.[10] The *SKILD* quality index is thus set at a round 50 in the South, but subjected to sensitivity analysis in Section 4.4.2.

A1.7 Cost of Capital

The gross (of depreciation, interest, and tax) profit rate in Northern manufacturing is a 1985 average of nine countries, derived from OECD data.[11] For the South, where data on manufacturing profitability are scarcer, the gross profit rate is an average of estimates for Korea and Taiwan, derived from national accounts

---

[9] The tests were conducted by the International Association for the Evaluation of Educational Achievement (see the references in Inkeles 1979, n. 1). In reading comprehension, for example, the average score of the four developing countries covered was 30–40% (lower for older children) of the developed-country average.

[10] Based on an unweighted average of the scores for Chile, India, Iran, and Thailand in IEA (1973, table 7.2). Heyneman and Loxley (1983, table 2) summarise a wider range of Southern science scores, which confirm that they are substantially lower than in the North. However, the adjustments made by these authors to render the data more suitable for their particular purposes make it hard to calculate an average gap from their summary table. In particular, their rendition of the IEA numbers differs greatly from the original source.

[11] More specifically, it is a manufacturing-capital-stock-weighted average of gross operating surplus divided by net fixed capital stock (both in manufacturing) for the nine developed countries for which the relevant data are available in OECD *National Accounts* 1973–85, Vol. 2, adjusted for self-employment income as described in Section A1.2.

data similar to those used in breaking down the cost of manufactured exports.[12] The capital goods price index for the North and the South is derived from Kravis *et al.* (1982, table 6-8).[13]

[12] It is a simple average of the 1985 rates in Korea (31.6%) and Taiwan (34.7%). Both rates are estimated from national accounts data on net operating surplus and capital consumption in manufacturing, assuming the ratio of capital consumption to net capital stock to be the same as the Northern average (10.8%), and adjusting for self-employment income. The Korean data are from Bank of Korea *National Accounts* 1970–86, supporting table 1. Those for Taiwan are from the Directorate-General of Budget, Accounting and Statistics, *National Income in Taiwan Area, Republic of China*, supplementary table 1.

[13] More specifically, it is based on line 109–145 of this table (domestic capital formation). The figure for the North is an average of Groups V and VI, weighted by the US and non-US shares of total Northern GDP from World Bank (1987, indicators table 3). The figure for the South is an average of Groups I and II (unweighted because the two numbers are similar). Both figures are rescaled to make North = 100.

Appendix A2
Changes in Relative Sectoral Skill Intensities

This appendix reports on an attempt to quantify the impact of defensive innovation on the skill composition of the demand for labour in Northern manufacturing (discussed in Section 4.4.3 of the main text). It outlines the method used, describes the practical problems encountered in applying it, and presents a selection of results.

A2.1 Method

The approach is to estimate the impact of defensive innovation jointly with the impact of the trade-induced reallocation of labour among manufacturing subsectors of differing skill intensity. (The latter can be measured, and hence separated off, by factor content calculations.) The method described here is applicable to the South as well as the North, but the problems with Southern data are even more serious (Wood 1991a: 170–4), and there is less reason to suppose that trade-induced technical change is important.

The method involves comparing changes over time in the skill intensity of (a) manufacturing (as a whole) and (b) nontraded sectors. Both defensive innovation and reallocation among subsectors must have tended to raise the average skill intensity of manufacturing (its ratio of skilled to unskilled workers). However, the skill intensity of manufacturing must have been raised also by increases in the economy-wide supply of skilled relative to unskilled labour as a result of educational expansion. The comparison with nontraded sectors is intended to control for this supply shift: more trade with the South should have caused skill intensity to rise *faster* in manufacturing than in nontraded sectors.[1]

It is possible that, even in the absence of trade, the skill intensity of manufacturing might have risen faster (or slower) than in nontraded sectors, for example because of a difference in their elasticities of substitution between skilled and unskilled labour, or because of a long-term difference in the bias of autonomous technical progress. For this reason, the present method is to look not simply for divergent movements in the skill intensity of manufacturing and the nontraded sectors, but for *changes* in the rate of divergence after the North started to import manufactures on a large scale from the South.

In principle, the impact of more trade with the South is thus estimated as the difference between the actual ratio of skilled to unskilled workers in manufacturing at the end of the period (ϵ_i) and the level this ratio would have attained (ϵ_i^*) if

---

[1] The manufacturing–nontraded comparison should in principle control for *all* economy-wide changes in the relative demand and supply of skilled and unskilled labour. The validity of the control should not be affected by the reduction in the unskilled relative wage caused by expansion of trade, which increases the incentive to employ unskilled labour both in traded and in nontraded sectors, without affecting their *relative* skill intensities. However, if unskilled wages were less flexible downwards in manufacturing than in nontraded sectors, these calculations would exaggerate the impact of trade, and vice versa.

there had been no change in the rate of divergence between manufacturing and the nontraded sectors. The calculation involves dividing the time-series on skill intensity in each sector between 'pre-trade' and 'post-trade' sub-periods. The without-trade counterfactual skill intensity of manufacturing at the end of the period is then calculated as

$$\epsilon_i^* = \epsilon_{nt}(\epsilon_i/\epsilon_{nt})^*$$

where ϵ_{nt} is the actual end-period skill intensity of the nontraded sectors, and $(\epsilon_i/\epsilon_{nt})^*$ is the estimated end-period counterfactual ratio between the skill intensities of the two sectors, calculated by extrapolating the change in this ratio during the pre-trade sub-period.

In itself, this method clearly cannot distinguish between the effects of North–South and of North–North trade. However, as explained in Section 7.3.1, there is little reason to suppose that the latter sort of trade has raised the average skill intensity of Northern manufacturing, so that the observed changes can be attributed mainly to expansion of trade with the South. This attribution is vulnerable, however, to changes in other influences on the relative skill intensity of manufacturing and nontraded sectors. For example, an autonomous acceleration of skill-using technical change confined to manufacturing would have the same effect as more trade with the South. A simple way of testing whether the latter is truly the cause is to correlate variations among countries in the relative sectoral skill-intensity shift with variations in Southern import penetration.

The dividing line between traded and nontraded sectors is fuzzy, and in practice there is little choice but to define the latter as all sectors other than agriculture, mining, and manufacturing. Because this residuum includes traded services, whose skill intensity has also been increased by trade with the South (Section 4.4.3), the calculations tend to understate the impact of trade on the skill intensity of manufacturing, but the bias is probably small, because few services are traded. 'Nontraded' sectors also vary widely in skill intensity, and their relative sizes have altered over time, so the calculations are based on fixed-weighted averages.[2]

The application of this method ran into two practical problems. The first is that it turns out to be hard to make satisfactory comparisons between the skill intensity of manufacturing and of nontraded sectors, because they require different types of skill, and because of the shortcomings of most educational and occupational data as skill indicators. The second problem is simply that time-series on skill intensity by sector are scarce, and generally too short to permit changes in trends to be measured. The rest of this appendix discusses these problems in more detail, and summarises the results obtained with various different measures of skill intensity.

A2.2 Education

The limitations of length of schooling as a measure of skill (noted in Section 2.4.1) are less serious when comparing changes in sectoral skill intensities over

---

[2] However, the effective use of fixed weights was impeded by the 1968 revision of the International Standard Industrial Classification, which radically changed the boundaries between some of the nontraded sectors.

time than in most other contexts, such as international comparisons of skill levels). However, the omission of all other sources of skill—formal and informal training outside school—matters a lot in the present context, because these other sources of skill are particularly important for manual workers in manufacturing. The usual dividing lines between levels of education—primary, secondary, and tertiary—do not tell us enough about the skills of the manufacturing labour force. This problem of comparison is compounded by the heavy concentration of workers with tertiary education in the nontraded sectors (especially in education, health, law, finance, and public administration).

Availability of information is also a problem. Data on the educational qualifications of the labour force broken down by sector are not regularly compiled by any international agency, though OECD (1969*a*) pulled together national information for the 1960s. Virtually no information is available prior to 1960, and in later years there are some striking gaps (including France and Germany). Most of the information that is available refers only to decennial census years, and at the time of writing the 1990–1 results were not yet available, making 1980 usually the most recent available year. Finally, in some cases the educational categories used in census data have changed over time in such a way as to preclude comparisons between years, which is why the results for Canada in the next table are so limited.

Table A2.1 contains results based on two variants of what is probably the most useful skill breakdown available from the educational data, namely that between workers with and without post-upper-secondary education. An attempt has been made to standardise across countries for the differences in the time-periods covered by the data—by extrapolating in all cases to a 1960–85 basis—but the coverage is clearly unsatisfactory, with only one observation after 1981, and no data for some countries after 1970 or 1971. The table shows not only the education intensity of manufacturing relative to nontraded sectors, but also the absolute education intensity levels of manufacturing and the whole economy in the years concerned.

The results in the third column imply that the relative skill intensity of manufacturing increased between the early 1960s and the early 1980s. This is consistent with the expected effects of the expansion of trade with the South. The increases in relative skill intensity are mainly rather small—their weighted average is about 15 per cent in both cases—although this might be attributable to the lack of data for the 1980s, during which most of the increase in trade with the South occurred, as may be seen from Fig. 1.1 of the main text. Nor is there enough data to assess properly whether the increase in the relative skill intensity of manufacturing accelerated over the period, although this did happen in the USA.[3]

A2.3 Occupation

The geographical and temporal coverage of information on the occupational structure of employment in each sector are much better than for education.

---

[3] Using the 'university' definition, the relative skill intensity of manufacturing rose by 4% between 1960 and 1970, and by 13% between 1970 and 1983. Using the broader tertiary definition, there was a slight decline between 1960 and 1970, and a 6% rise during 1970–83.

TABLE A2.1. *Higher education intensity of Northern manufacturing, 1960–1985*

Country		Data period	Scope of education	As ratio of nontraded sectors			Absolute levels (×100)			
				Early level	Later level	Est. change 1985/1960	Manufacturing		Economy-wide	
							Early	Later	Early	Later
Education intensity = university-educated/other workers										
Belgium		1961–70	University	0.26	0.29	1.35	1.0	1.8	2.3	4.1
Finland	a	1960–80	University	0.28	0.35	1.35	0.7	3.0	1.2	6.2
Italy	b	1961–81	University	0.16	0.17	1.13	1.0	1.7	2.6	6.2
Japan		1960–80	University	0.60	0.62	1.03	3.9	10.2	3.6	13.0
Netherlands		1960–70	Doctorate	0.26	0.27	1.07	0.6	1.0	1.4	2.7
New Zealand	a	1966–81	University	0.28	0.36	1.52	3.0	5.5	6.5	11.5
UK	b,c	1961–81	Univ. sci.	0.81	1.01	1.33	0.6	2.6	0.7	2.6
USA		1960–83	16+ years	0.45	0.53	1.19	6.3	18.0	10.1	28.4
Weighted averages	d			0.45	0.50	1.16	4.6	12.7	6.7	19.5

Education intensity = tertiary-educated/other workers

Belgium	e	1961–70	Tertiary	0.23	0.33	2.55	1.9	4.5	4.6	9.2
Canada	a	1961–71	13+ years	0.54	0.51	0.88	15.0	16.8	19.5	24.5
Japan		1960–80	Tertiary	0.47	0.51	1.10	6.6	15.0	7.1	21.5
Norway	a,f	1960–80	Tertiary	0.24	0.40	1.87	1.2	8.7	2.6	17.2
UK	b,c	1961–81	Higher sci.	0.99	1.25	1.33	1.1	4.8	1.1	4.1
USA		1960–83	13+ years	0.50	0.53	1.05	16.2	45.2	23.8	70.6
Weighted averages	d			0.48	0.52	1.14	12.3	31.8	17.1	49.1

Notes: First two columns of data show education intensity of manufacturing relative to average education intensity of nontraded sectors in the first and last years available (see data period column). Third column shows the estimated 1960–85 change in this relativity, calculated by dividing the recent level by the early level and extrapolating the result over a standard 25-year period. The average education intensity of nontraded sectors is a fixed-weighted average of all sectors other than manufacturing, agriculture, and mining, weighted by mid-data-period shares of all nontraded sector employment. Last four columns of data show absolute education intensity (×100) in manufacturing and whole economy in first and last years available. All calculations omit workers with sector of activity 'not adequately described'. Workers whose educational level is unknown are also omitted, except where this category also includes workers with education below some specified level.

[a] Later year data include unemployed workers.

[b] Manufacturing includes mining.

[c] Higher-educated workers include only those with scientific, engineering, and technological qualifications. Data refer to Great Britain (UK less Northern Ireland).

[d] Weighted by early-1970s total employment. The UK is excluded from the averages of levels (see previous note), but is included in the average change in col. 3.

[e] Early and later coverage of non-university tertiary education may not be comparable.

[f] Early and later coverage not strictly comparable.

Sources: Most 1960s data from OECD (1969a). Otherwise directly from national population censuses and labour force surveys.

However, the standard international occupational classification has some serious limitations as an indicator of skill, the most notable being its failure to divide manual workers by level of skill. One of the available breakdowns is between professional and technical workers and other workers. Alternatively, the labour force can be split between white-collar and blue-collar workers (the former group including managerial, clerical, and sales, as well as professional workers), although this is unsatisfactory, because there are larger skill differences within than between the white- and blue-collar groups (see for example Table A1.4).

Table A2.2, which is laid out in much the same way as the previous table, uses both these occupation-based measures to assess changes in the skill intensity of manufacturing relative to nontraded sectors between the early 1960s and the mid-1980s.[4] Its upper panel shows that the professional and technical ratio in manufacturing generally increased by much more than in nontraded sectors—on (weighted) average by about 70 per cent more. Only in two countries (Canada and Sweden) did this relativity decrease.

The change in the relative professional intensity of manufacturing is in the direction that would be expected as a result of the expansion of trade with the South. It is not clear, though, how much of this change can be attributed to trade. Professional and technical workers are concentrated in nontraded sectors, and in some nontraded activities, such as education and health, the initial levels of professional intensity are so high that the scope for raising them seems bound to be less than in manufacturing. These doubts are reinforced by cross-country comparisons from the early 1960s (prior to the changes in trade) which suggest that there is a normal tendency, in the course of development, for the professional intensity of manufacturing to rise faster than that of services (OECD 1969*b*: 59–72).

The lower panel of Table A2.2, by contrast with the upper panel, shows a general decline in the relative white-collar intensity of manufacturing (which is especially striking because professional and technical workers are part of the white-collar group). The absolute white-collar intensity of manufacturing increased substantially, on average from thirty-one to forty-nine white-collar workers per hundred blue-collar workers. But the absolute white-collar intensity of the nontraded sectors increased even more, and so the relative white-collar intensity of manufacturing fell—on average by about 10 per cent—with only three exceptions (Germany, New Zealand, and Norway).

The change in this relativity is inconsistent with the expected effects of the expansion of trade with the South, which should have made manufacturing relatively more skill-intensive, but not much significance can be attached to this inconsistency. The general limitations of the white-collar ratio as a measure of skill intensity were mentioned above. It seems especially inadequate for compar-

---

[4] Two minor complications should be mentioned, neither of which makes much difference to the results. One is that transport has to be excluded from the nontraded average, because its occupations were radically reclassified by the 1968 revision of the ISCO. The other is that the self-employed are excluded from the calculations, because of doubts about their allocation to occupational categories, with the exception of self-employed professional and technical workers in the service sectors, who are not excluded. These adjustments for self-employment, which are only approximate, are based on data on the 'employment status' of workers in each sector and occupation.

ing the skill intensity of manufacturing and nontraded sectors, because their occupational structures are so different, with a far smaller proportion of blue-collar workers in most nontraded sectors. (This disparity may be understated in Table A2.2, which classifies managerial and sales workers in commerce as blue-collar.)[5]

The inherent difficulty of comparisons between the occupational structures of manufacturing and the nontraded sectors suggests that it may be better to focus simply on changes in absolute levels within manufacturing (shown in the fourth and fifth columns of the table). There is a positive cross-country correlation between increases in Southern import penetration and the absolute increases in both the professional intensity and the white-collar intensity of Northern manufacturing.[6] However, these correlations are not statistically significant unless one excludes Canada, where there was little change in either skill indicator, despite a large rise in import penetration, and even then only for the white-collar measure.[7]

A2.4 Wages

Comparison of trends in average sectoral wages is another way of measuring changes in relative skill intensity. If the proportion of skilled workers rises faster in manufacturing than in nontraded sectors, the average wage in manufacturing should tend to rise relative to that in nontraded sectors. It may thus be possible to work backwards, and to measure the change in the relative proportion of skilled workers from the change in the relative wage, given information on the proportion of skilled workers at the end of the period and on the size of the skilled–unskilled wage ratio.

This approach is vulnerable to changes over time in the skilled–unskilled wage ratio: an economy-wide increase in this ratio would raise the average wage in a more skill-intensive sector, relative to a less skill-intensive sector, even if the proportions of skilled workers in each sector did not change. It is also vulnerable to changes in the wages of particular skill categories in one sector relative to

[5] This treatment of managerial workers in commerce was the only available solution to major inconsistencies of definition among countries and time-periods. Sales workers in commerce were deliberately categorised as blue-collar, on the grounds that their average levels of education and training are more similar to those of manual than of clerical workers.

[6] The import penetration variable, which refers to 1970–85, is the same as in Fig. 5.6 (and others in Chs. 5–8), except that the denominator of the ratio is manufacturing value added rather than GDP (the data are shown in Table A2.5). Probably because of the way in which this variable is defined, the correlations are stronger if the changes in skill intensity are measured as the *differences* between the later and the early levels (rather than as the ratios of the later to the early levels). There is no correlation whatsoever between import penetration and changes in the occupational measures of the *relative* skill intensity of manufacturing.

[7] The weaker correlation with changes in professional intensity could be because these are more affected by cross-country variations in the rate at which higher education has expanded. The case for excluding Canada is that it is the only developed country in which, according to these occupational measures, there has not been a substantial increase in the absolute skill intensity of manufacturing (the same is true of the education measures in Table A2.1). The cause of this unusual pattern is unclear, but part of it could have been the 1965 US–Canada Automotive Products Agreement, which caused rapid expansion of blue-collar-intensive automobile manufacturing.

TABLE A2.2. *Occupational structure of manufacturing employment in the North, 1960–1985*

Country		Data period	As ratio of nontraded sectors			Absolute level in manufacturing (×100)	
			Early level	Later level	Est. change 1985/1960	Early	Later
Occupational structure = professional and technical/other employees							
Canada	a	1961–81	0.25	0.23	0.88	6.1	6.4
Denmark		1960–85	0.12	0.20	1.73	3.0	10.2
Finland	a	1960–80	0.22	0.28	1.34	7.5	11.2
France	c	1962–82	0.30	0.42	1.48	5.9	12.2
Germany		1961–84	0.26	0.42	1.65	5.9	11.4
Ireland		1961–85	0.06	0.22	3.67	1.9	8.7
Italy	d	1961–81	0.14	0.21	1.65	3.1	6.2
Japan		1960–85	0.10	0.22	2.09	2.0	4.8
Netherlands		1960–85	0.16	0.28	1.74	4.9	12.1
New Zealand	a	1961–81	0.08	0.17	2.47	2.8	5.4
Norway		1960–86	0.14	0.26	1.75	4.4	12.0
Sweden	e	1960–86	0.36	0.27	0.77	11.5	20.9
UK	f	1961–81	0.33	0.36	1.13	5.9	12.5
USA		1960–86	0.31	0.58	1.84	8.4	13.6
Weighted averages			0.24	0.39	1.71	5.7	10.5

Occupational structure = white-collar/other employees

Canada	a	1961–81	0.45	0.32	0.64	42.2	44.7
Denmark		1960–85	0.29	0.26	0.91	18.2	40.0
Finland	a,b	1960–80	0.34	0.29	0.84	21.2	31.4
France	c	1962–82	0.34	0.23	0.61	25.8	38.8
Germany		1961–84	0.32	0.46	1.48	27.6	52.2
Ireland		1961–85	0.32	0.29	0.91	20.7	42.5
Italy	b,d	1961–81	0.20	0.20	0.97	13.7	26.9
Japan		1960–85	0.40	0.32	0.79	27.1	39.7
Netherlands		1960–85	0.34	0.33	0.98	28.1	52.8
New Zealand	a	1961–81	0.22	0.26	1.22	24.0	33.8
Norway		1960–86	0.29	0.32	1.11	19.1	42.0
Sweden	b,e	1960–86	0.53	0.24	0.46	34.5	51.9
UK	f	1961–81	0.44	0.37	0.80	29.3	46.2
USA		1960–86	0.50	0.45	0.89	40.6	62.3
Weighted averages			0.41	0.36	0.89	31.2	48.7

Notes: Definitions and principles of calculation as set out in general notes to previous table, except (*a*) transport excluded from nontraded sectors average (see n. 4 in text), and (*b*) economy-wide columns omitted because of noncomparability of occupational categories in agriculture. White-collar workers are professional and technical, managerial, sales, and clerical, except in commerce, where managerial and sales workers are excluded (see n. 5 in text).

^aLater year data include some or all unemployed workers.

^a replaced:
aLater year data include some or all unemployed workers.
bWhite-collar workers in commerce include managers.
cNon-ISCO occupational classification.
dManufacturing includes mining.
eManufacturing includes mining and electricity.
f1961 data refer to Great Britain.

Sources: Most 1960s data from OECD (1969*a*), and most 1980s data from ILO *Yearbooks*. Otherwise directly from national population censuses and labour force surveys.

another: for example, if competition from Southern imports temporarily depressed skill-specific wage rates in manufacturing relative to those in nontraded sectors, the increase in the proportion of skilled workers in manufacturing would be underestimated by this method.

The results of such 'backward' calculations are also very sensitive to errors in measuring the change in sectoral relative wages. For example, with an end-period share of skilled workers in manufacturing of one-half and a skilled–unskilled wage ratio of 2 (roughly as in Table A1.4), a mere 5 per cent rise in the average wage in manufacturing relative to nontraded sectors would imply that the relative demand for unskilled labour in manufacturing had been reduced by 25 per cent (and a 10 per cent wage rise that it had been reduced by 44 per cent).[8]

Relevant data are also scarce. The wage data in the ILO *Yearbook* are not usable for this purpose because they cover only manual workers. Censuses of industrial production often include all categories of workers, but cover at most two sectors other than manufacturing. The best source of wage data is thus national income accounts, which give the total wage bill in each sector, from which the average wage can be calculated with the aid of data on employment by sector. However, series from this last source rarely go back beyond 1970 (when the breakdown of each sector's value added by class of income was introduced into the UN system of national accounts).

Table A2.3 shows movements in the relative wages of manufacturing between the early 1970s and the mid-1980s in all the developed countries for which the necessary data are available. These results suggest a general rise in the relative skill-intensity of manufacturing (the only exception is Japan, where there was no change). However, the two alternative results for the USA expose a likely source of upward bias in the calculations, which is that the share of part-time employees in the labour force has been rising faster in nontraded sectors than in manufacturing (which would depress the average annual wage per worker in nontraded sectors even if there were no change in the average hourly wage or the skill composition of employment). The USA is the only country in which this bias can be measured, by using data on full-time-equivalent employment by sector. The difference between the USA(1) and USA(2) results in the table suggests that this bias exists, but also that it accounts for only part of the rise in the relative wage of manufacturing.

The rise in the relative skill intensity of manufacturing implied by these wage movements is consistent with the expected effects of more trade with the South. However, to be more confident that trade was in fact the cause (either wholly or in part), it would be necessary to compare these results with relative wage trends before 1970, which is not possible, as explained above. The US data do not sug-

---

[8] The average wage in manufacturing (as a ratio of the unskilled wage) is

$$w = ew_E + (1 - e)$$

where e is the proportion of skilled workers in the manufacturing labour force, and w_E is the skilled wage as a ratio of the unskilled wage. This expression can be rearranged as

$$e = (w - 1)/(w_E - 1)$$

which with $w_E = 2$ simplifies conveniently to $e = (w - 1)$. An end-period e of 0.5 (and $w_E = 2$) implies $w = 1.5$. To make w 5% lower (1.4286), e would have had to be about 0.43, implying a reduction in the demand for unskilled relative to skilled labour of $(1 - (0.50/0.57)/(0.50/0.43))$, or about 25%.

TABLE A2.3. *Manufacturing wage relative to nontraded sectors,*
1970–1985

	Data period	Early level	Recent level	Est. change 1985/1970
Finland	1970–85	0.95	0.98	1.03
Germany	1973–84	0.97	1.13	1.23
Italy	1973–85	0.98	0.99	1.01
Japan	1973–85	0.97	0.97	1.00
Netherlands	1973–83	0.94	1.02	1.13
New Zealand	1971–81	0.87	0.98	1.20
Norway	1970–85	0.95	0.99	1.04
Sweden	1970–83	1.07	1.12	1.05
UK	1973–85	1.07	1.21	1.17
USA (1)	1971–86	1.29	1.38	1.07
USA (2)	1971–86	1.17	1.23	1.05
Weighted average excl. USA (2)		1.11	1.18	1.08

Notes: Definitions and principles of calculation as in two previous tables, except that the changes are standardised over the period 1970 (rather than 1960) to 1985, and that the absolute level columns are omitted.

The wage in each sector is calculated by dividing total employee compensation by the number of employees. The USA (2) calculation is based on full-time-equivalent employment (extrapolated back from 1977 to 1971 using data on hours worked). In the US calculations, the 1971 and 1986 figures are 1970–2 and 1985–7 averages.

In Italy, manufacturing includes mining.

Sources: OECD *National Accounts*, Vol. 2, Detailed Tables, 1970–82, 1973–85, 1975–87, and 1976–88 edns., tables 13 and 15.

gest acceleration *within* the 1970–85 period, as the trade explanation would lead one to expect, although this could be because a proxy for the full-time-equivalent employment series has to be used prior to 1977.[9] None the less, there is a weak positive cross-country correlation between the extent of the rise in the relative manufacturing wage and the extent of the rise in Southern import penetration.[10]

Supposing for the sake of argument that the whole of the 1970–85 increase in the relative manufacturing wage were due to more trade with the South, what would a 'backwards' calculation imply about the size of the induced reduction in the relative demand for unskilled workers? From Table A2.3, the weighted average increase in the relative wage was 8 per cent, or perhaps 6 per cent on a full-time-equivalent basis (judging from the US results). A 6 per cent rise in the relative wage would imply a reduction of 29 per cent in the demand for BAS-ED

[9] From 1970–2 to 1976–8, the rise in the relative manufacturing wage was 2.9% (using data on hours worked), while from 1976–8 to 1985–7, it was 2.3% (using data on full-time equivalent employment).
[10] The import penetration variable is as specified in n. 6. The correlation is almost significant at the 10% level.

relative to SKILD labour within manufacturing.[11] This is roughly twice as large as the reduction of 15 per cent estimated by the modified factor content method for the period up to 1985.[12] This result provides a little support for the contention (in Section 4.4.3) that including defensive innovation would at least double the factor content estimates of the impact of trade.

A2.5 Nominal Value Added

Changes in the average wage in a sector are associated, other things being equal, with changes in nominal value added per worker in that sector (see equation 3.5 in the main text). Changes over time in the average wage in manufacturing relative to nontraded sectors might thus, in principle, be inferred from changes in relative levels of nominal value added per worker. The advantage of this approach would be that one could assemble time-series back to the early 1950s, and so ascertain whether the rise in the relative wage in manufacturing was correlated with the expansion of trade with the South, rather than being a trend of longer standing.

The problem with this approach is that changes in average wages are by no means the only cause of changes in nominal value added per worker. Other possible causes include variations in profits per worker (which may arise from movements either in the profit rate or in the value of capital per worker), and changes in indirect taxes (which are included in value added in the national accounts of most countries). The approach is particularly risky in the present context, because the profitability of manufacturing fluctuated substantially during the period concerned (see Section 5.4.1), and because of the sensitivity of inferences about changes in skill ratios to errors in the measurement of wage trends.

It was hoped to overcome these problems by adjusting the data on nominal value added to allow for the fluctuations in manufacturing profitability (with data from Armstrong *et al.* 1991). However, experiments for the 1970–85 period, when actual movements in relative sectoral wages can be compared with estimates based on adjusted nominal value added, suggested that the latter are not an acceptably accurate proxy for the former. The approach was therefore abandoned.

A2.6 Real Value Added

An alternative approach is to examine trends in real (rather than nominal) value added per worker, or, more precisely, to compare changes in sectoral labour productivity trends. Expansion of trade with the South should have raised real output per worker in manufacturing, relative to the nontraded sectors, because of

---

[11] See n. 8 for the method of calculation.

[12] This is based on the second of the A1 experiments in Table 4.10, the level of the South's manufactured exports in 1985 having been \$120bn. (Table 4.6). The relative demand shift shown in Table 4.10 refers to the economy as a whole, rather than (as here) to manufacturing alone, and is expressed as an *increase* in the demand for skilled labour.

increased specialisation in skill-intensive activities and because of defensive innovation. There is a longstanding tendency for labour productivity to grow faster in manufacturing than in services, but trade with the South should have accelerated the rate of divergence.[13]

The real value added approach does not permit a direct assessment of the impact of trade on the skill composition of employment. However, it seems reasonable to infer from the factor content calculations in Chapter 4 that acceleration of relative labour productivity growth in manufacturing would be mainly a reflection of reduced employment of unskilled workers, without much of an offsetting increase in skilled employment. (Within the skilled category, some of the data in Sections 3.3.1, 3.4.2, and A1.5 suggest that increases for professional, technical, and skilled manual workers might be offset by declines for managerial and skilled clerical workers.)

In comparison to the other approaches discussed above, the real value added approach has two main shortcomings. One is that it is difficult to measure output (and hence labour productivity) in services, which account for most of the non-traded sectors.[14] If the errors of measurement remained constant over time, they would not affect the accuracy of the proposed calculation, which is based on *changes* in the productivity growth differential between manufacturing and services. However, because of the changing composition of the service sectors, and the rapidity of innovation in all sectors, the measured growth of productivity in nontraded sectors may not be an adequate control for non-trade influences on productivity growth in manufacturing.

The second objection to the proposed calculations is that their inability to distinguish between the effects of North–South and of North–North trade is more serious when the indicator is labour productivity than when it is a measure of skill intensity. This is because North–North trade, although it is unlikely to raise the skill intensity of manufacturing, is highly likely to raise average manufacturing labour productivity, through realisation of scale economies and greater competitive pressure. Moreover, there has been a massive expansion of North–North trade over the past few decades, partly because of successive GATT rounds of trade liberalisation and the formation of the European Community. Calculations based on widening of the gap in labour productivity growth between manufacturing and the nontraded sectors are thus likely to overstate the impact of more trade with the South alone.

Table A2.4 presents the results of some calculations of this sort for the North as a whole. The first four columns show labour productivity growth rates in manufacturing and (a fixed-weighted average of) nontraded sectors in an early sub-period and a later sub-period. The manufactured exports of the South started to expand rapidly in the early 1960s (see Fig. 5.1 in the main text): the upper panel of the table thus breaks the full period 1950–85 at 1960, the lower panel at 1965. In each panel, there is one set of estimates for the nontraded sectors, and three for manufacturing, based on alternative sources of data. The first of these three is probably the most reliable, because it is based on the only source (the UN

---

[13] That productivity normally increases relatively slowly in services is argued by Balassa (1964) and Kravis *et al.* (1982: 332–6, and 1983). For a contrary view, see Bhagwati (1984).

[14] See e.g. Blades *et al.* (1974). But measuring real output growth in *manufacturing* is also hard, and sometimes controversial (de Leeuw 1988).

TABLE A2.4. *Relative acceleration of manufacturing productivity growth in the North*

| Data source | Labour productivity growth (% per year) | | | | 'Excess' manufacturing productivity in 1985 (%) |
| | Manufacturing | | Nontraded sectors | | |
	1950–60	1960–85	1950–60	1960–85	
UNISY	2.9	3.8			27
UNNAY	2.3	4.3	1.7	1.7	65
UNIDO	2.9	3.3			13
	1950–65	1965–85	1950–65	1965–85	
UNISY	3.5	3.6			17
UNNAY	2.9	4.3	2.1	1.4	48
UNIDO	3.4	3.1			8

Notes and sources: Labour productivity series are derived from output and employment series covering the whole of the UN statistical category 'developed market economies'. The growth rates are calculated between 3-year averages centred on the years mentioned.

UNISY: UN *Industrial Statistics Yearbook* (formerly titled *The Growth of World Industry*).

UNNAY: UN *National Accounts Yearbook*. The manufacturing productivity growth rates use data on growth of real manufacturing value added from this source, but the manufacturing employment data are the same as for the UNISY estimates.

UNIDO: output and employment series for 1963 to 1986 from the UN Industrial Development Organisation data base, combined with UNISY series for 1950–63.

Nontraded sector productivity growth rates: (i) the output index is a weighted average of electricity, gas, and water (EGW), commerce, transport, and other services. The EGW output data are from UNISY, the output data for the other nontraded sectors from UNNAY; (ii) the employment index is a weighted average of EGW and services (the sum of commerce, transport, and other services). Construction is excluded from the productivity growth calculations for lack of suitable data on employment. The EGW employment data are from UNISY. The services employment data for 1950–60 are from ILO *Economically Active Population Estimates 1950–80* Vol. 5, and for 1960–85 from OECD *Labour Force Statistics*.

'Excess' manufacturing productivity in 1985 is the percentage by which actual labour productivity in manufacturing exceeded the level that would have been attained if the gap between the productivity growth rates of manufacturing and the nontraded sectors had been the same in the later sub-period as in the early sub-period.

Industrial Statistics Yearbook) that provides data for the whole period on both output and employment in manufacturing.

The upper panel of the table shows that growth of labour productivity in manufacturing accelerated after 1960—whichever source or combination of sources is considered—while in the nontraded sectors the productivity growth rate scarcely altered. In the lower panel (with the break at 1965) there is much less of an acceleration of manufacturing labour productivity growth, and a deceleration in nontraded sectors, reflecting the familiar slowdown of productivity growth in the 1970s and 1980s. In both panels, however, the growth of labour productivity in manufacturing accelerates *relative* to nontraded sectors in the latter part of the period.[15]

[15] This is likely to be associated with the real appreciation of Northern exchange rates from the early 1960s to the early 1980s discovered in Wood (1991e: 329), which also links this trend with increased openness to trade.

The last column of the table, headed 'excess manufacturing productivity in 1985' shows how much higher manufacturing productivity was in 1985 than it would have been in the absence of this relative acceleration. To put it another way, these percentages measure the cumulative effect up to 1985 of the acceleration of productivity growth in manufacturing relative to that in nontraded sectors. They vary in size, depending on the source and the break-point. The most reliable source suggests that output per worker in manufacturing in 1985 was 27 per cent greater than it would have been if the 1950s gap in productivity growth rates between manufacturing and the nontraded sectors had been maintained, and 17 per cent greater than if the 1950–65 gap had been maintained. The other estimates are spread from 8 per cent to 65 per cent, which is an unsatisfactorily wide range.

These results can be compared with those obtained by the factor content method up to 1985, which suggest that trade with the South raised labour productivity in Northern manufacturing by 4–5 per cent.[16] This estimate is only about half of the lowest figure in Table A2.4, and about one-fifth of the 27 per cent figure obtained with the most reliable source and a 1960 break-point. It is not possible to assess how much of this difference is due to more trade with the North, rather than to defensive innovation in response to more competition from the South. But even with a generous allowance for the effect of North–North trade, the extent of the difference seems large enough to be consistent with the contention that defensive innovation was at least as important as the trade-induced reallocation of labour among manufacturing subsectors (as measured by the factor content method).

Table A2.5 contains the results of similar calculations for the individual countries of the North. The first four columns show the growth rates of labour productivity in manufacturing and the nontraded sectors in 1950–60 and 1960–85. The next three columns show changes between the earlier and later sub-periods, for manufacturing and the nontraded sectors separately, and for manufacturing relative to the nontraded sectors. The acceleration of productivity growth in manufacturing relative to the nontraded sectors that is documented for the North as a whole in Table A2.4 is also observed in all but one of the individual countries, Italy being the exception.

The last column of Table A2.5 shows the rise in Southern import penetration of each country's manufacturing sector between 1970 and 1985. There is no cross-country correlation between the rise in import penetration and the extent of the *relative* acceleration of manufacturing productivity growth, but this is apparently because of large errors in the data on productivity growth in the nontraded sectors, whose variation among countries and over time is clearly erratic. For there is a strong positive correlation with the *absolute* change in the growth of manufacturing productivity between the earlier and the later sub-periods.[17] In other

---

[16] See n. 12. In the experiment concerned, trade with the South reduces Northern gross manufacturing output by 3.6%, manufacturing value added by 4.8%, and total manufacturing employment by 8.5% (expressing all three reductions relative to actual 1985 values). The implied rise in labour productivity is 4.7% on a gross output basis, and 3.5% on a value added basis.

[17] The OLS regression is $PVCH = -1.13 + 0.37IMPCH$, with $R^2 = 0.44$, and the coefficient on $IMPCH$ significant at the 1% level on a two-tailed t-test.

TABLE A2.5. *Labour productivity growth in Northern manufacturing and nontraded sectors*

	Labour productivity growth (% per year)				Change in productivity growth rate between 1950–60 and 1960–85			Southern import penetration change 1970–85
	Manufacturing		Nontraded sectors		Manu-facturing	Nontraded	Manuf./ nontraded	
	1950–60	1960–85	1950–60	1960–85				
Australia	4.3	2.6		1.6	−1.7			2.8
Austria	5.6	5.0	6.4	2.3	−0.5	−4.1	3.5	9.6
Belgium	3.8	6.6	1.4	2.0	2.8	0.6	2.2	6.1
Canada	2.8	4.0	0.0	0.9	1.2	0.8	0.3	4.6
Denmark	2.1	4.1	3.0	1.0	2.1	−2.0	4.0	2.0
Finland	3.9	3.5	3.3	1.1	−0.4	−2.2	1.8	4.0
France	4.6	4.5	3.6	2.3	−0.2	−1.3	1.1	4.0
Germany	4.9	4.8	5.1	2.6	−0.2	−2.5	2.3	4.5
Italy	6.9	5.5	2.8	2.2	−1.4	−0.6	−0.7	3.9
Japan	8.8	8.5	5.1	1.7	−0.3	−3.4	3.1	1.8
Netherlands	4.3	5.1			0.9			8.3
Norway	3.7	3.1	6.1	0.5	−0.6	−5.6	4.9	3.1
Sweden	2.3	4.4	2.8	0.2	2.1	−2.6	4.7	3.6
UK	2.2	4.6	1.4	1.7	2.3	0.3	2.0	5.8
USA	2.2	3.9	2.0	1.5	1.7	−0.5	2.2	7.7

Notes and sources: These labour productivity growth rates are calculated in much the same way as those in the previous table. One minor difference is that electricity, gas, and water (as well as construction) are omitted from the nontraded average, for lack of suitable employment data. The sources of data for the manufacturing productivity growth rates are not exactly comparable with any of the three alternatives in the previous table, but are closest to the UNIDO series.

Labour productivity growth in manufacturing 1950–69 derived from output and employment series in UN *Industrial Statistics Yearbook* (and its predecessor *The Growth of World Industry*), and for 1968–85 taken directly from World Bank *World Tables* 1988–9 (based on data from UNIDO).

Nontraded sectors real output data for 1950–60 from the 1969 UN *National Accounts Yearbook*, for 1960–80 from World Bank *World Tables* (3rd edn.), and for 1980–5 from OECD *National Accounts*, Vol. 2, Detailed Tables, 1975–87. Data on employment in services for 1950–60 from ILO *Economically Active Population Estimates 1950–80*, and for 1960–85 from OECD *Labour Force Statistics*.

For a few countries, the 1950–60 data are from other sources; for France they are from Carré *et al.* (1976), for Japan from Ohkawa and Rosovsky (1973), for the UK from Feinstein (1972), and for the USA from Kendrick and Pech (1973).

The Southern import penetration change is the difference between 1970 and 1985 imports of narrowly defined manufactures from developing countries, expressed as a percentage of manufacturing value added in the Northern country concerned (see n. 6 in text).

words, productivity growth in manufacturing speeded up more (or slowed down less) in countries where there was a larger rise in Southern import penetration.

This correlation supports the proposition that more trade with the South accelerated the growth of productivity, and reduced the demand for labour, in Northern manufacturing as a whole. It also allays possible doubts about the accuracy and relevance of the 1950s data on manufacturing productivity growth. However, the absence of correlation with the *relative* productivity acceleration variable casts further doubt on the accuracy of the all-North calculations in Table A2.4, since it exposes the limitations of nontraded sector productivity growth as a control for influences other than trade.

This cross-country correlation with Southern import penetration is subject to another source of ambiguity, namely collinearity between the independent variable and changes in *Northern* import penetration (see the cross-country variation subsection of Section 5.4.2).[18] The ambiguity is most acute for these real value added calculations, because, as mentioned earlier, intra-North trade is likely to raise productivity in manufacturing by realising scale economies. It is less acute for the correlations with measures of skill intensity reported earlier in this appendix, since, as mentioned in section A2.1, there is little reason to expect intra-North trade to raise the relative skill intensity of manufacturing.

A2.7 Conclusions

Taken together, the results of the various calculations described above strongly imply that the relative skill intensity of Northern manufacturing has increased in recent decades, and are also consistent with the view that expansion of trade with the South has contributed to this increase in skill intensity. This causal connection, predicted by theory, is corroborated both by the timing of the increase, and by its correlation across countries with the extent of the rise in Southern import penetration.

However, none of these calculations provides an acceptably precise and reliable measure of the *size* of the impact of more trade with the South, and in that sense they fail to attain their original objective, which was to quantify the effects of defensive innovation. All that can be said is that the results do not contradict the contention (in Section 4.4.3 of the main text) that the effects of defensive innovation were at least as large as those of the reallocation of labour within manufacturing. The results of the wage and real value added calculations give more active support to this contention, but their accuracy is open to serious doubt.

Further work along the lines described in this appendix would be possible, and might yield more conclusive results. There is scope for more analysis of changes between sub-periods, especially in individual countries, and the emergence of data from the 1990–1 round of national censuses will provide a valuable extension of some key time series. The basic method applied in this appendix could also be

[18] The discussion in Sect. 5.4.2 refers to import penetration as a ratio of GDP, but applies also where the denominator is manufacturing output (as in this appendix); e.g. there is a cross-country correlation (R) of 0.67 between the import penetration changes shown in Table A2.5 and the change over the same period in the ratio of broad manufactured imports from the North to gross manufacturing output (from Berthet-Bondet *et al.* 1988).

Appendix A3
Returns to Education and Experience

This appendix reviews recent trends in skill differentials in the North, using education and age as indicators of skill. In the first subsection, changes in relative wages are examined, in the second, changes in relative unemployment rates. The third subsection asks whether and to what extent demographic and other supply-side changes could have accounted for the observed movements in skill differentials.

Education, usually measured by years of schooling, is the most commonly used indicator of skill, often in conjunction with experience, usually measured by age. Education and experience together explain a substantial part of the variance of wages among individuals in most countries (see Willis 1986 and the surveys in Psacharopoulos 1987). Moreover, in the present context, differences in wages and unemployment rates among groups of workers with varying amounts of schooling and experience are probably the best of the three available measures of skill differentials. Education and age give a more direct and precise indication of differences in the amounts of skill that workers have acquired than do occupational categories (Appendix A4) or wage levels (Appendix A5). It is of course necessary to suppose for this purpose that there is a fixed relationship between the amount of skill acquired and the amount of time spent acquiring it, but because the present emphasis is on changes in skill differentials over time within particular countries, this supposition is much less unreasonable than it would be for cross-country comparisons.

To say that this is the best of the three available indicators is not to ignore the many problems, conceptual and practical, of measuring and interpreting the associations among education, age, and earnings (which are discussed at length in the sources mentioned in the previous paragraph). Of particular relevance in the present context is the fact that highly educated workers (for example, college graduates) are only a subset of the *SKILD* labour category, which also includes workers with extensive training of other sorts, such as manual craftsmen. The estimates of the trade-induced demand shift reported in Part A generally lump all *SKILD* workers together, so that it is not possible to predict whether the increase in the wage premium over *BAS-ED* workers should have been larger or smaller for the highly educated than for *SKILD* labour in general.

Another problem in the present context is country bias. Mainly because the relevant data have been collected there more regularly and for longer, the relationships among education, age, and earnings are much better documented, and have been more closely studied, for the USA than for the rest of the North put together. Although a considerable effort has been made to assemble data covering as many countries as possible, the evidence remains somewhat lopsided.

A3.1 Relative Wage Trends

Fig. A3.1 shows movements in the wages of workers with higher education (usually a university degree), relative to those of workers with secondary education

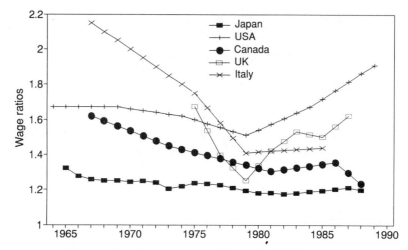

Fɪɢ. A3.1 Wage differential for workers with higher education in five large
countries (relative to workers with secondary education)

Notes and sources: Cross-country differences in the *levels* of wage differentials are
not accurately reflected in this graph, which is intended only to illustrate trends
over time. The coverage of the data varies substantially across countries. In addition, to make the graph easier to read, 0.08 has been added to the figures for
Italy and 0.25 to those for the USA, while 0.06 has been subtracted from the
Canadian figures.

Canada: full-time males 40–45 years of age (from Table A3.3, with interpolation).

Italy: university and secondary graduates (from Table A3.1, spliced at 1979–80
and interpolated).

Japan: male university and high-school graduates 35–39 years of age (from
Table A3.4, extrapolated to 1988 using all-age data).

UK: adult males with degree relative to those with O-levels (from Moll 1991,
table 3, interpolation of two-year averages).

USA: white males with 6–10 years of experience (from Table A3.2, with interpolation).

(variously defined), in five large countries from the mid-1960s to the late 1980s. In
four of the five cases the data refer only to males, and in three of these cases only
to a particular age or experience group. Table A3.1 includes more fragmentary
information of a similar kind on four other developed countries, though only for
two of these do the data cover the 1980s. The table also presents some additional
information on two of the countries in the figure (the other three countries have
more detailed tables of their own below).

The trends revealed by the figure and the table are remarkably clear and consistent. Skill differentials, as measured by education, tended to narrow until the late
1970s or early 1980s, after which they tended to widen. This pattern is observed
in all the countries for which data are available, with only one notable exception

TABLE A3.1. *Wage differential for workers with higher education in other countries*
(ratio of earnings of less-educated workers)

Country	Definitions of (1) higher-educated, (2) less-educated.					
Australia	(1) Degree (2) Left school at 17	**1969**	**1974**	**1979**		
	Aged 25–34	1.81	1.63	1.44		
	Aged 45–54	2.46	2.10	1.65		
Denmark	(1) Government employees with academic degree	**1971**	**1974**	**1978**		
	(2) Other salaried employees	1.94	1.76	1.67		
	(2) Wage-earners	2.22	1.96	1.72		
France	(1) Bachelor's degree (2) Office workers	**1962**		**1972**		
	Males under 35	1.97		1.88		
	(1) Higher			**1979**		**1985**
	(2) Secondary			1.35		1.39
	(2) Primary			1.66		1.63
Italy	(1) University graduates	**1967**	**1975**	**1979!**	**1980**	**1985**
	(2) Secondary school graduates	2.07	1.67	1.33!	1.45	1.48
	(2) Elementary school graduates	2.63	1.96	1.54!	1.60	1.61
Netherlands	(1) Higher			**1979**		**1985**
	(2) Secondary			1.32		1.42
	(2) Primary			1.51		1.80
UK	(1) Male applied science graduates (starting salary)	**1968**		**1978**		
	(2) All male non-manual workers	0.71		0.67		
	(2) All male manual workers	0.92		0.86		
	(1) University graduates with 6 years' experience	**1966**		**1976**		**1986**
	(2) Economy-wide average earnings	1.75		1.33		1.41

Sources: Derived from Freeman (1982, table 1), except: 1979 and 1985 France and The Netherlands (Eurostat 1990, tables 5.6, 5.9); 1980 and 1985 Italy (Wolleb 1989, table 4.5); 1966, 1976, 1986 UK (Dolton and Makepeace 1990, table 2). The additional France, Italy, and The Netherlands data refer to household per capita income or expenditure classified by education level of household head.
! = discontinuity in source of data.

(the drop in the last two years of the Canadian series).[1] The magnitudes of these trends, however, appear to vary among countries. Though differences in the measures used make comparison even of trends hazardous, the pre-1980 declines seem to have been particularly large in Italy, the UK, and Australia, and the post-1980 increase particularly large in the UK. In Japan, the movements in both directions seem particularly small. (The timing of the change in trend also appears to vary among countries, but this cannot be assessed properly because of differences in the years for which data are available.)

The general impression of a decline in returns to education in the 1970s followed by a rise in the 1980s is confirmed by Davis (1992, table 3 and figs. 6–7),

[1] This drop is discussed later in the text. Another minor exception to the general U-shaped pattern is the higher/primary series for France in the 1980s. A third series for the UK (IER 1989: 3) shows that the rate of return for all graduates declined from the mid-1950s until the late 1970s, after which it remained roughly constant until the series ends in 1985. It is not clear why this indicator remains constant in the 1980s, whereas the other two indicators for the UK rise (Fig. A3.1 and Table A3.1).

who presents data on eight Northern countries. He includes information on three countries or periods not covered in Fig. A3.1 and Table A3.1: Australia in the 1980s, showing an increase in the wage of men with a university degree relative to 'trade qualified' men; Germany in the early 1980s, where there was a rise in the wage of men with 14–18 years of education, relative to those with 11–13 years; and Sweden, where the wage of men with a university education, relative to those with post-secondary education, fell during the 1970s but rose in the early 1980s.

The data used by Davis suggest that the increase in wage differentials by education was largest in the USA, followed by Germany and then by the UK. The increase was smaller in Canada, slight in Sweden and Australia, and zero (on average across all age groups) in Japan. In The Netherlands, the Davis data show a decline in returns to education during the 1980s, which is in contrast to all the other countries, and conflicts with the data in Table A3.1 (although neither source of data is satisfactory).

As mentioned above, the trends in the USA are well documented. The rate of return on secondary relative to primary schooling apparently fell between 1939 and 1959, then showed no clear trend up to the mid-1970s (Psacharopoulos 1980, table 5). The wage differential between college and secondary education did not change much in the 1940s and 1950s (ibid.), and rose in the 1960s (Davis 1992, fig. 6A). During the 1970s, the returns to college education declined: some studies suggest a steep decline (Psacharopoulos 1980), and others a more moderate decline (Freeman 1976: 26; 1980, table 1; Murphy and Welch 1992, table V), while one study suggests little or no decline (Willis 1986: 537).

During the 1980s, by contrast, there was a 'remarkable rise in the economic returns to schooling' (Kosters 1990: 309). Juhn, Murphy, and Pierce (1989: 22 and fig. 12), using weekly wage data for males, find that the education premium fell by about 10 per cent between 1963 and 1979, but 'skyrocketed' after 1979, and by 1987 was 25 per cent above its 1963 level. The direction and size of this change are evident in Table A3.2, and confirmed by several other studies, which use a range of different methods and data sources, and cover females as well as males (Freeman 1987, table 1.9; Murphy and Welch 1989: 9–10; Bound and Johnson 1992, figs. 1 and 2).

More information on the relative earnings of males in Canada is presented in Table A3.3, which defines both college and secondary education more broadly than the USA table. In all age categories, there was a marked decline in the returns to higher education between 1967 and 1981 (noted in the earlier studies of Freeman 1982 and Dooley 1987). As in other countries, this trend was reversed between 1981 and 1986, but 1986–8 saw a further decline, except in the oldest age group.[2] This terminal drop seems to be genuine, and is observed also in the other Canadian skill indicator series in Appendices A4 and A5. The most likely explanation is the cyclical boom between the two years, which favoured less-skilled workers. (The Canadian data up to 1986 refer to selected years at similar points in the cycle, while 1988 is simply the most recent year available.) Among females, the rise in the return to college education was smaller than among males during

---

[2] Katz and Loveman (1990: 4) cite a study by Freeman and Needels which confirms that educational wage differentials widened in Canada during the 1980s, though less than in the USA.

TABLE A3.2. *Wages of college graduates relative to high-school graduates in the USA* (white males, hourly earnings, smoothed data)

No. of years' work experience	1964	1969	1974	1979	1984	1989
1–5	1.59	1.52	1.39	1.30	1.63	1.74
6–10	1.42	1.42	1.37	1.26	1.42	1.66
26–35	1.40	1.43	1.43	1.43	1.40	1.49
All levels	1.43	1.44	1.41	1.37	1.44	1.58

Source: Murphy and Welch (1992, table V). Experience is measured by adjusting age to allow for differences in length of schooling.

1981–6, but continued during 1986–8, perhaps because fewer females work in the cyclically sensitive mining, manufacturing, and construction sectors.

Table A3.4, which refers to male university and high-school graduates, provides more detail on wage differentials by education within age groups in Japan.[3] As in the USA, the initial narrowing and later widening of these differentials is most pronounced for the entry-age group. For older groups, and for all age groups together, this pattern is less marked or nonexistent.[4] The change in trend also occurs earliest for the entry-age group, around 1975, which is about five years

TABLE A3.3. *Wages of college-educated relative to secondary-educated workers in Canada*

(average annual labour income of full-time full-year males)

Age	1967	1973	1981	1986	1988
25–30 years	1.32	1.10	1.11	1.23	1.10
40–45 years	1.68	1.51	1.36	1.42	1.29
55–60 years	1.78	1.50	1.40	1.26	1.34
All age groups	1.63	1.38	1.30	1.35	1.28

Notes: Labour income includes wages and salaries and self-employment income; 'college' refers to all post-secondary education; secondary includes incomplete as well as complete post-elementary education.

Source: *Survey of Consumer Finances*, special tabulation from Analytical Studies Branch, Statistics Canada.

[3] Similar calculations were also made using data (from the same sources) on elementary and lower secondary graduates rather than high-school graduates. This least-educated group is now an ageing minority in Japan. On average across all age groups, their earnings were similar to those of high-school graduates throughout the period covered by the table. Within particular age groups, the high–lower secondary earnings ratio shows some tendency to decline in the earlier part of the period and to rise in the later part, but this pattern is neither consistent nor strong.

[4] Thus Katz and Revenga (1989), like Davis (1992), conclude that educational wage differentials in Japan did not widen in the 1980s.

TABLE A3.4. *Wages of university graduates relative to high-school graduates in Japan*

(males: average monthly cash earnings of regular workers)

Age	1965	1970	1975	1980	1985	1988
Starting rate	1.33[a]	1.26	1.19	1.23	1.25	1.28
25–29 years	1.08	1.03	1.05	1.01	1.04	n.a.
35–39 years	1.32	1.24	1.24	1.18	1.19	n.a.
40–44 years	1.46	1.43	1.30	1.29	1.22	n.a.
50–54 years	1.56	1.57	1.45	1.51	1.43	n.a.
All age groups	1.31	1.27	1.24	1.19	1.18	1.19

[a] refers to 1968.

Sources: *Historical Statistics of Japan* (Vol. 4, 1987, tables 16-12, 16-13); *Statistical Yearbook of Japan* (1990, tables 3-29, 3-31).

sooner than in the USA. The change then seems to have worked its way up the age structure, in a more muted form, occurring later for older groups. But even in the entry-age group, where the initial narrowing was similar in magnitude to that in the USA, the subsequent widening has been smaller than in the USA.

In many Northern countries, there was also a widening of wage differentials between experienced (or older) and less experienced (or younger) workers, especially among those with less education. Most of the available evidence is summarised by Davis (1992, table 2 and figs. 4–5). He shows that age-earnings differentials among males widened during the 1980s in all nine of the countries for which there is information. The increases appear huge in Germany and tiny in Sweden, but in the other countries (Australia, Canada, France, Japan, The Netherlands, the UK, and the USA) were between 6 per cent and 14 per cent over a 5-year period.[5] Among females, too, age-earnings differentials widened in the 1980s, at least in Canada, France, the UK, and the USA.

In some countries, the rise in age-earnings differentials started before the 1980s. Davis (1992, table 2A) puts the 'trough year' for the USA at the end of the 1960s, for France, Japan, and the UK in the mid-1970s, and for Canada in 1979 (though earlier for females). Myles, Picot, and Wannell (1988: 90–5) view the widening of age-earnings differentials in Canada as a trend established in the 1970s. Another study concludes that during the two decades before the early 1980s youth relative wages declined in the USA (after the late 1960s), and in Canada (except in 1973–7), but remained constant or increased slightly in Australia, France, Germany, Japan, Sweden, and the UK (OECD-EO 1986: 119–20).

The rise in age-earnings differentials was more pronounced among workers with low levels of education in the USA, Canada, Sweden, and Japan (Davis 1992:

[5] Davis does not provide a numerical estimate for Japan in the 1980s, but his fig. 4B suggests a 5-year rise of 6–7% for approximately the same age group ratio as in his table 2B.

10).[6] Among people with a college education, indeed, age-earnings differentials narrowed during the 1980s in both Japan and the USA (having widened substantially during the 1970s—see also Bound and Johnson 1992, table 1; and Murphy and Welch 1992, table IV). In the UK, age-earnings differentials among both manual and non-manual workers widened until the late 1980s, and then narrowed (Davis 1992, fig. 5C). Other studies of the UK suggest widening during 1973–82 among more educated groups (Wright 1989), but approximate constancy after 1982 (Moll 1991, sect. 2.4).

A3.2 Relative Unemployment Trends

During the 1970s, the relative unemployment rates of highly educated workers, like their relative wages, appear to have deteriorated in many Northern countries.[7] During the 1980s, the opposite happened. Table A3.5 shows the percentage distribution of total unemployment among education categories in seven countries in two different years—as widely separated as possible—during the

TABLE A3.5. *Adjusted distribution of unemployment by education level* (%)

		Males					Females				
		Level A	Level B	Level C	Level D	Level E	Level A	Level B	Level C	Level D	Level E
Belgium	1970	44.4	33.3			22.2	81.8	9.1			9.1
	1986	89.6	6.5			3.8	84.9	9.6			5.6
Canada	1975	12.4	49.9		22.9	14.7	18.4	57.5		19.4	4.3
	1987	30.7	50.0		15.5	3.9	19.4	57.1		19.5	4.1
Germany	1978	43.3	6.0	47.0	1.4	2.3	51.1	4.8	41.3	1.0	1.7
	1987	42.8	4.9	49.0	1.2	2.2	62.1	2.8	33.2	0.6	1.3
Italy	1980	54.8	39.8			5.1	58.8	35.6			5.6
	1987	75.2	22.2			2.5	69.9	26.7			3.4
Norway	1972	80.0	20.0			0.0	76.9	23.1			0.0
	1987	77.6	20.5			1.9	78.6	18.5			2.9
Sweden	1971	77.3	8.5	10.3	2.5	1.4	78.9	5.4	11.3	2.6	1.8
	1987	75.6	9.3	11.0	1.8	2.2	80.8	5.0	10.8	1.7	1.7
USA	1972	51.0	32.1		11.3	5.7	44.6	39.8		10.3	5.4
	1988	58.1	30.6		7.8	3.5	51.9	37.6		7.0	3.5

Note: to render the distribution in the second year comparable with that in the first year, it is adjusted to allow for changes in the relative numbers of people in the labour force at different education levels.

Level A: less than complete upper-secondary school
Level B: complete upper-secondary school
Level C: post-school vocational education
Level D: less than university degree post-school education
Level E: university degree

Source: OECD-EO (1989, table 2.4).

---

[6] However, Murphy and Welch (1992, table 4) find that wage differentials by age narrowed during 1979–89 for white males with less than 12 years of schooling, while widening among those with 12 to 15 years of schooling.

[7] Freeman (1982: 19–29). However, the 1970s results for the USA seem to depend on the choice of years and groups (Freeman 1991*a*, tables 8.1–8.2).

1970s and 1980s. The distribution in the second year is adjusted to allow for alterations in the educational composition of the labour force. Hence the change in the *share* of unemployment in a given education category also indicates a change in the unemployment *rate* of that category relative to the average unemployment rate for all categories. Separate information is provided for males and females.

In most cases, the unemployment rate among less-educated workers rose relative to that among workers with more education. In category A, which contains those with no more than an incomplete secondary education, the share of unemployment rose in all seven countries for females, though in only four of the seven for males. In the two highest education groups, D and E, the share of unemployment fell for both males and females in nine of the eleven cases for which data are available. There are thus seven (out of thirty-six) exceptions in categories A, D, and E, of which Norway accounts for three, Sweden for two, and Canada and Germany for one each. However, even where skill differentials in unemployment rates widened, the changes varied widely in size: for males, the increases in category A were large in Belgium, Canada, and Italy, but modest in the USA; while for females in category A, the increases were trivially small in Belgium, Canada, Norway, and Sweden.

In addition to the problem of skill differences within education categories (which in general do not cover out-of-school training), the statistics in Table A3.5 may be distorted by variations in the definition or measurement of unemployment, both among countries and between males and females. In particular, those who cannot find work may withdraw from the labour force and consequently not be counted as unemployed. Freeman (1991*a*, fig. 8.1) thus examines ratios of employment to population as well as unemployment rates for males in three education categories in the USA during 1970–87. There was a general tendency for unemployment to rise and employment to fall. But these adverse trends were much slighter for college graduates than for high-school graduates and particularly for high-school dropouts (as is confirmed by Juhn 1992: 87–91).

The OECD study summarised in Table A3.5 did not include the United Kingdom. However, measures similar to those of Freeman (1991*a*) are calculated for the UK by Moll (1991, table 4) for males and females over the period 1977–88, and by Balls, Katz, and Loveman (1991, tables 1 and 2) for males by region and age over the period 1979–89. Among people with formal educational qualifications, there is not a consistent ranking of proportional changes in unemployment (or non-employment) rates by level of qualification. For example, people with a university degree did not experience the smallest proportional rise in unemployment in all the demographic sub-categories for which results are presented. In every case, though, the unemployment and non-employment rates among those with no formal educational qualifications rose relative to the average, in most cases by a substantial amount.[8]

A more recent study of Germany, which also allows for non-employment other than recorded unemployment, arrives at a different conclusion from the OECD

---

[8] The un(non)employment rate among those with no qualifications as a ratio of the average rate rose by only 4% in the case of female *un*employment, for which the data are unreliable. In every other category this ratio rose by at least 17% (the average rise in these other categories was 36%).

study. Franz (1991, table 3.3) defines the unskilled as those with less than a complete vocational education: he shows that between 1976 and 1987 their share of total unemployment remained at about one-half (which is consistent with Table A3.5), but that their share of total *employment* fell from one-third to one-quarter, implying a marked deterioration in their relative unemployment or non-employment rate.[9] Data for The Netherlands show a similar strong trend.[10] Between 1979 and 1985, the unemployment rate among people with only a basic education rose from 1.47 times to 1.88 times the overall unemployment rate. The (unweighted) average unemployment rate of the three lowest education categories rose over this period by 45 per cent relative to the average rate in the four highest education categories.

Unemployment rates by age group are a further source of evidence on changes in skill differentials. In most Northern countries, the unemployment rates of younger, less experienced, workers rose more than those of adults between the early 1970s and the mid-1980s, although the trend was reversed in the last few years of the period (OECD-EO 1986, chart 17). There was apparently also a trade-off against changes in relative wages: the increase in the relative unemployment rate of young workers was smaller in countries where their relative wages declined (ibid. 120–1). Similarly, the activity rate of males aged 20–4 declined during the 1980s in France, where there was a high minimum wage, but not in the UK.[11] In Canada, a trade-off over time is discerned by Myles, Picot, and Wannell (1988: 90–5): rising youth unemployment in the early 1980s was reversed after a fall in the relative wages of young people.

A3.3 Supply-side Explanations

To summarise, trends in the relative wages and unemployment rates of different education groups suggest that skill differentials in most Northern countries narrowed in the 1970s, but widened in the 1980s. There was also a widespread tendency for the relative wage and/or the relative unemployment rate of younger people to deteriorate during part or all of these two decades. Workers who were both less-educated and younger thus fared particularly badly. In assessing the causes of these changes, an important first step is to ask whether they could have been generated by shifts in the relative supply of skilled and less-skilled workers.

The decline in the returns to higher education during the 1970s is agreed to have had a supply-side cause, namely accelerated growth of the number of college graduates. This acceleration was due partly to demographic trends, which expanded the college-age population, and partly to higher enrolment rates. One or both of these two forces appears to have operated in most developed countries (Freeman 1982: 30–6), but they are best documented for the USA (Freeman 1976: 69–73, 1987: 23; Murphy, Plant, and Welch 1988: 42–3). Their combined effect

---

[9] The OECD data in Table A3.5 imply that their relative *unemployment* rate (recorded unemployment/labour force) did not alter much. If so, the deterioration must have been mainly in other forms of non-employment.

[10] Reported in the *IMF Survey* (30 May 1988: 172).

[11] Edward Balls, 'Youth "non-employment" in Britain and France', *Financial Times*, 30 Sept. 1991.

can be seen for example in Table A3.2 from the larger decline in the relative earnings of younger than of older college graduates.

The widening of wage and unemployment differentials by education level during the 1980s was probably amplified by supply-side forces, including lower spending on education in the 1970s and slower growth of the number of young people in the labour force (Murphy, Plant, and Welch 1988; Kosters 1990: 310–11). However, several studies of the USA concur that this rise in the returns to higher education must have been caused predominantly by a shift in relative demand. Above all, the supply-shift prediction that changes in the relative numbers of people in different education categories should be inversely correlated with changes in their relative wages does not hold for most groups in the 1980s (Bound and Johnson 1992: 375; Murphy and Welch 1992: 287). Moreover, although all the available formal studies refer to the USA, it is highly likely that their main conclusion applies also to other Northern countries, in all of which the share of the labour force with higher educational qualifications has been rising, not falling.

Shifts in relative demand likewise appear to have contributed to the widening of age-related earnings and unemployment differentials. The influence of supply-side forces, and particularly of baby booms, has been extensively studied (OECD-EO 1986; Wright 1989). There is compelling evidence that generational crowding depressed the relative economic position of young people in most developed countries at some time during the 1970s and 1980s. But it is clear, too, that this only partly explains the observed deterioration of youth relative wages and unemployment. High rates of unemployment among young people were a problem even in countries where there was little generational crowding, and persisted long after youth bulges had passed (OECD-EO 1986: 126–7). A multi-country econometric study of the relative unemployment rate of young people during 1966–83, which controlled for the relative size of the youth cohort and for youth relative wages, found that the coefficient on the time trend variable was significantly positive (ibid., table 43). Myles, Picot, and Wannell (1988: 90) likewise note that the relative wages of young people in Canada fell sharply in the 1980s despite shrinkage of their relative numbers.

The evidence on the education and age measures of skill thus strongly suggests that the widening of differentials during the 1980s in most Northern countries was caused by an increase in the relative demand for skilled labour. Moreover, relative demand seems to have been shifting in this direction also during the 1970s, even though wage and unemployment changes during that decade were dominated by supply-side shifts. Katz and Murphy (1992: 37, 54) conclude that 'fluctuations in the rate of growth of the relative supply of college graduates combined with smooth trend demand growth in favor of more-educated workers can largely explain fluctuations in the college/high school differential over the 1963–87 period', although there was 'some acceleration in the rate of growth of demand for women and more-educated workers in the 1980s'. Murphy and Welch (1992: 287) arrive at a weaker conclusion: their 1963–89 data cannot discriminate between the three hypotheses (*a*) that there was no trend in demand prior to the 1980s, (*b*) that a pre-existing trend continued in the 1980s, and (*c*) that a pre-existing trend accelerated in the 1980s.

Appendix A4
Occupational Relativities

This appendix continues the review of recent trends in skill differentials in the North (started in Appendix A3), using occupation as the indicator of skill. The first section looks at the relative wages of white-collar and blue-collar workers, the second at more finely specified occupational wage relativities. The third and fourth sections examine movements in relative unemployment and vacancy rates, and in employment levels. The last section documents the sources of data used.

Although detailed occupational classifications are concerned mainly with differences in the nature of work (nurses versus librarians, plumbers versus electricians), some of the broad categories involved can be used as indicators of skill, because they are associated with differences in required amounts of education, training, and experience—for example, the distinctions between professional and clerical workers, or craftsmen and labourers.[1] Moreover, occupational data have a potential advantage over educational measures of skill, which is that they may also capture training undertaken outside the formal schooling system, such as apprenticeships.

It is important to recognise, however, that occupational categories are at best a proxy for differences in education and training. This matters in the present context because the required amounts of skill in particular occupations are likely to alter over time, which makes changes in wage relativities among occupations an inaccurate guide to movements in the rewards to different levels of education and training. For example, the wage gap between two occupations could widen or narrow even in the absence of change in true skill differentials if the amount of skill needed in one or other occupation were to alter. Similarly, a rise in the relative skill content of lower-paid occupations might conceal an increase in the wage differential between skilled and unskilled workers.

In addition to this limitation of principle, there are some troublesome practical problems in using occupational wage data to measure changes in skill differentials. It is rarely possible to control for differences and changes in age structure—for example, fast growth of employment has tended to reduce the average age and experience of professional workers, making their average earnings growth slower than it would appear if data for specific age groups were available. Sometimes it is not even possible to distinguish males from females, so that movements in the relative wages of different occupations may also be affected by differences and changes in the relative numbers of men and women employed, or in their relative wages. Moreover, occupational categories are often coarse and changing mixtures of activities with widely varying skill requirements and wages.

---

[1] In the USA and Canada there are also estimates of the amounts of General Educational Development and Specific Vocational Preparation required in detailed occupational categories (see e.g. Myles 1987).

A4.1 Relative Wages of White-collar and Blue-collar Workers

The coarsest of all occupational breakdowns is that between white-collar (non-manual) and blue-collar (manual) workers. Its particular weakness in the present context is that the white-collar and the blue-collar groups are both mixtures of *SKILD* and *BAS-ED* labour (see Section A1.5). On average, non-manual workers have more education and training than manual workers, but many blue-collar jobs require more training than many less-skilled white-collar jobs. For about half the countries in the North, however, this is the only breakdown of wages by occupation for which time series are available.

The trends in the relative wages of white-collar and blue-collar workers in fifteen Northern countries are summarised in three graphs, whose design and data owe much to earlier work in OECD-EO (1987, ch. 3).[2] In most cases (and unless otherwise mentioned), the data refer only to males and only to manufacturing or 'industry', but the coverage of the white- and blue-collar categories varies among countries. Moreover, in these and in subsequent graphs, as detailed in the notes, some of the lines have been shifted upwards or downwards to improve readability. At best, then, these figures give only a rough indication of movements over time.

Fig. A4.1 refers to relative wage levels in five of the largest countries: for France, the UK, and the USA, the data are not confined to industry. In three of the five countries (Germany, the UK, and the USA), white-collar wages rose faster than blue-collar wages after the late 1970s, which suggests a widening of skill differentials. In Germany, there was such a rise also in the early 1970s, but from 1975 to 1979, and in the UK and the USA during most of the 1970s, the white-to-blue-collar wage ratio was constant or declining. In Japan, this ratio declined from the early 1960s to the mid-1970s, after which it changed very little. In France, there was a steep decline from the late 1960s, which slowed down but did not altogether cease in the 1980s. However, part of the downward trend in France was due to changes in age structure and 'classification drift' among managers (Marsden 1989*b*: 1.4, 2.5; Cases and Lollivier 1989).

The next figure needs to be interpreted more cautiously. It does not show relative wage levels, but ratios of wage indices for white- and blue-collar workers. Moreover, in most cases (and unless otherwise mentioned) the two indices of which the ratio is shown here are based on different payment periods, usually hourly wages for blue-collar workers and monthly salaries for white-collar workers. Thus if weekly or monthly hours of work were to fall over time, as they did in most countries during part or all of this period, this ratio of indices would decline even if there were no change in the true ratio of (hourly or monthly)

---

[2] Since the OECD study covered occupational differentials in general, this indebtedness applies also to the following sections. David Grubb, one of the authors of the study, kindly supplied much of the underlying data. David Marsden, the other author, generously provided some recent unpublished data of a similar kind (Marsden 1989*b*). As is explained in Sect. A4.5, it was possible in some cases simply to update the OECD series from the original sources, but in other cases they had to be extended (and sometimes replaced) with data from different sources.

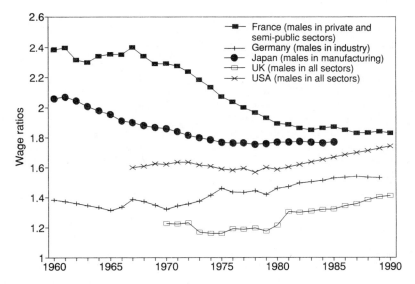

FIG. A4.1 Relative wages of white-collar and blue-collar workers
Notes and sources: Cross-country differences in the *level* of wage differentials are not accurately reflected in this graph, which is intended only to illustrate trends over time. The coverage of the data varies across countries. In addition, to make the graph easier to read, 0.05 has been added to the figures for Germany, 0.45 to those for Japan, and 0.15 to those for the USA. For more detailed definitions and sources of data, see Sect. A4.5.

white-collar to blue-collar wages. To get a better idea of what has really been happening to this wage ratio, the graphs should be mentally tilted anti-clockwise (OECD-EO 1987, n. 15).

Fig. A4.2(*a*) covers two large countries (Canada and Italy) and three smaller ones. For Canada, Denmark, Finland, and Sweden (after 1980), the sectoral coverage extends beyond industry. In Denmark, the first few years include both males and females, as do all the data for Finland and (probably) Italy: this may impart a downward bias, because of the increasing share of (lower-paid) females in the white-collar group.[3] In all five countries, the white-collar index rose more slowly than the blue-collar index during most of the 1970s, although in three of them (Canada and Italy after 1974 being the exceptions) this probably partly reflects a fall in hours of work. In Sweden after 1980, working hours have no further effect (because of a change in the source of the data), but the white-collar to blue-collar wage ratio continued to decline. In the other four countries, however, the earlier trend ceased or was reversed. In Finland, the change occurred soonest (1975), but the subsequent upward tendency was only slight. In Canada and Denmark, there was an upturn after about 1980, although in both cases with a drop in 1986–8.

---

[3] This depends of course on how the indices are constructed, which is rarely specified in the sources on which these graphs are based.

(a)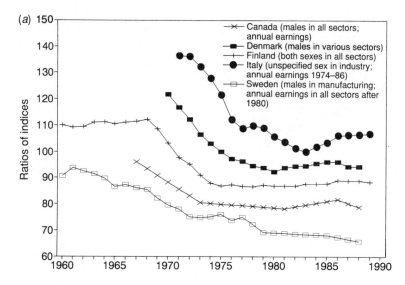

Notes and sources: see previous figure. To improve the readability of the graph, 4 has been subtracted from the Canadian index and 14 from the Swedish index.

(b)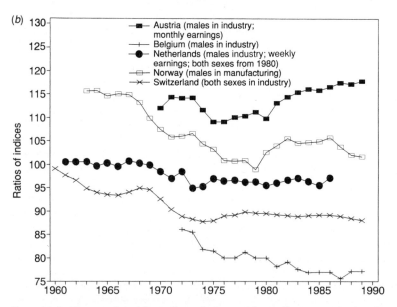

FIG. A4.2 Changes in white-collar relative to blue-collar wages (ratio of monthly salary to hourly wage indices unless otherwise indicated)

Notes and sources: See Fig. A4.1. To improve the readability of the graph, 12 has been added to the index for Austria and 7 to the index for Norway, while 20 has been subtracted from the index for Belgium, 2 from the index for The Netherlands, and 5 from the index for Switzerland.

And in 1983 the relative wage of white-collar workers began to rise in Italian industry.[4]

Fig. A4.2(*b*) covers a further five small countries: in The Netherlands (after 1980) and Switzerland, females as well as males are included. In all five countries, the ratio of white-collar to blue-collar wage indices tends to decline in the earlier part of the period, even in Austria and The Netherlands, where the series are not affected by changes in working hours. In the latter part of the period, although the general downward tendency ceases, the pattern is mixed. Only in Austria is there a sustained subsequent upward trend (from 1975). In Norway, there is a marked upward movement from 1979 to 1986, but then a decline to 1989. In The Netherlands and Switzerland, there is little change after the mid-1970s. And in Belgium, the earlier decline continues during the 1980s.

In summary, the data on white- and blue-collar wages suggest that skill differentials in many Northern countries widened after the late 1970s or early 1980s, though not as consistently as the data on wages by education and age.[5] In five of the fifteen countries, the graphs show clear and sustained increases (Austria, Germany, Italy, UK, USA). In seven countries, there was a less clear uptrend, or merely cessation of a previous downward tendency, but in four of these (Denmark, Finland, Norway, Switzerland), the indices may be biased downward by reductions in working hours. Only in three countries (Belgium, France, Sweden) did the downward tendency continue in the 1980s. Moreover, these series may understate or conceal widening of skill differentials because of the lack of control for age (and in a few cases also for sex) mentioned earlier.

A4.2 More Specific Occupational Wage Relativities

Looking more closely at the blue-collar category, Fig. A4.3 presents evidence for six countries on trends in wage differentials between skilled and unskilled manual workers (variously defined). The data refer to males, except in Denmark, where the skilled group includes a few females, in Italy, where sex is not specified, and in the USA, where both sexes are included from 1970 onwards. For Denmark, Germany, and Italy, the coverage is limited to industry, but elsewhere other sectors are also included.

The figure suggests striking differences among countries. In both the UK and the USA, there is a steep increase in the skilled-to-unskilled manual wage ratio after the late 1970s. In the USA (where the rise in the 1980s is similar in the male-only data in Table A4.3), this continued a trend that began in the early 1970s. In the UK, by contrast, the increase merely reversed a steep decline during

---

[4] The change in trend in 1983 coincided with the partial de-indexation of wages (Marsden 1989*b*: 2.4). However, the 1986–9 data are not comparable with those for 1974–86, and may understate the rise. Like the data for 1971–4, they are based on wage index series whose pay-period basis is not stated in the source, but may well refer to monthly salaries and hourly wages. The 1974–86 data refer to annual earnings, and thus are not affected by changes in working hours.

[5] Jackman, Layard, and Savouri (1991, table 2.16) present similar data on white- and blue-collar wages for seven European countries, but conclude that in general skill differentials did *not* widen during the 1980s.

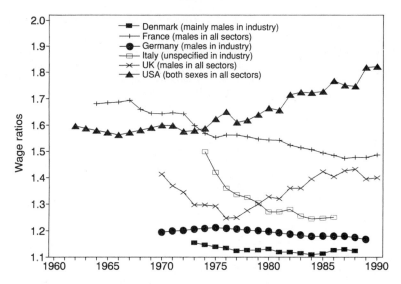

Fɪɢ. A4.3 Relative wages of skilled and unskilled blue-collar workers
Notes and sources: See notes to Fig. A4.1 and Sect. A4.5. To improve the readability of the figure, 0.20 has been added to the ratio for France, 0.05 to the ratio for Italy, and 0.17 to the ratio for the USA, while 0.06 has been subtracted from the ratio for Germany.

the earlier part of the 1970s, when incomes policies discriminated in favour of lower-paid workers, so that in 1990 the skilled–unskilled wage ratio was no higher than it had been in 1970.[6] In France and Italy, this ratio declined for most of the period for which data are available, with a particularly steep decline in Italy during the 1970s (a pattern also observed in Sweden 1975–80).[7] But in both countries it eventually levelled off, and may even have risen in the 1980s in Italy.[8] In Germany and Denmark, there was much less change, though the German data suggest a slight decline from the mid-1970s to the late 1980s. In Austria in the 1980s, too, there was little change in the relative pay of skilled and unskilled manual workers.[9]

The pay of lower-level white-collar (mainly clerical) workers is generally similar to that of blue-collar workers. During the 1970s, moreover, there was little change in the wage ratio between these two groups (OECD-EO 1987, table 3.2 and chart 3.3). Relative to blue-collar workers, lower white-collar workers became slightly

---

[6] This decline and recovery can be seen also in chart 3.4 of OECD-EO (1987), which is based on a different (and no longer published) source of data.

[7] See chart 3.4 of OECD-EO (1987).

[8] Of the three alternative series for Italy cited by Marsden (1989*b*), one rose in the 1980s (ibid. 2.4), and two did not (ibid. 2.4 and table 2.6).

[9] The median standard income of *Facharbeiter* as a ratio of that of *Hilfsarbeiter* in the private sector was 1.15 for males in both 1983 and 1989. For males and females together, this ratio declined from 1.29 in 1981 to 1.23 in 1989. (Calculated from table 9.24 of the 1990 *Statistiches Handbuch für die Republik Österreich* and similar tables in earlier issues.)

worse off in France and Italy, slightly better off in Germany and the USA, and held their ground in the UK after 1973. During the 1980s, too, as shown in Table A4.1, there were only small movements in this wage ratio, and not in any consistent direction. In both decades, therefore, the movements in the average white-collar to blue-collar pay ratio charted in the previous section mainly reflected the changing relative position of higher-level (professional, technical, and managerial) white-collar workers.

TABLE A4.1. *Relative wages of lower white-collar and middling blue-collar workers in 1980s*

(ratio of male white-collar to blue-collar)

		Early ratio	Late ratio	Late/ early
Austria	1983–9	1.11	1.09	0.99
Canada	1981–8	0.96	0.95	0.99
France	1980–5	1.24	1.22	0.98
	1987–90	1.15	1.15	1.00
Germany	1980–9	1.22	1.22	1.00
UK	1980/1–89/90	0.92	0.94	1.02
USA	1984–90	1.18	1.15	0.97

Notes and sources: sources as in Sect. A4.5 except where otherwise specified below.

Austria: *Angestellte mit gelernter Tätigkeit* versus *Angelernte Arbeiter*.

Canada: clerical versus non-farm manual workers.

France: 1980–85, *employés* versus *ouvriers specialisés* in private and semi-public sectors; 1987–89, *employés* versus *ouvriers non-qualifiés* in private sector.

Germany: *Kaufmannische Angestellte Leistungsgruppe* III versus *Arbeiter Leistungsgruppe* II in industry (including trade and finance for *Angestellte*). *Arbeiter* × 4.34 for weekly/monthly wage comparability.

UK: clerical workers (group VII) versus processing, making, and repairing workers, mechanical and engineering (group XIV).

USA: administrative support workers versus machine operators: source as in Table A4.3.

The next figure looks more closely at relativities within the white-collar category. Except for the USA, where females are also included after 1970, the data refer only to males, and cover quite a range of sectors, except in Norway and Sweden, where they refer to manufacturing. In three of the four large countries in Fig. A4.4(*a*), the wage differential between higher and lower white-collar workers widened during the 1980s. This movement is more marked in the UK and the USA (see also Table A4.3) than in Germany (where most of it arises from a discontinuity in 1982–3). In France, there was a slight decrease in this wage ratio during the 1980s, but it too might have increased slightly if controlled for changes in age structure (Cases and Lollivier 1989, table 2). Moreover, the virtual constancy of the high-to-low white-collar wage ratio in France during the 1980s contrasts sharply with its previous steep decline, which started in the late 1960s. In Germany there was also a decline from the early 1960s until the mid-1970s, and a similar but slighter decline in the USA during most of the 1970s. In the UK, there was a marked dip and recovery during 1974–8, prior to the rise in the 1980s.

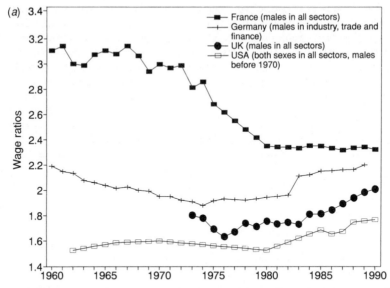

Notes and sources: See notes to Fig. A4.1 and Sect. A4.5. To improve readability, 0.5 has been subtracted from the ratio for France, 0.1 from the ratio for Germany, and 0.06 from the ratio for the USA, and 0.1 has been added to the ratio for the UK.

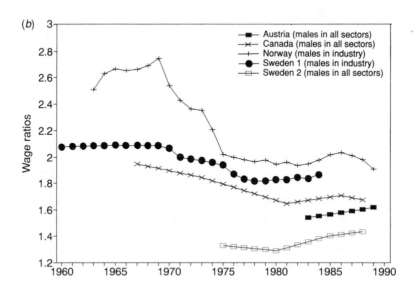

FIG. A4.4 Relative wages of higher and lower white-collar workers
Notes and sources: See notes to Fig. A4.1 and Sect. A4.5. To improve readability, 0.26 has been added to the Canadian ratio, and 0.25 subtracted from the Sweden 1 ratio.

Fig. A4.4(*b*) includes five series covering four other countries. In Austria and Sweden, there appears to have been a modest widening of wage differentials within the white-collar group during the 1980s, which in the case of Sweden was preceded by a narrowing in the 1970s and little change during the 1960s. In Canada, there was also a decline in the 1970s and a rise in the 1980s (though with a drop in 1986–8, as in the other Canadian series). In Norway, there was a sharp fall in the ratio of higher-to-lower white-collar wages from the late 1960s to the mid-1970s, but no clear subsequent trend. Age-controlled calculations for Norway in the 1980s reveal that, as in France, the increasing youthfulness of higher-level white-collar groups imparts a downward bias to the all-age series shown in the graph. In Italy, the higher-to-lower white-collar wage ratio fell steeply between 1974 and 1983, but rose slightly in 1983–6 (OECD-EO 1987, chart 3.3).

In summary, the behaviour of the more precisely defined occupational wage differentials examined in this section is quite consistent with that of the coarser white-collar-to-blue-collar ratios looked at earlier. But there are variations among countries in magnitude and in some cases in direction. The UK and the USA apparently experienced the most substantial widening of wage differentials, within as well as between the white- and blue-collar groups. In most of the other countries covered by the data, intra-white-collar wage differentials widened after the late 1970s or early 1980s, but by less than in the UK and the USA. However, movements in intra-blue-collar differentials were more varied, with no evidence of substantial widening in the 1980s outside the USA and UK, and if anything some narrowing in France and Germany. Even in the UK, the gains of skilled manual workers were largely a recovery of ground lost during the early 1970s, though in Italy similar losses during the 1970s were only partially recouped later.

That many occupational wage relativities in many Northern countries had started to widen or ceased to narrow in the late 1970s and early 1980s was first noted and documented in OECD-EO (1987, ch. 3). That these 'new trends' (ibid. 93) continued into the mid-1980s was later confirmed for a number of countries by one of the authors of the OECD study (Marsden 1989*b*). The widening of occupational skill differentials has also been noted in studies of individual countries, particularly of the USA and the UK, where the trend seems to have been most pronounced.

In the USA, Freeman (1987: 16) was apparently the first person to observe that 'in the 1980s, white-collar, especially professional, workers have enjoyed much greater wage increases than blue-collar workers, especially the lower-skilled (laborers)', and that this represented 'a sharp break from historic patterns'. Mishel and Simon (1988, fig. 6) record that the widening gap between white-collar and blue-collar pay applied to both male and female workers. Ryscavage and Henle (1990: 12–13) not only confirm that wage gaps among broad occupational categories have widened, but also examine trends in pay for different skill categories within selected white-collar occupations. In nine out of ten occupations, pay increases were proportionally larger in the higher-skilled categories, both in the 1980s and in the 1970s, but in only two out of seven occupations in the 1960s.

For the UK, Adams, Maybury, and Smith (1988, charts 1–4) and Katz and Loveman (1990, fig. 7) compare changes in pay with initial levels of pay in more than a hundred detailed occupational categories, for males and females separately. During 1973–9, the association was generally negative, indicating an improvement in the relative position of lower-paid occupations, but during 1979–88 it became strongly positive. Moll (1991, sect. 2.3) confirms that occupational wage differentials in the UK widened throughout the 1980s for both males and females.

A4.3 Relative Unemployment and Vacancy Rates

Data on occupational unemployment and vacancy rates are subject to more than the usual number of problems of interpretation. The most obvious is that unemployed people literally have no occupation. Where they are allocated among occupational categories, this is done either on the basis of their last job or in accordance with their wishes (or an administrative judgement) concerning their next job. Such allocations are unsatisfactory in the present context, partly because higher-level occupational skills are often specific. For example, a craftsman or manager who has lost his job in a declining industry may be skilled in retrospect and in intention, but in reality have only unskilled job opportunities.[10] Occupational vacancy rates do not suffer from this problem of principle, but have several more practical limitations (Walsh 1982).

Jackman, Layard, and Savouri (1991, table 2.4) present two sorts of series of relative unemployment rates by occupation for several countries during the 1970s and 1980s. One refers simply to the ratio of the unemployment rate among blue-collar workers to that among white-collar workers. The other sort of series refers to the dispersion of unemployment rates among occupations. These (relative) dispersion indices are calculated with data on a few broad occupational categories (between five and eight categories, depending on the country). The authors interpret these series as showing remarkable stability of relative unemployment rates (ibid. 46). However, regressions against time (whose results are shown in Table A4.2) suggest a different conclusion: both series appear to be rising in all countries but Spain, which is not included in the North in this book.

In the left-hand half of Table A4.2, the positive coefficients are highly significant in three out of six countries, though barely significant in two of them. These differences in significance levels mainly reflect differences in the size of the coefficients: in Germany and the UK, for example, the ratio of blue-collar to white-collar unemployment rates rose over the period by 40 per cent or more, but in Canada by only about 5 per cent. It should be recalled, however, that the white-collar and blue-collar groups are both mixtures of skilled and unskilled workers: the true rise in the ratio of the unskilled to the skilled unemployment rate was thus probably greater than the rise in the blue-collar to white-collar ratio suggests.

In most countries, the significance levels of the trend coefficients are lower in the right-hand half of Table A4.2 than in the left-hand half. However, this could well be because the occupational classifications are not closely related to skill levels. A similar problem of interpretation arises with respect to an earlier study (Jackman and Roper 1987, table 7) which uses occupational unemployment and

---

[10] Nor is it meaningful with occupational categories (unlike education and age groups) to calculate employment-to-population ratios to overcome the limitations of official unemployment statistics.

TABLE A4.2. *Trends in relative occupational unemployment rates, 1973–1987*

	Ratio of blue- to white-collar unemployment rate		Dispersion of occupation-specific unemployment rates	
	Period	Estimated trend coefficient	Period	Estimated trend coefficient
Australia	1977–86	0.036 (*)	1977–85	1.002**
Canada	1975–87	0.011 (*)	1975–87	0.093
Germany	1976–85	0.069****	1976–85	0.720**
Spain	1976–87	–0.017*	1977–86	–0.473
Sweden	1973–87	0.022*	1973–84	0.624****
UK	1974–85	0.066****	1974–85	0.268
USA	1973–87	0.046****	1973–82	1.007**

Notes and sources: Based on time series of relative unemployment rates from Jackman, Layard, and Savouri (1991, table 2.4). See present text for a fuller description of the series.

For each country, each of the two relative unemployment rate series was regressed against time (using OLS) over the period shown, which in each case is the longest for which consistent series are available in the source.

The estimated trend coefficients shown above are the coefficients on the independent (time) variables in these regressions. The significance levels of the estimated coefficients (on the basis of *t*-tests) are indicated as follows: **** = 1% (two-tailed test); *** = 2% (two-tailed test); ** = 5% (two-tailed test); * = 10% (two-tailed test); (*) = 10% (one-tailed test).

vacancy data for eight countries to calculate skill-mismatch indices (discussed further in Section 8.2). These indices reveal no general tendency for occupational differentials to widen, at least up to 1982 or 1983, when the series end. But again, the occupational classifications involved are not specifically related to skill level, and in some countries are quite detailed (up to forty occupations), which probably exacerbates this problem.[11]

Another international comparative study of occupational unemployment and vacancy rates, in eight developed countries between the early 1970s and the mid-1980s, is OECD-EO (1987, ch. 3, sect. E), some of whose results are further analysed in Marsden (1989a). It notes that relative occupational unemployment rates are cyclical.[12] This makes it harder to detect trends, especially because there was a severe recession in 1980–2 and the OECD series stop in the middle of the decade. An additional problem is that some of the series refer to absolute numbers unemployed, rather than to rates of unemployment, and thus understate the

[11] The 327–occupation calculation for Germany by Franz (1991: 119–21) is a more extreme illustration of this point. It suggests a decline in skills mismatch, whereas his more reliable two-category education-based calculation shows a marked increase in mismatch.

[12] The cyclical pattern has several different causes. One is arithmetic: uniform proportional reductions in employment cause larger proportional increases in unemployment rates in occupations where the unemployment rate was initially lower (see n. 14, Ch. 8). Thus recessions tend to raise relative unemployment rates in more skilled occupations. This effect is compounded within the blue-collar group by the fact that recessions tend to displace fewer unskilled than skilled manual workers, since the skilled workers are concentrated in two cyclically sensitive sectors—construction and manufacturing. However, white-collar workers tend to be less affected by recessions than blue-collar workers.

relative improvement, or exaggerate the relative deterioration, in the position of skilled occupations, whose share of the labour force is rising.

The ratio of professional and managerial to clerical unemployment shows no clear trend in most of the countries, although it declines in France and rises until 1977 in Italy (absolute numbers). The trends in the ratio of white-collar to blue-collar unemployment *rates* are reasonably consistent with the Jackman, Layard, and Savouri (JLS) series described above: there are declines in Australia, France, and the USA, and approximate constancy in Canada and Sweden. The more dubious series based on *absolute numbers* of unemployed white-collar and blue-collar workers give a different impression from the JLS series, though in all cases the discrepancy is in the anticipated direction. Thus the OECD series for Germany is more or less constant, and for the UK rises, whereas the JLS series for both countries imply a steep fall. There is also a rise in the OECD absolute numbers series for Italy, where the data refer only to managers and labourers.

The ratio of skilled to unskilled manual unemployment rates shows little trend in Canada and the USA. In the other four countries in the OECD study with skilled and unskilled manual series, the ratio is based on absolute numbers: it falls in Italy, but rises steeply in France, Germany, and the UK (implying that skilled workers have become relatively more unemployed). These apparent rises are again open to doubt, since they do not allow for the rising ratio of skilled to less-skilled manual employment, but they might be genuine. In all three of these countries (unlike Canada, Italy, and the USA), the absolute level of blue-collar employment in manufacturing declined.[13] Manual craftsmen with industry-specific skills in contracting sectors were particularly hard-hit: reluctant to accept lower-paid work, and too old to retrain, they had even fewer alternative job opportunities than their less-skilled colleagues.

This problem of reabsorbing skilled workers displaced from contracting sectors may explain why Micklewright (1984) found in the UK that the rate of unemployment among unskilled manual workers, though high, rose less than in more skilled occupations during 1972–80. During 1982–8, by contrast, the unemployment rates of male unskilled and semi-skilled manual workers declined less than the average rate (Moll 1991). Skilled manual workers improved their position relative to other manual groups, though not so much as managers, intermediate non-manual workers, and (especially) professionals. In France, too, unemployment increased more slowly during 1975–84 for professional than for male manual workers (Malinvaud 1987), and 'the unemployment rate for the unskilled was nearly double the overall rate in 1989 (compared to a gap of only about one-third in the late 1970s)'.[14]

The OECD study has data for relative occupational vacancies for only three countries (France, Germany, and the UK). In all cases, moreover, the data refer to absolute numbers, not vacancy rates, which imparts an upward bias to the trend of the skilled-to-unskilled ratio because of the rising share of skilled

[13] See fig. 3 of Wood (1991*a*). This figure does not include Canada, where the absolute level of manufacturing employment increased by more than 50% over the period, with little change in the ratio of white- to blue-collar workers (see Table A2.2), implying a similar proportional increase in the absolute level of blue-collar employment.

[14] The quotation is from the OECD *Economic Survey* of France (1990–1: 56). 'Unskilled' is not defined.

employment. In all three countries, the ratio of non-manual to manual vacancies has an upward trend. In France and Germany, the ratio of professional and managerial to clerical vacancies is also rising, while in the UK it has no clear trend. The ratio of skilled to unskilled manual vacancies is rather volatile, but it appears to have an upward trend in France and the UK, and a downward trend in Germany. This last result is the only one of the nine to imply an improvement in the relative position of less-skilled workers, although in all cases, as mentioned above, there is a bias in the other direction.

However, there is another study of Germany which does not suffer from this bias (Franz 1991, table 3.3). Defining unskilled workers as those with less than a complete vocational education, it finds that between 1976 and 1987 their share of all vacancies declined faster than their share of total employment, indicating a deterioration in their position relative to skilled workers. In The Netherlands, too, vacancy rates for jobs requiring higher education rose much more in the 1980s than for jobs requiring lower qualifications (van Ours and Ridder 1989, fig. 3.3). This tendency was observed within two separate occupational groups (clerical or business, and technical), whose overall vacancy rates moved in parallel (ibid., fig. 3.1). It suggests that occupational classifications may conceal more than they reveal about shortages and surpluses of labour of differing skill levels.

For the UK, there are also data on the proportion of manufacturing firms which expect their output to be constrained over the next few months by shortages of skilled and unskilled labour. Bean and Pissarides (1991, fig. 7.2) infer from a plot of the annual series that there was only a slight upward shift in the ratio of skilled to unskilled labour shortages in the second half of the 1980s. By contrast, Layard, Nickell, and Jackman (1991, table 19) calculate period averages, and discover a much stronger and longer-term trend: the skilled–unskilled shortage ratio rose from 2.7 in 1960–73 to 3.8 in 1974–80 and 6.6 in 1981–9.[15]

In summary, the data on unemployment and vacancy rates by occupation tend to confirm that the relative position of less-skilled workers deteriorated in the late 1970s and 1980s. Several series give a different impression, either of no clear trend, or of a contrary trend, but in most of these cases the accuracy or relevance of the underlying data is open to doubt. It is also hard to make inferences from the occupational data about the magnitude of the relative deterioration in the position of less-skilled workers. This is partly because there are important differences among skill groups within broad occupations, partly because some workers classed as skilled may no longer have marketable skills, and partly because the data do not capture induced exit from (or entry into) the labour force.

A4.4 Demand, Supply, and Employment Trends

With education and age measures of skill, simultaneous changes in the proportions of the labour force in different education and age groups can reveal whether changes in relative wages are caused predominantly by shifts in relative demand

---

[15] The 1960–73 and 1981–9 figures given here are weighted averages of two sub-period figures in the original source. This averaging does not affect the conclusion.

or by shifts in relative supply (Section A3.3). With the occupational measure of skill, this sort of analysis is not so straightforward. One reason for this is again the difficulty of allocating people who are not working, but are actual or potential members of the labour force, among occupational groups. For at the present time such people have no occupation, and prospectively most of them could work in a wide range of occupations. Moreover, many of those who currently *are* working in particular occupations form part of the labour supply to other occupations, in the sense that they could and would move if relative wages and job opportunities ' changed. So although the labour force obviously can be divided exhaustively among a set of mutually exclusive education and age groups, this is in principle not possible for occupational categories.

An alternative approach is to compare relative wage changes instead with changes in relative *employment* levels in different occupations, which do not suffer from this problem of principle, although in practice comparable wage and employment data are not often available. For movements of relative wages and employment in the same direction clearly tend to imply predominance of demand shifts—and in opposite directions, supply shifts. However, such inferences can be made only when markets clear, or (if they do not clear) when movements in excess demand and excess supply indicators are consistent with the pattern of change in relative scarcities implied by relative wage movements. Thus although there are few actual contradictions of the wage data, the mixed signals from trends in occupational unemployment and vacancy statistics require some caution in interpreting the evidence.[16]

The share of more skilled occupations in total employment has generally been rising for a long time throughout the North. This trend was documented in an earlier appendix (Table A2.2) for the period between the early 1960s and the mid-1980s for professional and technical relative to other workers, and for white-collar relative to blue-collar workers.[17] Within the blue-collar category, there is less information on the relative employment shares of skilled and less-skilled workers, and some ambiguity about the (often large) 'semi-skilled' category. But most of the available evidence suggests a long-term trend in the same direction.[18] For example, in the USA, the share of craftsmen among male blue-collar workers rose from about one-third in 1900 to just under one-half in 1982, and the share of

[16] Marsden (1989*a*) finds only weak evidence of an inverse short-term association between changes in the relative pay of different occupational groups and changes in their relative unemployment levels or rates.

[17] The last two columns of Table A2.2 show increases in the professional and white-collar employment ratios of manufacturing in all countries. It can be inferred from the table that these ratios rose also in nontraded sectors, except for the professional ratio in the USA and New Zealand. The table refers to changes in specific sectors, and therefore understates the economy-wide increases in these two ratios, since it does not capture the effects of the increased share of total employment in nontraded sectors, where both ratios are relatively high.

[18] In the UK, the share of skilled jobs in total manual employment was 42% for males both in 1911 and in 1951, but had risen to 51% in 1970 (Routh 1965, table 1; *New Earnings Survey* 1970, table 162; classifications only roughly comparable). Among females, this share declined from 30% in 1911 to 20% in 1951, and had risen only to 23% by 1970. The share of skilled workers in total male manual employment in the UK engineering industry rose from 46.7% in 1970 to 49.0% in 1980 (Marsden 1989*a*, table 6.A.3). In France, population census data show that the share of qualified workers in total manual employment (*ouvriers*

labourers declined from two-fifths to under one-fifth, though with little change between 1960 and 1982. The share of semi-skilled 'operatives' rose until 1960, but then declined.[19]

What happened during the 1980s is a matter of some controversy, and hard to assess accurately because of changes in occupational classifications and long intervals between censuses. It is agreed by all that the share of white-collar jobs, and especially of professional and technical jobs, continued to expand. But it has also been argued that the share of middle-level-skill jobs declined, and thus that there was a rise in the share of low-skilled as well as high-skilled jobs.[20] This 'hollowing-out' thesis has been advanced (and disputed) mainly in North America, where the low-skilled jobs in question are usually said to be in fast-food restaurants and similar services. However, some data for the UK also suggest a fall in the employment share of middle-paying occupations, especially among male manual workers in manufacturing, the group whose relative decline has been emphasised also in the US debate (Adams, Maybury, and Smith 1988: 81–2).

The debate over hollowing-out in the lower reaches of the wage hierarchy will be considered further below (and in Appendix A5). But the evidence on the causes of change in the pay of higher-level white-collar occupations, relative to lower-level white-collar and to blue-collar occupations, is fairly clear-cut. The coexistence during the 1980s of rising relative wages and rising relative employment among professional, technical, and managerial workers strongly suggests a shift in relative demand towards these more skilled groups. Likewise, the decline in their relative pay in most countries during the 1970s, when their share of total employment was also rising, strongly suggests that the predominant influence then was an increase in the relative supply of these more skilled workers. In neither decade do changes in relative unemployment and vacancies contradict the wage movements. And in both decades, the pattern is consistent with (and closely related to) that for college graduates described in Appendix A3.

The change in the fortunes of the higher-level occupations in the 1980s appears more striking when it is recognised that the 1970s combination of declining relative pay and rising relative employment represented the continuation of a much longer-term trend. This trend was neither uniform across occupations nor smooth across decades. But for most professions, and probably also for managers, it had apparently been the usual direction since at least the beginning of the twentieth century, and as in the 1970s was probably caused largely by the relative expansion of upper-secondary, technical, and higher education. (The introduction of

and *manoeuvres* of both sexes) rose from 38% in 1962 to 55% in 1982. Between 1972 and 1978, the ratio of skilled to total manual employment rose among males in Belgium, France, Germany, and Italy, but fell in The Netherlands (OECD-EO 1987, table 3.5). For females, it rose in France and The Netherlands, remained constant in Germany, and fell in Belgium and Italy. Other more recent data for various countries are cited later in the text.

[19] Data for 1900–60 refer to the labour force and are from *Historical Statistics of the USA* (1975, Series D 182–232). Data for 1960–82 refer to employment and are from *Statistical Abstract of the USA* (1984, table 693). In both cases, manual workers exclude farm and service workers, and operatives include transport workers. The occupational classification differs from that in Table A4.3.

[20] Recent contributions to the debate, with references to earlier studies, include Wolfson (1989), Harrison and Bluestone (1990), and Picot, Myles, and Wannell (1990).

free and compulsory lower-secondary schooling had also contributed to a long-term decline in the pay of clerical relative to blue-collar workers.) Among manual workers, too, the long-term increase in the proportion of skilled jobs had generally been associated with a secular narrowing of skill differentials in wages. (See for example the studies surveyed in Wood 1978: 181–202; Williamson and Lindert 1980; and Saunders and Marsden 1981.)

As explained earlier, movements in the relative pay of higher-level white-collar workers were the main ingredient of movements during the 1970s and 1980s in the average white-collar to blue-collar wage ratio. So the assessment above that a supply shift narrowed higher-level occupational skill differentials in the 1970s, while the widening in the 1980s was caused by a demand shift, must apply also to the coarser wage relativity between white-collar and blue-collar workers. The white-collar share of employment increased during both decades, which is consistent with this assessment. Moreover, trends in the relative unemployment and vacancy rates of white-collar and blue-collar workers, though somewhat mixed, do not generally contradict this interpretation of the evidence.

However, in some countries there are clear indications, both for white-collar workers in general and for higher-level groups, that institutional forces also had an effect on relative wage movements (Marsden 1989*b*: 3.5–10). In the United Kingdom during the 1970s, when incomes policies discriminated against higher-paid workers, Figs. A4.1 and A4.4(*a*) show sharp dips in the relative pay of white-collar and professional workers. In Italy, the reversal of the downward trend in the relative pay of these two groups started when the official system of wage indexation was amended in 1983. In France, minimum wage (SMIC) policy, and in Sweden union wage bargaining policies, may have contributed to the observed narrowing of these wage differentials during the 1970s and much of the 1980s. And in other countries it seems likely that the tendency for these differentials to widen during the 1980s was inhibited, albeit to varying degrees, by some combination of union action by lower-paid white-collar and blue-collar workers, minimum wage legislation, and social security income floors.

It is harder to assess the causes of the observed behaviour of wage relativities between skilled and unskilled blue-collar workers during the 1970s and 1980s, even in particular countries, and impossible to generalise about the North as a whole. For these intra-blue-collar wage differentials moved in different ways in different countries (Fig. A4.3). The evidence on changes in relative unemployment and vacancies for these occupational groups is likewise mixed. And there is less information, and more dispute (connected with the hollowing-out argument), about trends in the relative employment of more and less skilled manual workers. Some conclusions may none the less be extracted from the limited data available.

Table A4.3 shows employment and wage changes in selected occupations in the USA during the 1980s. The above-average increases in employment and wages for managerial, professional, and technical workers are apparent for both males and females. The table also confirms that, among blue-collar males, the wages of craftsmen went up faster than those of machine operators, who in turn did better than labourers. (The corresponding ranking for females is less meaningful, since there are so few in the highest and lowest categories.) However, the relative employment levels of craftsmen and machine operators did not change. Moreover, employment among labourers increased relative to these two other

TABLE A4.3. *Employment and wages in selected occupations in the USA in the 1980s*

(full-time wage and salary workers)

	Wage level 1990 (ratio of handlers etc.)	Employment share 1990 (%)	Employment increase (1990 level/ 1984 level)	Money wage increase (1990 level/ 1984 level)
Males				
Executive, administrative, managerial	2.45	12.9	1.08	1.32
Professional specialty	2.37	12.1	1.10	1.33
Technicians and related support	1.85	3.5	1.17	1.28
Administrative support, including clerical	1.44	6.6	1.08	1.17
Precision production, craft, and repair	1.57	20.6	1.00	1.24
Machine operators, assemblers, and inspectors	1.25	9.2	1.00	1.20
Handlers, equipment cleaners, helpers, laborers	1.00	6.0	1.18	1.16
Service except household and protective	0.91	6.1	1.26	1.29
Other occupations*	n.a.	23.0	1.07	n.a.
Total	n.a.	100.0	1.07	n.a.
Females				
Executive, administrative, managerial	1.92	13.3	1.46	1.34
Professional specialty	2.11	16.5	1.27	1.38
Technicians and related support	1.60	3.8	1.20	1.28
Administrative support, including clerical	1.29	30.9	1.07	1.28
Precision production, craft, and repair	1.21	2.4	1.02	1.20
Machine operators, assemblers, and inspectors	1.01	7.8	0.93	1.20
Handlers, equipment cleaners, helpers, laborers	1.00	1.9	1.23	1.23
Service except household and protective	0.90	11.1	1.21	1.27
Other occupations*	n.a.	12.2	1.18	n.a.
Total	n.a.	100.0	1.16	n.a.

*Sales, private household and protective service, transport, farming.

Source: US Bureau of Labor Statistics, *Employment and Earnings*, Jan. issues, table A-75. Data refer to fourth quarter: apparently not published in comparable form prior to 1984 (occupational classification changed in 1982). 'Wages' are median weekly earnings.

blue-collar groups, which seems inconsistent with a shift of relative demand against the unskilled. And for (male and female) service workers, the lowest-paid group, both wages and employment increased relative to other manual occupations.

The table clearly gives some support to the hollowing-out hypothesis. Among both males and females, employment in the two lowest-paid groups (labourers and service workers) expanded faster than for the three groups immediately above them (clerical workers, craftsmen, and machine operators). But its implications regarding the causes of the widening of skill differentials in wages among blue-collar workers are less clear, because the occupational classification is a mixture of skill-related and sectoral characteristics. For both males and females, the relative employment decline has been most pronounced in the two occupational categories most closely associated with manufacturing (craftsmen and machine operators).

In the UK, the other country where wage differentials among manual workers clearly widened during the 1980s, the occupational classification does not provide a general categorisation of blue-collar workers by skill (the wage differential in Fig. A4.3 refers to two narrow occupations). As in the USA, the share of employment in occupations associated with manufacturing (groups XII to XV) declined during the 1980s, from 35 per cent to 30 per cent for males and from 18 per cent to 13 per cent for females.[21] Unlike the USA, however, the share of total employment in the low-paid catering, cleaning, and personal service category increased only slightly for males and declined for females. This might reflect the relatively higher reservation wage of less-skilled labour in the UK, because of the general income floor provided by the social security system (which has no counterpart in the USA). But the differences between the occupational classifications preclude a proper comparison of the degree of hollowing-out in the two countries.

Layard and Nickell (1986: 40–1) combine data from different sources to show that the relative demand for less-skilled manual workers declined sharply in the UK during 1979–85. They infer from Micklewright (1984) that the unemployment rate among semi-skilled and unskilled manual workers is roughly double that among skilled manual workers, and that these two rates have risen over time by roughly the same proportion. This implies that employment of less-skilled manual workers has fallen by proportionally twice as much as employment of skilled manual workers. Since the relative wage of less-skilled workers has also fallen, as evidenced by the increased dispersion of manual wages, relative demand must have shifted against them. Assuming an elasticity of substitution between skilled and less-skilled workers of 2.5 (on the basis of another study), Layard and Nickell estimate the size of the shift during this period at one-third, which they rightly describe as 'huge'. If, as argued in Section 6.1.2, the elasticity were about unity, the implied shift would be smaller (about one-fifth), but still substantial. Moreover, the unemployment rate of less-skilled workers actually deteriorated relative to skilled manual workers during the 1980s (Moll 1991), implying an even faster relative decline in their employment.

This decline in the employment of less-skilled relative to skilled manual workers in the UK is in contrast to the USA, where, among males, employment of craftsmen did not change relative to machine operators, and declined relative to both labourers and service workers. But the limited data available for other Northern countries generally show the same trend as in the UK. In France the ratio of skilled to semi- and unskilled male manual employment in the private and semi-public sectors rose from 1.22 in 1970 to 1.66 in 1980 and 1.73 in 1985, with a similar trend for females (Marsden 1989a, table 6.3). In Germany the share of skilled workers in male manual employment in industry increased steadily from 41 per cent in 1970 to 48 per cent in 1985, but for females remained constant at about 1 per cent (ibid.). In Sweden the ratio of skilled to non-skilled full-time manual employees rose from 0.65 in 1975 to 0.84 in 1984 (Marsden 1989b, table 2.9). In Austria this ratio also went up between 1983 and 1989 for females, but declined for males.[22] In Denmark the male manual skilled–unskilled ratio in manufacturing and construction appears to have been constant from 1975 to 1988, perhaps because of the sampling procedure used.[23]

[21] These results are from an earlier version of Moll (1991), and are based on data from the *New Earnings Survey*.
[22] Source as in Sect. A4.5. The same result obtains whether 'skilled' workers are defined to include only *Facharbeiter* or also *Meister und Vorarbeiter*.
[23] Source as in Sect. A4.5. The share of skilled workers in the total is between 41% and 43% throughout the period.

In these other countries, however, there was no general or strong tendency for wage differentials among manual workers to widen. In principle, this association between rising relative employment and unchanging relative wages of skilled manual workers might reflect a declining relative supply of less-skilled workers. But this interpretation is not at all plausible, given the high levels of unemployment among less-skilled workers in most of these countries. For even though the evidence on *changes* in relative unemployment and vacancy rates for skilled and less-skilled manual workers is mixed (as noted earlier), the undisputedly much higher unemployment rates among less-skilled than among skilled manual workers make it hard to believe that increasing scarcity of less-skilled workers could be behind the decline in their employment with maintenance of their relative wage. A more plausible explanation is that the lack of change in the relative wage reflects institutional pressures, while the relative reduction in less-skilled employment reflects an adverse movement of relative demand.

To sum up, the evidence on trends in relative wages and employment by level of skill among blue-collar workers is scanty, open to various doubts, and does not all point in the same direction. But most of it seems consistent (like the evidence on other occupational categories) with the hypothesis of an increase in the relative demand for skilled workers, in conjunction with differing degrees of relative wage flexibility. In the USA, the shift in demand appears to have emerged mainly as a widening of wage differentials, perhaps facilitated by the relative decline of the federal minimum wage after 1981, rather than as a change in relative employment.[24] In most European countries, the opposite seems to have happened, with rather rigid wage differentials, and a decline in less-skilled employment. In the UK, powerful institutional constraints on relative wages were deliberately weakened during the 1980s, but by no means eliminated, so that among blue-collar workers there was both a widening of skill differentials and a decline in less-skilled employment. What happened in Japan is not known.

A4.5 Annexe: Definitions and Sources of Wage Data

This section contains detailed information, organised by country, on the data used in compiling the figures in earlier sections (and Table A4.1). In many cases, the figures are updated versions of those in OECD-EO (1987, ch. 3), with no change in definitions or sources. More detail is provided below where the coverage, definitions, or sources differ from those in the OECD study. Table numbers are cited for only one recent (usually 1990) issue of annual national statistical yearbooks, although some of the data may have been drawn from corresponding tables in earlier issues. The labels (*a*), (*b*), and (*c*) refer to the same occupational groupings in all countries, though data on all three are not available in all countries.

Austria

The data are from various issues of the annual *Statistiches Handbuch für die Republik Österreich.*

---

[24] On the trend in the minimum wage, see Mishel and Simon (1988: 43) and Marsden (1989*b*: 3.7).

(*a*) White-collar and blue-collar workers. An update of the OECD series, which refer to the monthly earnings of male *Angestellte* and *Arbeiter* in industry. (Table 9.06 of the 1990 *Handbuch*.)

(*c*) Higher and lower white-collar workers. Median standard net personal income of male *Angestellte mit hochqualifizierter Tätigkeit* and *Angestellte mit gelernter Tätigkeit* in all sectors, in 1983 and 1989 (interpolated). (Table 9.24 of the 1990 *Handbuch*.)

Belgium

The data are from various issues of the annual *Statistiques Sociales*.

(*a*) White-collar and blue-collar workers. An update of the OECD series, which refer to indices of the monthly salaries of male *employés* and the hourly earnings of male *ouvriers* in industry. (1990 issue no. 3, p. 70.)

Canada

The data are from the Survey of Consumer Finances, and are drawn from a special tabulation provided by the Analytical Studies Branch of Statistics Canada. They refer to full-time full-year males in all sectors, and to annual labour income, which includes self-employment income as well as wage and salary income.

(*a*) White-collar and blue-collar workers. Blue-collar workers are non-farm manual, and white-collar workers a fixed-weighted average of professional and technical and clerical.

(*c*) Higher and lower white-collar workers. Professional and technical workers, and clerical workers.

Denmark

The data are from various issues of the annual *Statistisk Årbog*.

(*a*) White-collar and blue-collar workers. Monthly earnings of male salary-earners in all sectors, and hourly earnings (including overtime) of male manual workers in manufacturing and construction. (Tables 201 and 203 of the 1990 *Årbog*.) Extended backwards in 1970–5 using OECD series, which is based on salary and wage indices for both sexes in manufacturing.

(*b*) Skilled and unskilled blue-collar workers. Hourly earnings (including overtime) of skilled (mainly male) and unskilled male wage-earners in manufacturing and construction. (Table 201 of the 1990 *Årbog*.)

Finland

The data are from various issues of the annual *Statistisk Årsbok*.

(*a*) White-collar and blue-collar workers. An update of the OECD series, which refer to indices of the monthly earnings of salaried employees and the hourly earnings of wage earners of both sexes in all sectors. (Table 350 of the 1990 *Årsbok*.)

France

The data are from various issues of the *Annuaire Statistique de la France, Economie et Statistique*, Marsden (1989*b*, table 2.7), Lhéritier (1990), and Girard and Lhéritier (1991).

(*a*) White-collar and blue-collar workers. A modification (males rather than both sexes, except in 1975–80) and update of the OECD series. Annual earnings of full-time workers in private and semi-public sectors. White-collar workers are a fixed-weighted average of *cadres supérieures, cadres moyens*, and *employés*; blue-collar workers are *ouvriers*. After 1985, the series is not strictly comparable: the occupational classification changes, and the data apparently refer only to the private sector.

(*b*) Skilled and unskilled blue-collar workers. Ratio of annual earnings of male *ouvriers qualifiés* to *manoeuvres* in 1980–5 in private and semi-public sectors (table C.03–2 of 1986 *Annuaire*), extrapolated back to 1973 using hourly wage indices for level 5 and level 1 manual workers (both sexes 1977–80, males 1973–7), and then back to 1964 using hourly wage indices for male *ouvriers qualifiés* and level 1 *manoeuvres*. Extrapolated forward to 1990 using data on the annual earnings of male *ouvriers qualifiés* and *non-qualifiés*.

(*c*) Higher and lower white-collar workers. As for (*a*), using the ratio of *cadres supérieures* to *employés*. Extrapolation after 1985, when coverage of *cadres* alters.

Germany

The data are from various issues of the annual *Statistiches Jahrbuch*.

(*a*) White-collar and blue-collar workers. An update of the OECD series, which refer to the monthly earnings of male *Angestellte* and *Arbeiter* in industry. The updating used indices of monthly earnings of *Angestellte* and weekly earnings of *Arbeiter*. (Tables 22.2 and 22.6 of the 1990 *Jahrbuch*.)

(*b*) Skilled and unskilled blue-collar workers. From Marsden (1989*b*, table 2.8, males), interpolated and updated using data on the weekly earnings of *Leistungsgruppe* 1 and 3 of male *Arbeiter* in industry. (Table 22.3 of the 1990 *Jahrbuch*.)

(*c*) Higher and lower white-collar workers. An update of the OECD series, which refer to the monthly earnings of male *Angestellte* in industry, trade and finance. Ratio of *Leistungsgruppe* II to V. Extrapolated to 1987 from Marsden (1989*b*, table 2.8), and to 1989 using average wage increases of *kaufmannische* and *technische Angestellte*. (Table 22.7 of 1990 *Jahrbuch*.)

Italy

(*a*) White-collar and blue-collar workers. An update of the OECD series, which refer to the average annual earnings of *impiegati* and *operai* of unspecified sex in manufacturing. This series was converted into an index and extrapolated to cover 1971–4 and 1986–9 using indices of earnings for unspecified pay-periods for workers of unspecified sex in industry. (Table 18.1 of the 1990 *Annuario Statistico Italiano*.)

(*b*) Skilled and unskilled blue-collar workers. This is the OECD series, which refer to the typical annual pay of *Livello* 5 and *Livello* 2 manual workers of unspecified sex in manufacturing.

Japan

(*a*) White-collar and blue-collar workers. This is the OECD series, which refers to the monthly earnings of male non-production (or salaried) and production workers in manufacturing.

Norway

The data are from various issues of the annual *Statistisk Årbok*.

(*a*) White-collar and blue-collar workers. An update of the OECD series, which refer to (white-collar) a fixed-weighted average of the monthly earnings of male technical, supervisory, office, and warehouse employees, mainly in manufacturing, and (blue-collar) the hourly earnings of adult male manual workers in manufacturing. (Tables 189 and 194 of the 1990 *Årbok*.) The 1987–9 values of the index were adjusted for a reduction in weekly working hours (with full compensation) from 40 to 37.5 in January 1987. (OECD *Economic Survey* of Norway 1987–8: 75.) Had this adjustment not been made, the index would have dropped sharply (and misleadingly) between 1986 and 1987.

(*c*) Higher and lower white-collar workers. Also an update of the OECD series, using the ratio of male managers (chief engineers and those in management positions) to simple routine workers, mainly in manufacturing. (Table 194 of the 1990 *Årbok*.)

Sweden

(*a*) White-collar and blue-collar workers. For 1960–80, the OECD series, which refer to salaries (presumed monthly) of full-time male technical and office staff, and hourly earnings of male workers in manufacturing. Extrapolated 1980–8 using data on the annual earnings of full-time males in the public and private sectors; white-collar workers are a fixed-weighted average of *högre tjänstemän* and *tjänstemän på mellannivå*, and blue-collar workers are *arbetare och lägre tjänstemän*. (Data from table 25 of the *Income Distribution Survey* 1988.)

(*c*) Higher and lower white-collar workers. Series 1 (1960–84) is the OECD series, using the ratio of male managerial to clerical workers in manufacturing. Series 2 (1975–88, interpolated) is the ratio of the annual earnings of male *högre tjänstemän* to those of *tjänstemän på mellannivå* in the public and private sectors. (Table 25 of the *Income Distribution Survey* 1988.)

Switzerland

The data are from various issues of the annual *Statistiches Jahrbuch*.

(*a*) White-collar and blue-collar workers. An update of the OECD series, which refer to indices of the monthly salaries of *Angestellte* and the hourly wages of *Arbeiter* of both sexes in industry. (Table 3.16 of the 1991 *Jahrbuch*.)

The Netherlands

(*a*) White-collar and blue-collar workers. An update of the OECD series, which refer to the weekly earnings of male *employés* and *arbeiders* in industry. The update used indices for non-manual and manual workers of both sexes. (*Statistical Yearbook of the Netherlands* 1988, sect. V, table 3.)

United Kingdom

The data are from various issues of the annual *New Earnings Survey*, and refer to the median weekly earnings of full-time adult males whose pay was not affected by absence, in all sectors.

(*a*) White-collar and blue-collar workers. Non-manual and manual workers. Includes overtime pay. (From the summary volume of the *NES*.)

(*b*) Skilled and unskilled blue-collar workers. Maintenance fitters (non-electrical) from group XIV, and general labourers (including engineering and shipbuilding) from group XVIII. Excludes overtime pay after 1971. (From table 98 of Vol. D of the 1990 *NES*.)

(*c*) Higher and lower white-collar workers. Professional and related supporting management (group II) and clerical and related (group VII). Excludes overtime pay. (From table 98 of Vol. D of the 1990 *NES*.)

United States of America

(*a*) White-collar and blue-collar workers. For 1967–80, the OECD series, which refer to the annual earnings of full-time males in all sectors. Extrapolated to 1990 using private industry employment cost index data from Freeman (1987, table 1.8), Ryscavage and Henle (1990, table 11), and *Monthly Labor Review* (Dec. 1990, table 22).

(*b*) Skilled and unskilled blue-collar workers. For 1970–83, the OECD series, which refer to the median weekly earnings of craft and kindred workers and non-farm labourers of both sexes in all sectors. Extrapolated forward using data from *Current Population Survey* (1984–7) and *Employment and Earnings* (1988–90) on 'precision production, craft and repair' and 'handlers, equipment cleaners, helpers and laborers'. Extrapolated backwards to 1962 using data on the median annual earnings of males from the *Statistical Abstract*.

(*c*) Higher and lower white-collar workers. Professional and clerical workers of both sexes in all sectors, from Freeman (1987, table 1.8), interpolated and extended to 1990 using data from *Employment and Earnings* for 'professional specialty' and 'administrative support including clerical'. Extrapolated backwards to 1962 as in (*b*), using data on 'professional and technical' and 'clerical and kindred'. (Freeman bridges the occupational classification change in 1982.)

Appendix A5
Wage Dispersion and Income Inequality

This appendix completes the review of recent trends in skill differentials in the North (initiated in Appendix A3 and continued in Appendix A4). It examines movements in overall wage dispersion (Section A5.1), and possible causes of these movements (Section A5.2). It concludes by looking also at trends in the distribution of income among households (Section A5.3).

The two preceding appendices examined movements in the relative wages of skilled and less-skilled workers, using education, age, and occupation as measures of skill. This appendix uses a rather different measure of skill, namely the wage itself. It attempts to make inferences about movements in skill differentials from changes in the dispersion (or inequality) of the size distribution of wages among workers. The underlying assumption is that high- and low-earning groups of workers correspond roughly with more- and less-skilled groups (cf. Williamson and Lindert 1980: 327). If so, a rise (say) in the wages of skilled workers relative to less-skilled workers would clearly tend to increase wage dispersion. Conversely, other things being equal, greater wage dispersion would imply wider skill differentials.

This measure of skill has some advantages over the education, age, and occupation measures used earlier, which fail to capture the large and obvious diversity of skill levels among people with a given number of years of schooling and experience, or in particular occupational categories. By contrast, differences in wages are in principle capable of reflecting the differing economic value of all sorts and gradations of work-related abilities, whether innate, or deliberately or fortuitously acquired. In practice, however, changes in wage dispersion are at best an imperfect indicator of changes in skill differentials, and are more reliable in this regard when (as here) studied in conjunction with other cruder indicators.

The most obvious limitation is that not all wage differences among workers are caused by differences in skill. Some of the other causes can be controlled for: for example, using data on the earnings only of full-time workers eliminates most of the effect of differences in hours worked. But many non-skill-related causes of wage differences cannot be controlled for in size distribution data. These include differences in the nonpecuniary attractiveness of particular jobs, obstacles to labour mobility, unions, and other direct institutional determinants of wage rates. Observed movements in wage dispersion could thus arise from changes in these other influences.

Even if skill were supposed to be the sole influence on wages, movements in wage dispersion would not necessarily be a good indicator of changes in the relative wages of workers with specific degrees of skill. Such movements could also arise from changes in the skill distribution of the population of workers concerned. Even with no change in skill differentials, for example, wage dispersion would increase if the gap between the amounts of skill possessed by higher-paid and lower-paid workers widened over time. Wage dispersion would likewise tend to diminish if unskilled workers were given relatively more training, or if they ceased to work, and hence vanished from the wage statistics. Moreover, such

changes in the skill composition of the work-force might be causally associated
with changes in skill differentials, and might thus amplify or muffle the effects of
changes in skill differentials on wage dispersion.[1]

A5.1 Trends in Wage Dispersion

Fig. A5.1 and Table A5.1 summarise information on changes in wage dispersion
in eleven Northern countries during the 1970s and 1980s. In almost all cases the
data refer only to full-time workers. Inclusion of part-timers would not only make
the distribution appear more dispersed at any given time, but would also tend to

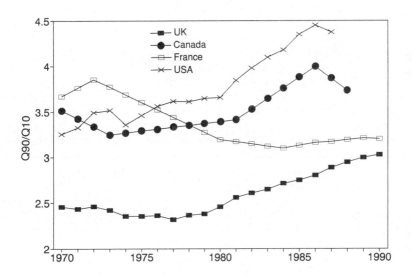

FIG. A5.1 Wage dispersion in four large Northern countries, 1970–1990
(Q90/Q10 for full-time males)
Note: Because the coverage of the wage and of the work-force differ somewhat
across countries, *levels* of dispersion are not strictly comparable.

Sources: Canada (annual earnings): from Table A5.1, with interpolation. France
(annual earnings): from Table A5.1, with interpolation. UK (weekly earnings):
New Earnings Survey summary volumes; refers to adults unaffected by absence,
and includes overtime pay. USA (weekly earnings): Juhn, Murphy, and Pierce
(1989); forward and backward extrapolation of 1970 (1968–72) Q90/Q10 ratio
derived from table 1, using indices in fig. 3.

---

[1] e.g. training or exit of unskilled workers might be induced by widening of skill
differentials, and might thus offset a tendency towards greater wage dispersion.
Alternatively, such training or exit might be autonomous, and hence cause skill differentials
to narrow, which would further diminish the dispersion of wages.

increase its dispersion over time, because of the rising share of part-time employment. Where possible, the sample is also limited to males, in order to eliminate
the effect of the rising share of (generally lower-paid) female workers. The measure of dispersion is in most cases dictated by the sources used, and varies among
countries, adding to the difficulty of these international comparisons.

The figure contains information for four large countries—Canada, France, the
UK, and the USA—on the ratio of the ninth to the first decile of full-time male
wages. Increased dispersion during the 1980s is apparent in all four countries.
This tendency was strongest in the USA, where it represented the continuation of
a milder and less steady trend in the same direction during the 1970s. In Canada,
the pattern was similar to the USA (though with a 1986–8 drop, explained in
Section A3.1 above). In the UK, the increase in dispersion seems to have started
in 1977, prior to which there had been a modest downward trend. In France, the
increase in wage dispersion started only in 1984, and was much slighter than in
the other countries. Before then, dispersion had been diminishing from the early
1970s (the pre-1980 numbers are not strictly comparable, but the trend during the
mid-1970s is corroborated by other data in Marsden 1989*b*, table 2.2).

Table A5.1 covers seven other countries. The coverage of the data, the time-
periods, and the measures of dispersion vary considerably. But the impression
that consistently emerges is of reduced dispersion in the 1970s and increased dispersion in the 1980s. This U-shaped pattern is most evident in Sweden, where the
data include females, and the trough appears to have been in 1983. The data for
Denmark hint at a similar pattern, though the coverage and the dispersion measure are unsatisfactory. There were increases during the 1980s also in The
Netherlands and New Zealand (the data for both these countries include females).
In both Germany and Italy, there was declining dispersion in the 1970s, although
it was only slight in the former country. The limited data on full-time workers for
Austria show increasing dispersion in the 1980s. (The longer Austrian series,
which includes part-timers, exhibits an entirely different pattern, with rising dispersion in the 1970s and no change in the 1980s.)

Davis (1992, figs. 1A and 1B) compares trends in wage dispersion among full-
time males in eight Northern countries from the early 1960s to the late 1980s. For
the USA, Canada, the UK, and Sweden, the Davis series show much the same
movements as in Fig. A5.1 and Table A5.1. For France, the timing and size of
the upturn in the 1980s is similar to that in Fig. A5.1, but the prior downtrend is
much milder in the Davis series. In The Netherlands, the Davis series show little
change between 1983 and 1987 (compared with the 1980–6 increase in Table
A5.1, which is suggested by another source to have continued to 1988—Marsden
1990, n. 11).[2] Two extra pieces of information in the Davis study are that wage
dispersion rose steeply in Germany between 1981 and 1984, and in Australia
between 1981 and 1987.

Davis also makes some illuminating cross-country comparisons of the upper
and the lower halves of the wage distribution. He notes that the levels of dispersion in the top half tend to be more similar across countries than in the bottom
half. In particular, there is less lower-half dispersion in the UK and France than

---

[2] The Davis series for The Netherlands have the advantage of being limited to males, but
exclude the top 5% of earners (Davis 1992, table 1).

TABLE A5.1. *Changes in wage dispersion in the North, 1970–1990*

Country	Indicator (definitions below) and coverage						
Austria		**1970**	**1975**	**1980**	**1983**	**1987**	**1989**
	Q75/Q25: full-time males				1.47		1.52
	Q75/Q25: all males	1.70	1.74	1.81		1.79	1.81
Canada		**1967**	**1973**	**1981**		**1986**	**1988**
	Q90/Q10: full-time males	4.08	3.55	3.71		4.29	4.03
Denmark			**1975**	**1980**	**1983**	**1986**	**1989**
	Mean/median: full-time male salary-earners		1.10	1.08	1.08	1.08	1.10
	Q75/Q25: all males				1.60	1.59	
France		**1970**	**1972!**	**1980**	**1984**	**1986**	**1990**
	Q90/Q10: full-time males	3.67	3.85!	3.19	3.10	3.16	3.20
Germany		**1972**	**1978**				
	Q90/Q10: full-time manual males	1.59	1.57				
	Q90/Q10: full-time non-manual males	2.13	2.10				
Italy		**1972**	**1978**				
	Q90/Q10: full-time manual males	1.88	1.58				
	Q90/Q10: full-time non-manual males	2.99	1.51				
Netherlands			**1978**	**1980!**	**1985**	**1986**	
	Q75/Q25: all full-time employees		1.47	1.46!	1.52	1.54	
New Zealand				**1980**	**1983**	**1986**	**1990**
	Top/bottom quintile groups mean income indices: all full-time employees			100	101	102	103
Sweden			**1975**	**1980**	**1983**	**1984!**	**1988**
	Top/bottom decile groups mean earnings: all full-time employees aged 20–64		3.53	2.98	2.87	3.01!	3.65

Note: Q75/Q25 = ratio of upper to lower quartile; Q90/Q10 = ratio of 90th to 10th percentile.
! = discontinuity in source of data.

Sources:
   Austria: full-time (standard income) figures from *Statistiches Handbuch* 1990 (table 9.24), 1984 (table 9.18); all-males figures from 1990 *Handbuch*, table 9.05 (1989 number spliced over 1987 break).
   Canada: *Survey of Consumer Finances*, special tabulation from Statistics Canada.
   Denmark: *Statistisk Årbog* 1990 (tables 193, 203) and corresponding tables of earlier issues.
   France: Sawyer (1982, table 7.12), Marsden (1989*b*, table 2.3), Girard and Lhéritier (1991).
   Germany and Italy: Marsden (1989*b*, table 2.2).
   Netherlands: *Statistical Yearbook* (1980: 352; 1981: 358; 1986: 347; 1988: 350).
   New Zealand: *Pocket Digest of Statistics* (1988: 80); *Key Statistics* (Dec. 1990, table 4.02). Data in table generally refer to September, but in 1990 to June.
   Sweden: Marsden (1989*b*, table 2.4); for 1988 calculated from *Income Distribution Survey* (1988, table 28).

in the USA and Canada, which corroborates other evidence that institutional pressures tend to prop up low wages much more in Europe than in America. Moreover, Davis (1992, figs. 3A and 3B) shows that in France the two halves of the wage distribution moved in different ways, with increasing dispersion in the upper half from about 1973, but declining dispersion in the bottom half until 1984. In Canada, the two halves also moved in opposite directions in the 1970s, but with declining dispersion in the top half and increasing dispersion in the bottom half. In the USA and the UK, the two halves of the distribution behaved more symmetrically.

   There are many other studies of trends in wage dispersion in the USA. Their findings vary somewhat, as do their methods and choice of data, but it is apparently agreed by all that wage dispersion among both male and female full-time workers increased in the 1980s. The study by Juhn, Murphy, and Pierce (1989) from which the US data in Fig. A5.1 are drawn focuses on male wage- and salary-earners with strong labour force attachment, and adjusts for a change in census procedures that may have reduced dispersion between 1974 and 1975. It concludes that there was little change during the 1960s, but an accelerating trend increase in dispersion after 1968 or 1969. Other authors interpret the unadjusted data as indicating a U-turn in dispersion, with its trough in 1975 for full-time males and females (Bluestone 1990, and Harrison and Bluestone 1990).

Blackburn and Bloom (1987) stress the differences among earlier studies of the USA. Their own calculations for full-time year-round workers during 1967–85 (ibid., table 4) indicate a U-shaped pattern for females with a trough in the mid-1970s (which the authors interpret as no trend), and for males little change until the late 1970s, after which there was a marked increase in dispersion. Ryscavage and Henle (1990, table 3) also examine the earnings, including self-employment income, of year-round full-time workers. Between 1968 and 1978, they discover no change in dispersion for males, and a decrease in dispersion for females. Between 1978 and 1988, earnings dispersion increased substantially among both males and females.

In Canada, Picot, Myles, and Wannell (1990) discover that the earnings distribution of full-time full-year employees became increasingly polarised between 1967 and 1986. Up to 1981, much of this increase was due to the rising labour force participation of females (which is consistent with the lack of a clear trend for males during the 1970s in the analysis of Dooley 1987, table 5). But in the 1980s changes in the sex and age composition of employment contributed little to the marked increase in polarisation. The source of the Canadian data for males in Table A5.1 confirms that earnings inequality increased also among full-time females during the 1980s, and suggests that the increase for females started earlier, in about 1973.

In the UK, the J-shaped movement of wage dispersion among full-time males during the 1970s and 1980s shown in Fig. A5.1 has been widely noted, and occurred also among full-time females, although for them the trough appears to have been in 1979 rather than 1977 (Adams, Maybury, and Smith 1988, table 3).[3] If the ratio of the upper to the lower quartile, rather than the top to the bottom decile, is considered, the trough appears earlier and wider: 1974–7 for males and 1977–9 for females (Moll 1991, table 2). There are no comprehensive data on the distribution of earnings for the UK prior to the 1970s, but Saunders and Marsden (1981: 159–66) infer that its dispersion had generally been declining in the 1950s and 1960s.

Movements in wage dispersion in other countries have received much less attention than in North America and the UK. Anticipating Davis (1992), Marsden (1989b) and Harrison and Bluestone (1990) suggest, each on the basis of data for a couple of other countries, that this trend may have been ubiquitous. Marsden notes, however, that the increase in dispersion appears to have been later and milder in France and Sweden than in the USA and the UK, although the more

---

[3] Katz and Loveman (1990) note an important difference between UK and US experience. In the USA, the increase in wage dispersion has been associated with a marked absolute decline in the real wages of the lowest decile, while in the UK the real wages even of this decile rose in the 1980s.

recent data for Sweden in Table A5.1 and in Davis (1992) show a steep rise. In the two other countries with separate data for each sex (Austria and France), the sources for Table A5.1 show that the increase in dispersion among males in the 1980s was paralleled among females.

A5.2 Causal Interpretations

In summary, wage dispersion among full-time workers, both male and female, appears to have increased during at least part of the 1980s in all eleven of the Northern countries for which relevant data exist. What happened earlier, and when, is more varied by country and by sex. However, as explained above, causal interpretation of these trends is not entirely straightforward. The increase in dispersion during the 1980s is consistent with widening wage differentials between skilled and less-skilled workers, but it could also reflect changes in other determinants of wage differences, or in the shape of the skill distribution of employment.

The hypothesis that the increase in dispersion was caused *solely* by these other forces can be rejected with considerable confidence. For there is strong evidence, presented in Appendices A3 and A4, of a simultaneous widening of wage differentials among skill-related education, age, and occupational categories. It is also clear, though, that the enlargement of these inter-group wage differentials was responsible for only part of the increase in overall wage dispersion, to which increased dispersion *within* these groups also made a substantial contribution.

As usual, the increase in intra-group wage dispersion is best documented for the USA. Juhn, Murphy, and Pierce (1989, fig. 11) show that rising returns to education and experience explain only about half of the increase during the 1980s in the overall dispersion of wages among full-time males. The other half reflected rising inequality within education and age groups, a trend which had been strongly in evidence since the late 1960s, and had accounted for virtually all the pre-1980 increase in overall inequality. Ryscavage and Henle (1990, tables 7 and 8) also discover that the Gini coefficients of the earnings distribution of full-time year-round workers increased between 1982 and 1988 in all six broad occupational categories, both for males and for females, though only in one category was the increase statistically significant. The same authors had earlier noted significant trend increases in earnings inequality among full-time year-round males in eight out of ten occupational groups during 1958–77 (Henle and Ryscavage 1980, table 3).

The evidence for other countries is more limited, but most of it points in the same direction. Davis (1992) examines movements in wage dispersion among full-time males within education, age, and occupational groupings in the USA and seven other Northern countries. During at least part of the 1980s, he finds increases in intra-group dispersion in Australia, Canada, Germany, The Netherlands, Sweden (from 1984), and the UK, but not in France. During the 1970s, too, there was an increase in Canada (as in the USA), but in France, Sweden, and the UK (until 1977) intra-group dispersion declined (and there are no earlier data for the other three countries).

Picot, Myles, and Wannell (1990: 15) likewise conclude that almost all the increase in earnings polarisation among full-time workers in Canada during

1967–86 'took place *within* industries and occupations'.[4] In the UK, Adams, Maybury, and Smith (1988, table 3) record that earnings dispersion increased during the 1980s among both manual and non-manual full-time workers of both sexes. Moll (1991) notes increased wage dispersion in this period also within the ten largest manual and non-manual occupations for men and women. In France between 1982 and 1986 earnings dispersion increased among males in all three broad non-manual occupations, but decreased among male manual workers and among females in three of the four occupations (Marsden 1990, table 3B). In Sweden between 1980 and 1984 wage dispersion increased among both skilled and unskilled manual workers, and in the two lower non-manual occupational groups, but decreased among both higher and intermediate non-manual workers (ibid., table 4).

The increases in wage dispersion within education and occupation groups are of course subject to the same problem of interpretation as the increase in overall dispersion, since they too could have been caused partly by changes in other determinants of wage differences or in the distribution of skills. Juhn, Murphy, and Pierce (1989) argue that increased intra-group dispersion largely reflects rising returns to aspects of skill that cannot be measured with conventional census data. They also argue that this has been caused by increased relative demand for these unobservable skills, on the grounds that observed changes in industry and occupation mix suggest a simultaneous rise in the skill intensity of employment. This interpretation is highly plausible, but obviously is not amenable to direct verification. For one of the limitations of the wage as a measure of skill (unlike, say, years of schooling) is that it is not possible to juxtapose changes in the relative wages and relative numbers of people in different skill categories.

To some extent the observed movements in wage dispersion, both overall and intra-group, must have reflected pressures on wage differentials unrelated to skill. In particular, as noted in Section A4.4, incomes policies, minimum wage legislation, and union wage policies appear to have compressed all wage differentials in the UK, France, Italy, and Sweden in the 1970s (and in the latter three countries also at the beginning of the 1980s). It is therefore likely that the increase in wage dispersion during the 1980s partly reflected the restoration of differentials to their previous levels (Marsden 1990). But wage dispersion in the UK had by the late 1980s risen well above its level of the early 1970s. More generally, the pervasiveness across countries of the increase in dispersion, and its persistence over time, make it impossible to believe that relaxation of egalitarian constraints was the main cause. And there is no other obvious non-skill-related explanation for this general increase in wage dispersion.[5]

It remains to consider the possibility that the increase in dispersion was partly, though clearly not entirely, caused by a change in the shape of the skill distribution, rather than in the relative wages of skilled and less-skilled workers.[6] This

[4] However, Dooley (1987, table 6) finds only a slight tendency for wage dispersion within education and age groups to increase during the 1970s among full-time Canadian males.

[5] Increased labour-market mobility due to the abolition or weakening of union or legislative restrictions on entry and exit may have been another institutional feature of the 1980s, but this should presumably have tended to narrow wage differentials rather than to widen them.

[6] This distinction is particularly well explained by Adams, Maybury, and Smith (1988),

hypothesis is often connected with the debate over 'hollowing out' or the 'disappearing middle' referred to in Section A4.4, but it needs some disentangling. It also demands closer attention to the concepts and measurement of dispersion, inequality, and polarisation. The term 'dispersion', which has been heavily used in this appendix, is general but rather vague. 'Inequality' is a more precise concept, although it is well known that different formal measures of inequality may give different results. The term 'polarisation' is formalised by Wolfson (1989) as the proportion of people in the tails of the distribution, with wages beyond some specified range around the median.[7] He shows that standard measures of inequality and polarisation need not move in the same direction.

The distribution whose middle is said to be disappearing is often simply the size distribution of wages among individual workers. However, changes in the shape of this *wage* distribution, which also reflect changes in the relative wages of skilled and less-skilled workers, are a poor guide to changes in the shape of the *skill* distribution. Moreover, a tendency for the middle of the wage distribution to disappear could be entirely due to wider skill differentials in wages, which would make the distribution more polarised. Whether the distribution would also become more unequal is less clear, and would depend on the measure of inequality. But inter-quantile wage ratios, which are used to measure dispersion for most of the countries in Fig. A5.1 and Table A5.1, would usually move in the same direction as measures of polarisation.[8] So there need be no conflict between the trends described here and those emphasised in other studies which have focused on the disappearing middle of the wage distribution.

Where there *is* a potential conflict is between the present view that the middle has shrunk mainly because skill differentials in wages have widened (as argued also, for example, by Juhn, Murphy, and Pierce 1989) and the view that this has happened mainly because the proportion of jobs or workers with middling levels of skill has declined. But there is unfortunately little direct evidence on changes in the shape of the skill distribution. The best available study is that of Myles (1987), who uses four measures of occupational skill requirements, and data on the occupational composition of employment, to assess changes in Canada between 1961 and 1981. His results (ibid., tables 1 and 2) give no support to the

who note that the disappearance of workers from the middle of the wage distribution would be sufficient to increase inter-quantile wage ratios even if there were no change in the wages of those who remained in the distribution. This is because the absolute number of workers in the (say) upper quarter of the distribution would decline, and hence the wage threshold of this quarter (the quartile) would rise.

[7] Subsequently, Wolfson and Foster (1991) have devised a different measure of polarisation, which can be conceptually related to the Lorenz curve.

[8] Inter-quantile ratios, as Wolfson (1989) notes, are poor measures of inequality in a strict sense, since they omit a lot of information and are not necessarily consistent with the usual minimum criterion of ranking by Lorenz curves. For this reason, these ratios may not move in the same direction as more formal measures of inequality. Fig. 1 of Wolfson (1989) also happens to provide an exception to the proposition that inter-quantile ratios will usually move in the same direction as measures of polarisation. This hypothetical counter-example, in which polarisation increases but the inter-quartile ratio does not alter, depends on rather unusual assumptions, namely bimodality and movement of some people towards as well as away from the mean. But such contradictions could arise even with more usual distributions, e.g. if the quantiles were extreme while the income range used to define the tails was narrow.

view that middling-skill jobs have expanded more slowly than low- and high-skill jobs.[9] On the contrary, with very few exceptions, his calculations indicate a general upgrading of the skill distribution: progressively fewer jobs with low skill requirements and more jobs with higher skill requirements. This upgrading, moreover, proceeded faster in the 1970s than in the 1960s.

All other studies of this issue appear to have been forced to rely on changes in the distribution of jobs ranked by their wage levels. In Section A4.4, it was noted that the distribution of employment among coarse occupational categories suggests some shrinkage of middle-wage jobs relative to lower-wage jobs, both in the USA during 1984–90 and in the UK during 1973–86, and that this shrinkage was concentrated on occupations associated with manufacturing. Juhn, Murphy, and Pierce (1989, fig. 13) calculate the effects of changes in the industrial and occupational composition of employment on the proportions of workers at different relative wage levels in the USA during 1967–87. Over the whole period these structural changes would have increased the relative demand for highly paid workers and reduced the demand for workers with average or below-average wages. This shift began in the early 1970s. In 1979–87 demand for the lowest-paid workers fell less than for lower-middle-wage workers, but only slightly. The authors conclude that increased wage dispersion has been caused by relative shrinkage, not expansion, of the number of low-wage jobs.

Picot, Myles, and Wannell (1990) likewise conclude from an analysis of Canadian data that people who attribute increased wage dispersion in the 1980s to the growth of low-wage jobs in consumer services are mistaking the symptom for the cause. The basic change, as they see it, has been a decline in the relative wages of young people, which 'is simply more *visible* in consumer services because of the concentration of young workers there' (ibid. 25). It should be emphasised that not all studies of the changing shape of the distribution of jobs have interpreted the wage as a proxy for skill. Moreover, since there are other influences on wages, it would in principle be possible to have a decline in the share of middle-wage jobs without a decline in the share of middle-skill jobs. In any event, there is little or no empirical support for the proposition that increased wage dispersion has been caused mainly by polarisation of the skill distribution of workers or of employment opportunities. Widening skill differentials in wages appear to have been the main or sole cause.

A5.3 Income Inequality

The principal reason for concern about greater wage dispersion is the undesirable social effects of increased income inequality. But there are several intervening linkages between the distribution of wages among full-time workers of a particular sex (as in Fig. A5.1 and Table A5.1), and the distribution of income among households, which is the usual way of looking at inequality. So although wider skill differentials tend to increase income inequality, the connection between movements in the two sorts of distribution is not necessarily close.

[9] However, data from another source suggest that the skill distributions of blue-collar and lower white-collar jobs may be bimodal (Myles 1987, table 11).

The intervening linkages include the gender balance of employment, the female–male wage ratio, and the extent of part-time work. Also important are variations among households in the number of wage-earners, and for the distribution of per capita income, variations also in the number of non-earners (which depends partly on the level and pattern of unemployment). Moreover, there are other sources of household income, both from capital and from the state in the form of pensions and other social security benefits. Finally, some data on household income distribution are also net of the effects of taxation.

Not all these linkages are independent of changes in skill differentials. For example, a reduction in the relative wages of unskilled males may push their wives out to work. Increased unemployment among unskilled workers may augment the effect of wider wage differentials on income inequality. Greater wage dispersion adds cumulatively, via savings, to inequality in the ownership of (and income from) capital. But most of the intervening linkages are governed by other forces, changes in which may thus offset or amplify the influence of wider skill differentials on income inequality.

Table A5.2 summarises the available information on household income distribution in eleven Northern countries between 1960 and 1990.[10] It draws on many different sources, which use a wide variety of concepts and measures of income inequality. Comparing the level of inequality across countries is thus in some cases impossible, and in all cases risky. However, comparisons of the direction of trends in inequality can be made with more confidence, although in some countries this requires looking at two or more overlapping series.

The data strongly suggest that trends in the 1980s were different from those in the two earlier decades, and in a direction consistent with the influence of wider skill differentials. In none of the nine countries for which information is available did household income inequality increase significantly during the 1960s or early 1970s, and in seven it decreased. In the 1980s, by contrast, inequality increased in six out of eleven countries, and in only three did it decrease. There are eight countries whose data span the periods before and after 1980. In four of them there was a change in trend towards greater inequality (in the 1970s in the UK and the USA, and around 1980 in Japan and The Netherlands). In three (France, Germany, and Italy) the former trend of decreasing inequality continued during the 1980s, and in Canada there was no trend in either sub-period.

The detailed data that would be necessary to prove the connection between wider skill differentials and greater household income inequality—and to ascertain why in some cases there is no such connection—are not readily available for any of these countries. However, other studies cast some light on this issue. Wolleb (1989: 12–18) analyses trends in household income inequality in France, Germany, and Italy—the three countries in which there was a continuing decrease in the 1980s—as well as in the UK. In France, he notes that wage differentials continued to narrow until the mid-1980s, and argues that this was an important

---

[10] The table does not include all the available data. Other series which simply confirmed the trends shown in the table were omitted. Additional information on trends in relative poverty in the early 1980s in eleven countries is provided in Eurostat (1990, tables 4.4 and B7): for France, Germany, The Netherlands, and the UK, it confirms the trends shown in Table A5.2; but for Italy it suggests that inequality may have increased. In Belgium, relative poverty decreased, and in Denmark it remained unchanged.

TABLE A5.2. *Changes in household income inequality in the North, 1960–1990*

Country	Indicator and coverage							
Australia	Gini: gross income among households	1980 0.40	1985 0.42					
Canada	Gini: gross income among households	1967 0.40	1973 0.41	1981 0.40	1986 0.40	1988 0.40		
France	Gini: gross income among households	1962 0.51	1970 0.44	1975 0.42	1979 0.40			
	Gini: a–e expenditure among households				1980 0.33	1985 0.29		
Germany	Gini: net income among households	1960 0.38	1964 0.38	1970 0.39	1975 0.37	1980 0.37	1985 0.34	1988 0.33
Italy	Q5/Q1 shares: net income among households	1967 9.58	1972 8.48	1975 7.08				
	Gini: expenditure among households			1975 0.34	1980 0.35	1985 0.35	1987 0.35	
	Gini: gross income among households				1980 0.32	1985 0.31	1987 0.30	
Japan	Gini: gross income among employee households	1963 0.22	1968 0.20	1974 0.20	1982 0.20	1986 0.21	1989 0.21	
	Gini: gross income among households	1963 0.36	1968 0.35	1974 0.34	1982 0.34			
Netherlands	Q5/Q1 shares: net income among households	1959 7.96	1967 6.60					
	Q5/Q1 shares: net income among individuals		1967 4.38	1975 4.02	1981 3.98			
	Q5/(Q1+Q2) shares: net income among individuals				1981 2.29	1985 2.98		
New Zealand	Gini: gross income among households	1980 0.35	1985 0.35					
Sweden	Maxeq%: factor income among economically active households	1975 21.6	1980 22.2	1984 24.4	1988 24.8			
	Maxeq%: net income among all households	1975 22.9	1980 21.8	1984 23.4	1988 23.7			

		1959	1965	1970	1977	1979	1985	1988
UK	Gini: gross income among households	0.40	0.39	0.39	0.37	0.37	0.41	0.37
	Gini: a-e gross income among households				0.29	0.30	0.32	0.37
		1960	1965	1970	1973	1979	1985	1988
USA	Q5/Q1shares: gross income among households	8.60	7.87	7.57	7.47	8.02		9.57
	Gini: gross income among households/individuals			0.41	0.40	0.41	0.43	

Definitions:

Q5/Q1shares = income share (or mean income) of top quintile group as ratio of bottom quintile group.

Gini = Gini coefficient of inequality.

Maxeq% = maximum equalisation percentage (larger value indicates more inequality).

Factor income = income from all sources except government transfers.

Gross income = income from all sources (including transfers) before tax.

Net income = income from all sources, after direct taxes.

Expenditure = expenditure out of net income.

Among households = distribution among household or family units.

Among individuals = distribution among individual income recipients.

a-e = household income or expenditure adjusted to an adult-equivalent basis.

Sources:

Australia, New Zealand: Saunders, Hobbes, and Stott (1989, table 10).

Canada: Wolfson (1989, table 1), updated to 1988 in a personal communication.

France: 1962–70 Sawyer (1976: 27); 1970–9 Wolleb (1989: 41); 1979–85 Eurostat (1990, table 5.6).

Germany: net income series 1960–80 Wolleb (1989: 67); 1985–8 calculated from DIW *Wochenbericht* (1986 No. 51–2, and 1990 No. 22).

Italy: gross income and expenditure 1975–87 Wolleb (1989: 110, updated in a personal communication; net income 1967–77 Sawyer (1982, table 7.14, figure in 1975 col. refers to 1977).

Japan: employee household series 1962–74 Mizoguchi and Takayama (1984, table 1–4); 1982–9 calculated from table 5 of the *Annual Report on the Family Income and Expenditure Survey* (current income row); all household series Mizoguchi (1985*b*, table 8, overall household column).

Netherlands: 1959–67 Sawyer (1982, table 7.14); 1975–85 net income among individuals *Statistical Yearbook of The Netherlands* (major coverage change 1981–2; Q5/(Q1+Q2) figure in 1981 col. refers to 1982).

Sweden: Statistika Meddelanden, *Income Distribution Survey* (1988, tables 19, 20).

United Kingdom: a-e series *Economic Trends* (March 1991: 118, table O); gross income series *Economic Trends* May 1978, July 1984, Nov. 1987 (data in 1970 col. refer to 1970–71, those in 1977 col. to 1975–6, those in 1978 col. to 1978–9, and those in 1985 col. to 1984–5).

United States: households (families) Mishel and Simon (1988, table 14), Bureau of the Census P-60 Reports (No. 97 table 22 and No. 166 table 5); households/individuals (families plus unrelated individuals) Blackburn and Bloom (1987, table 1).

contributor to reduced income inequality, as were increases in social security benefits and tax progressivity, while demographic forces had mixed effects.

In Germany, Wolleb recognises that rising wage dispersion after 1978 tended to increase household income inequality. But this was more than offset by a rise in the proportion of households with more than one wage-earner (a group within which there is a relatively low degree of income inequality), so that there was on balance a further reduction of inequality. In Italy, too, income inequality did not increase despite widening wage differentials after the early 1980s, but it is less clear what changes in the structure and behaviour of households broke the connection. In the UK, the marked widening of skill differentials surely contributed to the sharp increase in household income inequality during the 1980s, which was exacerbated by regressive tax and social security changes.

Widening wage differentials must also have contributed to rising household income inequality in the USA, though once again the connection is not well documented (Freeman 1987: 43; Mishel and Simon 1988). Blackburn and Bloom (1987: 37) find that increased wage dispersion among male principal earners was one cause of greater household income inequality, but put more emphasis on other influences. However, Danziger and Gottschalk (1989) note the insufficiency of several possible explanations of increased inequality, including cyclical forces, cohort size, and the extent of female headship of households. In Canada, where wage dispersion among full-time workers increased after 1970, the stability of income inequality is the net outcome of various conflicting economic and demographic pressures (Wolfson 1986a, 1989). The level of household income inequality in Japan is disputed, but all sources agree that it increased after the late 1970s, and there is some evidence that wider wage differentials contributed to this shift (Ishizaki 1985–6; Ozawa 1985–6).

References

This list excludes articles from newspapers and standard statistical sources, to which full references are given at the points where they are cited in this book.

Abraham, K. G. (1991). 'Mismatch and Labour Mobility: Some Final Remarks', in Schioppa (1991).

Adams, Mark, Ruth Maybury, and William Smith (1988). 'Trends in the Distribution of Earnings, 1973 to 1986', *Employment Gazette* (Feb.): 75–82.

Addison, Tony, and Lionel Demery (1989). 'Labour Standards or Double Standards? Worker Rights and Trade Policy', *Overseas Development Institute Briefing Paper* (Apr.) (London).

Adelman, Irma (1984). 'Beyond Export-Led Growth', *World Development*, 12/9: 937–50.

—— and Cynthia Morris (1973). *Economic Growth and Social Equity in Developing Countries* (Stanford University Press, Stanford).

—— and Sherman Robinson (1978). *Income Distribution in Developing Countries* (Oxford University Press, Oxford).

—— —— (1989). 'Income Distribution and Development', in Chenery and Srinivasan (1989), Vol. 2.

Akerloff, G. A., and J. C. Yellen (1990). 'The Fair Wage-Effort Hypothesis and Unemployment', *Quarterly Journal of Economics*, 105/2: 255–83.

Amsden, Alice (1989). *Asia's Next Giant* (Oxford University Press, Oxford).

Appleyard, R. T. (1977). 'Major International Population Movements and Policies: An Historical Review', *International Population Conference*, Vol. 2, IUSSP, Liège: 291–305.

Armstrong, Philip, Andrew Glyn, and John Harrison (1984). *Capitalism Since World War II: The Making and Breakup of the Great Boom* (Fontana, London).

—— —— —— (1991). *Capitalism Since 1945* (Blackwell, Oxford).

Arrow, K. J. (1962). 'The Economic Implications of Learning by Doing', *Review of Economic Studies*, 29/1: 155–73.

—— H. B. Chenery, B. S. Minhas, and R. M. Solow (1961). 'Capital–Labor Substitution and Economic Efficiency', *Review of Economics and Statistics*, 43/3: 225–50.

Ashenfelter, Orley, and Richard Layard (eds.) (1986). *Handbook of Labor Economics*, 2 vols. (North-Holland, Amsterdam).

Azariadis, Costas, and Allen Drazen (1990). 'Threshold Externalities in Economic Development', *Quarterly Journal of Economics*, 105/2: 501–26.

Baily, M. N. (1981). 'Productivity and the Services of Capital and Labor', *Brookings Papers on Economic Activity*, 1: 1–57.

—— (1984). 'Will Productivity Growth Recover? Has it Done So Already?', *American Economic Review, Papers and Proceedings*, 74/2: 231–5.

—— and R. J. Gordon (1989). 'Measurement Issues, the Productivity Slowdown and the Explosion of Computer Power', *Discussion Paper* 305 (Centre for Economic Policy Research, London).

Balassa, Bela (1964). 'The Purchasing-Power Parity Doctrine: A Reappraisal', *Journal of Political Economy*, 72/6: 584–96.

—— (1979a). 'The Changing International Division of Labor in Manufactured Goods', *Banca Nazionale del Lavoro Quarterly Review*, 130: 243–85.

—— (1979b). 'The Changing Pattern of Comparative Advantage in Manufactured Goods', *Review of Economics and Statistics,* 61/2: 259–79.

—— (1981). 'The Process of Industrial Development and Alternative Development Strategies', in Bela Balassa, *The Newly Industrialising Countries in the World Economy* (Pergamon, New York).

—— (ed.) (1982). *Development Strategies in Semi-Industrial Economies* (Johns Hopkins Press for the World Bank, Baltimore, Md.).

—— (1986a). 'The Employment Effects of Trade in Manufactured Goods Between Developed and Developing Countries', *Journal of Policy Modelling*, 8/3: 371–90.

—— (1986b). 'Comparative Advantage in Manufactured Goods: A Reappraisal', *Review of Economics and Statistics*, 68/2: 315–19.

—— (1988). 'Essays in Development Strategy', *Occasional Paper* 5 (International Center for Economic Growth, Panama).

—— (1989). *New Directions in the World Economy* (Macmillan, London).

—— and Luc Bauwens (1988). *Changing Trade Patterns in Manufactured Goods: An Econometric Investigation* (North-Holland, Amsterdam).

Balasubramanyam, V. N. (1983). 'Transnational Corporations, Choice of Techniques and Employment in Developing Countries', in Helen Hughes and Burton Weisbrod (eds.), *Human Resources, Employment and Development* (Macmillan, London).

Baldwin, R. E. (1984). 'Trade Policies in Developed Countries', in Jones and Kenen (1984), Vol. 1

Ballance, R. H., J. A. Ansari, and H. W. Singer (1982). *The International Economy and Industrial Development: Trade and Investment in the Third World* (Wheatsheaf, Brighton).

Balls, E., L. F. Katz, and L. H. Summers (1991). 'Britain Divided: Hysteresis and the Regional Dimension of Britain's Unemployment Problem', unpublished paper.

Barro, R.J., and J-W. Lee (1993). 'International Comparisons of Educational Attainment', *NBER Working Paper* 4349 (National Bureau of Economic Research, Cambridge, Mass.).

Battese, G. E., and S. J. Malik (1987). 'Estimation of Elasticities of Substitution for CES Production Functions using Data on Selected Manufacturing Industries in Pakistan', *Pakistan Development Review*, 26/2: 161–77.

—— —— (1988). 'Estimation of Elasticities of Substitution for CES and VES Production Functions using Firm-level Data for Food-processing Industries in Pakistan', *Pakistan Development Review*, 27/1: 59–71.

Bean, C. R., and C. A. Pissarides (1991). 'Skill Shortage and Structural Unemployment in Britain: A (Mis)Matching Approach', in Schioppa (1991).

Beenstock, Michael (1984). *The World Economy in Transition*, 2nd edn. (George Allen & Unwin, London).

Behrman, J. R. (1982). 'Country and Sectoral Variations in Manufacturing Elasticities of Substitution between Capital and Labour', in Krueger (1982).

Berger, M. C., and M. A. Webb (1988). 'Exchange Control Regimes and the Size Distribution of Income', unpublished paper (Dept. of Economics, University of Kentucky).

Berndt, E. R., and M. S. Khaled (1979). 'Parametric Productivity Measurement and Choice among Flexible Functional Forms', *Journal of Political Economy*, 87/6: 1220–45.

Berry, A., and R. H. Sabot (1978). 'Labor Market Performance in Developing Countries: A Survey', *World Development*, 6/11–12: 1199–249.

Berthet-Bondet, Claude, Derek Blades, and Annie Pin (1988). 'The OECD Compatible Trade and Production Data Base 1970–1985', *Working Paper* 60 (Dept. of Economics and Statistics, OECD, Paris).

Best, Michael (1990). *The New Competition: Institutions of Industrial Restructuring* (Polity Press, Oxford).

Bhagwati, Jagdish (1984). 'Why are Services Cheaper in the Poor Countries?', *Economic Journal*, 94 (June): 279–86.

—— (1990). 'The International Trading System', *IDS Bulletin* (University of Sussex), 20/1: 8–15.

Bhalla, A. S. (1985). *Technology and Employment in Industry: A Case Study Approach*, 3rd edn. (ILO, Geneva).

Bienefeld, Manfred (1982). 'The International Context for National Development Strategies', in Manfred Bienefeld and Martin Godfrey (eds.), *The Struggle for Development* (John Wiley, Chichester).

—— (1986). 'Growing up in a Hostile World: Which NICs can Advance in the International Economic Hierarchy?', published in German in Alfred Pfaller (ed.), *Der Kampf um den Wohlstand von Morgen* (Verlag Neue Gesellschaft, Bonn).

Bigsten, Arne (1983). *Income Distribution and Development: Theory, Evidence and Policy* (Heinemann, London).

—— (1987). 'Poverty, Inequality and Development', in Norman Gemmell (ed.), *Surveys in Development Economics* (Blackwell, Oxford).

Black, J., and A. I. MacBean (eds.) (1989). *Causes of Changes in the Structure of International Trade 1960–85* (Macmillan, Basingstoke and London).

Blackburn, M. L., and D. E. Bloom (1987). 'The Effects of Technological Change on Earnings and Income Inequality in the United States', *Discussion Paper* 1339 (Harvard Institute of Economic Research, Cambridge, Mass.).

Blades, Derek, *et al.* (1974). *Service Activities in Developing Countries* (OECD, Paris).

Blanchflower, D. G. (1990). Review of Lindbeck and Snower (1989), *Economic Journal*, 100 (Dec.): 1370–73.

Bliss, Christopher (1989). 'Trade and Development', in Chenery and Srinivasan (1989), Vol. 2.

Bluestone, Barry (1990). 'The Impact of Schooling and Industrial Restructuring on Recent Trends in Wage Inequality in the United States', *American Economic Review, Papers and Proceedings*, 80/2: 303–7.

Blundell, Richard (1988). 'Consumer Behaviour: Theory and Empirical Evidence: A Survey', *Economic Journal*, 98 (Mar.): 16–65.

Borooah, V. K., and K. C. Lee (1988). 'The Effect of Changes in Britain's Industrial Structure on Female Relative Pay and Employment', *Economic Journal*, 98 (Sept.): 818–32.

Bound, John, and George Johnson (1992). 'Changes in the Structure of Wages in the 1980s: An Evaluation of Alternative Explanations', *American Economic Review*, 82/3: 371–92.

Bourguignon, François, and Christian Morrisson (1989). *External Trade and Income Distribution* (OECD, Paris).

Bowen, H. P., E. E. Leamer, and L. Sveikauskas (1987). 'Multicountry, Multifactor Tests of the Factor Abundance Theory', *American Economic Review*, 77/5: 791–809.

Bowles, S., D. M. Gordon, and T. E. Weisskopf (1986). 'Power and Profits: The Social Structure of Accumulation and the Profitability of the Postwar US Economy', *Review of Radical Political Economics*, 18/1–2: 132–67.

Brauer, D. A. (1991). 'The Effect of Imports on US Manufacturing Wages', *Federal Reserve Bank of New York Quarterly Review* (Spring): 14–26.

Brecher, Richard (1974). 'Minimum Wage Rates and the Pure Theory of International Trade', *Quarterly Journal of Economics*, 88/1: 98–116.

Brittan, Samuel, and Steven Webb (1990). *Beyond the Welfare State* (Aberdeen University Press for David Hume Institute, Aberdeen).

Brown, D. K. (1988). 'Trade Preferences for Developing Countries: A Survey of Results', *Journal of Development Studies*, 24/3: 335–63.

Carré, J. J., P. Dubois, and E. Malinvaud (1976). *French Economic Growth* (Oxford University Press, Oxford).

Cases, Chantal, and Stefan Lollivier (1989). 'En 1988, les salaires nets ont gagné 0.7% de pouvoir d'achat en moyenne', *Economie et Statistique*, 221 (May).

Champernowne, D. G. (1973). *The Distribution of Income between Persons* (Cambridge University Press, Cambridge).

Chan-Lee, J. H. (1986). 'Pure Profit Rates and Tobin's q in Nine OECD Countries', *Working Paper* 34 (Dept. of Economics and Statistics, OECD, Paris).

—— and H. Sutch (1985). 'Profits and Rates of Return in OECD Countries', *Working Paper* 20 (Dept. of Economics and Statistics, OECD, Paris).

Chau, L. C. (1984). 'Economic Growth and Income Distribution of Hong Kong since early 1950s', *Discussion Paper* 38 (Dept. of Economics, University of Hong Kong).

Chenery H. B., M. S. Ahluwalia, C. L. G. Bell, J. H. Duloy, and R. Jolly (1974). *Redistribution with Growth* (Oxford University Press, Oxford).

Chenery, Hollis, and Moshe Syrquin (1975). *Patterns of Development 1950–1970* (Oxford University Press, Oxford).

—— Sherman Robinson, and Moshe Syrquin (1986). *Industrialization and Growth* (Oxford University Press for the World Bank, Oxford and New York).

—— and T. N. Srinivasan (eds.) (1988, 1989). *Handbook of Development Economics*, 2 vols. (North-Holland, Amsterdam).

Chiplin, B., and P. J. Sloane (1988). 'The Effect of Britain's Anti-Discrimination Legislation on Relative Pay and Employment: A Comment', *Economic Journal*, 98 (Sept.): 833–43.

Choo, Hakchung (1985). 'Estimation of Size Distribution of Income and its Sources of Change in Korea, 1982', *Korean Social Science Journal*, 12: 90–105.

Chow, S. C., and G. F. Papanek (1981). 'Laissez-Faire, Growth and Equity: Hong Kong', *Economic Journal*, 91 (June): 466–85.

Clague, C. K. (1991). 'Factor Proportions, Relative Efficiency and Developing Countries' Trade', *Journal of Development Economics*, 35/2: 357–80.

Clements, B. J., and K. S. Kim (1988). 'Foreign Trade and Income Distribution: the Case of Brazil', *Working Paper* 108 (Helen Kellogg Institute for International Studies, University of Notre Dame, Notre Dame, Ind.).

Colclough, Christopher, with Keith M. Lewin (1993). *Educating All the Children: the Economic Challenge for the 1990s* (Clarendon Press, Oxford).

Corbo, Vittorio and Patricio Meller (1982). 'Substitution of Labour, Skill and Capital: Its Implications for Trade and Employment', in Krueger (1982).

Crafts, N. F. R., and M. Thomas (1986). 'Comparative Advantage in UK Manufacturing Trade 1910–35', *Economic Journal*, 96 (Sept.): 629–45.

Danziger, Sheldon, and Peter Gottschalk (1989). 'Increasing Inequality in the US: What We Know and What We Don't', in Paul Davidson and Jan Kregel (eds.), *Macroeconomic Problems and Policies of Income Distribution* (Edward Elgar, Aldershot).

Davis, S. J. (1992). 'Cross-Country Patterns of Change in Relative Wages', *NBER Working Paper* 4085 (National Bureau of Economic Research, Cambridge, Mass.). Later published in the 1992 *NBER Macroeconomics Annual*.

de Grauwe, P., W. Kennes, T. Peeters, and R. van Straelen (1979). 'Trade Expansion with Less Developed Countries and Employment: A Case Study of Belgium', *Weltwirtschaftliches Archiv*, 115/1: 99–115.

de Leeuw, Frank (1988). 'Gross Product by Industry: Comments on Recent Criticisms', *Survey of Current Business* (July): 132–3.

de Melo, Jaime, and David Tarr (1988). 'Welfare Costs of US Quotas on Textiles, Steel and Autos', *Trade Policy Working Paper* 83 (World Bank, Washington, DC).

—— and Sherman Robinson (1980). 'The Impact of Trade Policies on Income Distribution in a Planning Model for Colombia', *Journal of Policy Modelling*, 2: 81–100.

de Meza, David, and Piergiovanna Natale (1989). 'Efficient Job Creation in LDCs Requires a Tax on Employment', *Economic Journal*, 99 (Dec.): 1112–22.

Deardorff, A. V. (1982). 'The General Validity of the Heckscher–Ohlin Theorem', *American Economic Review*, 72/4: 683–94.

—— (1984a). 'Testing Trade Theories and Predicting Trade Flows', in Jones and Kenen (1984), Vol. 1.

—— (1984b). 'An Exposition and Exploration of Krueger's Trade Model', *Canadian Journal of Economics*, 17/4: 731–46.

Denison, E. F. (1983). 'The Interruption of Productivity Growth in the United States', *Economic Journal*, 93 (Mar.): 56–77.

Dervis, Kemal, Jaime de Melo, and Sherman Robinson (1982). *General Equilibrium Models for Development Policy* (Cambridge University Press, Cambridge).

DGBAS (1977). *Yearbook of Labor Statistics 1977* (Directorate-General of Budget, Accounting and Statistics, Republic of China, Taipei).

—— (1979, 1991). *Statistical Yearbook of China* (Directorate-General of Budget, Accounting and Statistics, Republic of China, Taipei).

—— (1986). *Survey of Personal Income Distribution 1986* (Directorate-General of Budget, Accounting and Statistics, Republic of China, Taipei).

DGBAS (1990). *Yearbook of Earnings and Productivity Statistics* (Directorate-General of Budget, Accounting and Statistics, Republic of China, Taipei).

Dicken, Peter (1986). *Global Shift* (Harper & Row, London).

Dilnot, A. W., J. A. Kay, and C. N. Morris (1984). *The Reform of Social Security* (Clarendon Press, Oxford).

Dolton, P. J., and G. H. Makepeace (1990). 'The Earnings of Economics Graduates', *Economic Journal*, 100 (Mar.): 237–50.

Dooley, M. D. (1987). 'Earnings Inequality among Canadian Men: Recent Changes and Possible Demographic Causes', QSEP *Research Report* 189 (McMaster University, Hamilton, Canada).

Dosi, Giovanni, Keith Pavitt, and Luc Soete (1990). *The Economics of Technical Change and International Trade* (Harvester Wheatsheaf, London).

Driver, Ciaran, Barry Naisbitt, and Andrew Kilpatrick (1984). 'The United Kingdom Employment Effects of Trade Expansion with EEC and NICs', *Working Paper* 17 (National Economic Development Office, HMSO, London).

Eatwell, John, Murray Milgate, and Peter Newman (eds.) (1987). *The New Palgrave*, 4 vols. (Macmillan, London).

EC (1987). *Schemes with an Impact on the Labour Market and their Statistical Treatment in the Member States of the European Community*, Theme 3, Series D (Commission of the European Communities, Brussels).

Edin, Per-Anders, and Bertil Holmlund (1991). 'Unemployment, Vacancies and Labour Market Programmes: Swedish Evidence', in Schioppa (1991).

Ethier, W. J. (1984). 'Higher Dimensional Issues in Trade Theory', in Jones and Kenen (1984), Vol. 1.

Eurostat (1990). *Poverty in Figures: Europe in the Early 1980s* (Statistical Office of the European Communities, Luxembourg).

Evans, H. D. (1989*a*). 'Alternative Perspectives on Trade and Development', in Chenery and Srinivasan (1989), Vol. 2.

—— (1989*b*). *Comparative Advantage and Growth: Trade and Development in Theory and Practice* (Wheatsheaf, Brighton).

Fei, J. C. H., G. Ranis, and F. W. Y. Kuo (1979). *Growth with Equity: The Taiwan Case* (Oxford University Press, New York).

Feinstein, C. H. (1972). *National Income, Expenditure and Output of the United Kingdom 1855–1965* (Cambridge University Press, Cambridge).

Fields, G. S. (1990). 'Poverty and Inequality in Latin America: Some New Evidence', unpublished paper (Dept. of Economics, Cornell University).

—— (1980). *Poverty, Inequality and Development* (Cambridge University Press, Cambridge).

—— (1984). 'Employment, Income Distribution and Economic Growth in Seven Small Open Economies', *Economic Journal*, 94 (Mar.): 74–83.

—— (1988). 'Income Distribution and Economic Growth', in G. Ranis and T. P. Schultz (eds.), *The State of Development Economics: Progress and Perspectives* (Blackwell, Oxford).

—— (1989). 'A Compendium of Data on Inequality and Poverty for the Developing World', unpublished paper (Dept. of Economics, Cornell University).

—— and G. H. Jakubson (1990). 'The Inequality-Development Relationship in

Developing Countries', unpublished paper (Dept. of Economics, Cornell University).

Findlay, Ronald (1978). 'Relative Backwardness, Direct Foreign Investment and the Transfer of Technology: A Simple Dynamic Model', *Quarterly Journal of Economics*, 92/1: 1–16.

—— and Henryk Kierzkowski (1983). 'International Trade and Human Capital: A Simple General Equilibrium Model', *Journal of Political Economy*, 91/6: 957–78.

Fischer, Bernhard, and Dean Spinanger (1986). 'Factor Market Distortions and Export Performance: An Eclectic Review of the Evidence', *Kiel Working Paper* 259 (Institut für Weltwirtschaft an der Universitat Kiel).

Forstner, Helmut, and Robert Ballance (1990). *Competing in a Global Economy: An Empirical Study on Specialisation and Trade in Manufactures* (Unwin Hyman, London).

Franz, Wolfgang (1991). 'Match and Mismatch on the German Labour Market', in Schioppa (1991).

Freeman, R. B. (1976). *The Overeducated American* (Academic Press, New York).

—— (1980). 'The Facts About the Declining Economic Value of College', *Journal of Human Resources*, 15/1: 124–42.

—— (1982). 'The Changing Economic Value of Higher Education in Developed Economies: A Report to the OECD', *Discussion Paper* 874 (Harvard Institute of Economic Research, Harvard University, Cambridge, Mass.).

—— (1986). 'The Demand for Education', in Ashenfelter and Layard (1986), Vol. 1.

—— (1987). 'Factor Prices, Employment and Inequality in a Decentralised Labour Market', in *Analysis of the Dynamics of the Job Creation Process in the United States and an Evaluation of Medium and Long Term Prospects*, iii, Programme for Research and Actions on the Development of the Labour Market (Commission of the European Communities, Luxembourg).

—— (1991*a*). 'Labor Market Tightness and the Mismatch between Demand and Supply of Less-Educated Young Men in the United States in the 1980s', in Schioppa (1991).

—— (1991*b*). 'Crime and the Employment of Disadvantaged Youths', *NBER Working Paper* 3875 (National Bureau of Economic Research, Cambridge, Mass.).

—— and L. F. Katz (1991). 'Industrial Wage and Employment Determination in an Open Economy', in J. M. Abowd and R. B. Freeman (eds.), *Immigration, Trade and the Labor Market* (University of Chicago Press, Chicago).

Fröbel, Folker (1984). 'The Current Development of the World Economy', in Herb Addo (ed.), *Transforming the World Economy* (Hodder & Stoughton, London).

—— Jürgen Heinrichs, and Otto Kreye (1980). *The New International Division of Labour* (Cambridge University Press, Cambridge).

—— —— —— (forthcoming). *Recasting the World Economy*, unpublished type-script of book.

Galbraith, J. K., and P. D. P. Calmon (1990). 'Relative Wages and International Competitiveness in US Industry', *Working Paper* 56 (LBJ School of Public Affairs, University of Texas at Austin).

Gasiorek, Michael, Alasdair Smith, and Anthony Venables (1991). 'Completing the Internal Market in the EC: Factor Demands and Comparative Advantage', in Alan Winters and Anthony Venables (eds.), *European Integration: Trade and Industry* (Cambridge University Press, Cambridge).

Gershenkron, Alexander (1966). *Economic Backwardness in Historical Perspective* (Harvard University Press, Cambridge, Mass.).

Girard, Jean-Paul, and Jean-Louis Lhéritier (1991). 'L'Evolution des Salaires en 1990 dans le Secteur Privé', *INSEE Première*, 145 (June).

Glismann, H. H., and D. Spinanger (1982). 'Employment and Income Effects of Relocating Textile Industries', *The World Economy*, 5/1: 105–9.

Godfrey, Martin (1985). *Global Unemployment* (Wheatsheaf, Brighton).

Goldin, C., and R. A. Margo (1992). 'The Great Compression: the Wage Structure in the United States at Mid-Century', *Quarterly Journal of Economics*, 107/1: 1–34.

Goldsbrough, D. J. (1981). 'International Trade of Multinational Corporations and its Responsiveness to Changes in Aggregate Demand and Relative Prices', *IMF Staff Papers*, 28: 573–99.

Goldstein, M., and M. S. Khan (1982). 'Effects of Slowdown in Industrial Countries on Growth in Non-Oil Developing Countries', *Occasional Paper* 12 (International Monetary Fund, Washington, DC).

—— —— (1985). 'Income and Price Effects in Foreign Trade', in Jones and Kenen (1985), Vol. 2.

Gray, J. P. (1985). *Free Trade or Protection? A Pragmatic Analysis* (Macmillan, London).

Gregory, Peter (1986). *The Myth of Market Failure: Employment and the Labor Market in Mexico* (Johns Hopkins University Press for the World Bank, Baltimore, Md.).

Griliches, Zvi (1980). 'R&D and the Productivity Slowdown', *American Economic Review, Papers and Proceedings*, 70/2: 343–52.

Grossman, G. M. (1982). 'The Employment and Wage Effects of Import Competition in the United States', Working Paper 1041, NBER (Cambridge, Mass.). Repr. in *Journal of International Economic Integration*, 1987, 2: 1–23.

—— (1986). 'Imports as a Cause of Injury: the Case of the US Steel Industry', *Journal of International Economics*, 20/2: 201–23.

—— and E. Helpman (1991). *Innovation and Growth in the Global Economy* (MIT Press, Cambridge, Mass.).

—— and J. A. Levinsohn (1989). 'Import Competition and the Stock Market Return to Capital', *American Economic Review*, 79/5: 1065–87.

Hahn, F. H., and R. C. O. Matthews (1965). 'The Theory of Economic Growth: A Survey', in *Surveys of Economic Theory*, ii (Growth and Development), published for the American Economic Association and the Royal Economic Society (Macmillan, London).

Hamermesh, D. S. (1986). 'The Demand for Labour in the Long Run', in Ashenfelter and Layard (1986) Vol. 1.

Hamilton, C. B. (1989). 'The Political Economy of Transient "New" Protectionism', *Weltwirtschaftliches Archiv*, 125/3: 522–46.

—— and L. A. Winters (1992). 'Opening Up Trade with Eastern Europe', *Economic Policy*, 14 (Apr.): 78–116.

Harberger, A. C. (1977). 'Perspectives on Capital and Technology in Less Developed Countries', in M. J. Artis and A. R. Nobay (eds.), *Contemporary Economic Analysis* (Croom Helm, London).

Harrison, Bennett, and Barry Bluestone (1990). 'Wage Polarisation in the US and the Flexibility Debate', *Cambridge Journal of Economics*, 14/3: 351–73.

Helpman, Elhanan (1984a). 'Increasing Returns, Imperfect Markets and Trade Theory', in Jones and Kenen (1984), Vol. 1.

—— (1984b). 'The Factor Content of Foreign Trade', *Economic Journal*, 94 (Mar.): 84–94.

—— (1989). 'The Noncompetitive Theory of International Trade and Trade Policy', in *Proceedings of the World Bank Annual Conference on Development Economics*, Washington, DC: 193–216.

Henle, Peter, and Paul Ryscavage (1980). 'The Distribution of Earned Income among Men and Women, 1958–77', *Monthly Labor Review* (Apr.): 3–10.

Heyneman, S. P., and W. A. Loxley (1983). 'The Effect of Primary-School Quality on Academic Achievement across Twenty-Nine High- and Low-Income Countries', *American Journal of Sociology*, 88/6: 1162–94.

Hill, T. P. (1979). *Profits and Rates of Return* (OECD, Paris).

Hoffman, Kurt, and Raphael Kaplinsky (1988). *Driving Force: the Global Restructuring of Technology, Labour and Investment in the Automobile and Components Industries* (Westview Press, Boulder, Col.).

Holland, D. M. (ed.) (1984). *Measuring Profitability and Capital Costs: An International Study* (Lexington Books, Lexington, Mass.).

—— and S. M. Myers (1984). 'Trends in Corporate Profitability and Capital Costs in the United States', in Holland (1984).

Hufbauer, G. C., D. T. Berliner, and K. A. Elliot (1986). *Trade Protection in the United States: 31 Case Studies* (Institute for International Economics, Washington, DC).

—— and H. F. Rosen (1986). *Trade Policy for Troubled Industries* (Institute for International Economics, Washington, DC).

Hughes, Helen, and Jean Waelbroeck (1981). 'Can Developing-Country Exports Keep Growing in the 1980s?', *The World Economy*, 4/2: 127–48.

IEA (1973). International Association for the Evaluation of Educational Achievement, *International Studies in Evaluation I, Science Education in 19 Countries: An Empirical Study* (Wiley, New York).

IER (1989). Institute for Employment Research, *Bulletin* 4 (University of Warwick).

Ikemoto, Yukio, and Kitti Limskul (1987). 'Income Inequality and Regional Disparity in Thailand, 1962–81', *The Developing Economies*, 25/3: 249–69.

Inkeles, Alex (1979). 'National Differences in Scholastic Performance', *Comparative Education Review*, 23/3: 386–407.

Ishizaki, Tadao (1985–6). 'Is Japan's Income Distribution Equal? An International Comparison', *Japanese Economic Studies*, 14/2: 30–55.

Jackman, Richard (1986). *A Job Guarantee for Long-Term Unemployed People* (Employment Institute, London).

—— Richard Layard, and Savvas Savouri (1991). 'Mismatch: A Framework for Thought', in Schioppa (1991). Repr. without substantive change in Layard, Nickell, and Jackman (1991, ch. 4).

Jackman, Richard, and Stephen Roper (1987). 'Structural Unemployment', *Oxford Bulletin of Economics and Statistics*, 49/1: 9–36.

Jain, Shail (1975). *Size Distribution of Income: A Compilation of Data* (World Bank, Washington, DC).

Johnson, George, and Richard Layard (1986). 'The Natural Rate of Unemployment: Explanation and Policy', in Ashenfelter and Layard (1986) Vol. 2.

Johnson, H. G. (1968). *Comparative Cost and Commercial Policy Theory for a Developing World Economy*, Wicksell Lectures (Almqvist and Wiksell, Stockholm). Repr. in *Pakistan Development Review*, Spring 1969.

Jones, R. W. (1980). 'Comparative and Absolute Advantage', *Schweizerische Zeitschrift für Volkswirtschaft und Statistik*, 3: 235–260; also available as Reprint Series 153 (Institute of International Economic Studies, University of Stockholm).

—— and P. B. Kenen (eds.) (1984, 1985). *Handbook of International Economics*, 2 vols. (North-Holland, Amsterdam).

—— and J. P. Neary (1984). 'The Positive Theory of International Trade', in Jones and Kenen (1984), Vol. 1.

Jorgenson, Dale (1985). 'Technical Change', in Michael Intriligator and Zvi Griliches (eds.), *Handbook of Econometrics*, Vol. 3 (North-Holland, Amsterdam).

Juhn, Chinhui (1992). 'Decline of Male Labor Market Participation: the Role of Declining Market Opportunities', *Quarterly Journal of Economics*, 107/1: 79–121.

—— Kevin Murphy, and Brooks Pierce (1989). 'Wage Inequality and the Rise in Returns to Skill', unpublished paper, University of Chicago. To appear in the *Journal of Political Economy*.

Julius, DeAnne (1991). 'Direct Investment among Developed Countries: Lessons for the Developing World', *IDS Bulletin* (University of Sussex), 22/2: 15–20.

Kaldor, Nicholas (1956). 'Alternative Theories of Distribution', *Review of Economic Studies*, 23/2: 83–100.

—— (1957). 'A Model of Economic Growth', *Economic Journal*, 67 (Dec.): 591–624.

—— (1966). 'Marginal Productivity and the Macroeconomic Theories of Distribution', *Review of Economic Studies*, 33/4: 309–19.

Kaneko, Motohisa (1986). 'The Educational Composition of the World's Population: A Database', *Education and Training Series Discussion Paper* EDT29 (World Bank, Washington, DC).

Kaplinsky, Raphael (1984). 'The International Context for Industrialisation in the Third World', *Journal of Development Studies*, 21/1: 75–96.

—— (1987). *Microelectronics and Employment Revisited: A Review* (ILO, Geneva).

—— (1991a). 'Direct Foreign Investment in Third World Manufacturing: Is the Future an Extension of the Past?', *IDS Bulletin* (University of Sussex), 22/2: 29–35.

—— (1991b). 'The New Flexibility: Promoting Social and Economic Efficiency', paper prepared for conference on The Efficient Society: Competition, Cooperation and Welfare, Budapest, 20–2 Sept.

Katz, L.F., and A. B. Krueger (1992). 'The Effect of the Minimum Wage on the Fast Food Industry', *NBER Working Paper* 3997 (National Bureau of Economic Research, Cambridge, Mass.).

—— and K. M. Murphy (1992). 'Changes in Relative Wages 1963–1987: Supply and Demand Factors', *Quarterly Journal of Economics*, 107/1: 35–78.

—— and G. W. Loveman (1990). 'An International Comparison of Changes in the Structure of Wages: France, the United Kingdom and the United States', unpublished paper, Harvard University.

—— and A. L. Revenga (1989). 'Changes in the Structure of Wages: the United States versus Japan', *Journal of the Japanese and International Economies*, 3: 522–53.

—— and L. H. Summers (1989). 'Industry Rents: Evidence and Implications', *Brookings Papers on Economic Activity: Microeconomics 1989*: 209–90.

Keesing, D. B. (1965). 'Labour Skills and International Trade: Evaluating Many Trade Flows with a Single Measuring Device', *Review of Economics and Statistics*, 47/3: 287–94.

—— (1966). 'Labour Skills and Comparative Advantage', *American Economic Review, Papers and Proceedings*, 56/2: 249–58.

—— (1974). 'Income Distribution from Outward-Looking Development Policies', *Pakistan Development Review*, 13/2: 188–204.

—— (1979). 'Trade Policy for Developing Countries', *World Bank Staff Working Paper* 353 (Washington, DC).

Kendrick, J. W., and M. Pech (1973). *Postwar Productivity Trends in the US 1948–69* (National Bureau of Economic Research, New York).

Kim, K. S., and P. Vorasopontaviporn (1989). 'Foreign Trade and the Distribution of Income in Thailand', *Working Paper* 124 (Helen Kellogg Institute for International Studies (University of Notre Dame, Notre Dame, Ind.).

Kindleberger, C. P. (1963). *International Economics*, 3rd edn. (Irwin, Homewood, Ill.).

King, Mervyn, and Jacques Mairesse (1984). 'Profitability in Britain and France 1956–1975: A Comparative Study', in Holland (1984).

Knight, J. B., and 'R. H. Sabot (1983). 'Educational Expansion and the Kuznets Effect', *American Economic Review*, 73/5: 1132–6.

Koekkoek, A. A., and L. B. M. Mennes (1984). 'Revealed Comparative Advantage in Manufacturing Industry: the Case of the Netherlands', *De Economist*, 132/1: 30–48.

Kol, Jacob (1986). 'Key Sectors, Comparative Advantage and International Shifts in Employment', paper presented at the Eighth International Conference on Input-Output Techniques, in William Peterson (ed.), *Advances in Input–Output Analysis: Technology, Planning and Development* (Oxford University Press, New York, 1991).

—— and L. B. M. Mennes (1983). 'Trade and Industrial Employment: An Accounting for Growth Approach with an Application to the Netherlands', in I. Dobozi and P. Mandi (eds.), *Emerging Development Patterns: European Contributions* (EADI, Budapest).

Kosters, M. H. (1990). 'Schooling, Work Experience and Wage Trends', *American Economic Review, Papers and Proceedings*, 80/2: 308–12.

Kravis, I. B., A. Heston, and R. Summers (1982). *World Product and Income: International Comparisons of Real Gross Product* (Johns Hopkins University Press for the World Bank, Baltimore, Md.).

Kravis, I. B., A. Heston, and R. Summers (1983). 'The Share of Services in Economic Growth', in B. G. Hickman and F. G. Adams, *Global Econometrics* (MIT Press, Cambridge, Mass.).

Krueger, A. B. (1991). 'How Computers Have Changed the Wage Structure: Evidence from Microdata 1984–89', *NBER Working Paper* 3858 (National Bureau of Economic Research, Cambridge, Mass.).

Krueger, A. O. (1977). 'Growth, Distortions and Patterns of Trade Among Many Countries', *Princeton Studies in International Finance*, 40; repr. with minor revisions as Krueger (1983, ch. 4).

—— (1978). *Foreign Trade Regimes and Economic Development: Liberalization Attempts and Consequences* (National Bureau of Economic Research, New York).

—— (1980). 'LDC Manufacturing Production and Implications for OECD Comparative Advantage', in I. Leveson and J. W. Wheeler (eds.), *Western Economies in Transition* (Westview Press, Boulder, Col.).

—— (ed.) (1982). *Trade and Employment in Developing Countries: 2 Factor Supply and Substitution* (University of Chicago Press, Chicago, Ill.).

—— (1983). *Trade and Employment in Developing Countries: 3 Synthesis and Conclusions* (University of Chicago Press, Chicago, Ill.).

—— H. B. Lary, T. Monson, and N. Akrasanee (eds.) (1981). *Trade and Employment in Developing Countries: 1 Individual Studies* (University of Chicago Press, Chicago, Ill.).

Krugman, Paul (1979). 'A Model of Innovation, Technology Transfer and the World Distribution of Income', *Journal of Political Economy*, 87/2: 253–66.

—— (1991). *Geography and Trade* (MIT Press, Cambridge, Mass.).

Kuo, Shirley (1989). 'Income Distribution and Foreign Trade: the Case of Taiwan', in Bourguignon and Morrisson (1989).

Kuznets, P. W. (1988). 'Employment Absorption in South Korea: 1970–1980', *Philippine Review of Economics and Business*, 25/1–2: 41–70.

Kuznets, Simon (1955). 'Economic Growth and Income Inequality', *American Economic Review*, 45/1: 1–28.

Kwack, S. Y. (1987). 'Economic Development in South Korea', in L. J. Lau (ed.), *Models of Development: A Comparative Study of Economic Growth in South Korea and Taiwan*, revd. edn. (ICS Press, San Francisco).

Lary, H. B. (1968). *Imports of Manufactures from Less Developed Countries* (National Bureau of Economic Research, New York).

Lawrence, R. Z. (1984). 'Sectoral Shifts and the Size of the Middle Class', *The Brookings Review* (Fall): 3–11.

Layard, Richard (1985). 'How to Reduce Unemployment by Changing National Insurance Contributions and Providing a Job Guarantee', *Discussion Paper* 218 (Centre for Labour Economics, London School of Economics).

—— (1986). *How to Beat Unemployment* (Oxford University Press, Oxford).

—— and Alan Walters (1978). *Microeconomic Theory* (McGraw-Hill, New York).

—— and Stephen Nickell (1986). 'The Performance of the British Labour Market', paper for presentation at the Conference on the British Economy, Isle of Thorns, Haywards Heath, Sussex, 18–21 May.

—— —— and Richard Jackman (1991). *Unemployment* (Oxford University Press, Oxford).

Leamer, E. E. (1984). *Sources of International Comparative Advantage: Theory and Evidence* (MIT Press, Cambridge, Mass.).

—— (1987). 'Paths of Development in the Three-Factor, n-Good General Equilibrium Model', *Journal of Political Economy*, 95/5: 961–99.

Lecaillon, Jacques, Felix Paukert, Christian Morrisson, and Dimitri Germidis (1984). *Income Distribution and Economic Development: An Analytical Survey* (ILO, Geneva).

Lee, Eddy (1984). *Export Processing Zones and Industrial Employment in Asia*, Asian Employment Programme (ARTEP) (ILO, Bangkok).

Lee, J. K. (1989). 'Why are Koreans not Happy about their own State of Distribution', *Seoul Journal of Economics*, 2/4: 367–81.

Lee, J. W. (1986–7). 'Economic Development and Wage Distribution in South Korea', *Korean Social Science Journal*, 13: 78–94.

Lee, T. H., and K. S. Liang (1982). 'Taiwan', in Balassa (1982).

Lee, W. D. (1991). 'Economic Growth and Earnings Distribution in Korea', in Mizoguchi (1991).

Lee, Y. S. (1986). 'Changing Export Patterns in Korea, Taiwan and Japan', *Weltwirtschaftliches Archiv*, 122/1: 150–63.

Leontief, Wassily (1982). 'The Distribution of Work and Income', *Scientific American*, 247/3: 188–204.

Lewis, W. A. (1954). 'Economic Development with Unlimited Supplies of Labour', *Manchester School of Economic and Social Studies*, 22/2: 139–91.

Lhéritier, Jean-Louis (1990). 'L'Evolution des Salaires dans le Secteur Privé en 1989', *INSEE Première*, 85 (June).

Lim, Linda (1980). 'Women in the Redeployment of Manufacturing Industry to Developing Countries', *Working Paper on Structural Change* 18 (UNIDO, Vienna).

—— and Pang Eng Fong (1982). 'Trade, Employment and Industrialisation in Singapore', *International Division of Labour Working Paper* 17, World Employment Programme (ILO, Geneva).

Lin, T. B. (1985). 'Growth, Equity and Income Distribution Policies in Hong Kong', *The Developing Economies*, 23/4: 391–413.

Lindbeck, Assar (1983). 'The Recent Slowdown of Productivity Growth', *Economic Journal*, 93 (Mar.): 13–34.

—— and Dennis Snower (1989). *The Insider–Outsider Theory of Employment and Unemployment* (MIT Press, Cambridge, Mass. and London).

Lipsey, R. E., I. B. Kravis, and R. A. Roldan (1982). 'Do Multinational Firms Adapt Factor Proportions to Relative Factor Prices?', in Krueger (1982).

Little, I. M. D., D. Mazumdar, and J. M. Page (1987). *Small Manufacturing Enterprises: A Comparative Study of India and Other Economies* (Oxford University Press for the World Bank, Oxford and New York).

Lluch, C., A. A. Powell, and R. A. Williams (1979). *Patterns in Household Demand and Saving* (Oxford University Press for the World Bank, Oxford and New York).

LNJ: see Layard, Nickell, and Jackman (1991).

Lovell, M. C. (1978). 'The Profit Picture: Trends and Cycles', *Brookings Papers on Economic Activity*, 3: 769–88.

Lydall, H. F. (1975). *Trade and Employment* (ILO, Geneva).

Machin, Stephen and Alan Manning (1992). 'Minimum Wages, Wage Dispersion and Employment: Evidence from the UK Wages Councils', *Centre for Economic Performance Discussion Paper* 80 (London School of Economics).

Mahler, V. A. (1989). 'Income Distribution Within Nations: Problems of Cross-National Comparison', *Comparative Political Studies*, 22/1: 3–32.

Malinvaud, Edmond (1987). 'The Rise of Unemployment in France', in C. R. Bean, P. R. G. Layard, and S. J. Nickell (eds.), *The Rise in Unemployment* (Blackwell, Oxford).

Markusen, J. R., and R. M. Wigle (1990). 'Explaining the Volume of North–South Trade', *Economic Journal*, 100 (Dec.): 1206–15.

Marsden, David (1989a). 'Occupations: the Influence of the Unemployment Situation', in Willem Molle and Aad van Mourik (eds.), *Wage Differentials in the European Community: Convergence or Divergence* (Avebury, Aldershot).

—— (1989b). 'The Flexibility of Relative Wages and Changing Economic Conditions', unpublished paper, London School of Economics.

—— (1990). 'Merit Pay: the Decline of Rate for the Job Systems?', unpublished paper, London School of Economics.

Martin, J. P., and J. M. Evans (1981). 'Notes on Measuring the Employment Displacement Effects of Trade by the Accounting Procedure', *Oxford Economic Papers*, 33/1: 154–64.

Metcalfe, J. S., and I. Steedman (1981). 'On the Transformation of Theorems', *Journal of International Economics*, 11/2: 267–71.

Micklewright, John (1984). 'Male Unemployment and the Family Expenditure Survey 1972–80', *Oxford Bulletin of Economics and Statistics*, 46/1: 31–53.

Minford, Patrick (1989). 'A Labour-Based Theory of International Trade', in Black and MacBean (1989).

Mishel, Lawrence, and Jacqueline Simon (1988). *The State of Working America* (Economic Policy Institute, Washington, DC).

Mizoguchi, Toshiyuki (1985a). 'Economic Development Policy and Income Distribution: The Experience in East and Southeast Asia', *The Developing Economies*, 23/4: 307–24.

—— (1985b). 'Economic, Sociological and Industrial Factors in Changes of Size Distribution of Household Income: Japanese Experience in a Century', *Discussion Paper* 120 (Institute of Economic Research, Hitotsubashi University, Tokyo).

—— (ed.) (1991). *Making Economies More Efficient and More Equitable: Factors Determining Income Distribution* (Kinokuniya Company, Tokyo, and Oxford University Press, Oxford and New York).

—— and Noriyuki Takayama (1984). *Equity and Poverty Under Rapid Growth: The Japanese Experience*, Economic Research Series 21 (Institute of Economic Research, Hitotsubashi University, Tokyo).

—— et al. (1980). 'Appendix: Statistics for Studies on Poverty in Asian Countries', *Philippine Economic Journal*, 19/2: 296–357.

Mohan, Rakesh, and Richard Sabot (1988). 'Educational Expansion and the Inequality of Pay: Colombia 1973–78', *Oxford Bulletin of Economics and Statistics*, 50/2: 175–82.

Moll, Terence (1991). 'Why is Earnings Inequality in the United Kingdom Rising?', forthcoming in *Labour*.

—— (1992). 'Mickey Mouse Numbers and Inequality Research in Developing Countries', *Journal of Development Studies*, 28/4: 689–704.

Moore, Mick (1990). 'Economic Liberalisation, Growth and Poverty: Sri Lanka in Long Run Perspective', *IDS Discussion Paper* 274 (Institute of Development Studies, University of Sussex).

Morawetz, David (1976). 'Elasticities of Substitution in Industry: What Do We Learn From Econometric Estimates?', *World Development*, 4/1: 11–15.

Murphy, Kevin, and Finis Welch (1989). 'Wage Differentials in the 1980s: the Role of International Trade' (University of Chicago, UCLA and Unicon Research Corporation). Subsequently published in Marvin Kosters (ed.), *Workers and Their Wages: Changing Patterns in the United States* (American Enterprise Institute, Washington, DC, 1991).

—— —— (1992). 'The Structure of Wages', *Quarterly Journal of Economics*, 107/1: 285–326.

—— Mark Plant, and Finis Welch (1988). 'Cohort Size and Earnings in the United States', in R. D. Lee, W. B. Arthur, and G. Rodgers (eds.), *Economics of Changing Age Distribution in Developed Countries* (Clarendon Press, Oxford).

Murray, Robin (1992). 'Flexible Specialisation in Small Island Economies: the Case of Cyprus', in F. Pyke and W. Sengenberger (eds.), *Industrial Districts and Local Economic Regeneration* (International Institute for Labour Studies, Geneva).

Muscatelli, V. A., T. G. Srinivasan, and D. Vines (1992). 'Demand and Supply Factors in the Determination of NIE Exports: A Simultaneous Error-Correction Model for Hong Kong', *Economic Journal*, 102 (Nov.): 1467–77.

Myles, John (1987). 'The Expanding Middle: Some Canadian Evidence on the Deskilling Debate', *Research Paper* 9 (Analytical Studies Branch, Statistics Canada).

—— Garnett Picot and Ted Wannell (1988). 'Wages and Jobs in the 1980s: Changing Youth Wages and the Declining Middle', *Research Paper* 17 (Analytical Studies Branch, Statistics Canada).

Nickell, Stephen (1990). 'Unemployment: A Survey', *Economic Journal*, 100 (June): 391–439.

Niroomand, Farhang (1991). 'Factor Inputs and US Manufacturing Trade Structure 1963–1980', *Weltwirtschaftliches Archiv*, 127/4: 744–63.

North–South Institute (1989). *Trade, Protectionism and Industrial Adjustment: Three North American Case Studies* (Ottawa).

OECD (1969a). *Statistics of the Occupational and Educational Structure of the Labour Force in 53 Countries* (OECD, Paris).

—— (1969b). *Occupational and Educational Structures of the Labour Force and Levels of Economic Development, Possibilities and Limitations of an International Comparison Approach* (OECD, Paris).

—— (1979). *The Impact of the Newly Industrialising Countries on Production and Trade in Manufactures* (OECD, Paris).

—— (1985). *Costs and Benefits of Protection* (OECD, Paris).

—— (1989). *Trade and Employment*, unpublished report (OECD, Paris).

OECD-EO (various years). *Employment Outlook* (OECD, Paris).

Ohkawa, Kazushi, and Henry Rosovsky (1973). *Japanese Economic Growth* (Stanford University Press, Stanford, Calif.).

Ohlin, Bertil (1933, 1967). *Interregional and International Trade* (Harvard University Press, Cambridge, Mass.). (1st edn. 1933; page references are to revd. edn., 1967.)

Ozawa, Masako (1985–86). 'Myths of Affluence and Equality', *Japanese Economic Studies*, 14/2: 56–99.

Pack, Howard (1987). *Productivity, Technology and Industrial Development: A Case Study in Textiles* (Oxford University Press, Oxford).

—— (1988). 'Industrialisation and Trade', in Chenery and Srinivasan (1988), Vol. 1.

Papanek, G. F., and O. Kyn (1987). 'Flattening the Kuznets Curve: The Consequences for Income Distribution of Development Strategy, Government Intervention, Income and the Rate of Growth', *Pakistan Development Review*, 26/1: 1–54.

Paqué, Karl-Heinz (1989). 'Is Structural Unemployment a Negligible Problem? A Critical Note on the Use of Mismatch Indices', *Working Paper* 357 (Kiel Institute of World Economics).

—— (1990). 'Unemployment in West Germany: A Survey of Explanations and Policy Options', *Working Paper* 407 (Kiel Institute of World Economics).

Park, Se-il (1988). 'Labour Issues in Korea's Future', *World Development*, 16/1: 99–119.

Pasinetti, L. L. (1981). *Structural Change and Economic Growth* (Cambridge University Press, Cambridge).

Patel, Pari, and Keith Pavitt (1991). 'Europe's Technological Performance', in Christopher Freeman, Margaret Sharp, and William Walker (eds.), *Technology and the Future of Europe* (Pinter, London).

Pavitt, Keith, and Pari Patel (1988). 'The International Distribution and Determinants of Technological Activities', *Oxford Review of Economic Policy*, 4/4: 35–55.

Phelps Brown, E. H. (1977). *The Inequality of Pay* (Oxford University Press, Oxford).

Picot, Garnett, John Myles, and Ted Wannell (1990). 'Good Jobs/Bad Jobs and the Declining Middle: 1967–86', *Research Paper* 28 (Analytical Studies Branch, Statistics Canada).

Pilgrim Trust (1938). *Men Without Work* (Cambridge University Press, Cambridge).

Posner, M. V. (1961). 'International Trade and Technical Change', *Oxford Economic Papers*, 31/3: 323–41.

Psacharopoulos, George (1980). 'Returns to Education: An Updated International Comparison', in T. King (ed.), 'Education and Income', *World Bank Staff Working Paper* 402 (Washington, DC).

—— (ed.) (1987). *Economics of Education: Research and Studies* (Pergamon, Oxford).

—— (1988). 'Education and Development: A Review', *World Bank Research Observer*, 3/1: 99–116.

—— and Ana Maria Arriagada (1986). 'The Educational Composition of the Labour Force: An International Comparison', *World Bank Reprint Series* 402 (Washington DC).

Ramanayake, Dennis (1984). 'Sri Lanka: The Katunayake Investment Promotion Zone', in Lee (1984).

Ranis, Gustav (1991). 'The Political Economy of Development Policy Change', in G. Meier (ed.), *Politics and Policy Making in Less Developed Countries* (International Center for Economic Growth, San Francisco, Calif.).

Rao, V. V. B. and M. K. Ramakrishnan (1980). 'Economic Growth, Employment Expansion and Reduction in Income Inequality: the Singapore Experience 1966–1975', in Kazushi Ohkawa and Bernard Key (eds.), *Asian Socioeconomic Development* (The University Press of Hawaii, Honolulu, Ha.).

Reati, Angelo (1986). 'The Rate of Profit and the Organic Composition of Capital in West German Industry from 1960 to 1981', *Review of Radical Political Economics*, 18/1–2: 56–86.

Reich, R. B. (1989). 'As the World Turns', *New Republic*, 1 May: 23–8.

—— (1991). *The Work of Nations: Preparing Ourselves for 21st Century Capitalism* (Simon and Schuster, New York).

Renshaw, Geoffrey (1986). *Adjustment and Economic Performance in Industrialised Countries: A Synthesis* (ILO, Geneva).

Revenga, A. L. (1990). 'Wage Determination in an Open Economy: International Trade and US Manufacturing Wages', unpublished paper (Harvard University).

—— (1992). 'Exporting Jobs? The Impact of Import Competition on Employment and Wages in US Manufacturing', *Quarterly Journal of Economics*, 107/1: 255–84.

Rhee, Y. W., B. Ross-Larson, and G. Pursell (1984). *Korea's Competitive Edge: Managing Entry into World Markets* (Johns Hopkins University Press, Baltimore, Md.).

Riedel, James (1988). 'The Demand for LDC Exports of Manufactures: Estimates from Hong Kong', *Economic Journal*, 98 (Mar.): 138–48.

Robinson, Sherman (1976). 'A Note on the U Hypothesis Relating Income Inequality and Economic Development', *American Economic Review*, 66/3: 437–40.

Romer, P. M. (1986). 'Increasing Returns and Long-Run Growth', *Journal of Political Economy*, 94/5: 1002–37.

—— (1992). 'Two Strategies for Economic Development: Using Ideas and Producing Ideas', *Proceedings of the World Bank Annual Conference on Development Economics 1992*, Washington, DC.

Rosen, Sherwin (1986). 'The Theory of Equalizing Differences', in Ashenfelter and Layard (1986), Vol. 1.

Routh, Guy (1965). *Occupation and Pay in Great Britain 1906–60* (Cambridge University Press, Cambridge).

Rowthorn R. E., and J. R. Wells (1987). *Deindustrialisation and Foreign Trade* (Cambridge University Press, Cambridge).

Roy, D. J. (1987). 'Eurosclerosis, Productivity Slowdown and Technological Gap: Myth and Reality', unpublished paper (Strategic Studies Department, Central Electricity Generating Board).

Ruffin, R. J. (1984). 'International Factor Movements', in Jones and Kenen (1984), Vol. 1.

Ryscavage, Paul, and Peter Henle (1990). 'Earnings Inequality Accelerates in the 1980s', *Monthly Labor Review* (Dec.): 3–16.

Sachs, J. D. (1979). 'Wages, Profits and Macroeconomic Adjustment: A Comparative Study', *Brookings Papers on Economic Activity*, 2: 269–332.

Salvadori, Neri (1987). 'Non-Substitution Theorems', in Eatwell *et al.* (1987), Vol. 3.

Samuelson, P. A. (1948). 'International Trade and the Equalisation of Factor Prices', *Economic Journal*, 58 (June): 163–84.

—— (1949). 'International Factor-Price Equalisation Once Again', *Economic Journal*, 59 (June): 181–97.

Sapir, André, and Dieter Schumacher (1985). 'The Employment Impact of Shifts in the Composition of Commodity and Services Trade', in *Employment Growth and Structural Change* (OECD, Paris).

Sarkar, Prabirjit, and Hans Singer (1989). 'Manufactured Exports and Terms of Trade Movements of Less Developed Countries in Recent Years', *IDS Discussion Paper* 270 (Institute of Development Studies, University of Sussex).

Saunders, Christopher, and David Marsden (1981). *Pay Inequalities in the European Community* (Butterworth, London).

Saunders, Peter, Garry Hobbes, and Helen Stott (1989). 'Income Inequality in Australia and New Zealand: International Comparisons and Recent Trends', paper presented to the 21st general conference of the International Association for Research on Income and Wealth, Lahnstein, Germany.

Sawyer, Malcolm (1976). 'Income Distribution in OECD Countries', *OECD Economic Outlook, Occasional Studies* (July): 1–36.

—— (1982). 'Income Distribution and the Welfare State', in Andrea Boltho (ed.), *The European Economy: Growth and Crisis* (Oxford University Press, Oxford).

Schioppa, Fiorella Padoa (ed.) (1991). *Mismatch and Labour Mobility* (Cambridge University Press, Cambridge).

Schultz, T. P. (1988). 'Education Investment and Returns', in Chenery and Srinivasan (1988), Vol. 1.

Schumacher, Dieter (1983). 'Intra-Industry Trade Between the Federal Republic of Germany and Developing Countries: Extent and Some Characteristics', in P. K. M. Thakaran (ed.), *Intra-Industry Trade* (North Holland, Amsterdam).

—— (1984). 'North-South Trade and Shifts in Employment', *International Labour Review*, 123/3: 333–48.

—— (1989a). 'Employment Impact in the European Community Countries of East–West Trade Flows', *International Employment Policies Working Paper* 24, World Employment Programme (ILO, Geneva).

—— (1989b). 'Employment Effects of the European Internal Market', *Intereconomics* (Nov./Dec.): 259–67.

—— (1992). 'A Note on the Human Capital Intensity of EC Trade', *Cahiers Economiques de Bruxelles*, 133 (1er trimestre): 3–19.

Scott, M. F. (1989). *A New View of Economic Growth* (Clarendon Press, Oxford).

Seers, Dudley (1983). *The Political Economy of Nationalism* (Oxford University Press, Oxford).

Singh, Ajit (1987). 'Manufacturing and Deindustrialisation', in Eatwell *et al.* (1987), Vol. 3.

Sinn, Stefan (1992). 'Saving-Investment Correlations and Capital Mobility: On the Evidence from Annual Data', *Economic Journal*, 102 (Sept.): 1162–70.

Slade, M. E. (1989). 'Modeling Stochastic and Cyclical Components of Technical Change: An Application of the Kalman Filter', *Journal of Econometrics*, 41/3: 363–83.

Smith, M. A. M. (1984). 'Capital Theory and Trade Theory', in Jones and Kenen (1984), Vol. 1.

Solow, R. M. (1990). *The Labor Market as a Social Institution* (Blackwell, Oxford and Cambridge, Mass.).

Soskice, David (1991). 'Skill Mismatch, Training Systems and Equilibrium Unemployment: A Comparative Institutional Analysis', in Schioppa (1991).

Steedman, Ian (1979a). *Trade Amongst Growing Economies* (Cambridge University Press, Cambridge).

—— (ed.) (1979b). *Fundamental Issues in Trade Theory* (Macmillan, London).

Stevens, Christopher, and Jane Kennan (eds.) (1992). *Reform in Eastern Europe and the Developing Country Dimension* (Overseas Development Institute, London).

Stewart, Frances (1978). *Technology and Underdevelopment*, 2nd edn. (Macmillan, London).

Summers, L. H. (1988). 'Relative Wages, Efficiency Wages and Keynesian Unemployment', *American Economic Review, Papers and Proceedings*, 78/2: 383–94.

Sundrum, R. M. (1990). *Income Distribution in Developing Countries* (Routledge & Kegan Paul, London and New York).

Swamy, Gurushri (1985). 'Population and International Migration', *World Bank Staff Working Paper* 689 (Washington, DC).

Syrquin, Moshe (1988). 'Patterns of Structural Change', in Chenery and Srinivasan (1988), Vol. 1.

—— and Hollis Chenery (1989). 'Patterns of Development: 1950 to 1983', *World Bank Discussion Paper* 41 (Washington, DC).

Tan, A. H. H., and O. C. Hock (1982). 'Singapore', in Balassa (1982).

Taubman, P., and M. L. Wachter (1986). 'Segmented Labour Markets', in Ashenfelter and Layard (1986), Vol. 2.

Terasaki, Yasuhiro (1991). 'Distributional Consequences of Laissez-Faire Policy and Inequality Structure in Hong Kong 1976–1986', in Mizoguchi (1991).

UNCTC (1983). *Transnational Corporations in World Development: Third Survey* (United Nations Center on Transnational Corporations, New York).

—— (1988). *Transnational Corporations in World Development: Trends and Prospects* (United Nations Center on Transnational Corporations, New York).

UNDP (1990, 1991, 1992). United Nations Development Programme, *Human Development Report* (Oxford University Press, Oxford).

UNIDO (1978). 'The Impact of Trade with Developing Countries on Employment in Developed Countries', *Working Paper on Structural Change* 3 (UNIDO, Vienna).

—— (1985, 1986, 1987). *Industry and Development Global Report* (UNIDO, Vienna).

van Ours, J. C., and G. Ridder (1989). 'An Empirical Analysis of Vacancy Durations and Vacancy Flows: Cyclical Variation and Job Requirements', *Research Memorandum* 325 (Institute of Economic Research, Faculty of Economics, University of Groningen).

Varian, H. R. (1978). *Microeconomic Analysis* (Norton, New York).

Venables, Anthony (1985). 'International Trade, Trade and Industrial Policy, and Imperfect Competition: A Survey', *Discussion Paper* 74 (Centre for Economic Policy Research, London).

Ventura-Dias, V., and Sorsa, P. (1985). 'Historical Patterns of South–South Trade (Statistical Handbook)', paper prepared for informal UNCTAD symposium on South–South Trade, Geneva (June).

Vernon, Raymond (1966). 'International Investment and International Trade in the Product Cycle', *Quarterly Journal of Economics*, 80/2: 190–207.

Wade, Robert (1990). *Governing the Market: Economic Theory and the Role of Government in East Asian Industrialisation* (Princeton University Press, Princeton, NJ).

Walsh, Kenneth (1982). *Vacancies Notified: Methods and Measurements in the European Community* (Commission of the European Communities, Luxembourg).

Wang, Z. K., and L. A. Winters (1991). 'Eastern Europe's Trading Potential', *Discussion Paper* 610 (Centre for Economic Policy Research, London).

Watts, H. W. (1987). 'Negative Income Tax', in Eatwell *et al.* (1987), Vol. 3.

Weisskopf, T. E. (1988). 'An Analysis of Profitability Changes in Eight Capitalist Economies', *Review of Radical Political Economics*, 20/2–3: 68–79.

Westphal, L. E., and K. S. Kim (1982). 'Korea', in Balassa (1982).

—— Y. W. Rhee, and G. Pursell (1981). 'Korean Industrial Competence: Where It Came From', *World Bank Staff Working Paper* 469 (Washington, DC).

White, Gordon (1988). *Developmental States in East Asia* (Macmillan, London).

White, Lawrence (1978). 'The Evidence on Appropriate Factor Proportions for Manufacturing in Less Developed Countries: A Survey', *Economic Development and Cultural Change*, 27/1: 27–59.

Williamson, J.G. (1985). *Did British Capitalism Breed Inequality?* (Allen & Unwin, London).

—— and P. Lindert (1980). *American Inequality: A Macroeconomic History* (Academic Press, New York).

Willis, R. J. (1986). 'Wage Determinants: A Survey and Reinterpretation of Human Capital Earnings Functions', in Ashenfelter and Layard (1986), Vol. 1.

Wilson, R. A. (1984). *Impact of Information Technology on the Engineering Industry* (Institute for Employment Research, University of Warwick).

Winters, L. A. (1987, 1989). 'Patterns of World Trade in Manufactures: Does Trade Policy Matter?', *Discussion Paper* 160 (Centre for Economic Policy Research, London). Repr. in Black and MacBean (1989).

Wolf, Martin (1979). 'Adjustment Problems and Policies in Developed Countries', *World Bank Staff Working Paper* 349 (Washington, DC).

—— (1983). 'Fortress Europe and Collective Self-Reliance', *Weltwirtschaft und Internationale Beziehungen, Sonderdrucke: Neue Folge 5* (Deutsches Übersee-Institut, Hamburg).

Wolfson, M. C. (1986*a*). 'Stasis Amid Change: Income Inequality in Canada 1965–1983', *Review of Income and Wealth*, 32/4: 337–69.

—— (1986*b*). 'A Guaranteed Income', *Policy Options* (Jan.): 35–45.

—— (1987). 'The Arithmetic of Income Security Reform', in S. B. Seward and M. Iacobacci (eds.), *Approaches to Income Security Reform* (Institute for Research on Public Policy, Halifax, Nova Scotia).

—— (1989). 'Inequality and Polarisation: Is There a Disappearing Middle Class in Canada?', unpublished paper (Analytical Studies Branch, Statistics Canada).

—— and J. Foster (1991). 'Inequality and Polarisation: Concepts and Recent Trends', unpublished seminar notes (Analytical Studies Branch, Statistics Canada).

Wolleb, Guglielmo (ed.) (1989). *Trends and Distribution of Incomes: An Overview*, Programme for Research and Actions on the Development of the Labour Market (Commission of the European Communities, Brussels).

Wood, Adrian (1975). *A Theory of Profits* (Cambridge University Press, Cambridge).

—— (1978). *A Theory of Pay*, (Cambridge University Press, Cambridge).

—— (1988). 'How Much Unemployment is Structural?', *Oxford Bulletin of Economics and Statistics*, 50/1: 71–81.

—— (1991*a*). 'North–South Trade and Female Labour in Manufacturing: An Asymmetry', *Journal of Development Studies*, 27/2: 168–89.

—— (1991*b*). 'How Much Does Trade with the South Affect Workers in the North', *World Bank Research Observer*, 6/1: 19–36.

—— (1991*c*). 'What Do Developing-Country Manufactured Exports Consist Of?', *Development Policy Review*, 9/2: 177–97.

—— (1991*d*). 'The Factor Content of North–South Trade in Manufactures Reconsidered', *Weltwirtschaftliches Archiv*, 127/4: 719–43.

—— (1991*e*). 'Global Trends in Real Exchange Rates 1960–84', *World Development*, 19/4: 317–32.

—— (1991*f*). 'A New–Old Theoretical View of North–South Trade, Employment and Wages', *IDS Discussion Paper* 292 (Institute of Development Studies, University of Sussex).

World Bank (1985a). *China: Long-Term Development Issues and Options* (Johns Hopkins University Press for the World Bank, Baltimore, Md.).

—— (various years). *World Development Report* (Oxford University Press for the World Bank, New York).

Wright, R. E. (1989). 'Cohort Size and Earnings in Great Britain', *Discussion Paper in Economics* 89/8 (Birkbeck College, University of London).

Yeats, A. J. (1989). 'Developing Countries' Exports of Manufactures: Past and Future Implications of Shifting Patterns of Comparative Advantage', *The Developing Economies*, 27/2: 109–45.

Index

Abraham, K. 272 n., 296–7, 301, 304
accounting decomposition of employment changes 9–10, 106–9
Adams, M. 444, 449, 462, 464
Addison, T. 186 n.
Adelman, I. 220, 224 n., 225–7, 232, 243 n.
agriculture 214, 226, 244; employment in 199, 201–2, 204–5, 208, 209, 216; *see also* trade in primary products
Aid to Families with Dependent Children 371
Akerloff, G. 57, 298, 305
America 23–4, 379, 380–3, 389; *see also* USA
Amsden, A. 230, 232
Ansari, J. 46 n.
Appleyard, R. 179
Argentina 84, 86, 90–1, 93, 189, 400
Armington elasticities 73 n.
Armstrong, P. 192 n., 193, 418
Arriagada, A. 114, 149, 232 n.
Arrow, K. 43 n., 111, 133 n.
Australia 399, 422; deindustrialization 204–5; income inequality 254, 468; skill differentials 256, 262, 264 n., 267–8, 293 n., (by education and age) 248, 427–8, 430; unemployment 301–2, 309, 444–6; wage dispersion 252, 460
Austria 399, 422; deindustrialization 203–6; skill differentials 256, 262, 268, (by occupation) 250, 302, 438–9, 440–3, 452, 454; unemployment 302, 309, 314–15, 318; wage dispersion 253, 460–1
Azariadis, C. 53 n.

baby boom, *see* crowding, generational
Baily, M. 280 n., 281 n.
balance of trade; intra-North 276 n.; North–South 69–70, 110, 139, 142–3, 155, 199 n.; and unemployment 292 n., 386; of USA 270
Balassa, B. 41, 69 n., 92 n., 98 n., 99, 101, 103 n., 104 n., 105–6, 117 n.,

109–10, 112–16, 130 n., 148, 218, 341, 419 n.
Balasubramanyam, V. 133 n.
Baldwin, R. 108, 269, 354 n.
Ballance, R. 46 n., 80, 111–18, 172 n., 188
Balls, E. 260 n., 296 n., 306 n., 317 n., 432 n., 433 n.
Bangladesh 222
barriers to trade 144, 209, 221, 310; duration of effects of changes 217, 229, 233, 242, 257–8; future prospects 19, 330–7; recent changes 7–8, 27, 162–4, 171–4, 181–2, 206; *see also* export-oriented industrialization; protectionism
Barro, R. 266 n.
BAS–ED labour, definition and measurement 6, 49, 343, 365, 402–4
Battese, G. 133 n.
Bauwens, L. 112–16
Bean, C. 270 n., 278 n., 283–4, 298, 447
Beenstock, M. vii, 3, 70, 108, 177, 192 n., 198
Behrman, J. 132 n.
Belgium 399, 467 n.; changing sectoral skill intensities 410–11, 422; deindustrialization 203–7; factor content of trade 98, 102, 104; skill differentials 256, 262, 267–8, 274, (by occupation) 250, 438–9, 449 n., 454; unemployment 300, 302, 309, 311, 315, 431–2
Berger, M. 220
Berliner, D. 144 n., 161 n.
Berndt, E. 283 n., 285
Berry, A. 186
Berthet-Bondet, C. 97, 125 n., 208 n., 422
Best, M. 161 n., 344 n.
Beveridge curve 296–7
Bhagwati, J. 173 n., 419 n.
Bhalla, A. 133 n.
Bienefeld, M. vii, 3 n.
Bigsten, A. 243 n.
Blackburn, M. 462, 469 n., 470
Blades, D. 97 n., 419 n.